THE CAMBRIDGE HISTORY OF ISLAM

VOLUME 2A

THE CAMBRIDGE HISTORY OF ISLAM

VOLUME 2A

THE INDIAN SUB-CONTINENT, SOUTH-EAST ASIA, AFRICA AND THE MUSLIM WEST

EDITED BY

P. M. HOLT

Professor of Arab History in the University of London

ANN K. S. LAMBTON

Professor of Persian in the University of London

BERNARD LEWIS

Institute for Advanced Study, Princeton

CAMBRIDGE UNIVERSITY PRESS

CAMBRIDGE

LONDON · NEW YORK · MELBOURNE

Published by the Syndics of the Cambridge University Press
The Pitt Building, Trumpington Street, Cambridge CB2 1RP
Bentley House, 200 Euston Road, London NW1 2DB
32 East 57th Street, New York, NY 10022, USA
296 Beaconsfield Parade, Middle Park, Melbourne 3206, Australia

Library of Congress catalogue card number: 73-77291

Hardcover edition
ISBN 0 521 07567 x Volume 1
ISBN 0 521 07601 3 Volume 2

Paperback edition
ISBN 0 521 29135 6 Volume 1A
ISBN 0 521 29136 4 Volume 1B
ISBN 0 521 29137 2 Volume 2A
ISBN 0 521 29138 0 Volume 2B

First published in two volumes 1970
First paperback edition (four volumes) 1977

First printed in Great Britain by
Spottiswoode, Ballantyne & Co. Ltd
London and Colchester
Reprinted in Great Britain
at the
University Printing House, Cambridge

CONTENTS

A dynastic list, bibliography, glossary and index will be found at the end of Volume 2B.

LIST OF MAPS

PREFACE

The aim of these volumes is to present the history of Islam as a cultural whole. It is hoped that in a single concise work the reader will be able to follow all the main threads: political, theological, philosophical, economic, scientific, military, artistic. But *The Cambridge history of Islam* is not a repository of facts, names and dates; it is not intended primarily for reference, but as a book for continuous reading. The editors believe that, while it will not be despised by the expert orientalist, it will be useful to students in other fields of history, and particularly to university students of oriental subjects, and will also appeal to those who read history for intellectual pleasure.

A standardized system of translation has been employed for proper names and technical terms in the three principal Islamic languages—Arabic, Persian and Turkish. Some anomalies have, however, been inevitable, and place-names which have a widely accepted conventional spelling have been given in that form. Dates before the nineteenth century have normally been given according to both the Islamic (*Hijrī*) and Christian eras. Footnotes have been used sparingly; principally to give references for quotations or authority for conclusions in the text. The bibliographies are not intended as an exhaustive documentation of the subjects to which they refer, but as a guide to further reading. For this reason, and to avoid extensive repetition of titles, many of the bibliographies have been consolidated to cover two or more related contributions.

The editors are responsible for the planning and organisation of the work as a whole. They have tried to avoid gaps and overlaps, and have given general guidance to contributors, designed to secure some consistency of form and presentation. The individual authors are, of course, responsible for their own opinions and interpretations.

The editors wish to express their thanks to all who have assisted in the preparation of this work. They are particularly grateful to those who undertook the translation of contributions or gave advice and sub-editorial assistance, especially Mr J. G. Burton-Page, Professor C. D. Cowan, Dr J. F. P. Hopkins, Dr A. I. Sabra, Professor H. R. Tinker, Col. Geoffrey Wheeler and Dr D. T. Whiteside. They would also like to thank members of the staff of the Cambridge University Press for their invariable patience and helpfulness.

THE EDITORS

INTRODUCTION

P. M. Holt[1]

A reader taking up a work entitled *The Cambridge history of Islam* may reasonably ask, 'What is Islam? In what sense is Islam an appropriate field for historical enquiry?' Primarily, of course, Islam is, like Christianity, a religion, the antecedents, origin and development of which may, without prejudice to its transcendental aspects, be a legitimate concern of historians. Religious history in the narrow sense is not, however, the only, or even the main, concern of the contributors to these volumes. For the faith of Islam has, again like Christianity, been a great synthesizing agent. From its earliest days it displayed features of kinship with the earlier monotheisms of Judaism and Christianity. Implanted in the former provinces of the Byzantine and Sasanian empires, it was compelled to maintain and define its autonomy against older and more developed faiths. Like Judaism and Christianity before it, it met the challenge of Greek philosophy, and adopted the conceptual and logical tools of this opponent to expand, to deepen, and to render articulate its self-consciousness. In this connexion, the first three centuries of Islam, like the first three centuries of Christianity, were critical for establishing the norms of belief and practice, and for embodying them in a tradition which was, or which purported to be, historical.

The Islamic synthesis did not stop at this stage. The external frontier of Islam has continued to move until our own day. For the most part, this movement has been one of expansion—into Central Asia, into the Indian sub-continent and south-east Asia, and into trans-Saharan Africa—but there have also been phases of retreat and withdrawal, notably in Spain, and in central and south-eastern Europe. But besides this external frontier, which has largely been the creation of conquering armies, (although with important exceptions in Central and south-east Asia and Africa) there has also been throughout Islamic history an internal frontier—the invisible line of division between Muslim and non-Muslim. Here also over the centuries there has been an expansion of Islam, so that, for example, in the former Byzantine and Sasanian lands the Christian and Zoroastrian communities were reduced to numerical insignificance, and became minority-groups like the Jews. This two-fold expansion has brought new elements into the Islamic synthesis,

[1] I should like to thank my co-editors, Professors Lambton and Lewis, for reading and commenting on this Introduction in draft.

some permanent and widely accepted, others more transient or local in their effects.

The process of synthesization has not gone forward in a political vacuum. Unlike the early Christian Church, the Islamic *Umma*, or community of believers, achieved political power from the outset, and was organized for mutual support in the maintenance of the faith. This concern of the community for the faith survived the break-up of the caliphate and the emergence of new and often transitory régimes. It has taken various forms. Two of the principal institutions of Islam, *Sharī'a* and *Jihād*, the Holy Law and the Holy War, are expressions of the concern in its conservative and militant aspects respectively—aspects moreover which are not wholly distinct, since the Holy War is fought in defence of the Holy Law against its external and internal enemies. In political matters as in others, Islam adopted and incorporated contributions from many sources. The successors of the Prophet as heads of his community drew on the customs of Arab tribal leadership, as well as the usages of the Meccan trading oligarchy. They inherited the legacy of Byzantine administration, as well as the traditions of the Sasanian monarchy. Later rulers were influenced by other political concepts: those brought into the medieval Islamic world by Turkish and Mongol immigrants from the steppes, and in the latest age the constitutional and legal doctrines of liberal Europe, followed by the seductive panaceas of totalitarianism.

Islam, then, as it will be examined in the following chapters, is a complex cultural synthesis, centred in a distinctive religious faith, and necessarily set in the framework of a continuing political life. The religion, the culture, and the political structures alike present many features which seem familiar to an observer whose own background is that of Christian Europe. It could hardly be otherwise, since elements derived from Judaism and Hellenism are common to both the Islamic and the Christian syntheses; since, furthermore, the histories of the Islamic community and of Christendom have touched so often and at so many points. But consciousness of the similarities must always be balanced by an awareness of the characteristic and substantial differences. Like Christianity, Islam is a monotheism with an historical founder and a sacred book; although its theology in regard to both differs essentially from Christian theology. There is also a perceptible difference in the criteria of membership of the community. Whereas in Christianity acceptance of the catholic creeds has been the basic criterion, in Islam credal theology has been of less relative importance; adherence to the Holy Law is the characteristic manifestation of faith, and hence orthopraxy rather than orthodoxy has been the usual token of membership. Another difference is that Islam has no equivalent to the Christian sacraments (although certain practices, notably the Fast of Ramaḍān and the Pilgrimage, appear to have an unacknowledged quasi-sacramental character), and no priesthood, although the *'ulamā'* (the religious scholars) and the leaders of the Ṣūfī orders (two groups at some times and in some places closely interconnected) have often played a part in Muslim societies analogous to that of the clergy amongst Christians. The absence of a sacerdotal hierarchy, or of any conciliar system, to define the faith, linked with the primacy ascribed to orthopraxy, has made Islam more tolerant of variations of belief than Christianity. It is in general true to say that heresy (to use a term not quite appropriate in Islam) has been repressed only when it has been manifested as political subversion: it is also true to say that, since Islam is both a religious and a political community, the distinction between religious and political dissent is not clearcut.

Another question which the reader of this work may ask is, 'What are the sources on which knowledge of the history of Islam is based?' The Islamic civilization of the first three centuries (in this as in other respects the seminal period) evolved two characteristic types of historical writing. The first of these was the chronicle, of which the outstanding classical example is that composed by al-Ṭabarī (d. 310/923). But behind the chronicle lay diverse historiographical elements—the sagas and genealogies of the pre-Islamic Arab tribes, the semi-legendary narratives of the Persian kings, and, serving as the central theme to which all others were subservient, the career of the Prophet and the vicissitudes of the *Umma* which he founded. The early historians were primarily religious scholars: the traditions which they recorded were in part Traditions in the technical Islamic sense, i.e. *Ḥadīth,* the memorials of the alleged acts and sayings of the Prophet, as transmitted by a chain of informants. There was no formal distinction between the historical *Ḥadīth* and the main body of Traditions which formed a principal element in the elaboration of the Holy Law; indeed it is clear that many items ostensibly of an historical nature had in fact legal and social purposes. There is also a fundamental problem of criticism; namely, the difficulty of establishing how much of this copious *Ḥadīth* material is a veritable record of Muḥammad's activities, and how much is of subsequent and extraneous origin, assimilated in this form into Islam. The early Muslim scholars were keenly aware of the problem, although the criteria they adopted for discriminating between the authentic and the feigned Traditions seem artificial and insufficiently rigorous by modern standards of historical investigation. The whole subject is highly controversial at the present day, with, on the whole, non-Muslim scholars adopting a more radical, and Muslim scholars a more conservative attitude in *Ḥadīth* criticism.

Thus the motive which led to the development of Islamic historiography was primarily religious. In nothing does Islam so clearly demonstrate its kinship with Judaism and Christianity as in its sense of, and attitude towards, history; its consciousness of the existence of the world under a divine dispensation, and its emphasis on the significance of human lives and acts. Muḥammad saw himself as the last in a sequence of prophets who were God's apostles to mankind. The Qur'ān abounds in references to sacred history. Hence Islamic historiography assumes as axiomatic the pattern already evolved in Judaeo-Christian thought: a succession of events in time, opening with the creation, culminating in a point of supreme divine revelation (when, in effect, there is a new creation of a holy community), and looking prospectively to a Last Day and the end of history. In this connexion, it is significant that, in spite of the contacts between Islamic and late Hellenistic civilization, and of the Muslim reception of much of the Graeco-Roman cultural heritage, the Islamic historians were almost totally uninterested in their Classical predecessors, whether as sources of information, or as models of historiography. The Roman Empire played no part in the *praeparatio evangelica* for Islam as it did for Christianity.

This conception of Islamic history as sacred history was a factor in the development of the second characteristic type of historical writing, a type original in Islam—the biographical dictionary. The earliest of these to survive is a collection of lives of Companions of the Prophet, and, in the words of Sir Hamilton Gibb:

> it is clear that the conception that underlies the oldest biographical dictionaries is that the history of the Islamic Community is essentially the contribution of individual men and women to the building up and transmission of its specific culture; that it is these persons (rather than the political governors) who represent or reflect the active forces in Muslim society in their respective spheres; and that their individual contributions are worthy of being recorded for future generations.[1]

[1] H. A. R. Gibb, 'Islamic biographical literature', in *Historians of the Middle East*, ed. B. Lewis and P. M. Holt (London, 1962), p. 54.

Although both the chronicle and the biographical dictionary changed and developed as, after the third Islamic century, historical writing ceased to be the special field of the religious scholars, as the caliphate was fragmented, and as new states and dynasties arose, the two persisted as the standard forms of historical writing until recent times. From Arabic they were carried over into the Persian and Turkish literatures, and from the heartlands of the Middle East to the fringes of Islam. Only during the last century, and partly at least in consequence of the reception of Western historical objectives and techniques by Muslim scholars, have they become moribund.

One important class of source-material, familiar to the student of Western history, is almost completely lacking for the history of Islam—namely, archives. Certain documents are to be found transcribed in chronicles, as well as in collections of model letters and the encyclopaedic handbooks written for the guidance of government officials, but these are at least at one remove from their originals, and as isolated pieces are of diminished evidential value. Climatic conditions in Egypt, and chancery practice in Europe, have preserved some documents, more or less at random, but only with the records of the Ottoman Empire does a rich and systematically maintained government archive become available. With the nineteenth century, archival material increases. As in other fields of historical study, important contributions have been made by the auxiliary sciences of archaeology, epigraphy, palaeography, diplomatic and numismatics.

The modern study of Islamic history goes back to developments in Europe during the sixteenth and seventeenth centuries. Throughout the previous millennium, the peoples in the lands of Western Christendom and Islam had remained in almost total ignorance of each other's history; but whereas the Muslims almost without exception chose to ignore events which seemed to them extraneous and irrelevant, the Christian writers elaborated what has rightly been called a 'deformed image' of Islam and its founder.[1] In the sixteenth and seventeenth centuries, this came to be challenged. The contacts of trade and diplomacy were increasing between Muslim and Christian states. The study of Arabic was established in European universities for a variety of reasons, not least that it was seen to be the key to the writings of the Muslim philosophers and scientists, hitherto known only in imperfect medieval Latin translations. A knowledge of Arabic was also important in the

[1] See N. Daniel, *Islam and the West: the making of an image* (Edinburgh, 1960).

study of the Hebrew Bible—a study which flourished in the age of the Renaissance and the Reformation. During the same period in Western Europe, the foundations of critical historical enquiry were being laid: ancient texts were being published, old documents were being brought out of neglected archives. The motive behind much of this activity was ardently polemic; nevertheless, controversialists both in Britain and on the Continent were fashioning the instruments and devising the methods of modern research.

A new approach to the study of Islam was one aspect of this 'historical revolution', as it has been called.[1] It was demonstrated in two principal respects. The first of these was the publication of texts. Here the initiative was taken by Dutch scholars, Erpenius and Golius, in the first half of the seventeenth century, to be followed shortly by the Englishman, Edward Pococke (1604–91). The greatness of Pococke, however, lies mainly in a second respect. He had for his time an unrivalled knowledge of Muslim history and Arab antiquities, of which he gave an exposition in a short but very influential work, *Specimen historiae Arabum* (1650). The book remained authoritative for a century and a half, during which time it served as a quarry for a succession of writers. Resting on an encyclopaedic range of Arabic sources, the *Specimen,* implicitly by its scholarship, as well as by the occasional explicit comment, prepared the way for a more accurate and dispassionate view of Islam than the 'deformed image', which was still commonly accepted—and indeed lingered for two centuries. A later generation of orientalists extended the new understanding of Islam, and, by writing in modern languages, conveyed it to a less academic readership. Three highly important works in this connexion were the *Bibliothèque orientale* (1697) of Bartholomé d'Herbelot, *The history of the Saracens* (1708, 1718) of Simon Ockley, and George Sale's Preliminary Discourse to his translation of the Qur'ān (1734). Besides the information thus made available on the Islamic (and especially the Arab) past, there was in the same period a growing body of literature on the contemporary Muslim powers, especially the Ottomans and the Safavids. Through such publications, as well as others which were works of controversy rather than of scholarship, Islamic history became more familiar to educated Europeans, and was established beside ancient and modern history as an accepted field of study. This expansion of the world-view of European historians is

[1] See F. S. Fussner, *The historical revolution: English historical writing and thought, 1580–1640* (London, 1962).

demonstrated by Edward Gibbon, who, in his *Decline and fall of the Roman Empire* (1776–88) devoted nine out of seventy-one chapters to Islamic history, ranging from Arabia in the time of the Prophet to the Mongol and Ottoman conquests, and viewed its course with the same ironical detachment as he did the establishment of Christianity and the barbarian invasions of the West.

In the space of nearly two hundred years that have elapsed since Gibbon wrote, the Renaissance, the Reformation and the Enlightenment have themselves passed into history, and new forces have emerged in the development of European society. Political, social and economic change, the new ideologies of liberalism, nationalism and Marxism, have contributed to form the outlook and to define the preoccupations of historians in the nineteenth and twentieth centuries. At the same time, the methods of historical study have continued to evolve. The source-materials available for research have immensely increased, and the range of techniques at the historian's disposal has been extended. The aims of the historian have changed in response to both of these factors. Where the pioneers in the field sought primarily to construct, from the best sources they could find, the essential framework of political history, and to chronicle as accurately as possible the acts of rulers, historians today are more conscious of the need to evaluate their materials—a critique all the more important in Islamic history since the control supplied by archives is so largely deficient. They seek to penetrate the dynastic screen, to trace the real sites and shifts of power in the capitals and the camps, and to identify, not merely the leaders and figure-heads, but the ethnic, religious, social or economic groups of anonymous individuals who supported constituted authority or promoted subversion. It is no longer possible, therefore, to segregate the political history of Islam from its social and economic history—although in the latter field especially materials are notably sparse over wide regions and long periods. As the study of Islamic history is now developing, many of the apparent certainties of the older Western historiography (often reflecting the assertions and interpretations of the Muslim traditional historians) have dissolved, and it is only gradually through detailed research that a truer understanding of the past may be attained. At the same time, the range of investigation has been extended from its older foci, the heyday of classical Islam, the great dynastic empires, and the areas of confrontation with Christendom, to other periods and regions, which as recently as ten or twenty years ago aroused little interest among serious historians.

The Cambridge history of Islam cannot therefore pretend to supply a definitive conspectus of its field: it seeks rather to offer an authoritative guide to the state of knowledge at the present day, and to provide a sound foundation on which to build. The majority of its chapters are devoted to political history—this is inevitable in view of the relative abundance of source-material, and of the comparatively large amount of work that has been done here. Similar reasons explain the generous proportion of space allotted to the Muslim lands of the Middle East—which were, moreover, the region in which the classical Islamic synthesis evolved. Yet the picture which the work as a whole seeks to present is of the great and diversified community of Islam, evolving and expanding throughout thirteen centuries, creating its characteristic religious, political and social institutions, and making through its philosophy, literature and art a notable contribution to civilizations outside its own household of faith.

PART V

THE INDIAN SUB-CONTINENT

CHAPTER I

MUSLIM INDIA BEFORE THE MUGHALS

THE GHAZNAVIDS AND GHURIDS

When Alptigin rebelled against the Samanids he established himself at Ghazna in 352/962, where his slave and son-in-law Sebüktigin succeeded him in 367/977 and started vigorously to expand his dominions. Jayapāla of Waihind saw danger in the consolidation of the kingdom of Ghazna and decided to destroy it. He therefore invaded Ghazna, but was defeated and agreed to pay an indemnity. He defaulted, took the field again and was once more defeated. This was the beginning of the struggle between the Ghaznavids and the Hindu Shāhīs.

Sebüktigin died in 387/997 and in the following year was succeeded by the famous Maḥmūd. The latter defeated Jayapāla (391/1001), who immolated himself by fire because his subjects thought that he had brought disaster and disgrace to the dynasty. Jayapāla's son Ānandapāla carried on the struggle, and in a few years succeeded in organizing a confederacy of the Hindu rulers of Ujjayn, Gwalior (Gwālyār), Kālinjar, Kannawj, Delhi (Dihlī) and Ajmēr. This powerful confederacy was defeated at Peshāwar in 399/1008, despite the fact that during the greater part of the battle Maḥmūd and his army were hard-pressed. The tide turned when Ānandapāla's elephant was hit by an arrow, took fright and ran away. On this the Hindu army broke and fled. The Hindu Shāhī dominions came into Maḥmūd's possession and a governor was appointed to reside at Lahore (Lāhawr). He decided to teach the Hindu rajas a lesson so that they should not venture to combine against him again. He soon discovered that they were incredibly rich, having vast hoards of treasures, and that the Hindu temples also were repositories of great wealth. This also must have whetted his appetite for expeditions. Nagarkōt ,Thānesar, Kannawj and Kālinjar were all conquered and left in the hands of the Hindu vassals. His last expedition was against Somnāth, which he captured in 415/1024 after a trying march through the desert. He returned to Ghazna in 417/1026. Four years later, in 421/1030, he died.

It would have been impossible for Maḥmūd to control all the vanquished Hindu kingdoms because of his involvement in Central Asia.

Therefore, he contented himself with the annexation of the Panjāb only. He was neither a mere robber nor a bloodthirsty tyrant, as some modern writers have called him, and shed no blood except in the exigencies of war. He did despoil and destroy many Hindu temples, but in his dealings with his own Hindu subjects he was tolerant, as is evident by his employment of Hindus, some of whom lived in Ghazna and rose to high posts. Maḥmūd's reputation as a great patron of culture and literature has remained undiminished throughout the ages. It was under his patronage that the well-known epic *Shāh-nāma* was written by Firdawsī. The story that Firdawsī was shabbily treated and wrote a poem maligning the sultan has been contested. One of the greatest scholars at his court was Abū Rayḥān Muḥammad al-Bīrūnī.

Maḥmūd's successor, Mas'ūd, maintained control over Lahore, and when he heard that its governor Aḥmad Niyaltigin had rebellious intentions he sent a Hindu general, Tilak, against him. Niyaltigin was defeated and killed. Mas'ūd decided to retire to Lahore after his defeat at the hands of the Seljuks but he was deposed by his guards near the Marghīla Pass between Attock (Ātak) and Rāwalpindī in 432/1040. The dynasty, however, continued to rule until Mu'izz al-Dīn Muḥammad b. Sām ousted them from Lahore in 582/1186. One of the Ghaznavid rulers of Lahore, Ibrāhīm (451–92/1059–99) deserves special mention because he was able not only to secure peace by entering into a treaty with the Seljuks, but was also to make inroads into the Hindu kingdoms of the Gangetic plain. Under him and his son Mas'ūd III (492–508/1099–1115) Lahore rose to be a great centre of culture.

The Ghaznavid monarch Bahrām (512–47/1118–52) came into conflict with the rulers of Ghūr. After a protracted conflict 'Alā' al-Dīn Ḥusayn (known as *Jahānsūz*) destroyed the city of Ghazna (545/1150) which was reduced to ashes. Bahrām was able to reoccupy a dilapidated Ghazna after *Jahānsūz* had been defeated and imprisoned by Sultan Sanjar of the Seljuk dynasty. When Bahrām died, the Oghuz Turks occupied Ghazna, and the dynasty once again moved to Lahore. The power of the Ghūrīs revived and prospered under Ghiyāṯ al-Dīn Muḥammad. His brother, Muḥammad b. Sām (who had the title of Shihāb al-Dīn as a prince) was destined to extend Muslim rule over the greater part of northern India. He took Ghazna, Mūltān and Ucch in 570/1175 and then turned towards Gujarāt in 573/1178. This expedition resulted in failure, and he decided to consolidate his position in the Panjāb which he did by capturing Peshāwar in 574/1179, Siālkot in

576/1181, Lahore in 582/1186 and Bhatinda in 587/1191. At this the Hindu raja of Ajmēr and Delhi marched upon Bhatinda and when the sultan went to meet the danger he was wounded and had to be hastily moved to Ghazna. The sultan, however, was not daunted and he defeated Prithvīrāja in 588/1192 at Nardīn, near Tarā'orī. Delhi and Ajmēr then passed to the sultan. Two years later he turned his attention to Kannawj and Banāras, which were added to the Muslim empire. His general Muḥammad b. Bakhtyār Khaljī conquered Bihār and Bengal. The conquest of Bengal is one of the romances of history. It was with the incredibly small force of eighteen troopers that Muḥammad b. Bakhtyār captured the capital city of Nadiyā. Ghiyās̱ al-Dīn having died in 599/1203, Shihāb al-Dīn Muḥammad assumed the title of Mu'izz al-Dīn and was officially invested as sultan. The major conquests, however, had already been made. The last few years of his life were mostly spent in dealing with difficulties in Central Asia, where in 602/1205 he suffered defeat at the hands of the Kara-Khitay. On rumours of this defeat reaching the Khokars they rose in rebellion which the sultan crushed in person. However, on his way back to Ghazna he was assassinated by an Ismā'īlī *fidā'ī* at Damīk in 603/1206. Mu'izz al-Dīn Muḥammad was not as brilliant as Maḥmūd of Ghazna, but he left a lasting impact on the history of India. He was reputed to be a mild and benevolent man, a good general and a just ruler.

THE ESTABLISHMENT OF THE SULTANATE OF DELHI

Three months later the sultan's slave and general, Quṭb al-Dīn Aybak, was enthroned as sultan of Delhi, and thus was ushered into existence the sultanate which gradually brought the greater part of the sub-continent under its sway, and established Muslim rule on a firm foundation. After a short reign of five years he died and was succeeded by his son Ārām Shāh, who proved incompetent. In his place was elected Shams al-Dīn Iltutmish, who was Aybak's son-in-law. A struggle between the powerful slaves and generals of Mu'izz al-Dīn Muḥammad was inevitable, and Iletmish had first to deal with his rivals. He was still in the throes of this struggle when Jalāl al-Dīn Mengübirdi of Khwārazm entered his dominions, being pursued by the famous Mongol conqueror Chingiz Khān. It was with some difficulty that Iltutmish was able to get rid of Jalāl al-Dīn, who ultimately left for Persia. In 632/1234 the Ismā'īlīs organized a *coup d'état* to assassinate the monarch and to establish their rule. They entered the mosque one Friday when the sultan was praying, and had hewed their way almost up to him when he made his escape. The effort was frustrated.

Iltutmish was one of the greatest sultans of Delhi. To him goes the credit of consolidating the empire. He was able to avert an imminent Mongol invasion by cold-shouldering Jalāl al-Dīn. He was ably assisted by Niẓām al-Mulk Kamāl al-Dīn Muḥammad Junaydī, who had considerable administrative talent and insight. About this time the Ṣūfī orders became very active, and contributed considerably to the growth of Islam in the newly-conquered areas.

Iltutmish died in 633/1236. He had thought highly of his daughter Raḍiyya as a possible heir, because she was more capable than her brothers. After her brother Fīrūz had ruled ineffectively for six months she then succeeded, but found it difficult to manage 'the Forty', a group of powerful officers who had rendered meritorious service in the reign of Iltutmish. After his death, however, they robbed the throne of all power and raised one prince after another to the throne. Raḍiyya showed some spirit and fought for her throne, but she was defeated, and, while in flight, was killed by some Hindus (637/1240). Her half-brother Bahrām was raised to the throne on promising that authority would rest in the hands of a group of high officials. This proved too irksome for the young sultan, who tried to free himself from tutelage, and was therefore deposed in 639/1242. Yet another son, Mas'ūd, was now raised to the throne and was deposed in 644/1246 because he too tried to assert his authority. Then came to the throne Nāṣir al-Dīn Maḥmūd, a pious and kindly prince, who reigned till his death in 664/1266 with all power vested in the hands of Balban, a capable slave of Iletmish and one of the powerful Forty.

The power of such a military oligarchy could not last. A modern speculation that if the Forty had exercised this power wisely they might have succeeded in establishing some constitutional precedents is baseless, because there was no ground of traditions or social institutions into which constitutionalism could have roots. The Forty were united neither in their outlook nor in their interests, the only binding factor was their aversion, for selfish reasons, to a powerful monarchy. This negative factor also disappeared when the Mongol pressure increased to such an extent that the very existence of the sultanate was threatened. The Mongols had penetrated Sind, Mūltān and the west Panjāb and had sacked Lahore in 638/1241, and some nobles had even begun to look to them for patronage and support. The Forty were divided into several groups because of mutual jealousies, their time and resources wasted in domestic quarrels. Hindu chieftains were discovering that the authority of the sultanate was not all-pervading, and the fear instilled by the rapid spread of Muslim power was wearing off. Gwalior and Ranthambor were lost and Katehr was giving trouble. Even the suburbs of Delhi had become unsafe, through the depredations of highwaymen, and the gates of Delhi had to be closed before dusk. Communications with Bengal were all but disrupted by Hindu robbers in the Do'āb. Bengal was under Muslim rule but virtually independent. It must have been obvious to all but the most selfish and short-sighted that the sultanate could not last long without vigorous effort and the strengthening of the central authority.

Nāṣir al-Dīn Maḥmūd entrusted all authority to Balban, and did not interfere with the administration throughout his reign except for a brief period of two years (651–3/1253–5) when, as the result of a palace conspiracy, Balban was removed from office. Balban was too circumspect to use his power in a manner that would alienate any strong group which might try to oust him with the help of the monarch. When Maḥmūd died in 664/1266, Balban ascended the throne with the title Ghiyās̱ al-Dīn, and began to assert himself fully. He belonged to a noble family of Ilbārī Turks of Central Asia, but was carried away as a slave during a Mongol incursion to Baghdād. He was ultimately sold to Iletmish at Delhi. He showed capacity and steadily rose to a position of eminence.

After his accession, Balban's first concern was to instil a sense of discipline into the officers. He strengthened the central army by reorganizing the department of recruitment and salaries—the office of the *'āriẓ-i mamālik*. After having strengthened the central army, he turned to the Forty and reduced their power. Those who resisted were heavily punished, and others soon saw the advantage of conforming to the new discipline. Balban established an exacting court etiquette. He deported himself with great dignity, never permitting anyone to take any liberty with him. It is said that even his personal valet did not see him half-dressed, bare-headed, or without his socks and shoes. He strengthened his intelligence system, and kept himself informed of the doings of his officers to stop them from indulging in any rebellious activities.

He limited himself to the area that he had inherited and made no effort even to recover parts of Mālwā which had been conquered earlier and then lost. He turned his attention to the improvement of peace and order. The forest near Delhi was cleared, and nests of robbers were rooted out. Katehr was again reduced to submission. Balban spent about a year in the districts of Patiālī, Bhojpur and Kampil in the Do'āb to punish the robbers and to suppress rebellions. He built forts and established townships of Muslims so that they might look after the security of the region. He then turned his attention to the Mongols and reorganized the administration of Sind and the west Panjāb. The capable Shēr Khān Sunqar was given command of the area and, on his death, Balban's eldest son, Muḥammad Khān, was appointed governor. These preparations kept the Mongols in check, though their incursions, in one of which the prince was killed, did not stop completely.

Balban decided to bring Bengal under his control. The main reason seems to be that the sultans of Delhi were dependent on Bengal for their supply of elephants, and an unfriendly Bengal could cut off these supplies. Two expeditions sent against the rebellious governor, Ṭughril, were defeated. Then Balban took the field in person in 679/1280. Ṭughril fled and took shelter in the forest of Orissa, from where he was captured and executed with his main supporters. The governorship was entrusted to Balban's second son, Bughrā Khān.

In 684/1285, when the news of the death of his eldest son, Muḥammad Khān, reached Balban, he heard it with fortitude and conducted his business as if nothing had happened, but at night he was disconsolate. He sent for Bughrā Khān with the intention of keeping him near the throne, so that he might succeed him without difficulty, but the prince left Delhi without permission. Balban died in 686/1287. He was succeeded by his worthless grandson, Kay-Qubād, who had been brought up under strict control, but who, when he was no longer under the tutelage of his grandfather, completely lost control over himself, and gave himself up to pleasure. His father, Bughrā Khān, marched from Bengal, and reached the river Ghāgrā (Gogra) at the same time as Kay-Qubād; because of the intercession of some nobles there were no hostilities. Bughrā Khān gave fatherly advice to Kay-Qubād, who seems to have made an effort to reform himself, but, even before he reached Delhi, he had been enticed back to his old ways. When shortly afterwards he was struck by paralysis his infant son Kayūmarṯ displaced him, as a puppet in the hands of first the Turkish faction and then of the Afghān party; his Khaljī deputy, Fērōz, defeated his rivals, and ascended the throne in 689/1290 under the title of Jalāl al-Dīn Fērōz Khaljī.

THE KHALJĪ SULTANATE IN DELHI

The Khaljīs were Turks by origin, but had resided in Afghanistan so long that they were no longer regarded as Turks. Their rise, therefore, was disliked by the Turks. Gradually the animosity wore off; but not before Jalāl al-Dīn had suppressed the rebellion of Chhajjū Khān (690/1291), a scion of the house of Balban, and executed a *darwīsh*, Sīdī Mawlā, who had become a centre of rebellious conspiracies. Fērōz had distinguished himself as a general and administrator, but was more than seventy years old at the time of his enthronement. He was mild, and did not like to take stern measures even when they were necessary. Many of his followers were dissatisfied because they saw in his mildness a danger to their own position. Apart from his solitary action against Sīdī Mawlā, Fērōz's nature led him to abstain from executing even robbers and thugs, who were deported instead. He treated Chhajjū Khān with quixotic mildness to the consternation of his supporters. Towards the close of Fērōz's reign in 694/1294 his nephew and son-in-law, Muḥammad, set out from Karā, at the head of 8,000 horse, crossed the Vindhyās and after a march of two months through difficult terrain, appeared before Devagiri and captured it. A huge booty of gold, silver, pearls, jewels and silk fell into his hands. When he returned he was summoned to court, but he pretended that he was afraid of punishment, having undertaken the expedition without royal permission. Fērōz was persuaded to go to Karā and reassure Muḥammad. He was also motivated by the hope of obtaining some of the wealth that Muḥammad had brought with him. He was, however, assassinated and Muḥammad proclaimed himself sultan as 'Alā' al-Dīn Muḥammad Khaljī in 695/1296.

Despite the circumstances in which he came to the throne, 'Alā' al-Dīn made a great impact upon the history of India. He was efficient, imaginative and strong. His expedition against Devagiri is in itself one of the boldest military ventures in history. His murder of Fērōz is no doubt a blot on his character, but he was motivated in this as much by the desire to maintain the authority of the Khaljīs as by self-interest.

'Alā' al-Dīn was soon able to make a correct assessment of the political situation. He undertook the task of securing his dominions from Mongol inroads and to extend his sovereignty further afield. This needed considerable organization and great resources. He therefore tightened his control over his officers as well as over Hindu chiefs, raised large sums of money through additional taxation, and built up a large army through rigid economy and establishing successfully a system of price-control. He introduced great austerity, and frowned upon any laxity in morals or indulgence in loose talk and intrigue. He further improved the intelligence services, and made them so efficient that the possibility of treasonable talk and association was eliminated. To stop the officials from organizing themselves into groups, he prohibited intermarriage without royal permission. He stopped convivial and drinking parties, so that the officers would not become too familiar with one another and establish relationships injurious to the state. He raised the state levy of agricultural produce from twenty per cent to fifty per cent in many areas and, to reduce any ensuing hardship, he eliminated the perquisites which Hindu chiefs used to extract from the peasantry. He also stopped the commission which the state paid them on the realization of the revenue. He examined the titles of rent-free grants of land given in previous reigns for pious purposes, and resumed them wherever they were no longer justified. In the same way, he abolished all grants in money which were no longer deserved. For the purpose of increasing his army and equipping it properly, he fixed salaries at a level lower than previously. His grants to poets and scholars also were not lavish.

For the purpose of removing any difficulty which smaller salaries might entail to public servants and others, he fixed prices at a reasonably low level, and was able to maintain them successfully throughout his reign. The system adopted was scientific and sensible. By lowering salaries he reduced the circulation of money, which had been artificially stimulated by the treasure that poured into Delhi as a result of the conquest of rich Hindu kingdoms. By raising the state levy on agricultural produce, he induced the peasant to cultivate more land, to enable him to make up for the lost margin in his net income. He ensured a continuous supply of food by the purchase of all surplus grain from the peasants, and bringing it to the town to ensure a constant supply. The cultivator was encouraged to pay the state in grain, which was stored at numerous places, and if, through a natural disaster or some unforeseen circumstance, the normal supply failed, the state granaries were able to make up the deficiency. Storage seems to have been managed skilfully, because as late as Ibn Baṭṭūṭa's visit to Delhi (1334–42), when the city was in the grip of a famine, rice stored in the reign of ʿAlāʾ al-Dīn Khaljī was given to the public. The prices of other articles were also fixed, and they could be sold only in the *Sarā-yi ʿadl* where royal officials supervised the transactions. The measures succeeded extremely well, and there is complete unanimity amongst the authorities of the period that throughout the reign prices were maintained at the low level fixed by the sultan.

He fixed the salaries of his troopers at levels where they would not face any difficulty. The horses were regularly examined and branded so that a horse could not pass muster twice, nor could horses be changed for fraudulent purposes. The reforms introduced by him in his agrarian administration were also effective. He eliminated middlemen, and insisted that the area cultivated should be properly assessed through a system of measurement.

The sultan succeeded in creating sufficient resources to secure his dominions from Mongol invasions. The need had indeed become pressing. As early as 702/1303, the Mongols reached Delhi itself, and a large army laid siege to the city. However, they raised the siege after two months. The sultan was quick to see that it was necessary to take proper steps to deal with the menace. The fortifications built by Balban were repaired, new forts were built and the frontier province of Dīpālpur was put under the charge of Tughluq. Ultimately the Mongols developed a wholesome respect for the sultan's army.

In the south he was equally successful. His general, Malik Kāfūr, a slave of Hindu origin, defeated Rājā Rāmadeva of Devagiri who had withheld tribute. The raja had to come to Delhi to renew his allegiance. The sultan wisely treated him with marks of favour, bestowed upon him the title of *ra'i rāyān* (raja of rajas) and sent him back to his capital. In 709/1308 Malik Kāfūr conquered Warangal. In this expedition Rājā Ramadeva rendered much help, which showed that 'Alā' al-Dīn's policy of reconciliation had borne fruit. In 710/1310 Malik Kāfūr conquered Madura and Dvārasamudra, and thus extended the boundaries of the sultanate to the sea-coast in the extreme south. 'Alā' al-Din's treatment of the rulers of southern India was conciliatory: he permitted them to retain their former kingdoms as vassals. Bengal, Sind, Mālwā and Gujarāt also were brought under control.

The historian Baranī,[1] for whom the sultan was wicked although strong and successful, has recorded a somewhat dramatized story of 'Alā' al-Dīn's intention to set himself up as a prophet, and to undertake the conquest of the world like another Alexander. There can be little doubt that the sultan did have the ambition to be a great conqueror, an

[1] Żiyā' al-Dīn Baranī (of Baran, i.e. Bulandshahr), a historian and writer on government in the style of Mirrors for Princes, was probably born *c.* 680/1279 and died *c.* 758/1357.

ambition in which he was remarkably successful. It is quite possible that the scheme of conquests was discussed at a time when there were other dangers besetting the sultanate, and the sultan was wisely persuaded not to undertake them until he had properly organized the resources of the sultanate, and established full control over it. The story regarding the intention to be a prophet seems difficult to believe because no other authority mentions it, nor is it in keeping with the sultan's actions and policies. The idea may have crossed his mind in a moment of weakness, and perhaps have been mentioned to one or two officers, but it does not seem to have been entertained seriously, and was, therefore, discarded when the folly of such an intention was pointed out.

The sultan's rule made a good impression upon the people. His crime of assassinating his uncle seems to have been forgotten, and, after his death, the people remembered him with gratitude and affection. His tomb was visited by large numbers like the tomb of a saint. 'Alā' al-Dīn died in the year 716/1316 as the result of illness. A great name of the period is that of the Chishtī mystic Shaykh Niẓām al-Dīn, whose influence was responsible for a great upsurge in religious and moral fervour among the people. It is said that 'Alā' al-Dīn's achievements would have been impossible but for the moral stamina among the Muslims engendered by Niẓam al-Dīn. The prayers of Niẓām al-Dīn were popularly believed to have brought about the raising of the Mongol siege of Delhi in 702/1303.

On 'Alā' al-Dīn's death, Malik Kāfūr, whose relations with the heir-apparent, Khiżr Khān, and his mother, the queen, had been unfriendly, caused the prince and his brother to be blinded and his mother to be imprisoned. He then sent some soldiers to blind the third son, Mubārak Khān, as well. This prince, however, persuaded the soldiers, who were by now probably tired of Malik Kāfūr's excesses, to return and avenge the wrongs perpetrated on the family. Kāfūr was killed, and Mubārak Khān ascended the throne with the title of Quṭb al-Dīn Mubārak Shāh in 716/1316. He showed some firmness in dealing with disorders in Gujarāt and Devagiri. However, he soon surpassed the limit in severity, and had some high officials wantonly executed. He also indulged in gross licentiousness. One of his favourites was Khusraw Khān, a low-born slave, who at last murdered the sultan and assumed the royal title himself in 720/1320. Under him, a large number of his Hindu kinsmen gained ascendancy, and openly insulted and vilified Islam. At last Ghāzī Malik Tughluq, who was a veteran general and warden of the marches in the Panjāb, could tolerate such a state of affairs no longer and set out for Delhi to punish the usurper. The battle which was fought in the suburbs of Delhi in 720/1320 ended in a victory for Tughluq.

THE TUGHLUQ SULTANATE IN DELHI

Tughluq adopted the title of Ghiyās̱ al-Dīn Tughluq. He applied himself to putting the administration in order again. He restored public works of utility such as forts and canals. Order was re-established, and severe action was taken against robbers. He encouraged agriculture, planted gardens, and took steps to safeguard the cultivator from the exactions of middlemen and officers.

He had to turn his attention to the Deccan when the ruler of Warangal rebelled, and Tughluq's son, Jawnā Khān, was sent to bring him back to his allegiance. This expedition, however, failed because a mischievous rumour was spread to the effect that Tughluq had died, which was generally believed in the absence of contradiction from Delhi. The prince, therefore, returned to Delhi. In 723/1323 he was again sent to the Deccan and, after capturing Bīdar, he marched on Warangal, reduced it, and annexed the surrounding regions, Telingānā.

Bengal was still under the descendants of Balban. Civil war broke out on the death of Balban's grandson, Shams al-Dīn Fērōz Shāh, in 718/1318. One of the parties, Nāṣir al-Dīn, appealed to Tughluq, who considered this to be an excellent opportunity for intervention. He marched to Bengal and placed Nāṣir al-Dīn as a vassal monarch on the throne of west Bengal. East Bengal was annexed and administered as a province. Tughluq then returned to Delhi in 725/1325. Preparations were made, as was normal, to accord the sultan a warm reception. Jawnā Khān built a special pavilion to entertain the monarch. When he had just finished the meal, the prince suggested that the elephants brought from Bengal might be paraded. The pavilion collapsed, killing Tughluq. It has been suggested by some later historians that the pavilion was specially designed to cause the monarch's death, which, instead of being an accident, was really parricide on the part of Jawnā Khān. The authority for this story is Ibn Baṭṭūṭa, but it seems that there is not much truth in the allegation. Historians of the period mention it as an unexpected accident, and evidence to the contrary is not convincing. Baranī, who fiercely condemns Muḥammad b. Tughluq for very much of his policy, makes no suggestion of parricide and sees Tughluq's death as a 'thunderbolt and heavenly calamity'.[1]

Jawnā Khān ascended the throne with the title of Muḥammad Shāh and is generally known to historians as Muḥammad b. Tughluq, a style used in contemporary literature and inscriptions. He was well educated and was equally at home in Islamic law, philosophy, mathematics, logic and medicine. He had a sharp intellect, and few could win a point in arguing with him. He had brilliant ideas, but often was blind to difficulties in implementing them. He was impatient, and did not tolerate inefficiency. He looked upon every failure to carry out his orders as wanton disobedience, which he punished sternly. He confused the officials by a succession of orders which they found difficult to enforce, and were sometimes heavily punished for this failure. His punishments were notoriously severe, for he could not see that not every little failure or delinquency was an act of rebellion. The virtue of moderation was absolutely foreign to him. He was not unjust. He had a scrupulous regard for law and justice, yet he was ruthless in punishment, and, once an offence was proved to his satisfaction, he knew no mercy. So great was his regard for justice that he would appear personally in the court of the *qāẓī* whose orders he would carry out, even though they were against him. There are at least two occasions on record when he did so. He was liberal in making gifts, but he was unforgiving, and executed a large number of men. He was perhaps embittered by rebellions, and he thought that the only way of dealing with them was inordinate severity. Some of his measures were well conceived, but they failed for the lack of obvious precautions. It also seems that he was not ably assisted, which made him more furious.

As the result of the annexations in the south Muḥammad b. Tughluq was convinced that a new imperial centre was needed there. He selected Devagiri which he named Dawlatābād, and decided to establish a metropolis there in 727/1327. He built a beautiful city with well laid out streets and imposing buildings, and strengthened the rock-built citadel, the circumference of which, about 500 yards, had under the Hindu kings been scarped smoothly, so that scaling was impossible, with a deep ditch dug in the solid rock. This city was intended to be a second capital, or, as some historians assert, to replace Delhi completely as the capital of the empire. Many government officials, scholars and others went to Dawlat-

[1] For a full discussion, see Syed Moinul Haq, 'Was Mohammad bin Tughlak a parricide?' *Muslim University Journal,* Aligarh, v/2, (October, 1958), 17–48.

ābād to settle, and others whose livelihood depended upon the court followed. Anyone who voluntarily decided to settle at Dawlatābād was encouraged to do so. Efforts were made to facilitate the journey by providing food and rest at convenient distances, the two cities having first been connected by a good and shady road. It seems that the sultan was not satisfied with the results of the voluntary migration and, therefore, he used compulsion after two years. Even then the story that Delhi was reduced to utter desolation does not seem to be true.[1] The non-Muslim population was not forced to migrate, as this would have been pointless. The sultan's action proved to be extremely unpopular. There is little doubt, however, that, but for his foresight, Muslim influence in southern India would have received a serious setback when the sultanate of Delhi was involved in difficulties and the rise of independent provincial dynasties reduced the extent of its dominions. But for Dawlatābād, there would have been no Bahmanī kingdom to check the rising power of Vijayanagara. The sultan's compulsion, however, seems to have embittered his relations with his Muslim officials to such an extent that he was involved in a series of rebellions.

In 729/1329 the sultan raised the state demand on agricultural produce in the Ganges-Jamnā Do'āb. Here again it has been stated that the demand was increased tenfold and twentyfold, others have said that it was raised threefold and fourfold. The truth seems to be that the demand was increased by five to ten per cent.[2] This increase was resented by the population, who left their holdings and took to robbery. As the thick forests were impenetrable to cavalry it was customary for recalcitrant peasants to leave their hamlets and enter the forest with all their belongings. The sultan sent punitive expeditions, which made it more difficult to restore agriculture in this fertile province, and produced famine in the area right up to Delhi.

The sultan in 731–2/1130–2 introduced a 'forced' currency, replacing gold, silver and bullion coins by tokens of copper and brass. Intrinsically this was not unsound, but he forgot that craftsmen could forge the token coins: there was large-scale forgery, and the entire scheme failed. The sultan redeemed all the token coins at face value, which caused considerable loss to the treasury. It has been suggested that the sultan had grandiose ideas of conquest, and he thought that the introduction of

[1] A. Mahdī Ḥusain, *The rise and fall of Muḥammad bin Tughluq* (London, 1938), 116 ff.

[2] For fuller discussion, see I. H. Qureshi, *The administration of the sultanate of Dehlī* (Karachi, 1954), 115–17.

brass and copper coins would give him the means for carrying out his projects. This does not look plausible, because the sultan could not be so ignorant as to imagine that brass and copper could completely replace gold and silver. Another explanation, more credible, has been offered that there was scarcity of specie during this period, but the sultan's ability to redeem both genuine and forged token coins counters this argument.

The sultan had to march to the south from Delhi in 735/1335 because Sayyid Jalāl al-Dīn Aḥsan of Kaythal, who had been appointed governor of Ma'bar, had rebelled at Madura. When Muḥammad b. Tughluq reached Warangal, an epidemic of cholera spread in the army. The sultan himself was taken ill. The expedition was, therefore, abandoned, and Ma'bar was lost to the sultanate. The kingdom of Ma'bar or Madura lasted to 779/1378, when the dynasty came to an end. It had to fight constantly against its Hindu neighbours, and ultimately was destroyed by the forces of Vijayanagara.

Muḥammad b. Tughluq returned to Delhi and was, it seems, hard-pressed for funds, the treasury having been emptied by rebellions, lavish grants and unwise measures. He therefore started farming out revenues of large areas. Men of no substance, and with little experience of revenue matters, offered unrealistic sums of money, which they were unable to pay. Being afraid of the dire consequences, they rebelled. The resultant deterioration in agriculture was aggravated by the failure of the monsoons in the area around Delhi, where famine conditions prevailed. The sultan first introduced a daily ration of grain to the citizens, and tried to conciliate and encourage the peasants by making grants of money for bringing land back into cultivation. The scheme failed, mostly because of lack of rainfall, but also because by now the peasants were puzzled and had lost confidence. The sultan, therefore, went with his court and a large number of people of Delhi to the fertile province of Oudh (Awadh) which had prospered under the wise administrator, 'Ayn al-Mulk. The sultan established a camp on the west bank of the Ganges about 165 miles from Delhi, a city of straw sheds and walls, which he called Svargadvāra, 'the gate of Paradise'.

This gave the sultan some respite, but, despite all his difficulties, he had not given up the idea of further conquests. For a considerable time he had kept alive his ambition of conquering Transoxania and Khurāsān. When the situation in those areas did not warrant such an undertaking, he thought of bringing the mountain area of Kāngrā and beyond under his sway. He sent an army of 100,000 horse and a large number of foot into the mountains by way of Kāngrā. After the conquest of Kāngrā, the army marched into the mountains beyond and secured considerable success. However, when the rains came, the army was cut off. There was disease among men and horses and it decided to retreat. This was difficult, partly because of bad weather and landslides, and partly because the local population was hostile, and hurled stones when the army was marching through narrow passes and valleys. The army was almost completely annihilated. Some writers have thought that the sultan's intention was to invade China, but there seems to be little justification for this conclusion because the objective is clearly mentioned as Himāchal or Qarāchal, the Himālaya or 'black mountains'. The destruction of such a large army and the consequent dwindling of the sultan's prestige now made rebellion even easier.

From many sides came news of risings and rebellions. East Bengal became independent in 739/1338. In 740/1339 an officer 'Alī Shāh Kar rebelled and occupied Bīdar after having taken possession of the treasury at Gulbargā. This rebellion, however, was suppressed by Qutlugh Khān who had charge of Dawlatābād. It has been noted that the sultan had established a camp at Svargadvāra, where all arrangements were made by 'Ayn al-Mulk. A number of fugitives from the sultan's anger had taken shelter with the governor. The sultan's mind was poisoned, and he decided to transfer him from Oudh to the Deccan. This was unwise, as 'Ayn al-Mulk was popular because of his good administration, and was reluctant to go to the Deccan, which was in turmoil. But the sultan insisted and 'Ayn al-Mulk was advised to rebel. The sultan, despite his difficulties, gave battle and 'Ayn al-Mulk was defeated. He was carried before the sultan, who, instead of executing him, ordered his imprisonment. Later he was pardoned and reinstated in his government of Oudh. In 741/1340 Malik Shādū Lodī, governor of Mūltān, rebelled, and when the sultan marched against him he fled into Afghanistan. In 743/1343 there was a rebellion in the areas of Sunām, Sāmāna, Kaythal and Guhrām in the Panjāb. Before it could be properly suppressed there was a rebellion of the *amīrān-i ṣada*[1] in Gujarāt.

The sultan had come to think that the *amīrān-i ṣada* were responsible for all mischief. Eighty-nine of them were executed by 'Azīz Khammār,

[1] Sing. *amīr-i ṣada:* literally 'commander of a hundred', is often taken to mean commander of a hundred horse, and misleadingly translated 'centurion'. They commanded small contingents to maintain order in the countryside.

the governor of Mālwā, under the sultan's instructions. This spread horror among the *amīrān-i ṣada* of Gujarāt and the Deccan. The first to take up arms were those in Gujarāt. Muḥammad b. Tughluq appointed a council of regency at Delhi and marched towards Gujarāt. 'Azīz Khammār in the meanwhile had been defeated and put to death by rebels. The *amīrān-i ṣada* in Gujarāt were defeated with heavy losses. The sultan ordered the governor of Dawlatābād to send the *amīrān-i ṣada* of that province to Gujarāt. They were despatched, but at the end of the first day's march they decided to rebel. Then they imprisoned the governor, seized the fort and proclaimed Ismā'īl Mukh sultan of the Deccan under the title of Nāṣir al-Dīn Shāh. Those *amīrān-i ṣada* who were imprisoned in Gujarāt escaped, and joined Ismā'īl Mukh. The sultan marched against Dawlatābād, where the citadel held out. In the meanwhile there was another serious rebellion in Gujarāt under Ṭaghī, a cobbler, who had gathered around himself a considerable following. The sultan left Dawlatābād and marched against Ṭaghī.

Ṭaghī was a capable leader and the monarch was not able to corner him. In the meanwhile the situation in the Deccan deteriorated. Another *amīr-i ṣada*, Ḥasan, had shown greater initiative and Ismā'īl Mukh abdicated in his favour. This Ḥasan became sultan under the title of Abu'l-Muẓaffar 'Alā' al-Dīn Bahman Shāh. Muḥammad b. Tughluq abandoned the idea of recovering the Deccan, and decided to devote his entire energy to Ṭaghī, who escaped to Thatthā in Sind, where he joined the local rulers who were also in revolt. The sultan, having summoned reinforcements from Delhi and other places, marched to Sind, and was within a short distance from Thatthā when on 10 Muḥarram 752/9 March 1351 he was taken ill. Ten days later he died.

When Muḥammad b. Tughluq was worried because of his growing unpopularity amongst the Muslims, he thought that recognition from the caliph would strengthen his position. Therefore, after making diligent inquiries, he applied for recognition from the 'Abbasid shadow-caliph in Egypt. For three years the Friday prayers and the observance of the two '*Īds* were suspended and coin was issued in the name of the caliph. It was in 745/1344 that Ḥājjī Sa'īd Ṣarṣarī came from Egypt bearing a letter from the caliph. The envoy was received with the utmost respect and the Friday prayers and the '*Īds* were restored. Another important event of the reign was the visit of the well-known traveller Ibn Baṭṭūṭa, who was at the court from 734–43/1334–42.

Muḥammad b. Tughluq's reign was a complete failure. After initial success, in spite of his great ability and perseverence, his harshness and ill-advised measures ruined the sultanate, which in the early days of his reign had reached its climax. He was a man of great ability, but his genius was of a kind that takes no account of realities. A poor judge of men, he was unbalanced in his views, and knew no compromise.

When Muḥammad b. Tughluq's army found itself in difficulties in Sind, being left without a leader, it started retreating in disorder, and was harassed both by its Mongol allies and the local population. The sultan's cousin, Fērōz, was present in the camp, but he was unwilling to take up the responsibilities of the throne. Ultimately, because of the sad plight of the army, he was persuaded to ascend the throne under the title of Fērōz Shāh, on 24 Muḥarram 752/23 March 1351. The minister Khwāja Jahān had proclaimed at Delhi a child whom he called Muḥammad b. Tughluq's son, but whose claims are dismissed by the writers of the period. While still on his way he was joined by several important officials from Delhi. One of these was the able Malik Maqbūl, a converted Brahman of Telingānā, subsequently entitled Khān Jahān Maqbūl Telingānī. He was appointed *wazīr*. Khwāja Jahān was able to gather little support and came as a suppliant. He was received with kindness, but later was nevertheless killed. Five months after his succession Fērōz entered Delhi.

He was confronted with a colossal task. The general dissatisfaction engendered by Muḥammad b. Tughluq's policies had to be removed, and the people reconciled. In addition there was the difficulty of suppressing widespread rebellion. Fērōz Shāh recognized the futility of trying to reconquer all the lost provinces. This proved to be wise, because the sultan could use his forces in consolidating the areas that he controlled.

Fērōz Shāh made a good beginning by remitting outstanding debts to the state which had been mostly incurred by rash tax-farmers and government servants who had been given advances for the purposes of improvement of agriculture. He did not try to recover even the large sums of money which had been freely spent by Khwāja Jahān when seeking support for his nominee to the throne. Fērōz Shāh appointed Khwāja Ḥusām al-Dīn Junayd for the purpose of making a new assessment of the revenues of the sultanate. This had become necessary because Muḥammad b. Tughluq's measures had created chaos in the revenue records. However, with the help of local records, this task was completed in a period of six years, and many unjust cesses which had grown up as the result of the breakdown in administration were abolished. These measures were rewarded with success, agriculture was restored to its original condition, and a greater area was brought under cultivation. The townsfolk were not forgotten, and a number of small but vexatious taxes were abolished. With the increase in productivity prices came down, and maintained a steady level for the greater part of the reign. It is interesting to note that the level was almost the same as in the days of 'Alā' al-Dīn Muḥammad Khaljī, which shows that the Khaljī monarch's measures were economically sound. The difference was that Fērōz Shāh did not have to use any extraordinary administrative machinery for the purpose of maintaining prices. Further to improve cultivation, he dug a number of important canals and sank wells. The failure of monsoons during Muḥammad b. Tughluq's reign must have brought home to Fērōz Shāh the necessity of artificial irrigation. Canals had been constructed earlier, especially by Ghiyās̱ al-Dīn Tughluq, but Fērōz Shāh's canals were more important, and some of them have survived even until today.

Fērōz Shāh was a great builder. He restored a large number of old monuments which had fallen into disrepair, one of these being the famous Quṭb Mīnār at Delhi. He repaired a large number of towns and cities, which, because of rebellions and maladministration, had suffered during the last reign, and he founded several new cities, of which Ḥiṣār and Jawnpur are the most famous. The latter became the capital of the Sharqī kingdom, and developed into a great seat of learning. He built a new 'city of Delhi' called Fērōzābād, and created south of that Delhi a vast *madrasa* beside the large reservoir called Ḥawż Khāṣṣ. The imposing remains of pavilions and lecture halls are still intact. He is credited with the construction of three hundred towns, which perhaps is not an exaggeration if the restoration of townships which had suffered under Muḥammad b. Tughluq is taken into consideration. In addition, he built four large mosques, thirty palaces, and many other public works and buildings.

Fērōz Shāh displayed an interest in the past by removing two of Ashoka's pillars. One was re-erected inside the citadel of Fērōzābād, and the other set up near Kushk-i Shikār on the Ridge north of Delhi. Around the former was built a double-storeyed pavilion, and the monolithic pillar was mounted on a solid base so that it seemed to the casual observer that it stood on the vaulted roof of the building. It was gilded, and therefore came to be known as Mīnāra-i Zarrīn. It is interesting to note that the Brahmans in the reign of Fērōz Shāh were not able to read the inscriptions, and falsely told the sultan that they contained a prophecy about his coming to the throne, and promised him great success as a monarch.

In the process of conciliation, Fērōz Shāh had to secure the co-operation of the Muslim *'ulamā'* and religious leaders. Many of Muḥammad b. Tughluq's difficulties had arisen because of his alienation of this class, first by ordering many of them to migrate from Delhi to Dawlatābād and, later, by punishing some of them heavily because of their reluctance to identify themselves with his measures. Partly because of his own temperament, and partly because of need, Fērōz Shāh went out of his way to reconcile the religious leaders, and showed the utmost respect to them. Some of his intolerant actions can be ascribed to their influence. Though the sultan abolished discretionary capital punishment, a Brahman was burnt to death for insulting Islam and the Prophet. The accepted practice whereby priests, recluses and hermits of other religions are exempt from paying *jizya* had been liberally interpreted in India, and no Brahman, however wealthy, was asked to pay the tax. Fērōz Shāh imposed the tax, in all probability, on those Brahmans who were not engaged in religious work. This measure was unpopular, and a large number of Brahmans assembled in front of the palace, and threatened to burn themselves alive. The sultan did not relent, and ultimately other Hindus voluntarily undertook to pay the tax on behalf of the Brahmans. He also dealt severely with the Ismā'īlīs, who had become active once again. This animosity was as much due to their reputation for underground political work as to doctrinal differences.

Fērōz Shāh had no military ambitions, but for the purpose of the consolidation of his empire he had to undertake a number of campaigns. He had extricated Muḥammad b. Tughluq's army from a desperate situation with considerable success. He first turned his attention to Bengal, which had become independent. He would perhaps have left that kingdom alone but for the fact that its ruler, Ilyās, who had made himself master of west Bengal in 745/1345 and then annexed east Bengal in 752/1352, invaded Tirhut. Fērōz Shāh could not tolerate this invasion of his territories, and therefore marched from Delhi in 753/1353 and chased Ilyās away from Tirhut to his capital Pānduā, and from there into Ikdalā, which stood on an island in the Brahmaputra. As the monsoons would have cut his communications, Fērōz Shāh retreated and reached

Delhi in 755/1354. In 760/1359 he again invaded Bengal. Now the ruler was Sikandar Shāh, who had succeeded to the throne in 758/1357 and who, like his father Ilyās, had entrenched himself in Ikdalā. Fērōz Shāh, finding it impossible to reduce Ikdalā, ultimately agreed to negotiations which resulted in the recognition of Sikandar as a tributary on the annual payment of forty elephants. On his way back, Fērōz Shāh led an expedition from Jawnpur into Orissa, which he occupied. The raja of Orissa sued for peace, and was restored as a tributary on surrendering twenty elephants and promising to send the same number annually to Delhi. On the way back the sultan's army lost its bearings in the jungle, and reached Delhi only after considerable hardship.

Khān Jahān Maqbūl Telingānī died in 774/1372 and was succeeded by his son, who also received the title of Khān Jahān. Next year Fērōz's eldest son, Fatḥ Khān, died. After this Fērōz Shāh was gradually reduced to utter senility, and became incapable of exercising control or judgment. The minister now started on a career of intrigue which ultimately resulted in civil war. Fērōz Shāh died in 790/1388 at the age of eighty-three. As the result of a prolonged struggle between the nobles and the princes of the royal family, the dynasty sank into insignificance and all the good work done by Fērōz Shāh was destroyed. It was in this state of chaos that Tīmūr marched upon Delhi in 801/1398. The forces of the sultanate were decisively beaten in a battle near Delhi, although even in this decrepit state they gave a good account of themselves. Tīmūr won huge booty, not only from Delhi but from the entire area on his route. Internal dissensions had demolished the structure of a mighty empire within a period of less than two decades. The last monarch of the dynasty, Maḥmūd, earned the satire that 'the writ of the lord of the world runs from Delhi to Pālam', Pālam being about nine miles from the city.

THE SAYYID AND LODĪ DYNASTIES IN DELHI

A certain Khiżr Khān had been appointed governor of Mūltān by Fērōz Shāh. When Tīmūr invaded the sultanate, Khiżr Khān cast his lot with him and was appointed governor of the Panjāb and Upper Sind. He consolidated his power, and ultimately absorbed Delhi. Thus he laid the foundation of the Sayyid dynasty, so named because Khiżr claimed to be a *sayyid*, i.e. a descendant of the Prophet. The history of his reign is mostly a narrative of expeditions against recalcitrant chiefs for the collection of revenue and their reduction to allegiance. He died in 824/1421, and was succeeded by his son Mubārak Shāh who, by constant fighting, was able to keep his territories together. Mubārak was assassinated at the instigation of his minister, Sarwar al-Mulk, who was annoyed at the curtailment of his powers, and was succeeded in 837/1434 by his nephew Muḥammad Shāh who, through his folly, alienated the sympathies of the supporters of the dynasty. His son 'Alā' al-Dīn 'Ālam Shāh succeeded him in 847/1444. 'Ālam Shāh displayed little interest in his office, and lived in comparative obscurity enjoying the income of the area settled upon him by Buhlūl Lodī.

One of the contestants for power, the minister Ḥamīd Khān, invited an Afghan noble, Buhlūl, to Delhi. He seized power, and, after 'Ālam Shāh's abdication in 855/1451, enthroned himself. Bahlūl was successful in obtaining powerful Afghan support. He used tact and foresight, and treated the Afghan nobles with consideration and did not assume airs of superiority. Gradually he built up so much strength that he was able to defeat Ḥusayn Shāh of Jawnpur, and to absorb the Sharqī kingdom into the sultanate (see p. 24). He died in 894/1489 and was succeeded by Sikandar Lodī, who was a capable monarch. His brother Bārbak, appointed governor of Jawnpur by Buhlūl, refused to recognize Sikandar's authority, and was defeated at Kannawj; but he was treated with leniency and was permitted to rule Jawnpur as a vassal. Bārbak showed little capacity for administration and was twice unable to control rebellions. At last he was arrested and Sikandar took over the administration. Ḥusayn Sharqī, who had been ousted by Buhlūl and was in exile, tried to create trouble. At last he took the field, was defeated near Banāras, and fled to Bengal where he lived as a pensioner. Sikandar was able to bring Bihār under his complete control. The raja of Tirhut also submitted. Sikandar next led an expedition into Bengal, where Ḥusayn Shāh of Bengal sent his son Dāniyāl for negotiations. Sikandar wisely entered into a treaty by which the two rulers agreed to respect each other's frontiers. Sikandar conquered Dholpur, and, to extend his authority over Rājpūtānā, he established his capital at Āgrā in 910/1504.

The sultan took great interest in the welfare of his subjects. He put the administration on a sound foundation. His intelligence system was so good that the credulous believed that he had supernatural powers. He was firm and tactful, and, without weakening their support, he kept the Afghans under discipline. He displayed intolerance in suppressing some Hindu religious practices. He died in 923/1517 and was succeeded by Ibrāhīm Lodī who alienated the sympathies of the Afghan nobles. One of them called upon Bābur, who ousted the dynasty in 932/1526.

PROVINCIAL DYNASTIES DURING THE TIME OF THE DELHI SULTANATE

The Sharqī dynasty of Jawnpur was established (796/1394) by Malik Sarwar, who was given the titles of Khwāja Jahān and Malik al-Sharq, and appointed governor of the eastern provinces by Nāṣir al-Dīn Maḥmūd, whom Sarwar had put on the throne of Delhi (795/1392). When Tīmūr invaded Delhi, Sarwar found it convenient to become independent. At his death he left a kingdom extending from 'Alīgarh in the west to Bihār and Tirhut in the east, which early received tribute from the Bengal sultans, for whom it was a convenient buffer-state between themselves and Delhi. Malik Sarwar was succeeded by his adopted son, Qaranful, who ascended the throne as Mubārak Shāh in 802/1399. His son Ibrāhīm Shāh, who came to the throne in 804/1402, was a cultured prince and a great patron of learning. His reign established the Sharqī sultanate as one of the major powers of north India. Because of the disturbed conditions in Delhi, a large number of scholars migrated and built up Jawnpur as a great seat of art, letters and religion as well as of a distinguished building activity. There were constant but always indecisive hostilities with Mālwā, which continued under Ibrāhīm's son Maḥmūd (844–61/1440–57); the latter even besieged Delhi in 856/1452 in an attempt to oust Buhlūl Lodī, and extended the kingdom to the south. The last sultan, Ḥusayn, whose army was possibly the strongest in India, and who had married the daughter of 'Ālam Shāh, the last Sayyid king of Delhi, made several attempts on her behalf to capture Delhi until decisively beaten by Buhlūl in early 884/spring 1479. Delhi thereupon annexed the Sharqī territories, and Ḥusayn was thereafter capable of no more than fomenting dissensions between rival Lodī nobles after Buhlūl's death.

It has already been noticed that Balban's son, Bughrā Khān, established himself as an independent ruler of Bengal (see above, p. 8). On the death of Shams al-Dīn Fērōz there was a war of succession and Ghiyās̱ al-Dīn Tughluq installed Nāṣir al-Dīn on the Bengal throne at Lakhnawti and annexed the rest of the kingdom (see above, p. 13). During Muḥammad b. Tughluq's reign, Bahādur, who had been displaced by Ghiyās̱ al-Dīn Tughluq, was placed on the throne of Sonārgāon under the tutelage of an official. Bahādur rebelled and was executed. Once again, because

Muḥammad b. Tughluq's attention was diverted by rebellions elsewhere, there was civil war in Bengal, which lasted until Fērōz Shāh invaded Bengal to chastise Ilyās. We have seen (pp. 21–2) that Fērōz recognized the independence of Bengal under Sikandar Shāh, who was wounded when his son A'ẓam rebelled in 795/1393. Sikandar Shāh died in the arms of A'ẓam, who ascended the throne with the title of Ghiyāṯ al-Dīn A'ẓam Shāh. He was a patron of learning and is also known for his sense of justice. He died in 798/1396. A Hindu official, Rājā Ganēsh, became *de facto* ruler, and is said to have persecuted Islam; at any rate a well-known Muslim saint, Quṭb al-'Ālam, invited Ibrāhīm Shāh of Jawnpur to attack Bengal for this reason. When Ibrāhīm's forces invaded Bengal, Ganēsh gave his son Jādav to the saint for conversion to Islam, and this son was raised to the throne under the title of Jalāl al-Dīn Muḥammad after Ganēsh's death (818/1415). The saint now interceded with Ibrāhīm, who reluctantly retired. Jalāl al-Dīn's reign seems to have been a time of peace and prosperity: architecture is to some extent a political barometer, and the buildings of this period are renowned for their magnificence. There is also some evidence for the growth of maritime trade with China. Then follows a period when the history of Bengal offers little beyond a tale of constant internecine warfare and intrigue. The conflict between Delhi and Jawnpur removed the threat from the west, although the east was troubled by disturbances in the Arakan province. The Ilyās Shāhī dynasty, restored in 837/1433, was finally superseded by a succession of Ḥabshī rulers, descendants of a large colony of Abyssinian slaves imported by the Ilyās Shāhīs. Ultimately the nobles raised Sayyid Ḥusayn to the throne in 898/1493. It was in his reign that Ḥusayn Shāh of the Sharqī dynasty took refuge in Bengal. Sayyid Ḥusayn recovered several lost parts of his kingdom and extended its frontiers by annexing Assam; he died in 924/1518. Some of the sultans of Bengal were enlightened patrons of literature. They showed a liberal attitude towards their Hindu subjects, especially those belonging to the lower castes, who reciprocated by depicting them in literature as their liberators from the tyranny of the Brahmans.

Islam was introduced into Kashmir by Shāh Mīr or Mīrzā of Swāt in 713/1313. He entered the service of the Hindu ruler Sūhadeva, and eventually, in about 739/1339, became the ruler with the title of Shams al-Dīn Shāh. The rule of his third (?) son Shihāb al-Dīn (755–74/1354–73 ?) saw Kashmir victorious over most of her Hindu neighbours. The next important ruler was Sikandar (*c.* 791–815/1389–1413), commonly called

Butshikan (idol-breaker) because of his intolerance of Hinduism. He made Kashmir a predominantly Muslim state. Four years after his death came Zayn al-ʿĀbidīn (823–75/1420–70), who reversed Sikandar's policies of persecution by recalling the exiled Brahmans and permitting the observance of Hindu practices, which had been prohibited during the reign of Sikandar, subject to their conforming to the Hindu scriptures. He suspended the *jizya,* abolished illegal taxes, and besides extensive patronage of literature and music was distinguished in public works and buildings. He maintained friendly relations with other rulers both Muslim and Hindu. But after his death the royal power declined, and a succession of puppet kings was eventually displaced by one of the powerful tribes.

When the Ghaznavid hold in Sind weakened because of Masʿūd's difficulties, the local dynasty of Sūmrās who were Ismāʿīlīs by faith established themselves in Sind. They were succeeded by the Sammās, a Sunnī dynasty, about 736/1335. They were of local origin and used the indigenous title of *Jām*. In Fērōz Shāh's reign, Jām Banhbina and Jām Jūnān, who were joint rulers owing allegiance to Delhi, instigated some Mongols to raid the sultan's dominions, causing Fērōz's Sind expedition of 767/1366 in which the Mongols were defeated and the rulers brought captive to Delhi. They were later released, and Jūnān returned to rule in Sind. After the death of Fērōz Shāh the Sammas became independent of Delhi. Little is known of events in Sind after this, and the chronology is uncertain; but the later Sammā kings are known to have been connected by marriage to the royal house of Gujarāt, and received support from Gujarāt when rebels, mostly Mongols of the Arghūn tribe, rose against the *Jām*, and again when reports came of persecution of Muslims by local Hindus. The dynasty, however, continued to rule until 933/1527, when the Arghūns gained control of Sind.

In Gujarāt Muẓaffar Khān, who had been appointed governor in 793/1391, declared his independence after five years. He was imprisoned by his son Tātār Khān, who proclaimed himself sultan under the title of Muḥammad Shāh in 806/1403, but the latter was poisoned and Muẓaffar was released in 810/1407. Muẓaffar was succeeded (813/1410) by his grandson, Aḥmad Shāh, who ruled for a period of thirty-two years and spent a good deal of his time in consolidating and extending his kingdom and improving its administration, building his capital of Aḥmadābād, and establishing Islam throughout his dominions. The most famous ruler of this dynasty was Maḥmūd I (862–917/1458–1511). It was during his reign that Gujarāt made common cause with the Mamluks of Egypt and defeated the Portuguese fleet off Chaul in 913/1508. The Portuguese, however, appeared with a stronger force next year and defeated the Muslim navies near the island of Diu (Dīw). This defeat destroyed Muslim trade in the Arabian Sea. Bahādur Shāh, 932–43/1526–37, who was engaged in war against the Mughal Humāyūn as well as continually against the Portuguese, was the last great sultan of Gujarāt, for he was followed by more puppet kings supported by rival nobles. The local Ḥabshī community rose to much power, as did the minor Mughal princelings known as the Mīrzās; and there was virtual anarchy for a few years before Akbar's conquest of the province in 980–1/1572–3.

Malik Rājā, an able official appointed by Fērōz Shāh of Delhi to an *iqṭā*ʿ near Thālnēr, in the Sātpura hills between the rivers Narbadā and Tāptī, established himself sufficiently to act independently of Delhi, after the death of Fērōz, from about 784/1382, and sought alliance with Mālwā through a royal marriage. On his death in 801/1399, his state of Khāndēsh was divided between his two sons, of whom the elder, Naṣīr Khān, receiving scant support from Mālwā against his younger brother, had to recognize the overlordship of Gujarāt in 820/1417—a necessity in the case also of some later rulers, for alliances by marriage with neighbouring states gave little guarantee of their support. The rulers of this house, the Fārūqīs, were not recognized as equals by their stronger neighbours, and bore only the title of khan; yet the state was not interfered with much by its neighbours, partly because of the strength of its fortress Asīrgarh, partly because it formed a natural buffer-state between the great powers, Mālwā/Gujarāt and Mālwā/Bahmanī (later, after the fragmentation of the Bahmanī sultanate, between Mālwā and Aḥmadnagar also). Gujarāt later became a powerful ally, especially in the time of Muḥammad Khān I (926–43/1520–37) whose uncle, Bahādur Shāh, designated him his heir. By 972/1564 Khāndēsh had to accept the Mughals as overlords, as Gujarāt was in anarchy; Mālwā had been annexed by the Mughals, Aḥmadnagar was more concerned with her southern neighbours, and the balance of power had so changed that Khāndēsh's position as a buffer state was no longer tenable. Khāndēsh at first connived at the Mughal manipulation of the Aḥmadnagar throne, but eventually was annexed by the Mughals in 1009/1601.

The sultanate of Mālwā was established in 794/1392 at Dhār by Dilāwar Khān Ghūrī, who had been appointed governor of Mālwā by Fērōz Shāh or his successor. He died in 808/1405, and was succeeded by his son, Alp Khān, who assumed the title of Hōshang Shāh and transferred the capital to Māndū. Hōshang was a capable monarch who extended his kingdom and brought considerable prosperity. He died in 838/1435 and was succeeded by his son Muḥammad Shāh, who alienated the sympathies of his nobles because of cruelty. At last Maḥmūd Khān, a general and counsellor of Hōshang and the son of the *wazīr*, poisoned the sultan and made himself monarch in 839/1436. During his long reign the Mālwā sultanate reached its greatest extent, and he attacked not only his neighbours but also Jawnpur, the Deccan, and even Delhi. He was a good Muslim and a patron of the arts. He was succeeded by Ghiyāṯ al-Dīn (873–905/1469–1500), a man of peaceful disposition, and several minor kings, under whom Mālwā fell in 937/1531 to Gujarāt, then to Humāyūn, next to Shēr Shāh, and finally to Akbar in 968/1561.

Muḥammad b. Tughluq's loss of hegemony over Dawlatābād and the rise of 'Alā' al-Dīn Bahman Shāh to independence in the Deccan has been mentioned above (p. 18). After extensive campaigns of conquest which brought the Deccan—roughly the boundaries of the old Ḥaydarābād state before the 1956 reorganization of Indian provinces—under his control, he established his permanent capital at Gulbargā, where it remained until *c.* 827/1424. The second sultan, the dignified Muḥammad I (759–76/1358–75), set the kingdom on a sound footing, bringing in careful and extensive administrative reforms, both civil and military. The sultanate, peaceful internally, was involved in continual skirmishing with the Hindu state of Vijayanagara to the south, the *do'ab* of the Rāychūr district being a constant bone of contention; but the introduction of gunpowder gave the Bahmanīs the advantage over the numerous but less organized Vijayanagara forces. The fifth sultan, Muḥammad II (780–99/1378–97), did for Bahmanī culture what Muḥammad I had done for its administration, attracting numerous Persian and Arab poets and theologians (even Ḥāfiẓ of Shīrāz was invited), foreign civil and military architects, tile-workers and calligraphers, and not neglecting certain elements of Hindu culture. On his death a Turkish slave seized power and installed a puppet ruler, but Fērōz, a grandson of the first sultan, restored the dignity of the royal house, and succeeded as sultan in 800/1397. with his brother Aḥmad as *amīr al-umarā'*. In a reorganization of the administration Fērōz employed Brahmans extensively, probably to balance the high proportion of influential 'foreigners' (Persians and 'Irāqīs). He took pains to maintain good relations with his Hindu neighbours, taking wives from several prominent Hindu houses, not excluding Vijayanagara (being persuaded, although a Sunnī, that he could contract *mut'a* alliances: Shī'ī doctrines were being popularized in the Deccan at this time), although he was involved in border struggles with Vijayanagara and the Gond kings. Some opposition to Fērōz at the end of his reign centred round the Chishtī saint, Gēsū Dārāz, who favoured his brother Aḥmad, to whom Fērōz assigned the throne in 825/1422. The Gulbargā period ended in an atmosphere of constant intrigue.

Aḥmad soon moved his capital to Bīdar; Gulbargā, besides being a centre of intrigue, was also too near to the Vijayanagara kingdom for comfort. He strengthened his northern frontiers in order to attack Mālwā, Gujarāt and Khāndēsh in pursuit of the Bahmanīs' putative sovereignty over those regions 'conferred' on Fērōz by Tīmūr in 803/1401 (not recorded by Tīmūr's historians, but apparently confirmed by the actions of the Bahmanīs' neighbours at the time); and there were indeed hostilities with Mālwā and Gujarāt, and matrimonial alliances with Khāndēsh. Aḥmad Shāh, pious enough to have been generally known as *walī*, was sufficiently strong to manage the rival factions; not so his son Aḥmad II (839–62/1436–58), under whom faction between local (Dakhnī) and foreign Muslims crippled the stability of the state. A third party of importance was formed by the Ḥabshīs, who as Sunnīs generally supported the Dakhnīs against the predominantly Shī'ī foreigners, but were not invariably so aligned. The next king, Humāyūn, tried to maintain a balance between Dakhnīs and foreigners and to consolidate the kingdom in his short reign. In the reign of two minors the regent, the brilliant Persian Maḥmūd Gāwān, was able to pursue a similar policy of conciliation at home, in spite of much military activity against Vijayanagara. Maḥmūd Gāwān was the real power in the state until his assassination in 886/1481 by a Dakhnī-Ḥabshī conspiracy, after which there was political chaos. The reign of Maḥmūd, from 887/1482, saw the gradual decline of the Bahmanī state, which had earlier been a much greater force, politically and culturally, than the Delhi sultanate. The king became completely subservient to a Sunnī Turkish *wazīr*, Qāsim Barīd, in Bīdar, The provincial governors Niẓām al-Mulk (Aḥmadnagar), 'Imād al-Mulk (Barār), and Yūsuf 'Ādil Khān (Gulbargā and Bījāpur), breaking away from the Barīdī ascendancy in about 895/1490, became autonomous in their own territories where they founded respectively the Niẓām Shāhī, 'Imād Shāhī and 'Ādil Shāhī dynasties. The governor of Telingānā at Golkondā, Sulṭān Qulī Quṭb al-Mulk, who became virtually independent of Bīdar after 924/1518, was similarly the founder of the Quṭb Shāhī dynasty. Bahmanī sultans held the throne as Barīdī puppets until 934/1528, when the Barīd family succeeded as the Barīd Shāhī dynasty of Bīdar.

ADMINISTRATION

In the beginning, the sultans of Delhi recognized the suzerainty of the caliphs of Baghdād. The first investiture took place under Iltutmish, when in 626/1229 the emissaries brought a diploma from the Caliph al-Mustanṣir. On al-Musta'ṣim's death in 656/1258, the sultans were confronted with a difficulty, because the office of the caliph was not filled. They continued al-Musta'ṣim's name on the coinage until Jalāl al-Dīn Fērōz Khaljī's death in 695/1296, nearly forty years later. It has been suggested that 'Alā' al-Dīn Khaljī claimed to be caliph within his own dominions, but the evidence is not conclusive. His son, Mubārak Shāh, definitely claimed to be caliph. After his death there was no revival of the claim. Muḥammad b. Tughluq was persuaded to believe that recognition from the caliph was absolutely essential. He therefore applied to the caliph in Cairo, and received a diploma in 745/1344. Fērōz Shāh also received a diploma. The historian Firishta says that the Bahmanī kingdom also received recognition from Cairo, but this is doubtful in view of a clear statement by Fērōz Shāh to the contrary. The Sayyids and the Lodīs made vague references to the caliph on their coins.

The sultans of Delhi adhered to the legal conception of the position of the sultan which was common throughout the Muslim world. They also adhered to the form of an election by the *élite*. After the nobles had formally elected a monarch, they swore allegiance and later, the oath was taken by the people in the mosques of the state. The election of a sultan was in fact often purely nominal, because the candidate had already decided the issue by conquest or by the possession of superior force. The sultan was virtually bound by the election to control the state, defend Islam and its territories, protect his subjects and settle disputes between them, collect taxes and rightly administer the public treasury, and enforce the criminal code. It follows that an elected sultan could also be deposed for breach of those conditions, and a number of sultans of Delhi were in fact so removed for incompetence; loss of the mental faculties, physical infirmity, or blindness, were also held to render a ruler liable to dethronement. There was no prescriptive hereditary right of succession, and not many sultans were succeeded by their sons; but the nobles frequently limited the choice of successor from among members of the ruling house. In the Bahmanī sultanate, however, primogeniture became normal after Aḥmad Shāh Walī. As in other Islamic states, the mention of the ruler's name in the *khuṭba* and the minting of coins in his name were considered the most important attributes of sovereignty.

The administration of the sultanate was based upon models which had already developed under the 'Abbasids and their successors. All matters relating to the royal household were in the hands of the *wakīl-i dār*, while court functions and audiences were in the hands of *ḥājibs* under an *amīr ḥājib* or *bārbak*. The imperial household required a large commissariat which was divided into departments called *kārkhānas*. Some of these manufactured articles of use, others maintained stables, of which the *pāygāh* (stud) and the *fīl-khāna* (elephant-stables) were more important. Possession of elephants in India was a royal prerogative, not confined to Muslim kings. The *fīl-khāna* was maintained in the capital; for no ruler would permit a concentration of elephants in a distant town, from where they might have been used against him. The slaves were at first an integral part of the royal household, and the Turkish slaves of the early rulers of Delhi were well treated, given minor household offices, and promoted to such high posts as their merit fitted them—no office in the state being beyond their reach. But their power could be dangerous to the state, as both Iltutmish and Balban found when they had to deal with powerful slave nobles of previous reigns. Yet monarchy had often to rely on its slaves to counter the high-handedness of nobles, and many a battle, besides more domestic conflicts, was won for a sultan by the large force of slaves under his command. In the time of Fērōz Shāh, when prisoners of war and captive rebels were also enslaved, a separate department was organized to deal with their vast numbers. Ibn Baṭṭūṭa notices Ḥabshī[1] slaves employed in large numbers all over India, including many employed at sea.

The civil administration was mostly in the hand of the *wazīr*, who was the finance minister and chief adviser of the monarch. The *wazīr* (later often known by the honorific *khwāja jahān*) was assisted by two officers of ministerial rank, the *mushrif-i mamālik* and the *mustawfī-i mamālik*. The former was the accountant-general and the latter the auditor-general.

[1] Nominally Abyssinian, certainly African. For an account of them in India, see *EI2*, s.v. Ḥabshī (J. Burton-Page).

All affairs relating to the recruitment and maintenance of the army were dealt with by the *'āriẓ-i mamālik*. The *dabīr-i khāṣṣ* was in charge of state correspondence in the *dīwān-i inshā'*. The *barīd-i mamālik* was the head of the state information agency, including intelligence. Religious affairs were under the *ṣadr al-ṣudūr*, who generally was also the *qāẓī-i mamālik*, the chief judge of the empire.

The main source of income was the state demand on agricultural produce, most of the area being treated as *kharājī* land. Lands granted for religious purposes were generally treated as *'ushrī*. Assessment was mostly made on the basis of schedules of average produce applied to the area cultivated, which was measured. In case of a dispute, the peasant could demand crop-sharing. The demand was levied mostly in kind, and varied from area to area, depending upon local tradition. The level was generally one-fifth of the gross produce, which was raised by 'Alā' al-Dīn Khaljī to a half. It was again lowered to a fifth by Ghiyās̱ al-Dīn Tughluq. When Muḥammad b. Tughluq tried to enhance the demand in the Do'āb, there was disaffection and even rebellion. An important part was played by Hindu chiefs who acted in many areas as intermediaries between the government and the peasants. They, however, had their functions strictly defined, and care was taken that the peasant, who was recognized as the owner of the land, did not have to pay more than the prescribed demand.

The sultans maintained an excellent standing army, in which cavalry played the central role. Descriptive rolls of soldiers and their mounts were maintained, horses were branded, and annual reviews held to prevent fraud. Elephants were considered to be a great asset. There was infantry as well, recruited mainly from Hindus and others who could not afford a horse, and frequently not maintained as a permanent cadre except for the body-guards. The army was organized on a decimal basis.

The departments of justice, *ḥisba* (public morals) and police functioned in accordance with the general pattern that had developed elsewhere in the Muslim world. Justice was dispensed through *maẓālim* (governmental and administrative), *qaẓā* (civil), and *siyāsa* (martial law and cases of rebellion) courts. The chief of the police in the city was known by a term of Hindu origin—*kotwāl*.

The provincial government was under governors known as *wālīs* or *muqṭi's*. The provinces were divided into *shiqqs*, the *shiqqs* into *parganas*, and *parganas* into collections of *dihs* or villages. A *dih* was not only the residential part of a village but also included the agricultural land attached to it. The *pargana* was the main unit of local administration. Later the *shiqqs* came to be known as *sarkārs*. The pattern of the central government was repeated at the provincial level and the provincial departments corresponded directly with their counterparts at the centre. The head of the *pargana* administration was a *mutaṣarrif* who was also called an *'āmil*.

For most of the period the administration worked smoothly and a change of dynasty did not seriously affect its efficiency. However, it broke down under Muḥammad b. Tughluq with disastrous consequences. This system prevailed with only minor alterations in the provincial kingdoms as well when they became independent.

ASPECTS OF CULTURE

Among the great names associated with the Ghaznavids at Lahore are those of Abu'l-Faraj Rūnī, whose *dīwān* has been published in Persia. Mas'ūd Sa'd Salmān (441–515/1048–1121) was born and educated at Lahore and wrote in Persian, Arabic and the local dialect, but only his Persian poetry has been preserved and published. The famous author of *Kashf al-maḥjūb*, Sayyid 'Alī Hujwīrī, also belongs to this period. He died in 463/1071 and was buried at Lahore. *Imām* Ḥasan al-Saghānī, born at Lahore in 576/1181 and educated there, was a well-known lexicographer and jurist, and his *Mashāriq al-anwār* is a standard book on *Ḥadīth*. The greatest writer associated with Delhi is Amīr Khusraw (651–725/1253–1325), who wrote voluminous works in poetry and prose on historical subjects. His friend Ḥasan Sijzī is also famous as a poet, though not so prolific as Amīr Khusraw. Muḥammad b. Tughluq's court was also adorned by Badr-i Chāch, who has left a number of *qaṣīdas* in his praise which contain some historical information. And no account of Muḥammad b. Tughluq's court would be complete without mention of that acute observer, the Moorish traveller Ibn Baṭṭūṭa, whose *Riḥla* presents an invaluable view of fourteenth-century India through independent eyes. A good amount of historical writing was also produced in this period.[1]

The contribution to music made by Muslims in India is considerable. They certainly brought to India a number of Persian, Central Asian and Arab instruments, and introduced new musical modes and forms. In the absence of exact evidence of the period the Muslim contribution can

[1] For a detailed study of historians of this period, see P. Hardy, *Historians of medieval India* (London, 1960).

perhaps be appreciated only by the expert, who can evolve some sort of calculus from the evidence of the ancient Sanskrit texts on the original Indian music, and the divergences from this standard of modern north Indian music; with the proviso, however, that ancient, *folk*-music, not specifically dealt with in the old texts, may have persisted into the Muslim period.[1]

This period saw a great effort on the part of the Ṣūfīs to reconvert the Ismāʿīlīs in Sind to Sunnī Islam and to spread Islam amongst non-Muslims as well. Ismāʿīlī effort did not come to an end and there are many communities, some Hindu in origin, who still retain their Ismāʿīlī beliefs. The four main Ṣūfī orders in the sub-continent were the Chishtiyya, the Qādiriyya, the Suhrawardiyya and the Naqshbandiyya. It was through the efforts of these orders that a Muslim community grew up. This community did not consist only of converts, as is often imagined, but included a fair element of descendants of migrants from various regions, especially Central Asia and Persia. The school of jurisprudence which found favour was the Ḥanafiyya. Islam, especially some aspects of Sufism, had some impact upon the thought of some Hindu religious reformers from the fifteenth century.

[1] For a discussion on the nature of the Muslim contribution to music in India, see now N. A. Jairazbhoy, article 'Music', in *EI2*, s.v. Hind.

CHAPTER 2

INDIA UNDER THE MUGHALS

THE MUGHAL EMPERORS

Bābur

A Timurid prince, 'Umar Shaykh Mīrzā, ruler of Farghānā, died in 899/1494, leaving little more than a title to his principality for his son Bābur, then eleven years old. Bābur had to fight not only to defend Farghānā but also to fulfil his ambition of possessing Samarqand because of its prestige as the main city of Central Asia. His adventures described in his excellent memoirs read like a romance. He did succeed in occupying Samarqand, only to lose it again. His lasting possession proved to be Kābul which he occupied in 910/1504, and which became his headquarters. All else, including Farghānā, he lost in the struggle.

The rise of the Özbegs and the Safavids affected Bābur's career deeply. The Özbegs were able to extinguish the power of the Timurids because they proved incapable of serious and joint effort. The Safavids came into conflict with the Özbegs and defeated them. Bābur was restored to the kingdom of Samarqand as a vassal of Shāh Ismā'īl I after the defeat and death of Muḥammad Shaybānī Khān Özbeg (917/1511). The Safavids were defeated in the battle of Ghujduwān, and Bābur lost all hope of ruling Samarqand, and returned to Kābul (918/1512). When Bābur felt secure, his mind turned towards India. Ibrāhīm Lodī, the sultan of Delhi, had alienated his nobles. Dawlat Khān, the governor of Lahore, sent messengers to Kābul offering allegiance in return for help. Ibrāhīm's uncle, 'Ālam Khān, also went to Kābul seeking assistance to capture the throne of Delhi. Bābur, who had made some incursions into the Panjāb before, now marched, ostensibly to help Dawlat Khān, and captured Lahore. Dawlat Khān, finding that Bābur had no intention of handing over Lahore to him, turned hostile. In the meanwhile 'Ālam Khān attacked Delhi with the help of some Mughal troops without success. Bābur, whose attention had been diverted because of the siege of Balkh by the Özbegs, returned and heard at Siālkot of 'Ālam Khān's failure. Dawlāt Khān surrendered and died soon after, Ibrāhīm marched from Delhi, while Bābur occupied Pānīpat and waited for Ibrāhīm.

The first battle of Pānīpat (932/1526) is remarkable because Bābur succeeded in defeating an army of 100,000 men and 1,000 elephants with a small force of about 25,000. Bābur entered Delhi and his eldest son, Humāyūn, was sent to Āgrā. Bābur's name was read in the *khuṭba* as the emperor of Hindustan. Thus was established the Mughal empire.

Bābur had still to contend with formidable forces. The remnant of the Afghan nobles elected Ibrāhīm's brother, Maḥmūd, as sultan. Rānā Sāngā of Chitor, the head of a strong Rajput confederacy, saw in the débâcle of the Lodīs the opportunity of gaining vast territories; but Bābur defeated him at Khānua in 933/1527.

Bābur then turned his attention to Maḥmūd Lodī. The decisive battle was fought in 936/1529 near the confluence of the Gogra (Ghāgrā) with the Ganges, where Bābur was once again victorious. He was also able to conclude a treaty of peace with Nuṣrat Shāh, the king of Bengal. A year afterwards Bābur was taken ill, and died in 937/1530, nominating Humāyūn as his successor.

Bābur was not only a valiant soldier and a capable general but also an accomplished writer and a poet of merit. His memoirs are famous. Because of his preoccupations, some entries are sketchy as if made in a diary, but in other places the reader is fully compensated by Bābur's excellent pen-pictures of important contemporaries. He has also recorded a considerable amount of natural data of which he seemed to be a keen observer. In addition there are his essays in criticism of literary works and paintings, buildings and institutions. Outstanding is his great sincerity, which prevents him from indulging in self-praise or hiding his shortcomings. He emerges as a lovable, generous, capable and brave man, who wins the admiration and sympathy of the discerning reader by telling all about himself, whether creditable or otherwise.

Humāyūn

Humāyūn succeeded to the throne without any trouble, but later his younger brothers, Kāmrān, 'Askarī and Hindāl, created difficulties. After his defeat at the hands of Bābur, Maḥmūd Lodī had fled to Bengal. Now he invaded the Mughal territories and took Jawnpur. Humāyūn marched against him and gained a decisive victory.

The sultan of Gujarāt, Bahādur Shāh, thought it opportune to send three columns against various points in Mughal territories, all of which were defeated. Bahādur Shāh, who had been besieging Chitor, turned after its fall towards Humāyūn, who had reached Mandasor, only sixty miles away, in pursuit of one of the Gujarāt columns. Bahādur Shāh, instead of attacking Humāyūn, entrenched himself in a camp. The Mughals cut off all supplies, and ultimately Bahādur Shāh had to escape to Māndū (941/1535).

Humāyūn followed him. The fort fell, and Bahādur once again escaped with the Mughals in pursuit. He succeeded in reaching Diu (Dīw). Humāyūn, leaving 'Askarī at Aḥmadābād, returned to Māndū to organize the administration of Mālwā. 'Askarī did nothing to oust Bahādur Shāh from Diu, nor did he organize the administration. Bahādur Shāh was soon able to collect a force, and marched upon Aḥmadābād. 'Askarī retreated in the direction of Āgrā. Thus Gujarāt was won and lost in a little over one year. It was reported to Humāyūn that 'Askarī's followers had treasonable designs, so Humāyūn left Mālwā and marched towards Āgrā, meeting 'Askarī's forces on the way, but did not punish 'Askarī because, in addition to the loss of Gujarāt, there had come news of difficulties with the Afghans in the east. After Humāyūn's march from Māndū, Mālwā was seized by Mallū Khān who had been governor before the Mughal occupation.

At this juncture Humāyūn encountered a formidable rival in the Afghan, Shēr Khān, the son of Ḥasan Khān who held the *parganas* of Sahsarām, Ḥājīpur and Khawāṣpur Tāndā. Farīd, as Shēr Khān was originally called, fled from Sahsarām to Jawnpur because of his father's coldness, as Ḥasan was completely under the influence of Farīd's step-mother. At Jawnpur he devoted himself to his studies, and, when his father once visited Jawnpur, he was so struck with Farīd's capacity that he invited him back and put him in charge of his *parganas*. Here he showed his great talent for good administration.

This further excited his step-mother's jealousy, and he was soon forced to leave again, and seek service in Āgrā at the court of Ibrāhīm Lodī. After the sultan's defeat at Pānīpat, Farīd attached himself to the self-appointed Sultan Muḥammad of Bihār. It was in his service that, one day, while accompanying the monarch in a hunt, Farīd slew a tiger with a sword, and received the title of Shēr Khān. He was also appointed tutor to the sultan's young son, Jalāl Khān. After an interval in the service of Bābur, he returned to the court of Sultan Muḥammad, where he was restored to his former position. The sultan died shortly after; his son, Jalāl Khān, being a minor, his mother became the regent and appointed Shēr Khān as her agent. Thus he became the ruler of Bihār. When the queen died he was virtually king.

Sultan Muḥammad of Bengal sent a force against Bihār which was defeated with heavy losses. He sent another army, and this time the nobles persuaded Jalāl Khān to dismiss Shēr Khān. He retired to Sahsārām, and Jalāl Khān joined forces with Bengal. At this Shēr Khān enlisted more troops, advanced against the Bengal army, and defeated it. Jalāl Khān escaped into Bengal, and Shēr Khān's power became absolute. The treasures, animals and equipment left by the two Bengal armies had enriched and strengthened him. He then acquired the strong fort of Chunār on the Ganges through marriage with the widow of its commandant. Maḥmūd Lodī now took possession of Bihār, leaving only his *parganas* to Shēr Khān, who reluctantly joined him, but refrained from actively supporting the sultan against the Mughals. Maḥmūd Lodī was defeated and, being unable to raise a new army, retired to Orissa, where he died in 949/1542.

During all this time Shēr Khān had been quietly building up his power. He accumulated arms and devised a plan to seize the hoarded treasures of the rulers of Bengal. When reports of Shēr Khān's activities reached Humāyūn, he marched against Chunār, which was captured after a difficult siege in 944/1537. While Humāyūn was busy besieging Chunār, Shēr Khān marched into Bengal and took Gawr. Shēr Khān, knowing full well that Humāyūn would follow him into Bengal, lost no time. He removed his booty to the hills of southern Bihār, which he intended to use as a base against the Mughals. He also gained by a strategem the fort of Rohtās, where he put his family and his newly acquired treasures. Humāyūn marched into Bengal and, delighted with its verdure, prolonged his stay. He posted Hindāl on the north bank of the Ganges to guard his line of communication. Southern Bihār is hilly, and, being covered with thick jungle, is impenetrable by cavalry. The sole means of communication was through the Teliyāgahrī pass. Shēr Khān, who knew the terrain well, harassed the Mughal communications, so that Hindāl deserted his post; he retired to Āgrā with rebellious intentions. Shēr Khān took all the area between Banāras and Teliyāgarhī. Bengal was thus turned into a prison for Humāyūn by the superior strategy of Shēr Khān. At last Humāyūn realized his danger, marched out and reached Chawsa, where he halted, unaware of Shēr Khān's position.

Shēr Khān's forces soon appeared, and, instead of attacking them when they were tired, the Mughals waited. After resting his troops, Shēr Khān attacked Humāyūn, who was taken by surprise. The Mughal army was thoroughly beaten (946/1539). After the battle, Shēr Khān proclaimed himself sultan, with the title of Shēr Shāh.

While Humāyūn was in difficulties in Bengal, Hindāl had failed to help him, and had indulged in treasonable activities at Āgrā. Kāmrān also moved from Lahore, and established himself in Āgrā. Humāyūn and 'Askarī were able to reach Āgrā with difficulty, and Shēr Shāh occupied Bengal. Kāmrān left Humāyūn in this desperate situation and retired to the Panjāb. Shēr Shāh after having consolidated his position in Bengal, marched against the Mughals. Humāyūn advanced from Āgrā and stopped near Kannawj, with Shēr Shāh on the other bank of the Ganges. Defections forced Humāyūn into crossing the river. The Mughals fought a half-hearted battle, and Shēr Shāh's 10,000 troops put a Mughal force of 40,000 to flight (947/1540).

After this defeat Humāyūn reached Āgrā, but there was no chance of taking a stand. He evacuated Āgrā and, after a halt at Delhi, hurried on to Lahore, followed in close pursuit by the Afghans. Lahore was abandoned. His progress towards Afghanistan being barred by Kāmrān, Humāyūn turned towards Sind, where he had no success. He received an invitation from Rājā Māldeva of Mārwār, and faced grave difficulties in reaching there, only to discover that the raja had turned against him. He returned facing even greater hardships. Ultimately he reached 'Umarkōt, where the ruler gave him shelter. It was here that Akbar was born in 949/1542. Humāyūn could not stay long at 'Umarkōt and decided to go to Qandahār. 'Askarī, who was the governor of Qandahār on behalf of Kāmrān, strengthened his defences, and instigated some Balūch chiefs to arrest Humāyūn, who escaped, but Akbar fell into their hands and was sent to 'Askarī. Humāyūn entered Persia as a refugee, and, after many humiliations and difficulties, secured small reinforcements in 952/1545 from Shāh Ṭahmāsp to fight against Kāmrān. A protracted struggle ensued, until Humāyūn succeeded in ousting Kāmrān. 'Askarī, who had remained faithful to Kāmrān, was captured and was sent to Mecca, where he died in 965/1558. Hindāl was killed in a night attack by an Afghan (959/1551). Kāmrān joined, for a while, the court of Shēr Shāh's son, Islām Shāh, but disappointed with his contemptuous reception he ran away, and finally fell into Humāyūn's hands. In spite of pressure from the courtiers, Kāmrān was not executed, but was blinded and sent to Mecca, where he died in 964/1557.

After Humāyūn's departure from Lahore, Shēr Shāh occupied the Panjāb, Mālwā and Ranthambhor. He punished Pūranmal of Rāysēn for having massacred the Muslim inhabitants of Chāndērī and enslaving Muslim and Hindu women. He brought Mārwār and Mēwār under his control. Then he marched against Kālinjar, which he besieged. A rocket, rebounding from the gate of the fort, fell into a heap of ammunition in proximity to the sultan. He was severely burnt, and was carried to his tent. The officers were summoned and commanded to take the fort, and before sunset he received the news of its capture by storm. Then he died (952/1545).

Shēr Shāh was a good general and a great strategist, as the way he trapped and defeated Humāyūn shows. He has been highly praised for his efficient administration. The lessons learnt in his youth in administering the *parganas* of his father were never forgotten, and he stands out as one of the greatest administrators who ever sat on the throne of Delhi. He was just, tolerant and benevolent. He took an interest in the welfare of his subjects, improved communications, built and repaired caravanserais, and took steps to maintain peace and order. He rose from being a student in exile to be first the ruler of Bihār, and then the sultan of Delhi. Afghan writers, who naturally wrote with considerable nostalgia in the days of Akbar, exaggerated his originality, though not his capacity as an administrator. Shēr Shāh had very little time at his disposal to create new institutions. He was, however, a keen student of history, and succeeded in putting into action the administrative machinery, which had been considerably damaged by disturbed conditions.

He was succeeded by his son, Islām Shāh, who was brave and determined, but suspicious by nature, and harsh in his dealings. Because of his harshness, his brother ʻĀdil Khān was favoured by some nobles, which set Islām Shāh against him. ʻĀdil Khān was defeated, and fled towards Patnā where he disappeared, but Islām Shāh's campaign against the nobles continued, and there is little else to narrate about the reign. On his death (961/1554) his son Fērōz was raised to the throne. His brother-in-law, Mubāriz Khān, marched at the head of a strong force towards Gwalior, where he forced his way into the presence of the young king and, despite the entreaties of the mother, murdered the boy and ascended the throne under the title of ʻĀdil Shāh. He displayed little tact and even less capacity. Relations between the nobles and the sultan were embittered because of his harshness. A cousin of the sultan, Ibrāhīm Khān Sūr, came to know that an attempt was to be made on his life. He fled from Gwalior, occupied Delhi and assumed the royal title. ʻĀdil Shāh then grew suspicious of another cousin, Aḥmad Khān, whom he intended to remove, but who was warned by his wife, the sultan's younger sister. He left Gwalior and escaped to Delhi. There he quarrelled with Ibrāhīm, and, having defeated him near Āgrā, occupied Delhi, and proclaimed himself sultan as Sikandar Shāh in 962/1555. There were now three sultans: 'Ādil Shāh, whose authority extended over Āgrā, Mālwā and Jawnpur; Sikandar Shāh, who was supreme from Delhi to Rohtās in the Panjāb; and Ibrāhīm Shāh, who ruled the foothills of the Himalayas in the Panjāb. A fourth contender for position was a petty shopkeeper of Rewārī called Hēmū who had gathered all local power into his hands.

The power of the Sūrs being thus divided, Humāyūn decided to try his luck again. He captured Lahore, Jullundar (Jālandhar), Sarhind, Ḥiṣār and Dīpālpur. Sikandar marched with an army of thirty thousand, was defeated at Māchiwārā, and retired into the hills. Sāmānā fell soon after, and from there Humāyūn marched upon Delhi, which he occupied. Forces were sent into the Do'āb. However, before much could be achieved, he fell from the stairs of his library, and died two days later in 963/1556.

Akbar

Akbar was little more than thirteen years old when he succeeded to the throne. Bayram Khān, a tried officer and friend of Humāyūn, was appointed his guardian. The reign began with difficulties. Apart from the three Sūr contestants, there was the ambitious Hēmū. He advanced from Gwalior to Āgrā, which was lost. Hēmū then marched upon Delhi, from which the Mughal governor, Tardī Beg, fled. Such areas in the Do'āb as had been occupied were evacuated. Bayram marched against Hēmū, at the second battle of Pānīpat. The Mughals were greatly outnumbered, but after an archer succeeded in piercing Hēmū's eye with an arrow, he was captured and executed. Āgrā and Delhi were recovered. 'Ādil Shāh was still in Chunār when he was attacked by his cousin Jalāl al-Dīn Bahādur Shāh of Bengal, and was slain. Sikandar surrendered in 964/1557, and the Do'āb was soon brought back under control.

When Akbar was eighteen years old, a number of his foster-relatives and others persuaded him to break with his guardian. Akbar left Āgrā and went to Delhi, from where he informed Bayram Khān that he was no longer needed as a regent and tutor. Bayram, rejecting all advice to rebel, announced his intention of going on Pilgrimage to Mecca. However, he wanted to dispose of his property in the Panjāb. Akbar showed impatience, and sent a former servant and personal enemy of Bayram Khān to hasten him. This goaded Bayram Khān into rebellion; he was defeated, and took refuge in Tilwārā, a hill fortress, from where he sent a messenger to Akbar expressing repentance. Bayram appeared before Akbar at Ḥājjīpur. He then departed for Mecca, and was killed by some Afghans near Pātan in 967/1560. Bayram deserved better treatment because of his services to Humāyūn and Akbar. He was an able, sincere and wise servant.

Mālwā had acted independently of its Mughal governor since 954/1547. In 968/1561 Akbar sent an expedition under Adham Khān, his foster-brother and the son of his chief nurse, Māham Anāga, who, along with other foster-relatives, had come to wield great influence in matters of state. Mālwā was under Bāz Bahādur, the enthroned son of a Khaljī noble, who is still remembered as an accomplished musician and for the famous romance between him and a beautiful Hindu girl, Rūpmatī. He was easily defeated and sought safety in flight. Rūpmatī took poison to save herself from Adham Khān, whose misbehaviour brought Akbar to Mālwā, but Adham Khān was permitted to continue as governor.

In the meanwhile ʿĀdil Shāh's son, Shēr Khān, marched on Jawnpur and was defeated. Āṣaf Khān was sent against Chunār, which surrendered. The eastern provinces were now relieved of any serious danger. Adham Khān continued to misbehave in Mālwā, and had to be recalled. His lieutenant, left in charge of the province, was even worse, and Bāz Bahādur recovered Mālwā. Akbar then sent ʿAbd Allāh Khān Özbeg, who reorganized the province.

Akbar invited Atga Khān from Kābul to take up the duties of chief minister, to the disappointment of the harem party. When Adham Khān reached the court he murdered Atga Khān (969/1562). Akbar executed Adham immediately, and Māham died of grief forty days later. This brought Akbar complete emancipation from the harem influence. Henceforth, Akbar, who had already shown considerable initiative, mostly followed his own counsel.

Āṣaf Khān was ordered to conquer the Hindu kingdom of Gondwānā, which was annexed (971/1564). Khān Zamān, along with several other Özbegs, was posted in the east, and extended the frontiers of the empire to the borders of Bengal. Because of their absence from the court, the interests of the Özbegs were neglected. This created disaffection, and ultimately revolt broke out in 973/1565. The rebellion was quelled when Khān Zamān was trampled to death by an elephant in a hard-fought battle near Karā (975/1567).

In the same year Akbar marched against the *rānā* of Chitor. Bihārī Mall of Ambēr had already allied himself with the Mughals by marrying his daughter to the emperor, which was the beginning of the intimate relationship between the Mughal dynasty and the Rājpūts. Uday Singh, the *rānā* of Chitor, however, had not offered submission, hence the campaign against Chitor. The fortress was considered impregnable, and the defence was left by the *rānā* to one Jay Mal, who put up a spirited fight. Akbar, however, succeeded in shooting Jay Mal with his musket when he was out on a round of the defences. The Rājpūts then committed the terrible rite of *jawhar*, in which they burnt their women, donned saffron robes, and rushed upon the enemy to be killed. Chitor thus fell into Akbar's hands. Ranthambor and Kālinjar were also taken, and Gujarāt, which had fallen into a state of anarchy, as mentioned above (p. 27), was conquered in 981/1573.

Akbar next turned his attention to Bengal. Sulaymān Karārānī had been the governor under Shēr Shāh, and, after the decline of the Sūrs, had become independent. He died in 980/1572. His son Dā'ūd invaded the Mughal dominions. This resulted in war, ending only when Dā'ūd was captured in battle and executed (984/1576).

Akbar's strictness in the enforcement of regulations regarding the maintenance of troops by local officers resulted in a rebellion in the eastern provinces. It was aggravated by Akbar's attitude towards orthodox Islam, which will be discussed later. Simultaneously his younger brother, Muḥammad Ḥakīm, marched into the Panjāb, and reached Lahore. He did not receive much support, and when he heard that Akbar was marching against him, he retreated. Akbar followed him to Kābul, where Ḥakīm was forgiven. He died four years later. The area around the Khyber pass was occupied by the fanatic sect of Rūshanā' īs. The campaign against them proved difficult, but they were ultimately defeated in 996/1586.

Akbar was disturbed by the rise of 'Abd Allāh Khān Özbeg in Central Asia. The province of Badakhshān was torn with internal dissensions. The tribal area, as has been mentioned, was in a state of unrest, and Kābul itself was badly administered by Ḥakīm. Akbar therefore moved to Lahore to be closer to the scenes of trouble and to plan the control of Kashmir as well. 'Abd Allāh Khān, to whom one of the contestants in

Badakhshān had appealed for help, took hold of that province. Shortly afterwards Muḥammad Ḥakīm died, and Kābul was occupied for Akbar (993/1585). Another Mughal force marched into Kashmir, where it received the homage of its ruler, Yūsuf Shāh, in 994/1586; subsequently Kashmir was formally annexed and Yūsuf was detained as a state prisoner. Sind was annexed in 999/1590 and the ruler, Jānī Beg, appeared at court in 1002/1593. There he won Akbar's favour by becoming his disciple, and was appointed governor of Sind.

Having secured the whole of northern India, Akbar started taking definite steps to bring the Deccan under his control. (An account of the Deccan sultanate is given later in the Appendix.) Missions were sent to different rulers who had sent gifts, these were treated as tribute and gave the Mughals a pretext to interfere in the affairs of the Deccan whenever it suited them. After a protracted war the imperial troops succeeded in occupying Aḥmadnagar (1009/1600), and then annexing the small principality of Khāndēsh. The fall of the Niẓām Shāhī sultanate of Aḥmadnagar demonstrated to the other rulers of the Deccan that it would be difficult for them to resist the might of the Mughal empire.

Salīm, Akbar's eldest son, later the Emperor Jahāngīr, was dissatisfied because his position as heir-apparent had not been recognized. His behaviour at Allahabad, where he was governor, caused some anxiety and in the view of some historians amounted to rebellion. He was reconciled with Akbar and forgiven in 1012/1603. Two years later, in 1014/1605, Akbar died.

By all standards Akbar was personally brave, a good general and an excellent administrator. He was responsible for converting a small kingdom into a resplendent and mighty empire. His name passed into legend and folklore as the embodiment of the qualities associated with great monarchs. However, a good deal of what Akbar did contributed to bringing about the destruction of the fabric that he had built. His patronage of architecture and literature will be discussed elsewhere, as also his peculiarities as a religious thinker.

Jahāngīr

Salīm succeeded to the throne as Nūr al-Dīn Muḥammad Jahāngīr Ghāzī. His son, Khusraw, had also been a claimant. Khusraw was influential, and had the quality of attracting devoted friends. Mān Singh, Khusraw's uncle, was his main supporter. When Jahāngīr ascended the throne, he tried to conciliate Mān Singh and Khusraw. However, Khusraw escaped to the Panjāb, where he attracted some support. An incident of far-reaching consequences was that the Sikh *gurū* Arjun gave his blessings to Khusraw; this embittered the relations between Jahāngīr and the Sikhs, and Sikh-Mughal animosity developed. Khusraw laid siege to Lahore. Jahāngīr marched in pursuit of Khusraw who, leaving a contingent in front of Lahore, turned to fight, and was defeated at Bhairowāl. He was captured in an attempt to cross the Jhelum. Jahāngīr imprisoned the prince, but his followers were punished severely. While in confinement Khusraw hatched a plot, which was revealed, and the ringleaders were executed. Jahāngīr refused to read the entire correspondence for humane reasons. The leading officials thought it unfair that whereas the supporters were punished heavily, nothing happened to the prince who was the root of the trouble. They, therefore, put pressure upon Jahāngīr, and induced him to blind Khusraw to stop him from any further mischief. Soon, however, Jahāngīr relented, and asked physicians to treat the prince whose eyesight was partially restored, but he was not released.

Jahāngīr's queen, Nūr Jahān, was the daughter of Mīrzā Ghiyās̱ Beg, a well-born man of talent, who migrated to India, and rose steadily in the imperial service. She was lady-in-waiting to Akbar's senior widow. Jahāngīr saw her for the first time in 1020/1611, fell in love with her, and married her. Nūr Jahān, beautiful and capable, proved to be a devoted wife. When Jahāngīr's health declined because of asthma, he came to rely more and more upon her. She was supported by her father who was given the title of I'timād al-Dawla. He would have risen anyhow, but his promotion was more rapid because of Nūr Jahān's influence. Her brother Āṣaf Khān was learned, a good administrator, and an expert financier. Her group included Prince Khurram, later the Emperor Shāh Jahān, the most capable of Jahāngīr's sons, and the one obviously marked out for succession. He was Āṣaf Khān's son-in-law.

Jahāngīr's reign can be divided into two parts. The first extends from 1020–32/1611–22 when Jahāngīr still had complete control over affairs. I'timād al-Dawla was alive and exercised a moderating influence, and Nūr Jahān and Khurram were in agreement. During the second period, from 1032/1622 to 1037/1627, Jahāngīr began to lose his hold on the administration because of his ill-health. I'timād al-Dawla was dead, while Khurram and Nūr Jahān became hostile to one another.

In 1021/1612 an Afghan revolt in Bengal gave considerable trouble until a young officer, Islām Khān, was made governor, and succeeded in defeating the rebels. After this the Afghans never gave trouble. Disturbances also broke out in Mēwār where the *rānā*, Amar Singh, had gradually increased his power. The Rājpūts waged guerrilla warfare in the hills. After some time in 1022/1614 Khurram was appointed to Mēwār, to whom Amar Singh submitted and promised not to occupy Chitor again. He was excused from attendance at the court because of his old age, but his son was sent as a hostage for his father's loyalty.

In 1024/1616 Jahāngīr received Sir Thomas Roe. The English had been trying to secure some concessions from the Mughals, and William Hawkins had visited the court eight years earlier. The Mughals had a poor opinion of the English, who were considered to be uncouth and unruly. Roe was unable to obtain any concession, but did succeed in securing permission to carry on trade from Khurram, who was the viceroy of the Deccan.

The situation in the Deccan had taken a turn for the worse, as far as the Mughals were concerned, because of the rise of a Ḥabshī officer, Malik ʿAnbar, to power in Aḥmadnagar. He recruited Marāthās and organized them into guerilla troops, and recovered a good deal of the territory lost to the Mughals. After initial difficulties, the command was given to Prince Khurram. Malik ʿAnbar thought it wise to cede the territory that he had captured. Khurram visited his father after this successful campaign, and was awarded the unprecedented rank of 30,000 (see below, p. 55) and given the title of Shāh Jahān.

By 1033/1623 all power had passed into the hands of Nūr Jahān. She could foresee that Shāh Jahān was not likely to remain under her influence and, therefore, she thought of advancing the incapable Shahryār, Jahangīr's youngest son, as her candidate. With this in view, she married her daughter by her first husband to him in 1030/1620. Iʿtimād al-Dawla died in 1032/1621 and, as Āṣaf Khān was Shāh Jahān's father-in-law, he was not likely to turn against him. Thus Nūr Jahān was isolated. Shāh Jahān's position was strengthened by Khusraw's death in 1031/1622.

In 1016/1606 Shāh ʿAbbās I of Persia instigated his officers to besiege Qandahār, but it was ably defended, and the Persians retired when Mughal reinforcements arrived. Shāh ʿAbbās disowned the campaign. In 1031/1622 Shāh Jahān was asked to march to its relief, but, being afraid of Nūr Jahān's intrigues in his absence, he laid down conditions which were rejected by Jahāngīr. When Shāh Jahān felt that he was likely to be punished, he rebelled. After a tedious campaign he was defeated. He had to send his sons, Dārā Shikōh and Awrangzēb, to court and was demoted to the governorship of Bālāghāt.

The general Mahābat Khān, who had been instrumental in defeating Shāh Jahān, was alienated by Nūr Jahān, and, while Jahāngīr was marching towards Kābul in 1036/1626, Mahābat Khān brought off a *coup* and captured the person of the emperor. Nūr Jahān's attempt to rescue him failed, and Mahābat Khān became the dictator though all appearances of Jahāngīr being at the helm of affairs were kept up. Nūr Jahān, however, was busy throughout, and finally succeeded in getting Mahābat Khān dismissed.

Shāh Jahān made another attempt when he heard that his father had fallen into Nūr Jahān's hands. He received no support, and his progress was stopped at Thatthā. Nūr Jahān, however, administered a strict warning, reminding him that Mahābat Khān's power had been broken. Shāh Jahān was sick, and was carried in a litter through Gujarāt, where Mahābat Khān joined him with a force of two thousand. Thus the two most capable and brilliant generals of the empire were united, but both of them were without resources. They waited for an opportunity. Jahāngīr died in 1037/1627 on his way back from Kashmīr, and his body was carried to Lahore, where he was buried.

Jahāngīr was a sensible, benevolent and generous man. In his beliefs he was a conforming Muslim, although he had in later life a weakness for alcohol. He was responsible for a number of minor reforms. He was a great patron of painting, of which he was a connoisseur, and his coinage is the most distinguished of all Indian issues. He was a simple and straightforward man with no cunning. He retained his affection for Khusraw despite his repeated rebellions, was a devoted husband to Nūr Jahān, was fond of sports, a great lover of nature and desirous of proving a benefactor to his people.

Shāh Jahān

Shāh Jahān was the elder surviving, and the more capable, son and his succession would have been without trouble but for Nūr Jahān's opposition. Āṣaf Khān, however, was in his favour and acted with great circumspection. He put Nūr Jahān under guard, removed Shāh Jahān's son from her charge, and put Khusraw's son on the throne as a stopgap. Shahryār, who proclaimed himself emperor at Lahore, was easily defeated. In the meanwhile Shāh Jahān marched through Gujarāt and reached Āgrā, where he was proclaimed emperor in 1038/1628. Nūr Jahān was given a good pension and lived near Lahore, building Jahāngīr's tomb and engaging in charitable works.

In the Deccan Mahābat Khān had captured Aḥmadnagar, which passed under Mughal rule in 1041/1631. The imperialists had already been encroaching upon Golkondā territory and by 1040/1630 about one third of it had passed into their hands. As Golkondā and Bījāpur were both creating trouble for the Mughals in Aḥmadnagar, Shāh Jahān decided to punish them. In 1047/1636 Golkondā agreed under pressure to remove the name of the shah of Persia from the *khuṭba* and to insert Shāh Jahān's name instead; to abolish the Shīʿī formula on the coins, because the association of a Shīʿī formula with Shāh Jahān's name might have created difficulties for the emperor within his own dominions; to pay an annual tribute, and to help the Mughal troops against Bījāpur.

In 1047/1636 Shāh Jahān demanded that Bījāpur should clearly recognize Mughal sovereignty, pay regular tribute, and cede the territories that had belonged to Aḥmadnagar. As Bījāpur took no action, Shāh Jahān decided on an invasion. Bījāpur sued for peace, which was granted on its acceptance of the demands. After the death of Muḥammad ʿĀdil Shāh in 1067/1656, when his son ʿAlī ʿĀdil Shāh found himself too young to control the factions at the court or suppress rebellion in the kingdom, Shāh Jahān decided to intervene. One of his sons, Awrangzēb, led a successful campaign but at the intervention of Dārā Shikōh, Shāh Jahān's eldest son, much to the chagrin of Awrangzēb, peace was granted on the surrender of some territory.

The Portuguese had established themselves at Huglī in Bengal and, with the help of a large number of converts and half-castes, carried on piracy and kidnapping children to sell them into slavery. In 1049/1639 an expedition freed a large number of slaves, and the Portuguese were forced to pay a large indemnity and evacuate the settlement.

Qandahār was restored to the Mughals through its Persian governor, who came over to them (1048/1638). The Mughals had never given up their dream of recovering their ancestral territories in Transoxania, where internal difficulties encouraged Shāh Jahān to send an expedition. His second son, Murād Bakhsh, was able to occupy Balkh, but because he disliked the climate he was replaced by Awrangzēb, who was able to defeat an Özbeg force in a pitched battle. In 1058/1648, however, Shāh ʿAbbās II intervened openly, and demanded the evacuation of Qandahār and the restoration of Balkh to the Özbegs. Shāh 'Abbās took Qandahār: it was lost to the Mughals, and the Central Asian adventure also came to an end.

In 1068/1657 Shāh Jahān fell ill and was not able to hold public audience. There were wild rumours, and the princes thought that they should make a bid for the throne. Murād Bakhsh proclaimed himself emperor in Gujarāt; Shāh Shujā', a capable administrator and then governor of Bengal, advanced towards the capital; Awrangzēb, with imperial troops under his command, was in correspondence with both, and Dārā Shikōh tried to reduce his power by recalling those troops. One army was sent against Shāh Shujā', another against Murād, and a third was despatched to keep Awrangzēb in check. Shāh Shujā' was defeated and fled to Bengal. Awrangzēb completed his preparations, and marched from Awrangābād in 1069/1658. Murād came and joined him and the two marched on Āgrā. A Rājpūt commander sent to stop Awrangzēb's progress was defeated at Dharmat. Then Dārā had to take the field himself at Sāmūgarh, ten miles east of Āgrā. Awrangzēb won the battle despite his inferior resources, and then marched on Āgrā and took the city. Shāh Jahān tried to lay a trap for him, but an intercepted letter addressed to Dārā Shikōh revealed the plot to Awrangzēb. Murād Bakhsh was arrested and confined, and Awrangzēb ascended the throne with the title of 'Ālamgīr. Shāh Jahān was deposed and confined in Āgrā at his son's order.

'Ālamgīr I (Awrangzēb)

Dārā Shikōh was pursued into Kachh. He crossed into Gujarāt, mustered sufficient resources, and marched northwards. He was captured, tried for heresy, and beheaded, Murād Bakhsh also was executed. Shāh Shujā' marched from Bengal, was defeated in pitched battle near Karā, and was pursued into Bengal. After continuous warfare he escaped into the Arakān, where he was killed in 1072/1661.

In 1072/1662 Mīr Jumlā, the governor of Bengal, led a campaign into Assam because the raja had taken hold of some Mughal territory. In spite of the difficulties of the terrain the raja was defeated.

In 1078/1667 the Yūsufzāy, a Pathān tribe, rose in rebellion. They were defeated near Ātak and were brought under control. Then in 1083/1672 the Afrīdīs revolted. They were inspired by the famous poet Khushḥāl Khān Khatak, who had served Shāh Jahān faithfully, but was disappointed with Awrangzēb when he extended imperial patronage to another tribe. Awrangzēb established himself at Ḥasan Abdāl and systematically brought the tribes under control. In 1086/1675 he left the campaign in the hands of Amīr Khān, who completed the work of pacifying the tribes.

Jaswant Singh, maharaja of Mārwār, had tried to plunder the imperial camp at night on the eve of the battle of Karā when Shāh Shujā' was defeated. He was forgiven and posted at Jamrūd. After his death without heirs in 1089/1678 Awrangzēb brought Mārwār under direct administrative control, and on a posthumous heir being born soon afterwards seized the infant, Ajīt Singh, and his mother. The child was rescued and conveyed to a place of hiding, while the Rājpūt national leader in Mārwār, Durgā Dās, after unsuccessfully opposing the Mughals openly, carried on guerrilla warfare from the hills. The neighbouring Mēwār, which tried to stand by the Mārwār Rājpūts, was no match for the imperial army with its European artillery. Awrangzēb's third son, Akbar, was left in command of Mēwar while Awrangzēb returned to the Mārwār campaign. Akbar ultimately joined forces with the Rājpūt contingents, and marched against his father who was almost defenceless at Ajmēr. However, Prince Mu'aẓẓam managed to join the emperor, who took up a position at Dorāhā to give battle. Through the familiar stratagem of addressing a letter to the prince, commending him for laying a trap for the Rājpūts, and taking care to see it fall into the hands of the enemy, he isolated Akbar who, deserted by his troops, wandered from one place to another until he made his way to the Deccan and joined the Marāthās. Later he made his way to Persia. The war against Mēwār was pursued until the *rānā* secured peace on surrendering three *parganas* in lieu of *jizya*. The campaign against Mārwār went on a little longer until ultimately Durgā Dās was reconciled.

It has been mentioned (p. 46) that Malik 'Anbar organized Marāthā guerillas to harass the Mughals. Even earlier the Marāthās had sought service in Muslim armies, and were prized for their hardihood. Shāhjī Bhonsle had risen to the position of king-maker in Aḥmadnagar. When Shāh Jahān captured that sultanate, Shāhjī migrated to Bījāpur, where also he became powerful. His son, Shivājī, was born in 1037/1627. After the death of Muḥammad 'Ādil Shāh in 1067/1656 Bījāpur declined rapidly, and its control over the mountainous areas so relaxed that Shivājī was able to take many forts, mostly by stratagem. His power went on increasing. In 1075/1664 he sacked Sūrat, two-thirds of the city being destroyed by fire or plunder. In 1076/1665 Awrangzēb sent

Rājā Jay Singh of Ambēr, who forced Shivājī to yield four-fifths of his territory and to acknowledge the sovereignty of the emperor. In 1077/1666 he visited Āgrā and was given command of 5,000 (see below, p. 55). He considered this inadequate, created a scene, and was confined but escaped. After three years of preparation he resumed his activities, occupied large areas, and crowned himself king in 1085/1674. He continued to harass the Mughals until he was attacked by an imperial force, and was forced to fight. The Marāthās suffered heavy losses, though Shivājī escaped. Soon afterwards he died in 1091/1680, and was succeeded by his son, Shambhūjī.

The rapid decline of the Deccan sultanates (see Appendix) and the creation of anarchic conditions, which contributed to the growth of the Marāthā power, could no longer be ignored by Awrangzēb. Bījāpur and Golkondā had not only encouraged the Marāthās, but had actually entered into secret alliances with them. The emperor, therefore, decided to conquer the sultanates so that the Marāthās should not thrive upon their decadence, and moved camp to the Deccan. In 1100/1689 Shambhūjī was defeated, captured and brought before Awrangzēb, when he abused the emperor and the Prophet. He was executed. His family was kept at court, and properly maintained.

The Mughals besieged Bījāpur in 1097/1686, and the ruler, unable to put up a long defence, waited on the emperor, was received kindly and enrolled as a *manṣabdār* with a large pension. All Bījāpurī officers were enrolled in the imperial service.

In 1083/1672 Abu'l-Ḥasan had come to the throne of Golkondā. The power was in the hands of a Brahman minister, Madanna, who entered into a secret alliance with Bījāpur and Shivājī. In 1097/1685 a secret letter to Bījāpur was intercepted in which all help was promised against the Mughals. At this Prince Mu'aẓẓam, now styled Shāh 'Ālam, was sent against Golkondā. He took Ḥaydarābād and Abu'l-Ḥasan fled to Golkondā. Abu'l-Ḥasan, however, made his peace by the payment of an indemnity and a cession of territory. He promised to dismiss Madanna, but, because the dismissal was put off, the Muslim nobles, who were tired of his tyranny, brought about his assassination. Conditions in Golkondā did not improve, and ultimately Awrangzēb decided to put an end to the dynasty. He therefore annexed the kingdom by proclamation. Despite the fact that a mine under the fort misfired, and killed many of the assailants, the emperor stood firm and saved the situation. The fort was captured. Abu'l-Ḥasan was sent to Dawlatābād with a handsome pension. Awrangzēb was now free to devote his entire attention to the Marāthās. Rājā Rām, who had succeeded Shambhūjī, retired to Jinjī on the east coast, which became the centre of Marāthā activities. It was captured by the Mughals in 1110/1698.

In 1112/1700 Rājā Rām died, and Shivājī III was put on the throne. Between 1110/1689 and 1112/1700 the Mughals conquered the whole of the north Konkan from the Marāthās. Awrangzēb himself patiently went on conquering one fort after another between 1111/1699 and 1117/1705 but he fell ill and died in 1118/1707. The Marāthā snake had been scotched but not killed, and was to give considerable trouble to the Mughals (and to the British) in subsequent years.

Awrangzēb was a pious Muslim. He was an excellent general and possessed the qualities of determination and perseverance to a remarkable degree. The last great monarch of the dynasty, he took his responsibilities as an orthodox Muslim ruler seriously, and endeavoured to make Islam once again the dominant force in the realm. After the policies of the three previous reigns, this brought him into conflict with the forces arrayed against such a revival.

ADMINISTRATION

The Mughal emperors claimed to be fully independent monarchs, and to be caliphs within their dominions. After the abolition of the ʿAbbasid caliphate in Baghdād, some jurists had already come to believe that a universal caliphate was no longer necessary, and that every independent monarch should discharge the duties of a caliph inside his realm. However, the rulings of the jurists regarding the functions of the caliph were applicable to independent monarchs as well. The monarch was the chief executive of his realm, and the commander of its forces. His power was limited by the *Sharīʿa*.

Akbar, however, made a correct analysis of the situation and decided that if he allied himself with the non-Muslims and the heterodox elements in the Muslim population, he could reduce orthodoxy to helplessness. He succeeded, and became virtually a temporal sovereign outside the practice of Islamic kingship. Orthodoxy, however, rallied towards the end of his reign, and gradually built up a power which could not be ignored. Jahāngīr, therefore, had to restore such institutions of orthodox Islam as had been put in abeyance, the only exception being the *jizya*. The orthodox reaction did not subside, and ultimately resulted in the policies of Awrangzēb, who was not only personally orthodox like Shāh Jahān, but also relied heavily upon orthodox support.

The Mughal emperor was in a very real sense the head of the government. He had all authority centered in his hands. Next to the

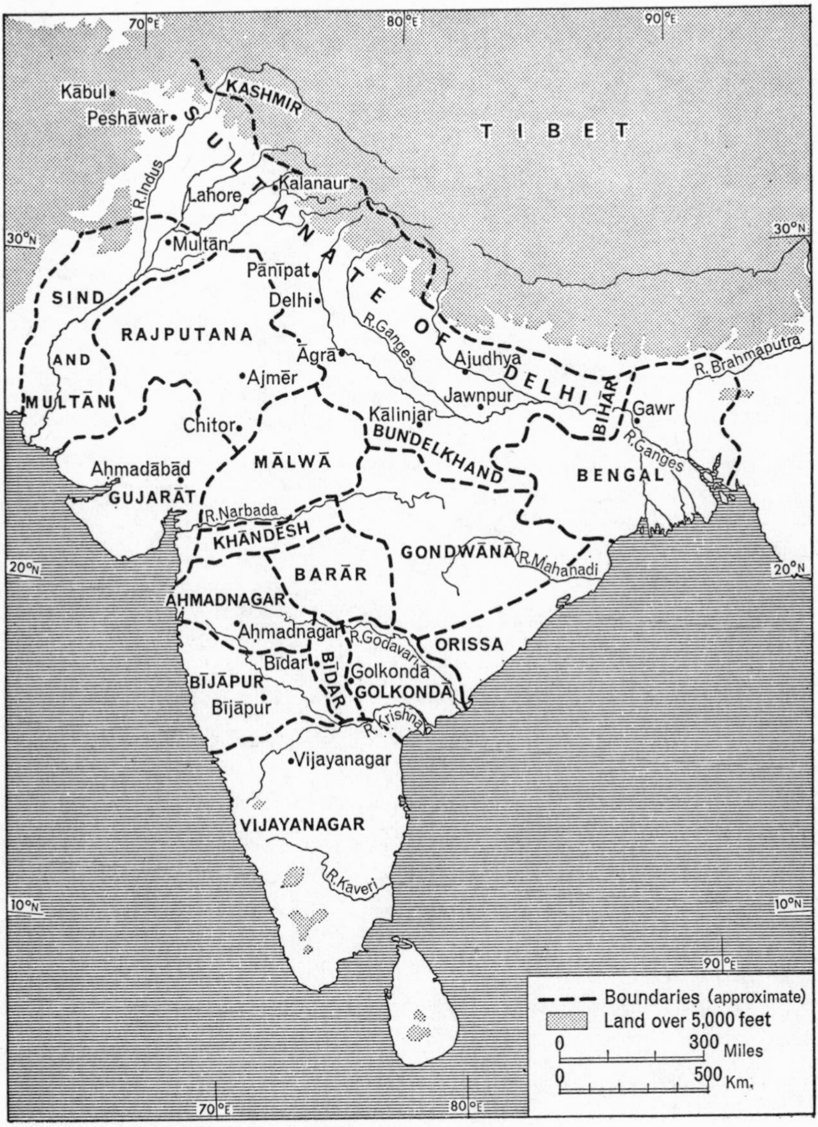

Map 10a. The Indian sub-continent in 1525.

monarch was the *wakīl al-salṭana*, who was theoretically the lieutenant of the monarch in all civil and military matters. During the period of Akbar's minority, this office possessed real authority. Later, because of the active role played by the emperors themselves, the post became an empty honour. The *wazīr* or *dīwān*, as he came to be called, was the head

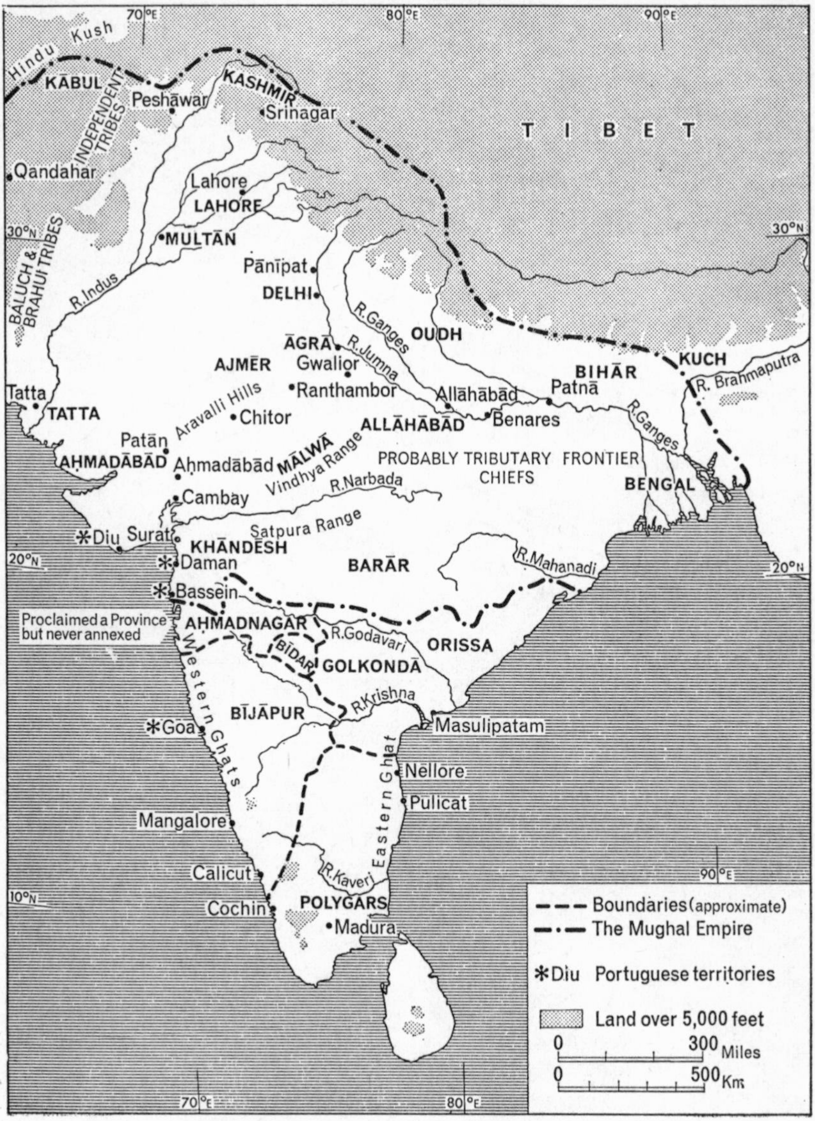

Map 10b. The Indian sub-continent in 1605.

of the fiscal administration. He was assisted by a *dīwān-i khāliṣa*, who looked after the unassigned lands and cash salaries; a *dīwān-i tan*, who was responsible for all assignments in land, called *jāgīrs*. The *mīr bakhshī* was responsible for the proper organization of the army, and was the chief recruiting officer and paymaster. He also controlled the various agencies that kept the central government informed of the happenings in the provinces. He was assisted by three assistants: the second, third, and fourth *bakhshīs*. The *ṣadr al-ṣudūr* was responsible for religious affairs, pious foundations, grants to scholars and men of merit. He was also the chief judge with the dual function of *qāẓī al-quẓāt*.

The public services were organized under a unified system called *manṣabdārī*. An official's rank was fixed within a complex cadre by his *manṣab*. In the beginning, officers were grouped into ranks ranging from commanders of ten (*dah bāshī*) to commanders of 5,000 (*panj hazārī*). Later the *manṣabs* were increased and commands of 7,000 (*haft hazārī*) were created. Sometimes very large *manṣabs* were conferred, for instance, Jahāngīr bestowed the unprecedented rank of 30,000 upon Khurram when he was awarded the title of Shāh Jahān. Within the same rank, however, were variations based upon the additional rank of *sawār* (troops). Thus a commander of 5,000 might have the rank of 5,000 *ẓāt* (personal) and 5,000 *sawār*. The *sawār* rank could vary from nil to the figure of the *manṣab*. Those officers whose *sawār* rank corresponded to the *ẓāt* rank belonged to the first class; those whose *sawār* rank was less than the *ẓāt* rank but half or more than half of the *ẓāt* rank to the second class; and the rest to the third. A further complication was introduced by the number of horses in the contingent. Thus, for instance, an officer could be 5,000 *ẓāt*, 5,000 *sawār*, 3,000 *dō aspa sih aspa*. The *dō aspa sih aspa* rank meant that a certain proportion of the contingent assigned to the officer contained, in a prescribed proportion, troopers with two horses and three horses each. The *dō aspa sih aspa* rank determined the number of months in the year for which the *manṣabdār* drew his salary. The system was further complicated by the fact that none of the figures denoted the actual number of troopers maintained by the *manṣabdār*. In Shāh Jahān's reign, for instance, many *manṣabdārs* were expected to maintain only a fifth of the *sawār* contingent. Another complication was created by the fact that sometimes all the ranks were purely fictitious and a *manṣabdār* was not expected to maintain any soldiers at all; this was merely a convenient device to fix the position of civilian officers in the cadre. So long as the emperors were vigilant, the *manṣabdārī* system, despite its cumbersome nature, served them well, because all appointments and promotions were made on merit.

The finances were provided mainly by the state demand upon agricultural produce. Other sources of revenue, such as the customs, were not so important. *Jizya*, never a great source of revenue, was abolished by Akbar and reimposed by Awrangzēb.

The agrarian administration of the Mughals was scientific and benevolent. Although Akbar's *dīwān* Todar Mall is given much credit for bringing the Mughal provinces within a unified system of administration, his principles were in fact those first applied in the extensive reforms of Shēr Shāh. Apart from the old systems of crop-sharing by division of the harvested yield, the division of the standing crops, or by appraisement of the estimated yield after harvesting, the system mainly in use was that of measuring the area cultivated and calculating the yield on the basis of schedules of produce. These were kept up to date through the maintenance of a record of the 'medium' produce of an area and taking a fresh decennial average of it every year. Sample cuttings were made of good, middling and poor crops, by which the figure of 'medium' produce was determined for the entire area which formed the basis of the schedule. Akbar raised the state demand from a fourth to a third of the gross produce, though in certain provinces, because of long-standing traditions, it varied from one-tenth to a half. Payments to public servants were made in cash or through *jāgīrs*, i.e. grants of land. The assignee collected the state demand, but maintained the same machinery of assessment and collection for the assigned area. The *jāgīrs* were not the property of the assignee; they were transferred, resumed or awarded to new assignees. The *manṣabdārs* were servants of the state, the salaries were fixed in cash and the assignment was only a method of payment.

All disputes between citizens were within the jurisdiction of the *qāẓī*. All complaints against servants of the government came within the purview of *maẓālim* courts. The *maẓālim* court at the centre was presided over by the monarch himself and was attended by the *qāẓī al-quẓāt* to tender advice on legal matters. The monarch acted as a *siyāsa* (summary) court in dealing with rebels and prisoners of war. No death-penalty could be enforced without the previous consent of the emperor.

The provincial government was organized on the pattern of the central government. Every department dealt with the corresponding department at the centre and was under its control. The head of the provincial government was the *ṣūbadār*. The provincial *maẓālim* courts consisted of the *ṣūbadār*, the *dīwān*, the provincial *bakhshī* and the provincial *qāẓī*. The provinces (sing., *ṣūba*) were divided into *sarkārs*, and the *sarkārs* into *parganas*. The units of administration were the village and the *pargana*.

ASPECTS OF CULTURE

Literature

Literary activities flourished under the patronage of the emperor as well as the nobles, some of whom were *littérateurs* themselves. Akbar's court poet was Fayẓī. Other important poets were 'Urfī, Naẓīrī and Ẓuhūrī, all of whom hold a high position in the history of Persian poetry. Ṭālib Āmulī was the poet laureate in Jahāngīr's reign. Ṣā'ib came into prominence under Shāh Jahān. Under Awrangzēb, Bēdil's philosophical fancies and insight earned him great popularity amongst intellectuals. The poetry of this period is characterized by its polished and elegant diction and its remarkable insight into psychology, a complexity of thought, combined also with a concern for the philosophy of life. A Hindu poet of great eminence who wrote in Persian was Brahman, whose poems enjoy popularity even today. Translations were also made into Persian of the sacred writings of the Hindus.

The Mughal courts saw also a great development in the literatures of Indian languages: Mughal rulers and nobles were active patrons of Indian literature, especially Hindī, and there is a small but important corpus of Hindī works by Muslim writers. In addition, the toleration shown to Hindus by some Mughal courts, especially under Akbar and Jahāngīr, led to the production of fine devotional poetry by Hindus. The Ṣūfīs' allegorical poems in Hindī, known from the late eighth/fourteenth century, continued into Mughal times, and Malik Muḥammad Jāyasī's *Padmāvāt* of 947/1540, an allegory of the search of man's soul for wisdom cast in a delightful love-story, is the finest such epic of the period, of the calibre of Spenser's *Faerie Queene*. This and similar allegories are of a form resembling the Persian *masnavī*, but in Indian metres. A very different *genre* of poetry was in favour at the courts, a deliberately cultivated display of the poetic art, as originally formulated in Sanskrit court-poetry, on erotic themes. At Akbar's court the cultivated general and minister 'Abd al-Raḥīm, the Khān-i Khānān, was a leading Hindī poet under the pen-name Raḥīm, and popularized a new metre.

Other languages similarly produced fine literatures in the courts of the Deccan. At Bījāpur, especially under Ibrāhīm II, Kannada and Dakhnī poetry were as esteemed as Persian; while at Golkondā, besides some cultivation of Telugu verse, excellent Dakhnī poetry was written by members of the royal house.

Historiography was well represented, and except for the later part of Awrangzēb's reign there are reliable histories for every reign. The *Akbar-nāma* and *Ā'īn-i Akbarī* of Abu'l-Fażl, in spite of their difficult and rhetorical style, constitute the greatest historical works of Akbar's period, coloured throughout by excessive adulation of the emperor. In addition, a number of religious and literary biographies throw considerable light upon the period. Two autobiographies are famous: Bābur's memoirs are considered to be one of the most revealing and sincere autobiographies ever written; different in nature and style, Jahāngīr's memoirs are an excellent record of the period.

Awrangzēb himself was a master of style, and various collections have been made of his letters. The letters of Shaykh Aḥmad of Sirhind collected in *Maktūbāt-i imām-i rabbānī* form source-material for writing on his mission. A remarkable book is the *Dabistān-i maẓāhib*, which is almost an encyclopaedia of the various religions and sects found in the subcontinent during the period. The author, Muḥsin Fānī, was a Zoroastrian.

Painting

There is some evidence to show that painting was practised under the sultans of Delhi, and a well-defined school of miniature painting grew up in Gujarāt. Painting, however, received great impetus under the Mughals. Bābur was a critic and has relevant observations on the artists of his period. His son Humāyūn found time during his exile in Persia to go to Tabrīz and meet some of the leading artists of the city. He was able to attract Mīr Sayyid 'Alī and Khwāja 'Abd al-Ṣamad to his court after Shāh Ṭahmāsp's loss of interest in the arts, and these two artists joined him in Delhi after his return. They were entrusted with the task of illustrating the epic of Amīr Ḥamza. Some of these paintings on cloth are still extant though unfortunately many have been mutilated. Under Akbar the school was developed further. A large number of artists were employed to work under the direction of Mīr Sayyid 'Alī and later of Khwāja 'Abd al-Ṣamad, and a large number of books were illustrated, using new techniques and materials, under the emperor's personal interest. Because of the employment of a number of Hindu artists a new spirit entered the pictures. The growth of new trends soon freed the Mughal school from purely Persian conventions. Under

Jahāngīr, who while still a prince maintained his own *atelier*, the school developed further. It achieved maturity and distinctiveness. It retained its vigour but it was softened with grace and aesthetic sensitiveness. As Jahāngīr was fond of birds and flowers, more of the local environment entered into the paintings, especially in the background. Western influence also began to make itself felt through Jahāngīr's interest in the paintings brought from Europe by the Jesuit missions. It showed itself in the adoption, in some paintings, of linear and aerial perspective called *dūrnumā*. One typical Mughal canon of perspective was of one plane superimposed on the other with a plurality of vanishing-points, so that all details were shown equally clearly; but European unitary perspective was also introduced.

Under Shāh Jahān, though the excellence of the pictures was unaffected, there was a ripeness that felt baffled in seeking new avenues of excellence. It expressed itself in the richness of materials and especially in elaborately ornate margins. It is wrongly believed that painting languished under Awrangzēb. The ripeness of Shāh Jahān's reign, however, turned into decay and, though some excellent pictures were painted, art lost its vigour; certainly there was less patronage, and the status of the artist was much degraded.

The Mughal school of miniature painting reached an excellence which has seldom been surpassed. In spite of the handicaps of the conventions which admitted only profiles or three-quarter faces, and mostly stiff postures, the Mughal portrait painter was somehow able to depict the very soul of the subject. Even in large groups, this quality is maintained in drawing the individuals. The pictures were drawn in three styles: *rangīn qalam* (full colours), *nīm rang* (one prevailing colour, mostly sepia), and *siyāhī qalam* (black and white). The figures have the rhythmic beauty of the calligraphic curve, and the composition of groups, as well as the distribution of colours, is excellent. It was not uncommon for the outlines to be done by one artist and the colourings by another. Copies on vellum (*charba*) were taken of the linework of portraits and groups, from which further paintings might be made in later years. It is a remarkable testimony to the realism of the school that Awrangzēb, feeling concerned about his son Mu'aẓẓam, when he was placed in confinement in 1098/1687, asked the painters to send him regularly pictures of the prince so that the emperor could see himself that the prince's health had not suffered. Mughal art was entirely secular, and concerned itself mainly with the court, though sometimes pictures relating to the life of the people were also painted. Jahāngīr had the habit of having painted a new bird or a new flower that he came across, and his favourite painter, Manṣūr, has been acclaimed as one of the greatest nature painters of the world. The influence from Muslim countries was kept alive by the employment of painters from outside. One of the most outstanding of these was Farrukh Beg, who arrived in the last years of Akbar's reign.

The Rājpūt schools of painting, which grew up under the inspiration of the Mughal school, also deserve mention. Their themes were strikingly different: Hindu epics and religious themes, and also symbolic representations of the sentiment of musical modes (*rāgas*).

Calligraphy was looked upon as an allied art and received generous patronage. It was practised on a much wider scale and the period produced some outstanding calligraphists.

Music

The difficulties of the interpretation of the evidence concerning Indian music mentioned in the previous chapter are no less in the Mughal period. The greatest name, perhaps, of this period is that of Tānsēn, a converted Hindu who became a disciple of the saint Muḥammad Ghawṯ of Gwalior, near whom he is buried. Everyone knows of him and pays lip-service to him; yet it is now almost completely impossible to form any idea of why he was so highly praised or of what contributions to music he made.

RELIGION

The first millennium of the Hijra came to a close in the sixteenth century. Many Muslim minds were attracted to the idea of the advent of the *mahdī*, a leader who would breathe new life into Islam. This idea had become common and was accepted even in orthodox circles. Sayyid Muḥammad, a pious and learned professor in the university town of Jawnpur, came to believe that he was the *mahdī* and proclaimed his mission. His teachings were not heretical. He demanded greater conformity with the *Sharī'a*. His claim, however, was rejected by the orthodox '*ulamā*', and he met with such opposition that he had to emigrate from the sub-continent. He died in exile in 911/1505. Two of his disciples carried on his mission. The first was Shaykh 'Abd Allāh Niyāzī who settled near Bayānā. A young scholar, Shaykh 'Alā'ī, became his disciple, and gathered a large following, who did not limit themselves to preaching, but tried to enforce the *Sharī'a* through coercion. This brought conflict with the officials. Makhdūm al-Mulk, the *ṣadr al-ṣudūr*, asked for a trial of Shaykh 'Alā'ī. The ruling sultan, Islām Shāh, despite his strictness, did not want to push matters to extremes, but on Makhdūm al-Mulk's insistence, Shaykh 'Alā'ī was flogged. Already weak and emaciated through austerity and wandering, Shaykh 'Alā'ī collapsed and died at the very first stroke. 'Abd Allāh Niyāzī also was flogged, and was removed by his followers, who nursed him back to health. Later a message was received from Sayyid Muḥammad that he had repented at the time of his death and seen his error. 'Abd Allāh gave it credence and recanted. Many others, however, refused to believe the message. The followers of the sect are still found in the Deccan and in Gujarāt, though their numbers are small. The orthodox hostility to these Mahdawīs led to systematic persecution which made the theologians in power unpopular.

There was some impact of Islam on Indian religious thought at this time. Certainly some Ṣūfī teachers, especially those of the Chishtī order, had made a popular front for their own views through their allegorical romances in Indian vernaculars; probably with some acceptance, for Ṣūfī mysticism often has much in common with the pantheistic mysticism of the Indian *Vedānta*. To their influence, both from their teachings and on account of the popular respect they commanded as saints and thaumaturges, may be attributed the partial conversions amongst the lower strata of Indian society—communities with more or less of Muslim belief on particular points of doctrine but generally faithful also to the godlings of popular Hinduism, its rites, festivals, social implications and prescriptions. On a higher level of influence comes the strictly monotheistic thought of such teachers as Kabīr—who in spite of his Muslim name preached strongly against what he considered to be the fallacies of both Hinduism and Islam—and Nānak, who added to Kabīr's monotheism a discipline of religion which he so much admired in Islam. But his Sikhs later developed an antagonism to the Mughal rulers, and Sikhism became the implacable adversary of Islam in north India.

Akbar, who was tired of subservience to the leaders of orthodox Islam, sought political support from non-Muslims and heterodox sectors of Islam. They gradually led him away from orthodoxy. Akbar instituted discussions on religious topics, to which in the beginning only Muslims were invited, but later men of all faiths participated, and discussions took place regarding the very fundamentals of Islam.

Amongst those who participated were Hindu pandits, Jain anchorites, Zoroastrian *mūbids* and Catholic priests. Akbar was persuaded to believe in his own spiritual attainments and he began to enrol members of different faiths as his disciples. His views were certainly not those of orthodox Islam, though the charge that he denounced Islam and ceased consciously to be a Muslim is not proved. Too much importance has been attached to the reports of the Catholic fathers by some modern writers and errors have crept into the translations of Badā'ūnī's cryptic and ambiguous statements.[1] Akbar built up a superstructure of eclectic pantheism upon the heretical views of some heterodox Ṣūfīs and others, which he perhaps only partially understood. The system he promulgated is generally called *Dīn-i Ilāhī* (Divine Faith), which attracted a little support in his court. Towards the end of his life, Akbar's enthusiasm for religious innovation considerably cooled down and we do not find any exercise in religious speculation after the assassination of Abu'l-Fażl who, along with his brother Fayżī the poet, has been credited by some for turning Akbar away from orthodox Islam. There were so many complex influences at work that even Akbar was more the recipient of ideas than a thinker.

The political repercussions of Akbar's religious thought have been mentioned earlier. At the instigation of Abu'l-Fażl's father, Shaykh Mubārak, a manifesto was drawn up to which the leading *'ulamā'* of the court were forced to affix their signatures saying that Akbar was a just ruler (*imām-i 'ādil*), and as such empowered to choose any interpretation which was in accordance with the Qur'ān and good for the realm if the *mujtahids* disagreed. This has been wrongly termed a decree of infallibility, but it was intended to weaken the position of orthodox Islam. Akbar could not be termed *imām-i 'ādil*, because he was not equipped to adjudicate between the differences of opinion of learned lawyers. However, the decree was never utilized, and Akbar relied upon the political device of appointing to high religious and legal offices his own nominees, men with pliant consciences who would carry out his wishes.

At the time of Jahāngīr's accession the orthodox party had gained sufficient influence to defeat the machinations of their rivals, and extracted from him a promise that he would restore the institutions of Islam. The movement gained momentum under the leadership of Shaykh Aḥmad of Sirhind, who is known as the *mujaddid* (renewer of the faith)

[1] For a fuller discussion, see I. H. Qureshi, *The Muslim community of the Indo-Pakistan subcontinent* (The Hague, 1962).

of the second millennium. He was a practising Ṣūfī of the Naqshbandī order, but he was able to see the harm that was being done by the views of the monists of the Shaṭṭārī and Qādirī orders. He relied upon his mystic experience to state categorically that the sensation of monism (i.e. union with the godhead) was not the highest expression of mystic progress because it was experienced in a state of ecstasy which he called *sukr* (intoxication). The higher stage was when a person was able to have this experience without losing his own sense of identity. This doctrine was reinforced with philosophical arguments. The philosophy of *waḥdat al-shuhūd* (feeling of monism through mystic experience) as opposed to *waḥdat al-wūjūd* (monism as a reality) was used for the purpose of eliminating heterodox doctrines (mainly based upon monism) from Sufism. The shaykh's influence was considerable, and we find that gradually orthodoxy was able to recapture the minds of the people as well as the leaders and this expresses itself in its growing strength until it culminated in the orthodox measures of Awrangzēb. This was no doubt partly political: his popular elder brother, Dārā Shikōh, was a disciple of a Ṣūfī of the Qādiriyya, had studied Hindu philosophy and mysticism, and in his *Majma' al-baḥrayn* sees a 'mingling of the two seas' of Hindu pantheism and Muslim mysticism, of a type similar to Ibn al-'Arabī's. Shaykh Aḥmad's influence was not limited to the sub-continent: through the Mujaddidiyya branch of the Naqshbandīyya order it spread as far as Turkey in the west and Indonesia in the east. It was through his efforts that Sufism gradually turned away from heterodoxy, and became one of the main supporters of orthodoxy.

APPENDIX

THE SULTANATES OF THE DECCAN, SIXTEENTH TO EIGHTEENTH CENTURIES

The rise of the five Deccan sultanates from the chaos of the Bahmanī empire, through the assertion of autonomy by the provincial governors, has been mentioned in the previous chapter. Their subsequent political history is largely a record of continuous strife between them, with occasional and variously aligned alliances but only on one significant occasion a community of interest. Internally, however, in spite of their border troubles, they developed major literary, religious and cultural centres.

To some extent all the sultanates inherited the factionalism of local and foreign elements which had led to the disruption of the Bahmanī empire; although the religious tensions implicit in this faction were less prominent, as the influential Shī'a tended to be concentrated in the Shī'ī sultanates, Bījāpur and Golkondā. The Barīd Shāhīs in Bīdar and the 'Imād Shāhīs in Barār were Sunnī, as were the Niẓām Shāhīs of Aḥmadnagar until Burhān I adopted Shi'ism in 944/1537. The sultanate of the Barīd Shāhīs was gradually encroached upon in the north and west by Bījāpur, against which Bīdar made occasional alliances with the other sultanates; Bījāpur was subject to continual pressure on the south from the Vijayanagara kingdom, and the only occasion on which all the sultanates, except the northern Barār, acted jointly was when their confederation defeated Vijayanagara at the battle of Tālīkota in 972/1564–5. Bīdar was finally annexed by the 'Ādil Shāhīs of Bījāpur in 1028/1619.

The 'Imād Shāhīs were remote enough in Barār to avoid most of the Deccan inter-sultanate conflicts, although there were occasional clashes with the Niẓām Shāhīs. Eventually, after the battle of Tālīkota, when Bījāpur was able to enlarge its dominions by the annexation of former Vijayanagara possessions, Aḥmadnagar was anxious to achieve a similar increase of strength. She therefore invaded Barār in 981–2/1574–5, and extinguished and absorbed the 'Imād Shāhī power.

The Niẓām Shāhīs were generally in a state of dispute with the two large sultanates, Bījāpur and Golkondā; one sultanate was always eventually compelled to intervene in a war between any two others lest one should become victorious, and so upset the balance of power to the disadvantage of the original non-belligerent. It was indeed in this way that these three sultanates were able to remain in existence where the single Bahmanī sultanate had failed. Part of the Aḥmadnagar-Bījāpur dispute arose from a royal marriage in 927/1521 when the Bījāpur princess's dowry was stipulated as the border fort of Sholāpur, which Bījāpur consistently failed to cede. In 937/1531 Burhān I of Aḥmadnagar, alarmed by the growth of the power of Bahādur Shāh of Gujarāt, who had just annexed Mālwā and with whom Khāndēsh was now closely allied, offered him his allegiance. The aim of Bahādur was to enlist Aḥmadnagar's support against the Mughals, but Burhān secretly suggested to Humāyūn that he attack Gujarāt. A compact between Aḥmadnagar and Bījāpur to annex Barār and Golkondā respectively in 941/1534 was pursued, but abandoned on the death of the Bījāpur sultan, Ismā'īl. His successor, Ibrāhīm, instituted Sunnism as the official faith, dismissed most of the 'foreign' element, and by substituting Marāthī and Kannada for Persian allowed the free employment of Brahmans in his administration. Shortly afterwards Bījāpur-Aḥmadnagar relations worsened when the Niẓām Shāhī ruler embraced Shi'ism. Bījāpur was faced also with rebellion in its Konkan provinces, fomented by the Portuguese at Goa which they had taken from Bījāpur in 915/1510. From the 960s/1550s the 'Ādil Shāhīs actually turned to Vijayanagara for assistance against their rivals; but Vijayanagara soon became the dominant partner in the Bījāpur/Golkondā/Vijayanagara confederacy, offended allies and enemy alike by the insults it offered Islam, and made arrogant demands on the sultanates as the price of its assistance in arms, and their excesses led to the battle of Tālīkota already mentioned.

Aḥmadnagar, constantly at war with Bījāpur and weakened by wars of succession, had further trouble from a Mahdawī faction in 999/1591. On the death of the ruler some four years later, four contending factions were leading towards anarchy when an appeal was made to the Mughals for help. They were in fact preparing for an invasion of the Deccan when the appeal arrived, and Aḥmadnagar was soon under siege from them. The dowager queen, Chānd Bībī, purchased its liberty by the cession of Barār; but Mughal ambition was not to be denied, and the city fell to them in 1009/1600. Within ten years the Ḥabshī minister, Malik 'Anbar, had ousted the Mughals and restored a nominal Niẓām Shāhī dynasty, but the state was still under heavy Mughal pressure and Bījāpur was able to acquire much of the southern Aḥmadnagar lands. The defection of a Mughal nobleman to Aḥmadnagar led to a renewed Mughal attack in 1039/1630, and the kingdom finally fell to the Mughals three years later.

In Bījāpur a Mughal force had in 1046/1636 forced a peace compelling the acknowledgment of Mughal suzerainty, and the land remained peaceful for some twenty years thereafter until the Marāthās under Shivājī commenced a series of depredations on the north and west. This did not prevent Bījāpur from retaining its position as a great cultural centre; but politically it was almost a spent force when it finally fell to Awrangzēb in 1097/1686.

The Quṭb Shāhī kingdom of Golkondā was less disturbed than its neighbours, and knew less internal party and religious faction. The city of Hyderabad (Ḥaydarābād), built with much magnificence at the end of the tenth/sixteenth century, had for six years a Persian embassy from Shāh 'Abbās, and was a leading centre of Shī'ī scholarship. The Dutch established themselves at Masulipatam, on the Madras coast, in 1024/1615, and the English seven years later. In the 1040s/1630s the Golkondā possessions to the south were extended, but the Mughals were pressing on the north and in 1045/1635–6 Shāh Jahān forced the payment of tribute. The Golkondā minister Mīr Jumlā having aggrandized himself in the east, the sultan appealed to Awrangzēb for aid; this led to the Mughal siege of Golkondā in 1066/1656, which was bought off. But the later rise of two Brahman ministers provoked Awrangzēb to renewed attack, and Golkondā finally fell in 1098/1687.

CHAPTER 3

THE BREAKDOWN OF TRADITIONAL SOCIETY

By the beginning of the eighteenth century, Muslim society in India was composed of descendants of Turkic, Afghan, Persian and Arab immigrants, and of Indian Muslims who had embraced Islam in different regions and circumstances, and under varied pressures. The immigrants, who themselves belonged to distinct culture groups, brought with them the characteristic features of their ethnic and non-Islamic religious backgrounds. In the course of time, the interaction of their various ideas and values contributed to the rise of cultural traditions which were radically different from those of their birthplaces; Muslims, while retaining the broad basic framework of their religion, evolved healthy traditions of toleration, and of peaceful coexistence with the indigenous population. A great deal of similarity developed in the dress and ornaments of Hindus and Muslims. Though the eating habits of the members of the two religious groups differed in important respects, especially in the eating of meat, these difficulties did not undermine their social relations. They appreciated each other's religions and social taboos and adjusted their lives in an atmosphere of social amity and mutual understanding. Hindu and Muslim peasants, artisans, craftsmen and merchants worked in close co-operation with each other. Hindu bankers, merchants and money-lenders controlled trade and commerce and exercised considerable influence over the finances of the government. They were the backbone of society.

The use of Persian served as a strong unifying bond between the Hindu and Muslim upper classes. Translations of some Hindu religious works into Persian widened the outlook of those Hindus who were linked with the Mughal administrative machinery; and an atmosphere of sympathetic understanding of the spiritual problems of the two major religions of India was thus created. The verses of Sa'dī, Rūmī and Ḥāfiẓ regulated the patterns of social behaviour of Hindus and Muslims alike. The educational policy and the translation scheme undermined Brahmanical superiority in the interpretation of Hinduism. The obscurantism and bigotry of Awrangzēb disturbed the Hindu and Muslim nobility alike. The control of the Hindus over the revenue and the financial policies and administration of the Mughals had made even the Muslim theologians and other religious functionaries dependent upon them for the verification of their land grants. The occasional outbursts of the theologians and the Ṣūfīs against the Hindu administrative officers of the Mughals should be ascribed to their failure to make the administrative machinery subservient to their demands.

The system of state employment evolved by Akbar, known as the *manṣabdārī* system, absorbed all types of landed interests such as Rājpūts, Bundēlās, hill rajas, Jāts, Marāthās, and the Muslim tribes and ethnic groups, into the same graded hierarchy, with definite salaries either in the form of a *jāgīr* (assignment of land) or partly in cash and partly in *jāgīr*, for each *manṣab* (rank) and for the number of horsemen maintained. They constituted the upper crust of society. Their tribal, racial, or ethnic interests conditioned their alliances and enmities; religion played hardly any significant role in political and official dealings. The secular laws of the government exercised an overriding control over the administration.

The *zamīndārs* were those who held various types of hereditary land rights. From the highest Rājpūt chieftains down to the petty 'intermediaries' at village level, all were known as *zamīndārs*. They were ambitious, restless and given to intrigue. Akbar assimilated them to the Mughal administrative machinery by offering them *manṣabs* commensurate with their status and ability. The emperor's paramount authority to appoint, depose, or reduce rank kept them under proper control and various other restrictions ensured their loyalty to the emperor. They collected the revenue from the cultivators and credited the state's share to the imperial treasury through the official revenue collectors. They maintained law and order in their jurisdiction, protected the roads and other means of communication and were required to promote cultivation. Their rights and privileges were superior to those of the other cultivators in the village. The dispossessed Afghan nobles among the Muslims enjoyed large and compact *zamīndārī* interests. Under them, a considerable number of other Afghans and their retainers controlled many villages. The *zamīndārs* of other caste groups also held compact areas under their control. This enabled them to rebel without much inconvenience and on the slightest provocation. Religious and racial questions added to the confusion. The system itself was responsible for the frequent Jāt, Sikh and Afghan revolts in the north and those of the Marāthās and the Deccan Muslims in the south.

Grants were also made for religious and charitable purposes to scholars, theologians, and members of respectable families who had no other means of livelihood. The descendants of the Muslim saints, and of the Prophet, were the greatest beneficiaries under this system. Subsequently they also came to hold compact *zamīndārī* interests in different villages. These grants were liable to be resumed at the death of the assignee, though some grants were hereditary. The conditions under which grants were made were not always complied with by grantees; and any interference on the part of the administrators to curtail the privileges of the beneficiaries met with strong resistance.

The peculiar features of the Mughal administrative system produced three types of villages. There were villages consisting exclusively of a Hindu or Muslim population, and there were others with a mixed population. The exclusively or predominantly Muslim villages had their mosques with *imāms*, *mullās* and other religious functionaries, who played a vital role in directing village life into healthy channels, and exhibited restraint, understanding and sympathy in the celebration of religious festivals and other communal functions. The tomb of a genuine or legendary saint or a martyr was an object of veneration to Hindus and Muslims alike. Revivalistic and puritanical movements could not eradicate all syncretic tendencies.

The pressure on the supply of *jāgīrs*, the demand for which increased at the end of the seventeenth century because of the costly military campaigns of Awrangzēb (ʻĀlamgīr I) in the impoverished Deccan, and the need to reconcile Deccani nobles, unbalanced the Mughal administrative machinery. Awrangzēb's policy of breaking the *zamīndār* cliques by encouraging them to embrace Islam, and thus driving a wedge into their ranks, strengthened their parochial and separatist tendencies. Those *zamīndārs* who did not pay revenue unless military force was applied against them, were a perpetual source of trouble to the Mughal administration. At the end of the seventeenth century, in combination with other recalcitrants, such people rose in rebellion in several places. Some of them used religious slogans to rally support for their cause, and ambitious religious leaders lent a willing ear to them. In the eighteenth century these *zamīndārs* assumed the role of autonomous chiefs.

The war of succession after the death of Awrangzēb dealt a heavy blow to the straitened resources of the empire; and the prodigality of Shāh ʻĀlam Bahādur Shāh (1119–24/1707–12) shattered the basis of the *jagīr-*

dārī system. Subsequently, to the detriment of the interests of the central government, encroachments were made on crown land which began to be assigned as *jāgīrs*. An attempt to replenish the treasury by introducing a revenue-farming system aggravated the crisis. The powerful factions at the court began to bid for the profitable and most easily manageable *jāgīrs*, and the leading aspirants for power embarked upon a scramble for the key positions of the empire. Gradually some *manṣabdārs* also acquired permanent *zamīndārī* rights.

Formerly the Mughal nobles had intrigued to gain the favour of their masters; now they assumed the position of king-makers. The leading Muslim factions unhesitatingly set out to seek the protection of the Marāthās, the Rājpūts and the Jāts whenever it suited their purpose. Ẕu'l-Faqār Khān, the all-powerful *wazīr*, obtained the abolition of the *jizya* through Jahāndār Shāh, whom he raised to the throne in 1124/1712. Even the reversal of the policy of Awrangzēb did not save the Mughal empire from dissolution. Failure to keep pace with technological developments in other parts of the world and to introduce much-needed administrative reforms precipitated its downfall. Nādir Shāh's invasion of 1152/1739 left the imperial capital, Delhi, bleeding and prostrate. The surrender of Sind, Kābul and the western parts of the Panjāb to the invader made the Mughal frontiers vulnerable to successive invasions by the Afghan chief, Aḥmad Shāh Durrānī (1160–87/1747–73). His rise contributed to the encouragement of the Indian Afghans, who began to make a fresh bid for supremacy over the ruins of the Mughal empire. The Afghan chief Najīb al-Dawla assumed the role of a fifth columnist. A headlong collision between the rising Marāthā power and the ambitious Afghans, both of whom were making a bid for political supremacy in northern India, became inevitable. On 14 January 1761, a fierce battle was fought between Aḥmad Shāh Durrānī and the Marāthās at Pānīpat in which the Marāthā power was worsted. The Durrānī invasion drained the impoverished Mughal empire of its entire resources; Najīb al-Dawla suppressed the Jāt incursions, but the Sikhs, who had gradually consolidated their power, obtained supreme control of the whole of the Panjāb. In less than ten years the Marāthās reappeared before Delhi; but neither they nor the Mughals could withstand the gradual penetration of the British into India. The battle of Pānīpat exposed the weakness of the Indian powers.

On the decline of the central authority at Delhi, there arose along with the Hindu states a number of Muslim principalities which pretended to owe nominal allegiance to the Mughal emperors, but to all intents and purposes were independent. Of these the most important in the north were Bengal, Oudh (Awadh) and the trans-Gangetic powers, and in the south, the Āṣaf Jāhī state of Ḥaydarābād (Deccan). They tried to reorganize their administrations on traditional lines, and their courts became the rendezvous of unemployed artists, craftsmen, musicians and poets, mainly Muslims.

RELIGIOUS CHALLENGES

Except for the Mujaddidī Naqshbandīs, all the mystic orders in India followed the principles of *waḥdat al-wujūd*. At the end of the eleventh/seventeenth century, Shāh Kalīm Allāh Jahānābādī (d. 1142/1729) revived the past glories of the Chishtīs at Delhi. He tactfully but firmly opposed the religious outlook of Awrangzēb, denounced him as presumptuous, and sought to stimulate the interest of all sections of Indians in his own preachings. His disciple, Shaykh Niẓām al-Dīn Awrangābādī (d. 1142/1730), preached the humanitarian teachings of the Chishtīs in the Deccan. His activities in Awrangzēb's camp in the Deccan stifled the Naqshbandī influence. About 1160/1747, his son, Shāh Fakhr al-Dīn, moved to Delhi, and plunged himself into the teaching of *Ḥadith* and Sufism. The Mughal emperor, a large number of important nobles, princes and princesses vied with one another in exhibiting their devotion to him. Till his death in 1199/1785, his teachings inspired many of the Sunnīs of Delhi, and were acceptable to Shīʿīs, as well as to many Hindus. The influence of his disciples extended from Delhi to the Panjāb in the west and to Ruhīlkhand in the east.

The most eminent Ṣūfī and the theologian of the twelfth/eighteenth century was Shāh Walī Allāh of Delhi. He was born on 4 Shawwāl 1114/3 March 1703, and received his early education from his father, whom he succeeded in 1131/1719 as the head of the *madrasa* which he had founded in Delhi. In 1143/1731 he visited Mecca on Pilgrimage, and studied *Ḥadīth* under some eminent scholars at Medina; he came back to Delhi on 14 Rajab 1145/31 December 1732. His studies in Arabia and contacts with other scholars of the Islamic world sharpened his intellectual faculties and extended his outlook. He began to feel a mystical confidence which enabled him to discard *taqlīd* (acceptance of religious authority) without compromising his belief in the innate perfection of the *Sharīʿa*: he asserted that the pursuit of Islamic ordinances conferred far-reaching social and individual benefits upon Muslims. His *magnum opus, Ḥujjat Allāh al-bāligha,* draws extensively upon the works of Ibn Miskawayh, al-Fārābī and al-Ghazālī; it reflects a deep understanding of the importance of the process of historical change and socio-economic challenges. His *Sharīʿa*-state, which he sought to reorganize on the model of the government of the first four caliphs, was the *sine qua non* of a peaceful and prosperous life for all ages and times. *ʿAdl* (justice) was the golden mean which preserved the framework of all political and social organizations. *Tawāzun* (equilibrium) in economic life ensured the proper development of a healthy society. An excessive burden of taxation on the revenue-producing classes—peasants, merchants and artisans—undermined the health of the body politic.

In a letter addressed to the Mughal emperor, the *wazīr* and the nobles, he gave practical suggestions for the remedying of the defects in society and the administration. His letter to Aḥmad Shāh Durrānī details the chaotic condition of the imperial court, and includes a brief account of non-Muslim powers such as the Jāts, the Marāthās and the Sikhs. It was written mainly to seek the goodwill of the conqueror; and it would not be realistic to interpret it as an invitation to that adventurer to invade the country and restore the glory of Islam. Aḥmad Shāh Durrānī, who had already invaded India on four earlier occasions, hardly needed any invitation for the invasion of 1174/1761, or briefing about the state of affairs of the non-Muslim powers. Mīrzā Maẓhar Jān-i Jānān, another eminent saint of the times, had no respect for the Durrānī army and for him it was a scourge of God.

Shāh Walī Allāh was wholly sincere in his devotion to the cause of Islam, and had a firm faith in its power. 'If it so happens', he wrote, 'that the Hindus are able to obtain complete domination over India, the Divine Mystery would force their leaders to embrace Islam in the same manner as the Turks formerly did.'[1] Though his ancestors had migrated to India in the seventh/thirteenth century, he considered himself an alien, and exhorted his followers to abandon 'the customs of ʿAjam and the habits of the Hindus'.[2] His Arabic works subsequently found considerable popularity in Egypt and other Arabic-speaking countries which were experiencing an increasing tension because of the conflicts between eclecticism and revivalistic movements. His disciple, Sayyid Murtaḍā of Bilgrām (near Lucknow), achieved immense celebrity in Egypt. He

[1] Walī Allāh, *Tafhīmāt-i Ilāhiyya* (Delhi, 1936), I, 215–16.
[2] Walī Allāh, *Waṣiyat Nāma* (Lucknow, n.d.), 7.

wrote commentaries on al-Ghazālī's *Iḥyā' 'ulūm al-dīn* and other works on *Ḥadīth* and *fiqh*. Shāh Walī Allāh died in 1176/1762.

His son, Shāh 'Abd al-'Azīz (1159–1239/1746–1824), vigorously followed the traditions of his father. He wrote a detailed refutation of the beliefs of the Twelver Shī'a, which aroused considerable sectarian bickering. Mawlānā Sayyid Dildār 'Alī, the contemporary Shī'ī *mujtahid* of Lucknow, and his disciples, published several polemical works in refutation. His younger brothers, Shāh Rafī' al-Dīn, Shāh 'Abd al-Qādir and Shāh 'Abd al-Ghanī, co-operated with him in strengthening the cause of Sunnī orthodoxy. The first two translated the Qur'ān into Urdu. Students from Western Islamic countries also attended their seminaries.

The *fatwā* which he wrote after the Emperor Shāh 'Ālam was taken under the protection of the East India Company (1803) is regarded as a very revolutionary document, but it hardly solved any of the problems of the contemporary Muslims. In the *fatwā* he addressed the puppet Mughal emperor as the *imām* of the Muslims, and accused the British of wantonly demolishing the mosques and restricting the freedom of *dhimmīs* and Muslims alike. Their non-interference with practices such as the Friday and *'Īd* prayers, the call to prayer, and cow-slaughter, did not according to him merit any respect, because they felt no obligation to show such tolerance. He therefore declared that India was now *dār al-ḥarb* (the abode of war, i.e. outside the Islamic oecumene). The fact that he did not take the same view of the domination of the Marāthās, who had previously exercised supreme control over the emperor, cannot be defended on theological grounds. It seems that he examined the situation historically. Instances of Hindus exercising absolute control over the Muslim powers were not wanting in Indian history; but the supremacy of a foreign power was unprecedented. Neither Shāh Walī Allāh nor Shāh 'Abd al-'Azīz realized the strength of the challenge of the West, and they left Muslim society in a backward condition, torn with sectarian strife and groping in the dark.

Shāh 'Abd al-'Azīz's nephew, Ismā'īl Shahīd, and his disciple Sayyid Aḥmad Barēlwī (1201–46/1786–1831) made further contributions to the practical and theoretical aspects of the *jihād*. Sayyid Aḥmad was born at Rāe Barēlī, in the Shī'ī state of the nawabs of Oudh. He was not interested in literary education. In about 1804, he travelled to Delhi, and studied there under Shāh 'Abd al-Qādir, one of the sons of Shāh Walī Allāh. After approximately two years' stay he left for his native land.

In 1810 he joined the Pathān chief, Amīr Khān, and obtained considerable training and experience in guerrilla warfare. When Amīr Khān surrendered and was recognized as the ruler of Tōnk (November 1817), Sayyid Aḥmad came back to Delhi. His experience as a soldier and his achievements as a mystic elicited the immeasurable admiration of Shāh 'Abd al-'Azīz. Shāh Ismā'īl, son of Shāh 'Abd al-Ghanī, and Shāh 'Abd al-'Azīz's son-in-law, 'Abd al-Ḥayy, both became Sayyid Aḥmad's disciples. Like a roving missionary, accompanied by his disciples, he visited a number of towns in modern Uttar Pradesh, Bihār and Bengal, where they militantly sought to suppress popular religious practices, and combated the prejudice against the re-marriage of widows.

In 1821 Sayyid Aḥmad came to Calcutta, and set off for Mecca. A study of the Wahhābī movement there seems to have strengthened his zeal for militant Muslim revivalism; and in 1824 he returned to India with his mind full of ideas of *jihād*. A large number of disbanded sepoys of the East India Company, unemployed Pathān followers of Amīr Khān, Ruhillās and the supporters of the rulers of Sind warmly responded to his declaration of *jihād* against the Sikhs, whom he imagined he would be able to overthrow easily. In 1826 he left for the North West Frontier; patched up alliances with some tribal chiefs; and obtained considerable success in early skirmishes against the Sikhs. On 11 January 1827 he assumed the title of *imām*; he then wrote to the rulers of Bukhārā and Herat, explaining the differences between an *imām* and a sultan, and urging them to help him without any fear for their own thrones. Shāh Ismā'īl also wrote a treatise on the subject. Their arguments did not convince the Central Asian rulers, and their activities aroused considerable suspicion among the neighbouring Islamic powers and tribal chiefs. Yār Muḥammad Khān, the chief of Pēshāwar, strongly opposed Sayyid Aḥmad, whose followers defeated him heavily in 1830. The Sayyid formed a government in accordance with his ideas of a pious Islamic state. His attempts to stamp out the practice of giving daughters to the highest bidders, the enforcement of Islamic taxes on the poor tribes who had joined him in the lust for gold, and other rigorist judicial and economic laws, estranged the tribes from his followers, who were known as the *mujāhids* or 'fighters in the *jihād*'. His decree permitting his Indian disciples to take the young girls of the tribes as wives, provoked a violent storm of hostility against the *mujāhids*, and the tribes began to desert them. In the beginning of 1831 the Sayyid made a dash as far as Muẓaffarābād in Kashmir, was defeated, and returned to Bālākot, where he fell fighting against a strong force of Sikhs in May 1831. The claims of Sayyid Aḥmad to the imamate, his assumption of a status akin to that of the Rightly-guided Caliphs, his schemes for puritanical reforms, and the indiscreet interference of his followers with the lives of the tribes, brought rapid disaster to his plans of conquest and of founding an ideal Islamic empire extending from Pēshāwar to Calcutta. His schemes were too narrowly based to fit into the framework of contemporary Islamic society. The British authorities actively welcomed unrest on the frontiers with the Sikhs, and connived at the flow of arms, money and men from their Indian possessions to the Sayyid. The movement of Sayyid Aḥmad, though known as a Wahhābī movement, had no organic connexion with Muḥammad b. 'Abd al-Wahhāb's movement, and was called by its followers the *Ṭarīqa i-Muḥammadīyya*. His followers were divided into several branches; some even went to the extent of calling him a messiah.

THE IMPACT OF THE BRITISH ADMINISTRATION

Political distintegration and social degeneration after the death of Shāh 'Ālam Bahādur Shāh I brought little economic dislocation, and was not a corollary of intellectual or moral decay. The traditional seminaries of Delhi, and the *dars i-niẓāmī*, or the curriculum of the oriental learning evolved at Lucknow in the eleventh/seventeenth century, produced some eminent scholars in several branches of the traditional learning, and regional literatures were also greatly enriched. The development of Urdu was a singular contribution of the period. Scholars like Tafaḍḍul Ḥusayn Kāshmīrī who flourished in the reign of Āṣaf al-Dawla (1188–1212/1775–97) in Oudh, learnt English and Latin, and compiled some valuable mathematical works. Mīrzā Abū Ṭālib Khān, also called Abū Ṭālib Landanī ('the Londoner'), who was born at Lucknow in 1166/1752–3, served the court of Oudh and the East India Company in various capacities. In the years 1798–1803 he travelled to Europe and wrote a detailed account of his experiences in the *Masīr-i ṭālibī fī bilād-i Afranjī*, which he completed in 1804. He took a keen interest in British social, political and economic institutions, and assessed them in his work with a remarkable degree of comprehension.

The Rājpūts, Jāts, Marāthās and Sikhs who carved out independent principalities followed the broad pattern of the Mughal administration and welcomed the presence of talented Muslims at their courts; thus the general economic equilibrium of the Muslims remained undisturbed.

The battles of Plassey (Palāsī) in 1170/1757 and Buxar (Baksar) in 1178/1764 put an end to the independence of Bengal. The series of revenue legislative measures passed between 1772 and 1790 culminating in the permanent settlement (1793) of Lord Cornwallis replaced the old class of *zamīndārs*, mainly Muslims, with speculators comprising Calcutta *banians* (bankers), moneylenders and subordinate employees of the East India Company. The Muslim aristocracy, which took pride in its extravagance, had not the ready cash to profit by the new regulations as did the Hindus. The high-handedness of the Company's agents undermined the monopoly of the Muslim weavers, who possessed hereditary looms and adhered to the traditional system of manufacture. Subsequently the unfair competition of the manufacturers in England and the unwillingness of the Company either to protect the Bengal cotton industry from the repercussions of the Industrial Revolution, or to share with the Indians the widened horizon of their industrial experience, reduced the region to a plantation for the production of raw materials and a dumping-ground for cheap manufactured goods from the West.

A large section of the Muslim artisan class fell back upon the land for its livelihood. The Company's increasing interest in commercial crops such as jute, indigo, tea and opium, and the rapid development of a money economy undermined, especially in Bengal, the basis of Indian cultivation. A considerable number of Muslim agriculturists disposed of their land to Hindu bankers, and were soon reduced to the position of landless labourers. Suspicion of the British, their indifference towards the lot of the Muslims, and the high-handedness of the newly emerged landed aristocracy, prepared a breeding ground for several militant Muslim revivalist movements, which were regarded as offshoots of the Wahhābī movement.

The movement which Ḥājjī Sharī'at Allāh (1781–1840) started in East Bengal after his return from Mecca in 1818 was popularly known as the Farā'iżī movement, because of the emphasis which the adherents of the movement laid on the observance of *farā'iż* or obligatory religious duties. Sharī'at Allāh's long stay in the Ḥijāz (1799–1818) had imbued him with the spirit of the Wahhābī reforms, and driven him away from the mainstream of Bengali life. He set himself the task of restoring the puritanical customs of early Islam in rural Bengal. His followers emphasized that India under British rule was *dār al-ḥarb*, and therefore it was not lawful to perform Friday prayers or those of the two *'Īds*. A section of the Muslim peasantry became hostile to their uncompromising and fanatical attitude, and Hindu landlords helped the recalcitrants. In 1831 a major clash between the parties dealt a severe blow to the plans of Ḥājjī Sharī'at Allāh and he retired into seclusion. His son Ḥājjī Muḥsin, alias Dūdū Miān (1819–62), who after 1838 led the movement started by his father, divided most of East Bengal into districts and appointed a *khalīfa* (agent) to each. He took a determined stand against the levying of illegal cesses by landlords and indigo planters. Copying the Arabs, who ate locusts, he insisted that his disciples should eat grasshoppers. The cultivators and the village artisans responded enthusiastically to his preaching. The Hindu *zamīndārs* and his Muslim opponents, whom he forcibly tried to convert to his mission, implicated him in a number of criminal suits; he served several terms of imprisonment and died on 24 September 1862.

A similar revivalist movement based on socio-economic grievances was started in West Bengal by Mīr Nithār 'Alī, popularly known as Tītū Mīr, a well-known Calcutta wrestler who in 1821 had come under the influence of Sayyid Aḥmad of Rāe Barēlī. His followers wore a distinctive dress and would only eat with members of their own brotherhood. The landlords imposed a tax which was quite heavy for a poor peasant on each of them, which came to be known as the Beard Tax, for all of them wore beards. This gave rise to a number of minor riots and ultimately Tītū Mīr fell fighting against a military contingent sent to crush his uprising on 19 November 1831. The revivalists had little success in eradicating superstitions and backwardness in rural Bengal, and made themselves a target of attack by British officials and Hindu *zamīndārs*. Their zeal for reforms was praiseworthy, but they were antiquated and short-sighted.

The changes introduced into the revenue and judicial administration by Hastings and Cornwallis between 1772 and 1793 deprived the Muslims of all the higher posts that they had so far retained. By the end of the 1820s, the anglicization of Indian institutions, and the increased opportunities for the British to obtain home comforts, including the presence of their families in India, tended to set British administrators apart from Indian life. They became increasingly authoritarian and race-conscious, and the need to read and understand Persian or Hindustani was hardly felt. They regarded the use of native languages as a necessary aid to administration; few, indeed, took any cultivated interest in them.

Muslim scholars in India, who during the previous centuries had depended entirely on state patronage, suffered from its disappearance.

Until the end of the eighteenth century, the Muslims took a considerable interest in the service of the East India Company. Some of them wrote historical works of singular importance under the patronage of their English masters. Between 1800 and 1804, the encouragement of John Gilchrist of the Fort William College, Calcutta, contributed to the publication of works of outstanding value. Scholars from all over northern India applied to the authorities of the College for appointment. Even Mīr Taqī Mīr, the distinguished Urdu poet, applied for a position, but did not succeed because of his advanced age.

In 1835 the 'anglicizers' defeated the 'orientalists' and all the funds appropriated to education were directed to English education alone. In 1826 an English-language class was started in the Calcutta *madrasa*, which had been established in 1781; but already the Bengali Hindus had made considerable headway in learning English. The potential control by missionaries of the English education made the Muslims suspicious of the intentions of the government. They protested in vain against English being made an official language. Gradually there emerged in Bengal a class of uncovenanted government servants, medical practitioners, lawyers and their clerks, printers and publishers, who had acquired English as a commercial investment, and came to possess an outlook and ideology vitally different from that of previous generations. The Persian poets no longer stimulated the interest of the Bengali Hindus—in fact, Persian and Arabic words were deliberately purged from Bengali and a Sanskritized dialect was evolved for literary purposes. This effectively disqualified Muslim Bengalis from acquiring even minor posts in the government.

Bombay and Madras, the two other Presidency towns, did not witness the same process of economic distress. The influential and well-to-do Muslims in these towns, particularly in Bombay, were mostly descendants of Arab merchants. The Khōjās and Bohrās, who for centuries past had controlled trade in Gujarāt and Bombay, maintained an independent organisation for the betterment of their own communities. They also spent a portion of their obligatory religious taxes for the advancement of the Muslims in general. They kept their solidarity intact, and responded to the need to acquire an English education as far as it promoted their commercial interests. The Muslim landed nobility of the North-Western Provinces (created in 1843) and other parts of India that subsequently came under the control of the British, were not, as in Bengal, supplanted by a new class of Hindu *zamīndārs*; but they long remained suspicious of the government's intentions in spreading English. James Thomason, the lieutenant-governor of the North-Western Provinces[1] (1843–53) realized the potential dangers of the predominance in the public service of Bengalis educated in English. He designed a scheme of vernacular education which helped the Muslims to maintain their position in the lower ranks of government service. To all intents and purposes, the vernacular in that province meant Urdu, the language of Muslim intellectuals and Hindus who served Muslim chiefs.

Delhi College, founded in 1824, where English was also taught as a subject, stimulated considerable interest among Muslims; some of its pupils obtained commanding importance in the last years of the nineteenth century. It was primarily an institution of oriental learning, and used Urdu as the medium of instruction. The teaching of physics and chemistry and the experiments in laboratories stimulated considerable interest among the pupils. A body of scholars under its auspices translated a number of books from English and Persian into Urdu, which were published in Delhi, Āgrā and Lucknow. The College produced a galaxy of outstanding scholars who made singular contributions to the healthy development of the social and intellectual life of the second half of the nineteenth century.

RESISTANCE TO BRITISH IMPERIALISM

The most formidable resistance to British imperialistic designs was made by the Marāthās and the court of Mysore. The latter owed its glory to Ḥaydar ʻAlī, a man of humble origin, who with resourcefulness and admirable courage took control of the Hindu state of Mysore, overthrew his rivals, and in a very short time reorganised the administration on sound lines. After his death on 7 December 1782, his son, Tīpū Sulṭān, succeeded him. He introduced military reforms of far-reaching importance, created a navy, established armament factories, promoted trade and industries and reorganized the civil administration. His efforts to make alliances with the Ottomans, Persia and Kābul were in vain. The French did not respond to his overtures, and the *niẓām* of Ḥaydarābād and Marāthās found his power a challenge to their own existence. Yet he effectively resisted the British, and died defending his independence on 4 May 1799.

[1] The former name of the old province of Āgrā, later incorporated in the United Provinces (*sc.* of Āgrā and Oudh), and not to be confused with the North-West Frontier Province.

Oppressive revenue policies, the recklessness of unimaginative and inexperienced British settlement officers, the hardships of the artisans, economic distress, annoying delays in judicial proceedings, indiscreet evangelical preaching by Christian missionaries after their admission to the Company's territories in 1813, and the insular habits and prejudices of many British officers, all made the British power detestable in the mind of a large number of Indians, particularly the emotional and economically backward Muslims. The annexation of a number of states by Lord Dalhousie (1848–56) in pursuance of his policy of the 'Doctrine of Lapse', and the annexation of Oudh on the grounds of inefficient administration, precipitated a crisis. The introduction of Enfield rifles and greased cartridges sparked off the revolt. The rising began on 10 May 1857, when the sepoys at Meerut in the North-Western Provinces mutinied. Soon the leadership and initiative passed into the hands of dispossessed chiefs, *zamīndārs*, priests, civil servants and their supporters. Among the principal leaders were Khān Bahādur Khān in Rohīlkhand, Bēgam Ḥażrat Maḥall and Mawlawī Aḥmad Allāh Shāh in Oudh, Bēnī Mādhō Singh to the east of Lucknow, Kunwar Singh in Bihār, Nānā Ṣāḥib in Kanpur, Tatyā Tōpē and the *rānī* of Jhānsi in Bundēlkhand, and Bahādur Shāh II at Delhi. This concerted action cut across all barriers of caste and creed and of linguistic and regional prejudices. British officers, despite their active efforts, failed to stir up communal frenzy. The Muslims gave up cow-sacrifice in Delhi and other places to demonstrate their goodwill towards Hindus, and the latter exhibited due consideration towards the religious sentiments and prejudices of the Muslims. At many places in the North-Western Provinces, Oudh, Bihār and the Central Provinces, the entire population rose in a body against British domination. In Delhi, Barēlī and Lucknow, constitutions were hurriedly drafted, designed to ensure a sort of democratic government. The attempt to fight with antiquated weapons against forces trained on modern lines and using the hated Enfield rifles, lack of control over the means of communication and a want of proper organising capacity among the leaders shattered their hopes of expelling the British from India.

The failure of the revolt saw a complete liquidation of the old classes of *zamīndārs* throughout the British territories wherever they had been active in the rising. They were replaced by those who had loyally served the British. A horror of rebellion and its ruthless suppression made the new class of the *zamīndārs* and their supporters timid, suspicious, and dependent on the local British officers. Control of the Indian government was finally assumed by the British crown, and the perpetuation of the princely order under British paramountcy was ensured. The *ta'alluqdārī* order of big landlords was retained in Oudh; a number of influential *ta'alluqdārs* were Muslims. Some Muslim states, such as Rāmpur and Bhōpāl in northern India, and Ḥaydarābād in southern India, extended considerable patronage to talented Muslims from British India, and became centres of Islamic learning, art and literature. They retained Urdu as the court language. A considerable number of Muslims found important posts in the Hindu states too. The *ta'alluqdārs* of Oudh and the *zamīndārs* also offered minor posts to the Muslims, who gradually adjusted themselves to the changed circumstances and the new order.

A large number of Muslim sepoys escaped to the North West Frontier, joined the Indian *mujāhids* who lived round about Pēshāwar, and organized raids against the British. After a number of skirmishes they were badly crushed in 1863. Trial proceedings between 1864 and 1870 established the presence of close links between some Indian followers of Sayyid Aḥmad Barēlwī in India and the Frontier rebels, and dozens of them were sentenced to capital punishment. The publication of W. W. Hunter's *The Indian Mussalmans* in 1871 greatly alarmed many British officials but the lieutenant-governor of the North-Western Provinces denounced it as 'not only exaggerated but misguiding' and 'calculated to do much mischief, and create panic and alienation on both sides'.[1]

MUSLIMS AND ENGLISH EDUCATION

Before the outbreak of the revolt of 1857, some enlightened Muslims in Calcutta had realized the importance of English education for their community. The National Mohammedan Association, established in Calcutta in 1856, with Nawwāb Amīr 'Alī (1817–79) as president, and the Mohammedan Literary Society founded by Nawwāb 'Abd al-Laṭīf (1828–93) in April 1863, tried to overcome the difficulties that hindered the spread of English education among the Muslims. Karāmat 'Alī of Jawnpur (d. 1873) advocated the study of European languages in order to acquire a knowledge of the sciences. Throughout the greater part of his life he preached in eastern Bengal.

In 1806 Ḥājjī Muḥammad Muḥsin, a prominent Persian philanthropist,

[1] Mayo Papers, Cambridge University, Add. 7490 (56).

had established an endowment yielding an annual income of Rs. 45,000 for religious purposes. For some time the trustees mismanaged the income, and subsequently the government used it for other purposes. As a result of the efforts of Nawwāb 'Abd al-Laṭīf and some others, the income of the fund was directed in 1873 towards the establishment of *madrasas* in Dacca, Chittagong and Rājshāhī. A substantial portion of the fund was assigned to the payment of fees of Muslim students in the modern schools and colleges of Bengal. Scholarships for education in England were also granted out of the fund.

The Anjuman-i Islām of Bombay played an active role in the promotion of English education in Bombay. Badr al-Dīn Ṭayyibjī (1844–1906), a leader of the Khōjā community, worked for many years as its secretary and for about sixteen years was its president. He ardently advocated the higher education of Indian women, particularly Muslims. His own daughters graduated from Bombay University with distinction, and one of them trained as a teacher in England on a government scholarship.

The increasing interest taken by the British in the Middle East after the completion of the Suez Canal (1869) made them conscious of the need to win the hearts of the Muslims. The viceroy, the earl of Mayo (1869–72), observed 'There is no doubt that, as regards the Mohammedan population, our present system of education is, to a great extent, a failure. We have not only failed to attract or attach the sympathies and confidence of a large and important section of the community, but we may even fear that we have caused positive disaffection, as is suggested by Mr O'Kinealy and others'.[1]

The benefits of this change were adequately reaped by Sayyid Aḥmad Khān (1817–98) whose loyal and fearless services to the cause of the British in 1857 had won him their favour. He had already written several works of outstanding merit. After the restoration of peace and order, he plunged into the task of removing misunderstandings between the British and the Muslims, and of promoting education and Western thought. He started schools at Murādābād and Ghāzīpur in the North-Western Provinces, and tried to bring English works within the reach of his fellow-countrymen through translations into Urdu. He also urged patronage of vernacular education. The translations of the Scientific Society, founded by him in 1864, were warmly welcomed by the govern-

[1] Note by H.E. the Viceroy, Simla, 26 June 1871; Mayo Papers, Cambridge University, Add. 7490 (12).

ment. He strove for the establishment of a vernacular department in Calcutta University, or alternatively the creation of a vernacular university in the North-Western Provinces. Lord Mayo also supported the demand for patronage of the vernacular.[1]

The Bengalis, however, strongly opposed the movement, and asked what was really meant by 'the vernacular.' With Sayyid Aḥmad, it amounted to the introduction of Urdu. His Hindu associates, particularly Rājā Jaikishan Dās Chaubē of Murādābād, belonged to western United Provinces, where Urdu was spoken by Hindus and Muslims alike. Sayyid Aḥmad had insufficient experience of the sentiments of the Hindus of eastern United Provinces and Bihār, though he had served at Ghāzīpur and Banāras for about five years. He failed to realize that the new educated Hindu middle class rapidly emerging there was resilient and vitally different from the landed nobility of medieval days. The emphasis on vernacular education on the part of the government coincided with a movement for the introduction of Hindi, written in *Devanāgarī* characters, as the official language of the courts. In 1867, Hindi written in *Kaithī* characters (a running hand for keeping accounts in Bihār somewhat similar to *Devanāgarī*) was approved by the lieutenant-governor of Bengal as the official vernacular of Bihār. This change encouraged the protagonists of Hindi in Banāras. Sayyid Aḥmad came into headlong conflict with them. Both Urdu and Hindi prose were in a preliminary stage at that time. Sayyid Aḥmad was himself a founder of simple modern Urdu prose writing. The main controversy revolved around the question of a script. The use of both the scripts, or of Roman script, was suggested to him but he maintained a rigid attitude on the subject and transformed the *Scientific Society's 'Alīgarh Gazette* into a forum for the defence of Urdu. His successor, Nawwāb Muhṣin al-Mulk (1837–1907), suggested that he should also publish the translations of the Scientific Society in Hindi, as a compromise; but the Sayyid scornfully rejected the proposal.

During his visit to England (1869–70) he came in close contact with the conservative section of the country; studied the educational system of Cambridge; and was deeply impressed by the cultural and material progress of the West. In 1870 he started an Urdu journal entitled *Tahdhīb al-akhlāq* to educate the Muslims for modernism, and to prepare the ground for the establishment of the Mohammedan Anglo-Oriental

[1] Letter of Lord Mayo to Sir E. Perry, India Office, July 1870, Cambridge University, Add. 7490 (40).

College at 'Alīgarh, which he started in the form of a school in 1875. Separate arrangements were made for teaching Sunnī and Shī'ī theology on traditional lines. Opposition to his religious views impelled Sayyid Aḥmad to keep himself aloof from the management of the teaching of theology in the College. The foundation-stone was laid by Lord Lytton in 1877, and it started functioning in 1879 on the lines of the colleges of Cambridge. In 1877 Sayyid Aḥmad supported the cause of simultaneous examinations for the Indian Civil Service in England and India. In a speech delivered during his tour of the Panjāb in 1884 he referred to India as one nation. Yet he was devoted to the cause of the education of Muslims, mainly of the upper classes, throughout the rest of his life. He was strongly opposed to the system of representation by election and was 'convinced that the introduction of the principle of election, pure and simple, for representation of various interests on the local boards and district councils, would be attended with evils of greater significance than purely economic considerations'.[1]

The establishment of the Indian National Congress alarmed some landlords of the North-Western Provinces. Its lieutenant-governor, Sir Auckland Colvin, was strongly opposed to A. O. Hume, the moving spirit behind the Congress movement. Sayyid Aḥmad was alarmed. He thought that political agitation was likely to take a violent turn, and that if Muslims joined Congress the second phase of their ruin would begin; he imagined that the success of Congress would bring the domination of the Bengali Hindus throughout India. In speeches delivered at Lucknow in 1887, and at Meerut in March 1888, he strongly opposed the policies and programmes of Congress and advocated the strengthening of the hand of the British government. He advised the Muslims to concentrate their energies upon the acquisition of higher English education, and to rely upon the good sense of the government to safeguard their rights. He earnestly desired that 'The Crescent and the Cross being united should shed their light over India'.[2] He formed the Indian Patriotic Association and later on the United Indian Patriotic Association to mobilize the opinion of the landlords and influential sections of Indian society against Congress. He issued circular letters to Muslim associations all over the country urging opposition to the National Congress. His appeal did not receive a satisfactory response,

[1] C. H. Philips, *The Evolution of India and Pakistan* (London, 1962), 188–9.

[2] Sir Sayyid's address to Sir Auckland Colvin, 10 March 1888. '*Alīgarh Institute Gazette*, 15 March 1888.

and he soon decided to found a separate Mohammedan Anglo-Oriental Defence Association of Upper India to mobilize Muslim public opinion there in support of his point of view.

The contradictory and irreconcilable aims and objectives of his new association failed, like all his political preachings, to arouse the interest of the Muslims. The Muslim *ta'alluqdārs* of Oudh did not sympathize with the educational movement of 'Alīgarh, which was generally dominated by the *zamīndārs* of the North-Western Provinces, Delhi and the Panjāb. The raja of Maḥmūdābād was planning to establish a separate Shī'ī College, which his son founded in 1919. Several Urdu periodicals were pitted against his activities. His Mohammedan Educational Congress, founded in December 1886, which was renamed the Mohammedan Educational Conference in 1890, held its sessions mainly in the North-Western Provinces and the Panjāb. His '*Alīgarh Institute Gazette* had a circulation of no more than four hundred. During the last years of his life, it was virtually controlled by the principal, Theodore Beck (1885–99), who regarded the Indian universities as centres of native rebels and a political evil of the first magnitude, and had a particular aversion to Bengalis. The strings of the student organizations in the College were always in the hands of Beck or some other English professor who never let slip any opportunity of instilling the benefits of loyalty to the British government into the minds of Muslim youth, and of injecting them with anti-Hindu communal views. The European staff considered themselves more in the capacity of residents accredited to the native states than as members of the teaching profession. In collaboration with the district officers, they played a leading role in the establishment of the Board of Trustees and in the selection of Sir Sayyid's successor. The private life of Sir Sayyid was embittered by the resignation in 1892 of his own son, Sayyid Maḥmūd, from the Allahabad High Court Bench because of his disagreements with the chief justice of Allahabad. Sir Sayyid Aḥmad died broken-hearted on 27 March 1898.

Modern Muslim scholars in India, drawing upon the thesis of Mawlānā Muḥammad 'Alī and other nationalists, tend to depict him as a great nationalist and a well-wisher of all Indians, while the Pakistani scholars find in him one of the fathers of their nation. In fact he did not advocate separatism but tried to seek safeguards for the Muslims under indefinitely continued British rule.

As long as Britain remained friendly to the Ottoman empire, the claims of Sultan 'Abd ül-Ḥamīd II (1876–1909) to be the caliph of the

Islamic world did not disturb him and his followers. Indeed, he popularized the use of the Turkish fez in India, and extolled the Ottoman Tanẓīmāt. But the change in British policy after 1880 alarmed him; and he very strongly denounced the claims of Sultan 'Abd ül-Ḥamīd, and urged that the sultan's sovereignty or caliphate should be confined to his own territories.

The rise of Muḥammad Aḥmad b. 'Abd Allāh, who claimed to be the Expected Mahdi in the Egyptian Sudan (1881), caused considerable panic among European officials in India. The religious significance of the movement was closely examined, and the intelligence service was alerted to discover where the sympathies of Indian Muslims lay. Sir Sayyid and Muḥsin al-Mulk wrote articles theorizing on the rise of *mahdīs* in Islam, and convinced the European officials that Indian Muslims had no sympathy for the Mahdi of the Sudan. Pan-Islamic ideas were reinforced, mainly among the younger generation, by the successive visits of reformers such as Jamāl al-Dīn al-Afghānī to India, and by the sufferings and misfortunes to which the Muslims of the Middle East were thought to be exposed. Sir Sayyid was too much concerned with the present to pay attention to the future. He therefore fought incessantly against all ideologies which tended to arouse British suspicion about the loyalty of the Muslims. He advocated the cause of Muslim landowners, and had little sympathy with the common Muslims, though he occasionally shed tears of sympathy for them. He clung to the antiquated policy of the East India Company that education would 'filter down' to the lower classes from their 'leaders'. He drew inspiration from the political ideals of John Stuart Mill, and did not sufficiently realize the importance of contemporary political and economic forces.

His far-fetched interpretations of Qur'anic verses to prove his thesis that *waḥy* (revelation) and 'natural law' or 'reason' were not conflicting and irreconcilable, failed to convince many of his closest associates. But his plea for a close examination of the Traditions ascribed to the Prophet Muḥammad, even if they were embodied in the classical collections of *Ḥadīth*, stimulated great interest amongst members of his own generation and among his successors too. They, like him, applied the theory to suit their interpretations of such institutions as polygamy and slavery, which were becoming more and more distasteful to Western opinion. One of his close associates, Chirāgh 'Alī, who had studied the reform movements of the contemporary Middle East, and had come in contact with Jamāl al-Dīn al-Afghānī, elaborated Sir Sayyid's thesis with great confidence. He powerfully advocated the view that all the wars of Muḥammad were defensive, and that aggressive wars or forced conversion was not allowed in the Qur'ān. The *Spirit of Islam* by Sayyid Amīr 'Alī (1849–1928) is not defensive in tone but uses the findings of contemporary Western scholarship and a powerful mode of expression to establish the contributions made by Islam to the betterment of mankind. Such works equipped Muslims to carry out a dialogue with the critics of Islam.

Among the galaxy of scholars that supported Sayyid Aḥmad Khān in his educational programme but who pulled in different directions so far as his apologetics were concerned were Ḥālī, Shiblī and Nadhīr Aḥmad. Shiblī (1857–1914) wrote a large number of works in Urdu, including a detailed biography of the Prophet Muḥammad, in which for the first time he applied Western methods of research to historical writings in Urdu, and tried to demonstrate that Islam strongly protected the rights of non-Muslims. He passionately justified the levy of *jizya* on non-Muslims, and sought to prove that it was not a discriminatory tax, and did not seek to humiliate the *dhimmīs*. In 1879 Ḥālī (1837–1914) published his celebrated *Musaddas,* presenting in very appealing verse an account of the rise and fall of the Muslims. This work had a singular success and filled the Indian Muslims with pride in the past, and lamentations for the present. The work was intended to prepare them for the battle for life with understanding and confidence. Nadhīr Aḥmad (1831–1911) strongly defended the position of women in Islam, and urged their education on traditional lines. He endeavoured to reconcile the *Sharī'a* with the everyday needs of Muslims, and urged that the laws of the British government, being the source of peace and prosperity for Muslims, deserved the same implicit obedience as the *Sharī'a*. He did not hesitate to lend money on interest, and glossed over the injunctions concerning its illegality. He was a very good orator, and his subtle humour exercised great influence over his audience.

The traditional theologians strongly opposed the modernism of Sir Sayyid and his associates. They also were deeply concerned with the challenges that the Christian missionaries and the Arya Samāj movements offered to Islam, but they found the pseudo-intellectual fads of the westernized Muslims unsound and risky. The theologians trained at Deōband faced the above challenges on traditional lines. *Dār al-'Ulūm*, a seminary of traditional Islamic learning at Deōband in the North-Western Provinces, was established by a famous theologian, Mawlānā Muḥammad Qāsim Nānawtawī in 1867, and gradually attracted students from Afghanistan, Turkey and other Islamic countries. Since government rules did not permit assistance to theological institutions, *Dār al-'Ulūm* depended on donations from Muslims. Mawlānā Muḥammad Qāsim himself took an active interest in defending the traditional Muslim position in all polemical discussions. After his death on 14 April 1880, he was succeeded by Mawlānā Rashīd Aḥmad Gangōhī who passionately believed that the study of philosophy undermined theological beliefs. He urged the Muslims to co-operate with the Hindus in wordly matters, and to participate in the activities of the Indian National Congress as long as the basic principles of Islam were not violated. On his death in 1905, Mawlānā Maḥmūd Ḥasan (1851–1921) a man of courage and great organizing capacity, succeeded him. He organized former students of Deōband from India, Afghanistan and Turkey into a body known as the *Jam'iyyat al-Anṣār*. The theologians of this school made important contributions to the idea of Islamic brotherhood and the unity of Islamic countries.

The Barēlwīs, or the followers of Mawlāwī Aḥmad Riḍā Khān (b. 1855) of Barēlī, strictly adhered to the orthodox practices enjoined by the traditional theologians and the Ṣūfīs, and made a very strong impact upon the religious beliefs of the Muslim masses in the United Provinces and the Panjāb. *Nadwat al-'Ulama'* was started at Lucknow in 1894, with the avowed objectives of bridging the gulf between the old and the new ideals of Islamic learning, and of rousing the '*ulamā'*, as custodians of the interpretation of the *Sharī'a*, to the need for facing the challenges of the times effectively. The Shī'ī theologians also copied the example of *Nadwat al-'Ulamā'*, and organized a similar body at Lucknow.

Early in his career, Mīrzā Ghulām Aḥmad (1839–1908) of Qādiyān in the eastern Panjāb, took an active interest in the polemics directed against the Arya Samajists and the Christian missionaries. In 1889, he experienced a mystical urge which led him to declare himself to be the promised Mahdi or Messiah. His followers, who are known as the Aḥmadiyya or the Qādiyānīs, developed an organized and trained community in Qādiyān, which was upset after the partition of 1947. There they tried to restore the pristine purity of Islam, and endeavoured to solve economic and social problems within the framework of their brotherhood. They are keen missionaries, and actively propagate Islam in Europe, Africa and America.

Expanding facilities for higher education in the third quarter of the nineteenth century contributed to the rapid multiplication of Muslim graduates everywhere in India, but most of the native Muslim princes and richer *zamīndārs* sent their children to 'Alīgarh for higher education. The mere fact that a man's son was at 'Alīgarh enhanced his social prestige; many students there did not devote themselves seriously to studies but lived in idle elegance, willingly supported by their families. Some of them enthusiastically emulated English ways of life, etiquette and social behaviour. Most of them detested the compulsory theology classes and prayers; only a negligible number took an interest in them. This horrified the conservative Muslims, and a wide gap opened between them and the English-educated youths. The verses of Akbar of Allahabad (1846–1921) reflect the cultural tensions of the period. He bitterly mourned the fate of Muslims who acquired an English education in order to obtain higher government posts, but who were ultimately frustrated and disillusioned because of the want of adequate patronage from the British. He mercilessly criticized the growing indiscipline and neglect of parental authority among those who were educated in English. Unfortunately for him, his own son whom he sent (with most careful instructions about his behaviour) to London for higher education, threw his teachings overboard and married an English woman.

From the last decades of the nineteenth century, the Western style began to infiltrate systematically into the life of the English-educated Muslim aristocracy. Their village homes conformed to the traditional style of the eighteenth century, but those who possessed means tended to build bungalows of bastard Baroque or mock Gothic in Simla and other places where the European community retreated during the summer. There they found adequate opportunities for winning the favour of influential British officers. They were more than satisfied if their efforts won them the petty titles which, they imagined, established their superiority over the rest of the aristocracy, and certainly enabled them to obtain minor posts for their dependents.

Those who possessed resources sent their sons to England for higher education, where most preferred to seek admission to the bar, rather than to qualify as doctors, scientists or engineers. Those who did not possess adequate wealth or talents to read law in London, qualified themselves to practise in the district courts. Their strong links with the villages, most of them being themselves of *zamīndār* families, enabled them to earn a comfortable living and sufficient prestige in their own society. Soon these legal practitioners acquired more proprietary rights in the villages because of the ease with which they could learn about and profit from the financial difficulties of others. Thus, in 1901, of the seventeen barristers practising at Patna, twelve were Muslims. Of the eighteen advocates of the Allahabad High Court in 1901, ten were Europeans or Anglo-Indians, six Muslims, one Hindu, and there was one other.[1]

Since a literary education provided adequate opportunities for such ambitions as the Muslim youth then possessed, hardly any one in those days evinced any interest in technical education. So it was but natural that they should oppose the introduction of competitive examinations for services, and demand special privileges on the basis of their loyalty to the British government as a class, or of their links with the Muslim aristocracy.

THE MUSLIM POLITICAL AWAKENING

The political upheaval in the country, plague, famine, communal riots, movements relating to the protection of the cow, the Arya Samāj movement, and militant Marāthī and Bengali nationalism were all factors which drove the Muslims closer to the British government. The language question, however, shook the faith of a large section of the ʿAlīgarh youth on the advisability of blind reliance on British protection. In 1900 Hindi was accorded the status of the court language in the North-Western Provinces and Oudh. The Muslims were naturally agitated; but the militant attitude of the lieutenant-governor silenced them.

Muhṣin al-Mulk infused considerable life into the activities of the Mohammedan Educational Conference. Its Bombay session, held in December 1904, was presided over by Badr al-Dīn Ṭayyibjī, who did not fail to criticize the policy of the Muslims of ʿAlīgarh and their College. He also tried to mobilize the support of Muslim theologians in favour of the ʿAlīgarh educational movement. The *Anjuman-i Ḥimāyat-i Islām* of Lahore also made considerable efforts to invigorate the lives of the Muslims on the lines suggested by Sayyid Aḥmad Khān. These efforts, however, did not go far towards satisfying Muslim youths not belonging to the landed nobility. Muslim graduates of other universities were intolerant of the preferential treatment accorded to the products of ʿAlīgarh and the need for political awakening and political education was increasingly felt.

[1] B. B. Misra, *The Indian middle classes* (London, 1961), 329–30.

Lord Curzon's partition of Bengal (October 1905) which created a separate Muslim province of Eastern Bengal and Assam, promised fresh avenues to success, chances for higher education, and increased rank and responsibility to the Muslims of Eastern Bengal, particularly to those of Dacca, the capital. Nawwāb Salīm Allāh of Dacca, who, according to Sir Bampfylde Fuller (the lieutenant-governor of the new province and a most enthusiastic supporter of Curzon), was 'not a wise man' but 'exhibited courage and loyalty in the attitude he maintained' on partition,[1] became the leader of the Muslims overnight. The popular agitation that followed in the wake of the partition made the Muslims of other provinces restive. The Swadeshī movement, which among other aspects promoted the use of the handlooms and spindles of the Muslims of Bengal, was a significant challenge to the ideology of 'Alīgarh. Realizing its importance, Muḥsin al-Mulk urged Muslims to develop their handicrafts on the lines suggested by the agitators with a view to saving themselves from being left behind in the handicraft race as they had been left behind in others.

On 3 August 1906, Fuller offered his resignation in the hope of impressing the central government with the urgency of an unimportant matter. To his surprise, it was at once accepted; and as he had publicly stood forth as a champion of the Muslims, some turbulence seemed likely. The sensation was shortlived, however, and according to the viceroy was not 'so acute as to necessitate heroic measures'.[2] The excitement died down more quickly than was expected. However, the partition was accepted as a *fait accompli*. Lord Minto urged, 'in fact the Mohammedan community, when roused, would be a much stronger and more dangerous factor to deal with than the Bengalis'.[3]

The budget speech of the secretary of state for India, Lord Morley, (August 1906) embodying broad outlines of the introduction of reforms, evoked considerable interest on the part of Muḥsin al-Mulk who was finding it exceedingly difficult to pursue the policy of Sir Sayyid any longer. The factors leading to the presentation of an address embodying Muslim demands by a deputation to the viceroy on 1 October 1906, the formation of the Muslim League in December 1906, and the acceptance

[1] Letter of Fuller to Curzon, 18 October 1905, Curzon Papers, Mss. Eur. F. III (212); India Office, London.

[2] Reply to the letter of Archbold, principal of the Mohammedan Anglo-Oriental College 'Alīgarh; Dunlop Smith to L. Hare, 24 August 1906, Minto Papers, National Library of Scotland, Edinburgh.

[3] Letter of Minto to Arthur Godley, 17 October 1906, Minto Papers.

of the principle of a separate Muslim electorate have recently been examined at some length on the basis of the Minto and Morley papers by Wāsṭī and Das[1] from their respective points of view. An evaluation of the entire correspondence and the contemporary literature shows that the importance which the viceroy attached to Muḥsin al-Mulk's letter (which led to the deputation) and the manner in which the suggestions for the deputation were worked out indicate that such an opportunity was eagerly awaited. Certainly, no time was lost in exploiting the situation to the full.

The battle for reforms was fought mainly in London by Amīr 'Alī, the Aga Khan (Āghā Khān) and 'Alī Imām, who subsequently appeared on the scene, though Theodore Morison, the former principal of 'Alīgarh, played a leading part. The newly formed Muslim League was dominated mainly by members of the Mohammedan Educational Conference, and thus embodied the landed nobility and its protégés. Its permanent president, the Aga Khan (the *imām* of the Ismā'īlīs) was born in 1877 and had come in contact with Sir Sayyid Aḥmad Khān and Muḥsin al-Mulk as early as 1896. His appointment to the Legislative Council of Lord Curzon at the end of 1902 immensely enhanced his prestige among the Muslims, though he was warned by the governor of Bombay, with the approval of the viceroy, 'of the adverse effects of his lack of orthodoxy, his being over-anglicized and his fondness for European women'.[2] Of the younger generation, closely in touch with the youth of 'Alīgarh, was Muḥammad 'Alī (1878–1931). At the suggestion of the lieutenant-governor of the province, the Aga Khan transferred the League's headquarters from 'Alīgarh to Lucknow: the lieutenant-governor was frightened, 'lest the lawyer party, consisting of young and irresponsible persons, would attain a predominant position in the League, and that they might at some time coalesce with the advanced Hindu politicians against the Government on one or more questions, and later on rue the fact that they have done so'.[3]

The achievements of the Muslim League did not satisfy the educated Muslim youth. They were increasingly imbued with those pan-Islamic sentiments which had been so carefully controlled by Sir Sayyid Aḥmad and his followers. Faḍl al-Ḥasan Ḥasrat Muhānī, one of the most

[1] S. R. Wāsṭī, *Lord Minto and the Indian Nationalist movement 1905 to 1910* (Oxford, 1964); M. N. Das, *India under Morley and Minto* (London, 1964).

[2] Letter of Curzon to Lemington, 4 January 1904, Curzon Papers, India Office Library, London, F. 111 (209).

[3] Letter of Hewett to Minto, 3 February 1910, Minto Papers.

influential students of the period at 'Alīgarh, who edited a literary journal, was imbued with the revolutionary doctrines of Tilak, preached them fearlessly, and was convicted of sedition in 1908. Muḥammad 'Alī, although in the service of Baroda, frequently visited 'Alīgarh after his return from Oxford in 1902, and aroused political consciousness among the students.

The transfer of the headquarters of the Muslim League from 'Alīgarh to Lucknow (1 March 1910) brought it under the greater control of leaders from Oudh, eastern United Provinces and Bihār. The Aga Khan and his associates in their efforts to retain their leadership hurriedly launched a scheme for raising the College at 'Alīgarh to the status of a university, with a view to diverting the attention of Muslims from politics to educational progress. The funds collected exceeded two million rupees. The younger generation did not favour government control over the proposed university. They wanted to make it a central institution with power to affiliate Muslim institutions all over India. The Muslims of Eastern Bengal were also lukewarm in their support. The secretary of state refused to grant the power of affiliation and the scheme petered out. These events would not have proved more than short-lived ripples on the waters of Muslim politics, if the situation had not been aggravated by the successive misfortunes befalling the Ottoman empire, Persia and Morocco in 1911, 1912 and 1913.

Shiblī, who had come to believe that an oligarchy of the '*ulamā*' under his own leadership might control Indian Muslim politics, was bitterly opposed to the policies and programmes of the Muslim League. On the basis of first-hand knowledge of the affairs of the Middle East, he aroused the sympathies of Indian Muslims for their co-religionists. His disciple Muḥammad 'Alī, who had left the Baroda service towards the end of 1910, took up a journalistic career and in January 1911 started the publication in Calcutta of the *Comrade* with the motto, 'the comrade of all and partisan of none'. The paper was financed mainly by the Aga Khan and 'Alī Imām, and shifted to Delhi with the transfer there of the seat of government. *Hamdard*, its Urdu 'stable-companion' as Muḥammad 'Alī called it, was started at the close of 1913.

Mawlānā Abu'l-Kalām Āzād (1888–1958), who had obtained considerable journalistic experience under Shiblī, also travelled through Cairo and Turkey in 1908, and came in contact with the leaders of the Young Turk movement and other revolutionaries. He commenced a scheme for revitalizing Indian Muslims through his journal *al-Hilāl* which began in June 1912, marked a turning-point in Indian journalism, and soon reached a circulation of 26,000. Āzād utilized pan-Islamic feelings to whip up religious frenzy and arouse political consciousness among the Muslim masses. He strongly supported the need for a universal caliph and entertained the ambition of himself assuming the status of *imām* of all Indian Muslims. His immense learning, and mastery of the contemporary reform movements of the Middle East, endeared him even to the theologians, though most of them were envious of his increasing success and prestige. The Mawlānā himself regarded them as conservative and backward, but he could not ignore them if he was to realise his own dreams. He was in close touch with a number of Indian revolutionaries. Indeed, *jihād* and armed revolution to overthrow foreign domination were, in his opinion, identical in all respects. *Al-Hilāl* and its sister-journal *al-Balāgh* preached the notion of the Qur'anic state, which the Mawlānā's spiritual radicalism gradually transformed into a highly potent living force. He ridiculed the modernism of 'Alīgarh, as well as the backwardness of the traditional theologians, and denounced them both as blind copyists. He emphasized that the development of the sciences in the West did not necessarily undermine religious beliefs. What was needed by the Muslims was a resilient attitude towards the true Islamic values.

Intellectually much inferior but even more popular was the *Zamīndār* of Ẓafar 'Alī Khān, who never let slip a single opportunity to make capital of even the pettiest Muslim grievance. A number of other Urdu journals and newspapers in the United Provinces and Bihār also aroused political awakening among the Muslims. Dr (later Sir) Muḥammad Iqbāl (1876–1938), who formerly strove to worship in a *naya shiwālā* (new temple) of Hindu-Muslim amity and concord, set a new tone for their thinking by preaching 'that Islam as a spiritual force would one day dominate the world, and with its simple nationalism purge it of the dross of superstitions as well as of Godless materialism'.[1] His occasional verses were quoted *ad infinitum* by public speakers and whipped up the sentiments and emotions of the simple, intensely religious and sincere Muslim masses.

Amīr 'Alī, the founder of the London branch of the Muslim League and an uncompromising fighter for a separate electorate, was disillusioned after the reversal of the partition of Bengal (December 1911). He regarded it as a conspiracy between the Aga Khan, the nawab of

[1] Afzal Iqbal (ed.), *Select Writings and Speeches of Maulana Mohammed Ali* (Lahore, 1944), 51.

Dacca and the British government. He wrote to Lord Curzon on 4 January 1912, 'A telegram, copy of which I beg to enclose, reached the London League yesterday from the Honorable Syed Nawab Ally Choudhry for the East Bengal Provincial League. It was a very clever move to attempt to muzzle Salimollah with a G.C.I.E. and Aga Khan with a G.C.S.I. and it has partially achieved its objects'.[1] His proposals for closer cooperation between the Hindus and the Muslims because of the Italian aggression upon Tripoli, and Russian moves against Persia, evoked a sharp rebuff from Muḥammad 'Alī. An appeal to religion to arouse Muslim sentiments against foreign domination, became a convenient weapon in the hands of an important group of Muslim politicians in India, and retarded political awakening on a rational basis.

The Balkan War of 1912 inflamed Muslim feelings in India against the Western powers to the highest intensity. Funds were raised, and a medical mission was despatched. After the Russian bombardment of Mashhad, in 1912 and an absurd Italian threat to attack the Ka'ba from the air, all the holy places were conceived to be in danger. Their protection made a stronger appeal to the Indian Muslims than the difficulties of the Ottoman empire and Persia. Shawkat 'Alī, the elder brother of Muḥammad 'Alī, in collaboration with Mawlānā 'Abd al-Bārī, the head of the theologians of the Firangī Maḥall in Lucknow, founded the *Anjuman-i Khuddām-i Ka'ba* (Society of the Servants of the Ka'ba) with a view to uniting 'Mussalmans of every sect in maintaining inviolate the sanctity of the three *ḥarams* of Islam at Mecca, Medina and Jerusalem'.[2] Theologians of the Firangī Maḥall, who had hitherto kept themselves aloof from modern politics, became increasingly important; Muḥammad 'Alī and Shawkat 'Alī did not respond to Mahatma Gandhi's programme until 'Mawlānā 'Abd al-Barī of Firangī Maḥal had meditated and sought divine grace'.[3]

The demolition of a corridor of a mosque in Kanpur, on 1 July 1913, in order to improve the alignment of a road, named after the lieutenant-governor, stirred the resentment of the Indian Muslims very strongly. Several Muslim papers wrote passionately about the high-handedness of the government. Sir James Meston, the lieutenant-governor in question, conveniently laid the entire blame on the rising generation of the Muslims who according to him found 'a remunerative employment in agitation'.

[1] Curzon Papers, Eur. F. 111 (434). India Office Library, London.

[2] *My life: a fragment*, 67.

[3] A. K. Āzād, *India wins freedom* (Calcutta, 1959), 9.

Indeed, the incident was 'the first internal pretext',[1] but the resentment was not confined to one particular section.

After the Ottoman declaration of war against Britain, the Indian Muslim press was intensely agitated. The confiscation of the papers and presses of Muḥammad 'Alī, Abu'l-Kalām Āzād and Ẓafar 'Alī Khān, and their internment along with Shawkat 'Alī, suppressed the expression of pan-Islamic feelings for the time being. The Aga Khan, who could not accept the policies and programmes of the pan-Islamists, left the League after 1912, and it had to depend mainly on the raja of Maḥmūdābād for its finances. A Congress-League *rapprochement* was exceedingly helpful for satisfactory recruitment and the prosecution of the war. No one was better suited to achieve this than the raja of Maḥmūdābād and Sayyid Wazīr Ḥasan (later knighted), the secretary of the League from 1912 to 1919, who sincerely treasured the values of traditional Hindu-Muslim amity which the court of the nawabs of Oudh had fostered. Muḥammad 'Alī Jinnah (1876–1948), a leading Bombay barrister who was invited to join the Muslim League by Muḥammad 'Alī and Wazīr Ḥasan in London in 1913, became a trusted leader of the Congress and the League.

In 1915 Congress and the League held their sessions simultaneously at Bombay. The Congress-League scheme of 1916, whereby Congress agreed to a scheme for separate Muslim electorates (which it hitherto had strongly condemned) was the outcome of the co-operation and amity that developed in the wake of rising pan-Islamic feelings. The League and Congress worked in close co-operation for six more years. Congress, though dominated by Tilak's Hinduism and his Home Rule movement, did not arouse a sense of danger to Islam in the minds of the Muslim Leaguers of those days. Both Hindus and Muslims expressed their dissatisfaction with the Montagu-Chelmsford Report, published in July 1918. The establishment at Delhi by 'Ubayd Allāh Sindī, a student of Deōband, of an institution named *Niẓārat al-Ma'ārif al-Qur'āniyya*, to train the Muslim youth of 'Alīgarh, educated on Western lines, in the Qur'anic ideology of Shāh Walī Allāh, lent a romantic colour to the union of Deōband and 'Alīgarh. The Silk Letter conspiracy of 1915, in which the students, teachers and the principal of Deōband took an active part, adequately reflect revolutionary trends in the Deōband theologians.

[1] Minute by Sir James Meston, Lt. Governor of the U.P., 21 August 1913, Home Department, Political Proceedings No. 100/118, October 1913, Paras. 30–31, National Archives, New Delhi.

CHAPTER 4

INDIA AND PAKISTAN

Soon after the First World War, Muslim India was involved in a mass political convulsion of a composite nature. Its components were two parallel and mutually linked agitations: a tense and explosive pan-Islamic emotionalism apprehensive of the fate of the defeated Ottoman empire, of the Arab lands (especially the Ḥijāz), and of the institution of the caliphate; and an alliance with the Hindus in the nationalist and anti-imperialist mass-movement led by the Indian National Congress. These two elements of the agitation were directed against linked objectives: pressure on the government in Britain for a more sympathetic approach in deciding the fate of the vanquished Ottoman empire; and pressure on the British government in India for greater concessions towards self-determination.

The way for a working alliance with Congress had been prepared since 1911 by a series of national and international developments. The annulment of the partition of Bengal (1911), which deprived the Muslims of that province of the political and economic advantage conceded to them earlier, had convinced the Muslim leadership of the instability of British patronage. British action, inaction, or indifference on such developments as the Italian occupation of Libya, or the extension of French control over Morocco, the Balkan War, the suspected designs of a partition of Persia (and possibly Turkey) between Russia and Great Britain, had built up the image of British imperialism as an ally of all European imperialist thrusts directed against the Muslim lands. The annulment of the partition of Bengal had also taught the Muslim political leaders the lesson that the policy of loyalism, initiated by Sayyid Aḥmad Khān and followed ever since, did not pay as rich political dividends as the organised movement of political opposition conducted by Congress, or even the terrorism of extremist Hindus. The Muslim League's overtures for an alliance with Congress had begun in 1911, and had matured in the so-called 'Lucknow Pact' (1916) drafted by Muḥammad 'Ali Jinnah (Jināḥ) and approved by the Congress leaders including Tilak, whose policies had so far been unsympathetic, and occasionally actually hostile, to the Muslims. From 1917 to 1921 Congress and the Muslim League held their annual sessions simultaneously and in the same cities. Most Muslim leaders belonged to both these organizations, and naturally co-ordinated their policies.

As early as 1913 the *'ulamā'* had shown their concern over the possible fate of the Ḥijāz in the event of the dismemberment of the Ottoman empire, and Mawlānā 'Abd al-Bārī of Farangī Maḥall had founded the *Anjuman-i Khuddām-i Ka'ba*. After the war he and some other *'ulamā'* entered the political scene openly. In 1919 Muḥammad 'Alī, formerly editor of the *Comrade*, who had been imprisoned during the war for having written a fiery editorial supporting the Ottoman decision to enter the war against the Allies, was set free. In that highly tense atmosphere of Muslim political frustration, he soon emerged as the most eloquent and most influential leader of Muslim India. The Muslim League, which, despite its alliance with Congress, had followed a policy of caution when it came to open defiance of British rule in India, receded into the background. Its place in Muslim political life came to be taken by the Khilāfat Conference founded by Muḥammad 'Alī in 1919 with the objective of organizing Muslim mass-agitation to exercise pressure on the British government, to restore to the Ottoman empire its former frontiers. It was especially concerned with the independence of what it called *Jazīrat al-'Arab* (Arabia, including Iraq, Syria, Transjordan, Palestine, and especially the Ḥijāz) from non-Muslim domination, control or influence. The Khilāfat Conference was essentially a party of pan-Islam rather than of Indian Islam. The Ottoman Caliphate was its political symbol. In these policies the Khilafat Conference was supported by an organization of the *'ulamā'*, the *Jam'iyyat al-'ulamā'-yi Hind*, dominated by the theologians of Dēoband, who had a long tradition of resistance to British rule. Its leader, Maḥmūd al-Ḥasan, had contacted Enver and other Ottoman leaders in the Ḥijaz during the war, and agreed to work as an agent of the Turkish cause in India. He was arrested by the *Sharīf* Ḥusayn of Mecca, handed over to the British, and imprisoned in Malta, but released and allowed to return to India after the war.

The political philosophy of the Indian Khilāfat movement was formulated by Abu'l-Kalām Āzād, editor of the influential religious and cultural weekly, *al-Hilāl*, and a liberal theologian, who had come deeply under the influence of the pan-Islamic ideas generally attributed to Jamāl al-Dīn al-Afghānī. Āzād considered the concept of the Muslim *jamā'a* as a cohesive and monolithic social organism, the antithesis of which was *jāhiliyya*, a state of social chaos and confusion. The powers of the effective direction of the *jamā'a* had to be invested in the hands of a central authority, the caliph. Though after the four Patriarchal Caliphs the institution of the caliphate became monarchical, nevertheless under the Umayyads, the 'Abbasids and the Ottomans, the caliph still remained the rallying-point of the whole of the Sunnī Muslim community. The foundation of pan-Islamic society rested on this and on four other pillars: the rallying of the community to the call of the caliph, its obedience to the caliph, *hijra* or the migration of Muslims from a land conquered by non-Muslims to *dār al-Islām*, and *jihād* which in the modern context could be violent or non-violent according to the exigencies of the situation. For the Indo-Muslim section of the *jamā'a*, he favoured a regional *imām* or *qā'id*, a kind of a religious viceroy of the Ottoman caliph, and tried to persuade Maḥmūd al-Ḥasan of Dēoband to accept that responsibility. His concept of the Ottoman caliphate was that of a political sovereignty, and not a religious one like that of the pope; but still the monarchical caliph remained the only political symbol of the unity and coherence in the Muslim community. He commanded its obedience, which could be denied to him only if he acted in a way contrary to the Qur'ān and the *Sunna*.

But it was Muḥammad 'Alī who developed the Khilāfat movement of the Muslim masses, the first political agitation which carried almost the entire Muslim Indian population with it. From 1919 to 1922 the Khilāfat Conference and the Indian National Congress worked as twin organizations with a common leadership. Never before, and never afterwards, was Congress able to mobilize Muslim public opinion in its favour on any considerable scale.

In 1919, Mohandas Karamchand Gandhi, a London-trained barrister lately returned from South Africa, was effectively assuming the leadership of Congress, and replacing Tilak. Just then Indian nationalists were bitterly incensed against a repressive statute, the Rowlatt Act, which sought to perpetuate war-time restrictions on civil liberties. Tactless and unimaginative measures by local civil and military authorities in the Panjāb further exacerbated the situation. General Dyer, a military commander at Amritsar, had ordered firing at a public meeting held in defiance of the law, killing nearly four hundred people. Others were later made to crawl out of the area on all fours. This episode made the name of its venue, the Jaliānwāla Bāgh, the symbol of a sense of injustice and humiliation. Finally the Government of India Act of 1919, which had introduced some political reforms, modelled to some extent on the Congress-League 'Lucknow Pact' of 1916, had not come up to Indian expectations of a greater share in government and administration.

Gandhi developed at that stage the shrewd and incomparable technique of non-violent non-cooperation, a peaceful but revolutionary weapon which the vast millions of India could wield against the world's mightiest commercial empire. He took full advantage of the Muslim support which was available to him in the form of the Khilāfat unrest; lent it his full and unqualified support; used it as a testing-ground for his new technique of non-cooperation; and was able to create for a few years a monolithic structure of Hindu-Muslim solidarity, of which he was the first and undisputed leader. He pledged himself in support of the caliphate, and the territorial integrity of the Ottoman Empire. He swayed the Hindu masses towards the same political alliance and towards the mystique of the Khilāfat, a word which they considered to be derived from *khilāf*, meaning in Urdu 'opposition' and therefore implying 'opposed to the government'.

It was a Hindu-Muslim rather than an Indian nationalism. Jawaharlal Nehru describes it as 'a strange mixture of nationalism and politics and religion and mysticism and fanaticism'[1] in which the Hindu and the Muslim strains were clearly distinguishable. Gandhi's spiritualism, as described by a Hindu historian, was 'grounded in the theology of Hinduism and the ethics of Jainism'.[2] Muḥammad 'Alī was quite frank about the pull of his mind in opposite directions: 'I belong to two circles of equal size, but which are not concentric. One is India and the other is the Muslim world'.[3]

In its international role the Khilāfat movement achieved little. A deputation led by Muḥammad 'Alī visited London early in 1920, and laid before Lloyd George and H. A. L. Fisher the demands that Turkey might be allowed to retain her pre-war frontiers, and especially should not lose her control of the Ḥijāz. On 10 August 1920, the Allies sought to impose upon Turkey the treaty of Sèvres, which, if implemented, would have left her mutilated and shorn of her sovereignty. Some moves of the Khilāfat Conference in India were not only unsuccessful but disastrous in the larger interests of the Indian Muslims. The *hijra* from the British-occupied Indian *dār al-ḥarb* to the land of Islam in Afghanistan, counselled by Āzād, uprooted 18,000 Muslims, who were turned back

[1] Jawaharlal Nehru, *An autobiography* (London, 1942), 75.

[2] Beni Prasad, *The Hindu-Muslim questions* (Allahabad, 1941), 49.

[3] Afzal Iqbal (ed.), *Select Writings and Speeches of Maulana Mohammed Ali, passim.*

at the frontier by the Afghan government. From 1919 to 1924 Muḥammad 'Alī consistently expressed the view that in the event of an Afghan invasion of India, Indian Muslims should support it even if it turned against the Hindus; a view from which Āzād dissociated himself at an early stage, signalling a parting of the ways between the separatist and nationalist trends in Indian Muslim politics. These statements, encouraging, or at least expressing, wishful thinking in favour of an Afghan invasion were resented by Tagore and Gandhi. In the case of extreme Hindu communalists like Lala Har Dayal, they led to utopian polemics, envisaging a purely Hindu India, and the total conversion of all Indian Muslims and Afghans. The political confusion in the mind of the *élite* soon came to be reflected among the Hindu and Muslim masses in the form of communal riots. The sanguinary riots of Chauri Chaura in 1921 depressed Gandhi to such an extent that he called off the civil disobedience movement, which could have been very troublesome to the government. Lack of organized guidance by the Khilāfat workers in the south resulted in the ugliest and most violent of the series of riots, when, in 1922, Moplah Muslims started an anti-British agitation. This got out of control, and was turned violently against the Hindus. Hindu reaction to Islam and the Muslims stiffened soon to bitter hostility in the vigorous province of the Panjāb, where the revivalist organization Arya Samāj resumed with a reinforced fury the task of converting Muslims to Hinduism. Counter-conversion organizations of the Muslims sprang up in the same province with the propagation of Islam as their objective. Another violently anti-Muslim organization, the Hindu Sanghatan, was started by a former member of Congress, Moonje. Finally the extremist Hindu political organization the Hindu Mahasabha upheld a triple ideal consisting of the complementary concepts: Hinduism or the Hindu faith, *Hindutva* or 'Hindu-ness', being the linguistic, cultural and political aspects of Hinduism, and 'Hindudom' a novel concept of the unity and solidarity of the whole Hindu (including the Buddhist) world corresponding to the Muslim *dār al-Islām*.

By 1924 the communal atmosphere had become so poisonous with polemic, abuse and riot that Gandhi fasted for twenty-one days to enforce some moral restraint over the movements of conversion and reconversion. But the communal poison had by now reinfected the Indian National Congress itself. During the last decade of the nineteenth century and the first of the twentieth, two rival factions, under the leadership of Tilak and Gokhale, represented the anti-Muslim and pro-Muslim trends within the Congress leadership, of which the former had been the more powerful, and had alienated the Muslims from that organization during those decades. Between 1919 and 1924, under the undisputed leadership of Gandhi the two factions had merged, and the Muslims had been won over through support of the Khilāfat movement. By 1924, Hindu exclusivists, Madan Mohan Malviya and Lala Lajpat Rai, revived the anti-Muslim faction under the name of the Nationalist Party within Congress, and were more than a match for the liberal and pro-Muslim wing of Congress led by Motilal Nehru and C. R. Das. The overall moderate leadership of Gandhi, though in firm control of Congress policies relating to political resistance against the British, on the Muslim question barely held the two rival factions from falling apart. On the whole the inner pattern of Congress's attitude towards the Muslims had already in 1924 taken a polarized form, which it continued to retain, with adjustments and reorientations, until 1947.

The failure of the Congress-Khilāfat alliance almost synchronized with the collapse of the Khilāfat movement itself. Muṣṭafā Kemāl's successful revolution had put Turkey back on the map of the world; but it was a Turkey different from the one to which the Khilāfat Conference was emotionally attached. Turkish secularism, even in its earlier stages, was quite unpalatable to the Indian *'ulamā'*. The image of the Turkish hero which appealed to the Indian Muslim mind was that of Enver Pasha and not Muṣṭafā Kemāl. However, the Turkish Grand National Assembly's decision to appoint 'Abd ül-Mejīd as a caliph shorn of the Ottoman monarchy was reluctantly accepted. Supreme humiliation came with the abolition of the caliphate by the Turks on 3 March 1924, leaving the Indian Khilāfat Conference without a *raison d'être*. It had lost by now its national as well as international platform, though it continued to exist nominally for a few more years and showed some fervour in its denunciation of the caliphal claims of King Ḥusayn of the Ḥijāz, who was suspected of being a British tool. It was intellectually too unsure of itself and too disorganized to participate in the Caliphate Conference held in Cairo in 1926. It did participate in a conference of Islamic countries held in Mecca under the auspices of Ibn Su'ūd in the same year, but the question of the caliphate was not even on its agenda. In 1933 the Khilāfat Conference, now a shadow of its former self, ceased to exist. The theory of caliphate received a decent burial in the political philosophy of Sir Muḥammad Iqbāl (1876–1938), who, endorsing the approach of Żiyā Gökalp, added that though the concept of a universal Muslim caliphate was a commendable ideal, each Muslim nation should first try to put its own house in order, striving in due course for an Islamic multi-national free association.

With the collapse of the Khilāfat movement and the growing distrust of Congress, Muslim politics in India entered the phase of its *Wanderjahre* from 1924 to 1937. Separatist trends born in the 1880s now re-emerged as the predominant political impulse. This separatism was voiced in the mass orations of Muḥammad 'Alī, and Jinnah gave it a constitutional formulation. In this journey of resentment and apprehension into the political unknown, the Muslim leaders were concerned primarily with setting up safeguards for their community, to preserve its distinct religious, cultural and economic identity. As time elapsed, the focus came to be fixed more and more on securing for the Muslims a position of predominant political power in the provinces of Bengal and the Panjāb where they were numerically in a majority. With this was linked a demand for the creation or development of other Muslim regions as full provinces. In short, rather vaguely, Muslim separatism in the subcontinent was already taking a territorial form.

The next landmark in these developments was formed by the controversy over the recommendations of the committee appointed by Congress in 1928 to determine the principles of a future constitution for India (popularly known as the Nehru Report). It presented the constitutional image of a secular state as a solvent for inter-communal tensions, and in doing so, it rejected the method of separate electorates for the Muslims in favour of joint electorates.[1] To Muslims, it appeared as a repudiation of the 'Lucknow Pact' of 1916, by which Congress had accepted the principle of separate electorates. Muslim political reaction to the Nehru Report was rather confused in the beginning, but in the wake of an All-Parties Muslim Conference held under the chairmanship of the Aga Khan, Muslim counter-proposals were formulated by Jinnah in fourteen points and remained the sheet-anchor of Muslim demands for a share in political power until 1937. These envisaged a federal structure for the future India with residuary, almost autonomous, powers vested in the provinces; effective representation of minorities in the provinces 'without reducing the majority in any province to a minority or even equality' (to safeguard the chances of Muslim predominance in Bengal and the Panjāb); separate electorates, with a

[1] For this and other documents referred to in the next few pages see C. H. Philips (ed.), *The evolution of India and Pakistan 1858–1947* (London, 1962), 228–52, 290–334, 337–407.

proviso for the revision of this provision; and safeguards for the protection and promotion of Muslim institutions and personal law.

In 1930 the British Labour government invited Indian leaders to the first of a series of Round Table Conferences. Congress participated in the second Round Table Conference (1931) with Gandhi as its sole representative. Its Minorities Committee came to a dead end, as Gandhi's proposal that the problem of the relative representation of minorities should be postponed until after the framing of a constitution for India, and then referred to a judicial tribunal, was rejected alike by Muslims, Christians, Anglo-Indians and Hindus of lower castes.

The situation was summed up in the Report of the Joint Committee on Indian Constitutional Reforms (1934) in these words:

> Parliamentary government, as it is understood in the United Kingdom, works by the interaction of four essential factors: the principle of majority rule; the willingness of the minority for the time being to accept the decisions of the majority; the existence of great political parties divided by broad issues of policy, rather than by sectional interests; and finally the existence of a mobile body of political opinion, owing no permanent allegiance to any party and therefore able, by its instinctive reaction against extravagant movements on one side or the other, to keep the vessel on an even keel. In India none of these factors can be said to exist today. There are no parties as we understand them, and there is no considerable body of political opinion which can be described as mobile. In their place we are confronted with the age-old antagonism of Hindu and Muhammedan,...representative not only of two religions but of two civilizations.

The government's proposed solution for this situation was 'to translate the customs of the British constitution into statutory safeguards'.

In 1932 a British White Paper had upheld separate electorates. But the game of weightage cut both ways; depriving the Muslims of their parliamentary majority in the legislatures of Bengal and the Panjāb; and conceding them weightage in the provinces where they were, and, despite the weightage, still remained an insignificant minority. The Conservatives were in office in Britain when the Government of India Act of 1935 was passed. It invested the governor-general of the future Indian Federation, and the (British) governors of Indian provinces, with the special responsibility of safeguarding the legitimate interests of minorities. This provision, implying the perpetuation of the British presence as a third party, led to further recrimination between Congress and the Muslims. The former accused the latter of serving the cause of imperialism by their intransigence; the latter accused the former of a lack of generosity and fairness; both accused the British of a policy of 'divide and rule'.

In 1937 elections were held under the Government of India Act to implement its provincial sections. The Muslim League was revived by a new group of leaders; some of them, like Liyāqat 'Alī Khān, were members of the landed gentry, others, like Fażl al-Ḥaqq, were professional men. Jinnah was persuaded by them to return from his self-imposed retirement in Britain, and to assume the supreme leadership. The campaign and pledges of the Muslim League during these elections were not very different from those of Congress. Both stood for political independence. Both accepted, though with difference in emphasis, the principles of a diluted socialism. Both emphasized the need for industrial development and rural uplift. During the election campaign they worked, not in rivalry, but with arrangements that were co-operative. It was generally assumed that after the elections the provincial cabinets formed by Congress would include League members. Congress decided to reject the association of the Muslim League in its governments, and insisted as a pre-condition for a Muslim to be appointed as a minister, that he should resign from the League and sign the Congress pledge of membership. No similar condition required the would-be Hindu ministers to resign from the extremist Hindu Mahasabha. The Congress argument for refusing to share power with the Muslim League was that it could redeem its election pledges only by a programme of political and social reforms, which a homogeneous cabinet alone could implement by presenting a monolithic front to possible obstruction from a British governor. League members would introduce a divisible, if not a divisive factor. Against this position it is interesting to read the views of Beni Prasad: 'Orthodox parliamentarism led the Congress leaders to forget that the one-party theory, even if true of political agitation, was not, in the absence of an accomplished revolution, applicable to ministerial office.'[1]

In rejecting the Muslim League as an associate, Congress drove it in opposition to become its most fundamental adversary. By refusing to concede a minor political issue, Congress created between itself and the Muslim consensus an ever-widening political gulf. Had the Congress governments acted with restraint and foresight, and kept Hindu revivalist trends in control, this gulf could yet have been bridged. But a Hindu ideological and terminological shape was chosen for new educa-

[1] Beni Prasad, *The Hindu-Muslim questions*, 60.

tional and cultural schemes in some provinces. Hindi in the *Devanāgarī* (Sanskrit) script was given official encouragement by several Congress ministers at the expense of Urdu. In short, to the Muslims the pattern of the Congress's cultural policies seemed a substitution and a supersession of the British by Hindu institutions—a situation in which they feared the annihilation of their religio-cultural identity. The Muslim League, as the spokesman of Muslim separatism, marched from strength to strength, until it was able to justify its claim to be the sole representative of Muslim political opinion in India. Attempts by Congress to win over the Muslims by mass contact, or by creation and encouragement of mushroom anti-League parties proved quite ineffective except in the North-West Frontier Province, where the Muslim Red Shirt movement sided consistently with Congress. When the Congress governments resigned at the advent of the Second World War in 1939 (after the rejection by the British government of their ultimatum for immediate transfer of power as a prerequisite for their participation in the war effort), the political atmosphere in India as described by Sir Reginald Coupland was such that 'Indian observers agreed with the British officials that Hindu-Muslim relations had never in their experience been so bad'.[1]

During the crucial years between 1937 and 1939 the Indian Muslims in several provinces became for the first time familiar with the implications of the transfer of power from British hands into those of Congress, which had a predominantly Hindu membership. Under this impact, their political outlook underwent a final change. They ceased to regard themselves a minority community within a single, composite Indian nation. They claimed to be a nation by themselves, and, as such, felt their way towards accepting a doctrine of a separate national status, and a demand for a separate national homeland.

Though vague references to the possibility or feasibility of a separate Muslim state in India had been made from time to time since the 1920s, the first clear statement of this occurs in Sir Muḥammad Iqbāl's presidential address to the annual session of the Muslim League in 1930. He rejected the geographical, racial and linguistic criteria of nationhood in favour of Renan's definition that a nation is a spiritual principle, possessing a common and indivisible heritage of the past, which it consciously wills to hold together through the present for the future. Iqbāl argued that the Indian people as an ethnic conglomeration did not possess an indivisible heritage of the past. Hindus and Muslims

[1] Sir Reginald Coupland, *The Indian problem* (London, 1942–43), II, 132.

were in fact aiming at different, and more often than not, conflicting concepts of the future. 'Muslim demand for the creation of a Muslim India within India, was therefore perfectly justified.' Iqbāl further added 'I would like to see the Punjab, North Western Frontier, Sind and Baluchistan amalgamated into a single state'. This, he said, appeared to him as the final destiny of the Muslims.[1] Iqbāl did not specifically mention Bengal, but in all subsequent political thinking in Muslim India the same principle of separatist self-determination came to be applied to it. In 1937, the crucial year of the final parting of the ways between Congress and the League, Iqbāl wrote a number of letters to Jinnah, who observed:

> His views were substantially in consonance with my own and had finally led me to the same conclusions as a result of careful examination and study of the constitutional problems facing India, and finally found expression in due course in the united will of Muslim India as adumbrated in the Lahore resolution of All-India Muslim League (1940), popularly known as the 'Pakistan Resolution'.[2]

The name 'Pakistan', which fatefully captured the imagination of the Muslim masses because of its messianic connotations, was a contribution of Chawdharī Raḥmat 'Alī and a group of Indian Muslim students at Cambridge. It was explained that it did not represent its literal meaning 'the land of the pure', but was a mnemonic formation from the names of north-western Muslim regions. Panjāb, Afghania (for North-West Frontier), Kashmir, Sind and Baluchistan.

Iqbāl's concept of a separate Muslim state was still nebulous. The Muslim League resolution of 1940 sought to define it more precisely: '...that geographically contiguous units are demarcated into regions which should be so constituted with such territorial readjustments as may be necessary that the areas in which the Muslims are numerically in a majority, as in the north-western and eastern zones of India, should be grouped to constitute "independent States"'.[3]

From 1940 to 1947 the partition of the sub-continent on these lines remained an explosively controversial issue of Indian politics; and overshadowed all subsequent negotiations between Britain, Congress and the League. The principle of the secession of Muslim India as a separate

[1] Sir Muḥammad Iqbāl, 'The Presidential Address to the Annual Session of the Muslim League in 1930,' reprinted in *The struggle for independence* (Karachi, 1958), 16–17.
[2] M. A. Jinnah, Introduction to *The letters of Iqbal to Jinnah* (Lahore, n.d.), 4–5.
[3] Philips, *Evolution of India and Pakistan*, 353–4.

dominion was envisaged in the British Cabinet's proposals of transfer of power after the war, brought to India and discussed with the Indian leaders by Sir Stafford Cripps in March 1942, when a Japanese invasion of India seemed imminent.

Soon the concept of Pakistan as a solution of the problem of political deadlock came to be studied thoroughly by Muslims as well as non-Muslims. The case for Pakistan was perhaps argued much more convincingly by the Hindu Scheduled Castes leader, B. R. Ambedkar, and by the theorists of the Communist party of India, than by Muslim writers. A number of books were also written against the concept of Pakistan by non-Muslims, and by some nationalist Muslims; most significant of these is *India divided*, by Rajendra Prasad, who later became president of the Republic of India. The frustration which followed the failure of the Cripps Mission led a senior leader of Congress, C. Rajagopalchariyya, to introduce a resolution before the Congress Working Committee, in 1942, recommending the concession of an autonomous, if not independent, Muslim state, confined to the areas of Muslim majority, and with a confederal link with India. The Congress Working Committee rejected the resolution, but two years later it formed the basis of discussions between Gandhi and Jinnah which ended in failure. From 1942 onwards, however, Congress accepted in principle that it could not compel the people of any territorial unit to remain in a future Indian Union against 'its declared and established will'.

Elections to the legislatures, held at the end of the war in 1945, confirmed the Muslim League in its claim to be the sole representative of the Muslim consensus, as it captured all the Muslim seats in the Central Assembly, and 446 out of 495 Muslim seats in provincial legislatures.

The Labour government in the United Kingdom, which came into power at the end of the Second World War, applied itself sincerely to the problem of disengagement from India, and the transfer of power into the hands of the Indians. In 1946 a British Cabinet Mission was sent to India, which, in lieu of conceding a sovereign Pakistan, presented an alternative formula of a three-tier governmental structure consisting of a weak centre, the provinces, and between them a middle tier of provincial federal groupings. It envisaged three such groups: Group A was composed of the provinces with the Hindu majority in the middle and southern regions, and consisted of by far the greater part of India; Group B consisted of the provinces in the north-west with a large Muslim majority; and Group C consisted of the eastern provinces of Bengal and

Assam with a marginal Muslim majority. Against the feeling of the rank-and-file of the Muslim League which was now strongly in favour of a sovereign Muslim state, Jinnah accepted the Cabinet Mission's proposals. Congress also accepted them; but certain statements made, and certain stands taken by its leaders (such as Jawaharlal Nehru's proviso that the plan, including its scheme of groupings, could be subjected to future changes; and the general sympathy of the Congress leadership with the stand taken by Bordoloi, its chief leader in Assam, that the predominantly non-Hindu province of Assam should be a part of the Hindu Group A rather than the marginally Muslim Group C) filled the political atmosphere with uncertainty in so far as the Muslims were concerned. According to Abu'l-Kalām Āzād, this ambivalence in the attitude of Congress led Jinnah finally to believe that absolute separatism was the only alternative left for the Muslims, in view of the threat of revision by the Congress majority to any plan for a united India inherited from the British. The Muslim League revised its decision and rejected the Cabinet Mission plan. It reiterated its demand for a sovereign Pakistan, and launched upon a programme of direct action in an atmosphere which was already explosive with widespread communal riots.

British efforts for the transfer of power continued and a government was formed by Lord Wavell, the viceroy, with Jawaharlal Nehru as his deputy, and with Congress leaders for the first time in office at the centre. After an initial refusal the Muslim League also joined in, with the purpose of a divisive policy and an obstructionism which might serve as a pressure for the inevitable partition of the sub-continent. It was in this atmosphere that Earl Mountbatten succeeded Lord Wavell; and, as the head of a government divided against itself, it was possible for him to persuade first the anti-Muslim Patel, then the liberal Nehru and finally Gandhi himself of the inevitability of partition as the only solution.

On this basis the British government's proposal for the immediate transfer of power was announced by Earl Mountbatten on 3 June 1947, and accepted by the Indian National Congress and the Muslim League. The proposal envisaged the emergence of India and Pakistan as sovereign self-governing dominions of the British Commonwealth. The line of partition between them was to follow district boundaries (and later, according to the decisions of a Boundary Commission, sub-district boundaries) in the provinces of Bengal, the Panjāb and Assam, separating Muslim from non-Muslim areas.

British disengagement from India was largely a decision dictated by

Realpolitik and enlightened self-interest. During a debate in the House of Commons on 5 March 1947, Sir Stafford Cripps had pointed out that:

The exigencies of the war situation were such that it was not possible for the British Government to continue with the recruitment of Europeans, for the Secretary of State's Services [the higher cadres of the Indian Civil Service], while, at the same time, there was, of course, a great increase in the Indian Forces, accompanied by a rapid indianization of their officer cadre. This meant that, side by side with the growing demand for an acceleration of the transfer of power on the part of all parties in India, there was an obvious and inevitable weakening of the machinery of British control through the Secretary of State's Services.[1]

The British Parliament passed the Indian Independence Act on 18 July 1947. On 14 August 1947 the independent state of Pakistan came into existence as a dominion of the British Commonwealth with Muḥammad 'Alī Jinnah as its governor-general. India chose 15 August as the day of its independence, with Earl Mountbatten as its governor-general. The twin states were born in an atmosphere of the most sanguinary communal strife the sub-continent has known in historical times, this meant in the north-west the transfer of population involving millions in the regions on both sides of the frontier.

Hardly another state, except perhaps Algeria, was born to face from the very outset such overwhelming problems as did Pakistan. Whereas India had inherited the habitat and the smooth-geared machinery of the British administration, in the central government of Pakistan administrative institutions and offices had to start from the foundations. The two-way migration of refugees affected Pakistan adversely both ways. The exodus of non-Muslims from West Pakistan

included all the merchants, bankers and traders, most of the doctors and technical personnel, and a good proportion of teachers of higher education. In their place there arrived from East Punjab a flood of poor peasants, together with artisans and small shopkeepers from Delhi and other towns. On balance, there was an increase of almost a million out of this forced exchange. But those who came could not contribute anything vital to the economy, while those who were gone represented the whole network of commerce and exchange; the nerves and sinews of the economic system of West Pakistan...East Pakistan was crippled in a different way. The West was a viable economic unit, with a complete railroad system, a fully developed port, and an international airport: even if it entirely lacked an industrial base. The East had formed part

[1] *Parliamentary debates, House of Commons,* Vol. 434 (1946–7), cols. 497–508.

of the hinterland of Calcutta; its principal product, jute, was processed and exported from the Hooghley industrial nexus. Now, Calcutta with its mills was in another country. East Pakistan had no means of processing its staple crop, and only a second-rate port (Chittagong) through which to squeeze its exports.[1]

In 1949 neither East nor West Pakistan had any industries to speak of. This was partly due to the paucity of mineral deposits in these areas and partly to the British defence strategy of developing industrial centres at a safe distance from the frontiers. The economy of East and West Pakistan was to a certain extent complementary; but the distance of over a thousand miles between these two outlying territories made integrated economic planning very difficult from the very outset.

This geographical division of Pakistan in two far-flung units has been that country's most bewildering problem in several other ways. Situated at the opposite ends of the sub-continent, the two regions have only two elements of nationhood in common: Islam, and a dread of Indian aggression. These two elements of cohesion have to cope with a multiplicity of divisive factors. Fast air communication between these two regions has been possible only because of the courtesy of otherwise hostile India. The diet, the mode of living, the agricultural problems, the industrial requirements of the people of East and West Pakistan are different. West Pakistan is alive to the cultural pull of Shīrāz and Iṣfahān; East Pakistan to that of Calcutta. Urdu and the languages of West Pakistan are Persian-orientated; Bengali, on the other hand shares its cultural heritage with the Hindus of West Bengal, and is written in a Sanskritic script. West Pakistan itself is the home of a number of minor cultural communities, each with its own language, literature and traditions: the Pathāns, the Panjābīs, the Balūchīs and the Sindhīs who are only now beginning to merge into a single geographical and economic unity. Thus when Pakistan came into being it was a conglomeration of regional groups of peoples; it had yet to evolve into a nation.

Considering all these problems the emergence, survival and development of Pakistan has been a fairly creditable achievement. Into the vacuum created by the outgoing professional refugees entered fresh talent recruited from among the incoming middle class of Muslim evacuees. The civil service of Pakistan, though far less efficient than that of India—for under the British régime Muslim candidates who did not do so well in the competitive civil service examinations were selected to

[1] Hugh Tinker, *India and Pakistan. A political analysis* (London, 1962), 69, 71.

complete the Muslim quota—served as the steel frame which supported the superstructure of a hastily improvised administrative system. A Pakistan navy and an air force were built up *ab initio*. The army was reconstituted in the tradition of the British Indian army, which was taught to be loyal to the regimental flag, and to hold aloof from politics. In this process civil as well as defence officers received accelerated promotion, a development which to a certain extent weakened the calibre of government services. A foreign service was also created, which came to be regarded as the prize service, and therefore processes of selection to it reflected provincial rivalries and personal favouritism. Being of mediocre quality, it was less than a match for the highly professional Indian foreign service, which projected abroad a very favourable image of India in its disputes with Pakistan. Stabilizing factors in Pakistan were the vast masses of people, especially the refugees who had come in millions, and a new class of adventurous tradesmen and small-scale industrialists. The conservative religious lower middle class remained, in the years that followed, passionately loyal to the concept of Pakistan as an Islamic state. The Western-educated intelligensia, which was the real architect of Pakistan, presented a front of loyal patriotism to outside observers and in relation to all disputes with India; but within itself it had its frustrations in the way the things were going in the new state, the dangerous growth of religious fanaticism, which it used as a political instrument, and more especially in the chronic impact of provincial rivalries on the everyday life of the demoralized citizens.

In August 1948 Muḥammad ʿAlī Jinnah died. With him, Pakistan lost the only great leader it ever had. As long as he was alive, divisive trends, whether provincial or factional, were held firmly in control. Though theoretically a constitutional governor-general, he was given the title *Qāʾid Aʿẓam* (the Greatest Leader) and as such in practice, the prime minister, Liyāqat ʿAlī Khān, recognized him unofficially as a sovereign authority, and was directed by him on larger issues of policy.

On the death of Jinnah, the prime minister assumed in practice as in theory his rightful position as head of the government and administration, in accordance with democratic theory and practice; and the new governor-general (selected from East Pakistan in the interests of provincial balance), Khwāja Nāẓim al-Dīn, assumed his appointment as the constitutional head of the state with a mainly ceremonial role. Liyāqat ʿAlī Khān's Cabinet was responsible to the Constituent Assembly of Pakistan, which also acted as the national legislature. This government stabilized the country's civil, financial and economic life to some extent, with considerable emphasis on law and order. It evolved a foreign policy which envisaged close friendship with Islamic countries, especially Persia, and which, after some hesitation, moved in the direction of a closer approach towards the U.S.A. On the debit side there was a weakness on the part of Liyāqat 'Alī Khān in his sacrifice of competitive criteria of selection for the administrative services to provincial political pressure for quotas by provinces; in delay in the framing of a constitution and the holding of general elections; and in undue emphasis on the tightening of security measures. Liyāqat 'Alī Khan's assassination in 1951 was a national disaster for Pakistan, which has not since been able to produce a prime minister of his calibre. Between 1951 and 1956 the principle of a balance of power between the Panjāb and East Pakistan at the top determined the choice of the governors and the prime ministers. In itself not an unsound principle, within two years it degenerated into a manoeuvring for power, first provincial, then blatantly personal. The rivalries between the governors-general and the prime ministers sharpened the basically provincial nature of Pakistani politics, and dwarfed the chances of the growth of a healthy political life.

The economy of East and West Pakistan is essentially agricultural. Its two fundamental problems are to grow enough food for its teeming millions, and to produce cash crops for the much-needed foreign exchange, to strike a balance between the country's agricultural and industrial growth. The two main food crops of the country are rice, the staple diet of East Pakistan, which has a population of over fifty millions, and wheat, the staple diet of West Pakistan with a population of nearly forty-three millions. Its two cash crops are jute, of which East Pakistan has almost a world monopoly as raw producer; and cotton, grown mainly in West Pakistan. Acute food shortages have occurred since 1953, owing to a multiplicity of causes: steep rise in population, lack of modern fertilizers, land erosion, general encroachment of the desert on the sown land, salinity and waterlogging over vast stretches, as well as the restrictions imposed from time to time by India on the timing and supply of irrigation waters to the canals in West Pakistan.

This last problem, known generally as the Canal Waters Dispute, arose in 1948 with India's claim of proprietary rights over the waters of the eastern tributaries of the Indus that flow from India into Pakistan. India's case was that it was constructing vast irrigation headworks on the upper reaches of the rivers Rāvi and Satlaj to bring the deserts of

Rājāsthān, further south, under cultivation, and could ill afford to spare large supplies of water to its neighbour. Half of West Pakistan's irrigation depended on the waters of these rivers; it was therefore a life-and-death challenge to its agricultural economy. After three and a half years of acrimonious negotiation, a break-through was made in 1951 towards a solution sponsored by the World Bank, on the basis of a complicated and very extensive engineering project to construct dams and link canals running from west to east contrary to the natural drainage system of the Indus basin. The project was based on the political formula that the waters of the three western rivers of the basin would be used exclusively by Pakistan, and those of the three eastern rivers by India. Under the sponsorship of the World Bank, and after prolonged negotiations, a treaty was signed between India and Pakistan in 1960, with the provision that the enormous cost of the project would be met by a vast contribution from India, and financial assistance from the West.

On the general scale of the growth of industrialization in under-developed countries, Pakistan's industrial growth has been creditable, considering its political instability. The volume of industrialization has so far been weighted heavily in favour of West Pakistan. The government's policy has been to offer a lead through official or semi-official agencies, such as a Development Board set up in 1947, a Planning Commission founded in 1950, and chiefly through the Pakistan Industrial Development Corporation, which has set up a number of industrial units covering the production of jute manufactures, paper, heavy engineering and ship-building. The policy of the Corporation is to 'create' industries and then to sell them as going concerns to private enterprise—an industrial policy which almost reverses the process of nationalization. As in other under-developed countries, Pakistan's economic planning has had to lean heavily on foreign aid, received from the U.S.A., under the Colombo Plan, from the British Commonwealth, other countries of the West, and Japan. Since the establishment of Pakistan, several hydro-electric and irrigation projects have been completed, a cotton industry has been built up almost from scratch to meet the bulk of the consumer demand, and a number of other projects have contributed to some extent to the ultimate goal of economic self-sufficiency.

The partition of the sub-continent into the successor-states of India and Pakistan was confined specifically to British India. Interspersed in the British Indian Empire, there were also some 560 large or small princely states, ruled over by feudal chiefs or princelings under the suzerainty of the British Imperial Crown. The constitutional position taken by the British government, in the context of the transfer of power in 1947, was that the British suzerainty over the princely states would lapse, and they would be free to accede either to India or to Pakistan, or to remain independent. They were advised, however, to accede to the contiguous dominion, bearing in mind geographical and ethnic considerations. All the states followed this British advice with the exception of three: Jūnāgarh with a Muslim ruler and a Hindu majority acceded to Pakistan; it was soon overrun by the Indian army; Hyderabad (Ḥaydarābād) with a Muslim ruler, but an overwhelming majority of Hindu subjects, and landlocked between Indian provinces, chose independence, but was blockaded, invaded and occupied by the Indians; Kashmir, with a Hindu ruler but an overwhelmingly Muslim majority of population signed a 'standstill agreement' with Pakistan, wavered for a while, but under political pressure from India and faced with militant tribal uprising and infiltration signed an instrument of accession with India. This was accepted by India provisionally, pending a free and impartial plebiscite.

The state of Hyderabad, which was occupied by India in 1948 and later partitioned among three linguistic provinces, was the largest principality in India, and was ruled by the *niẓāms*, the descendants of the Mughal governor, Niẓām al-Mulk. Since the early eighteenth century it had preserved something of the splendour of Mughal culture; its rulers had been patrons of Islamic institutions, of intellectual *émigrés* from northern India, of Urdu literature, and promoters of Islamic studies. The most brilliant product of the Muslim culture of Hyderabad was the Osmania University which made a bold and successful departure from the traditions of the British Indian educational system in using Urdu as the medium of instruction for modern sciences at a high academic level.

Kashmir proved to be a very explosive problem. The Hindu ruler of Kashmir had disarmed the Muslim elements of his police and army in July 1947. The vast communal disturbances of the neighbouring provinces of India and Pakistan were soon reflected in southern Kashmir, where, according to a report in *The Times* (10 October 1947), '237,000 Muslims were systematically exterminated, unless they escaped to Pakistan along the border, by his Hindu troops'. In reaction the martial Muslims of the Poonch province of the state rose against the Hindu maharaja, and were soon joined by their kinsmen and associates across the Jhelum and the Indus, from the frontier and tribal territories of Pakistan. The advancing tribesmen reached the outskirts of the capital Srinagar, and could have taken it but for their proverbial preoccupation with loot, and the lack of the presence or guidance of any elements of the Pakistan army with them at that stage. Under Indian persuasion the maharaja of Kashmir acceded to India; Indian troops were flown across the Himalayas and drove the tribesmen outside the Vale of Kashmir. The front became stabilized in May 1948 when units of the Pakistan army took up certain defensive positions using artillery but no air cover.

While negotiations were in progress between India and Pakistan for a joint reference to the United Nations to create conditions for a fair plebiscite, India decided to avail itself of the technical legal advantage of the maharaja's accession, and submitted a complaint to the Security Council against what it described as Pakistan's aggression. The position was exactly the reverse of India's action in the case of Jūnāgarh and Hyderabad. From May to December 1948 the two dominions remained locked in an undeclared localized war. On 1 January 1949 a ceasefire was effected through the good offices of the United Nations' Commission for India and Pakistan; and a cease-fire line was demarcated which has since then been patrolled by U.N. officers. It leaves two-thirds of the state including the contested Vale of Kashmir to India, while frontier areas of northern Kashmir and a south-western strip are in Pakistani hands. The Commission's proposals for a truce, maximum military disengagement in the areas occupied by either party, and a fair and impartial plebiscite under the auspices of the United Nations were accepted by both parties, but with different interpretations. Since 1949 India policy has been to delay fulfilment of its commitments to a U.N.-controlled plebiscite. Successive proposals of compromise since 1949 have been accepted by Pakistan, and rejected by India. Direct negotiations have been equally ineffective, narrowing down to the question of the destiny of the Vale of Kashmir, and breaking down at that stage. Because of Pakistan's association with the Western defence alliances, several proposals in the U.N. Security Council were vetoed by the U.S.S.R.

Finally one comes to the position of Islam and Muslims in the Republic of India itself. The transfer of population which followed the partition of the sub-continent led to the migration of millions of Muslims to Pakistan. Millions who were left felt their lives, honour and property insecure in several Indian provinces. Delhi, the federal capital, a great seat of Islamic culture and containing a large percentage of Muslim population, was one of the worst victims of anti-Muslim violence. Hundreds of thousands were killed or driven away, 117 mosques in the city were occupied by Hindus and Sikhs, some of them converted into temples; and though under pressure from Gandhi the minister for Home Affairs took strong action to stop the genocide of Muslims, the great Mahatma paid with his life for the stand he had taken for humanity. He was assassinated during a syncretic peace prayer meeting by a Hindu fanatic, Godse, in 1948.

It was under these circumstances that a new pattern of Muslim political life in India emerged. Leadership of Muslim India passed, quite naturally, to those who were closest to Congress, especially Abu'l-Kalām Āzād. He and the *Jamiyyat al-'ulamā'* had evolved a theory of composite nationalism in the 1930s which in 1947 became the manifesto of Muslim Indian nationalism. This theory was based on the analogy of the Prophet's covenant with the non-Muslims of Medina, who were regarded as a single community (*umma*) with the Muslims. Not as leaders of the Muslim masses, but as prestige symbols for the Muslim community, there also emerged a coterie of intellectuals and civil servants. The Muslim University of 'Alīgarh was placed under Ẕākir Ḥusayn, to be diverted psychologically from Islamic separatism to Indian nationalism. Later there was an official move to change its name and its Muslim personality.

The separatist opposition, the Muslim League, remained very quiet in the years after the partition, but asserted itself on such points of economic survival as the falling ratio of Muslims in the new recruitment to the government services, or of static but popular conservatism as opposition to the reforms in personal law.

The first prime minister of India, Jawaharlal Nehru, from a family of persianized Kashmiri Brahmans, whose mother-tongue was Urdu, and whose education was English, was for a decade and a half the chief champion of the concept of the evolution of India as a secular state. The challenges he had to face were so overwhelming that a leader of lower calibre would have succumbed to them. These included Hindu communalist organisations like the Hindu Mahasabha, which in 1952 declared it would tolerate Muslims in India only if they adopted Hindu names, manner of dress and personal law; the Hindu orthodox wing in Congress itself, which frustrated a number of Nehru's policies in matters relating to a fair treatment of the cultural and linguistic interests of the Muslims; and especially certain state (provincial) governments which failed under the pressure of Hindu electorates to use their control over law and order to guarantee security to the Muslim minority.

Finally Indian secularism has been facing the problem of Muslim conservatism, as represented not only by the intransigent Muslim League, but also the Indian establishment's chief Muslim ally, the *Jam'iyyat al-'ulamā'-yi Hind,* on such matters as the extension of personal law reforms to the Muslim community. Muslimmarriage and divorce laws which have been modernized in Pakistan, still remain traditionally medieval in India, permitting polygamy and other inequalities for women. The traditionalist *Jam'iyyat al-'ulamā'*, opposed to any reforms in the Muslim personal law, regards India as a case distinct from Turkey. In Turkey the secularization of Muslim law, however repugnant to the *'ulamā'*, was done by the Muslims themselves. Any such action in India, where the law-making elements have a non-Muslim majority, would be regarded by them as a breach of the covenant of composite nationalism. The Muslims in India therefore run the risk of pitiable stagnation.

If legal and social stagnation are largely the responsibility of the Indian religio-political leadership, the responsibility for their cultural decline falls almost entirely on the predominant Hindu orthodox wing of Congress, and the policies of the state governments. Reversing all the pre-independence pledges of the Indian National Congress, the constitution of free India stated that Hindi in the *Devanāgarī* script alone would be the official language of the country; Urdu was reduced to a minor place among the fourteen languages of the country; and even in this category its position is very insecure. In the states of northern India it was eliminated as a medium of instruction. Various representations made by Urdu organizations and influential Muslim leaders, and finally the redistribution of states on a linguistic basis, elicited some response in theory which remained largely untranslated into practice. The position has been well summed up by W. Cantwell Smith: 'The [Muslim] community is in danger of being deprived of its language, than which only religious faith is a deeper possession. Nine years of gradual adjustment in other fields have brought no improvement in this, and little prospect of improvement.'[1]

The problem of employment, despite all the theoretical secular legislation, has progressively haunted the Muslim middle classes in India. On the top rungs of the federal government in India, in certain key ambassadorial positions there is a small constellation of civil servants

[1] W. Cantwell Smith, *Islam in modern history* (London, 1956), 266–7.

drawn from the Muslim *élite*. At the lower levels of public services, the Muslim percentage has considerably dwindled considering the ratio of their population. In the Indian parliament, Muslims, who make up ten per cent of the total population of the country, have only a four per cent representation. The flow of Muslim middle class *émigrés* has continued through these years not only to Pakistan, but to the United Kingdom and North America, showing signs of the beginning of an Indo-Muslim diaspora in the West.

PART VI

SOUTH-EAST ASIA

CHAPTER I

SOUTH-EAST ASIAN ISLAM TO THE EIGHTEENTH CENTURY

THE COMING OF ISLAM

On the whole, accounts of conversion to Islam in Malay and Indonesian literature and tradition are not very reliable, however numerous they may be. There is a kind of uniformity about them which does not ring true. Often the ruler, destined to be the first among his people to pronounce the 'Two Words' (the profession of faith), the mere utterance of which will make him a member of the Muslim community, has already received notification of this in a dream or vision, even before the apostle of Islam drops anchor off his shores. Generally his conversion is immediate, with his subjects following soon after. There is no lack of wonders and miracles: opponents are easily persuaded or overawed by magic.

Yet the historian cannot afford to ignore such accounts. They shed a great deal of light on the nature of these societies and their organization, as well as providing clues as to the way Islam was in fact introduced amongst them.

An analysis of these stories suggests that Islam was propagated in South-East Asia by three methods; that is by Muslim traders in the course of peaceful trade, by preachers and holy men who set out from India and Arabia specifically to convert unbelievers and increase the knowledge of the faithful, and lastly by force and the waging of war against heathen states.

The importance of the role of the trader, especially in the early years, arose naturally from the situation of Malaya and the Archipelago along the main trade-route between western Asia and the Far East and the spice islands of the Moluccas. In the ports of the Archipelago, already part of this trading system, the Muslim merchant and his goods were as welcome as other traders from India had always been. The conversion of Gujarāt and other Indian trading centres to Islam increased the numbers and wealth of the Muslim merchants, so that they came more and more into prominence as the commercial partners and political allies of local rulers, and the Hindus vanished from the seas.

The way was thus open for the preachers, teachers of religion, and holy men to establish themselves. They were known in South-East Asia by a variety of names: *kiyayi*, *'ulamā'*, *datu*, *maqdūm*, *mawlānā*, *walī*, and we find them moving untiringly from place to place. One moment they would be in the service of the great, acting as both spiritual and political advisers; the next founding a school in opposition to local secular authority. Their teaching was often noted for its element of Sufism. This had a strong appeal to a people whose pantheistic traditions offered it very fertile ground in which to grow. The scribes and preachers, some of whom had visited Mecca, put the local populations in touch with a wider world community than they had known until then. For even the circle limiting the world of Majapahit, the last great Hindu empire (1292–1527), hardly extended beyond the Archipelago, and during the ninth/fifteenth century it steadily crumbled away. Before these holy men from the West the waning glory of the last god-kings of Majapahit paled.

Finally, when the Muslim communities in South-East Asia had grown in cohesion and confidence, they had recourse to war on several occasions in order to spread the true faith among the *kāfirs*. The remnant of the state of Majapahit, for instance, was conquered and subdued by this means. In many cases, however, it is difficult to distinguish between the true *jihād*, or Holy War, and the efforts of a recently converted ruler to extend his realm by the new faith.

These three methods of conversion cannot always be clearly distinguished. It appears that scribes sometimes had strong commercial links, and had begun their careers as merchants. Or, if circumstances favoured it, they might emerge as statesmen or warriors in the Holy War against the unbelievers. So far as the chronology and geographical pattern of the spread of Islam is concerned, however, it is clear that the trading element was the most important in determining events. In this sense Islam followed trade. North Sumatra, where the trade-route from India and the West reaches the Archipelago, was where Islam first obtained a firm footing. Malacca, the main trading centre of the area in the ninth/fifteenth century, was the great stronghold of the faith, from which it was disseminated along the trade-routes, north-east to Brunei and Sulu, south-east to the north Java ports and the Moluccas.

SAMUDRA (PASAI)

Marco Polo, on his return from China to Persia in 1292, visited six of the eight 'kingdoms', into which he divided the island of Sumatra, and only one of them did he consider to be converted to Islam. This was Ferlec, now known as Perlak. Muslim merchants had islamized the urban population, but outside the heathen continued to live like beasts, eating human flesh and all sorts of unclean food and worshipping all day long whatever they set eyes on first thing in the morning. So here Islam was still very immature.

And yet its influence does not appear to have been as limited as Marco Polo thought. As early as 1282, according to Chinese sources, the small kingdom of Sa-mu-ta-la (Samudra) sent ambassadors, called by the Muslim names of Ḥusayn and Sulaymān, to the Chinese emperor, and the extant tomb of Sultan al-Malik al-Ṣāliḥ, who is reported to have been the first ruler of this kingdom, dates from 697/1297. So although tradition confirms that Perlak was the first to be converted to Islam, Samudra, though later than Perlak, certainly received the faith before 1282, even though this was not yet observed in 1292 by Marco Polo.

The kingdom of Samudra, before long to be known as Pasai, soon grew into an important state which was to have a powerful Muslim influence on its surroundings. In 746/1345–6 it was visited by the famous traveller Ibn Baṭṭūṭa. An orderly situation prevailed at the time; the inhabitants offered fruit and fish, a deputy harbourmaster appeared and granted permission to land. As an ambassador passing through from Delhi to China, the traveller was led by a deputation to the devout ruler al-Malik al-Ẓāhir. There was a great deal of pomp and circumstance with processions on horseback accompanied by a band, but further inland fighting continued against the unbelievers. These were made to pay tribute. This kingdom was to remain in existence till 1521. Then it was conquered by the Portuguese, who occupied it for three years. After that the Achehnese took possession.

Magnificent tombs of the rulers in Gujarātī style still bear witness to earlier greatness and point to the country of origin of Sumatran Islam.

MALACCA

From North Sumatra, Islam spread along the trade route to Malacca. The founder of this relatively new town (*c.* 1400) was Parameswara, a name which in no way indicates his Muslim convictions. We meet him also, however, as Muḥammad Iskandar Shāh, after his marriage to a daughter of the ruler of Pasai. His successors too, Muḥammad Shāh and Abū Sa'īd, or Rājā Ibrāhīm (1424–44 and 1444–5 respectively), are also better known by non-Muslim names, as Sri Maharaja and Sri Parameswara Dewa Shāh, so that one suspects a heathen reaction, or at least sees that the conversion of Malacca was at best incomplete.

Not until a palace revolution led by Indian Muslims had brought Sultan Muẓaffar Shāh (1445–59) to the throne did true Islam prevail, although a partisan legend attributes Malacca's conversion to the earlier Muḥammad Shāh. He is supposed to have been taught the profession of faith by the Prophet himself in a dream and been given the name of Muḥammad, and in the same dream the arrival of a ship from Jedda was foretold. When he awoke the ruler smelled of nard and found to his amazement that he had been circumcized. He continually repeated the 'Two Words' aloud, terrifying his wives. And true enough the next evening Sayyid 'Abd al-'Azīz's ship arrived while the crew was saying evening prayer. The ruler, mounted on an elephant, made his way to the ship and invited the faithful to climb on his mount and ride to his palace. It was then that everyone was supposedly converted to Islam. That Pasai long continued to be looked upon as Malacca's spiritual home is borne out by the account, be it historical or not, in the book that was ceremoniously presented and studied during Sultan Manṣūr Shāh's reign (*c.* 1457–77). The sultan had the work taken to Pasai, so that Tuan Pamatakan could write a commentary.

Just as Malacca owed a great deal to Pasai for its Islamic faith, so in its turn Malacca passed on the faith to its own dependencies. The first Muslim ruler of Pahang was a son of the sultan of Malacca. Trengganu adopted Islam on becoming a vassal of Malacca, as did Kedah. Patani was converted from Malacca, and Kelantan as Patani's vassal. On the western side of the Straits, in Sumatra, Rokan, Kampar, Siak, and Indragiri, all accepted Islam as clients or dependencies of Malacca during the fifteenth century.

The Portuguese conquest of Malacca in 1511 of course put an end to its role as a centre of Islam. The wandering descendants of the princes of Malacca no longer had much influence to wield, and from their changing capitals on the Johore River and in the Riau Islands only with difficulty held their own between Achehnese, Portuguese and Dutch, until the latter captured Malacca in their turn in 1641. Meantime Acheh had replaced Malacca as a centre of Islamic trade and a stronghold of the faith.

ACHEH

It is remarkable that in Acheh, which considers itself so resoundingly Muslim, no accounts of conversions have been handed down. It is certain that it received its Islam from Pasai which is now part of Acheh, and the conversion can be dated near the middle of the fourteenth century.

When, early in the tenth/sixteenth century, two small states, the very ancient Lamri and the Acheh Dār al-Kamāl, had agreed to unite, Acheh entered upon a period of great prosperity. This was furthered by the fact that Malacca had lost much of its attraction for the Muslim merchants now that the bastion of La Famosa flew the Portuguese flag. Moreover they could now fill their holds with pepper, a commodity produced in Acheh.

The first great ruler, 'Alī Mughāyat Shāh, captured Pasai from the Portuguese in 930/1524, and thereby laid the foundations of Acheh's power. His son 'Alā' al-Dīn, who reigned from 1548–71, having conquered Aru and Johore, ventured to lay siege to Portuguese Malacca. In this he was encouraged by his possession of heavy guns from the Ottoman Empire, where he had sent envoys in 971/1562. However, this Muslim attack, like all the others, was repelled.

Acheh experienced its greatest prosperity under Sultan Iskandar Muda (1608–37). His power extended along the east and west coasts of Sumatra, controlling the export of pepper. His fleet and army, however, suffered a crushing defeat by Malacca, a final triumph for the Portuguese. Even the Achehnese admiral, Laksamana Malēm Dagang, fell into their hands and only death saved him from transportation to Lisbon (1629).

In Acheh itself, Iskandar Muda ruled with a firm, severe, sometimes cruel hand. His palace, glittering with gold, aroused the admiration of the West, as did the great five-storey mosque. From Acheh the bordering Gayo-lands were islamized, and also Minangkabau. Only the heathen Bataks managed to repel the oncoming Islamic forces, even going so far as to call in Portuguese help.

Under Iskandar Muda's son-in-law and successor, the liberal Iskandar Thānī, Acheh continued to flourish for another few years. Mild and just, he encouraged religion and prohibited trials by ordeal. Religious learning also throve in this period.

His premature death, however, was followed by disastrous times, as a series of females occupied the throne (1641–99); conquered territories were lost, the state disintegrated. After this, the reinstatement of the sultans was of no avail, so that by the end of the eighteenth century the Acheh empire was a mere shadow of its former self, leaderless and disrupted.

MINANGKABAU

The Padang hills only received Islam fairly late. As recently as 1511 a heathen delegation from that area offered its credentials to the conqueror of Malacca, Affonso d'Albuquerque.

It is true that there is a tradition which ascribes the advent of Islam to a Minangkabau, Shaykh Ibrāhīm, who is supposed to have become familiar with Islam on Java, and they still point out the stone where this preacher used to sit when he attempted to convert the bathers to the new religion. But it is more plausible that they received Islam from Acheh, from Pidjië via Priaman. This is moreover the normal route along which new Muslim ideas reached Minangkabau during the nineteenth century. The statement that the popular Shaykh Burhān al-Dīn, pupil of Shaykh 'Abd al-Ra'ūf of Singkel, brought Islam to Minangkabau, is entirely incorrect, since the latter mystic belongs to the eleventh/seventeenth century.

A more likely connexion is provided by the accounts of wars between Acheh and the rulers of Minangkabau. One such ruler is said to have been married to the daughter of Acheh's prince and to have become unfaithful. This had caused a quarrel with his father-in-law, as a result of which he had to concede a large portion of coastal territory. Acheh's subsequent possession of this coast area must have advanced the Islamic cause.

NORTH-WEST BORNEO, SULU ARCHIPELAGO, MINDANAO

North-west Borneo, the Sulu Islands and the southern Philippines are all situated along a trade-route which connected Malacca with the Philippines. It is therefore mostly Arabs, calling in at Malacca or Johore on their merchant travels, who are reputed to have been the bearers of Islam to these three regions.

In 1514 the Portuguese de Brito reported that Brunei's king was still a heathen, but that the traders were Muslims. In 1567 the Spaniards encountered Muslims in the Philippine Islands. During this half century a certain amount of proselytizing must have taken place.

When Magellan's ship the *Vittoria* called at the coast of Brunei in 1521, the pilot Pigafetta found a town of pile-dwellings whose population he assessed at 25,000 families, probably an over-estimate. The sultan lived in a fortified residence on the shore. He gave the visitors a royal reception. Although they were supposed to be Muslims, it was apparent from the simplicity of their attire that the conversion could only have been very recent. Local tradition mentions various names: a Sultan Muḥammad, originally named al-Akbar Tata, and supposedly converted in Johore, was succeeded by his brother Aḥmad, who had become acquainted with Islam through an Arab from Ṭā'if. As a result this Arab had been allowed to marry the king's daughter.

The sultan referred to by Pigafetta was probably Bulkiah, though his earlier name seems to have been Nakoda Ragam. Under his rule Brunei, profiting like Acheh and Bantam from Malacca's fall (in 1511), came to great prosperity, and even sent out military expeditions. When the Portuguese visited its capital, it seemed to have grown and it had been surrounded by a stone wall. Islam, however, was restricted to the coast; it had made little or no headway among the Dayaks inland.

Spreading along the trade-route beyond Brunei, Islam reached the Sulu Islands. The first proselytizer is held to have been the Arab Sharīf Karīm al-Makhdūm, who supposedly devoted himself to magic and medicine, kindred crafts at the time. He is said to have settled in the old capital, Bwansa, where the people built a mosque for him of their own free will. Many flocked to the mosque and one or two chiefs were converted. He visited other islands too and his grave is reputed to be at Sibutu.

The next preacher of Islam is said to have been the Arab Abū Bakr, who can hardly have been the same man who taught in Malacca under Sultan Manṣūr Shāh (1458-77). He is supposed to have reached the Sulu archipelago via Palembang and Brunei. He married the daughter of the prince of Bwansa, Rājā Baginda, already a Muslim and probably a usurper from Minangkabau. His father-in-law appointed him his heir. With great self-assurance he then reigned over his subjects, calling himself sultan. He administered the government and legislation in an orthodox manner, though with due observance of the ancient customary law (*adat*; Arabic *'āda*).

Finally Islam reached the southern Philippines, in Mindanao. Here we meet Sharīf Kabungsuwan, originating from Johore, son of an Arab father, claiming descent from Muḥammad, and a Malay mother. The later *datu* of Mindanao claim to be descended from him. He is said to have been willing to land only after the people had become converted to Islam. Many embraced the faith, after having first washed. He married Putri Tunîna, who was found in a hollow bamboo, which could be a mythical allusion to his taking possession of the land.

Armed Spaniards under Legaspi, however, certainly put a stop to further penetration by Islam *c.* 1570 at Manila. There followed centuries of fighting against the unremitting and bellicose 'Moros'.

JAVA

Java's first Muslim community is referred to by the Chinese Muslim Ma Huan, who noted three kinds of people in East Java between 1415 and 1432: Muslims who had settled there from the West; Chinese, many of whom had already become Muslims; and natives, about whom he could say nothing good. They were ugly and dirty, they ate and slept with their dogs and believed in devils. So there was indeed a Muslim community, but very few members indeed belonged to the indigenous population. And it was Chinese Muslims who were to leave their mark on Islam in East Java for a long time to come; according to eye-witnesses, their descendants, Javanese-Chinese mestizos, can to this day be distinguished by their appearance from Muslims of unmixed Javanese blood.

The magnificent Gujarātī tomb of Mālik Ibrāhīm also dates from this first period (822/1419). Tradition has it that he was a preacher of Islam, but this is not borne out by reports from reliable sources; he was probably just a prominent Persian merchant.

Of equal fame is the tomb of the so-called *putri Tjempa* (princess of Champa), traditionally the wife of the last Majapahit ruler Bra-Wijaya. Her husband is supposed to have had her buried in the royal grounds according to Muslim custom. The grave attributed to her still bears the Javanese date 1370 (A.D. 1448), and she is popularly believed to have been an aunt of Raden Raḥmat of Ngampel-Denta, the foreign quarter of Surabaya. In the third quarter of the ninth/fifteenth century this scribe had been appointed *imām* of the Muslim community by a Majapahit authority. His numerous pupils spread Islam further across Java. By nature sensible and peaceable he attempted only pacific penetration, and in this he and his followers were to some extent successful. Several of the 'coastal lords' (rulers of regions along Java's north coast), who had grown tired of the yoke of the Majapahit god-prince, broke their ties with him by becoming Muslim converts.

It is about this time that the conversion of Java enters upon a new phase with the emergence of the so-called Islamic preachers. They were often outsiders, who tried to seek out a circle of devout sympathizers.

They were extremely active and very mobile but were scarcely noted

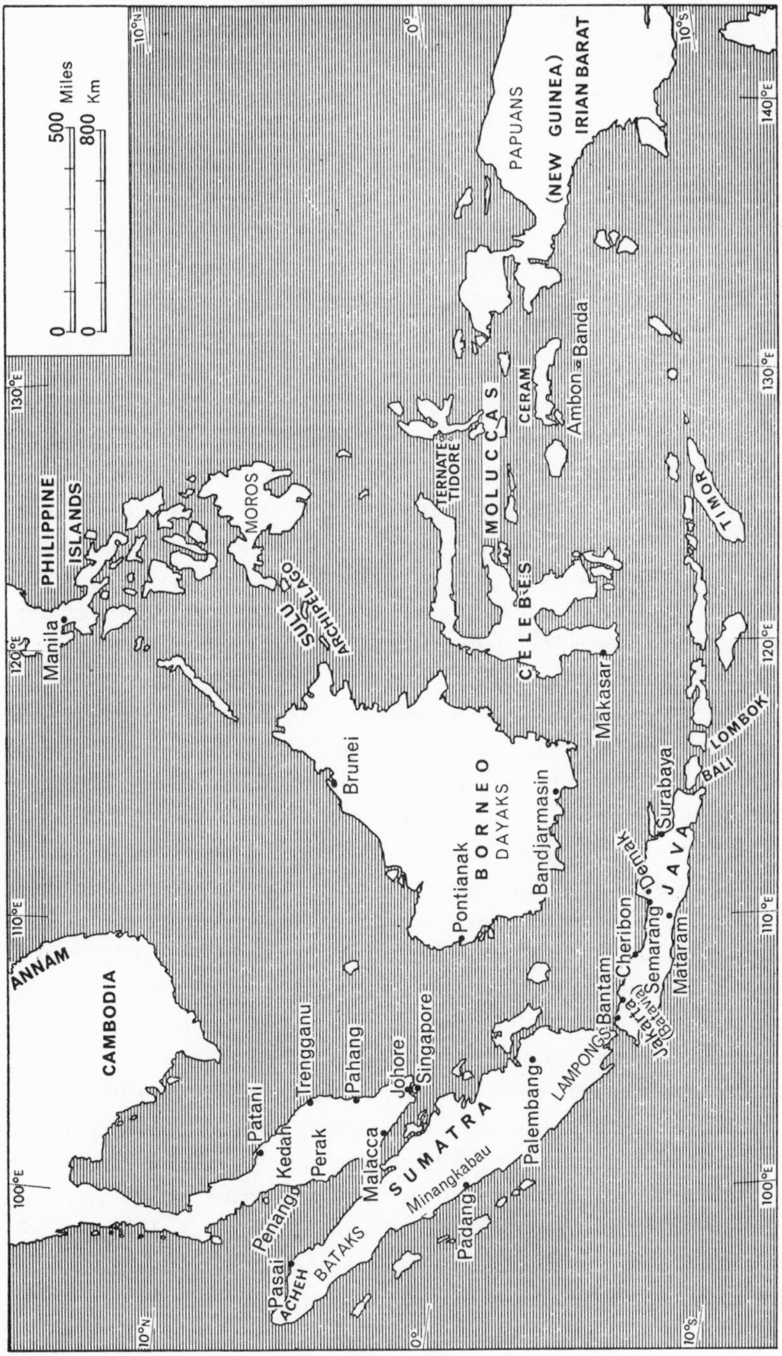

Map 11. South-East Asia

for their strict orthodoxy. Coming as they did from India, via Sumatra, they brought with them a mysticism which found an echo among the pantheistically-minded Javanese. Some Malay words and titles, such as *tuan* and *datu*, betray their Malay origin.

Sometimes they entered the service of Muslim potentates, but they were more often to be found looking for independence and a self-reliant, even obstinate, line of action. Some of them received estates from the rulers, others would withdraw with their pupils and followers into solitude and start separate communities. This would be in accordance with pre-Muslim traditions of independent spiritual sovereignties. Today we have the successors to these foundations in the *perdikan-desa* and the *pesantren*.[1] According to tradition they would regularly foregather in the sacrosanct mosque of Demak and discuss mystical-theological questions. It seems possible – though by no means proven – that there was a certain bond between them, e.g. a common political front against the languishing heathendom, the dying Majapahit empire, which is said to have received its death-blow from them (1527). On such occasions their followers and pupils often served them as armed supporters and the preachers' fanaticism and magic often inspired them to remarkable achievements.

The most prominent of the independent Muslim 'coastal lords' were those of Demak. They were probably of Chinese-Javanese origin and not, as is claimed by a later tradition, of Majapahit extraction.

At first, though Muslim, they still served the supreme ruler as customs officials. About 1475 they must have disengaged themselves to some extent and established connexions with other Muslim 'coastal lords'. Initially these lords of Demak extended their power westward and while still in Majapahit service they conquered Cheribon and the other places on their route. Then, at the instigation of a Malay adventurer who had captured Japara by a stratagem, they set out to conquer South Sumatra, ignoring the still heathen West Java. After heavy fighting Palembang and Jambi fell to them and were superficially proselytized. After that it was Malacca's turn, but the Portuguese anticipated the Javanese in 1511. Nevertheless they pressed on with the attack on the port, for according to the *mawlānā* the battle, now that they were fighting infidels, was all the more justified. This ambitious attack on Malacca, however, ended in a wretched débâcle (918/1512–13). This meant that the

[1] See below, pp. 152-54.

Javanese were powerless at sea, and it seemed as if the Portuguese were about to direct their offensive against the rising tide of Islam in Java.

In fact the Portuguese turned their attention to the Spice Islands, leaving Java in peace. This gave the Muslim Javanese a chance to recover from their defeat. The war against the infidels was resumed, but on land this time, against the heathen interior. In this campaign the holy men undoubtedly played an important role if they did not actually take the initiative.

After 927/1521 there appears to have been a sustained Muslim initiative throughout Java, and in our sources the figure of Shaykh Ibn Mawlānā, from Pasai, is conspicuous. When his native town had been captured by the Portuguese in 1521 he had made his pilgrimage to Mecca and on his return had settled in Japara and Demak. There he attracted so many pupils and won such esteem that the Demak ruler offered him his sister for a wife, and commissioned him to take Islam to the still unconverted West Java. In this he succeeded fairly rapidly.

He first gained possession of Bantam, and in 933/1526, perhaps on 12 Rabī II/17 December, he took the port of Sunda Kalapa and renamed it Djaja-Karta. Portuguese attempts to reopen communications with the Sunda state in the interior were thus completely foiled.

Cut off from the sea this empire succumbed to the Muslim forces fifty years later (1579). A small remnant of adherents to the ancient Sunda faith still hold their own as *Badui* in the Bantam interior.

In the meantime Demak had begun a long series of wars of conquest, to which the court and capital of Majapahit finally fell victim in 1527. In extensive areas of East Java, however, Javanese Hinduism held its own and fighting continued. When in 1546 a large-scale attack was made against the last important bulwark of Hinduism at Panarukan, it resulted in an utter failure. The Demak ruler Trengganu was murdered and his realm became the scene of endless confusion. The result was a temporary revival of East Javanese heathendom, from which it was never completely purged. The Tengger mountains still shelter worshippers of the mountain-god Brama, who have their own priests (*dukun*). Elsewhere Islam triumphed by force of arms.

In the south of Central Java the story is very different. Islam's peaceful penetration into this territory is the subject of the legend of Ki geḍé Panḍan-Arang. This erstwhile mundane and greedy ruler of Samarang was suddenly converted through the intervention of a holy man (the legend, probably wrongly, identifies him as the 'last of the *walīs'*, Sunan Kali-Jaga). Having given away all his treasures he set off in a southerly direction. According to the legend, he had many adventures and performed many miracles, until the hour of his calling came and he ascended Mount Jabalkat. There he built a mosque. He held long discussions with the holy men he found there and competed with them in the art of sorcery, always emerging as the victor. Now he rests on Mount Tembayat in a mausoleum, at the summit of a long flight of steps with magnificent archways. Each year thousands of pilgrims, chiefly from among the small tradespeople, come to worship this apostle of the southern part of Central Java, and invoke his assistance.

Likewise on a hill-top was the throne of Prabu Satmata, the first so-called priest-king of Giri (near Gresik). Tradition has it that he was the son of Mawlānā Iskak and a Balambangan princess from the most easterly part of Java. Mawlānā Iskak had cured her of a fatal disease. Since her father, the prince, refused to become a Muslim, Mawlānā Iskak left his bride and went to Malacca. When his son was born the cruel grandfather had him thrown into the sea in an iron box. He was hauled out of the sea by a fisherman and received tuition from Raden Raḥmat of Ngampel-Denta, together with the latter's own son. The teacher became aware of the boy's remarkable destiny because of the light emanating from him. After this course of instruction the young man, accompanied by his teacher's son, set out for Mecca, but he only got as far as Malacca, where he met his father. The latter advised him against the Pilgrimage, and finished his education. On his return to Java he entered commerce for a time and then applied himself to asceticism for forty days inside the corpse of a buffalo. When as a result he felt the need of a bath, his staff miraculously caused a spring to rise (an ancient sacred motif known too in Western Europe). His time had then come, and he ascended the Giri mountain. To this place, too, holy men flocked, but a punitive Majapahit column was also approaching. The attackers were miraculously hewn down by his pen, which had turned into a revolving *keris*. This *keris* became a sacred heirloom, and he himself now also rests in a sumptuous mausoleum on Mount Giri, the objective of many pilgrims.

During the reign of his successor, Sunan Dalem, the Hindu Javanese are said to have attempted another attack on Giri, so that the inhabitants fled in confusion. Only two watchmen remained loyally on guard at the tomb of the first saint. The attackers did not spare it and tried to exhume the body, but a huge swarm of bees burst out of the grave, driving the desecrators away, pursuing and killing them. Only the leader was spared because of his timely conversion to Islam. The reputation of Giri as a shrine of great sanctity is widespread throughout the Archipelago.

THE SPICE ISLANDS

Continuing eastwards along the trade-route, Islam reached the Spice Islands, now called the Moluccas, in the latter half of the ninth/fifteenth century.

According to local tradition there had been traces of Muslim influence a century before that. Ternate's twelfth ruler, Molomateya (1350–7) is said to have been very friendly with an Arab who instructed him in the art of ship-building, but seemingly not in the faith. And yet two Arabic names occur in the lists of rulers at this period; even on Tidor there was a ruler by the name of Ḥasan Shāh. Was it a passing fashion?

Not until the reign of Marḥūm (which is not really a name at all but the fragment of a title denoting a deceased ruler) did things really begin in earnest. His court was attended by the Javanese *datu*, Mawlānā Ḥusayn. His writings on the Qur'ān appealed to the inquisitive, who were fascinated by the mysterious letters and vainly attempted to imitate them. At their request the artful Javanese instructed them not only in Arabic script but also in the profession of faith. Only those who accepted this were allowed to learn the sacred letters. In this way he won many souls for Islam.

After Marḥūm's death religious fervour flagged, particularly when the Javanese Mawlānā also disappeared. Apparently Marḥūm himself never undertook the decisive step. The story is typical of a primitive society.

The first truly Muslim ruler was Zayn al-'Ābidīn (1486–1500). There was such an increasing flow of Muslim merchants that the ruler succumbed to their pressure and decided to study Islam at the source, which meant at the *madrasa* of Giri, probably with Prabu Satmata, whom we have already mentioned. He was known in Giri as Raja Bulawa, or king of the cloves, which he may have brought with him as an offering. On his return from Java the ruler brought with him Tuhubahahul, said to have become the main propagator of Islam.

In view of Islam's tender age on Ternate, the Portuguese, who had settled there in 1522, were hoping to replace it with Christianity. This proved an idle hope. Only very few were baptized, though it is true that some were members of the royal family. Eventually a Ternatan prince, Tabariji, was baptized, and he would have ascended the throne as Dom Manuel if he had not died suddenly (1545). Even the great apostle of Asia, Francis Xavier, who was in the Moluccas from 1546 until 1547, was unable to loosen Islam's hold there – all he could do was to strengthen the weak communities of Christians on Ambon. The Ternatans did adopt Portuguese culture and customs, their attire, armament, housing, and so on, but they would not be baptized.

Turning now to Ambon – the only Ambonese historian Rijali recounts how the Perdana Jamīlu, from Hitu (one of Ambon's two peninsulas), accompanied the ruler of Ternate, Zayn al-ʿĀbidīn, on his journey to Giri.[1] This account, however, implies too close a Ternate-Hitu co-operation for it to merit much credence. More plausible is the account of the arrival of a *Qāḍī* Ibrāhīm, who became judge of Ambon and from whom all the teachers of this island received instruction. Ambon even built a seven-storeyed mosque, reminiscent of Giri where a similar edifice was erected.

Local tradition also names Java as the source of Hitu Islam, although Pasai is named too, and even Mecca, with Banda as a half-way house. This is why the bearer of Islam to Rohomoni was called Pandita Pasai; he had been converted in Mecca. The founder of a village of Kailolo, by the name of ʿUs̱mān, had acquired Islam from a Pandita Mahu (Java), who had travelled from Mecca to Gresik and who had there come into contact with Sunan Giri and other holy men. He had then gone to Banda and finally to Kailolo and Tèngah-Tèngah. The people of Kailolo still point out his grave and pay homage to it. What is more, his descendants receive *pitrah* (religious tribute). This ʿUs̱mān is possibly the same as the Pangeran kalipah haji Ngusman, husband of the ascetic, later called Nyai ageng Moloko (Moluccas), who returned to Java after her husband's death.

At any rate communications between the Moluccas and Giri were maintained right up to the seventeenth century. Letters from the Giri priest-king to Hitu were welcomed with splendour; Giri fezzes showing magic formulae were much appreciated in Hitu and exchanged for spices (cloves), and for a long time the sons of prominent citizens continued to receive instruction in the *madrasa* of Giri.

Political and economic ties between the Moluccas and Java also survived. Demak and Japara were Hitu's allies in their fierce battle

[1] Rijali, *Hakajat Tanah Hitoe.* Malay MS. Leyden University Library, No. 3011.

against the Portuguese, when the latter had established themselves in Ambon's still heathen peninsula, Leitimor, and had introduced Christianity there.

SOUTH BORNEO

Borneo, too extensive to be under a single authority, has only in parts been converted to Islam; first the north-west, from Malaya, the south from Demak, the east from Makasar, and last of all the west, by an Arab adventurer. Since Brunei has been discussed earlier, we now turn to South Borneo, the state of Bandjarmasin. A. A. Cense's version of the chronicles, although not an early record, is probably the best account of the essential facts here.

South Borneo's accessibility from Java all through the year (the prevailing easterly or westerly winds do not seriously interfere with the north-south passage) encouraged Islamic expansion from there, and it also explains the presence in Bandjarmasin of many elements of Javanese culture.

The chronicle records a conflict between two pretenders, the *Pangerans* Samudra and Tumenggung, in which the former enlisted the help of Demak's ruler. This was promised on condition that he embraced Islam. He accepted and the Demak ruler dispatched 1,000 armed men under a *penghulu* (subordinate chief), which meant a considerable reinforcement for Samudra's 40,000 warriors. It was therefore decided to settle the dispute by a duel between the pretenders, but before they came to blows the two became reconciled. Amidst great festivities Samudra was made king.

The actual outcome was perhaps not quite so peaceful. In any event, 1,000 Demak fighters stayed behind while the *penghulu* converted all the inhabitants to Islam. An Arab gave Samudra the title *Surian Allāh*. After this the Demak contingent and the *penghulu* went home, laden with gifts (or perhaps booty). Subsequently all the rulers of Bandjarmasin boast Arab names.

SOUTH-WEST CELEBES

There is more information about the conversion of Gowa in South-west Celebes than about any other conversion in Indonesia. There are two reasons for this: firstly, the late date, the early eleventh/seventeenth century and secondly, the remarkably accurate accounts of the Makasar historians, who have kept countless diaries and chronicles. For instance, we know the exact date at which the prince of Tallo embraced Islam: 9 Jumādā I 1014/22 September 1605.[1] This was preceded by a long-established contact with Muslim merchants, so that Islam was not entirely unknown in Makasar.

In about 1591 the prince had already consulted the ruler of a neighbouring state on the subject of Islam, but since the latter was not a Muslim, this consultation had not been much help.

Then, just at the right moment, Dato'ri Bandang appeared on the scene. He was a Minangkabau, who had also received instruction in Giri. Conversion to Islam therefore was no mere gesture, but an action undertaken with full conviction. On the day mentioned the prince publicly made his profession of faith so that he could attend the Friday Prayer in the mosque of the Malay colony the next day. From then on he regularly read the holy books, and only illness would prevent him attending the Friday Prayer every week.

On 19 Rajab 1016/19 November 1607, two years after his conversion, the first Friday Prayer was held at Tallo, intended for a large number of inhabitants who had not previously made up their minds. Foreigners became aware of the conversion because of the shortage of pork which had been plentiful until then.

The very next year saw the start of religious wars against neighbouring states; Bone, Soppeng, Wajo'—one after the other they were forced to embrace Islam, though not without fierce opposition. One ruler, for instance, was dispossessed of all his offices by his lords for embracing Islam before the battle had been decided; he could have held out longer.

From then on the people of Makasar became the champions of Islam in East Indonesia. They played an important part in the battle between the Dutch and the Muslims in the Moluccas, which was not merely a religious conflict, but also a struggle for the monopoly of the spice trade. Muslim refugees from Ambon could be assured of a safe refuge in Makasar. This is how, in 1057/1647, it acquired the scholar Imām Rijali, who wrote the only Ambonese historical work, the *Hikayat Tanah Hitu,* while he was in exile in Makasar, on the advice of the studious prince Patingallowang.

Makasar's tough opposition to the Netherlands East India Company, which continued until 1656, was only the prelude to a war which the company began after another ten years against its troublesome rival.

[1] J. Noorduyn, *De Islamisering van Makassar.* B.K.I. CXII, 1956, 247–66.

Led by Admiral Cornelis Speelman this bitter struggle ended provisionally with the signing of the so-called Bongaais Treaty (1 Jumādā II 1078/18 November 1667). This put an end to the dominating position of Makasar in the trade and politics of East Indonesia.

EAST BORNEO

The conversion of Kutei in East Borneo followed hard on that of South Celebes, but would appear to have been at first somewhat superficial.

According to the Kutei chronicle,[1] two Muslim preachers arrived at Kutei during the reign of Rājā Makota. One of them was Tuan di Bandang, easily recognizable as the Dato'ri Bandang from Makasar; the other was Tuan Tunggang Parangan. Though they had already converted the people of Makasar, there is said to have been a relapse to heathendom, necessitating Tuan di Bandang's return to Celebes, but Tuan di Parangan remained in Borneo. He had been given this name after arriving in Kutei riding a swordfish (*jukut parang*). He buttressed his case for Islam by miracles: by becoming invisible, by making fire through sheer auto-suggestion, by bringing about the appearance of a *jukut parang*. After these three miracles Rājā Makota submitted to the new faith, stipulating only that the pork already on hand should first be eaten. In the meantime a mosque was erected so that their religious instruction could begin at once. Rājā Makota was first, then the princes, ministers, commanders and lords, and finally the common people.

From then on Rājā Makota did his best to propagate Islam by the sword, as a result of which the affairs of the state prospered. After some time Rājā Makota married, the marriage contract being concluded by Tuan di Parangan after a threefold votive offering to the Prophet. Yet all further games and festivities were arranged in accordance with the existing *adat*. The ruler's marriage too was solemnized by the Islamic preacher in the mosque. After this there is no more mention of Islam in the chronicle. There are no rulers with Arabic names prior to the eighteenth century.

RELIGIOUS JURISDICTION

The *Sharī'a* was in fact supposed to cover all aspects of life, but for practical reasons other rules of law were evolved, in many walks of life. The *Sharī'a* was confined to matters touching upon the intimate and

[1] Edited by C. A. Mees (Santpoort, 1935).

religious lives of the faithful, i.e. to questions of family and inheritance, as well as those related to *waqf*. This was the situation in South-East Asia as wherever there were Muslims.

There were, of course, local differences. In Minangkabau (Central Sumatra), where hereditary rights were decided by matriarchy, religious jurisdiction had to content itself with even less. The same applies to the Negri Sembilan in Malaya, where scattered Minangkabau had settled, taking their institutions with them.

In Bantam, on the other hand, during the eleventh/seventeenth and twelfth/eighteenth centuries, much more fell under the jurisdiction of the religious magistrate than was customary elsewhere. The *qāḍī* is said to have been in sole charge of juridical matters and the ruler intervened only in special cases.

In the principalities in Java and elsewhere in the Archipelago there existed, apart from the religious codes, statute books which, in parts, date back to pre-Muslim law and which included only very few Muslim elements. One of these is the *Pepakem Cheribon* (Handbook of Cheribon). Then there is the *Surja Alam* in Central Java, dating back to the time of the first Muslim Demak empire (tenth/sixteenth century) and perhaps even earlier. These manuals of jurisprudence were not used by the *qāḍī* or their deputies, but by secular magistrates, the *jaksa* (Sanskrit, *adhyaksa*). It is possible that during the ninth/fifteenth and tenth/sixteenth centuries in areas under spiritual authority, as in Kudus and Giri on Java's north coast, attempts were made to pass sentence according to Muslim law, but the sources leave us guessing on this matter.

THE RELIGIOUS TEACHERS

A quite remarkable part was played by the independent teachers, who appear under various names in the Archipelago: *'ulamā'*, *kiyayi*, *mawlānā*, *maqdūm*, *sunan*, *walī*. As a rule they did not belong to the mosque staff, yet they generally maintained their independence of the rulers. Many of them attracted pupils and became heads of schools. Their learning and piety assured them of the approval of the people who honoured them even after their death. To doubt their pronouncements was sometimes tantamount to unbelief. Some were mystics, others were conspicuous for their strict interpretation of the law. At times they caused trouble not only to Western but also to Muslim authorities because they became the rallying points of opposition. But this does not mean that there were no cautious and peaceful people among them.

Either way they certainly constituted the dynamic element in Indonesian Islam. The unattached scribes would inspire a fossilized religiosity with new life, thereby discrediting the institutions of the mosque. Their international contacts furthered co-operation between Muslims of different countries. They certainly deserve credit for their outspoken attitude towards the rulers, and in the fields of theology and law they made a very useful contribution.

After a brief consideration of the work of the Sumatran scribes, a fuller account will be given of the difficulties of the scribes on the island of Java. More detail is possible here because of the fullness of the historic sources, and the unique character of the relationship between ruler and *kiyayi* in Java deserves special attention.

SUMATRAN SCRIBES

Acheh, 'Forecourt of the Holy Land', was the field of activity of one or two theologians whose influence was felt far beyond the borders of the state. All were to some extent mystics and the names of several are honoured still.

Although Java can boast of countless anonymous mystics and of many others who concealed their identity behind famous pseudonyms, Sumatra's mystics were known by name, could be dated fairly accurately and were quite sharply defined personalities. The prosperity of the sultanate of Acheh during the late tenth/sixteenth and early eleventh/seventeenth centuries formed the background for their activities. We shall confine ourselves to the most important of these.

A few theologians from the Near East, tempted by the flourishing port of Acheh, had already brought their light to these parts when Ḥamza Fanṣūrī arrived there towards the end of the tenth/sixteenth century. He was a fervent supporter of the *wujūdiyya* doctrine, a doctrine of emanation, popularly known as *martabat tujuh*, or doctrine of the seven degrees. He was wise enough to wrap his dissenting views in a cloak of orthodoxy. For, while he declared that prayers and fasting were unnecessary, he wanted to maintain the *ṣalāt* (ritual prayer) as a pedagogic expedient to achieve unification with God. The power of his persuasive verses procured him many followers, and many enemies. His pupil and successor, Shams al-Dīn of Pasai, who died in 1630, was a contemporary of Sultan Iskandar Muda and he was in high favour with this powerful ruler. Various works of his have been preserved.

During the reign of Iskandar Thānī (1637–41) and his widow and successor 'Ināyat (1641–75) the tide turned. At that time Nūr al-Dīn al-Rānīrī, a native of Rander in Gujarāt, was residing at the court. In 1620 he made the Pilgrimage to Mecca, whence he returned to his native town, a declining trading-centre. In 1637 he travelled to Acheh, where he stayed until 1644. For unknown reasons he then returned to Rander, where he died in 1658.

During his stay in Acheh, al-Rānīrī, as he is generally known, displayed a fabulous industry. A stalwart of orthodoxy, he attempted to disseminate a fundamentalist faith by emphasizing such aspects as Hell and the Last Judgment; hence his popular book on eschatology. He fiercely contested the heretical mystics of the Shams al-Dīn school, committing their works and even their disciples mercilessly to the flames. And yet he he was not averse to mysticism: he believed in an orthodox doctrine of emanation. The number of his writings is vast, in Arabic as well as in Malay. One of his many works is the *Bustān al-salāṭīn* ('Garden of kings'), a voluminous mirror of princes in seven volumes.

The last of the great mystics and the most famous was 'Abd al-Ra'ūf of Singkel. He was probably born soon after 1024/1615 and died after 1105/1693. In 1643 he left for Arabia, where he studied for nineteen years in different places. When his teacher died in 1661, his successor gave him permission to do teaching duties himself. He then returned to Acheh where he remained active for many years. At the request of the sultan he wrote a legal work, for the purpose of which he first had to take lessons in Pasai-Malay from the sultan's private secretary. He wrote altogether twenty-one works. He was no follower of the excessive mysticism of Ḥamza Fanṣūrī but gave an orthodox reinterpretation of the *Wujūdiyya* doctrine. His fame was not confined to his native country and spread as far as Java. After his death the people venerated him as a national hero, so that later he came to be regarded as the first Muslim preacher in Acheh. Thousands still visit his grave, from which he derives his name, Teunku di Kuala.

The fame of these Achehnese scribes spread the more rapidly beyond Acheh and Sumatra because, prior to the era of steam-navigation, many pilgrims or student-pilgrims would spend some time in Acheh on their way to and from Arabia. In this way they became acquainted with the prevailing religious trends there. So it is clear that the wild excesses of Sumatra's heterodox mysticism were curbed by al-Rānīrī's energetic action, and that from then on the mystics thought along more orthodox lines.

The Javanese mystics, on the other hand, came up against resistance of quite a different kind, namely the strong arm of worldly authority. This would explain their frequently manifested contempt of this authority, on which subject many references have come down to us. This antithesis led to prolonged and bloody wars. In the end the Mataram ruler emerged as victor in this issue. This struggle deserves to be looked at rather more closely.

THE PRINCES AND ISLAM ON JAVA—SECULARIZED SPIRITUAL LORDS

When Prince Trengganu of Demak was killed in the battle of Panarukan in East Java in 1546, his empire fell apart, and some spiritual lords thought that the moment had come to achieve their own independence.

Shaykh Ibn Mawlānā, who, having married the prince of Demak's sister, ruled over Bantam on his behalf, made himself not only virtually independent of central authority, but also managed to lay hands on Cheribon, whence he is said to have moved *c.* 957/1550. His son Ḥasan al-Dīn took his place in Bantam and tradition regards him as the first genuine prince of this territory. His grave, situated near the great mosque in the ancient, now deserted, town of Banten, is, however, honoured primarily as the resting place of a saint. He is the patriarch of the Bantam princes, who remained in power till 1813.

The father, who had settled in Cheribon, ruled this province till 1570 and his remains are now in an impressive mausoleum, which is one of the most frequented places of pilgrimage in West Java. His successors also became temporal rulers, although perhaps not to the same extent as the Bantam branch of the family. Having, since 1091/1680, branched out in three directions, Kasepuhan, Kanoman and Kacherbonan, the descendants of the great saint retained their high standing locally till well into the twentieth century.

In general, West Javanese Islam has a more orthodox character than elsewhere in Java. This may be due in the first place to the fact that Hinduism had much shallower roots in West Java, but it could also be because Islam was initially introduced here by men who had come to know the faith in Arabia. The spiritual lords travelled a great deal in those days. Whereas the lords of Cheribon had little share in the propagation of Islam by force – they inspired devotion rather than awe – Bantam contributed a great deal.

In 1579 Pangeran Yūsuf, the second prince of Bantam (1570–80), using subterfuge as well as force, secured for himself Pajajaran, the heathen state in the Sunda lands, and Islam came to stay. In 1596 his son, the young Pangeran Muḥammad, attacked Palembang, which was still considered heathen. The prince was killed in the battle however, and was deeply mourned. Palembang remained independent, but the Lampongs (South Sumatra) were conquered and had to accept Islam.

In the meantime Bantam had become a station on the main traffic route, since Malacca, taken by the Portuguese in 1511, lost much of its importance as a trade centre for the Asians. Portuguese from Malacca now came to Bantam to do business and in 1596 the Dutch also appeared, followed by other Westerners. They found a strong Muslim state, a large mosque and much trade in the local crop, pepper.

The Muslim character of the Bantam rulers is further borne out by their acquiring the title of sultan in 1638, and by the Pilgrimage made by one of them, who, being a ruling prince, earned the title of *Sulṭān Ḥājjī* (1682–7). It was during his reign, however, that the state first came under Dutch influence.

Bantam, on the main trade-route and until 1682 frequented by foreigners, was more exposed to external orthodox influences than Central and East Java, and as a result traces of puritanical Islam are found here quite early. During the eighteenth century the Arabs were particularly influential, and none more than the renowned Ratu Sharīfa, wife of the mentally deranged Sultan Zayn al-ʿĀrifīn (1733–47) and daughter of an Arab father and a Bantam mother. She managed everything in her own way for so long that an Arab dynasty seemed inevitable. The intervention of the Dutch East India Company, however, precipitated a bloody war of succession, which at times was more like a religious war. It ended in 1753 with the restoration of the old dynasty, and its recognition of Dutch overlordship. Not until 1813, however, during the British interim government of Java, did Bantam disappear as a separate state. Nevertheless Bantam always remained true to Islam, and the colonial authorities considered it wise not to admit Christian missionaries.

During the period 1550–1625 Surabaya was probably ruled by the descendants of the holy Raden Raḥmat of Ngampel-Denta. The son of the last of the princes, Pangeran Pekik, who spent his last years as a revered exile in Mataram, was, according to Javanese historical tradition, descended from a *walī* and his descendants have always paid homage to the holy man's grave at the harbour mouth at Surabaya. At that time Islam in Surabaya was by no means as orthodox as West Java's and in Mataram Pangeran Pekik was reputed to have introduced non-Muslim cultural elements too. This civilized nobleman, murdered in 1659 at the instigation of his son-in-law, Sunan Mangku-Rat I, formed a link between the cultures of the coast and the interior of Central Java.

THEOCRACIES

The spiritual lords who came to the fore on the disintegration of the Demak state in 1546 maintained a truer Muslim character in their state government than elsewhere.

Traditionally the first of these is the fifth *imām* of Demak's holy mosque, who left the ancient, perhaps ruined, residency for a nearby place, since named Kudus. This is one of the few Javanese towns with an Arab name and this holy man is associated with it in his name, Sunan Kudus. There is no doubt that the word is derived from al-Quds, Jerusalem, and it must surely have been the *imām*'s intention to establish this settlement as a theocracy in a holy city. Like the mosque on the site of the Temple in Jerusalem, the mosque in Kudus is called al-Aqṣā and it differs from most Indonesian mosques in having a minaret. This was built in Hindu-Javanese style, but of course without any images of living creatures.

Possibly as early as 1549, this spiritual lord bore the title of *qāḍī*. Temporal lords paid him the utmost respect. Tradition has it that princes sat at his feet. His spiritual and political influence extended far beyond Kudus, as far, on one side, as West Madura. He also pursued a policy of his own, directed against the nascent state of Mataram in the interior of Central Java, and his choice of candidate to rule over the whole of Java was Pangeran arya Panangsang of Jipang, who was opposed by Sunan Kali-Jaga. The downfall and death of his protégé damaged his reputation as well as his authority, and, when Kudus finally fell, it was supposedly by the prince of Mataram, Panembahan Sénapati, *c.* 996/1588, that it was taken. Sunan Kudus's descendants then fled eastwards and led somewhat obscure lives until a female member of the family married Sunan Mangku-Rat IV (1719–27) of Mataram and had a son, Sunan Paku-Buwana II (1727–49), whereby the family regained its prestige. It was included in the right wing (*panengen*) of the official

Mataram family tree, the *Sajarah Dalem*. The Hindu princes of Majapahit belong to the left wing (*pangiwa*).

The line of rulers (commonly called priest-kings) of Giri (near Gresik) remained longer in power. We have already seen how their high reputation dates from Prabu Satmata, who established himself on Mount Giri, built a seven-storeyed mosque there and was finally buried in state on that spot. To this day thousands of pilgrims visit his richly ornamented mausoleum every year.

The family reached the height of its power under Sunan Parapen (1546–1605). His influence extended far beyond Java, due no doubt also to his prolonged rule. It was not only the Dutch who knew him as 'the Mohammedans' pope'; his fame as a seer and prophet travelled as far as China. His independence, which he achieved after the fall of the Demak empire in 1546, is well expressed in the magnificence of the regal residence he built.

He showed a surprising concern for the other islands of the Archipelago. According to historical tradition he was responsible for Lombok's conversion to Islam. Bali, on the other hand, would not accept Islam and all attempts to introduce it were emphatically rejected. But the Minangkabau, Dato'ri Bandang, who achieved Makasar's conversion to Islam, is said to have started as a pupil at Giri. Tradition has it that there were matrimonial ties with Pasir (Borneo), and that they had close contacts with the Hituese on Ambon (Moluccas), who were fighting the Portuguese. The master at Giri sent them Javanese auxiliaries, who stayed for three years at a place later named *kota Jawa* (Javanese town).

Like the lord of Kudus, Sunan Giri was treated with the utmost respect. As his subjects, the temporal rulers came and offered him their respects. The story goes that even the prince of Pajang in the interior visited Giri to obtain recognition of his sovereignty of Java. For it is a fact that these spiritual lords, until well into the eleventh/seventeenth century, arrogated to themselves the right to consecrate and accredit local princes. When, finally, the powers temporal allied themselves with the Dutch unbelievers, the divines had to submit to secular authority. In 1680, at the instigation of Sunan Mangku-Rat II of Kartasura (1677–1703), and with the assistance of the Dutch, Giri was conquered, and the last of these kings was killed.

The third and the most extraordinary was Sunan Kali-Jaga. Tradition credits him with a distinguished descent, a dissolute early life and a miraculous conversion. He is said to have devoted himself to asceticism in Cheribon. The prince of Demak sent for him and presented him with Adi-Langu, an estate adjacent to the residency, where he instructed countless distinguished pupils. It is possible that he replaced Sunan Kudus as *imām* or *qāḍī* of Demak, for those two spiritual lords disliked each other intensely. After the catastrophe at Demak in 1546 he seems to have travelled about, pursuing a policy opposed to Sunan Kudus. In fact he became the spiritual father and patron of the rising Mataram house of princes in the interior, and for some time after close ties were maintained between this house and Sunan Kali-Jaga's descendants. The princes looked after their graves with great care and visited them at times. Culturally, too, Mataram is greatly indebted to these lords of Adi-Langu, specifically for the important contribution which they are said to have made to the Mataram chronicle of princes, known as *Babad Tanah Jawi*. And by their inclusion in these annals of references to their forebear's glorious deeds, they ensured his abiding fame.

JAVA'S INTERIOR AND ISLAM

Sunan Bayat of Tembayat is known as the apostle of South Central Java, and this area regards many of the lesser saints as his disciples. And yet it is strange that there is nowhere any reference to a remarkable conversion of the rulers, as is so often reported in the Malay countries. It might be concluded from this that the lukewarm reaction to Muslim affairs, a commonplace in Java's interior today, is no new or recent phenomenon. Even in the official chronicle of princes there is no mention of Sunan Bayat's activities.

South Central Java was never subjected to Muslim Demak. An attempt by *Sunan* Kudus to lay his hands on the small state of Pengging (to the west of Surakarta) failed dismally. To this day the time-honoured grave of Ki Ageng of Pengging can be found, near an ancient-looking cemetery, still containing Hindu-Javanese remains. Of his two sons Ki Kebo Kanigara was then an unbeliever; Ki Kebo Kenanga lived according to Muslim precepts and even attended the Friday Prayer. But his teacher, Pangeran Siti-Jenar, was known to be a heretic, and he would not dream of paying his respects in Demak. These stories do not give the impression of a very orthodox Islam. And it is precisely in this area that Sunan Kali-Jaga became so politically active.

He is believed first to have connived at the preferment of Jaka-Tingkir, later prince of Pajang, and still a legendary figure in popular belief; then he appears to have favoured the founder of the Mataram dynasty. He seems to have been forever on the move, encouraging, advising, intriguing, and always, being himself a man of the coast, opposing the policies of the coastal spiritual lords. At last a soldier of fortune, his protégé Panembahan Sénapati of Mataram (1584–1601), was triumphant, and laid the foundation of a dynasty which was one day to rule over virtually the whole of Java.

Panembahan Sénapati, a *Realpolitiker*, showed little evidence of a true Muslim mentality. His thoughts and emotions were guided by the worship of mountains and sea, and in particular by his communion with the mysterious Goddess of the South Sea. Apparently he did pray to Allāh in moments of crisis, but on the whole Islam took second place in his life. The teaching that Sénapati gave to his younger friend and ally, Pangeran Benawa of Pajang, reveals the character of his religion. His disciple, he considered, ought to have three different categories of people at his disposal: teachers of religion for putting his realm in order; seers for predicting the future; and ascetics to give guidance on magic powers. What he appreciated in the Muslim spiritual leaders was in the first place their political gifts. Marriages between his own Mataram family and members of these other families indicate that he did really value contacts with them. Doubtless both parties hoped to profit by these contacts. And yet there was a mosque near Sénapati's residence. In 1601, after what was on the whole a prosperous reign, he was buried on the south side of the mosque.

SULTAN AGUNG, SPIRITUAL AND TEMPORAL RULER

The Mataram empire reached its zenith during the reign of Sénapati's grandson, generally known as Sultan Agung (1613–46). He conquered nearly the whole of Java, with the exception of Batavia, founded in 1619 by the Dutch governor-general Jan Pietersz, Coen, and Bantam, which managed to shelter behind Batavia. Thus the north coast, where Islam had been proclaimed for two centuries, came under Mataram rule – a significant development for heterodox Mataram. For now the prince had to deal with countless Muslim subjects in the districts along the north coast, whose spiritual leaders were able to fortify the ranks of the *kiyayi* further inland.

It must be assumed that Sultan Agung wanted to pursue a positively religious policy, and that, unlike his predecessors, he adopted a strict

Muslim attitude. Hence he offered his Dutch prisoners the choice of circumcision or death. One of them, Antonie Paulo, died a martyr to his Christian faith in 1642.

The prince also strove to enhance his wordly reputation, and in view of the fact that his family had no background at all, this was energy well spent. To this end he had only to follow the admirable example set by the erstwhile spiritual lords. In 1624 therefore, after the hard-won conquest of Madura, he conferred upon himself the title of *susuhunan*, which until then appears to have been reserved for a deceased *walī*. And like the spiritual lords who sat enthroned on mountain tops, he had a raised terrace built in front of his residency, on which he and his retinue appeared in glorious array. Finally he began the construction of a mountain tomb for himself and his successors, with his own grave nearest the top, again in imitation of the holy men. On the other hand he openly prided himself on a collection of objects with magical power, the *pusaka*, which (in a slightly different category) included the large guns which he sported at his palace.

After two unsuccessful sieges of Batavia (1628–9) he was faced with a serious crisis. There were threats of rebellion and fanatics were roaming the country. He warded off the dangers, not only by despotic force but also by a sensible approach to Islam. The Islamic calendar was now officially introduced in the realm, although he retained the ancient Shaka era, which began in A.D. 78. In 1633 he also visited the holy grave of Tembayat, which he embellished with magnificent monuments. Was he paying his respects at Canossa?

Following Bantam's example he managed in the end to acquire the title of sultan, thanks to the co-operation of the English, who provided transport to Mecca for his envoys. After 1641 he called himself Sultan 'Abd Allāh Muḥammad Mawlānā Mataranī (i.e. of Mataram). It is, however, as Sultan Agung that he is generally known. So this ruler not only managed to preserve his authority, but by his wise policy of courting the spiritual lords with their time-honoured traditions and great influence among the people, he actually added to it. He even went so far as to humiliate one of them, the ruler of Giri, who refused to bow to him. In doing so, he used his brother-in-law, the Pangeran Pekik, son of the last of the Surabaya rulers. After a fierce battle the refractory ruler was forced to leave his holy mountain and settle in Mataram for a time. This was a great triumph for the Mataram ruler, who now combined temporal and spiritual power in his residency.

THE DOWNFALL OF THE SPIRITUAL LORDS

Sultan Agung's son and successor, known as Susuhunan Mangku-Rat I Tegal-Wangi, did not follow his father's footsteps. He refused the title of sultan and preferred to be just *susuhunan*, as his father had been from 1624 until 1641, and as his successors were after him. Since he suspected the spiritual lords of conspiring with his brother in a rebellion, he carefully planned a mass-murder of the divines, hoping in this way to settle with them for good. But enough of them survived to preserve an aftermath of hostility against him. Nor did this prevent him from appealing to them for spiritual ministrations in times of crisis, illness and so on. It was not by prudent statesmanship, but by terror and force that this ruler, with his deranged mind, sought to maintain his waning authority. It was the north coast in particular that he is believed to have alienated by his policies.

It is not surprising, therefore, that the spiritual lords, in league with his rebellious son, the crown-prince, conspired against him. One religious family in particular, under the grey-haired *Pangeran* of Kajoran, nicknamed Ambalik (the turn-coat), laid the foundation for a general conspiracy. The revolt broke out in 1675 and it was seven years before peace was restored. In 1677 the Susuhunan had to find refuge with the Dutch. He died on the way and was buried in a 'fragrant field' (*tegal-wangi*), whence his nickname. His grave is another miniature imitation of a mountain.

His son, Mangku-Rat II (1677–1703), followed his father's policies and allied himself to the Dutch, also on the advice of the lord of Adi-Langu. And so his power was restored with the help of the Dutch East India Company. The leader of the rebels, Raden Truna-Jaya from Madura, and several of the spiritual lords had to pay for their revolt with their lives. Now that the prince could boast of having allies who were insensitive to the hidden powers of the *kiyayi*, he did not want to miss his chance of settling with these rebels. The Dutch commander, Jan Albert Sloot, was able to capture Ambalik of Kajoran, but none of the Javanese allies dared to kill the holy man. The wild Buginese from South-west Celebes had to be invited to perform this task. The Susuhunan next provoked a clash between the Dutch and the grey-haired ruler of Giri. After a fierce battle, the fiercest of the entire seven years' war, the old man was wounded and taken prisoner, and was later beheaded by order of the prince (27 Rabīʿ I 1091/27 April 1680).

Even after Sunan Mangku-Rat II had moved into his new palace Karta-Sura, in 1680—the old one having been desecrated by the rebels—fanatics continued to cause disturbances. This time it was Kiyayi Wana-Kasuma, related to Ambalik, who predicted that the end of the dynasty was near. According to this prediction, the succession would now, after seven generations, fall to another house. For years the battle raged to and fro, and more than once the Dutch troops had to intervene to save Karta-Sura. Peace was restored in the end, but a Dutch garrison was necessary to protect the Sunan (or ensure his adherence to the Dutch alliance). Again in 1719, Sunan Mangku-Rat IV (1719–27) took advantage of a new war of succession to wipe out the priestly line of the lords of Tembayat, and only after this does the political role of the *kiyayi* seem to have come to an end.

THE ESCHATOLOGY

That the *kiyayi* party, though beaten, never completely lost heart, is borne out by a story that was current in South Central Java until recently. Pangeran Puger, who later became Sunan Paku-Buwana I (1703–19), is said to have been a suppositious child, and in fact Ambalik's son. When the latter, even before his revolt, was asked to remove the caul of a child born to Sunan Mangku-Rat I Tegal-Wangi, the future rebel did so, at the same time, however, exchanging this child with his own of the same age. Thus the state was still ruled by a descendant of the *kiyayi*.

Nevertheless, as the chances of political success faded, there must have been among the devout, somewhere near the turn of the seventeenth century, a growing belief in the coming of a messianic *ratu adil*, 'just (*'ādil*) ruler'. To some extent this belief originated in Islamic eschatology. Hinduism contributed to it with the doctrine of the four world eras, which were to be followed by the end of all things. And it is quite feasible that ancient pre-Hindu native beliefs influenced the Javanese *ratu adil* complex too.

The Javanese eschatological speculations are attributed to a pre-Muslim ruler of Kaḍiri, Jaya-Baya, who lived in the twelfth century. Possibly the memory of his name was kept alive by the fact that he was mentioned in the ancient epic *Brata-Yuda* (1157) which is an episode of the Indian epic *Mahabharata*.

The first written records of such 'predictions of Jaya-Baya' date from 1719, and they have never failed to impress the Javanese people. Again and again someone would emerge who claimed to be the coming *mahdī*. Some of them acted in good faith, others were deceivers whose main concern was the sale of amulets and the collection of money. After a short while the police and the law usually put an end to their messianic careers. Some were indeed of high birth and were pretenders to the throne. Among them we can certainly place even the great rebel Pangeran Dipa-Negara who, at any rate during some stage in his career, was considered by himself and his followers as a *ratu adil*.

As far as the contents of the predictions are concerned, these mainly contain a compound of Muslim eschatology and Hindu-Javanese elements. They usually cover the complete history of Java, past, present and future. They have a strange knack of adapting themselves to the most recent events, so that the unprepared reader or listener is amazed at the completely correct description of the present by a so-called teacher from antiquity. This makes his predictions ring doubly true, and one forgets that earlier predictions of this kind sometimes did not come true at all, such as those published by Raffles.[1]

The fact is that these prophecies were coupled with dates which the world has survived completely unscathed.

SURVIVAL OF THE HOLY MEN

Kiyayi, with their miraculous gifts and secret teachings, have survived to the present, even though their numbers have gradually decreased. There were one or two very ancient institutions and customs which strengthened their social position.

In pre-Muslim times there had been religious villages whose inhabitants kept to certain strict rules. Later they became largely Muslim, and so they became Islamic holy villages, whose inhabitants kept strictly to Muslim precepts and to those of their *kiyayi*. The Muslim princes granted these villages privileges, thereby in fact merely extending or confirming privileges dating from pre-Muslim times. In later centuries these villages were called *pamutihan*, villages of the 'whites', or, since they were exempt from taxation, *perdikan-desa*. Colonial governments, with little concern for the religious ideals of these communities, tried to reduce them in number and size with an eye to a higher tax yield and the promotion of peace and order.

[1] *History of Java* (London, 1817) II, 40.

There were also *kiyayi* who established themselves outside the village communities in small settlements, accompanied by their relatives and their pupils. There they eked out a simple living from the produce of their fields. Where the *kiyayi* shed an odour of sanctity, others would join the settlement so as to receive instruction. In this way schools came into being, to this day known as *pesantren*, derived from *santri*, a *kiyayi* disciple. Life was lived according to earlier customs. The unmarried *santri* lived in small huts, the floor of which, according to ancient practice, was raised off the ground. It can be safely assumed that this type of teaching-establishment was to some extent a continuation of similar institutions in pre-Muslim times. They have also much in common with Indian ashrams.

Other relics from the distant past were retained in the ancient pre-Muslim dances and performances at the *pesantren*. Some of the members took instruction in magic, juggling and self-torture without shedding blood, in order to demonstrate their progress in Muslim mysticism. Music and dancing were effective in inducing an individual or communal trance. Some of these features may have originated in other parts of the Muslim world; the instruments of self-injury that are kept near the ancient mosque of Bantam, for instance, resemble similar implements in use among the mystics in Bosnia and Cape Town. From the *pesantren* these displays spread through the outside world, where they are still to be seen here and there.

The actual teaching in the *pesantren* was far from systematic. It consisted largely of reading and writing, and the memorizing of the Qur'ān, theological and legal texts, mystical proverbs and prayers, litanies and hymns in a corrupt form of Arabic. These things were written down in note-books which provide us with a glimpse into the spiritual life of these devout communities. Snouck Hurgronje was one of the first to draw attention to these particular writings.

The teaching is largely concerned with the unity of Lord and servant. To know oneself is to know the Lord. Unity of microcosm and macrocosm is taught along the same lines. All that exists can be summed up in the one word, *Ingsun*. This doctrine of the all-embracing self is the keystone of Javanese metaphysical speculations. Gradually this sometimes very tendentious heterodox mysticism was supplemented by the orthodox mysticism of some *ṭarīqas*, such as the Shaṭṭāriyya, and Naqshbandiyya. Various tracts stemming from these schools were put into Javanese. As time went on, even diehard *kiyayi* either became members of such *ṭariqas*, or imitated them, in this way gradually adapting themselves to their pattern and causing less offence to the orthodox. Despite this adjustment, however, the steady decline of the *pesantren* could not be halted. The princes resisted them because of their attitude of bold independence, while the colonial authorities, fearing their tendency to create factions, sought to suppress them. The orthodox shunned their heretical teaching and finally educational institutions on the European model deprived them of many of their pupils.

CHAPTER 2

SOUTH-EAST ASIAN ISLAM IN THE NINETEENTH CENTURY

Centuries, calendrically precise, are seldom as meaningful historiographically as historians are apt to make them seem. The nineteenth century in Islamic South-East Asia is no exception, and yet, with the need to see a pattern in a period of years, patterns do emerge. The Java and Acheh Wars stand like tombstones at either end of a series of violent and often bloody conflicts fought to renovate or defend Islam and the *ummat* (Arabic, *umma*) against the vitiating syncretism of local tradition and increasing colonial encroachment. The early years of the century saw the beginnings of a redefinition of the relationship of the West with the Archipelago which was to culminate before the beginning of the next in the complete subjection of Indonesian and Malay political and administrative authority to alien rule. And finally, the opening of island and peninsular South-East Asian societies to the west meant, in the literal sense, not merely the consolidation of European power and influence, but a considerable increase in the flow of communications with the heartland of Islam which did much to determine the nature and intensity of the conflicts which characterize these years.

The Java War of 1825–30, though from one point of view the first in a series of manifestations of social unrest in Java in which protest at socio-economic change brought about by the West played a determining role, must also be seen as yet another in the succession of conflicts which had punctuated the previous hundred years, arising in large part out of social tensions present within Javanese society itself. The eighteenth century in central Java had been marked by an efflorescence of specifically Javanese culture, and of Javanism, prompted in part, it has been suggested, by the severance of Mataram from the coast and from the vitalizing trade contacts which (among other things) had helped to bring and sustain Islam. The partition of the empire in the mid-century, followed as it was by a turning in upon the courts of Jogjakarta and Surakarta, led to an intensification of the hierarchical qualities already present in the Javanese social order, and set the pattern for an aristocratic and bureaucratic, *priyayi* civilization which found little time for the relative austerities of the 'Arab religion'. Doctrinally, the Javanese form of Islam, which had always been characterized by an idiosyncratic blend of indigenous, Hindu-Buddhist, and rather florid (mainly Shaṭṭāriyya) Ṣūfī mysticism, tended to move even further away from its 'orthodox' sources towards traditional religious beliefs. Organizationally, the ruling class relied for the administration of Islam upon what came to be an appointed hierarchy of officials who functioned more or less as adjuncts of secular rule, staffing mosques, prayer-houses and religious courts—the 'priesthood' of contemporary European observers. Below or beyond this, in the interstices of village society—where the *abangan* variant of Javanese religion, compounded largely of pre-Hindu mysticism with Muslim accretions in varying degree, held sway over peasant life—stood the rural *kiyayi* and '*ulamā*'. As teachers and propagators of the faith, as the nucleus of the pious *santri* civilization of the earnestly Muslim, they derived their authority not from the fiat of a secular power but from their knowledge of Islam and the Holy Word, their esotericism as initiates in Ṣūfī *ṭarīqas*, and their espousal of an outwardly as well as inwardly Islamic mode of life. The '*ulamā*' constituted a distinct if unorganized element in Javanese society, standing aloof from, and at times fiercely critical of, Islamically imperfect secular governments, much in the manner of similar groups in other times and places. For the most part of and from the rural community to which they ministered, they formed a powerful focus for peasant discontents with the harshness of the world in general, and with the exactions of the ruling class (and its symbiotic relationship with the *kāfir* Dutch) in particular, as had already been amply demonstrated. The dichotomy this points to, between the syncretic and compromising *priyayi élite* and their official religious establishment on the one hand, and the independent '*ulamā*' on the other, each competing for the allegiance of the *abangan* peasant majority, formed the dynamic for much that was now to take place in Java. The direct and forceful entry of the Dutch on the side of the *priyayi*, the increasing islamization of the peasantry, and the growth during the century of new, and especially urban, groups with interests served by a more individualistic Islamic ethic, served only to strengthen and deepen these tendencies.

With the demise of the Dutch East India Company in the last days of the old century, Java entered upon two brief periods of administrative experiment at the hands successively of the Dutch-Napoleonic Herman Daendels and Thomas Stamford Raffles, which set in motion new processes of Western penetration into Indonesian society and the indigenous economy. In the complex political history of these years, the wars, revolutions and alliances of Europe played a larger part than any consideration of Eastern affairs. What is of relevance here is the character and effect of the Daendels and Raffles régimes and of the restored Dutch system which succeeded them.

Whereas the Company, bent on trade and not dominion, had for the most part retained Javanese traditional authority intact as a means of exacting forced deliveries of agricultural products from a peasantry heavily obligated to their traditional chiefs, Daendels set out to break this system, at least partially in the interests of the ordinary Javanese, by instituting direct payments for produce and by declaring the Javanese regents (local rulers) to be Dutch government officials, with military rank and a fixed income. In the semi-autonomous states of Central Java, Daendels reduced the status and authority of the princely rulers by appointing ministers rather than residents to the courts of Jogjakarta and Surakarta and entitling these officials to royal insignia, and he divided the remainder of the island into administrative divisions directly controlled from Batavia, and linked where possible by improved communications. Many of these reforms, especially the economic ones, were only partially carried out, if at all; but the patterns of indirect Company control had been broken, and for the first time all Java was fused into something approaching a colonial system of rule.

When the British took Java in 1811, the policies instituted by Raffles followed similar lines, with a number of important additional innovations which affected even further the position of traditional authority. Daendels's attempts to curtail the powers of the regents had been limited by his inability to run the economy of Java without recourse to the taxation functions of the ruling class, even if revised, and to a variety of other expedients (including the lease of villages and the sale of large tracts of land to private individuals, Chinese and European) which meant that the burdens on the peasantry were if anything increased. Of liberal economic views, and anxious to continue the 'defeudalization' of Javanese society, Raffles instituted a land-rent system which brought the peasant cultivator into direct contact with the government, and removed the regents and other traditional authorities from the revenue-producing machinery in return for certain sorts of compensation. One consequence of this system, which did not, it may be said, work very well economically during the brief period of Raffles's administration, was to intensify the degree of interaction between Javanese village society and a centralized and increasingly European civil service. At the same time, though the privileges of the ruling class were in many areas scarcely touched, there was a general and irksome undermining of their position and (at least as important) an increase in their dependence for favour upon a foreign administration. Open conflict in the princely states, where Raffles put down a movement to throw the British out, and deposed the sultan of Jogjakarta in favour of his son, further fragmenting the state in the process, did nothing to improve this situation and left resentment which before long was to bear fruit.

When the Dutch returned to Java in 1816, under orders from the revived monarchy 'to establish a colonial system based upon principles of free trade and free cultivation', Raffles's economic and social policies were continued for the time being, despite the parlous financial situation in which the administration now found itself, and growing evidence of Javanese restlessness. The unsettling effects of two decades of experiment and uncertainty were widespread. In the principalities in particular, discontent with changing times affected all classes of society. The nobility and aristocracy, chafing under reduced incomes and shrunken territory which made it difficult to meet traditional obligations to kin and clients, turned more and more to the leasing of their lands (and the labour upon them) to foreign cultivators. When this process was stopped by the government in 1823, with the requirement that all lands be returned together with large financial indemnities for improvements made in the interim, this was for many *priyayi* the last turn of the screw. Secondly, from 1817 onwards, the sale of customary taxes and tolls to the Dutch government, promptly farmed out to Chinese entrepreneurs, may have helped to raise additional income for aristocracy and government alike, but resulted in an inhuman exploitation of the peasantry which provided much of the fuel for the risings that followed. And finally, Muslims of all degrees, but particularly the *kiyayi* and '*ulamā*', felt a special hatred for the increasing manifestations of infidel rule and desired to see both it and its Javanese allies put down, sentiments which linked them with irredentist sections of the nobility seeking to see Mataram reunited and restored to its former greatness.

Dipa-Negara, the 'Hamlet prince' of Java (as he has been called), and chief progenitor of the war that now ensued, is in many ways a strange and enigmatic, and certainly a tragic figure. Son of Sultan Hamengku Buwana III of Jogjakarta by a morganatic marriage, he was close to the throne but had been passed over in the succession (or had himself declined it) on two separate occasions. Of markedly religious temper and mystical leanings, he had been a frequent and sombre critic of the laxity of the court and its increasingly European ways, and also, it would seem, of the miseries inflicted on the peasantry by the current dispensation. He himself retired largely from court life and was accustomed to wander the countryside dressed in black, Arab-style clothing and (in an older tradition than that of Islam) to seek solitude for prayer and meditation in sacred tombs and cave-shrines, where he was vouchsafed visions and heard voices that taught him of his own eschatological mission as leader of a great movement to purify Islam and its practices among his people. Sayings and prophesies associated with the prince achieved wide currency and attached themselves to characteristically Javanese messianic expectations concerning the coming of the *ratu adil*, or 'just king', who would save the land from oppression, and lead it to plenty and peace.

The occasion for the outbreak of hostilities in July 1825 was relatively trivial—little more than a dispute concerning the building of a road across Dipa-Negara's property at Tegalreja and the high-handed behaviour of a Dutch official. In the confusion that followed, Dipa-Negara and those around him prepared for rebellion by retreating to a strategically situated village and issuing a call to arms. The word spread like fire in stubble and within the next few weeks supporters came to his side by the hundred. Messages sent by Dipa-Negara to the outlying districts in the north and east appealed to the people 'to take up arms to fight for the country and for the restoration of the true Islam'. Of those who came immediately to his side, one Indonesian account says, the greater number were *'ulamā'* and *santri*. Chief among several leading *'ulamā'* who appeared was Kiyayi Maja, a forceful figure of great popular reputation, who besides playing an important part in arousing the peasantry acquired before long considerable influence over Dipa-Negara himself. Urging the prince to assume the titles of sultan and *panatagama* (head of religion) through all Java, Kiyayi Maja gave the insurrection increasingly the character of a *jihād*, and swore not to cease fighting until every last *kāfir* (European) had been killed.

In the early stages of the war, many of the Javanese nobility and aristocracy loyal to the Dutch or inclined to stand behind the court party were also put to the sword, though increasingly the older pattern of '*ulamā*'-led, peasant-fortified conflict with a compromising and oppressive *priyayi élite* gave way to a holy alliance of Islam and the aristocracy against the infidels, as traditional chiefs came over to Dipa-Negara's side. The Dutch, caught on the wrong foot, with little in the way of military reserves, were able for a time, despite reverses, to exploit factions within the ruling class and levy armed assistance from within the state of Jogjakarta itself and especially from rival Surakarta, but they were forced eventually to recruit troops in Madura, the Celebes and elsewhere, and to call for reinforcements from Europe. As the struggle developed and the Dutch gradually gained the upper hand in the principalities, the guerrilla character of the warfare became more marked, and seeking to avoid a long drawn out campaign the Dutch sought directly to negotiate a settlement and later encouraged approaches from among the insurgents themselves. Almost all these attempts, which took place during the latter part of 1827 and in 1828, seem to have failed on one basic ground, the refusal of the Dutch to recognize Dipa-Negara's claims to be head of the Islamic religion. Though there is evidence that the authorities might have been prepared to accept the prince as ruler of Jogjakarta and perhaps make other concessions as well, they were adamant in holding that 'fanatical' Islam, upon which with some justice they blamed the fireiness of the present dispute, must be taken out of the hands of the prince and his advisers. And so the war dragged on for a further two years, causing great loss of life, as much from disease as from the fighting, and bringing untold distress to a harried peasantry disturbed in its usual occupations by the coming and going of government troops and insurgent bands alike. Ultimate Dutch victory was assured, and as the end neared Dipa-Negara was deserted one by one by his principal supporters (including Kiyayi Maja, who was captured while suing for a separate peace), until he himself was forced to accept an invitation to discuss, under safe conduct, terms of surrender. Treacherously taken prisoner during the talks that followed, his final request that he be permitted to make the Pilgrimage to Mecca was refused and he spent the remainder of his days in exile in the Celebes, dying only in 1855.

Full understanding of the Java War and its meaning for Javanese society and Islam must await proper monographic research, for though, fortunately, many of the materials still exist, there has as yet been no detailed study in any language of the crowded and complex events of these years. Certain things, however, seem clear. The paramount role played by Islam in providing the ideology for the revolt associated purified Islamic belief and practice once and for all with defence against alien rule. One result of this, it seems likely, was that the position of the *'ulamā'* in Javanese society among the peasantry was considerably strengthened—a tendency assisted by the growing countervailing identification of the *priyayi élite* with Dutch authority in subsequent years. Together these circumstances help to explain the marked increase in islamization of the peasantry which took place even before the mid-century. For the Dutch themselves, whose understanding of Islam was for some time to remain at best superficial, the Java War drove home the danger of permitting any alliance between the secular chiefs and the forces of Islam. Though this lesson had to be re-learnt towards the close of the century, in the context of the Acheh War, it formed for the next twenty or thirty years a cardinal element in, on the one hand, the exercise of severely repressive policies towards independent Islam, and on the other, the return to supportive, indirect rule policies towards the traditional ruling class.

In the period following the war in Java, the Dutch, with local treasuries exhausted to the point of large-scale indebtedness, the ruins of an ill-understood and ill-applied economic liberalism lying at their feet, and pressing financial problems at home as a result of the Belgian revolt, began afresh the task of making the Indies pay. The system devised to achieve this end—the lifebelt, it has been said, that was to keep the Netherlands afloat—came to be known as the Culture (or Cultivation) System. Under it, the peasant was required, in lieu of tax, to cultivate on one-fifth of his land designated export crops for surrender to the government, or alternatively to provide a proportionate amount of labour for government-owned estates and other projects. To ensure the success of the system, and at the same time to reassert a measure of custom-sanctioned control over a still unsettled populace, it was necessary for the Dutch to re-establish, under allegiance to themselves, the position and authority of the traditional aristocracy. Accordingly the next two decades saw not only the conversion of large areas of Java into something like a state-owned plantation system, but a restoration of the recently undermined status of the regents and the *priyayi élite*, and their gradual transformation into an hereditary class of officials functioning as the executive arm of the colonial power. The nature of the mutually advantageous association thus formed between traditional authority and colonial exploitation was not lost on the Javanese people, and widened further the gulf between rulers and ruled.

Alongside the bureaucratic *élite*, and under the combined surveillance of this *élite* and their Dutch overlords, there developed a parallel class of religious officials, hierarchically organized and fitting neatly into regional administrative patterns. Regency *penghulu*, appointed by and responsible to the regent (as were all other mosque officials, according to customary law), functioned mainly as *qāḍīs*, though their independent jurisdiction was limited to family law and *waqf*, and part of their time was spent sitting as advisers in the secular courts, where, however, it has been said, their tasks tended to be limited to the administering of oaths. District *penghulu* performed similar roles at the district administrative level, and at the village level lesser *penghulu* and their assistants carried out tasks related mainly to the supervision of marriage contracts and the upkeep of mosques. The incorporation of this class of religious officials (regarded by the Dutch as 'priests') into the general administrative framework of the state resulted in the emasculation of the *'ulamā'* taking part, subject as they were to a *priyayi élite* who to some extent shared the prevailing Dutch fear of religious fanaticism, and who in any case had no interest in maintaining anything like a separate Islamic authority.

In the circumstances, it is scarcely surprising that the independent *kiyayi* and *'ulamā'* should as a rule have held religious officialdom in disrepute, nor that most of the Islamic life of the community (and the prestige associated with its leadership) should rest in their hands—from the multitude of small-scale religious activities and occasions attendant upon the incidents of everyday life to the running of religious schools (*pesantren*) and the setting up and regulation of the Ṣūfī *ṭarīqas* which still shaped much of Javanese religious thought. This independent focus for peasant loyalties was feared by the Dutch, who, in the belief that the principle sources of 'unrest' among the peasantry were returned pilgrims and itinerant Arabs, placed, or attempted to place, restrictions upon the Pilgrimage and upon the movement of Arabs out of the urban areas. Nevertheless, unrest persisted. Though the Java War, marking the onset of intensive Western interference in Javanese life, was the last of the great conflagrations in the island, the thirties, forties and subsequent years continued to be disturbed by spasmodic peasant risings, invariably under the banner of Islam.

Elsewhere in South-East Asia, Islamic communities were left much more to themselves in the early nineteenth century than in Java. The absence of an external threat from Western expansion was not in all instances, however, accompanied by internal tranquillity. In Sumatra in particular, parts of which had long been amongst the most intensely islamized in the region, there occurred in Minangkabau at the start of the century an inner convulsion generated by powerful reform influences which derived their initial impetus, it is true, from outside the state, but were for nearly two decades to be fought out strictly within the society itself.

This conflict has usually been seen as a struggle between more or less clearly defined *adat* (custom-centred) and *agama* (Islamic-centred) parties; but the complexities of the Minangkabau social and political systems are so considerable that anything like a simplified account of their working is bound to be defective in one respect or another. The most that can be done here is to try to clarify a little of the background to the events of the early nineteenth century, and look at some of their consequences for Islam.

Minangkabau society at the close of the eighteenth century manifested several sets of oppositions which, though always potentially and sometimes actually in conflict, found more or less precarious resolution in a variety of integrative concepts and institutions. In the first place, the social structure presented two separate faces, that of the royal family of the old Minangkabau kingdom, which had a patrilineal descent system, and that of the independent commonality, which was matrilineal. Both, however, were inseparable parts of one whole, with a shared as well as a divided view of life. Kingship seems never to have functioned as an instrument of government in Minangkabau proper—that is to say, in the inland central highlands known as the *darat*—but despite implicit conflict between the two social systems, acceptance of the institution served to maintain equilibrium among the separate *nagari* (or 'village republics', as they have been called), the basic political units into which the state divided. Among the *nagari* themselves a further divisive principle existed, between two conflicting political systems based on separate *adat* traditions, which differed little in fundamentals but the balance between which was vital for the well-being of the society as a whole. Territorially, Minangkabau presented yet another complex dichotomy—between the *darat*, identified as the source of *adat* or the corpus of 'custom', where royalty had its seat but did not rule, and what was known as the *rantau*, the peripheral areas in general but particularly the coastal plain, which, though directly governed by representatives of the royal family, was historically and traditionally the source of Islam. Here again, potential strife between the two, sometimes realized, was lessened by a recognition of economic interdependence, and by an encapsulation of *adat* and Islam in a common system of coexisting principles, together necessary for the persistence of the society.

Within this continuum of actual and incipient conflict (and the list is by no means exhaustive) the key to understanding is perhaps provided by the notion of *adat* itself, which in Minangkabau society, it has been argued, contains important ambiguities. On the one hand, the *adat* may be taken to refer to the complex of local customary rules, derived from 'ancient times', which regulate relationships and behaviour within the society. On the other, *adat* in a larger sense may refer to the whole structural system of society, to its inner world view, of which local custom and institutionalized conflict between variants of local custom are themselves component parts. Provided the system as a whole, and its bases, are not seriously challenged, conflict can be contained by the expression of conflict, and the idealized pattern of life continue undisrupted, even if subject to change as element jostles with element. Thus the original penetration into Minangkabau society of an Islam which, as elsewhere in Indonesia, was accommodating and syncretic, and more influenced by *ṭarīqa* practices than by strict adherence to either doctrine or 'orthodox' ritual, had not greatly shaken the existing social order. Though the growth of Islamic influence, and of more Islamically oriented groups (especially the religious teachers) within Minangkabau society, challenged by their nature certain other elements in the society, they did so more in the way of contributing another dimension to existing conflict, the result of which seems to have been the restructuring of the larger *adat* in order to domesticate and contain the foreign body while permitting continuation of the dynamic opposition which its presence constituted. This somewhat hypothetical discussion may be given some content by pointing, for example, to the organization of the ruling institution of the *nagari*, the *balai* or council, which, though it was 'owned' by the secular leadership of the community (just as the mosque was 'owned' by the religious) had as members not only the *penghulu* (in Sumatra, *adat* chief) and his staff, but some of the '*ulamā*', with a neutral group of elders to hold the middle. Most importantly, perhaps, the Islam involved in this situation, though staking a claim to a share in the determination of idealized patterns of behaviour for the society, and though at odds with the matrilineality (most obviously) of the commoners, and with the rival 'great tradition' represented by the king, was not in general militantly concerned to subvert the existing order.

Towards the end of the eighteenth century, symptoms of social disintegration and an accompanying social demoralization appear to have begun to make themselves evident in Minangkabau, perhaps associated with the decline in the power of the king (politically on the coast and sacrally elsewhere), and with the rise of new centres of religion in the interior under the leadership of *tuanku* (the title given to leading '*ulamā*') independent of the traditional structure of authority. None of this, however, seriously threatened the existing order, despite an increase in detached elements of social and political discontent, until the return of the famous three pilgrims from Mecca in 1803 unleashed the first wave of the puritanical reform movement known to the Dutch as the *Padri* movement, from the Portuguese *lingua franca* term for cleric.

The *padri*, like the Wahhābīs in Arabia, whose example may to some extent have been fortuitous but was certainly influential, directed their energies in the first place to the extirpation of moral laxity and an insistence upon strict adherence to the duties imposed by the faith. They proscribed the popular pastimes of cock-fighting, smoking, taking intoxicants or stimulants, and the like, and enjoined strict observance of the ritual prayers at the appointed times (upon pain of death for the unrepentent apostate), requiring also that women should go veiled and men wear white, Arab-style clothing (from which derived the name by which the *padri* were known locally—*kaum puteh*, 'the white ones'). Despite this apparent absorption, however, with what may be regarded as externals, the real importance and disruptive effect of the *padri*, whose campaign was waged relentlessly, and frequently with violence, lay less in their scourging of a ritually and doctrinally lax community than in the threat they offered to the socio-political *status quo*, demanding for Islam the right not merely to correct from within but to coerce from without, and to seize the largest share in the determination of the principles by which the community was to live. Their attacks upon *adat* in its more restricted sense, embodied in specific, locally hallowed custom seen to be in conflict with Islam, constituted at the same time a more serious attack on *adat* in the larger sense, as the structural system of society, embodied in its custodians, the *adat* chiefs, and in the institutionalized balance achieved between them and other contending elements. It is no accident that the first act of violence in the *padri* explosion was the burning of a *balai*, the integrative institution par excellence of the *nagari*, by followers of Ḥājjī Miskīn (Haji Miskin), one of the three returned pilgrims.

Thus, though the *padri* conflict may readily be seen in terms of opposition between religion and custom, and though it must to some degree have represented frustration on the part of the independent *'ulamā'* as a group within a social system which did not accord them a satisfactory place in the structure of authority, the familiar dichotomy is not wholly satisfactory. The reality was certainly more complex, and allegiances perhaps fell more clearly along the lines of those for or against change of a variety of kinds. Ḥājjī Miskīn's chief supporter in the affair mentioned was a *penghulu* from the same area. When Tuanku nan Rentjeh, the leading figure in the *padri* movement in the central district of Agam, turned for assistance to his own teacher, Tuanku Kota Tua, the latter, while agreeing with the general aims of the movement, refused to countenance its abrupt, violent, and intolerant abrogation of past accommodations. Conversely, the first prominent adherent of the *padri* when the movement spread into the northern valley of Alahan Panjang (later famed as the stronghold of Tuanku Imām Bonjol) was a leading traditional chief, Dato' Bendahara, accompanied by several of his fellows. In more general terms, accounts of this prolonged disturbance, which speak even of families divided against themselves, make it plain that it must have answered or become attached to many other sorts of conflict.

As the agents of change, the *padri* pursued for fifteen years their campaign of reformation, taking over, by force, intimidation or persuasion, one village after another, installing their own functionaries (usually an *imām* who laid down the law and a *qāḍī* who saw it observed) and expelling or killing *adat* chiefs and others who opposed them. Opposition was, indeed, not lacking, but progressively much of the interior came under *padri* control, and in 1818 a group of *penghulu*, led by two members of the royal family, appealed to the British on the coast at Padang for military aid. Though Raffles established only one armed post in the interior, probably in the hope of obtaining influence there before the impending return of the Dutch, the Dutch themselves assumed wider responsibilities a year or so later and before long were thoroughly implicated on the side of the opponents of the *padri* in what now became known as the *Padri* War.

The guerilla fighting that ensued was to last for some sixteen years before ending in 1837 with the reduction of the stronghold of the last *padri* leader, the redoubtable Tuanku Imām Bonjol. During the final years of this struggle its nature changed. Already in the 1820s the fires of dispute between the *padri* and their opponents had died down, partly as a result of a lessening of the extremes of religious fervour (in consequence, to some extent, of continued contact with the Ḥijāz, where Wahhabism itself waned after the political defeat of the Su'ūdīs in 1818) and partly because much had in fact been gained. The increased involvement of the Dutch, and a recognition of the threat to independence that this implied, led to a closing of the ranks and the formation of a common Muslim front against the *kāfirs* under *padri* leadership. The royal ruler of Minangkabau was exiled to Java in 1833, thus destroying the last vestiges of the old kingdom, never to be restored, and eventual Dutch victory was achieved by superior force of arms and the gradual isolation and dismemberment of final pockets of resistance.[1]

The long course of the *padri* movement had as its principal result a marked increase in the penetration of Islam into the fabric of Minangkabau society, with consequent long-term implications of importance for related peoples elsewhere in Sumatra and in the Malay peninsula. In Minangkabau itself, religious doctrine acquired a redefined and larger acceptance within the *adat*, as the basic referent for idealised patterns of life, even though the social schism between defenders of *adat* and innovators, buried briefly during the anti-Dutch years, reappeared before long. The leading practitioners of religion, the teachers and '*ulamā*,' emerged from the struggle with much enhanced prestige, despite subsequent Dutch attempts to curb their influence in favour of that of the *adat* chiefs in the interests of law and order and economic exploitation. Politically, the conclusion of the war, which was followed by occupation of the central highlands, opened the way for further extension of Dutch authority in this potentially most valuable of the 'Outer Possessions'. Though the resulting forward movement was pursued somewhat hesitantly in the face of British hostility, it resulted in substantial Dutch control over all Sumatra south of Acheh by shortly after the mid-century.

During the second half of the nineteenth century, and particularly in

[1] See Taufik Abdullah, 'Adat and Islam: an Examination of Conflict in Minangkabau', *Indonesia* (Ithaca), 2 (Oct. 1966), 1-24.

the final quarter, Islamic South-East Asia underwent a religious revival—perhaps more properly an intensification of religious life—of large proportions. Some of the many causes for this have already been suggested or discussed. In more than one area, long-standing conflicts for peasant allegiance between traditional secular *élites* and independent '*ulamā*,' which had helped retard the reception of Islam, were resolved in favour of the '*ulamā*'. The power and influence of rural Islamic leadership had been augmented by the onset of alien (and *kāfir*) rule which, at the same time as it added to the complexities and burdens of people's lives, came to be identified more and more with an increasingly discredited ruling class turned colonial bureaucracy. The spread of the faith in many parts of Java previously only nominally Muslim, for example, was greatly assisted by the readiness with which Islam became the standard-bearer of protest against changing times and consolation amidst the ills of the world. The growth in numbers of village Qur'anic schools and *pesantren* throughout Java in the latter part of the century represents, it is perhaps fair to say, more a hopeful turning away from the harshnesses of everyday life than a means of remedying them. The Dutch themselves, though going in fear of Muslim 'fanaticism', did much to hasten the islamization of the Archipelago. As the new administration tightened its grip on Java, it was accompanied by improved communications which broke down isolation and rendered previously closed communities open to outside influence. In the outer islands, the spread of Dutch authority was attended by hosts of subordinate Muslim officials who acted as witting or unwitting proselytizers, as in some of the Batak areas north of Minangkabau and in parts of Borneo. And though, as we shall see, there continued to be sporadic outbursts of village unrest, the *Pax Neerlandica* in the settled areas, while contributing, for example, to the quadrupling of population in Java from seven to twenty-eight millions between 1830 and 1900, helped to create conditions favourable to the peaceful growth of religion.

In addition to this fairly general and widespread dissemination of Islam during the latter part of the century, other processes were at work, especially in Java, enlarging the pious *santri* nucleus of the community and intensifying its attachment to Islamic ideas and values. For the most part these processes relate to fundamental socio-economic changes at work in Indonesian society, and to the growth of direct contact with the Middle East. After the abolition of the Culture System (progressively from about 1870) and the substitution of 'liberal' economic policies aiming at a shift from state to private European capital enterprise, the Javanese peasant economy ceased to be governed by 'remote control' contracts between the government and village heads, and was drawn increasingly into a more direct relationship with export markets and with Western economic life. Though this change of policy failed to have the successful demonstration effect believed likely by many liberal theorists, some stimulus did seep through to the village level. Individuals were enabled to grow and sell commercial crops, to lease and to aggregate land, and to participate in small-scale trade. Opportunities were by no means unlimited, and were frequently subject to cramping restrictions, not to mention better organized and more highly capitalized competition, but some advantage at least was provided for those able to respond to it. Though the increasing monetization of the village economy meant for many simply a new form of servitude, others found in thrift, frugality and individual effort a liberating sense of personal fulfilment and a means of rising in the world. For these energetic and industrious people, Islam supplied a system of values which validated economic behaviour differing from that of their fellows, and a status system which gave expression to these values. Of paramount importance in the latter was the Pilgrimage to Mecca which, fulfilled as the last religious duty, at one and the same time set the seal on accumulated wealth and gave enhanced prestige in village society to the returned *ḥājjī*, who in general became revivified exemplars and propagators of the faith. In addition to thus strengthening the *santri* element in rural religious life, the Pilgrimage, by its very nature involving travel and detachment from the *desa* (village), helped to link urban (or port town) and rural Islam in a shared complex of social and economic attitudes which were to be of great importance in mediating further social change.

Though the increase in the Pilgrimage was by far the most significant element in the furtherance of large-scale movement between Middle Eastern Islam and South-East Asia (and will be discussed in greater detail shortly), it was not the only one. In the course of the mid-century, migrant Arabs also came to play a larger part than in the past in Indonesian religious life. Itinerant Arabs, mainly traders but including some divines, had of course been a feature of the port societies of the Archipelago for centuries, and some had formed settled communities. In more recent times, individuals were often found in advisory religious capacities at the courts of local rulers, and in some cases, usually by marriage, had acquired actual political power. During the Java and *Padri* Wars Arabs had been used as armistice negotiators by both sides, but principally by the traditional *élite* and the colonial power, in whose service they tended to be. In the mid-century, however, and especially after 1870, what had been a relatively casual movement turned into a steadily increasing flow, in response to new economic opportunities on the periphery of colonial rule. Between 1859 and 1885, when the first important study of the community was undertaken, numbers rose from perhaps 7,000 in the Dutch possessions to more than 20,000, with another 1,500 in the Straits Settlements. Though interpretation of these figures (which, apart from other confusions, include non-immigrant women, children, and part-Arabs) presents some problems, it is clear that a major movement was under way. By far the greater proportion of the Arabs in the region came from the Ḥaḍramawt, with which regular communication was maintained by all able to afford it. Though there was among them an important minority of *sayyids* and shaykhs belonging to ancient Ḥaḍramī traditions of learning, most were common folk from the towns with a primary interest in small-scale trade. With few exceptions, however, all were earnest and orthoprax adherents of the faith, and this together with the respect paid almost automatically to any Arab, kinsman of the Prophet or not, gave them considerable authority in the eyes of their co-religionists. Dutch restrictions upon Arab movement outside the urban areas (for fear of their presumed deleterious economic influence and probable agitatory effect) were not entirely successful, but, together with a propensity for urban living and trading, probably did limit their impact on rural society. In the growing towns, however, the nodal points for much that was new in South-East Asian Islam, they became and remained an influential section of the community, active agents for an austere if often rather conservative version of the faith.

Where contact with the Middle East was concerned however, and indeed in most other terms, the real shaping influence on the Islam of the late nineteenth century came from the Pilgrimage to Mecca. Dutch mistrust of, and hostility towards, the Ḥ*ajj*, based on the belief (by no means always erroneous) that returned pilgrims were the chief trouble-makers in rural village society, has already been referred to. Until late in the century, however, this fear was founded almost solely on the observable fact that leadership for village unrest was frequently exercised by the 'native priests', the independent '*ulamā*' (many of whom, of course, had made the Pilgrimage), and not on any understanding of the nature of the Pilgrimage, the sort of religious and social experience it constituted for participants, or the ideas with which they might be imbued. In short, the official attitude towards the Pilgrimage was determined by the almost complete ignorance with which the Dutch approached Islam in general. As a result, regulations passed in the early part of the century went as far in hindering the Pilgrimage as was possible without adopting the recognizably more dangerous alternative (if indeed this had been practicable) of suppressing it altogether. Thus by resolutions of 1825 and 1831 it was made obligatory in Java and Madura for intending pilgrims to obtain at enormous expense a special passport, failure to do so being visited by an even larger fine. At the same time, Dutch and higher Javanese officials were instructed to discourage passport applications, in the interests of reducing the dangerously idle and discontented class which returned pilgrims were believed to form. Nevertheless, numbers continued to rise; at least in part in consequence of the ready evasion of the regulations made possible by taking passage from Sumatra or Singapore. It was perhaps recognition of this evasion that led to the removal of the more draconian provisions in 1852, when the passport tax (though not the passport) was abolished, a step accompanied by fresh attempts to exercise surveillance over those making the Pilgrimage, and over their behaviour on return.

In 1859, after a brief period of liberalization, a further set of regulations was introduced in the Dutch territories, and remained in force till beyond the end of the century. The reasons for the change in policy at this time are not clear, but seem to have been related to anxiety over the manner in which the prestigious symbols of Pilgrimage-fulfilment (especially the title *ḥājjī* and the Arab-style dress assumed with it) were being used or abused, and presumably concern about the economics of the Pilgrimage for those remaining behind as well as those travelling. Under the new system the intending pilgrim had to prove that he possessed sufficient means both to complete the journey and to maintain his dependants in his absence, and on his return he had to undergo a special examination designed to show whether or not he had in fact been to Mecca. In passing it may be noted that the British in the peninsula were much less nervous, and consequently less restrictive, concerning the Pilgrimage, levying only a nominal fee for documents of identity provided to residents of their own directly controlled territories (until 1895, when even this charge was abolished), and imposing no hindrance at all on transit passengers from outside the 'protected states' and the Straits Settlements. One important consequence of this was the rapid growth of Singapore in the mid-century as the focal point of the Pilgrimage for the region as a whole.

During the 1850s, some 2,000 pilgrims were counted annually as leaving the Dutch possessions for Mecca, together with a smaller but unknown number from the Malay peninsula. After the opening of the Suez Canal in 1869, and the consequent increase and improvement in steamship services through the Red Sea area, the number grew steadily each year, until by the late 1890s the figure was fluctuating from more than 11,000 in 1895 (a 'Great Pilgrimage' year) to 7,000 in 1900, together with many hundreds more from the Malay peninsula, Acheh and elsewhere, comprising in all about twenty per cent of the total number of pilgrims from overseas. The great majority of pilgrims spent no longer out of South-East Asia than it took to make the voyage to the Ḥijāz, spend a month or so in and around the Holy Places at the time of the Pilgrimage, purchase a little religious literature, some Zamzam water, and a few locally-manufactured souvenirs, and take ship back again. Only a handful stayed on to study under a teacher, enter fully into the *ṭarīqas*, and become conversant with politically anti-colonial, pan-Islamic ideas. The distinction was important and hitherto unrecognized, if fairly obvious, as Snouck Hurgronje went to some pains to point out after 1889, and certainly fundamental to a proper appreciation of the influences exerted by Mecca. Nevertheless, the effect of even brief exposure to a wholly Muslim environment, in which all authority was subject to the law of God, and in which the universality of the faith was demonstrated by a congregation of pilgrims of all races, all levels of society, visibly joined in a levelling, if also exalting, religious experience, was by no means negligible. Even sojourners could hardly fail to be impressed by talk of the greatness of the Islamic peoples, or escape sharing in the common knowledge of the manner in which so much of Islam had become politically subordinate to the West and to Christendom. Returning to the Indies, to the towns and villages, the mosques and religious schools, they took with them not only a renewed zeal for purification of action and belief (and for the correction of their fellows), but a certain readiness to reject the colonial *status quo* if the occasion should present itself.

The effect on their own society of the *muqīm*, the permanent or semi-permanent residents from the Malay peninsula or the Archipelago, known collectively in Mecca as the *Jāwa*, was, however, certainly more profound and penetrating. Snouck Hurgronje remarked of the colony that it 'represents in essence the future of the peoples out of whom it is composed and increased', and his own detailed portayal of the community in the mid-1880s gives an invaluable account of the process at work. The core of the *Jāwa* was formed by the great teachers, of whom several commanded scholarly respect among the Meccans themselves. As instructors of their fellow-countrymen, as writers of formative and sometimes controversial religious works published in Arabic and Malay, which found their way in great quantity to the Indies, they fed a constant stream of revivified Islamic thought into the homeland. Lesser figures played a similar if less distinguished role, and themselves frequently moved back and forth between the Archipelago and the Ḥijāz, lecturing in the mosques, selling books and rosaries, gathering pilgrims, and in general inspiring their fellow Muslims.

Nowhere, perhaps, was the influence of the *Jāwa* more marked than in connection with the Ṣūfī *ṭarīqas* which flourished in Mecca. Countless hundreds of pilgrims and temporary settlers were inducted over the years into the Naqshbandiyya, Qādiriyya, and other orders, and on return home became active participants in *ṭarīqa* activity, and in some cases organizers of branches. In two areas in particular, though doubtless elsewhere as well, the consequences of this were considerable. In Minangkabau, 'orthodox' Naqshbandī influence originating with *Jāwa* shaykhs from the area, was responsible for reactivating *adat*-Islam conflicts within the society, by attacking the entrenched and somewhat decadent Shaṭṭāriyya *ṭarīqa*, closely associated with the *adat* religious officials and with old-style practices generally. Though the conflict acquired towards the end of the century other and modernist overtones, these also sprang from Meccan influence, by way of, amongst others, Shaykh Aḥmad Khaṭīb, who became the teacher of a whole generation of Minangkabau and Malayan reformers. In Banten, in West Java, the *ṭarīqas* (mainly Qādiriyya, and stemming largely from the great Bornean shaykh of the order, Khaṭīb Sambas, and his pupils) became the organizational framework for the revolutionary protest movement against the Dutch which resulted in the so-called Tjilegon risings of 1888. Though it may be argued that differences among the *ṭarīqas* helped to divide the community against itself quite as much as direct it against colonial rule, there can be no question that the appeal they exercised was a powerful force in raising and channelling popular feeling, especially in the rural areas.

So far in this account the Malay peninsula has received little more than incidental attention, as is perhaps appropriate to the relatively small proportion of the Islamic community it comprised. The increasing importance of Singapore after the mid-century, however, and the effects of British colonial control over the western states from the 1870s (which ratified the political cleavage of the Malay world foreshadowed in the 1824 treaty between the English and the Dutch, and for the first time began seriously to isolate Malayan experience from that of its neighbours) require more detailed discussion. As is well known, the British had established themselves on the periphery of the peninsula at the end of the eighteenth century, when Light occupied Penang, and had further consolidated this position by the acquisition of Singapore in 1819 and the receipt of Malacca from the Dutch a few years later. The three Straits Settlements thus formed were to mark the extent of British territorial control, though not of her political and commercial interest, for the next half-century. During this period, the Muslim states of the peninsula remained largely free from Western interference, though the northernmost (in particular Patani and Kedah) were brought under Siamese control in the early period, and experienced in consequence a largely Muslim-led reaction, the nature of which, however, has not so far been explored by historians.

Unlike the Muslim communities in Java and parts of Sumatra, the Malay states of the peninsula possessed little or nothing in the way of structured Islamic authority. It is true that the sacral powers of the rulers included responsibility for the defence and good governance of the faith, but in the realm of religion as of political organization these sparsely settled riverine states lacked either the resources or the stimulus for centralization of control. Though the theoretical association between the traditional secular *élite* (whether represented by the rulers or by the aristocracy) and the religious life of the people was never seriously questioned, it was seldom seriously tested either. From time to time individual rulers or chiefs did, from pious or other motives, appoint religious officials of a variety of kinds beyond those attached to their own mosques, but there was a marked absence of anything approaching hierarchical organization or systematic control. In these circumstances, religious authority tended to dwell in those members of village society who from piety, some pretence to learning, and perhaps through having made the Pilgrimage, were accepted as fit to exercise it—as *imāms* of mosques and religious teachers, as functionaries at Islamic occasions of one sort or another, and, increasingly in the nineteenth century, as *guru tarekat* (*ṭarīqa* teachers). The rural *'ulamā'* thus described constituted in no important sense a separate social class, and in the absence of anything more than a vestigial religious officialdom, the Malay states were markedly without the tradition of institutionalized opposition between independent *'ulamā'* and religious bureaucrats which formed such a persistent pattern elsewhere.

Though the use of the term 'protectorate' to describe the relationship contracted between the British and the Malay rulers during the forward movement of the 1870s carried in the long run a certain irony where the generality of Malay interests was concerned, it must in fairness be said that the expression was less inapt in relation both to the traditional ruling class (whose authority within Malay society was sustained), and to Islam. The Pangkor Engagement signed by the Perak chiefs in 1874, which became the model for all subsequent instruments of the sort, provided for the appointment to the state of a British resident, whose advice it was to be incumbent upon the ruler to ask for and act upon, in all matters 'other than those touching Malay Religion and Custom'. The bracketing together of religious and customary secular authority in the phrasing of this careful exclusion was not accidental, for to British observers and Malays alike the two were ultimately, at least on earth, inseparable. For the British in particular, they represented, in however ill-defined a way (and it is clear that by 'custom' they understood 'customs', as applied mainly to those ceremonial aspects of Malay life least likely to get in the way of colonial rule) the twin and associated areas in which direct interference was most likely to arouse discontent, and hence unrest. At the same time, the formal surrender to the ruling class of this joint authority seemed to the British, and doubtless to Malay observers as well, no more than testamentary recognition of an ideally as well as an actually existing state of affairs.

The extremely rapid growth of the export economy of the Malay states during the early years of protectorate rule, and the expansion of alien administration which accompanied and fostered this, did little to disrupt the patterns of peasant Malay economic and social life, conducted as most of the developmental activity was by means of Chinese and Indian immigrant labour. In the process, however, the Malay ruling class, its bases of authority within the society confirmed, found itself increasingly deprived of any real say in the running of affairs in general or in the direction of policy, and not unnaturally turned for compensation to the exercise of its sole remaining powers, those relating to religion and custom. British undertakings not to interfere in matters relating to religion were on the whole scrupulously observed, but the bureaucratic and legal apparatus of the colonial administration provided a model for organizational change, and administrators themselves were not averse to encouraging the systematization of Islamic law and practice. The last two decades of the century, therefore, saw the creation, piecemeal and largely at the instance of the traditional Malay *élite*, of a complex religio-legal bureaucracy, appointed by and dependent on the traditional *élite* itself. Restrictive Islamic legislation was enacted in the state councils, courts and legal procedures were established, and hierarchies of *qāḍīs* and other officials were brought into being, staffed for the most part from among the existing rural '*ulamā*'. Few of the measures were wholly innovatory in themselves; what was new was their systematic application, and the centralized organization that lay behind it.

The processes just described constitute the most striking developments in the Islam of the Malay states during the latter part of the century, and the movement they represent towards the growth of a series of doctrinally rather narrowly-based religious establishments, closely associated with the maintenance of the authority of the traditional secular *élite*, was to have considerable implications for the future. At the same time, however, other and perhaps less readily apparent changes were beginning to take place within the peninsular community, in response to those stimuli at work elsewhere in the region. In Malaya, as in the Archipelago at large, the Pilgrimage, with its feed-back of unpredictable energy, increased markedly in the last decades of the century, and the *ṭarīqas* (especially the Naqshbandiyya and Qādiriyya) made great advances in village society. As in other areas, some of the most obvious effects of ideas emanating from the Middle East (sometimes mediated by way of Acheh or Java) related to resistance to the advance of alien and infidel rule. It may be remarked that when, in 1875, the first British resident of Perak had been assassinated in the course of an attempt by a group of traditional chiefs to reject British control, Islam seems to have played no part whatsoever in the affair itself, or in the response to the subsequent punitive expedition. Less than twenty years later the disturbances which accompanied the extension of British rule to Pahang took much of their popular force from a rumoured document, said to have been signed by both the ruler and the principal rebel, appealing to the 'Sultan of Turkey' to help to throw the British out of southern and western Malaya, and also from religious appeals made by a famous Trengganu teacher and mystic, Ungku Sayyid Paloh, when the rebels sought refuge across the border in that state.

No influence on the peninsula was more important in the long run than that emanating from the remarkably heterogeneous Muslim community of the Straits Settlements, and especially from Singapore, which acted as the extremely dynamic metropolis for the region as a whole. As a result of a combination of circumstances—principally its strategic position on the sea-routes of South-East Asia and consequent focal role in the trade of both the British and the Dutch commercial empires, but also its labour-exchange functions for Java, Sumatra, and the peninsular and Borneo states, its lack of restriction on the movements of individuals and ideas, and its liberal (indeed commercial) attitude to the Pilgrimage—Singapore brought together a cross-section of the Muslim peoples of South-East and South Asia and the Middle East. Its reputation as a centre of Islamic life and learning rested primarily on its position in relation to the Pilgrimage and Arab migration, but was greatly contributed to by its role as a publication and distribution centre for religious writings and a gathering place for teachers. Students from all over the Archipelago wishing to further their studies in law or doctrine came, if not to Mecca, to Singapore, where they could meet and sit at the feet of itinerant scholars from the Ḥaḍramawt and the Ḥijāz, from Patani, Acheh, Palembang and Java—most of whom had themselves studied in Mecca. The city thus stood at the heart of that network of communications which, as we have seen, fed a constant stream of revitalized and revolutionary thought into the peninsula and Archipelago. It was the archetype of urban, mercantile society, piety and economic enterprise going hand in hand, which had for long—indeed, since the beginning—been important to Indonesian-Malaysian Islam. Markedly different in its way of life and thought from either its peasant or its aristocratic neighbours, by virtue of its insistence on fundamental Islamic values uncontaminated by excesses of innovation or impurities of customary belief, it offered an implied criticism of the syncretism which otherwise informed so much of its surroundings.

Not least in importance among the functions performed by Singapore in the late nineteenth century was that of providing a base for a variety of political activities associated with attempts to stave off the advance of European hegemony in the area. It was a place of frequent recourse for rulers and chiefs from the peninsula, seeking legal assistance, borrowing money, raising a following, or escaping from factional feuds, during the extension of British control over the western states and Pahang. As early as the mid-1860s the Dutch complained that there were too many malcontents and adventurers in the settlement, plotting against Netherlands interests in the Archipelago (especially in Sumatra), and organizing appeals to outside powers. Worse was to come, for after the onset in 1873 of the final large-scale and protracted conflict of the century, the Dutch subjugation of Acheh, Singapore (together with Penang) became the centre of opposition-in-exile for nearly thirty years.

The once great sultanate of Acheh, traditionally the most vigorously Islamic of Indonesian powers, had for much of the nineteenth century been in a state of suspended political decline, beset from within by periodic feuds surrounding the throne, and caught up in the commercial struggle being waged by the Western powers for control over the pepper trade of northern Sumatra. Under the political and administrative system which had obtained since at least the end of the seventeenth century, the sultanate itself, based on the port-capital of Kota Raja at the mouth of the Acheh river together with a small area of land surrounding this, did not represent any great concentration of power. Dependent almost for its existence upon the three largely autonomous confederacies of *hulubalang* (hereditary chiefs) which shared with it territorial control over Acheh proper (the northern coastal plain and the valley of the Acheh river, striking back up into the highlands), the sultanate derived what separate authority it had largely from residual tributary rights exercised over coastal dependencies on the eastern and western sides of the island. Within the confederacies, known in Acheh as the three *sagi*, or 'angles', of the state, there existed social and political structures resembling those already encountered in other parts of the Archipelago, with customary secular and religious authority concentrated in the hands of the *hulubalang* and their religious officials, and a countervailing power potentially of great strength present among the independent '*ulamā*', in most of Acheh distinguished by the honorific *teungku*. Several of the more forceful and prestigious of the latter were either Arabs or, more specifically, of Ḥaḍramī *sayyid* descent, and in general the '*ulamā*', highly receptive to the currents of the time, constituted a force to be reckoned with, as both the Dutch and the traditional chiefs were in due course to discover.

Under an arrangement made immediately subsequent to the 1824

Treaty of London (by which Britain and Holland staked out their respective areas of influence in the Straits) the Dutch had undertaken to secure the safety of trade with Acheh, while guaranteeing the continued independence of the state. This arrangement became in the course of time extremely irksome to the Dutch, as they were brought increasingly into conflict with Acheh by their own territorial expansion up the west and especially the east coasts, and as standards of international conduct deteriorated with the scramble for profits which took place around the riverine states in the northern part of the island. Matters were not helped when Acheh, after renewing in 1850 its ancient relations with the Ottoman empire, sought aid from the Sublime Porte (and other powers) in the 1860s, against Dutch interference in its affairs. Finally, in 1871, a fresh Anglo-Dutch treaty was concluded which gave the Netherlands a free hand in dealing with this unruly and recalcitrant state. Attempts at a negotiated settlement of points at issue having failed, the Dutch launched an armed invasion of Kota Raja in April 1873, and the Acheh War began.

From an early stage, Achehnese resistance to Dutch aggression assumed the character of a *jihād*, the prosecution of which came more and more to rest in the hands of those best fitted to organize and lead a Holy War, the independent '*ulama*'—who were, it may be observed, strengthened thereby in their own institutional conflict with the traditional chiefs, increasing in turn the strength of the appeals made by Islam. It is not of moment here to discuss the complex stages through which this long, tedious and often brutal conflict passed, but it is worth looking in a little more detail at the part played during the first few years of the war by specifically political pan-Islamic ideas. The unsuccessful appeal made in 1868 to Constantinople, which had been organized by a remarkable and dominant figure in Achenese politics during these years, the Ḥaḍramī Sayyid Ḥabīb 'Abd al-Raḥmān al-Ẓāhir, was followed by renewed attempts in 1873 to gain active support from the same quarter. Though these too failed, the belief that help would be forthcoming from the Ottomans gained ground in Acheh itself, in the Straits Settlements and throughout the Archipelago. Emissaries were sent from Singapore to Java and elsewhere to organize support for the Holy War, and rumours abounded that a general rising was imminent. Though in later years these hopes subsided, as a result of non-fulfilment, they played an important part in sustaining Achehnese resistance, and unrest elsewhere (in Banten, for instance), and millenarian expectations that a union of the Islamic peoples would shortly arise and defeat the West continued to manifest themselves at intervals in response to such events as the Russo-Turkish War of 1877–8, the Mahdist rising in the Sudan, and the passage through Singapore in 1890 of a Turkish warship on a courtesy visit to Japan.

Dutch fears of pan-Islam, which had in any case been gaining ground, were greatly stimulated by affairs in Acheh, where the course of the struggle continued to go against them until late in the century despite various attempts at holding actions and pacification, and long pauses in the fighting. Acheh was, of course, in one sense, merely the most recent (if also the most bitter) in a long series of colonial conflicts, in which the driving force of resistance had been supplied by Islam, and which together indicated to the Netherlands government a serious failure to elaborate a satisfactory Islamic policy, capable of assuring the peaceful continuance of Dutch rule. As the end of the century approached, the need to remedy this situation became increasingly imperative, partly as a means of ending the disturbance in Acheh, and partly to permit the diversion of Dutch energies to other social and economic tasks in what was now, effectively, the Netherlands Indies. It was in these circumstances, then, that a decision was made to appoint an Islamist to the newly created post of adviser on Arabian and Native Affairs.

C. Snouck Hurgronje (1857–1936) came to this office in 1889 possessed of a unique familiarity with certain aspects of Indonesian Islam, derived during a six-month stay in disguise (a pretence never really forgiven him by many Muslims) with the *Jāwa* community of Mecca a few years earlier. Despite a certain Christian superciliousness towards Islam, and an often disparaging attitude towards the Achehnese in particular, as displayed in his otherwise brilliant study of Achehnese life—both of which failings may, however, have been of the time as much as of the man—Snouck was a sensitive and highly intelligent observer of Indonesian society, equipped with insights into the religious life of the community which were far in advance of any owned by his contemporaries. In addition, he was a good nineteenth-century liberal, and an advocate not only of tolerance towards other systems of belief, but of a more positive and generous vision of a peaceful associative relationship between the Dutch and Indonesian peoples in the future.

Snouck's Islamic policy, as it came to be developed during the last decade of the century, was based on the replacement of the blindly restrictive and at times punitive measures of the past by a more discriminating analysis of the manner in which Islam worked in Indonesian society, and of the means necessary to control it. Arguing that in the absence of a professional religious hierarchy in Islam it was no more legitimate to see 'priests' in the '*ulamā*' than to find a 'pope' in Constantinople, he advocated that, though a proper and strict surveillance should be kept over ideological appeals to pan-Islam, it was not necessary to suppose all pious and enthusiatic Muslims, far less all returned pilgrims, to be sworn enemies of Dutch rule and unamenable to reason. He proposed, therefore, the removal of irritating restrictions upon the Pilgrimage together with increased but intelligent vigilance over and prohibitions upon any form of political activity directly connected with it. A policy of sympathetic religious neutrality would, it was believed, come to reassure Indonesian Muslims that they had nothing to fear from the colonial government, provided they forswore political propaganda, while at the same time it improved Holland's reputation in the Muslim world at large. Combined with these measures, Snouck proposed a more purposive return to the policy which had, indeed, been pursued by the Dutch at intervals since the days of the East India Company, the support of those elements in Indonesian society least zealously Islamic, the traditional *adat*-chiefs and the *priyayi élite*.

Even before the end of the decade, the last of these stratagems, combined with a newly organized military offensive against the independent '*ulamā*', was bringing the war in Acheh nearer its inevitable if long-delayed close, and though in general the effects of Snouck Hurgronje's policies were to be felt in the new century not in the old, another era had begun. The nineteenth century, with its dual set of conflicts for Islam—one within, between the forces of renewal and the traditional order; and one without, against the relentless political encroachment of the West—was over. In the process much had changed, often with violence, but other battles remained to be fought—in a sense had barely been joined.

CHAPTER 3

SOUTH-EAST ASIAN ISLAM IN THE TWENTIETH CENTURY

The nineteenth century had witnessed repeated and powerful commotion among the major Muslim communities in island South East Asia, especially in the Netherlands possessions. At considerable human and financial cost, the Dutch succeeded in defeating Muslim rebelliousness in the field. Pacification was followed by the implementation, at the end of the century, of a circumspect Islamic policy. Though Wahhābī-inspired Muslim 'puritanism' was to leave lasting marks in many parts of Indonesia—most notably, perhaps, in the gradual gains of orthodoxy at the expense of the mystical *ṭarīqas*—Islamic militancy in Indonesia had to all intents and purposes given way to relative stability and tranquillity in the opening years of the new century. But this tranquillity was short-lived and soon gave way to a virtual religious, social and political renaissance embracing many parts of the area. The impetus for this Islamic renaissance came, as so often before, from abroad; what lent it viability and a measure of cohesion were social changes resulting from accelerated modernization under colonial rule.

The sources as well as the development of South-East Asia's Islamic renaissance were varied. For one thing, the Pilgrimage continued to attract increasing numbers of South-East Asians. Thus in 1911, Dutch statistics recorded over 24,000 Indonesians, comprising almost thirty per cent of all overseas pilgrims in the Holy City. Ibn Su'ūd's conquest of Mecca in 1924 and the subsequent *Pax Wahhabica*—coinciding with temporary prosperity in the Indies—led to a dramatic augmentation in the number of pilgrims, culminating in over 52,000 Indonesians (over forty per cent of the overseas total) in 1926–7. During the same year over 12,000 pilgrims left Malaysia for the Holy City. These quantitative increments were obviously not the most significant aspect of Wahhābī rule. Heightened orthodoxy in Mecca could not but affect, more or less profoundly, the *Jāwa* colony in Mecca, the reservoir of Indonesian (and Malayan) Muslims who remained in the city for years, and whose returning members so often played an important role in South-East Asian Muslim affairs.

Of more far-reaching importance to the Islamic renaissance was

Muslim reformism and modernism, emanating from Shaykh Muḥammad 'Abduh in Egypt at the close of the nineteenth century. Reformism did not merely reinforce the trend toward greater Muslim self-awareness and orthodox militancy engendered by Wahhābī thought. It supplemented the negative onslaught on South-East Asian syncretism and Sufism by a positive appeal to adjust Islam to the requirements of the modern world, and in so doing it infused in the Islamic communities a new vitality and momentum, a clear orientation and a programme for action. Thus, side by side with pilgrims returning after years of study with Meccan shaykhs, Islam had found new and dynamic spokesmen from among Indonesian and Malayan youths returning from Cairo; by the mid-1920s, al-Azhar may have counted between two and three hundred students from the two countries, about two-thirds of them Indonesians. In addition to the traditional Middle Eastern religious literature, South-East Asian Muslims increasingly became acquainted with, and were influenced by, 'Abduh's writings, by *al-Manār* and a host of other periodicals and newspapers carrying the message of modernism.

Yet a third foreign influence, that of Indian reformism, came to exert a less spectacular, though intellectually perhaps not negligible, influence. The writings of Amīr 'Alī and Mawlānā Muḥammad 'Alī, if not those of Muḥammad Iqbāl, though rarely explicitly acknowledged as spiritual sources by Indonesian or Malay reformists, did not go unnoticed. Again, though the missionary enterprises of the Indian Aḥmadiyya movement—especially of its Lahore branch, brought to Java by Mīrzā Walī Beg in 1924—were, numerically speaking, far from successful, the Aḥmadiyya translation of the Qur'ān acted as a source of inspiration and even imitation to some outstanding Indonesian Muslims.

I

Both in origin and orientation, twentieth-century Islamic activities bore an intrinsically pan-Malaysian character largely transcending the political boundaries separating British from Dutch colonial possessions. Subjects of both powers freely intermingled in Mecca, in Cairo, and not least in the Straits Settlements. These contacts had some political significance in creating pan-Malaysian sentiments from the 1930s onward. But these common factors must not obscure the very real differences between Islamic developments in British Malaya and the Dutch East Indies. In part these differences were determined by divergences in social and political patterns and historical developments, in part also by the kind and degree of colonial rule. The Dutch colonial empire in the Indies comprised a far wider variety of peoples and cultures than did British Malaya. Again, Dutch rule in many parts of Indonesia antedated the British in Malaya by several decades, and in the case of Java by centuries. Western economic and administrative interference had thus been far more prolonged and thorough in the Dutch than the British colonial realm, with far-reaching consequences for Indonesian, and especially also Islamic, developments. Of at least equal importance, finally, were colonial policies regarding Islam, that of the Netherlands being elaborated and executed with a paternalistic sophistication altogether unparalleled in British Malaya.

In the opening years of the twentieth century, it was the small but important Muslim communities in the Straits Settlements, in Singapore at first, Penang later, that formed the intellectual nerve-centres of the Islamic renaissance; a role dictated by their rather unusual cosmopolitan composition, relative wealth and dynamism, by their location athwart the Pilgrimage route, and not least, by the freedom they enjoyed under direct British rule. At the opening of the century, Straits Muslims included some 1,500 Ḥaḍramawt Arabs, including several outstanding shaykhs and *sayyids*; though for the greater part locally born, they constituted a distinct, Arab-oriented minority of considerable affluence and prestige. Another economically influential group were the so-called *Jawi Peranakan*, Indo-Malays descended from Indian (largely Malabari) Muslims, who had pioneered Malay journalism in the mid-nineteenth century. To these groups must be added the constant flow of peninsular Malays, as well as the many Indonesians—primarily Sumatrans, but later on also Javanese—who made the Straits Settlements their temporary or permanent abode.

The most notable influence exerted by these pious mercantile communities in constant touch with the centres of Islamic life in the Middle East and with most parts of the Archipelago lay in the field of writing, especially in journalism. The first newspaper to carry the message of reformism to the Malayo-Indonesian world was *al-Imām*, founded in 1907, and closely modelled on Cairo's *al-Manār*. Its founder, Shaykh Muḥammad Ṭāhir b. Jalāl al-Dīn al-Azharī (1869–1957), a student of 'Abduh's and one of the most respected and influential reformers, was a Minangkabau. In fact, few peninsular Malays served on the paper's editorial and managerial staff, which reflected the ethnic variety—and the strong Indonesian component—among the Straits Muslim activists. They also pioneered in one other important field, that of education, by establishing, in 1908, an Egyptian-staffed *madrasa* in the city. It was soon followed by hundreds of such new schools throughout the Archipelago.

The outstanding role of Singapore and Penang, then, was that of cultural brokers, translating the new purity, rationalism, and vitality of Islam into the Malay language—the Archipelago's *lingua franca*—and also into terms relevant to a local, Malayo-Indonesian frame of reference. Great as this contribution was, the Straits Settlements provided too narrow a base for organizational experiment on a significant scale. Their vigorous and cosmopolitan Muslim groups were exceptional: small groups living in the shadow of thriving Western and Chinese mercantile communities that could afford to ignore Islamic activism, not being in the least challenged by it. But it was otherwise when this activism started, almost immediately, to radiate to the various parts of insular South-East Asia. Even though reformist spokesmen originally limited themselves to religious reform as such—especially to the purification of worship and ritual and the modernization of religious education—their teachings were bound to engender far-reaching social and political repercussions. These found expression in the fact that the appellations *Kaum Muda* ('The Young Group') and *Kaum Tua* ('The Old Group'), originally specifically used to designate Muslim religious reformers and their traditionally inclined religious opponents, before long came to stand for innovators and conservatives in a far wider sense.

On the religious plane, reformism's broad attack on traditional South-East Asian Islam posed a threat to old-fashioned *'ulamā'* and their practices. On the social plane, its target was—though selectively and thus by no means always consistently—customary social and legal usages as embodied in the *adat*, and hence also the upholders of the traditional order. Cautiously at first, but here and there with increasing vehemence, reformers finally and inevitably also came to criticize and challenge the political, colonial order. It was seen as the preserver of traditional indigenous, social systems, but also as the creator of plural societies in which foreigners, Western as well as Asian, had come to wield predominant commercial and economic power. No less invidious in Muslim eyes was the subtle penetration of Western values, carried into South-East Asia both by Christian missionaries and secular educators under the European overlords. Finally, intensified Muslim sentiment could not but look askance at *kāfir* overlordship.

In spite of the geographic proximity of the Straits Settlements, reformism was organizationally least successful in Malaya. Its failure to score noticeable successes in the Malay states was primarily due to the relatively slow pace of social change among the peninsular Muslim communities. Though economic modernization under the British aegis had been swift and impressive, its major impact fell on mostly non-Muslim immigrant groups, especially Chinese, rather than on the autochthonous, still predominantly rural Malays. Malay society therefore did not as yet provide adequate anchorages for innovation and reform. But the spread of reformism was also seriously inhibited by British colonial policy, the same policy which paradoxically did so little to inhibit Muslim activities in the Malayan areas under direct British rule. British policy towards Islam displays fairly consistent non-interference, implicitly as a matter of course in the Straits Settlements, and as a matter of explicit stipulation in the treaties concluded with Malay rulers. The pattern was established in the first such treaty, the Pangkor Engagement concluded with (in fact, forced upon) the sultanate of Perak (January, 1874); it stipulated that the only matters specifically to be withheld from the powers of the British resident were to be 'those touching Malay Religion and Custom'. When the Federated Malay States (Perak, Pahang, Selangor, and Negri Sembilan) were founded in 1895, reference to Malay customs was deleted from the terms of the formal agreement, but the 'Muhammadan religion' remained specifically outside the purview of the protecting power. Under the protective umbrella of an allegedly indirect rule the Malay sultans, endowed with unprecedented political stature and authority, embarked on institutional innovation by creating well-organized and salaried hierarchies of Muslim officials in charge of religious administration and law. The process was in similar fashion repeated in the Unfederated States (Johore, Kedah, Trengganu, Kelantan, and Perlis), where the rulers' authority was in any case far less fettered by British 'advisers'.

While the religious hierarchies and a good many of the regulatory and supervisory tasks entrusted to them were new, their personnel was almost exclusively recruited from among the vestigial, unorganized and poorly equipped religious dignitaries of earlier days, augmented by rural '*ulamā*'. The new establishments thus came to be staffed by proponents of traditional, syncretic, heterodox and often Ṣūfī-tinged Islam, solidly entrenched in positions of authority by their secular superiors. It was this combination of Muslim traditionalism with Malay secular power that placed such obstacles in the way of Islamic reformism in the peninsula. Moreover Malaya, unlike Java and Sumatra, was barely encumbered by a tradition of '*ulamā*' opposition to secular authorities, let alone by the legacy of Wahhābī radicalism that had elsewhere led to the sharpening of such opposition in the nineteenth century. The *Kaum Muda*, agitating from their sanctuaries in directly ruled territories, thus appeared as radical innovators threatening both the religious and the secular *status quo*. If individual reformers of stature, such as Ṭāhir, occasionally gained favour as advisers and companions to a Malay ruler, the posts of religious officialdom, such as *muftī* (*shaykh al-Islām*) or *kathi* (*qāḍī*), or membership in the newly created Councils of Religious and Malay Custom, almost without exception remained beyond their reach. By the same token, the *Kaum Tua*, from their positions of authority, not infrequently banned reformist literature and newspapers from the Malay states.

Thus, though reformism was by no means without its lasting effects on Malayan Islam (e.g., the adoption of the *madrasa*, the modern Islamic school, though more often as an institutional rather than an intrinsic innovation) it was prevented from growing into an organizational force led by a peninsular *élite*. These inhibitions also precluded the development of the stunted Islamic renaissance into a more clearly political, proto-nationalist movement as in other parts of the Malayo-Indonesian world. This relative tardiness of religious and political modernization to a large extent reflected the slow rate of social change in a still predominantly rural society.

Since the divergent course of the Islamic renaissance in colonial Indonesia was so closely affected by Dutch policies, they must be briefly dealt with. The architect of Netherlands Islamic policy in the Indies, Christiaan Snouck Hurgronje (1857–1936), left his stamp on Dutch dealings with Islamic problems for over half-a-century. His Islamic policy postulated toleration of the Muslim faith, combined with repressive vigilance towards Islamic, especially pan-Islamic, political activities. This divorce of religion and politics, however problematical in theory and later often also in practice, did at the outset reconcile the vast bulk of Indonesian believers, and indeed even a substantial number of '*ulamā*', to the foreign overlord. Snouck Hurgronje's principles had been laid down before the onset of the Islamic renaissance in Indonesia; Snouck himself actually left his post in 1906, never to return to the islands. His successors, and Dutch administrators in general, continued to adhere to his principles after the appearance of reformism, not even abandoning them as major guidelines when the rapid growth of Muslim activism increasingly threatened to blur the thin and artificial dividing line between the religiously tolerable and the politically intolerable. Confronted by new Islamic challenges, Dutch practice at times perforce came to deviate quite markedly from non-interference. But the impressive gains which reformism was to score in twentieth-century Indonesia are undeniably in no small measure traceable to a *Pax Neerlandica* that kept the door ajar—even if neither always nor consistently wide open—to religious innovators.

The contrast between British Malaya and the Netherlands Indies stems, then, in part at least from differences in colonial policies and practices. We have seen that British non-interference in matters religious, while allowing free play to the vigorous, but politically insignificant, Muslim minorities in the Straits Settlements, had at the same time encouraged alliances of secular and religious traditionalists able to stem the tide of reformism in the Malay states. Dutch non-interference, by contrast, introduced the European-derived principle of religious toleration into the Indies and superimposed it, so to speak, upon the Indonesian *cuius regio eius religio*. This was of especial significance in the areas under direct Dutch control, most notably in Java. The difference between the two colonial realms is the more striking since resistance to the *Kaum Muda* was not necessarily weaker in many parts of Indonesia than in the Malay peninsula, and since, moreover, Dutch colonial policy in general tended to favour and support the social, political, and legal *status quo*. Yet social evolution, incomparably more far-reaching here than in the Malay states, combined with direct rule, had in the course of time eroded the authority and the independence of the erstwhile bearers of political power in Java to a point where in the twentieth century they lacked the ability to build a viable alliance between religious and secular conservatives. In the areas outside Java under indirect colonial rule, Indonesian chiefs and Muslim *Kaum Tua* often enough attempted to forge such alliances; but the Dutch guardians of religious freedom, at times unwittingly if not unwillingly, inhibited the consummation of their 'Counter-Reformation'.

In the early years of the twentieth century, reformism rapidly spread to most parts of the Archipelago. Intellectually, especially in the realm of journalism and literature, the Straits Muslim community served as a model that found ready Indonesian imitators. The first modernist journal, *al-Munīr*, was established in early 1911 on the west coast of Sumatra by Ḥājjī 'Abd Allāh Aḥmad (Haji Abdullah Ahmad 1878–1933) and Ḥājjī 'Abd al-Karīm 'Amr Allāh (Haji Abdul Karim Amrullah 1879–1945), who became one of the most impressive and influential representatives of Indonesian reformism. During its five years of life, *al-Munīr* in turn served as a model for the burgeoning Islamic press, particularly in Java, which almost from the outset developed into Indonesia's centre of the new Islamic activities. It was there that reformism was given organizational forms which spread out to the other islands, unhampered by the barriers which it encountered on the Malay peninsula. But since Java, the most populous and most modernized island, also acted as a magnet which attracted large numbers of Indonesians from other parts of the Archipelago, reformism was not exclusively led by Javanese Muslims, but before long by an all-Indonesian core of leaders. Even then, Indonesia's Islamic renaissance proper was by no means uniform. To survive, it had to find local leaders able to adapt, modify and domesticate—and also to defend—it in each particular social setting.

In fact, Islam in Java was in at least two major respects unique: it had been profoundly affected by Indian religious, cultural and social influences; and it had similarly experienced the longest and deepest impact of Western economic penetration and colonial rule. Indian influences had caused the process of islamization to be retarded and partly deflected. A specifically Hindu-Javanese culture thus survived, epitomized by an at best nominally Muslim nobility and aristocracy—the *priyayi*—at one end of the social spectrum. and by a highly syncretic, and in many parts likewise nominally Islamic, folk religion at the other. It was only on the periphery of indianization—on the north coast and in the westernmost part of the island—that Islam had struck deep roots before the twentieth century. Dutch influences, for their part, had considerably weakened the political authority of Javanese rulers and of the *priyayi* aristocracy, many members of the latter having become salaried civil servants of the colonial régime. Increasingly intensive administrative and economic penetration into the countryside, commencing in the late eighteenth century, had made progressive inroads into the social fabric of the peasantry. In the twentieth century, a whole host of Dutch-inspired innovations—most notably in the field of welfare and education—made their appearance under the so-called Ethical Policy, inaugurated by the Netherlands in 1901. These manifold changes, accompanied by a very rapid increase in population, created an increasingly volatile social setting. If the partial monetization of the native economy and increasing governmental interference in village life led to considerable rural *malaise*, new economic as well as educational opportunities brought into existence *élite* groups. Given the indianized matrix of Javanese traditional society, the Western nature of social and educational innovation, and finally the manifold repercussions from the political and intellectual stirrings elsewhere in Asia, the Islamic renaissance was bound to be only one, albeit an important, facet of Java's response to a rapidly changing situation. Often Islamic and non-Islamic developments tended to interact and overlap, since Islamic innovation from the very beginning touched not only the religious and social, but also the political, spheres.

These complexities are well exemplified by the two major organizations born in the princely states of Central Java in the year 1912, *Muhammadiyah* and *Sarekat Islam* ('Islamic League'). Though they had been preceded by earlier and smaller Islamic associations, the modern era may be said to commence with these two. Unlike other religious groups of modernist tendencies, both in the course of time developed into island-wide, and ultimately nation-wide, movements involving hundreds of thousands of Indonesians.

Muhammadiyah was founded by Kiyayi Ḥājjī Aḥmad Dachlan (1869–1923), a pious businessman from the *kauman* (the predominantly Muslim urban quarters adjacent to the principal mosque) of Jogjakarta, who had twice made the Pilgrimage and studied with renowned shaykhs in the Holy City. *Muhammadiyah* shunned organized political activities, concentrating on a bold programme of religious innovation directed towards the purification of Javanese Islam, the reformulation of Islamic doctrine in the light of modern knowledge, the reform of Muslim education, and the defence of the faith against external influences and attacks. From slow beginnings, *Muhammadiyah* soon grew to a membership of over 4,000 in 1925, to count 852 branches with a total membership of a quarter of a million thirteen years later. From the early 1920s, through intensive missionary work it found acceptance in parts of the Outer Islands. In 1938, well over 800 mosques and smaller houses of worship and—more important still—more than 1,700 schools (including secondary schools and teachers' colleges) testified to *Muhammadiyah*'s pioneering part in modern Indonesian Islam. If 'Abduh's *Tafsīr* and *Risālat al-tawḥīd* provided the guideposts for reformist education, it was Western organizational and institutional models—not least those successfully copied from Christian missions—that turned reformism into a new social force.

Muhammadiyah and its smaller sister organizations relied for their major support on the island's petty bourgeoisie, mostly urban (and including the small but influential group of Indo-Arabs) but also rural. In its formative years, these groups also played a leading role in *Sarekat Islam*, which in fact had originated in the *Sarekat Dagang Islam* ('Islamic Trade League'), founded in Surakarta (Solo) in 1911 by a Muslim merchant, Ḥājjī Samanhudi. The economic impetus behind these organizational activities stemmed from Chinese commercial competition, recently unfettered from restrictive controls by the colonial government. Religious activism was, for its part, spurred by Christian missionary activities, accelerated since 1910. But where *Muhammadiyah* remained firmly rooted in the specifically Muslim culture of the *kauman* and of the pious landowning *ḥājjī*, *Sarekat Islam* before long reached out beyond these geographic and social confines. Within less than a decade, *Sarekat Islam* expanded from its Central Javanese base into a heterogeneous mass-movement, losing in the process its merchant progenitors who, appalled at the increasing radicalization of the movement, sought affiliation with *Muhammadiyah* and similarly non-political, religious groupings.

This startling metamorphosis was accomplished, almost unwittingly it would seem, by a group of younger leaders, none of them reared in the *kauman's* mercantile piety. What distinguished them as a group from the *Muhammadiyah* leadership was greater social and ethnic variety, but above all Western education. Raden 'Umar Sayyid Tjokroaminoto (1882–1934), the movement's charismatic and forensically brilliant leader, was a *priyayi* by birth who, like his less prominent lieutenant, 'Abd al-Mu'izz (Abdul Muis 1878–1959) had been trained for government service. These two Javanese were soon joined by Ḥājjī Agus Salīm (1884–1954), scion of a prominent Minangkabau family, who as a young man had served the colonial government in various capacities and became an ardent convert to modernist Islam while working in the Netherlands consulate at Jedda. But Salīm's was the only specifically Islamic voice in the upper councils of *Sarekat Islam*, whose increasingly vehement agitation bore a decidedly political, even secular, ring. For some time, the movement's leadership was heavily infiltrated by Marxist youths, who in the early 1920s threatened to gain supreme control over it. *Sarekat Islam*, that is to say, attracted an urban audience by no means limited to those in search of religious innovation. Hence its major significance did not lie in its peripheral contribution to the Islamic renaissance in Java, but rather in the organizational experimentation which it brought to the younger generation of Indonesians. Undeniably, the *Sarekat*'s meteoric rise—it claimed over half a million members in 1919—owed a good deal to the religious mass-appeal conveyed by its very name. But this appeal was not of the leaders' conscious making. It stemmed, rather, from the spontaneous rural support mobilized by hundreds of local *kiyayi* and '*ulamā*,' purveyors of a syncretic, Javanese folk-Islam which saw in Tjokoraminoto not the harbinger of organized modernity but the messianic redeemer from the burdens of earthly existence. For a few years, *Sarekat Islam* thus served as a social barometer registering the mounting disaffection prevalent among the island's rural population as a result of economic and administrative change.

From the mid-1920s on *Sarekat Islam* started to decline as rapidly as it had risen. Lack of a viable programme of concerted action, disunity in its leadership, and increased governmental vigilance combined to bring about the gradual demise of colonial Indonesia's first and last political mass-movement. The Marxist element, unsuccessful in its bid for the domination of the organization, was expelled, and for a few years endeavoured to supplant the *Sarekat* leadership as the main spokesman for social unrest in towns and countryside, its efforts culminating in a series of strikes and peasant uprisings between 1925 and 1927. With the suppression of these outbreaks by the colonial government, social turmoil and the young Communist party virtually ceased to exist. Salīm, who had steered the *Sarekat* away from both its messianic associations and Marxist affiliations, now tried to imprint a distinctly Islamic orientation on the movement. But the desired prestigious connexion with revived pan-Islam evaporated after the collapse of the short-lived Caliphate movement in Egypt and Sa'udi Arabia. Attempts to forge close links with the modernist Aḥmadiyya led to estrangement from the doctrinally more cautious *Muhammadiyah* reformists. Thus deprived of its mass base and kept at bay by Muslim leaders, *Sarekat Islam*, continually torn by internal dissensions, dwindled to insignificance from the late 1920s.

If the movement's initiative in religious matters was lost, so was its leading political role. Leadership in Indonesian political life passed from *Sarekat Islam* to the proponents of a strictly secular nationalism, most of them—like Sukarno, Muḥammad Hatta, and Sutan Sjahrir—recipients of higher modern education in the colony or abroad.

The centre of gravity thus shifted from the *kauman* to the modern capital, Batavia, where the pulse of Muslim life beat but weakly in spite of a considerable semi-proletarian Muslim community. This did not indeed inhibit the steady growth of *Muhammadiyah* and other groups. In fact, they benefited from the selective repression practiced by the colonial authorities in the years after 1927, which placed far greater obstacles in the way of political than religious movements. Yet Muslims, reared outside the political climate of the capital city, for very many years failed to adapt themselves to Indonesia's political modernization. It was Agus Salīm who first recognized the dangers of this situation. In late 1925, he founded the *Jong Islamieten Bond* ('Young Muslims' League'), designed—as its Dutch name and its domicile, Batavia, suggest—to provide Western-educated Indonesians with a religiously based political organization at the centre of the colony's political life. The *Bond* became one of the important recruiting grounds for the political consummation of the Islamic renaissance. Other politically conscious Muslims, who for some years had moved in and out of *Sarekat Islam*, finally founded in 1938 the *Partai Islam Indonesia*, which through participation in elective bodies strove to provide an adequate political base for Indonesian Islam. By then, however, non-Islamic movements and parties had come to predominate in the organized political life and in the various institutions created by the colonial government.

Limited and belated as was the political role of reformism in twentieth century Indonesian political history, its impressive educational and religious achievements had far-reaching social and ultimately also political consequences, not least in some of the Outer Islands. To the extent that *Muhammadiyah* succeeded in educating a new generation of self-reliant Muslims, it gave birth to an increasingly sophisticated political public. And to the extent that reformist spokesmen found themselves at odds with the colonial government's intrusions in matters affecting the Muslim community in the 1930s—such as the jurisdiction of religious judges and the attempted reform of Muslim matrimonial law—they fanned a growing restiveness to *kāfir* overlordship. Nor was this all. The very vigour of the reformers' onslaught elicited spirited responses which before long resulted in the crystallization of distinct social and, implicitly at least, political attitudes dividing Indonesian society, especially in Java.

Not unexpectedly, the most vehement reaction to reformist inroads came from the *Kaum Tua*, the thousands of rural *kiyayi* and '*ulamā*', for centuries the sole and undisputed spokesmen of Javanese Islam. Their opposition to the religious innovators was shared by the religious officialdom entrusted with the supervision of Islamic worship and the administration of the *Sharī'a*, but above all by the *priyayi* hierarchy which constituted the native segment of the Dutch administrative system on the island. For the greater part descendants of the royal office-holders of Mataram, the *priyayi* continued to hold a distinctly Hindu-Javanese world-view, barely tinged by Islam. Judging by Malayan developments, such dual opposition to religious innovation could have constituted a wellnigh insuperable barrier to Indonesian reformism, had not Dutch policy to a considerable extent neutralized administrative interference. The traditional religious leaders were thus forced to meet the *Kaum Muda* on their own ground, and in the process to accept a modicum of modernization. In January, 1926, several *kiyayi* from Central and East Java founded the *Nahdatul Ulama* ('The Awakening of the '*Ulamā*''), their first and foremost modern-style organization which attracted some outstanding and venerable men, such as its later chairman, K. H. Hasjim Asj'ari (1871–1947), head of the famous religious school (*pesantren*) at Tebu Ireng in east Java. *Nahdatul Ulama*, though not as spectacularly successful as its reformist counterpart, copied some of its innovations and before long also emulated its missionary drive beyond the island. Opposition to increasing governmental interference in Muslim affairs in the 1930s, no less than growing apprehensions concerning the spreading appeal of Indonesian secular nationalism, were instrumental in bringing modernists and traditionalists together in a federative body, the *Majlisul Islamil A'laa Indonesia* ('Higher Islamic Council of Indonesia'), better known as *M.I.A.I.*, founded in Surabaya in September, 1937.

But this loose alliance could by no means bridge the profound gulf that came to divide Javanese Islam. Differences outwardly centred, as elsewhere, on the controversy between *ijtihād* and *taqlīd*, between the traditional *pesantren* and the modern *madrasa*, and hence between two contenders for the leadership of the Muslim community. Doctrinal controversy was reinforced by a more far-reaching social and cultural polarization between urban and rural Islam, or rather, between a sterner, more recognizably Middle Eastern, Islam on one hand, and the syncretic heterodox Javanese Islam, on the other. Though the organizational balance was decidedly in favour of the reformers, and though foreign overlordship allowed them relatively free rein, traditional Islam could count on a vast following not only among '*ulamā*' clinging to a stubborn individualism outside *Nahdatul Ulama* and its smaller, local, imitators, but also among millions of peasants whose religious allegiances ran the gamut from pre-Islamic *abangan* orientations to the specifically Javanese forms of Muslim orthodoxy.

This internal Islamic controversy constituted only one, and that by no means the most important, aspect of a wider confrontation. The fact that the two wings of the Islamic movement could—however tenuously and temporarily—agree to make common cause reflected a measure of basic unity in the face of outside threats to Islamic interests in general. But Muslim claims to the contrary notwithstanding, twentieth-century Javanese society was not coterminous with the Muslim community: *abangan* beliefs and especially *priyayi* culture not only retained their identities, but these pre-Islamic, if not inherently anti-Islamic, traditions provided secular nationalism with its specifically Javanese roots. These were already evident in the *Budi Utomo* ('Noble Vision') of 1908, but more importantly in the *Taman Siswo* ('Garden of Pupils') school system, founded in 1922 by Soewardi Soerianingrat (better known by his adopted name, Ki Hadjar Dewantoro), of the princely family of Paku Alam in the realm of Jogjakarta in Central Java. Dewantoro's was perhaps the most successful endeavour to translate *priyayi* culture into a modern milieu, attempting to do for Javanese culture what *Muhammadiyah* did for Islamic reformism.

The polarization between Islam and Javanese culture—a polarization going back to at least the sixteenth century—thus received reinforcement and modern expression through the leaders of Islamic reformism and the intellectuals who, whether trained in *Taman Siswo* or government schools, became the standard bearers of Indonesian nationalism. Joint opposition to colonial rule, it is true, could at times mute the discord between Muslims and secular nationalists. Indeed, the only significant concession that Indonesians were jointly able to wrest from the colonial government was the withdrawal of an ordinance seriously threatening the functioning of native private schools in 1933. But the gulf separating them was too wide to be more permanently bridged by such brief interludes of harmony and unity of purpose. What separated Western-trained intellectuals and Muslim spokesmen was not only differences concerning the outward goal—the modern secular state as against the *Dār al-Islām*—but the identification of nationalists with the legendary grandeur of pre-Islamic Majapahit, of Muslims with an intrinsically non-Indonesian culture. The cleavage was deepened by the political imbalance between nationalists and Muslims, the former having, since the eclipse of *Sarekat Islam*, gained predominance in organized political activities and in the representative institutions—such as the *Volksraad* (People's Council) and the Regency Councils—created by the colonial power in the twentieth century.

For both geographic and cultural reasons, the growing cleavage between Islam and modern nationalism was far more pronounced in Java than in the other islands. The institutions of higher learning, as well as the instrumentalities for modern political life, were almost exclusively concentrated in Java. It was there that the secular intelligentsia, and hence Indonesian nationalism, found their main abode. It is true, of course, that that intelligentsia was no more exclusively restricted to Javanese (and Sundanese) than was the leadership of Islamic reformism on the island. But such ethnic diversity, however important it was for the development of a truly all-Indonesian nationalism, was nonetheless counterbalanced by a peculiar blending of Javanese and Western values which permeated many among the intelligentsia, regardless of their ethnic origin, and which set them apart from most of their Muslim counterparts. The splendour and refinement of Javanese culture, still powerful in spite of the political impotence of the central Javanese principalities, thus exercised a far from negligible influence on Indonesian nationalism.

No comparable, viable cultural traditions existed in most of the other islands, many of whose most enterprising and dynamic youths moreover tended to be drawn to Java. More than that, even, the destruction of some ruling houses (the most notable examples being the Minangkabau during the *Padri* War and the Achehnese sultanate in the course of the Acheh War) had created social and political vacuums which neither territorial nor kinship units could adequately fill. Indeed, Sumatran royalty had never enjoyed either the substance or the aura of Javanese kingship. Equally important, unlike the Javanese *priyayi*, the Minangkabau *penghulu* and the Achehnese *ulèebalang* (secular territorial chiefs) merely represented local and parochial traditions. The pattern of Dutch rule in the Outer Islands in fact strengthened this innate parochialism of petty chiefs and village heads, thus precluding their gradual modernization along lines similar to those in Java. The absence of central secular authority, and the relative weakness of indigenous royal tradition, significantly determined the course of modern Islamic history in Sumatra and elsewhere. In none of the more sparsely populated Outer Islands was there, in fact, a politically and culturally dominant ethnic group comparable to the Javanese. Wahhabism had, as we saw, struck deep roots among both Achehnese and Minangkabaus in the nineteenth century. Though the militant *'ulamā'* had been subdued by the colonial power, Muslim sentiment only needed the impetus of modern activism to be rekindled to new vitality. But whereas in Java the Islamic renaissance encountered competition from both pre-Islamic Javanese tradition and modern nationalism, in Sumatra (and not only there) it was for some decades virtually the only modern, supra-local, and indeed proto-nationalist force. As such, it evoked a strong reaction among both traditionalist *'ulamā'* and secular chiefs. Even though the challenge of the *Kaum Muda* effected a rapprochement between these two historically antagonistic groups, their joint opposition to reformism was not nearly as effective in the Netherlands Indies as it was in British Malaya. This was in part due to the fact that Sumatran petty chiefs did not possess the authority and prestige enjoyed by Malayan sultans, in part to the modicum of protection extended to religious movements under Dutch Islamic policy, circumscribed and modified as it was in Sumatra by a general inclination—born of the experiences of the nineteenth century—to rely on the traditional representatives of the social order.

Modern trends in Sumatran Islam made their first appearance in the Minangkabau region on the island's West Coast, where reformists had taken the initiative in the fields of journalism, modelled on Straits publications, in the early years of the century. In 1918, Amrullah, together with Shaykh Muḥammad Jamīl Djambek (1860–1947) and others, founded the *Thawalib*, a reformist association catering for *madrasa* students, which before long spread to other parts of the island. In the mid-1920s, *Muhammadiyah* entered the region, whence Minangkabau emissaries—among them Amrullah's subsequently famous son, the prolific writer and publicist Ḥājjī 'Abd al-Malik (Haji Abdul Malik), better known under his pen-name Hamka—carried it to other parts of the island, and even to Borneo and Celebes. Though their organizational models derived from Java, both associations found themselves inextricably drawn into radical political channels to a far greater extent than their counterparts there. This was due to the fact that in an area already in the grips of accelerated economic and social change, reformist-educated youths became the prime leaders of political, gradually more pronouncedly nationalist-tinged, protest. In early 1927, the west coast of Sumatra experienced a widespread rural rebellion in which—as in Java a few months earlier—young Communists, allied with both traditional *'ulamā'* and some *Thawalib* graduates, played a leading role. Suppressed by the colonial government, radicalism nonetheless continued to smoulder until the end of Dutch rule in Indonesia. In the mid-1930s, the place of the proscribed *Thawalib* was taken by another local organization, *Permi* (*Persatuan Muslimin Indonesia*, 'Union of Indonesian Muslims'), but it, too, was disbanded, leaving only *Muhammadiyah* in the field. Yet in spite of increased governmental vigilance exercised through *adat* chiefs, and in spite also of the insistence of the movement's executive in Java that its unruly Minangkabau branches desist from political involvements, the stubborn restiveness of West Sumatran reformism proved difficult to contain. This was clearly demonstrated when, shortly before the outbreak of the Pacific war, Amrullah was banished to Java.

Achehnese society had not undergone a similar degree of social innovation in the twentieth century, and its response to outside influences thus differed from the Minangkabau pattern. *Muhammadiyah* branches had, it is true, been established in parts of Acheh, too, but their founders—as well as most of their members—were outsiders, so that the organization did not establish proper roots among the local population at large. To become effective, Islamic activism had to find a suitable indigenous organizational mould. It was only in 1939 that such a mould was found in the establishment of the *Persatuan Ulama-Ulama Seluruh Atjeh* ('All-Acheh Union of *'Ulama'*') or *PUSA*, under the energetic and brilliant leadership of Teungku Muḥammad Dā'ūd Beureu'eh. *PUSA* raised the banner of modernism, combining it with the peculiar, Muslim-tinged patriotism of Acheh in its successful efforts to undercut the equally modernist, but 'alien' *Muhammadiyah*. In spite of its reformist tendencies, the new organization in fact attracted some *Kaum Tua* elements to its fold; Achehnese Islam was so all-pervasive and so much identified with regional patriotism that the rift between *Kaum Tua* and *Kaum Muda*, quite unlike in Java and on Sumatra's west coast, never assumed important proportions in Acheh. Indeed, even the opposition between *'ulama'* and *ulèebalang* was primarily a social and political, not a religious phenomenon. Through its leader's skill, *PUSA* avoided a head-on collision with the *ulèebalang* and their Dutch patrons as long as Western colonial rule lasted, but it was preparing itself for an ultimate confrontation with its *kāfir* overlords, a confrontation that would erase from Achehnese memories the lost Acheh War.

II

Cataclysm and catalyst, the Japanese occupation of South-East Asia during the Second World War was for all its brevity of vast significance to the peoples of the area. Harsh military rule, accompanied by brutal requisitioning of food supplies and human labour, the virtual destruction of the area's modern economy, and progressive inflation, wrought abrupt and often painful social changes. At the same time, adroit Japanese propaganda and the creation of mass-movements, especially among the youth, did much to detach these South-East Asian societies from traditional moorings still precariously preserved by Western rule. Within this general upheaval, a crude yet often effective Japanese Islamic policy propelled the Islamic renaissance far beyond its confines in colonial times. The Japanese interregnum thus accelerated both its local consummation in some areas, and the confrontation with its opponents in others.

In the Malaysian world, Japanese administrative changes temporarily at least destroyed the arbitrary boundaries drawn by Europeans in the nineteenth century. Thus Malaya's four northern principalities were ceded to Thailand while Malaya's British-created threefold division gave way to administrative unity. Sumatra was for well over a year united with Malaya, but subsequently placed under a separate army command. The area was, finally, administratively divided between the army and navy, the army controlling Java, Sumatra, and Malaya, the navy, Borneo, Celebes and the smaller islands in the east. The jealously guarded existence of separate military administrations for each major island truncated Malaysian developments until almost the end of the war, when the Japanese hurriedly sought to replace separateness by unification, not only among the islands, but—unsuccessfully—even between Indonesia as a whole and Malaya.

The Japanese envisaged the permanent incorporation of both Indonesia and Malaya, as vital raw-material suppliers in the Co-Prosperity Sphere. They foresaw outright colonial status for large parts of the area, while others, most notably Java, were to attain an increasing measure of political co-determination, if not ultimate autonomy. Though the invader loudly proclaimed himself the liberator of South-East Asia from the yoke of alien overlordship, adherence to these basic policies placed serious obstacles in the way of indigenous political activities. Western-style political institutions disappeared, and nationalist organizational life as such was forced to a standstill. The Japanese, it is true, allowed and even encouraged individual nationalist spokesmen to play sometimes prominent public roles, but almost to the end their activities remained closely controlled. In pursuit of their short-term goals, Japanese administrators wittingly and unwittingly laid the groundwork for far-reaching social revolutions whose roots were in part at least embedded in the recent colonial past. Inevitably, the fate of the Muslim communities became crucially involved in this partial re-ordering of the Malaysian societies. To a large extent this was due to the lack of emphasis on politics inherent in early Japanese policies, coupled as it was with a pronounced interest in, and concern for, religion as a major social and ideological force in rural Malaysia. Japanese preoccupation with Islam thus spelt the end of the non-interference practiced by both their British and Dutch colonial predecessors, but without necessarily reversing, in fact here and there accelerating, the trends of the past decades.

In spite of the rather radical redrawing of the administrative map of Malaya by Japan, the effects of military occupation upon the Malay people and their institutions, and hence upon Malayan Islam, remained relatively slight. Thanks to the early abandonment by the military government of original plans which called for the abolition of the Malay sultanates, no violent changes occurred in the country's social and political structure. Thus the intrinsically evolutionary character of Malayan developments was affected but little by the change of sovereign. This was especially true of the position of Islam, entrenched, as we have seen, in a solid and viable alliance of religious *Kaum Tua* and secular rulers. The Japanese in fact indirectly strengthened the intimate tie between religious and secular traditionalism through the abolition of the State Councils which, in British days, had endowed the rulers with at least nominal, symbolic prestige in the Federated States. The sultans' considerably more substantial powers in the Unfederated States suffered an even more serious eclipse. The waning of political authority heightened the importance of the rulers' religious position, in effect the sole remaining attribute of their sovereign status. With the reconstitution and reorganization of the Religious Councils towards the end of 1944, the Japanese gave further proof of the significance they attached to matters Islamic. Japanese support, however grudging, for the pre-war social *status quo* on one hand, and the absence of a viable, modern Muslim organizational base, on the other, combined to leave the Malayan Islamic renaissance in its pre-war retarded state. When the Japanese, in the face of imminent defeat, embarked on political experiment, they chose members of the small, Indonesia-oriented and radical Malay intelligentsia, rather than Muslim leaders, to become the standard bearers of a still-born independent Malaya within a Greater Indonesia of Japanese make.

Of far greater and more far-reaching importance was the Japanese interregnum in Java, where Muslim organizational strength, as we noted, had been considerably augmented in the course of the twentieth century. Apparently quite cognizant of this strength, the Japanese from the very outset took vigorous measures to bring Islam on the island under their direct control, using as part of their tactics the services of several Japanese Muslims (or in any case, of Japanese with experience and some training in the Middle East). A Religious Affairs Bureau was among the first administrative offices opened after the invasion (March 1942), and it was through it that the military government's Islamic policies were to be channelled until the end of the war. An interesting counterpoint to Dutch Islamic policy, that of Japan nonetheless operated within a strikingly similar frame of reference. While in contrast to the Dutch the Japanese actively sought to intervene in religious affairs, and to lend a large measure of governmental—especially organizational and financial—support to the Muslims in Java, this conditional support—partly welcome, partly embarrassing as it proved to be to the Islamic leaders—was apparently based on the tacit assumption that it would undergird a religious, rather than a potentially or incipiently political, force on the island. Yet Japanese policies not only stimulated the further growth of the Islamic renaissance, they also—indirectly if not inadvertently—strengthened its precarious political stature. Much of this enhancement occurred in the early period, when autonomous political action by non-religious nationalists was in enforced abeyance in accordance with Japanese planning. When in late 1944 the ban was lifted and Indonesian nationalism allowed increasingly free rein, Islamic organizational strength had become a *fait accompli*.

The initial Japanese moves regarding Islam showed clearly that the new rulers wished to draw the line of demarcation between religion and politics even more consistently than had the Dutch. They immediately proscribed Muslim political parties, the *Partai Sarekat Islam Indonesia* (*Sarekat Islam's* name since 1929) and the modernist *Partai Islam Indonesia*, founded in 1938. At the same time, they set out to reassure religious leaders of their benevolence towards, and support for, the Islamic faith as such. Their initial organizational contacts were channelled through the prewar Islamic federation, *M.I.A.I.*, but in late 1943, it was replaced by a new federative body, the *Masjumi* (*Madjlisul Sjuro Muslimin Indonesia*, 'Consultative Council of Indonesian Muslims'). The new federation constituted a Japanese-decreed collaborative union of the two major pre-war Islamic religious associations, *Muhammadiyah* and *Nahdatul Ulama*, which had, unlike political parties, in fact never been banned by the occupying power; two smaller, local, traditionalist groups were subsequently added. Apart from these corporate members, individual *'ulamā'* were urged to join *Masjumi*. While the Japanese kept many Muslim politicians, such as the intellectuals from the *Jong Islamieten Bond*, beyond the pale of the only officially sanctioned Islamic organization, they brought—or forced—the thousands of hitherto unaffiliated *kiyayi* and *'ulamā'* out of their traditional isolation, in part through special training courses in the capital city.

Masjumi was directly linked with the Religious Affairs Bureau, and in early 1944 was entrusted with some of its executive functions, progressively vacated by Japanese personnel; soon the Bureau set about establishing a network of regional branch offices. For the first time in the modern history of Javanese Islam, an official, administrative structure had been created charged with the supervision and direction of Muslim life, and staffed by members of Muslim movements. This administrative innovation greatly diminished the supervisory powers hitherto vested in the *priyayi* and the religious officialdom subordinate to it; it thus constituted a significant redressing of the age-old balance between secular authorities and the proponents of both traditionalist and reformist Islam on the island.

Until mid-1944, *Masjumi* had no true organizational counterpart among nationalist groupings. The Japanese at first permitted, but subsequently disallowed, a small nationalist-led movement, replacing it by a multi-racial mass movement—the so-called *Djawa Hōkōkai* (Java Service Association)—in which all leading functions were in effect performed by Japanese, relegating the Indonesian leadership, including Sukarno and Hatta, to nominal and subordinate status. Even the various advisory bodies created by the military government in 1943 provided little scope for nationalist agitation; strictly controlled and narrowly circumscribed as to their limited competence, the pale Japanese imitations fell far short of the more representative bodies of the Dutch colonial era.

By the autumn of 1944, Japan's situation had deteriorated to the point where an Allied counter offensive in the Malaysian waters appeared likely. The Japanese home government therefore decided on a reversal of its policies *vis-à-vis* the political status of Indonesia and Malaya. After the Tokyo announcement (7 September 1944) that Indonesia would be granted independence 'in the future', the local military authorities started to reorient their policies. Before long, the balance between religious and secular factions started to change. Nationalist leaders, hitherto restricted to public prominence virtually devoid of organizational substance, gradually moved into commanding positions of political strength, in particular gaining control over funds and over the *Hōkōkai*. Even though several key groups created by the Japanese in the preceding three years—notably the Volunteer Defence Corps, various youth groups and guerilla units, as well as the personnel of the mass media—for quite some time remained outside the control of the nationalist leadership, the overall redressing of the balance benefited the secular nationalists at the expense of the Muslims. Nationalists, unlike their Muslim competitors, had actually for some months already been allowed access to top-level advisory positions in the executive departments of the military administration; they had even formed a 'shadow cabinet'. Islamic leaders now bent all efforts towards persuading their Japanese sponsors to retain as much of their hitherto privileged position as possible in the face of increasingly loud demands for the abolition of *Masjumi*'s organizational autonomy. With the sudden demise of Japanese rule and the proclamation of Indonesian independence (August 1945), the controversy between nationalism and Islam—accompanied by other conflicts—moved into the limelight of the new-born Republic's political arena.

In other parts of Indonesia, Islam had also gained significant advances under Japanese aegis, and here and there even more significant ones than in Java. This was due to the virtual absence of modern non-religious political leaders in most of the Outer Islands, as well as to the Archipelago's enforced dismemberment during the war, which obviated contacts with Java. The area most profoundly affected by the interregnum was Acheh, where the *PUSA* had taken the initiative in the organization of a pro-Japanese fifth column on the eve of the invasion; it subsequently continued to support the new régime. Even though the Japanese were far from throwing their entire support to *PUSA*—in fact they consciously played a divide-and-rule tactic in the area—they did much to endow the '*ulamā*' with increasing positions of influence. At the war's end, *PUSA* had thus gained considerable momentum and it was only continued foreign overlordship that barred it from the consummation of its prominence if not dominance. Without adequate organization, the *ulèebalang*, who for decades had been forfeiting popular support on account of their political and economic opportunism *vis-à-vis* both Dutch and Japanese rulers, fell prey to a concentrated *PUSA* attack with wide popular backing (December 1945–February 1946) in which well over half of the *ulèebalang* families were exterminated. Under the banner of a distinctly Islamic local and ethnic patriotism, Acheh thus entered independent Indonesia as a virtually autonomous *imperium in imperio.*

Less far-reaching in its effects on Sumatra's west coast, the interregnum nonetheless considerably strengthened Minangkabau Islam too. *Muhammadiyah* and *Permi* continued to function, albeit under manifold restrictions. In addition, the Japanese took the initiative in creating a consultative body, called *Madjelis Islam Tinggi* (Supreme Islamic Council), which not only comprised Muslim organizations but also, like *Masjumi* in Java, individual '*ulamā*' of both traditionalist and reformist leanings. This prestigious federation in which leading '*ulamā*' occupied prominent positions laid the foundations for Muslim political strength, precariously kept at bay by Dutch rule for many decades. Its existence forced the secular *penghulu* into an increasingly defensive position; but the Minangkabau *adat* chiefs, who not only enjoyed greater popular support than the Achehnese *ulèebalang*, but who had also started to organize themselves since before the war, were not subjected to frontal attack when Japanese rule collapsed.

III

The kaleidoscopic course of South-East Asian history since the Second World War has been both too turbulent and too recent to allow proper historical perspective for the assessment of the place of Islam in the postwar Malaysian-Indonesian world. Yet it is safe to say that decolonization forms a very real watershed between old and new, and nowhere with greater significance than in the political sphere. At long last released from alien direction and restraints, South-East Asian societies have, with greater or lesser vehemence, erupted into dynamic action which has put the stamp of politics on a multitude of social forces. It is equally obvious that the area's Islamic communities were similarly forced into the political arena, not only to a far greater extent than before and during the war, but also in a very different setting.

The slow modernization of Malaya under both British and Japanese rule and the country's peculiar ethnic composition were together responsible for the limited role Islam was to play in post-war Malayan history. The Japanese interregnum had, as we saw, not seriously affected the *status quo* within Malay society; if anything, it had deepened the close alliance between the Malay rulers and the intrinsically tradition-oriented religious leadership in the peninsula. By contrast, the occupation had wrought considerable changes among the numerically and economically very strong Chinese community. It was from among that community that organized armed resistance to the Japanese régime had arisen, ably led by the Malayan Communist party, and supported by the Allies. Japan's sudden surrender coincided with an open bid for power by the young Chinese Communist leadership. Thwarted in their attempt by the reimposition of firm British control, the Communists thereafter continued guerilla warfare in the jungles until their virtual defeat a decade later. The radicalization of part of the Chinese population, and the portent it bore for the deepening of communal cleavages, was one important determinant of the postwar Malayan scene. Another was British plans envisaging a centralized Malayan Union which would have abolished the sovereignty of the Malay sultans and provided far-reaching political concessions to non-Malays.

Reaction to this apparent twofold threat mobilized in a very short time hitherto dormant Malay national sentiment. Yet, though provoked by communal fears and colonial policy, post-war Malay nationalism followed neither a racially exclusivist nor a politically and economically radical course. Its intrinsically conservative orientation was charted by a leadership largely recruited from among the Malay aristocracy especially its Western-educated members. Combining traditional prestige with modern skills, members of this group founded the United Malays' National Organization (UMNO) in March, 1946. Before long, UMNO established close political links with the equally conservative leadership of the Chinese mercantile community, organized in the Malayan Chinese Association, and with the leaders of the smaller Indian minority organized in the Malayan Indian Congress. The Alliance party, formed of these three constituent groups, became the predominant political force in the Federation of Malaya, founded in 1948, and granted independence by Britain in 1957. The Federation originally comprised only peninsular Malaya (including Penang and Malacca, hitherto parts of the Straits Settlements), Singapore becoming a separate colony enjoying a large measure of internal autonomy. Six years later, a new political entity, the Federation of Malaysia, came into being, which in addition to Singapore (until mid-1965) extended to North Borneo (Sabah) and Sarawak.

In spite of an agonizing guerilla war, Malayan constitutional and political evolution towards a parliamentary democracy had proceeded swiftly yet smoothly. Yet given the plural nature of Malaysia, and the constitutional recognition of at least temporary separateness among the diverse ethnic groups coupled with preferential treatment of Malays, the new state's political leaders have had to steer a careful course between national and sectional interests. In the case of the Malay sectional interest, the Islamic factor has, especially since independence, gained in significance, if for no other reason than that Islam—almost by default—became one of the major marks of Malay identity, if not indeed the only one. The modern Malay political *élite*, it is true, is not only predominantly Western-educated and secularly oriented, it has also sought to fashion a multi-racial and multi-religious nation. But it has encountered —and not infrequently yielded to—Muslim pressures.

In Indonesia, the Japanese surrender set in motion a series of complex developments unparalled in neighbouring Malaya. In a matter of days after the Japanese surrender, an Indonesian Republic was proclaimed in Djakarta (Batavia), able to exercise loose control over parts of Java and Sumatra. Several months elapsed before the Netherlands returned in strength to their former colonial domain, after an interlude of British occupation. Though in 1945 no viable Communist movement existed in Indonesia comparable to that of Malaya, resistance to the reimposition of Dutch rule in Republican-held territories was widespread. Protracted Indonesian-Dutch negotiations were twice interrupted by Dutch military action (1947 and 1948–9) against the republic. In some of the areas outside republican control, the Dutch had succeeded in re-establishing their administration in cooperation with the traditional political *élites*. But stubborn Indonesian opposition, including widespread guerilla warfare, combined with outside diplomatic pressure exerted upon the Netherlands, finally led to the transfer of sovereignty to an Indonesian federal state in December, 1949, excluding West New Guinea (Irian Barat); only in 1962 was this hotly disputed area placed under Indonesian administration, through the intermediary of the United Nations.

Chaotic as the road to Indonesia's independence was, its attainment did not inaugurate an era of tranquility. The Japanese interregnum and, worse still, the subsequent years of bitter fighting had, moreover, taken a high toll in terms of human misery, social disorganization and economic deterioration which left their marks on subsequent developments. Unlike Malaya, post-war Indonesia has been in the grips of a truly revolutionary readjustment of which the separation from the former colonial overlord was only one, albeit a centrally significant, facet. The political fortunes of Indonesia were, moreover, in the hands of a revolutionary intelligentsia headed by President Sukarno, and not, as in Malaya, of a well-entrenched aristocracy. Indeed, a string of social revolutions—among them the Achehnese events briefly referred to above—took place within the larger Indonesian Revolution of 1945–9, resulting *inter alia* in the large-scale elimination of traditional ruling houses in many areas, and in a greatly diminished role for the *priyayi* aristocracy in Java, all of them tainted by alleged or real pro-Dutch and more often also pro-Japanese, orientations, before and immediately after the war. Quite apart from these social upheavals, the new state was almost from its birth plagued by serious factional cleavages within the political *élite* which weakened the position and the prestige of successive Cabinets and of the political parties that provided their personnel. The smooth functioning of parliamentary government was thus rendered increasingly difficult, if not wellnigh impossible. These bitter political conflicts, based on serious ideological and often also personal cleavages, were further aggravated by hardening opposition between politicians and the leaders of the republic's armed forces, which, created during the Japanese occupation, had played a key role in the struggle for independence. Shortly after the transfer of sovereignty, this opposition was reinforced by tensions between the central government and regional interests in some of the Outer Islands, a reaction to the attempted centralization that was the concomitant of the liquidation of the artificial federal structure in 1950. For some years, the very survival of the national state was jeopardized by regional revolts, usually spearheaded by local military commanders in close co-operation with dissident political leaders.

PART VII

AFRICA AND THE MUSLIM WEST

CHAPTER I

NORTH AFRICA TO THE SIXTEENTH CENTURY

According to the tradition of the chroniclers, it was in 26/647 that the Muslims first came into contact with North Africa. The Caliph ʿUmar had in fact forbidden his conquering generals to proceed westwards beyond Tripoli, but his successor ʿUthmān authorized the military commander ʿAbd Allāh b. Saʿd to lead an expedition into Ifrīqiya to obtain plunder. This ended in victory for the Muslims over the Byzantine troops of the Patrician Gregory on the plain of Sbeitla.

The new conquerors found a complex country. It is true that they found a Byzantine power that they were beginning to know well, since they had already conquered the Byzantine provinces of Syria and Egypt. But Byzantine authority did not by any means extend throughout the whole of North Africa: it stopped at the meridian of the Chott el-Hodna (Shaṭṭ al-Ḥaḍna) in the west and did not begin again until Ceuta, (Sabta) where a Byzantine governor held on for better or worse until 92/711. The rest of the country was controlled by the Berbers. Some of them had come under Carthaginian, and later under Roman influence: this was the case with the Berbers of the present-day Tunisia and of the region of Constantine. Others had come under Roman influence only—those of the present-day Algeria and of northern Morocco; but many of them had no direct contact with either Carthaginians or Romans: this was the case with the majority of the Berbers of Morocco and those of the high western plains of Algeria.

The former remained part of an age-old civilization which was patriarchal, rural and pastoral, knowing nothing of the big urban centres, and divided into a myriad of small political entities, tribes or villages. The earliest known facts about this civilization are provided by Sallust in his *Bellum Jugurthinum* and include a number of details which were still applicable to Berber society at the beginning of the twentieth century. But it is questionable whether the Berbers who had lived for four or five centuries in direct and permanent contact with the Romans or the Carthaginians led a life which was very different. It would seem that the Roman ruins which are scattered throughout North Africa have led to an exaggerated idea of the extent to which the Romans influenced the

Berbers. It is true that they influenced an urban *élite* which had adopted the language, the ideas and the customs of the conquerors; but this *élite* was never very numerous, for the towns were not in general large[1] and were in any case inhabited largely by Romans. Furthermore, certainly after the Vandal conquest and perhaps well before this,[2] over the greater part of Africa Roman influence had ceased, and the ancient Berber civilization had gradually reasserted itself. In any case, in the rural districts the impact of the civilization of Rome was probably never as great as its economic influence. In short it can be said that first/seventh century North Africa was much more Berber than Byzantine, or even Roman.

Very little information is available on the Muslim conquest from the chroniclers, who are in any case rather late, the earliest of them dating from the second half of the third/ninth century, and are eastern writers little acquainted with North African affairs, and only indirectly interested in them; and from traditions, which diverge on many points, and which, with no means of control, merely create uncertainty. There is still uncertainty over the dates[3] since we are concerned with early events which were not recorded until a century and a half later. It is more surprising that there is so little information on a phenomenon so important from all points of view as the islamization of the Berber population; the chroniclers contribute practically nothing about this, particularly about the actions of the governor Mūsā b. Nuṣayr, who seems to have played a decisive role in the stabilization of the conquest and the dissemination of Muslim doctrine. We shall limit ourselves here to pointing out the main features of this conquest, at least so far as they can be traced from the existing documentation.

The spearhead of the Byzantine army in Africa was destroyed at the battle of Sbeitla, and was never formed again, for Africa was very far from Byzantium and the rulers there had seceded just before the Muslims overran it. Nevertheless the *Rūm*, as the Arabs called the Byzantines, remained in Africa for a further fifty years, entrenched behind the natural barrier of the Tunisian dorsal, and based on the fortified town and port of Carthage, whence they formed alliances with the Berbers, or some of them at least, against the invader from the east.

Moreover the Muslims did not return immediately: after Sbeitla they

[1] Christian Courtois, *Les Vandales et l'Afrique* (Paris, 1955), 107 f. G. Charles Picard, *La Civilisation de l'Afrique Romaine* (Paris, 1959), 171 f., presents a completely different view.

[2] C. Courtois, *ibid.*, 79 f.

[3] E. Lévi-Provençal, 'Un nouveau récit de la conquête de l'Afrique du Nord par les Arabes', *Arabica*, I (1954), 17–43.

had evacuated Ifrīqiya loaded with booty, and did not reappear there until long afterwards. With the exception of one or two raids which affected only the south of the country, they did not think seriously of occupying it until after the Umayyad dynasty was firmly established in the east.

It was then that there appeared the first real Muslim conqueror of North Africa, 'Uqba b. Nāfi' al-Fihrī, and it is a pity that more is not known of him. Was he in fact a propagator of the new faith, or a remorseless swordsman, or an intransigent and brutal governor? The information about him is so legendary that one hesitates to describe him. He was certainly a man of character and boldness. It was he who founded about 43/663–4,[1] on a plain which was almost entirely steppe, the first permanent Muslim settlement in the Maghrib, the military encampment Qayrawān (Kairouan) which later became for several centuries the capital of the Muslim West. It was he too who later made an extraordinary ride on horseback across the Maghrib which is said to have taken him through the territory of the Berber tribes as far as the western High Atlas and to the Atlantic coast.[2] The first Muslim impression on the Maghrib certainly came from him.

But he had to deal with considerable opposition, for several powerful Berber groups, at the instigation or at least with the help of the Byzantines of Carthage, resisted the invader with fierce energy. Of 'Uqba's chief adversary, the Berber Kusayla, even less is known than of the Muslim conqueror himself. The little that is known shows that his pride was wounded by the Arab leader, so that he made up his mind to wage a pitiless struggle against him. In fact he was able to take him by surprise in 63/682–3 to the south-west of the Aurès massif: the Muslims were outnumbered and suffered a crushing defeat near the oasis of Sīdī 'Uqba where today the tomb of the fighter for the faith is a venerated place of pilgrimage.

As a result of this battle the Muslims were driven out of Ifrīqiya for several years. They seem however to have left there the seeds of their faith and, in any case, the Umayyads did not accept this defeat as final. A new Muslim leader, Ḥassān b. al-Nu'mān was sent to reconquer the lost

[1] The traditional date for the founding of Qayrawān is 50/670. But E. Lévi-Provençal has shown (*art. cit.*, 26, 38) that there existed at least one other Arab tradition, an early and more probable one, according to which it was founded several years earlier.

[2] This exploit has been questioned by R. Brunschvig ('Ibn 'Abdalh'akam et la conquête de l'Afrique du Nord par les Arabes', *Annales de l'Institut d'Etudes Orientales de la Faculté des Lettres d'Alger*, Vol. VI (1942–7), 138). The text published by Lévi-Provençal (cf. note 3, p. 212) seems on the contrary to confirm it.

province. He encountered there a new Berber adversary, no less legendary than Kusayla, in the person of an old woman known as *al-Kāhina* ('the Soothsayer'), who for years made his life difficult and prevented him from progressing beyond the present frontiers of Tunisia. However, with the help of reinforcements and by persistent effort, he succeeded in eliminating the last Byzantines by taking Carthage (79/698) and finally got the better of al-Kāhina.

It was at this point that there took place the great mystery of the Muslim conquest of the Maghrib: suddenly the Berber resistance crumbled, and Muslim political domination and the propagation of Islam spread with extraordinary rapidity. This reversal of the situation is linked with the name of Mūsā b. Nuṣayr, and there is a temptation to see him as the true conqueror of North Africa. But even less is known of him than of his predecessors, and it is not clear how he achieved such a result. It is indeed surprising that the Arab chroniclers provide so little information about him, but the reason may be that the contemporary chroniclers judged it imprudent to expatiate on his exploits.

The fact remains that in 91/710, Mūsā judged that he had the Maghrib sufficiently under control to consider launching an attack on its neighbour, Spain, with an army which was composed chiefly of Berber contingents levied from the northern tribes of what today is Morocco. It is an obvious exaggeration to imply, as do most of the chroniclers, that this Maghrib was entirely Muslim. It is known in fact that it contained numerous Jewish communities, probably consisting mainly of Berber converts. A passage of Ibn Khaldūn even suggests that al-Kāhina belonged to the Jewish faith, and it is likely that Jews played a part in the resistance to the Muslim conquerors. There is no indication that the Christians of Africa, as Christians, did the same; this phenomenon is not peculiar to the Maghrib, since neither in the Fertile Crescent nor in Egypt did the Christians resist the Muslims in defence of their faith. But there are many indications that Christian communities continued to exist in North Africa until the seventh/twelfth century. They were certainly still important, although docile, even after Mūsā b. Nuṣayr's policy of islamization. Finally, there were many Berbers who had not been materially affected by the propagators of the new faith and there is no doubt that numerous groups of them remained pagan, particularly in Morocco.

Arabic certainly at once became the official language and was spoken, sometimes well and sometimes not, by all who came into contact with the conquerors; that is by the inhabitants of the main towns and a certain number of local chiefs, perhaps also by the peasants in the areas where the conquerors carved out domains for themselves, but not elsewhere. It can be said that Arabic quickly took the place of Latin, but made very little inroad on the Berber dialects.

Very little is known of the policy adopted by the new conquerors in relation to the local peoples. Such information as there is, however, indicates that they did not behave in the Maghrib with the moderation which they had shown elsewhere, and which they were soon to show in Spain. This was probably because in the Maghrib they were not surrounded by ancient societies which were coherent and organized, but by disparate primitive tribes, peoples in fact which they did not consider as civilized. This led to the attitude of arrogance and despotism which is apparent in some of the details related by the chroniclers, and explains the terrible Berber reaction which was to take place from 122/740 onwards.

The revolt began at Tangier (Ṭanja) under the leadership of a man of the people called Maysara, and from there it spread throughout North Africa like a train of gunpowder. The Umayyads sent reinforcements, but they were submerged by the Berber flood, and sought for help from the Umayyad governor of Spain. Within a few years, Muslim power was swept from almost the whole of North Africa. It was able to hold on—and there not without setbacks—only in the region of Qayrawān, which often gave the impression of a ship surrounded by waves, when powerful tribes attacked its walls.

However, all was not submerged in this tempest: on the contrary, Islam itself emerged from it with renewed vigour. This was because the revolt had been inspired by the Kharijite Muslim doctrine. It is not known how this doctrine penetrated to the Maghrib and spread there, but there is no doubt that its egalitarian character and its opposition to Umayyad rule reflected the aspirations of the Berber peoples. It can be said that in about 132/750 almost the whole of North Africa was Kharijite. This seems to have been a matter of expediency, since the Kharijite tide quickly ebbed, and in the middle of the fourth/tenth century there no longer remained many of its adherents, but it had important consequences, since it resulted in Islam becoming much more firmly rooted in North Africa, and being carried into areas which until then had been very little touched by it. Kharijism not only spread Islam but led to a deeper knowledge of it, producing a vast number of Berber theologians, particularly on the Jabal Nafūsa and in the region of Tāhart, the present-day Tiaret. It is from the Kharijite movement that the islamization of the Berbers really dates.

This islamization was still no more than superficial, if we are to judge it by the various Berber beliefs and practices of that time (of which little is known), such as those of the Barghawāṭa, but in certain places it was sound, for on the strictly doctrinal level Kharijism differed little from orthodoxy. Furthermore, the presence of Kharijism acted as a spur to orthodox theology, and probably contributed indirectly to the formation of the famous school of Qayrawān which shone so brilliantly in the third/ninth century. Thus from the point of view of the development of Islam, the Berber and Kharijite revolt must be considered on balance to have produced positive results. It is also possible that Kharijism, added to the natural self-restraint of the Berbers, has given North African Islam a touch of puritanism and rigour which is still conspicuous.

It is curious that the Kharijite egalitarianism existed side by side during this period with a particular veneration for the Muslims of the east, and especially for the descendants of the Prophet. It was thus that several of the 'Alids (for whom life in the east under the 'Abbasids, as under the Umayyads, was becoming impossible) not only found refuge in the Maghrib but succeeded there in directing political groups of greater or less importance. The best known of them is Idrīs b. 'Abd Allāh, who came and settled in Morocco at the end of the second/eighth century, became chief of the Berber tribe of the Awrāba and founded the town of Fez (Fās), which was to be developed by his son, Idrīs b. Idrīs.

From this time onwards for a century a certain political equilibrium was established in the Maghrib. The Arab family of the Aghlabids had had its authority recognized by the 'Abbasid caliph in 184/800, and ruled in Ifrīqiya. A Kharijite state, that of the Rustamids, had been founded in the neighbourhood of Tāhart by a Persian emigrant, and maintained itself there, though not without doctrinal and dynastic crises. Finally the Sharīfī state of Idrīs formed in Morocco a centre of orthodox Islam and of arabization among Berber tribes who remained very particularist. Around these three relatively important political centres there revolved a number of principalities and tribes who sought to avoid all political domination, and continued to lead the centuries-old life of the Berbers, scarcely tinged now with Islamic beliefs and practices. The least obscure and certainly one of the most important of these Berber groups was that of the Barghawāṭa. Friction existed among all these groups, but at no time during the century did it degenerate into outright wars.

The centre of this still precarious civilization was Qayrawān. The Aghlabids very soon made it into a city worthy of this name; it was there that Maghribī architecture was born, with a strong oriental influence in the general arrangement as well as in the decoration of the buildings. The great mosque dates from this period, as do the ramparts, Raqqāda, the residential town of the sovereigns not far from Qayrawān, and some large reservoirs, which served to irrigate the gardens and to supply water for the town, as well as being used for court entertainments.

But Qayrawān was not only the model for Muslim city life in North Africa; it was also an important cultural centre. The Aghlabid rulers, so much to be criticized from certain points of view, had the great merit of fostering the intellectual life of their capital: theology, jurisprudence, and Maghribī poetry began and first flourished there. It can even be said that towards the end of the third/ninth century, the school of Qayrawān could bear comparison with the other centres of Muslim culture of that time. It was there that jurists such as Saḥnūn worked out the Maghribī system of jurisprudence, the influence of which is still felt today. It was based on the Mālikī *madhhab*, the most formalist of the orthodox *madhhabs*, and offered a strict interpretation which was in harmony with the Berber inclination towards austerity and punctiliousness.

The Arabic language naturally spread: it was the official language of the three principal states of the Maghrib, and was spoken in towns of any importance, of which there were still few at that time, as also in some rural areas, particularly in the north-east of the country, where great numbers of Arabic-speaking colonists had settled and exerted a linguistic influence on the Berber peasants in the surrounding districts. Thus it was during the third/ninth century that the Arabo-Islamic Maghrib took shape and gave birth to an original type of civilization which still remains alive. This was the period in which the new civilization took root.

From the beginning of the fourth/tenth century, the Maghrib suffered serious upheavals which were to continue almost without ceasing until the middle of the fifth/eleventh century. They began with the installation in Ifrīqiya of the Fatimid dynasty. Already some descendants of the

Prophet, such as Idrīs, had found in Africa the possibility of playing a political role which the ʿAbbasid dynasty forbade them in the east; but they had come there as individuals and without any preconceived plan. The Fatimids on the other hand had long been preparing for their arrival in the Maghrib. They sent there at the end of the third/ninth century a specially trained propagandist, Abū ʿAbd Allāh al-Shīʿī, who found support among the Berber confederation of the Kutāma in the mountainous coastal region which extends from Bougie (Bijāya) to Djidjelli. After a slow and thorough preparation, he launched the Kutāma on an assault on the Aghlabid kingdom. The enthusiasm and religious zeal of the Berbers triumphed over the black mercenaries of the Aghlabids, and Qayrawān fell into the hands of the insurgents on 2 Rajab 296/27 March 909. Meanwhile the Fatimid claimant, ʿUbayd Allāh al-Mahdī, had reached North Africa by devious routes, and had gone, it is not known why, as far as Sijilmāsa, where he was held prisoner by the local prince. His precursor arrived to release him on 6 Dhu'l-Ḥijja 296/26 August 909, destroying as he passed the Kharijite kingdom of Tāhart. ʿUbayd Allāh made his triumphal entry into Qayrawān on 29 Rabīʿ II 297/15 January 910, and there proclaimed himself caliph.

The new dynasty was not interested in the Maghrib in itself: its ambition was to obtain recognition of its right to rule the whole of the Muslim world. It had settled in North Africa because this was a relatively easy thing to do, but saw it only as a springboard from which to embark on the conquest of the Near East: thus in the winter of 301/913–14, ʿUbayd Allāh launched an attack against Egypt, but it was a failure. After other unsuccessful attempts he realized that he needed time and meticulous preparations in order to achieve his aim: he made his capital in Mahdiyya, a new city built on the eastern coast of Ifrīqiya, then instituted a system of taxation which seems to have proved successful in raising the funds necessary for the maintenance of a powerful army.

As in addition to this the Shīʿī rulers behaved with intolerance towards the orthodox Mālikīs, there arose, in the towns as well as in the country districts, a sullen discontent which rapidly became concentrated around a Kharijite Berber, Abū Yazīd, nicknamed 'the man on the donkey'. Within a few weeks this extraordinary old man, at the head of enormous masses, hurled himself into the conquest of Ifrīqiya: by 333/944 all that remained of the Fatimid kingdom was Mahdiyya, which defended itself as best it could. However, the Fatimid rulers, al-Qā'im, the successor of 'Ubayd Allāh, and his son, Ismā'īl al-Manṣūr, managed to hold on, turned the tide, and ended by defeating the rebel in Muḥarram 336/August 947. This was the end of militant Kharijism in North Africa, and of all organized resistance until the time when, his army having conquered Egypt, the Fatimid al-Mu'izz moved to his new capital in Cairo (Ramaḍān 362/June 973).

Before achieving this, the Fatimids had had to face another adversary, the caliph in Spain. For a long time the two antagonists fought each other indirectly by setting one against the other the main tribal groups of the central and western Maghrib, the Ṣanhāja for the Fatimids, the Zanāta for the Umayyads of Spain; and it was only in 344–5/955–6 that their two fleets came into conflict, but without decisive results. The most important consequence of this sterile struggle was that it disturbed a large number of Berber tribes, and provoked migrations, the details of which are unknown. On the other hand it led the Muslims in Spain to interest themselves in the Maghrib, and to introduce a leaven of their brilliant civilization into the northern part of Morocco, which they occupied for about forty years (360–400/971–1010). At the same time the Fatimids strengthened eastern influence in Ifrīqiya as is proved by the sadly few monuments of this period which have survived.

When they moved to Egypt, the Fatimids did not intend to abandon North Africa to its fate; they entrusted the administration of it to the Ṣanhāja Zirids who had served them faithfully. Thus, after an oriental interlude of sixty years, North Africa came once again under the political control of the Berbers. But as regards civilization the oriental cause had triumphed: under the Zirids the Arabic language and Islamic culture progressed still further, at least in the towns and in the regions surrounding the royal residences.

The political situation soon deteriorated: the Spanish Muslims, oppressed by serious civil strife, abandoned Morocco in 400/1010, after which tribal rule once again became the norm. The Zirid state split into two; a strictly Zirid kingdom in the region of Qayrawān, and another ruled by a family, the Hammadids, which was related to the Zirids, but which threw off their authority by force of arms. The Hammadid kingdom established its capital at Qal'at Banī Ḥammād on the southern slope of the Hodna mountains. Thus gradually a return was made to the Berber political formula of relatively narrow groupings, made up of coherent ethnic groups. Such was the situation in the middle of the fifth/eleventh century, when a precarious equilibrium, which nevertheless seemed to be well on the way to establishing itself, was overturned by two nomad invasions.

Although they enjoyed a large measure of autonomy, the Zirid princes remained under the nominal suzerainty of the Fatimids, and retained Shiʿism as a state religion. Probably in 439 or 440/1047 or 1049,[1] the Zirid ruler, al-Muʿizz, repudiated the suzerainty of the Fatimids and placed himself under that of the ʿAbbasids, the worst enemies of the Cairo dynasty. This action was not prompted by strictly political motives, for at that time Fatimid control was as light as it had been at the beginning of the century, but it satisfied Mālikī public opinion as guided by the orthodox *ʿulamāʾ* of Qayrawān: the Maghribīs had never voluntarily subscribed to a doctrine which was prepared to denigrate and even to ridicule the Companions and the Successors of the Prophet with the exception of ʿAlī and his descendants.

The Fatimid state was no longer powerful enough to deal with this by resorting to arms, but it was nonetheless determined to avenge itself on its disloyal vassals. The *wazīr* al-Yāzūrī found a means of vengeance: he encouraged a number of bedouin tribes, whose encampments were close to the Nile valley, and who were making raids on the peasants there, to emigrate towards North Africa. By this means he rid himself of a troublesome people, and was certain that the bedouin would make life difficult for the Zirid rulers. In 442/1050–1 these bedouin, led by the Banū Hilāl, were in Cyrenaica; the next year they penetrated Ifrīqiya proper, and defeated the Zirids decisively on 11 Dhūʾl-Ḥijja 443/14 April 1052, at Jabal Ḥaydarān, a place which has not been identified.

From this time on the Arabs gradually spread like an irresistible tide throughout the country, where they found good pasture for their animals. Its fame spread through the tribes of Egypt and Arabia, to such effect that for three centuries there was a more or less continuous flow of immigration, bringing into North Africa an ever-increasing number of bedouin Arabs. There has been much controversy on this phenomenon, which became known as the Hilālī invasion. The majority of historians, chief among them Ibn Khaldūn, have seen it as a calamity which suddenly struck the Maghrib, devastating it in a flash. Recently, however, some historians have considered that the scope, the political, and still

[1] For a detailed study of the different dates put forward by the chroniclers, see H. R. Idris, *La Berbérie orientale sous les Zirides (Xe–XIIe siècles)* (Paris, 1962), I, 172–203.

more the economic, consequences of this migration have been greatly exaggerated, and that the Banū Hilāl and other tribes had arrived in a country which was already disintegrating rapidly.[1]

If the existing information is carefully analysed, it becomes apparent that the consequences of the Hilālī invasion became manifest only slowly: in about 462/1070, the geographer al-Bakrī describes a North Africa which, except for the region of Qayrawān, was still prosperous. Only the political system of the Zirids was disturbed, having broken up into several small principalities, but the economy had suffered hardly at all. Gradually however the demands of their pastoral economy caused the bedouin to encroach on the area of cultivated land, to disrupt the flow of trade, and to strangle the towns of the interior, and this was felt more and more the further the bedouin spread towards the west. The description of the Maghrib by the geographer al-Idrīsī (mid-sixth/mid-twelfth century) no longer paints such a cheerful picture as that of al-Bakrī. It now seems impossible to deny that the Hilālī invasion produced in the long run very serious political, economic and social consequences, and notably a fall in the level of civilization which had hitherto been attained by Ifrīqiya.

On the other hand, the Arabic language made great progress outside the towns where it had, so to speak, been confined until this time. It is to the bedouin that this arabization of the Maghrib is to be attributed; the exceptions were some mountainous massifs, where groups of Berbers had entrenched themselves, preserving their language and their customs almost intact. But many Berbers, both nomadic and settled, intermarried with the new arrivals, a phenomenon which does not appear to have occurred in the time of the earlier conquerors. The reason may be that the civilization which the bedouin Arabs brought to the Maghrib was as simple as that of the Berber cultivators or pastoralists. Thus there disappeared the barrier which was inevitably created by excessively unequal levels of civilization; as in addition the Arabs and the Berbers had the common religion of Islam, they found no difficulty in living together and in intermarrying. In this way there was gradually formed the Arabo-Berber population which today inhabits the greater part of North Africa.

[1] See especially the articles of Jean Poncet: 'L'évolution des genres de vie en Tunisie (autour d'une phrase d'Ibn Khaldoun)', *Les Cahiers de Tunisie,* no. 7–8 (1954), 315–23; 'Prospérité et décadence ifrikiyennes,' *ibid.,* no. 33–34–35 (1961), 221–43; 'Pays subdésertiques et exemple tunisien,' in *Annales (Economies-Sociétés-Civilisations),* Jan.–Feb. 1961. 104–6.

Some years later, North Africa suffered a second invasion by nomads which was to produce very different results from the earlier one. At first sight, however, there were many similarities between the two invasions. The second was that of a group of nomadic Berber tribes who for hundreds, if not thousands, of years had inhabited the western Sahara, subsisting entirely on their flocks and, according to al-Bakrī, ignorant even of how to grow cereals. The men had their heads veiled, as the Tuareg nowadays, and for this reason the people of the north gave them the general name of 'the veiled ones' (*al-mulaththamūn*). It was much later that, for reasons which are not well understood, they came to be called 'the people of the monastery-fortress' (*al-Murābiṭūn*), the Almoravids. The causes of their migration are obscure: almost all the chroniclers attribute it to religious zeal. In about 437/1045 one of the chiefs of the 'veiled ones' is said to have performed the Pilgrimage to Mecca, and there realized the state of religious ignorance in which his fellow-Berbers lived. He finally arranged, though not without difficulty, that a man of religion from southern Morocco, ʿAbd Allāh b. Yāsīn, should accompany him on his return to teach the 'veiled ones' what they did not know. After some disappointments, ʿAbd Allāh is said to have ended by inflaming his new adherents with reforming zeal, and to have led them against the masters of the oases of Darʿa and of Sijilmāsa who were leading a dissolute life. Without entirely rejecting these religious motives, it is possible to consider that there were others—perhaps a series of particularly dry years in the desert, certainly also the fact that ʿAbd Allāh, who seems to have been both energetic and skilful, was able to give the 'veiled ones' a sense of unity and a confidence in themselves which they had formerly lacked, and which now needed an outlet.

After conquering the Saharan regions of Morocco, the 'veiled ones' crossed the High Atlas during the summer of 450/1058, under the command of one of their great chiefs, Abū Bakr b. ʿUmar al-Lamtūnī. For many years they conducted wars in southern and central Morocco, fighting especially the Barghawāṭa whom they regarded as heretics. ʿAbd Allāh b. Yāsīn was killed in this fighting at the beginning of 451/1059, and from then on Abū Bakr was in complete power. Gradually this sort of sultanate grew, so that in 461/1069, Abū Bakr considered that the village of Aghmāt, where he had settled at first, was becoming much too small and decided to found a new township on the plain which extends to the north of the High Atlas. This was Marrakesh (Marrākush), the building of which seems to have begun in 462/1070.[1] Soon after this, Abū Bakr was summoned back to the Sahara by grave internal quarrels and left the power in Morocco in the hands of his cousin, Yūsuf b. Tāshufīn (1 Rabīʿ II 463/6 January 1071). The latter took his charge so seriously that he soon came to consider Morocco as his own, so that when Abū Bakr returned from the Sahara in Rabīʿ I 465/November 1072, he saw that he must abandon Morocco to Yūsuf, and himself resume command of the tribes remaining in the Sahara.

After this, Yūsuf b. Tāshufīn could give free reign to his genius for conquest, and took Fez finally in 462/1070, then Tlemcen (Tilimsān), and gradually extended his power to beyond Algiers, refraining from attacking the natural fortress of the mountain of the Kabyles. Soon the Muslims of Spain appealed to him to help them to put an end to the offensive of King Alfonso VI of Castile. He crossed the Straits and inflicted a severe defeat on the Castilians at Zallāqa on 11 Rajab 479/23 October 1086; but he soon grew tired of the incessant quarrels of the petty kings of Muslim Spain and annexed their territories one after another. This marks the turning point of the history of the Almoravids. Until this time these obstinate nomads had behaved purely and simply as conquerors. The vigorous impetus arising from their hardy life had overcome all opponents in Spain as elsewhere. But in Spain they found themselves surrounded by an ancient and refined civilization, and they found this pleasant. Gradually the luxury, the softness and the varied charms of life in Spain seduced them. Yūsuf had continued to belong to the Sahara; but his son ʿAlī, a child born to him late in life by a Christian concubine, was completely different. The result was that these magnificently wild 'veiled ones' were soon transformed into propagators of the Andalusian civilization, unlike the Hilālīs who remained shepherds, both physically and spiritually.

It was at this time that Marrakesh began to grow into a town, that Fez suddenly developed, and that monuments of a Spanish character appeared on the primitive soil of Morocco: the charming Qubbat al-Barūdiyyīn at Marrakesh, and the great mosque of al-Qarawiyyīn at Fez, are almost the only traces which now remain of a gracious and subtle architecture. At the same time, the first Moroccan chroniclers began to write. If it had not been for the still barbaric soldiery which

[1] On the controversial question of the date of the founding of Marrakesh, see E. Lévi-Provençal, 'La fondation de Marrakech (462–1070)', in *Mélanges d'art et d'archéologie de l'Occident musulman*, II (Algiers, 1957), 117–20 and G. Deverdun, *Marrakech des origines à 1912*, I, (Rabat, 1959), 59–64.

occupied Spain, the Almoravids could have been taken for a settled people who had long been civilized.

The Maghrib was thus cut into two: on one side the bedouin Arabs imposed their customs and their pastoral economy on a region where the Arabo-Islamic civilization had for long been implanted; on the other the Berber nomads appeared as harbingers of Andalusian civilization in the extreme western Maghrib. It is difficult to imagine a more complete reversal of the situation.

But in losing their former energy in the delights of Seville or elsewhere, the Almoravids lost their basic *raison d'être*. They soon became incapable of continuing their military exploits, and, on another plane, quickly became sunk in bigotry and narrowness of spirit, going so far as to burn in the public square in Cordova the masterpiece of the eastern theologian and mystic, al-Ghazālī, because they considered it to be heterodox.

They needed all their forces however to fight against the movement of the Almohads, which was growing up in a remote valley of the High Atlas. About 512/1118–19, Muḥammad b. 'Abd Allāh b. Tūmart returned from the east where he had been studying for some years. He was a Berber from Sūs, who, like many others of his period had been travelling 'in search of learning'. He returned to his country as a reformer of morals, convinced that the Maghribīs were not behaving as they ought, and went about acting on this conviction, smashing musical instruments and jars of wine, and giving to whoever wished to hear it teaching which must have been of high quality, for he was a man of eminence. He seems to have thought that the Almoravids would recognize their errors, and would reform as soon as they heard him speak. Realizing that he had been mistaken, he became a political opponent of the Almoravid ruler, 'Alī b. Yūsuf, and in 518/1124, founded in the upper valley of the Nafīs, in the heart of the High Atlas, a community in accordance with his ideas, which soon took the name of 'those who proclaim the unity of God' (*al-Muwaḥḥidūn*), the Almohads. The reason that Ibn Tūmart proclaimed so loudly the unity and the immanence of God was that he considered the Almoravids to be anthropomorphists who divided the godhead up into little pieces. He also stressed the necessity for moral reform, condemning the luxury of Marrakesh, and finally insisted so strongly on the idea of the *mahdī*, who was to come at the end of time to restore order in the world that at the end of 515/1121 he was himself recognized as *mahdī* by his disciples.

For a long time the Almohad community remained confined within a few valleys of the High Atlas, and when, in the spring of 524/1130, the Mahdi decided to attack Marrakesh, his troops suffered a resounding defeat. He died soon afterwards, and his successor, ʿAbd al-Mu'min, a Berber from the region of Tlemcen, was more prudent: in the space of several years he conquered numerous territories, but only in the mountains and in the Saharan regions of Morocco. It was not until 540/1145 that he decided to meet the Almoravid army in open country, gaining a complete victory. He was soon master of the whole of the Almoravid Maghrib, penetrated into Spain, then conquered the central Maghrib in 547/1152–3, and Ifrīqiya in 555/1160.

His son and successor, Abū Yaʿqūb Yūsuf, added still more to this huge empire by annexing the areas of Muslim Spain which had not been subjected from the outset to the Almohad rule. But above all, the Almohad caliphs favoured the development of a vigorous civilization. According to the accounts of the geographers of the period, notably al-Idrīsī, it would seem that in this empire prosperity and order reigned. Marrakesh was considerably enlarged and endowed with monuments which still exist, such as the famous al-Kutubiyya mosque. Fez, Tunis, Algiers and many other less important towns also expanded under the Almohads; the little fortress of Rabat (Ribāṭ al-Fatḥ), founded by ʿAbd al-Mu'min, became under his grandson, Abū Yūsuf Yaʿqūb al-Manṣūr, a huge fortified camp surrounded by a continuous wall, with monumental gates and a mosque which, if it had been completed, would have been one of the largest of the whole Muslim world. The little locality of Tinmāl in the upper valley of the Nafīs, which had served as a capital for Ibn Tūmart, was endowed with a fine mosque, surprising in such a remote place.

Nor were intellectual works behind those of architecture; it suffices to recall that two of the great Arabian philosphers, Ibn Ṭufayl and Ibn Rushd (Averroes) were welcomed and encouraged by the court at Marrakesh. In addition, the poets, historians and theologians were numerous and often notable. This can certainly be called the golden age of Maghribī civilization. Islamic civilization brought to it centuries of achievement, and the Arabic language with its remarkable means of expression, Spain added its delicate charm, and Berber austerity gave to the whole an original note of proud reserve and of indisputable grandeur. When the Arab East broke up after the death of Saladin, the Almohad West was ready to pick up and to carry the torch.

But not for long—for the Almohad empire crumbled in its turn, almost as quickly as it had grown up: within forty years all had vanished. As though exhausted by such an effort, the Maghrib once again split into fragments and its brilliance was lost. This decline can be attributed to the enormousness of the enterprise: like the 'Abbasid empire or that of Charlemagne, the Almohad empire was on too large a scale for the resources of its time, although it seems to have been provided with an efficient administration. Furthermore the conquerors had not been able to associate those whom they had conquered in their political affairs, and perhaps not in economic matters either. The Maṣmūda of the High Atlas, who had been the founders of the empire, kept everything in their own hands, leaving to the Berbers and the Spaniards whom they had subjugated only subordinate positions and modest profits. The Almohad discipline was imposed and submitted to, rather than accepted, with the result that the ruling group, on which were focused all the rancour and envy, gradually became worn out in subduing the revolts which broke out on every side. As soon as it showed signs of weakness, the bolder ethnic groups, such as the Marinids, endeavoured to shake off the yoke, and gradually succeeded.

It must also be remembered that the Almohad group in its strict sense suffered from a serious lack of balance between the *élite* and the masses. The ruling classes quickly became powerful and opulent men of culture, for whom Arabic was the most normal means of expression; they adapted themselves with ease to their new life at court, or at least in the cities. But the common people of the Almohads did not enjoy the same amenities: the Maṣmūda who had become soldiers had remained rough mountain Berbers. Being perpetually engaged in campaigns, they had scarcely had time to accustom themselves to city life, and still less to acquire even the elements of education. We may imagine, although the chroniclers do not mention this, that the former warriors hardly ever returned to their mountains, having forgotten the way of life they had led there, but congregated in towns, where they formed a proletariat living in wretched conditions. In any case there was a wide difference between the great families and the common people: the latter were hardly changed from what they had been before the establishment of the Almohad régime, while the great families had obtained access to a civilization and a culture which separated them more and more from fighting men. Any attempt to understand the decline of the Almohads must certainly take account of this social division.

The Maṣmūda were not only at the end of their strength; they had rapidly lost the spirit which had inspired them. ʿAbd al-Mu'min had perhaps thought he was doing well in changing the community movement of Ibn Tūmart into an hereditary monarchy. Certainly he had taken the precaution, followed by his successors, of leaving much of the authority and the profits in the hands of the principal leaders of the movement, in particular of the first companions of the Mahdi and of their descendants. Nevertheless the real power belonged henceforward to the clan of ʿAbd al-Mu'min to the exclusion of the others: the members of a community had become the subjects of a prince.

Still more serious, the Almohad faith, which had been so vigorous in the time of Ibn Tūmart, had rapidly become moribund: the homilies of ʿAbd al-Mu'min, to judge by those which have survived, had lost the vigour of the exhortations of the Mahdi, and become mere conventional sermons; faith had been replaced by ritual. The Almohad belief had ceased to be a driving force, and had become pure conservatism. Certain caliphs moreover went so far as to repudiate the doctrine of the Mahdi; among them was Yaʿqūb al-Manṣūr (580–95/1184–99), whose secret belief was not revealed until later, and al-Ma'mūn (625–9/1128–32), who did not hesitate to make his position publicly known. In short, for dynastic and doctrinal reasons, the unity of the Almohads, which had been the cause of the success of the Maṣmūda, was soon shaken, to the very great detriment of the empire.

To this can be added the defeats inflicted on the Muslims by the Christians of Spain, beginning with the battle of Las Navas de Tolosa (Ṣafar 609/July 1212), and the political instability of the bedouin Arab tribes, who had been transported by ʿAbd al-Mu'min, and then by Yaʿqūb al-Manṣūr, into the very heart of their empire, not far from the capital. But Christians and Arabs would have carried little weight had the Almohad empire been as solid as it had been in the time of Yaʿqūb al-Manṣūr.

Finally, the dynasty itself declined. After the first three rulers, who had shown exceptional qualities, the power descended to ordinary men who were not of a stature to undertake such responsibilities, sometimes even gay and careless youths, such as the fifth ruler, Yūsuf al-Mustanṣir (610–23/1213–26), who hardly left Marrakesh, or even his palace, during the thirteen years of his reign. Soon, moreover, the successor was not chosen from among the many claimants by the head of the family, as in the time of the first rulers, but raised to power, often with the aid of great violence, by various factions, which nearly always included some leaders of the régime, some military figures, and one or more Arab tribes.

With this régime, the local leaders ended by ceasing to obey such an unstable power. Thus, almost simultaneously, the Hafsid chief was in command in Ifrīqiya, and the chief of the Banū ʿAbd al-Wād, who held the power in the region of Tlemcen, ceased to obey the orders of the Almohad caliph; this happened in about 633/1235–6. All was still not lost however when in 646/1248, the Almohad Caliph al-Saʿīd at the head of a powerful army set out to reconquer the empire of his ancestors. He was about to besiege Tlemcen when he was killed in an ambush, the victim of his own boldness. The panic-stricken army then disbanded, and this was the end of the empire which ʿAbd al-Mu'min had founded. Al-Saʿīd's successor, al-Murtaḍā (646–64/1248–66), had to content himself with reigning over a territory bounded by the High Atlas, the river Umm al-Rabīʿa and the Atlantic Ocean, until the time when the Marinids conquered Marrakesh (667/1269) and forced the last Almohads to seek refuge in Tinmāl, the very place where Ibn Tūmart had founded the first community. They were annihilated there in 674/1275.

With the Almohad empire, the Maghrib saw its most brilliant period until the present day; never before had this immense territory been unified, even in the time of the Romans. Never, above all, had an autochthonous people succeeded in building up such a state by their own efforts, and in creating such a brilliant civilization. Although this enormous structure soon crumbled, it left behind it important influences in the life of North Africa.

The first paradox is that the Berber conquest led to an exceptional development of Arabic culture. There is of course no doubt that the bedouin Arabs, who by this time were dispersed throughout the whole of the Maghrib, helped to spread the Arabic language in the country districts, but this is not the point. Never until this time had there been such a flowering in the thought expressed in classical Arabic: theologians, jurists, chroniclers, poets, writers of memoirs, philosophers, all appeared in greater numbers even than when the school of Qayrawān was at its zenith, and many of them enjoyed the patronage of the sovereigns and the great families. During this period there was established a vigorous Maghribī literary tradition.

The second paradox is that the Almohad doctrine, which began as a reaction against the Malikism of the Almoravids, resulted in the victory of Malikism which then held undisputed sway for many centuries—a Malikism which was perhaps more rigorous and austere than in the time of the 'veiled ones', but Malikism nevertheless. Even more paradoxical is the success of popular Sufism. It was in fact towards the end of the Almohad period that there often began to appear in the country districts holy men who, in imitation of the oriental mystics, spread the observance of divine love and of asceticism. It would seem as though the dry intellectualism of the Almohad doctrine had produced this popular fervour as an antidote.

Even after its political decline, the Almohad movement must be considered as an essential factor in the history of North Africa, if only in having shown what the Berbers were capable of when stimulated and supported by Arabic and Islamic civilization.

The Almohad decline led to the division of North Africa into three kingdoms, a system which, within variable territorial frontiers, has remained until the present day. The Hafsids in Ifrīqiya, and the Banū 'Abd al-Wād in the region of Tlemcen had severed their ties with the threatened empire. The Marinids had to carve out their kingdom by force of arms. Like the Hafsids and the Banū 'Abd al-Wād, they were still Berbers—a nomadic tribe of minor importance which alternated according to the seasons between the central valley of the Mulūya and the region of Figuig. When the empire began to weaken, they infiltrated into eastern Morocco, searching for better pasture. There they they inflicted several successive defeats on the troops who had been commissioned to drive them out, and succeeded in remaining, without however seizing any town of importance or, it seems, harbouring any definite political ambitions. Nevertheless, when faced with the vigorous retaliation of the Caliph al-Sa'īd, they yielded, and were meekly returning to their former territory when their leadership was taken by a man of energy who certainly did have political ideas—Abū Yaḥyā Abū Bakr (642–56/1244–58). Impelled by him, they returned to northern Morocco, took Meknès, which at that time was no more than an agglomeration of villages (642/1244), and in particular took advantage of the Almohad disorder to seize Fez and form a state. After twenty-five years of fighting, they succeeded in eliminating the Almohads completely, and in gaining control of the whole of Morocco.

Such were the three kingdoms which took the place of the empire of 'Abd al-Mu'min, but not one of them was resigned to the division which had taken place. Each of them was to endeavour to restore the unity of

North Africa to its own advantage; the Hafsids because they considered themselves as the legitimate heirs of the lost caliphs, the ʿAbd al-Wadids because they found the region of Tlemcen too small for them, the Marinids because, having conquered Morocco by force, they expected to be able to do the same in the rest of North Africa. None of these power-groups succeeded in realizing its ambition with any lasting results, and we shall examine the reasons for this separately for each of them.

The Hafsids, who were the first to attempt it, seemed near to achieving it. The rulers Abū Zakariyyāʾ (625–47/1228–49) and his son al-Mustanṣir (647–75/1249–77), using alternatively diplomacy and arms, forced both the Banū ʿAbd al-Wād and the Marinids to recognize their sovereignty. Furthermore their fame spread far beyond the Maghrib: ambassadors flocked to Tunis from almost all the western Mediterranean states, but also even from countries as distant as Norway and Bornu. And, as the ʿAbbasid caliphate had disappeared in 656/1258 under the Mongol attacks, the Hafsid al-Mustanṣir was recognized as caliph by the *Sharīf* of Mecca, then by the Mamluk sultan of Egypt, until an ʿAbbasid who had escaped from the Mongol massacres was proclaimed caliph in Cairo in 659/1261.

With or without the caliphate, the power of the Hafsids was of short duration. The crusade organized by King Louis IX of France in 668/1270 gave a first savage blow to the prestige of the masters of Tunis; then, after the death of al-Mustanṣir, incessant dynastic rivalries plunged the kingdom into serious disorder, so that in 683/1284 it split into two parts and remained thus for a long time. The upheavals spread still further as the bedouin played an important part in them, always ready to embrace the cause of the side which offered them the most, and then to betray it when offered still more. In addition, the various claimants endeavoured to bring in on their side either the Zayyanids (the name of the reigning family of the Banū ʿAbd al-Wād), or the Marinids, and paid very heavily for these unstable alliances. It came to the point that the Marinids twice made themselves masters of Tunis for several months in 748/1347–8, then in 758/1357.

The Hafsid state did not collapse under so much misfortune however. The *Amīr* Abu'l- ʿAbbās (758–96/1357–94) succeeded in restoring its unity; his successors Abū Fāris (796–837/1394–1434) and Abū ʿAmr ʿUthmān (838–93/1435–88), owing in part to the length of their reigns, but also to their outstanding personal qualities, restored the greatness of their kingdom, to which once again ambassadors flocked to offer advantageous commercial treaties, or simply to bring the homage of distant countries. After this long and brilliant interval there broke out new dynastic quarrels which allowed the Spaniards and the Ottomans in the tenth/sixteenth century to gain a foothold in the country without difficulty.

If only because of its duration, the Hafsid dynasty left its mark deeply on the eastern section of the Maghrib. It maintained and accentuated the tradition of centralization which had already been introduced by the preceding dynasties; but while formerly the capital had alternated between Qayrawān and Mahdiyya, the Hafsids gave to Tunis a priority which it has retained until the present day; there concentrating the scholars in the district of the mosque of al-Zaytūna, the administration around the *Qaṣba*, the administrative and fortified quarter, and a large part of the army, including the sultan's Aragonese guard; while creating in the suburbs pleasant estates, supplied with fresh water by the Roman aqueduct leading from Jabal Zaghwān which was restored for this purpose. Tunis became also an economic capital, since it was separated from the sea only by a lake, which was fairly shallow but navigable by flat-bottomed boats. Thus there were united power, prosperity and learning.

Until the Zayyanids settled there, Tlemcen had occupied only a secondary position. With the advent of Yaghmurasān b. Zayyān (633–82/1236–83), it became a capital city and an important economic centre. Indeed, situated as it was close to the port of Ḥunayn and to the islet of Rashgūn at the mouth of the Tafna, which were frequented by Christian ships, it was able to serve as a terminus for the Sahara caravans. But although in its early days the Zayyanid kingdom benefited from the fact that the Hafsids and the Marinids had still to consolidate their power, it was soon caught between these two stronger powers, and spent its time in desperate battles to survive. It went through fairly long periods of occupation by the Marinids in the eighth/fourteenth century, and by the Hafsids in the ninth/fifteenth century, and had in addition to reckon with the bedouin, who were particularly numerous in the high plains in the region of Oran (Wahrān). It is almost a miracle that the dynasty which began with Yaghmurasān was able to last until the middle of the tenth/sixteenth century, when it was finally overthrown by the Turks.

It was to this dynasty and to the Marinids that Tlemcen owed its very real greatness and its relative prosperity; most of the monuments of which this town can boast date from the Banū 'Abd al-Wād or from the period of Marinid occupation, for the masters of Fez did a great deal to win the favour of the inhabitants of Tlemcen.

The rise of the Marinids was a difficult one. They were masters of the whole of Morocco only in 673/1274–5, after the capture of Ceuta, and immediately made vain efforts to arrest, if not to drive back, the Christian reconquest in Spain; and they were also troubled for more than a quarter of a century by the Zayyanids who were impatient to extend their power. It was only in the eighth/fourteenth century that their dynasty really flourished under two important rulers, Abu'l-Ḥasan 'Alī (731–52/1331–51) and his son Abū 'Inān (749–59/1348–58). Each of them thought he had realized the dream of all the heirs of the Almohads—to restore the unity of the Maghrib, but this dream lasted barely a few months, because the bedouin Arabs were strong enough to oppose it, and the Marinid troops too few to impose it. Nevertheless during the thirty years that these two sovereigns reigned, the prosperity of their kingdom was reflected in the monuments which were built there—less well-constructed than those of the Almohads, more profusely decorated, and with a greater affectation of style, but still charming, and the witnesses of a superior civilization.

After the tragic death of Abū 'Inān, who was strangled by one of his *wazīrs* because he was taking too long to die of an illness, the kingdom became entangled in the intrigues of the great families and of the bedouin Arab tribes, and in the foreign intervention of the Muslim rulers of Granada, of the kings of Castile and of Aragon, of the Zayyanids and Hafsids, and even of the Christian militia employed by the rulers at Fez. In theory the Marinids reigned until 869/1465, but in fact from 823/1420 the power fell into the hands of a family which was related to them, the Banū Waṭṭās (Wattasids), who for more than forty years were content actually to wield the power without having the title of ruler. But they could do no more than hold together with great difficulty a kingdom which was split up into several parts, and exposed to attacks by the Christians. Ceuta was captured by the Portuguese as early as 818/1415, and at the beginning of the tenth/sixteenth century the Atlantic coast of Morocco was occupied by a chain of Portuguese factories from Tangier to Agadir, while the Spaniards settled at Melilla in 902/1497. As with the Zayyanids, this was a slow decline which ended in the installation of the Sa'did dynasty in Fez in 596/1549.

Nevertheless the Marinid period was an important one in the history of Morocco. During these three centuries the country assumed the religious character, and its towns the aspect, which lasted until the establishment of the French protectorate. The Marinids were neither religious reformers nor descendants of the Prophet, and were anxious to compensate for these inferiorities by serving as well as they could the interests of Islam. They built mosques, but even more *madrasas*, where the young men of the town and from the country came to study the religious sciences from the point of view of the Mālikī *madhhab*. The importance and fame of the university of Fez dates from the Marinid period, as does that of the *madrasas* of Salé, Meknes and Marrakesh, among others. By thus developing orthodox scholarship, the Marinids were endeavouring to counteract the spread of the Ṣūfī movements which had taken root in Morocco, particularly in the country districts, towards the end of the Almohad period. As they had only moderate success in this, they resigned themselves to a compromise with the emotionalism of the masses by giving official sanction to the festival of the birth of the Prophet, and, later, by organizing the cult of Mawlāy Idrīs, the founder of Fez. Thus was formed Moroccan Islam, which was a blend of the scrupulous intellectualism of the *'ulamā'* of Fez and the sometimes frenzied emotionalism of the ordinary masses.

From the Marinids date also the towns of Morocco as they existed until the establishment of the French protectorate, the most typical of them being Fez. They had no written institutions, but a lively tradition which preserved a flexible social hierarchy, and an economic organization which was at the same time strict and liberal, in which competition played a major part, and in which the common people were hardly protected at all against its hazards. The town consisted of an agglomeration of buildings surrounded by ramparts and threaded by a maze of streets, divided into districts which at night were separated from each other, the whole clustered round its principal mosques and its central market. The development of towns had already been the policy of the Almoravids and the Almohads, and the Marinids concentrated on it still further, to the point that until the beginning of the twentieth century, no new town was added to those of the tenth/sixteenth century, apart from the Andalusian section of Rabat, and the town of Mogador (al-Ṣuwayra); the one built at the beginning of the seventeenth, the other in the second half of the eighteenth century.

Rather than cover in detail three centuries which were full of petty and complicated events, we shall examine the period as a whole, and trace in it the broad lines of the development of the Maghrib. None of the three powers which had for so long been on the scene had a very strong ethnic basis. The great strength of Ibn Tūmart and of ʿAbd al-Mu'min arose from the fact that they had won over to their cause a large number of Berber tribes of the High Atlas, among which there had formerly existed ethnic links and common customs. The Banū ʿAbd al-Wād and the Marinids on the other hand were tribes of only minor importance numerically, and the Hafsids were simply a family and its dependents. This was not enough to restore the Almohad empire, and they all exhausted themselves in a vain effort to do so.

On the other hand, the full importance of the bedouin phenomenon became apparent; it had already appeared at the end of the Almohad period, but then in the middle of a period of decadence. The three Maghribī kingdoms on the other hand, even at the height of their power had had to rely on the unstable support of the bedouin tribes: these tribes were spread out over a large part of the territory, and did not form compact groups in the same way as the groups of mountain Berbers, such as the Rīfīs, the Kabyles or the Maṣmūda of the High Atlas. Consequently each of them tended to act independently according to its immediate interests, and this gave a decided feature of uncertainty to the politics of the period.

The bedouin tribes did however help to arabize the areas in which they spread. As the Berber governments had on their side also adopted Arabic, following the example of the Almoravids and the Almohads, the use of this language expanded considerably during the period. This does not mean however that Arabic became the only means of communication among the inhabitants of the Maghrib. There remained a considerable proportion of Berber speakers, particularly in Morocco, where the Arabs had arrived late and lived only in restricted areas. Even in Ifrīqiya, where the Arabs were numerous, and where they had been settled since their first arrival in the Maghrib, there was still a considerable number of Berber speakers. All the same, the three centuries with which we are dealing were certainly the essential period in the arabization of the country.

There was also a certain stabilization of social conditions. Since the time of the invasion of the Hilālīs and of the Almoravids, in the course of barely two centuries, the ruling classes had several times completely changed. But once the Hafsid, Zayyanid or Marinid aristocracies were in power, that is from the middle of the seventh/thirteenth century, Maghribī society was to have three centuries relatively without change, with leaders taken from among the groups in power and the chiefs of the Arab tribes; the middle classes in the towns were themselves firmly established, except in the case of Marrakesh, where, even during the Almoravid and Almohad periods, there does not seem to have developed a local and firmly rooted bourgeoisie as was the case everywhere else. The only modification to be mentioned is the reinforcement of the local bourgeoisies by the arrival of Andalusian town-dwellers fleeing from the Christian reconquest.

In the cultural field also stabilization took place. If we except the genius Ibn Khaldūn (eighth/fourteenth century), it can be said that the intellectual works no longer possessed the fire of the Almohad period. There were many worthy chroniclers, poets, geographers or writers of travel accounts, as well as jurists, theologians and hagiographers; but among all their works there was nothing which had the feeling of novelty and discovery which characterized the preceding period. Similarly, Marinid art, the most successful among the Marinid achievements, was, as we have already said, only a sort of insipid version of Almohad art. Even the attractive *madrasas* of Fez cannot eclipse the monuments erected by ʿAbd al-Mu'min or Yaʿqūb al-Manṣūr. What they gained in charm, they lost in vigour and in majesty. It was, in short, a period when artists and intellectuals lived on the attainments which they had inherited, but showed no sign of any creativity.

Lastly, perhaps the most important phenomenon which characterized this period in the Maghrib was the European, or rather the Christian, invasion. Not until the end of the fifth/eleventh century did there appear in Muslim North Africa some Christian merchants, Italians for the most part. In the following century, the Normans of Sicily made, with Roger II, a first attempt to gain a foothold in Africa in an economic, military and even political form: an abortive attempt, since it encountered the decisive opposition of the Almohads. But no sooner had the latter become masters of Ifrīqiya than they authorized Christian merchants to settle there. At the beginning of the seventh/thirteenth century the last Almohad caliphs recruited Christian mercenaries, especially Spaniards, while Franciscan and Dominican missionaries penetrated into the Maghrib to preach Christianity. From the end of the same century, the Almohad empire having disappeared, this phenomenon grew in scale, for, in addition to the merchants, the mercenaries and the missionaries, several European powers sent military expeditions to seize various points on the coast of the Maghrib. None of these attempts achieved a permanent result until the capture of Ceuta by the Portuguese, but there were many of them and they constituted an almost continuous threat to the country.

The attempts of the missionaries resulted only in individual success, and these very few in number, and on several occasions ended in the violent death of the proselytizers. The part played by the mercenaries had hardly any effect. The commercial enterprises on the other hand achieved so great a success that it can be said that in the ninth/fifteenth century all the maritime commerce of the Maghrib was in the hands of the Europeans, mainly Italians and Catalans, also, to a lesser degree, Portuguese and natives of Provence. In the absence of any statistics we have to be content with vague and general impressions, but it seems reasonable to affirm that the Europeans were taking an increasing part in the commercial affairs of the Maghrib, not only as importers and exporters, but also in the impetus which they gave to the trans-Saharan trade. They traded in fact in a large part of the gold dust, ivory, ostrich feathers, and even the slaves which reached the Maghribī coast via the Sahara. This reappearance in force of the representatives of Christian Europe, which since the Muslim conquest had practically disappeared from the Maghrib, forms one of the essential elements of this period.

At the end of the ninth/fifteenth century therefore, the Maghrib appears as a territory completely islamized, except for the relatively few Jewish communities, and thoroughly arabized, in spite of the presence of compact Berber-speaking groups. But beneath this basic unity there existed great disparities. It was not only that the Maghrib itself, far from forming a political unity, consisted of three different powers which were often at war with each other; but that within each of the three kingdoms the superficial unity was maintained only with difficulty. The authorities in each case, often themselves unstable, had great difficulty in controlling a collection of very individualistic tribes, little inclined to obey the central power unless it showed itself to be strong and vigilant. On the other hand, the Maghrib was no longer merely a distant and autonomous part of the Muslim empire, but, since the return of the Europeans in the fifth/eleventh century, must be reckoned as one of the countries of the western Mediterranean. In short, after breaking away for several centuries from its natural geographical milieu, the western Mediterranean, it was drawn back into it by the spirit of enterprise of the Christian peoples; and was not to leave it again until the present day.

This short account, however incomplete, indicates the development of the peoples of the Maghrib from the time of the Muslim conquest. Once again they submitted to the domination of a civilization which was imported from outside, and which was at its zenith. But instead of remaining on the whole outside the country, as the preceding civilizations had done, the Arabo-Islamic contribution became an integral part of the life of the Maghrib. It is possible to consider that an affinity already existed, especially if one accepts the view that the majority of the Berbers came from the shores of the Red Sea. But the part played by Islam in this phenomenon cannot be denied. This religion gained adherents with much more vigour than Christianity, even when the latter had Saint Augustine as its spokesman. Simple and meticulous at the same time, Islam drew the Berbers to itself, and held them. Finally the Hilālī invasion had a great influence on the fate of the Maghrib; it was responsible for the amalgamation of the Berbers and the immigrants, and from it dates the present-day Arabo-Berber population. At any earlier time the Arab influence could have been swept away as the Roman influence had been; but two centuries after the advent of the first Hilālīs, Arabic civilization, culture and language had taken firm root in the country. Thus those who were really responsible for this phenomenon with its considerable consequences were less ʿUqba b. Nāfiʿ, Mūsā b. Nuṣayr or Idrīs b. ʿAbd Allāh than the poor and proud camel-drivers sent by a Fatimid *wazīr* to punish disloyal vassals.

CHAPTER 2

NORTH AFRICA IN THE SIXTEENTH AND SEVENTEENTH CENTURIES

GENERAL CHARACTERISTICS OF THE PERIOD

Before the end of the ninth/fifteenth century, the three great dynasties then in power in North Africa—the Marinids in Morocco, the ʿAbd al-Wadids in the central Maghrib and the Hafsids in Ifrīqiya—were either being displaced by a new dynasty or suffered the decline of their authority and the dividing up of their lands; so that at the beginning of the tenth/sixteenth century the Maghrib was in complete political decay. This situation allowed the penetration of Africa by the Portuguese and the Spanish on the one hand, and by Ottoman Turks on the other. The Portuguese and the Spanish were unable to remain in Morocco, where the Saʿdid dynasty succeeded in forming an indigenous government which lasted for a century before being supplanted by the ʿAlawid dynasty. On the other hand, in the central and eastern Maghrib the Turkish corsairs, after conquering the rival Spanish forces, introduced governments of military occupation. These transformed themselves into local powers which were recognized by the Ottoman sultan, but their existence was troubled by many palace revolutions.

One of the principal activities of these states was privateering, from the ports of Salé, Algiers, Tunis and Tripoli, which provided resources for the rulers, but resulted in difficulties with the European maritime powers. Nevertheless, foreign merchants settled in Algiers, in Tunis, and in some other places; political relations were established between the North African states and England, France and Holland. The Mediterranean, in spite of the discovery of new sea routes and new countries, continued to play an important part in world politics, especially as the Ottoman empire, which until then had held only the eastern shores, was henceforward established along the greater part of its African coast, from the Nile Delta to Mulūya. Even although the Ottoman domination of Algeria, Tunisia and Tripolitania was only nominal, it is nevertheless true that this domination created a new political situation against which the Western powers struggled for three centuries.

MOROCCO

The Wattasids, the Portuguese invasion and the appearance of the Sa'dids

The seizure of power by the Wattasid *wazīr* Muḥammad al-Shaykh from the last Marinid ruler and the Idrīsī *Sharīfs*, took place at a difficult juncture. Within Morocco he was able to impose his authority only on the region of Fez, for the Berbers of the Atlas and the religious fraternities of the south refused to recognize his authority. Furthermore, the Portuguese who, taking advantage of the upheavals, had seized Arzila in 876/1471 and had forced the Castilians to recognize their rights on the African coast (treaty of 1479), proceeded to Morocco and settled firmly at Ceuta, al-Qaṣr al-Ṣaghīr, Tangier and Arzila. Spain, however, was uneasy that Portugal should be the only country to obtain the advantages of settlement in Morocco, particularly after the Reconquista was completed; for this reason, with the agreement of Portugal, they seized in 902/1497 the Mediterranean port of Melilla which provided them with a base for further operations.

The Portuguese, in the reign of Dom Manuel, continuing methodically their occupation of the Atlantic seaboard, and thus depriving Morocco of all possibility of maritime relations, settled in Agadir (909/1504), Safi (914/1508) and Azemmour (919/1513), all outlets from Marrakesh on to the Atlantic. In 921/1515 a Portuguese expedition, supported by some local contingents, after having subdued the greater part of the Ḥawḍ, got as far as the gates of Marrakesh but was unable to take it. However, although they spread their domination fairly widely throughout the central coastal plains, they limited themselves elsewhere to a restricted area surrounding their strongholds, from which they carried out incursions towards the interior. From these they returned with booty of cereals, flocks, and also men, whom they either sold as slaves or released against the payment of a ransom. Of more importance is the fact that, being in control of all the seaboard, they secured for themselves the monopoly of the maritime trade, reducing Moroccan navigation to nothing, and depriving the Moroccan rulers of hitherto assured revenues, notably those derived from the export of sugar. This Portuguese pressure was not without its consequences for the Wattasid rulers, Muḥammad al-Burtughālī (910–31/1505–24) and Abu'l-'Abbās Aḥmad (931–55/1524–49); being occupied in keeping in check so far as they could the Portuguese incursions, they could not face effectively the attempts at expansion being made by the *Sharīfs* of the south.

As early as the ninth/fifteenth century, a religious and, to a certain extent, a national movement had arisen in different regions of Morocco, and had manifested itself in the spreading of more or less mystical doctrines and in the increase in the numbers of marabouts.[1] This movement, in which the Ṣūfīs and the shaykhs played an important part, drew part of its strength from the hatred of Christianity and of the Europeans, and was particularly powerful in the south. Being, however, unable to achieve any successful action against the Portuguese, it directed its efforts against the Wattasids, who were accused of having done nothing to hinder the progress of the Europeans.

At the beginning of the tenth/sixteenth century, southern Morocco, and in particular Sūs, found itself under the authority of the tribe of the Banū Saʿd who claimed descent from the Prophet through a grandson of Fāṭima and ʿAlī. Supported by the nomads of the south, and with the help of gold sent from the western *Bilād al-Sūdān*, which enabled him to obtain weapons, the chief of the Banū Saʿd—or Saʿdīs—fought against the Portuguese of the Agadir region, and proclaimed himself in 915/1509 independent ruler of Sūs, supported by the marabout of that country, Sīdī ʿAbd Allāh b. al-Mubārak. Bearing the impressive title of *Sharīfs*, the Saʿdīs rallied to their cause a fair number of the southern tribes, made Taroudant into a formidable stronghold, then, having secured their rear, occupied Tafilelt and all the southern fringe of the High Atlas. On the second stage of their progress the Saʿdīs encountered the sultan of the south, their former ally, who was assassinated in 932/1525. They then set up their capital at Marrakesh, and commenced a decisive struggle against both the Wattasids and the Portuguese simultaneously.

The Wattasid ruler, Abu'l-ʿAbbās Aḥmad, attempted to conclude an agreement with the Saʿdīs, and conceded to them the complete possession of southern Morocco; but they ignored his proposals. In order to protect his own domain he gave battle to them, was conquered, and had to yield to them the greater part of central Morocco (942/1536). The prestige of the Saʿdīs was increased still further by their campaigns against the Portuguese settlements: after the Cape of Aguer (Agadir) which fell into their hands in 947/1541, Safi and Azemmour succumbed in 948/1542, al-Qaṣr al-Ṣaghīr and Arzila in 955/1549. The Portuguese domination of the Atlantic coast came to an end, and from that time Moroccan privateering was resumed from the ports of Salé and Larache, while the

[1] Marabout (Arabic, *murābiṭ*) signifies a popular religious leader, regarded as a saint. Many marabouts were connected with the Ṣūfī orders.

export of the sugar of Sūs and the gold of the *Bilād al-Sūdān* to France and England enabled Moroccan navigation to make a beginning again, with renewed vigour.

Strengthened as he was by these successes, nothing hindered the Sa'dī *Sharīf*, Muḥammad al-Mahdī, from turning his attention to the Wattasid Bā Ḥassūn, the brother of Muḥammad al-Burtughālī, and driving him out of Fez (955/1549). Unable to obtain help from the Spaniards, Bā Ḥassūn turned to the Turks of Tlemcen and of Algiers. Ṣāliḥ Re'īs, at the head of a strong armed contingent, succeeded in retaking Fez in the name of Bā Ḥassūn (960/1553), and sent his fleet to occupy the Peñon de Velez. But Bā Ḥassūn was killed soon afterwards during a battle against the Sa'dīs (14 Shawwāl 960/23 September 1553), which put to an end to the Wattasid dynasty, and completed the success of Muḥammad al-Mahdī and the installation of the new Sa'did dynasty as rulers of the whole of Morocco. Muḥammad al-Mahdī, wishing to avenge himself on the Turks, attempted to seize Tlemcen, but an army sent from Algiers succeeded in pushing him back towards Morocco. Nevertheless the conflict between Sa'dīs and Turks was not finished.

Thus after nearly a century the Wattasid dynasty disappeared, having achieved distinction only with its first ruler. Occupied with the struggle against the *Sharīfs*, the marabouts, the religious fraternities and the Christians, it undertook nothing constructive and was able to remain on the throne of Fez only thanks to the dissipation of the various forces then existing in Morocco. During this same period, the Portuguese, hesitating between Africa and America, were unable to gain a solid foothold in Morocco for lack of military resources, but also through lack of understanding of the surrounding Muslim milieu. In short, this was a period if not of anarchy, at least of characterless government from which there stands out, from 1525 onwards, only the tenacious effort of the Sa'dīs to seize power and to drive out the Portuguese.

The Sa'dids (960–1065/1553–1654)

With the Sa'did dynasty there began what has been called the Sharifian empire, so-called because the Sa'dīs, like their successors the 'Alawīs, claimed descent from the Prophet and thus had the right to the title of *sharīf*. With one exception, the Arabic sources on the Sa'dī period are of only mediocre value, consisting of biased works glorifying the sultans in excessive panegyrics; the facts themselves are presented uncritically and are often distorted; the hagiographies written during this period are of very little historical interest. The European sources, on the other hand, begin with the Sa'did dynasty to show a certain degree of consistency, including documents from the Spanish, Portuguese, French and other archives, as well as travellers' accounts, the number of which increases gradually through the eleventh/seventeenth century. With the help of these sources it is possible to follow fairly accurately the events which took place, as well as the Sa'dī system of government, economic life and commercial intercourse—of all which little is known under the preceding dynasties.

Muḥammad al-Mahdī, the real founder of the dynasty, is revealed as a great ruler, possessing a high conception of his title and his duty. Firmly resolved to impose his power on the whole of Morocco, he eliminated all political opposition, but had nevertheless to face a religious opposition led by the religious fraternities and the marabouts. Against these opponents, who did not hesitate to seek the aid of the Turks, he used violent methods of repression, intended to reduce the influence of the marabouts to nothing: a number of them were banished or executed and some *zāwiyas* (i.e. convents of Ṣūfīs) were destroyed. This action of Muḥammad al-Mahdī was not due solely to religious motives; it was prompted also by the fact that the marabouts and the *zāwiyas* had opposed the financial measures which he had promulgated. He wanted in fact to oblige those who lived in the mountains, as well as those who lived in the plains, to pay the *kharāj* or land tax; he was unable to enforce this without disturbances, of which the religious movements tried to take advantage. As these movements were particularly powerful in the region of Fez, the Sa'dī ruler set up his capital at Marrakesh, where the population was loyal to him.

In external politics, in order to be better able to oppose the Portuguese, he adopted a conciliatory policy towards the Spaniards, who could have become dangerous neighbours, as they were settled at Melilla, Oran and Mers el-Kebir. This rapprochement with the Spaniards was also connected with Muḥammad al-Mahdī's struggle against the Turks of Tlemcen. He wished in fact to avenge himself on the Turks who had given help to Bā Ḥassūn; taking the offensive, he succeeded in capturing Tlemcen but not its citadel, and finally had to return to Morocco. The Turks avenged themselves in their turn, and had Muḥammad al-Mahdī assassinated in 964/1557.

His son and successor, al-Ghālib (964–82/1557–74), encountered the same adversaries: against the Turks, he formed an alliance with the

Spaniards and the French; against the supporters of the marabouts he too used violence, and ordered the massacre of the members of the fraternity of the Yūsufiyya. The rest of his reign proceeded without incident. Finding himself master of a kingdom which was apparently pacified, well under control and well administered, al-Ghālib devoted himself to the planning and adornment of Marrakesh, where he built a mosque and a *madrasa*, and transformed the palace and the *qaṣba*. The reigns of Muḥammad al-Mahdī and of al-Ghālib, by eliminating the elements of opposition and providing a solid foundation for Sa'did rule, made possible the brilliant reign of Aḥmad al-Manṣūr. During the early years of the dynasty the Portuguese had undertaken no measures against it because of the alliance concluded between the Sa'dīs and the Spaniards, and above all because of the policy of John III (1521–57) which was directed entirely towards Brazil, to the extent that the Portuguese at that time evacuated Ceuta, Tangier and Mazagan, and, no longer possessing the necessary bases in Morocco, ceased to be a serious threat to the Sa'dīs. But this policy received little support in Lisbon, where the idea of a war against Islam, and especially against Morocco, had still some fanatical adherents: these prevailed in the reign of King Sebastian (1557–78) who, filled with an exalted mysticism, and anxious to revive the former spirit of the Crusades, abandoned the Brazilian and Indian policy of John III, and resolved to bring Morocco under the banner of Christianity.

He was encouraged in this attitude by the events which followed the death of al-Ghālib. In fact the latter's successor, Muḥammad al-Mutawakkil, had from the time of his accession (982/1574) to face strong opposition from two of his uncles. Internal quarrels reappeared, fostered and reinforced by the religious fraternities who saw in them a possibility of renewing their influence, by the interventions of the Turks of Algiers, and by the intrigues of the European powers, who hoped to weaken the Sa'did dynasty. One of the uncles of the sultan, 'Abd al-Malik, with the co-operation of the Turks and the Spaniards, succeeded in defeating him, and he fled to Portugal. But al-Mutawakkil did not admit himself irrevocably defeated, especially as he had made great plans of reconstruction for Morocco. He found ready co-operation from King Sebastian; for intervention in Morocco favoured the Portuguese king's plans for conquest, though he took part in the campaign against the advice of his army leaders, and even against that of Philip II of Spain—who had just lost in Tunisia his last bases in eastern

North Africa—against the advice also of all those who had been able to judge at first hand of the progress of the Saʿdīs. Moreover Sebastian mustered only a very small army, ill-prepared and ill-equipped, and, even more serious, he wanted to command it himself, although he was almost incapable of directing its advance or its operations. One section of this army was left at Tangier and the rest disembarked at Arzila on 7 Jumādā I 986/12 July 1578. The Portuguese troops then advanced towards Fez and arrived at Wādi'l-Makhāzin where they encountered the troops of ʿAbd al-Malik near al-Qaṣr al-Kabīr. ʿAbd al-Malik had gathered round him not only the southern tribes, who were traditionally faithful to the Saʿdīs, but also the other tribes who had formerly been more or less hostile, but whom he had rallied in the name of the struggle against Christianity and the Portuguese. In the battle which ensued on 30 Jumādā I 986/4 August 1578, the Portuguese troops, outnumbered and badly deployed, suffered a crushing defeat by the Moroccans. Sebastian was killed in the battle, al-Mutawakkil was drowned and the greater part of the Portuguese nobility were taken prisoner: Portugal was never again to be a dangerous enemy to the Moroccans, especially as Spain, taking advantage of the circumstances, hastened to put Portugal under its domination.

The battle of al-Qaṣr al-Kabīr was fatal also for ʿAbd al-Malik, who died there, not from wounds, but probably from a heart attack. His brother Aḥmad was immediately proclaimed sultan without the slightest opposition, and the victory which was won over the Portuguese gained him the name of *al-Manṣūr* ('the Victorious'). In addition, a considerable booty was taken, and the ransoms paid for the deliverance of the Portuguese prisoners swelled considerably the treasury of the new sultan. Spain, France and England were impressed by the Moroccan victory and made efforts to enter into good political and economic relations with Aḥmad al-Manṣūr, who because of the difficulties and the upheavals then taking place in Algeria and Tunisia, was considered the greatest of the North African rulers.

It was in fact during his reign (986–1012/1578–1603) that the Saʿdid dynasty reached its zenith in political as well as in economic affairs. In addition, Aḥmad al-Manṣūr had the distinction of instituting an administrative system which lasted practically until the beginning of the twentieth century. It was he who created the administrative system called the *Makhzen* (*Makhzan*), a central organization which was placed under the authority of the sultan, and which included the *wazīrs*, the officers, the governors, the palace personnel, and the military tribes or *gīsh(jaysh)*, who were exempted from dues and taxes and provided with land. This organization administered the land, which was subject to land-tax and occupied by the tribes grouped in federations forming the *bled el-makhzen* (*bilād al-makhzan*). The unsubdued part of Morocco constituted the *bled el-siba* (*bilād al-sība*), which remained outside the sultan's authority. This centralized rule was directed energetically by Aḥmad al-Manṣūr, who, at the beginning of his reign, had had to face military insurrections and the opposition of the *zāwiyas* and the Berber tribes: all of them were vigorously suppressed. The sultan took advantage of the period of peace which followed to develop agriculture and the sugar industry, and then to increase the taxes, which were sometimes violently levied by his war-bands. This provoked in 1004/1595–6 the revolt of the Barānis Berbers, which was mercilessly crushed. At the end of the reign, however, the chiefs of some of the tribes began to free themselves from the sultan's tutelage, and, taking advantage of the growing discontent against the number of Christian renegades and of Jews in the sultan's entourage, found support among the religious fraternities and all the anti-Christian elements. They created again a mood of anarchy and of latent crisis, which came to a head on the very morrow of the death of Aḥmad al-Mansūr.

Wishing to restore to his capital, Marrakesh, its former splendour, al-Manṣūr had built there palaces and various monuments, and for their construction brought workmen and artists from every land, among them being Europeans. He also built the palace of Badīʿ, later to be destroyed by Mawlāy Ismāʿīl, on which he spent considerable sums of money, and the eastern section of the mausoleum of the Saʿdid sultans. His court was one of the most brilliant of the period: magnificent feasts were held there, and the sultan was followed, surrounded and protected by a numerous entourage and guards of honour in sumptuous uniforms, while around him thronged the foreign ambassadors, the Christian merchants, and the important figures of the administration, not all of Moroccan origin. The personality of Aḥmad al-Manṣūr made a striking impression on contemporary European rulers, but his prestige is explained also by the boldness of his foreign policy.

Having formed an army on the Ottoman model, incorporating a number of Spanish renegades, Andalusians, Turks and negroes, he sent it against the western *Bilād al-Sūdan*. This land, islamized in the time of the Almoravids, had since then maintained peaceful relations with Morocco, which exercised there a great intellectual and religious influence, especially during the period when the dynasty of the Askiyas of Gao was in power (898–999/1493–1591). But Aḥmad al-Manṣūr wanted to appropriate the salt-mines themselves, at least the trade-routes of the Sudanese gold. After the failure of a first expedition, a second, under the command of the Spanish renegade Jawdhar, reached the banks of the Niger, and was enabled by its musketry to rout the army of the Askiya ruler and to seize Gao (Jumādā I 999/March 1591), and then Timbuktu (1 Rajab 999/25 April 1591), where Jawdhar, who had received the title of pasha, made his residence. His successor, Maḥmūd Zarghūn, attempted to form an independent state, which he ruled by violence, massacre and terror. From 1021/1612 onwards, the sultans of Morocco lost interest in the pashalic of Timbuktu, which sank into anarchy, bringing with it the ruin of Sudanese trade, and the impoverishment and political decline of the country. Nevertheless Aḥmad al-Manṣūr had been able to gain from the Sudan enormous profits, in particular such a supply of gold as to enable him to pay his officials in pure gold, to give the Moroccan ducat supremacy on the money market, to maintain a large army and to undertake much building work, especially at Marrakesh. But he was the only Sa'dī who was able to do this, for his successors were unable to impose their authority on the pashas of Timbuktu.

Al-Manṣūr's power and wealth were a source of anxiety not only to his new Turkish neighbours but also to the Ottoman sultan, who saw him as a possible rival in the Mediterranean. For his part, the *beylerbeyi* of Algiers, Kılij 'Alī, would have liked to bring the Moroccan ports under his domination in order to extend the range of Algerian privateering. He prepared to invade Morocco, but al-Manṣūr, by diplomatic intervention at Istanbul and the offer of magnificent presents to the sultan, put a stop to this attempt, which was not repeated. With the departure of Kılıj 'Alī in 996/1587 and the ensuing period of anarchy in Algiers, Aḥmad al-Manṣūr was freed from any threat from the Turks and even in his turn considered invading Algeria, but he soon gave up this idea.

He maintained close relations with the English, who, taking advantage of the decline in the fortunes of the Portuguese, had in 1511 begun a commerce of exchange with Morocco: the barter of cloth for gold, sugar and leather. There was also an attempt to organize merchants in a

Barbary Company (1585), but this lasted only twelve years. In addition the sultan formed a non-aggression pact with Philip II of Spain, who handed over Arzila to him (997/1589). But the Spanish king's projects in Africa alarmed al-Manṣūr, who approached the English. Queen Elizabeth I and the Moroccan sultan planned to conquer Spain, but this came to nothing, because in 1603 both rulers died.

The question of the succession to Aḥmad al-Manṣūr gave rise to terrible strife between his three sons. Finally one of them, Mawlāy Zaydān, gained the throne, but he was never firmly in power, and in fact was unable to gain authority over the region of Fez; even at Marrakesh he was three times obliged to abandon his throne. During the civil war, the Spanish had occupied Larache (1610) and then al-Ma'mūra. The progress made by the Christians had set in motion a national and religious movement of which a marabout of the south, Abū Maḥallī, took advantage to seize Tafilelt, drive out the Sa'dīs, and occupy Marrakesh. Zaydān was able to overcome him only with difficulty. In addition to this, at Salé the marabout al-'Ayāshī organized privateer ing against the Spaniards, and received help from the Moors who had been driven out of Spain, and from the English corsairs. He succeeded in recapturing al-Ma'mūra and extended his authority over the hinterland as far as Tāzā. Zaydān was powerless against him and against Shaykh Abū Ḥassūn, who held Sūs and Tafilelt: all that remained to him were Marrakesh and Safi.

After the death of Zaydān (1036/1627), Morocco was in fact shared between the leaders of the fraternities, among which that of Dilā' was active in the region of Fez. Little by little it increased its territory, and finally succeeded in gaining power in central and northern Morocco, Sultan Muḥammad al-Shaykh al-Aṣghar being powerless to prevent this. But the Dilā'īs did not last long. When Muḥammad al-Aṣghar died (1064/1654), his son was unable to have himself proclaimed sultan, and was assassinated by the tribe of the Shabāna, who appointed its own shaykh as sultan. The Sa'did dynasty thus came to an inglorious end. There followed in Morocco a period of more than ten years of anarchy, from which there finally emerged the Fīlālī or 'Alawī *Sharīf* Mawlāy al-Rashīd who founded the 'Alawī dynasty: having eliminated one after another the various little local rulers, he was able to assert his rule throughout Morocco.

During the final period of the Sa'did dynasty, French influence increased, and a peace treaty was concluded between Morocco and

France in 1040/1631 and confirmed by Salé in 1045/1635. There had been established at Salé the independent republic of Bu Regreg, which became the principal privateering port of Morocco and, consequently an important centre of commerce. But the incursions which the Salé corsairs made into European waters brought them difficulties with the French (1038/1629) and later with the Dutch (1061–64/1651–54). The capture of Salé by the 'Alawīs certainly did not reduce the privateering, but from the end of the seventeenth century the Europeans began vigorous counter-measures and European privateering became a factor which impeded the progress of Morocco.

TURKISH ALGERIA AND TUNISIA

The rivalry between Spain and Turkey (914–82/1508–74).

In the same period as Morocco, there took place in Algeria and in Tunisia the weakening of the reigning dynasties and the intervention of foreign powers. At the end of the ninth/fifteenth century in Ifrīqiya the Hafsid rulers were no longer able to impose their authority either in Ifrīqiya proper or in eastern Algeria: with the exception of Tunis and its immediate suburbs, all their territory lay open to the nomadic Arab tribes who levied tribute on the coastal and inland towns. In Algeria, the 'Abd al-Wadids had lost control over the central Maghrib, and could exercise their authority only over Tlemcen and the western part of the country. Everywhere else there had arisen small autonomous states. The ports had also made themselves independent, and local governments had turned them into bases for corsairs who raided merchant ships and at the same time carried on the war against the infidels. This privateering, moreover, gained a new impetus at the end of the century when the Moors who had been driven out of Spain joined forces with the local corsairs. The central and eastern Maghrib was thus completely fragmented, and although it was not reduced to complete anarchy, it had no powerful rulers to control it. It was so weakened by its divisions as to be unable effectively to oppose the Spaniards, who at that time, under the pretext of a religious crusade, were trying to establish, as the Portuguese had done in Morocco, *presidios* (i.e. garrisons) in the main coastal towns; but the Spanish enterprise was soon to encounter, not so much local resistance as the simultaneous opposition of the Turkish corsairs, and then of the Ottoman government itself, which looked on Spain as its chief enemy in the Mediterranean.

Although the initial pretext for the Spanish crusade was the struggle of Christianity against Islam, particularly after the insurrection which flared up among the Moors of Granada in 906/1501, this soon became subordinate to the political and material considerations aroused by the breaking up of the Maghrib. The insurrection of Granada was used as a motive by the advocates of Spanish intervention in Africa, the most ardent of whom was Cardinal Ximenez de Cisneros. Ferdinand II decided to take action after an attack by the corsairs of Mers el-Kebir on south-eastern Spanish ports, and in October 1505 a fleet of considerable size captured Mers el-Kebir. Next the Spanish corsair, Pedro Navarro, occupied the Peñon de Velez (914/1508), Oran (915/1509), Bougie (Shawwāl 915/January 1510) and Tripoli (Rabīʿ II 916/July 1510), but was defeated off Djerba (917/1511). The success of the Spaniards led to the other Algerian ports paying them tribute, and the Algerians even surrendered to Navarro an islet on which he built the fortress of the Peñon commanding the entry to the port. Thus in a very short time the Spaniards had made themselves masters of the whole of the Algerian coast: it only remained for them to conquer the interior of the country, but it does not seem that such a project was ever launched. In fact Ferdinand was unable to divert a large proportion of his military force from his European, and especially his Italian, commitments, and he contented himself with a limited occupation in Africa. Garrisons were established in the conquered ports, and their defences considerably strengthened. The authority of these garrisons often did not extend beyond the walls which surrounded them, and some of them led a difficult existence with the risk of famine ever present. This was very different from the religious crusade and the Christian reconquest of Africa which had been envisaged.

The situation of the *presidios* became worse with the intervention of the Turks, whom the Algerians called to their aid. Algiers was at this time a town of about 20,000 inhabitants, governed by a bourgeois minority dependent on the support of the powerful Arab tribe of the Thaʿāliba. From the eighth/fourteenth century, one of its main activities was privateering and piracy, so that the threat of the Spanish fortress of the Peñon looking down on the town was not likely to please the corsairs and the merchants of Algiers. To rid themselves of the Spanish, they asked for the co-operation of the Turkish corsair ʿOruj, more often called ʿArūj. He, with his three brothers Ilyās, Khayr al-Dīn and Isḥāq (to all of whom has been attributed the nickname Barbarossa, which should in fact be given only to Khayr al-Dīn), had at first displayed his talents as a corsair in the Greek Archipelago, and then, after various adventures, transferred his attentions to the western and central Mediterranean, fighting especially against the Spaniards, and helping to establish many Moors from Spain in the central and eastern Maghrib. ʻArūj had gained great prestige, and he obtained permission from the Hafsid sultan to use the island of Djerba as a base for his activities. After failing twice to take Bougie, in 918/1512 and 920/1514, he succeeded in capturing Djidjelli in 920/1514. At the request of the inhabitants of Algiers, ʻArūj first occupied Cherchel, then entered Algiers (921/1515); but as he delayed in attacking the Peñon, the dissatisfied inhabitants tried to get rid of him. ʻArūj was warned of this, and exposed the conspirators, executed a number of them, and made himself completely master of Algiers (922/1516). Alarmed at this, the Spaniards attempted an attack on the town but were severely defeated (Shaʻbān 922/September 1516). Continuing his progress, ʻArūj gained control of Miliana, Medea and Tenes. Soon after this, at the invitation of the inhabitants of Tlemcen, he occupied this town also. But the Spaniards reacted to this growing menace: Isḥāq was captured and killed in a battle, and ʻArūj himself besieged for six months in Tlemcen; when he attempted to flee, he was overtaken and slain (924/1518). By this time he had succeeded in extending his authority throughout the north-west of Algeria.

After his death, his work was carried on by his brother Khayr al-Dīn, who at that time was in command of Algiers. Khayr al-Dīn was to become the founder of the *ojak* of Algiers, or, as it was called in the West, the Regency of Algiers. In order to combat the attempts to break up his embryo state, Khayr al-Dīn placed himself under the direct authority of the Ottoman sultan Selīm I who appointed him *beylerbeyi* (commander-in-chief of the *ojak*), conferred on him the title of pasha, and sent him reinforcements of men and supplies. But his situation remained difficult. Attacked by the Spaniards, betrayed by the inhabitants of Algiers, and abandoned by the local troops, he was defeated, withdrew from Algiers, and established himself at Djidjelli (926/1520) where he prepared his revenge. This was rapid and severe: in turn Collo, Bône and Constantine fell into his hands (927–928/1521–22), then Algiers was taken (931/1525) and the Mitidja reoccupied; the Arabs and the Kabyles who had betrayed him or who tried to revolt were mercilessly massacred. Algiers had for long not known such a master. To complete his domination, Khayr al-Dīn seized the Peñon of Algiers (19 Ramaḍān

935/27 May 1529), demolished the fortress, and, having joined to the town the islets which were situated very close to the shore, he created the port of Algiers which, in spite of the bad anchorage, he made the headquarters of Turkish privateering in the western Mediterranean—a base which was unrivalled in the Maghrib as long as the Spaniards held Oran and Bougie.

But between eastern Algeria and Djerba, Ifrīqiya still remained outside Turkish possession. Fearing perhaps that this part of the Maghrib would provide the Spaniards with a base for eventual action against the Ottomans (the antagonism between Süleymān the Magnificent and the Emperor Charles V was then at its height), and taking advantage of the anarchy among the Hafsids, Khayr al-Dīn decided to seize Ifrīqiya. He occupied Bizerta without difficulty, then La Goulette, and finally Tunis after a brief battle (7 Ṣafar 941/18 August 1534). From there he sent a body of troops to occupy Qayrawān, and obtained the support of the ports of the eastern coast. It was the turn of the Spaniards to be alarmed by this extension of Turkish dominion, and particularly by the Ottoman possession of numerous bases along the coast of the Maghrib. So Charles V, who found in Algeria no local elements on which he could rely, lost no time in responding to the request for help from the former Hafsid sultan, Mawlāy Ḥasan, and a Spanish expedition seized La Goulette; and shortly afterwards, Tunis (19 Muḥarram 942/20 July 1535). The Spaniards were particularly interested in the position of Tunis, for it allowed them to control the Sicilian Channel, and seriously hampered communications between Istanbul and Algiers. But the Emperor Charles V, like Ferdinand the Catholic too much occupied with fighting in Europe against the French and the Turks, did not wish to divert troops to conquer Ifrīqiya. He limited himself to establishing a garrison at La Goulette, the fortress of which was restored and strengthened, while Mawlāy Ḥasan was re-established on his former throne, though without much power. Moreover the fate of Ifrīqiya, like that of the central Maghrib, no longer depended on the local people, but on the results of the rivalry between Spain and the Ottomans.

Because of the Spanish attack, Khayr al-Dīn had withdrawn to Bône; but he was recalled to Istanbul by the sultan, who appointed him *kapudan pasha* (admiral-in-chief) of the Ottoman fleet in 943/1536. He left the direction of operations in North Africa to his second-in-command, Ḥasan Agha (943–50/1536–43), whose main task was to repel a powerful Spanish attack on Algiers (Rajab 949/October 1541). This victory gained him the support of the ruler of Tlemcen, in spite of Spanish efforts to prevent this. In western Algeria, however, Turkish authority was not yet firmly established, especially as the Spaniards and the Moroccans were each trying to create there a following for themselves. It took several years for the *beylerbeyi* Ḥasan Pasha the son of Khayr al-Dīn and the successor of Ḥasan Agha (951–9/1544–52), to eliminate his opponents and make Tlemcen into a military and administrative centre, controlled and commanded directly by the Turks, without the intervention or the intermediary of the former local rulers. The next *beylerbeyi*, Ṣāliḥ Re'īs, extended Turkish domination towards the south. An expedition in the Sahara achieved the submission of the chiefs of Touggourt and of Wargla, while a permanent Turkish garrison was established at Biskra. He also intervened in Morocco in support of the Wattasid Bā Ḥassūn, took Fez (960/1553) but was unable to hold it, and in the east, in spite of being defeated in Kabylia, took Bougie (962/1555), which until then the Spaniards had been able to hold. Ṣāliḥ Re'īs died in 963/1556 while attacking Oran. His death gave rise to a serious conflict in Algiers between the militia of the Janissaries and the corsairs, the former wishing to instal their leader Ḥasan Corso as *beylerbeyi* instead of the pasha nominated by Istanbul. The sultan was then obliged to send Ḥasan Pasha again to Algiers to restore order (Sha'bān 964/June 1557). The situation was grave also in the west, where the Sa'dī ruler, Muḥammad al-Mahdī was besieging Tlemcen, and where the Spanish governor of Oran was besieging Mostaganem: but the former was assassinated (964/1557) and the latter defeated and killed (August 1558). The Spaniards had to be satisfied with Oran and with Mers el-Kebir, which Ḥasan Pasha besieged in vain for three months (Ramaḍān-Shawwāl 970/April–June 1563). He was recalled to Constantinople in 974/1567 and replaced by the son of Ṣāliḥ Re'īs, Muḥammad, who endeavoured to restore calm to Algiers where the enmity between corsairs and Janissaries had gone on almost continuously: in particular he allowed the Janissaries to take part in privateering. In March 1568, he was replaced by another *beylerbeyi*, 'Ulūj 'Alī, better known under the name of Kılıj 'Alī,[1] who was to remain there for nearly twenty years and ensure the triumph of Turkish domination in Algeria and in Tunisia (975–95/1568–87).

[1] Kılıj 'Alī eventually became the official name of 'Ulūj 'Alī. The name of *Kılıj* (sword) was more suited to this warlike man than that of *'Ulūj* (rough, rustic, non-Muslim barbarian) which came from his Calabrian origins. It is he who is called by the western sources Euldj Ali or Ochialy.

In Ifrīqiya or Tunisia, Mawlāy Ḥasan, after being reinstated by the Spaniards, had found opposed to him his son, Mawlāy Ḥamīda (also called Aḥmad Sulṭān) and a large section of the population. Although, thanks to the Veneto-Spanish fleet of Admiral Doria, he was able to gain authority over several towns on the eastern coast, he was less fortunate in the interior, where he was defeated outside Qayrawān by the Shābbiyya Arabs, who had formed themselves into an independent state surrounding the town (Rajab 947/November 1540). Having obtained military reinforcements from the Spaniards, he launched a new campaign, this time against his son, but he was defeated, taken prisoner, blinded and deposed in favour of Aḥmad Sultān (950/1543). For twenty-five years, the latter vacillated between the Spaniards and the Turks in order to maintain power. Thus, he formed an alliance with the Turkish corsair, Ṭurghut (called Dragut in the Western sources), who held Djerba and Mahdiyya. But Ṭurghut was forced to yield Mahdiyya to the Spaniards (Ramaḍān 957/September 1550) and escaped defeat at Djerba only by a skilful stratagem (Rabīʿ II 958/April 1551).

Ṭurghut was recalled to the east until 960/1553, when he returned to the central Mediterranean as governor of Tripoli, and recommenced his activity against the Spaniards and against the Tunisians who had at that time allied themselves with them. He first recaptured Djerba, then occupied Gafsa in southern Tunisia, defeated the Shābbiyya and seized Qayrawān (Rabīʿ I 964/January 1558). Philip II then attempted to cut Ṭurghut off from his bases, and sent a Malto-Neapolitan fleet against Djerba, which was quickly occupied, and from which the Spaniards planned to undertake an expedition against Tripoli (Jumāda II 967/March 1560). But soon afterwards the Spanish fleet was defeated by the Ottoman fleet commanded by Ṭurghut and by Piyale Pasha, and, in spite of a stubborn resistance, the Spanish garrison at Djerba was reduced to famine and exterminated (Shawwāl 967/July 1560). From this time on the Spaniards, like the Shābbiyya, ceased to play any role in southern and central Tunisia, particularly as most of the ports on the eastern coast were reoccupied by the Turks.

There remained northern Tunisia, and Tunis in particular. Before attacking the latter, Kılıj ʿAlī Pasha and Ṭurghut made a vain attempt to besiege Malta, during which Ṭurghut was killed (973/1565). Kılıj ʿAlī Pasha then directed the action against Tunis from Algeria, and, in 976/1569, he occupied the Hafsid capital and expelled Aḥmad Sulṭān, who took refuge with the Spaniards. Kılıj ʿAlī had not, however, been able to capture the port of La Goulette (Ḥalq al-Wād), which remained in Spanish hands. The Spaniards seemed, moreover, to emerge victorious from their conflict with the Turks, when, after the victory of Lepanto (19 Jumādā I 979/9 October 1571), Don John of Austria, the brother of Philip II, seized Tunis and installed there a new Hafsid sultan. But these successes were short-lived, for in 981/1574, the Turkish forces, commanded by Kılıj ʿAlī Pasha and Sinān Pasha, took La Goulette and Tunis, definitively putting an end to the Hafsid régime and to the presence of the Spaniards. Henceforward Tunisia became a Turkish province, governed by a *beylerbeyi*. Philip II, overwhelmed by serious troubles in Europe, finally resigned himself to concluding with the Ottoman sultan a truce which in fact was the equivalent of a peace-treaty (989/1581). The Spaniards retained in North Africa only Melilla, Mers el-Kebir and Oran, while Algeria, Tunisia and Tripolitania, having become Turkish provinces, constituted the '*ojaks* of the West', and Morocco maintained its independence.

Turkish Algeria until 1123/1711

In spite of their foreign origin, and in spite of serious internal unrest, especially at the beginning of their occupation, the Turks created a characteristic and organized state, and a geographical and political entity, which became Algeria. Nevertheless, from its inception the *ojak* of Algiers was not without its difficulties, caused by the struggle for power which rapidly developed between the militia of the Janissaries and the corporation of the corsair-captains (*ṭāʾifat al-ruʾasāʾ*).

It was the Janissaries, i.e. the infantry troops of the *ojak*, on whom Khayr al-Dīn Barbarossa and his successors depended to impose their authority on the country. These soldiers were recruited in Anatolia and sent to Algeria as ordinary Janissaries (sing., *yoldash*), but they could hope for promotion to any rank. The *ojak* had its own jurisdiction: Janissaries who had committed a breach of the law or an offence did not have to appear before the ordinary tribunals but before the tribunal of the militia. The *ojak* had a governing organization, the *Dīvān* which, originally formed to protect the interests of the Janissaries themselves, came later to take a greater and greater part in the direction of the affairs of the *ojak*. Following the success of the Algerian privateers, the Janissaries claimed—and obtained—a part of the booty, and even the right of themselves participating in the privateering. They were a corps which was formidable in its violence and its cohesion, but outstanding in battle.

The other dominant element was that of the corsairs who, in contrast to the Janissaries, included only a small number of Turks. The majority of them were renegades, natives of Sicily, Calabria, Corsica, and even of more distant countries, who, having been taken prisoner, had allied themselves with their conquerors, considering, often rightly, that they had nothing to lose by so doing.

So long as the *ojak* of Algiers was governed by *beylerbeyis* of worth and courage, both Janissaries and corsairs submitted to their authority, especially as the essential task at that time was to establish Turkish power firmly in the country, and, by privateering, to provide it with the men, supplies and money which were indispensable for the life of the *ojak*. The *beylerbeyis*, who held the honorific title of pasha, were appointed directly by the Ottoman sultan, of whom they were the official representatives in the *ojak*, both as governors and as military chiefs. The first *beylerbeyis*, from Khayr al-Dīn to Kılıj ʿAlī, had authority even over Tunisia and Tripolitania, but after 1574 each of the three countries had its own *beylerbeyi*, an arrangement which accentuated the political separation between them.

The first *beylerbeyis* of Algiers devoted themselves to establishing their authority over the interior of Algeria by placing garrisons in the principal towns, organizing the distribution and the collection of the taxes among the city-dwellers, the peasants and the tribes, and by greatly increasing privateering activity. Although they encountered only limited opposition from the Algerian population, they quickly realized that the difficulties created by the Janissaries and, to a lesser degree, by the corsairs, constituted a serious threat to the stability and the continuance of their power. This threat showed itself particularly during the absence of Kılıj ʿAlī, when the *ṭāʾifa* of the corsair-captains, at one moment directed by the renegade Ḥasan Veneziano (990–6/1582–8), was practically in control in Algeria until the end of the tenth/sixteenth century. It had, however, to reckon both with the Janissaries and with the presence of a pasha, who was generally appointed for three years and was in theory governor of the province. These pashas, who after Kılıj ʿAlī were in fact deprived of all authority, contented themselves with limiting, when they could, the conflicts between the militia and the corsairs, and concentrated their main efforts on becoming rich during their stay in Algeria. One alone among them, Ḥaydar Pasha, tried to establish strong personal power by relying on the Kouloughlis (*Kul oghlu*, the offspring of Turks and local women) and on the Kabyles (1004/1596). He was unable to maintain himself in power for long, and during the whole of the first half of the eleventh/seventeenth century the power belonged in effect to the *Dīvān* of the Janissaries, whose decisions, ratified without opposition by the pashas, had the force of law. Soon after the middle of the eleventh/seventeenth century, the intention of Ibrāhīm Pasha to deduct a tithe from the gratuities given to the corsair-captains caused a revolt of the militia, and the *Dīvān* suppressed the last remaining prerogatives of the pasha. The effective power in Algeria was then held by the *agha* of the militia, assisted by the *Dīvān* (1069/1659). But this new régime could not command sufficient authority. Riots and assassinations became usual in Algiers; furthermore, the captains who had been excluded from power, took their revenge. In 1082/1671 they put an end to the rule of the *aghas* and of the *Dīvān* and entrusted the command of the *ojak* to one of their number, Ḥājj Muḥammad, who was provided with the title of dey (*dayı*). The first four deys were elected by them; the later ones, from 1100/1689, by the officers of the militia. At the beginning of the twelfth/eighteenth century, the tenth dey, ʿAlī Chavush (Shāwūsh), drove out the pasha sent by the sultan, and forced the Ottoman ruler to acknowledge him as pasha himself, thus amalgamating the titles and the power (1123/1711), and inaugurating a new régime, which nevertheless still owed allegiance to Istanbul.

Although the rulers of Algiers did not much concern themselves with Algeria itself, they concentrated all their efforts on the development of privateering. Because of the weakness of the European navies in the Mediterranean, this was a period of great prosperity for privateering which enriched the inhabitants of Algiers, and enabled them to adorn the town by building many mosques, palaces and private residences. Above all, it brought to Algiers gold, commodities and slaves. The latter were the object of an active trade, as much for their use in many professions, as for the ransom which could be hoped for from some of them; a certain number were also used as galley-slaves. The majority of the slaves were housed in bagnios where their fate was not an enviable one, though it was no worse than that of contemporary galley-slaves in Europe. The prisoners could continue to practise their religion, but some of them had no hesitation in apostatizing, hoping thus to obtain a better situation in Algerian society. Such apostasy was not, however, regarded favourably by their masters, as it deprived them of the hope of obtaining ransom for them. Certain religious orders, such as those of the Trinitarians and of Notre Dame de la Merci were devoted to ransoming these slaves. In the middle of the seventeenth century, St Vincent de Paul—who, whatever he may have said, was probably never a prisoner at Tunis—and the Lazarists founded a charity intended for the moral and physical succour on the spot of the slaves in the bagnios of Barbary.

This privateering, however, resulted in the opening of hostilities with Holland, England and France, but never simultaneously. The English bombarded Algiers in 1031/1622, in 1065/1655, and in 1083/1672; the French in 1071/1661, 1075/1665, 1093/1682, and 1094/1683. An attempt by the French to occupy Djidjelli failed lamentably. The French had tried, in the years 1640–70, to launch a crusade against Barbary, at first with a religious basis, but later with a purely political aim. This was a failure, and in 1100/1689 a treaty was signed between France and Algiers which established cordial relations and allowed the development of commerce between the two countries. As early as 967/1560, Thomas Lenche, a native of Marseilles, had obtained a monopoly of the coral-fishing between Cape Roux and Bougie, and the right to establish a factory at the Bastion de France, to the west of La Calle; but the inhabitants of Algiers seized it in 1568. Recaptured soon afterwards, the Bastion de France was again lost in 1604. A Corsican from Marseilles, Sanson Napollon, succeeded in 1037/1628 in concluding with the Algerians the Agreement of the Bastion which gave him the coral-fishing concession; he made use of the Bastion in particular to carry out an illegal trade in wheat. His death in 1042/1633 was followed by the destruction of the Bastion. A new agreement concluded in 1050/1640 allowed the repair of the Bastion and the establishment of warehouses at Bône and at Collo. After this, the Bastion Company had more difficulties with the merchants of Marseilles than with the Algerians. Finally, at the beginning of the eighteenth century the French companies of eastern Algeria and of Tunisia were combined into the *Compagnie d'Afrique*.

Elsewhere the Spaniards carried on commerce on a reduced scale from Oran. In Algiers, the intermittent hostilities with the Europeans hindered commerce; but some European merchants had established themselves there, and French, English and Dutch, either directly, or through the intermediary of the Jews of Algiers and of Leghorn, carried on there an exchange of commodities, which remained, however, on a rather limited scale.

Turkish Tunisia

When Tunisia became an Ottoman province, the administration was entrusted by Sinān Pasha to a *beylerbeyi*, Ḥaydar Pasha, who had to assist him a militia of Janissaries some 3,000 to 4,000 strong and commanded by an *agha*; as in Algiers, this militia was divided into *ortas* and *odas*. From 982/1574 to 999/1591, nine *beylerbeyis* succeeded one another; like his counterpart in Algiers, the *beylerbeyi* of Tunis had to reckon with the militia of the Janissaries, and hence there was instituted the *Dīvān*, formed by the senior officers of the militia. It is possible that, after the death of Ḥaydar Pasha at the end of his second term as governor, the *beylerbeyi* was nominated by the officers of the *ojak*, and that this nomination was later ratified by the sultan. Tunisia was then a province subjected to a military régime. There were Turkish garrisons in the principal towns of the country, and fresh Janissaries were sent regularly from Anatolia. This régime lasted until 1002/1594, but as early as 999/1591 there had been unrest in Tunis, stirred up by the militia and the local population. Finally it was the subaltern officers of the Janissaries who seized power and formed a new *Dīvān* at the head of which they put one of themselves, elected by them and with the title of dey. This dey became the real ruler of the province; not that the *beylerbeyi-pasha* ceased to exist, but he had now merely a representative role. Nevertheless the continuance of the office of *beylerbeyi* maintained the links between Tunis and Istanbul. To a greater extent than in Algiers, the Tunisian militia included non-Turkish elements, Levantines, *Kul oghlus* and renegades, and some of them even rose to the office of dey.

The first dey, ʿUthmān (1002–19/1594–1610), pacified the interior of Tunisia and created two important offices: that of bey, or commander of the land-troops, charged particularly with the collection of the taxes during tours made for this purpose (*maḥalla*), and that of *kapudan*, commander of the fleet. Yūsuf Dey (1019–46/1610–37), the son-in-law of ʿUthmān, also wielded great authority. He effectively curbed the unrest of the Arab tribes, repelled an Algerian invasion, gave a vigorous impetus to privateering, and erected many buildings. After him Ustā Murād (1046–50/1637–40), a Genoese renegade appointed by the militia, was to yield the direction of the affairs of the province for all practical purposes to the Bey Ḥammūda b. Murād. The latter's father had already succeeded in getting his office of bey made hereditary, and in addition had received the title of pasha. Henceforward it was the Muradid beys who ruled Tunisia, although the offices of dey and of *beylerbeyi-pasha* were not suppressed. Ḥammūda (1040–70/1631–59) was an energetic ruler: he was responsible for the attachment to Tunisia of Djerba, claimed by the Tripolitanians, and for the complete pacification of the country. He was also a great builder, and under his rule Tunisia, enriched by privateering, led a relatively peaceful existence. Ḥammūda maintained fairly close relations with the sultans, and Tunisian ships took part in the war waged by the Ottomans against the Venetians in Crete. His son Murād (1070–86/1659–75) behaved like an actual monarch, dismissing when necessary those deys who displeased him, and installed himself in the palace of the Bardo. One of the most important buildings for which he was responsible is the mosque of Sidi Mahrez at Tunis, in which the influence of Turkish architecture is clearly seen. But after his death the succession was disputed by his son and his brother, resulting in twenty years of civil war in which the Algerians intervened. By means of a military plot, the *agha* of the *sipahis* (cavalry), Ibrāhīm al-Sharīf, seized power after having assassinated all the Muradids (1114/1702). Having become bey, he had himself given the title of dey and was recognized as *beylerbeyi-pasha* by Istanbul, thus gathering all the powers into his own hands and giving to the régime a new character of unity and of monarchy. But Ibrāhīm was defeated and taken prisoner by the Algerians in 1705. His successor, Ḥusayn b. ʿAlī (1117/1705), also an *agha* of the *sipahis*, received from the sultan the title of *beylerbeyi-pasha*, but suppressed from his titles that of dey: from then on the office of dey became a minor one. With Ḥusayn b. ʿAlī there began a new hereditary dynasty, which was to rule in Tunisia for more than two centuries.

Throughout the twelfth/seventeenth century, Tunisia had a less anarchic and troubled political life than Algeria. It had the advantage of being governed by leaders who were capable, energetic, and conscious of their responsibilities and duties. In general the army was kept under control, and although its leaders had seized power, they had not allowed it to take advantage of this to create disorder. It may be that this more authoritarian and more orderly aspect reflected a quite distinct influence of the elements originating from Anatolia, who played a leading part in the army and in the administration; it was certainly a factor which helped to create a growing differentiation between Tunisia and Algeria. In addition, the peace which prevailed in the country, and especially in the northern part, attracted the Moors, driven out of Spain in 1609. Some of them settled along the whole length of the Medjerda valley, which they helped to develop, and others in Tunis itself, where they created new industries or revived the old, such as the manufacture and weaving of silk and woollen materials, the manufacture of tarbushes, faïence, and so forth.

The authority of the deys, then of the beys, was imposed in the province through the garrisons spread throughout the country and by the *qā'ids*; the collection of taxes, levied during the two annual expeditions, does not seem to have given rise to many or serious incidents. Tunisia was a prosperous country, made more so by privateering (though it was of less importance here than in Algeria), and there took place, especially in the towns of Tunis and Qayrawān, tremendous activity in the building of religious monuments (mosques and *madrasas*), palaces and works of a utilitarian character such as bridges over the Medjerda, and the repair of the aqueduct of Carthage.

There was much privateering, and many European renegades took part in it; one of them, the Englishman, Ward, was responsible for the renewal of the Tunisian navy at the beginning of the seventeenth century. The slaves were consigned to bagnios as in Algiers, but their treatment there was perhaps less harsh. They probably had more opportunities of being appointed to some office if they apostatized; in any case the slaves and the renegades held a real position in the life of the country. Opportunities for ransom were not infrequent because of the activities of religious missions, that of the Lazarists in particular after the vigorous propaganda of St Vincent de Paul. Such men as Père Le Vacher, for example, acquired a great reputation among both Christians and Muslims.

In addition to the immediate neighbours—Sicilians, Maltese, Neapolitans and Calabrians—who often called in at Tunis, foreign merchants settled permanently there: English, Dutch, and above all French—chiefly Marseillais—who had a consul (originally, as at Algiers, a cleric, although subsequently officials were appointed by the French government) and a *funduq*, built in 1069/1659. This was the centre of French commercial life in Tunis, where French nationals took refuge if there were any incidents in the capital. The French also formed a company for coral-fishing, and in addition for trade, illegal as well as legal; this company was installed at Cap Nègre, near to the island of Ṭabarqa, which itself belonged to the Genoese. They had received it as the price of the ransom of the Turkish corsair, Ṭurghut, and had later handed it over to the Lomellini family, who made it into an active centre of commerce with Algeria and Tunisia and a centre for the work of coral. Sanson Napollon tried several times to seize Ṭabarqa, which was an extremely advantageous position, and competed successfully with the French factories of the Bastion and of Cap Nègre; on his third attempt he was captured by the Genoese and executed (May 1633). The Cap Nègre factory suffered a number of vicissitudes. It passed into the control of the Marseillais in 1040/1631, was taken by the Tunisians in 1047/1637, and given up again to the Marseillais soon after, but it was not until 1077/1666 that the latter obtained formal authority to trade in cereals and in coral, with no territorial concession. At the end of the eleventh/seventeenth century, the English endeavoured to take the place of the French in Tunis, but without success. At the beginning of the eighteenth century, the new *Compagnie d'Afrique* took the factory of Cap Nègre under its control, as it had done the Bastion de France.

TRIPOLITANIA

At the end of the ninth/fifteenth century, the inhabitants of Tripoli had freed themselves from the tutelage of the Hafsids and had formed a government the direction of which was entrusted to a dignitary of the town. This peaceful régime, essentially preoccupied with maintaining close commercial relations with the Mediterranean states, lasted until the beginning of the tenth/sixteenth century. It was then that the Spaniards, led by Pedro Navarro, seized Tripoli in Rabīʿ II 916/July 1510, thus completing the campaign which they had begun in Algeria and Tunisia, but the following month they suffered a crushing defeat during an attempt to land on the island of Djerba. As in Algeria, the Spaniards did not try to extend their occupation, and limited themselves to fortifying Tripoli. But the town, being far from Sicily and further still from Spain, was difficult to defend, so in 1530 the Emperor Charles V handed over Tripoli, at the same time as the islands of Malta and Gozzo, to the Knights of St John of Jerusalem (the Knights Hospitallers), who shortly before had been driven out of Rhodes by Süleymān the Magnificent.

In Rajab 957/August 1551, the inadequately defended town was captured by Ṭurghut. In 961/1554, Ṭurghut was appointed *beylerbeyi* of Tripolitania and immediately set about submitting the interior of the country to Turkish rule. He occupied the island of Djerba, and made

Tripoli an active centre of privateering against the Spaniards. The latter, having decided to take action against Ṭurghut, seized Djerba (Jumādā II 967/March 1560) and prepared an expedition against Tripoli, but their fleet was defeated by the Ottoman fleet, and Djerba was reconquered by Ṭurghut and Piyale Pasha (Shawwāl 967/July 1560). After his death (973/1565), Ṭurghut was succeeded at Tripoli by a pasha called Yaḥyā, who was unable to maintain discipline among the Janissaries. Their excesses led to a revolt, and the sultan then sent Kılıj ʿAlī to restore order and peace (974–6/1566–8). The next *beylerbeyi*, Jaʿfar, was responsible for the conquest of the Fezzan in 985/1577. After him, Tripolitania was shaken by revolts of the Janissaries and the rebellion of the Arab population led finally by the marabout Niyāl, who succeeded for a brief time in becoming master of Tripoli (997/1589), but reinforcements sent from Istanbul enabled the Turks to get the situation under control again. The *beylerbeyis* of Tripoli made several attempts, particularly in 1006 and 1007/1598 and 1599, to gain control of the island of Djerba. This was contested by the deys of Tunis, who sent help to the inhabitants of the island, enabling them to repel the Tripolitanian attacks.

Until 1018/1609, Tripolitania was governed by *beylerbeyis* who were appointed directly by the Ottoman sultan, and who, as at Algiers and Tunis, were assisted in their task by the *Dīvān* of the Janissaries. Also as in these two towns, it was a revolt of the Janissaries which led to a change in the local régime. In 1609 the soldiers of the militia revolted against their superior officers and against the *beylerbeyi*, Aḥmad Pasha, and proclaimed as leader of the *ojak* one of their junior officers, Sulaymān, who thus inaugurated the régime of the deys, which lasted until 1123/1711. The sultan however continued to send pashas to Tripoli, their role being purely representational. To make more certain of his power, Sulaymān executed a number of senior officers, then re-established Turkish authority, which for a brief time had been shaken, over Jabal Nafūsa and the Fezzan. It was perhaps he also who about this time gave a fresh impetus to Tripolitanian privateering with the help of a Greek renegade. His authoritarian government, however, earned him enmity, echoes of which reached as far as Istanbul; perhaps also he tried too openly to free himself from Ottoman tutelage. In any case he was arrested at Tripoli by envoys of the sultan and put to death (1023/1614).

Little is recorded of the next years: it is known that in 1029/1620 one Muṣṭafā, who claimed to be a *sharīf*, succeeded in obtaining the confidence of the Janissaries, and was proclaimed dey. He was responsible for the pacification of the Arab tribes, and it was during his period of government that the first French consul was appointed in Tripoli, in 1630. Muṣṭafā Sharīf also met a violent death, in 1041/1631. After a year of unrest, it was one of the corsair leaders, Muḥammad Sakızlı, a renegade native of Chios, who seized power and, in return for certain concessions, obtained the support of the militia. Sakızlı formed a corps of cavalry, intended to maintain order among the Arab tribes who inhabited the hinterland of Tripoli; the command of this corps was entrusted to another renegade from Chios, ʿUthmān, who received the title of bey. But it was Sakızlı's wise administration, particularly in the assessment and collection of taxes, which did even more to ensure peace in the country. In addition he gave a new impetus to privateering, and his corsairs, not content with attacking Christian vessels, made incursions on the European coasts, from Spain to Italy, which provoked reactions, especially from the French, whose consul had been expelled in 1632. About the same time, ʿUthmān Bey had to suppress a revolt in the Fezzan, and obtained the submission of the inhabitants of Murzuk. Nevertheless there was a permanent state of insecurity in this region, and the caravans from the Sudan, which until then had travelled to Tripoli via the Fezzan, changed their route towards the towns of Benghazi and Derna in Cyrenaica, which at the end of the eighth/fifteenth and the beginning of the ninth/sixteenth century, were occupied by Andalusian emigrants and Tripolitanian refugees. In 1049/1639 Sakızlı, attacking by land and by sea, occupied without difficulty Benghazi, then Cyrenaica, and his lieutenant ʿUthmān extended Turkish domination to the south, as far as Awjila. From then on a permanent garrison was established at Benghazi.

During the period of Sakızlı's government, some French merchants came and settled at Tripoli; one of them, Bayon, performed there the function of consul and gained permission for two French clerics to succour the prisoners in the bagnio. Sakızlı died, probably poisoned, in Ramaḍān 1059/September 1649. He had surrounded himself by a large number of renegades who held the principal offices of the *ojak*. ʿUthmān Bey succeeded him. He had no difficulty in obtaining recognition from the sultan, who asked him for the co-operation of the Tripolitanian fleet (as he had already asked for that of the Tunisian and Algerian fleets) for the Cretan expedition. In 1068/1658 the English admiral John Stoakes came to Tripoli to sign a peace treaty with 'Uthmān, and from then on an English consul was established in the town. This treaty was renewed in 1072/1662 in the name of Charles II. During the years which followed, the corsairs of Tripoli distinguished themselves on several occasions, especially against Italian ships, and took part in the final assaults against the Venetian positions in Crete.

However, the inhabitants of Tripoli, the Janissaries, and the corsairs did not find it easy to endure the authoritarian rule of 'Uthmān, and in particular the stringency of his financial measures: he had increased the taxes, and increased his own personal share of the booty taken by the corsairs. He was overthrown by a revolution in November 1672. With this event there began a period of anarchy during which corsairs and Janissaries struggled for power, and the Tunisians attempted to intervene.

As the corsairs of Tripoli continued their ravages in the Mediterranean, the English sent a fleet which for several months blockaded the port of Tripoli (1086/1675–6), and destroyed part of the corsair fleet. Finally a treaty was signed in Dhu'l-Ḥijja 1086/March 1676. In 1092/1681, the Tripoli corsairs attacked the French ships, and even went so far as to ill-treat the French consul at Larnaca in Cyprus during one of their expeditions in the eastern Mediterranean; and then took refuge in the roads of Chios. At this the French fleet, under the command of Admiral Duquesne, destroyed the corsairs' ships and bombarded Chios. This incident caused lively repercussions in Istanbul, where the grand *vezīr*, Kara Muṣṭafā Pasha, remonstrated with the French ambassador. Finally peace was concluded between the French and the Tripolitanians, the latter undertaking to attack no more French ships and to free all the French slaves imprisoned in their bagnios, and allowing the appointment of a new consul at Tripoli (Ṣafar 1093/February 1682). But the Tripolitanians did not keep to their agreement, and imprisoned the delegates who came to arrange for the liberation of the slaves, so a French fleet was sent to bombard Tripoli, after which a new treaty was signed (27 Rajab 1096/June 1685). A similar peace treaty had been concluded earlier with the Dutch (Jumādā II 1094/June 1683).

There followed in Tripoli continual changes of government; the Janissaries or the corsairs, according to circumstances, put their own candidate in power, generally for only a short time. These incidents had their repercussions on the economic life of the country, and in the interior there was unrest among the Arab tribes. Tripoli was at this time, according to the description of Pétis de la Croix, a town of nearly 40,000 inhabitants, 3,500 of them Turks and Kouloughs, 35,000 Arabs and 2,000 Christians (including slaves). Although the deys were elected, or imposed, by the militia or the corsairs, the sultan continued to send a pasha as his representative; these pashas took no part in the affairs of the country and the Tripolitanians sometimes even refused to recognize them as such. One of them, Khalīl, did nevertheless intervene directly in governmental affairs in 1687, and helped to reinforce the powers of the Dey Muḥammad al-Imām in imposing discipline on the corsairs and in the clarification of the situation.

The Tripoli corsairs having in 1102 and 1103/1691 and 1692 resumed their activity against the French ships, and the dey having arrested the French consul, Tripoli was bombarded in Shawwāl 1103/July 1692 and a new treaty was signed in Ramaḍān 1104/May 1693. In 1704 there were clashes between Tripolitanians and Tunisians, who laid waste the oases around Tripoli, then besieged the town itself, but finally retreated without having achieved anything. The situation in Tripolitania was at this time a difficult one, both politically and economically; in addition the population of the capital was decimated by an epidemic of plague. It was then, after fresh palace revolutions which continued from 1117 to 1123/1706 to 1711, that a cavalry officer, Aḥmad Qaramānlī (the descendant of a Turkish corsair who had settled in Tripoli during the period of Ṭurghut), was put into power by the native population and, later supported by the *Dīvān*, was proclaimed dey and pasha (11 Jumādā II 1123/27 July 1711). With him began the Qaramānlī dynasty which was to rule Tripolitania for more than 120 years.

Thus, at the very beginning of the twelfth/eighteenth century, there arose in Algeria, and to a greater extent in Tunisia and Tripolitania, locally formed governments, created by the military classes which were all-powerful in these countries, but still preserving fairly close relations with the sultan's government, which regarded Algeria, Tunisia and Tripolitania as provinces of the Ottoman empire, distant provinces perhaps, but ones whose legal links with Istanbul had not been severed. In actual fact these provinces behaved like autonomous states, and this autonomy was made easier on the one hand by their remoteness and on the other by the increasing weakness of the Ottoman government. Nevertheless the fiction of Turkish suzerainty remained, and it was to remain until the nineteenth century.

CHAPTER 3

NORTH AFRICA IN THE PRE-COLONIAL PERIOD

In the last years of the eleventh/seventeenth and the first years of the twelfth/eighteenth century, the three countries of the Maghrib began almost simultaneously a new phase in their history. In 1076/1666, in Morocco, the ʿAlawī dynasty established itself on the ruins of the Saʿdid state; in 1082/1671, in Algeria, the authority of the deys replaced that of the pashas; and in 1117/1705, in Tunisia, the Husaynid dynasty was born in the midst of the unrest provoked by the defeat and capture of the Bey Ibrāhīm al-Sharīf by the Algerians.

The three states, whose modern history was really beginning at this time, had to face the same problems until the middle of the nineteenth century, when they were confronted with the impact of European expansion: the problems of their development as coherent national entities, of the building up of efficient institutions, and of economic and social progress. These problems were only imperfectly solved. Morocco, comparatively protected by its geographical isolation, developed slowly, leaving open the Berber question and the question of the modernization of the *Makhzan*. In the meantime, each of the two neighbouring states, starting with the same status as Ottoman provinces, developed in a different way: whereas in Tunisia, for reasons both of geography and of early and recent history, there arose a national monarchy within clearly defined territorial frontiers, Algeria remained, both as a nation and in its institutions, immature.

MOROCCO

Morocco under the first ʿAlawīs to 1822

The ʿAlawī dynasty which, about 1660, succeeded the Saʿdid dynasty, emerged, in the middle of the Tafilelt, from the rise of a family of *sharīfs* which had come from Yanbuʿ in the time of the Marinids. At the time when, in the anarchy which was overwhelming Morocco, separate little states were arising—principalities formed around *zāwiyas*, like that of Dilāʾ, or a republic of corsairs as at Salé—these *sharīfs* brought Tafilelt beneath their authority under Mawlāy al-Sharīf (1041–5/1631–5).

They then, under Mawlāy Muḥammad (1045–75/1635–64), spread towards eastern and northern Morocco where they encountered the Dilā'īs, who seemed to be in the best position to recover the Sa'did heritage in the north of the country. It was finally with Mawlāy al-Rashīd (1075–83/1664–72), the real founder of the dynasty, that the 'Alawīs imposed their authority on the whole of Morocco. In 1076/1666 this ruler seized Fez, and assumed the title of sultan; two years later he made himself master of the *zāwiya* of Dilā'; in 1079/1669 he occupied Marrakesh.

With the very long reign of Mawlāy Ismā'īl (1083–1139/1672–1727) the dynasty almost immediately reached its zenith. This intelligent and ostentatious sultan, whose temperament was full of contrasts, devoted his untiring energy to the subduing of his kingdom: he is said to have spent twenty-four years in his tent. The difficulties which he encountered at the beginning of his reign (it took him fifteen years to put an end completely to revolts among the tribes, and to movements instigated by his brothers) had proved to him the necessity of forming a strong army: he developed the Sa'did organization of the *Makhzan* tribes (the *gīsh*), incorporating into it in particular the tribe of the Udāya. Then from the Negro troops of Aḥmad al-Manṣūr, Mawlāy Ismā'īl organized his corps of slaves, the *'Abīd*: 150,000 Negroes, grouped together at Mashra' al-Ramal and at Meknes, and duly registered, formed the reserve from which each year he drew the future fighting soldiers. The sultan thus had at his disposal about 20,000 loyal and reliable men. *Qaṣbas* (fortified posts) allowed him to exercise control over the territories which were not entirely subdued, and to watch over the principal roads. By these methods, and by repeated campaigns against the Berbers of the Atlas, Mawlāy Ismā'īl was able to maintain internal order during the greater part of his reign. During the later years, however, the habit which the ruler formed of entrusting the government of the provinces to his sons provoked numerous revolts, and in 1130/1717–18 he had to make up his mind to deprive all except one of them of their commands.

The power of Mawlāy Ismā'īl was particularly brilliantly displayed in his relations with other countries. The sultan's attempted incursions into Algeria were thrice repulsed by the *ojak* but he met with more success in his effort to reconquer the coastal regions which were still in the hands of the Europeans: al-Ma'mūra (1681), Tangier (1684), Larache (1689) and Arzila (1691) were all regained by Morocco. The Portuguese retained only Mazagan, and the Spaniards their four small fortified towns near the Straits of Gibraltar. The sultan entered into continuous negotiations with the great powers, concluded treaties with Great Britain and France, and even conceived great diplomatic projects aimed against Spain, which met with little comprehension at Versailles. The development of commercial relations with which the sultan concerned himself, and the profits from which were to replace the gains from privateering, tended towards the establishment of more normal relations between Morocco and Europe. At the end of his reign, Mawlāy Ismā'īl left a Morocco which was respected from without, and unified and pacified within: however, the crisis which followed his death showed that this success was due chiefly to the outstanding personality of a sultan whose love of power found its permanent embodiment in the magnificent buildings of Meknes.

The causes of the thirty years of anarchy which followed in Morocco (1139–70/1727–57) can be found in a lack of balance in the structure of the country. This was due to the incompleteness of the political institutions, and problems set by the Berbers, who began again their drive towards the north after 1139/1727, to which was added the insubordination of the '*Abīd* and the *gīsh* of the Udāya, and finally the mediocrity of Ismā'īl's successors. Between 1139/1727 and 1170/1757 there were no fewer than twelve proclamations of sultans; Mawlāy 'Abd Allāh for instance, who reigned intermittently from 1141/1729 to 1170/1757, was proclaimed six times, and five times forced to abandon the throne. In a country ravaged by disorder, one of the few stabilizing factors was loyalty to the 'Alawī dynasty, to which all the claimants to the throne belonged, and around which unity was restored after 1170/1757.

Morocco found once again a relative stability under Muḥammad b. 'Abd Allāh (1170–1204/1757–90) and Mawlāy Sulaymān (1206–38/1792–1822) with a brief interval of disturbances under Mawlāy Yazīd (1204–6/1790–2). Muḥammad took advantage of the general desire for peace to achieve the reorganization and pacification of the country: he had to undertake numerous expeditions, however, in order to stem the revolts of the Berbers of the Middle Atlas. Master of the plains of the north and of the south, the sultan had to resign himself to the cutting of the direct route from Fez to Marrakesh by the Tādlā. It was as much to weaken southern Morocco, by concentrating its economic activity in a place easy to control, as to develop commerce, that the sultan founded in 1179/1765 the new town of Mogador (al-Suwayra). After having, it may be, envisaged the return to a policy of a Holy War (he attempted at the beginning of his reign to re-establish privateering, without much success), the sultan contented himself with retaking in 1182/1769 the port of Mazagan, an attempt next to take Melilla meeting with no success. Muḥammad, on the whole, attempted rather to normalize his relations with Europe: he concluded in 1775 a peace of *status quo* with Spain, and took measures to encourage trade, capable of furnishing new resources for the treasury, and to attract foreign merchants, such as the commercial treaty with France in 1767, the foundation of Mogador, and buildings at Casablanca in 1770.

After the crisis of 1204–6/1790–2, Mawlāy Sulaymān had some difficulty in establishing his authority, and in eliminating his rivals, who were other sons of Muḥammad. Although his reign was remarkably peaceful so far as relations between Morocco and Europe were concerned, within Morocco the sultan had to carry out continual police operations, particularly against the Berbers of the Middle Atlas, and his last years were shadowed by serious difficulties. The reason for this was largely the policy which the sultan followed concerning the religious fraternities. Himself a strictly orthodox Muslim, Mawlāy Sulaymān was influenced after 1810 by Wahhabism, which led him take a firm stand against maraboutism, at the very time when both the recently-founded order of the Darqāwa and the earlier order of the Wāzzāniyya were undergoing a great expansion in Morocco. The insurrection in which, from 1818 to 1820, the town of Fez (Fās) and the Darqāwa and Wazzānī Berbers revolted against the sultan, had therefore the three-fold character of an outburst of Ṣūfī reaction, and of a Berber and a Fāsī movement. The sultan died in 1238/1822 without having entirely succeeded in re-establishing his authority.

Within a century and a half, the ʿAlawī dynasty had established itself firmly and incontestably, but it had been unable to solve the problem of Moroccan institutions or the Berber question. At the beginning of the nineteenth century the situation concerning the latter had even deteriorated in comparison with what it had been under Mawlāy Ismāʿīl. The alternation of powerful rulers capable of imposing order and weak successors, which was to continue to be characteristic of the dynasty, was to a large extent responsible for this stagnation and ineffectualness.

European penetration in Morocco

The history of Morocco in the nineteenth century was dominated by the phenomenon of European penetration, the effects of which were felt in all aspects of the country's life. Faced with this new problem, the sultans hesitated between two courses of action: to increase the isolation of Morocco, closing it to outside influences—a solution which the strength of European pressure and the lack of unity within the country made difficult to apply; or to take the opposite course, of attempting to modernize the empire by a policy of reform, to which the archaic structure of the country presented obstacles, and the consequences of which the European powers were not really prepared to accept. Incapable of resolving this dilemma, the sultans clung to an impossible *status quo*, and Morocco drifted towards the crisis in which it was to lose its independence.

Under Mawlāy 'Abd al-Raḥmān (1822–59), who inherited a difficult situation, operations were carried out against the Berbers in the plains, but the mountains and the south (where the *Sharīfs* of the Tazerwalt constituted a veritable small state of their own) evaded the action of the *Makhzan* almost entirely. While, for economic reasons, Morocco opened itself about 1830 to European trade, the occupation of Algeria revived European interest in this part of the Maghrib. Almost immediately serious problems faced the sultan. After having attempted to seize Tlemcen and the west of Algeria (1830–2), he became involved in a conflict with France over the help given to 'Abd al-Qādir al-Jazā'irī in Morocco. The Moroccan defeat at Isly (1844) had no immediate consequences, but it made clear how weak Morocco really was. After having initiated an effort to limit the development of the European enterprises, or at least to place a more rigid control on foreign trade by a system of monopolies and privileges, the sultan was finally forced to resign himself to the opening of Morocco to European penetration. A treaty signed with Great Britain in 1856 established free trade and abolished monopolies. In the long run the result was that the *Makhzan* abandoned part of its jurisdiction.

The reign of Muḥammad b. 'Abd al-Raḥmān (1859–73) began with a war with Spain (1859–60), from which Morocco emerged defeated and obliged to pay a heavy indemnity which forced it to borrow, and to place a part of its customs revenue under foreign control. Soon afterwards, the Béclard Convention, signed with France, by consolidating the privilege of the protection of Moroccans by the consular authorities, caused Morocco to go one step further on the way to becoming dependent (1863). While the *Makhzan* divided itself into a progressive and a reactionary party, the sultan considered encouraging the evolution of Morocco towards modernization by means of public works, agricultural and industrial enterprises, and some administrative and fiscal reforms. This modest and desultory effort came to nothing, but after 1870, thanks to the decline of French and Spanish influence in Morocco (leaving the field clear for the British consul, Hay), and also to the accession of Mawlāy al-Ḥasan, the question of reforms seemed to present itself in a more favourable light.

A worthy, active and experienced ruler who was conscious of his responsibilities, Mawlāy al-Ḥasan (1873–94) fought ceaselessly to preserve the internal unity of his country and its sovereignty abroad. Although he did not succeed completely in this task, at least he postponed the arrival of the crisis. He spent a large part of his reign in travelling through the country in order to quell the forces of disorder. Some of these expeditions were particularly spectacular, although probably not very decisive: among them were the two great raids of 1882 and 1886 in Sūs, where the efforts at penetration by the British at Cape Juby, and the Spanish at Ifni and in the Rio de Oro, increased the habitual difficulties which the sultan had in imposing his authority. The same was true of the campaign in the Tafilelt in 1893. Mawlāy al-Ḥasan's policy of reform took the form chiefly of an attempt to modernize the army. The permanent troops were put under European instructors and equipped with European-type arms; future Moroccan officers were sent abroad for training, and an arsenal was created at Fez. The fairly modest results obtained were out of proportion to the cost to the government. To this were added, in other fields, the monetary reform of 1881, various industrial and agricultural projects, and some improvements in the functioning of the *Makhzan*. The sultan lacked the technical and financial resources to go any further. Morever, had he tried, he would have exposed himself to strong internal opposition, public opinion in general, and particularly among the religious fraternities, being hostile to the reforms, which appeared to be an effect of foreign penetration. The ruler's caution can also be explained by the fear of arousing further European interference and of seeing the number of the *protégés* increase in proportion with the development of the foreign enterprises.

The abuses of the protection had become for the *Makhzan* one of the most irritating problems in relations with Europe, and constituted in the long term one of the most serious threats to Morocco's sovereignty. Mawlāy al-Ḥasan persevered in negotiating to put an end to them, or at least to limit them. But the results of the international conference at

Madrid (1880) fulfilled Moroccan hopes only very imperfectly; furthermore the procedure chosen for the discussion of the problem was evidently dangerous, for it opened the way for the internationalization of the Moroccan Question. The reappearance on the scene of France about 1880, the entry of Germany, and Spain's attempts at peaceful penetration marked the beginning of intense European competition, in which Great Britain, which until then had adhered firmly to the principle of preserving the *status quo*, seemed at one moment in 1892 tempted to take an active part. All the great powers developed in Morocco a network of interests which were often no more than a pretext for political intervention, and could serve to stake a claim to an eventual colonial operation. The Europeans in Morocco (about 9,000 in 1894, mainly Spaniards) were beginning to extend the field of their activities, and to interest themselves in industrial enterprises, and in agricultural colonization. Sea trade had taken the place of the traditional commercial movements, and produced a demand for new products (tea, sugar, cotton-goods) some of which competed with the products of local artisans. The trade deficit, the indemnities paid out to the Europeans, and the expenses incurred by the modernization of the army, had deprived Morocco of its resources on the eve of the crisis which was to be its downfall.

The organization of Morocco in the last years of the reign of Mawlāy al-Ḥasan, had not developed greatly since Mawlāy 'Abd al-Raḥmān. Absolute monarchs, whose status as *sharīfs* earned them great religious prestige, the sultans had seen their authority consolidated during the nineteenth century, as there had been no crisis in the succession. Even the refractory tribes recited the *khuṭba* in their name, and thus recognized their legitimacy if not their authority. The *Dār al-Makhzan* which surrounded the sultan consisted of a court service (directed by the chamberlain (*ḥājib*) and the *qā'id al-mashwar*) and a state service. The *Makhzan* properly so-called, which was the government of Morocco, remained very rudimentary, in spite of a certain diversification of offices. The *wazīr* fulfilled the function of a prime minister and was in charge of the internal administration. The *wazīr al-baḥr* (minister of the sea) was entrusted with foreign affairs. A *nā'ib al-sulṭān* represented the sovereign at Tangier where the foreign representatives resided. The *'allāf* (paymaster) was a sort of minister of war. The *amīn al-umanā'* (chief commissioner) controlled the finances, which consisted of three sections (receipts, expenditure and accounts), each one being entrusted to an *amīn* (commissioner). Finally the *kātib al-shikāyāt* (clerk of the petitions) was responsible for justice, and received appeals against the decisions of the *Sharī'a* tribunal, complaints against the governors, and so forth. The work of the secretariat was carried out in nine offices (*banīqa*) which corresponded to the ministerial departments. They were large unfurnished rooms, facing on to the interior court of the *Dār al-Makhzan*, in which worked secretaries in varying numbers.

This central administration, which at the beginning of the nineteenth century consisted of a very small staff, increased in number until in about 1900 there were some eighty secretaries. The membership of the *Makhzan* was recruited from among the great families of the *gīsh* and the urban middle class: the legal personnel and the secretaries came from among the '*ulamā*', and the *amīns* were chosen from the merchants. Entry into the governing class was in principle open to all; in fact it became more and more difficult for new recruits to enter, and posts tended to become hereditary. The *Makhzan* became a caste, isolated from the rest of the country, and with a powerful *esprit de corps*. The officials received no salary: they were thus induced to make money out of their positions, and this constituted one of the chief faults of the administrative system.

The main instruments of the *Makhzan*—the army and the financial administration—were only moderately efficient. The modernization of the army had never been completed and the sultan continued to rely on the contingents (*gīsh*) supplied by the four *Makhzan* tribes and the five quasi-*Makhzan* tribes of the south: in all, about 10,000 men, chiefly of use as garrisons in the imperial towns of Marrakesh, Fez, Meknes and Rabat, or as police. To these were added contingents supplied by the non-military tribes and under the command of their *qā'ids*. After the defeat of Isly, the sultans had formed a corps armed and equipped in a modern way. This army, though formed and trained at great expense, was only of mediocre quality, but its arms, and particularly its artillery, gave it a great superiority over the bedouin troops. In any case, when circumstances demanded it, the sultan directed against the refractory tribes *maḥallas* or *ḥarkas*, in which he travelled around the country, accompanied by the contingents of the *Makhzan* tribes, and surrounded by the members of the government.

Another weakness of 'Alawī Morocco was its finances. In addition to the Qur'anic taxes (*zakāt* and '*ushūr*), that of the *nā'iba* from which the *gīsh* tribes were exempt, and the 'gifts' authorized at the times of the three great feasts, the sultan had some difficulty in imposing new taxes, which were considered illegal and were badly received by the population. Hence the importance for the government of the customs revenue, which in 1894 was supplying half of the financial resources. Furthermore these taxes were paid regularly only by the towns and the tribes of the plain, and there were numerous exemptions, including *sharīfs*, *zāwiyas* and *Makhzan* tribes. Finally, although the finance services were relatively well organized under the supervision of the *amīns*, the collection of taxes was chaotic, and extortion was rife, particularly at the level of the *qā'ids*.

The sultan had three *khalīfas*, who in his absence governed Fez and Marrakesh (the two alternative capitals), and the Tafilelt. The administration of the tribes was in the hands of *qā'ids* who were endowed with wide powers: the appointment of shaykhs, the dividing out of taxes, the levying of contingents of troops, and relations with the *Makhzan*. To ensure the docility of the tribes, the *Makhzan* divided them up into very small units, or re-grouped them according to its interests of the moment. For example, Mawlāy al-Ḥasan split the large areas of authority into more than 300 qa'idships. The sultan tried to appoint *qā'ids* who were alien to the tribes that they were to govern, and chosen from the *Makhzan*, but he was not always able to do this. In any case the sultan's authority was truly effective over only a part of his empire, the *bled el-makhzen* who alone paid the taxes and supplied contingents to the army. It consisted essentially of the Gharb and the Ḥawḍ (the communications between these two regions being constantly threatened by the tribes), of the plains of eastern Morocco, of Tafilelt and Sūs. There was moreover no real frontier between the submissive *bled el-makhzen* and the dissident *bled el-siba*: their respective areas varied according to the power of the government, and some tribes lived in an intermediate state between total submission and independence. On the other hand the *bleb el-siba* did recognize the sultan, at least nominally. The *Makhzan* extended its military action only to the border of the *bled el-siba*, in order to maintain as far as possible the state of equilibrium within the country, and it avoided attacking the Berbers in their mountains. It attempted instead to negotiate, using the means available to it (the orthodox Islam of the '*ulamā*' and of the *Sharī'a*, represented by the *qāḍīs* which it appointed, the influence of certain *zāwiyas*, and the support of the *sharīfs*), and fostering the traditional rivalries which existed between and within the tribes. It was ultimately the lack of unity within this huge Berber block which enabled the 'Alawīs to maintain their hold on the other half of Morocco.

The profound opposition which existed between rural Morocco, still medieval in its powerful tribal organization and its backwardness in economic development, and the towns, where society and occupations were infinitely more diversified, was traditional. Nevertheless, European penetration had helped to aggravate these differences by introducing into the coastal towns the seeds of modern activity, and by joining Morocco, with its agricultural economy, to a world-market, from whose fluctuations it was beginning to suffer, while the traditional currents of trade and activities were undergoing profound changes and entering a state of crisis. To a deeply divided and stagnating Morocco, Europe at first brought only additional causes of dissolution.

The Moroccan crisis of the first years of the twentieth century took a double form. The basic elements of the internal crisis, (the lack of organization and weakness of the *Makhzan*, and the Berber problem) had long existed, but it was made more serious by the effects of European penetration, and exploited by the imperialist powers to justify their colonial ambitions. The diplomatic crisis resulted from the rivalry between the various imperialisms: at first it developed simultaneously with the internal upheavals, then independently, so that the Moroccan crisis ended as a mere chapter in European diplomatic history.

Mawlāy 'Abd al-'Azīz (1894–1908), the younger son of Mawlāy al-Ḥasan, was at first prevented from holding any power by the *wazīr* Bā Aḥmad b. Mūsā, whose policy, conforming completely to tradition, aimed at controlling the tribes and warding off European influences. After his death in 1900, the sultan, then about twenty years of age, undertook to rule alone. The young ruler was not without good qualities, but he lacked character, and fell under the influence of European advisors, who exploited his curiosity and his love of novelties, and led him into costly extravagances and innovations which discredited him in the eyes of his subjects. This desire for modernization was not only a childish whim, and the principles which inspired certain changes were not mistaken, but the clumsiness with which they were carried out immediately prejudiced their chance of success.

This was the case with the fiscal reform of September 1901 which was prompted by the double wish to obtain greater revenue for the *Makhzan*, and to introduce into Morocco one simple tax, fixed and applicable to all without privileges or exemptions, the *tartīb*. The simplicity and the fairness of the *tartīb* made it seem attractive, but it was imprudent to abrogate the ancient fiscal system before the new one was established, and dangerous to harm with one single act so many varied traditions and interests. The reform immediately encountered general opposition. The tribes refused to pay the tax, and out of the agitation and anarchy there appeared a pretender to the throne, Jalālī b. Idrīs al-Zarhūnī, (*Bū Ḥmāra*, 'the man with the donkey'). Apart from the discontent provoked by the *tartīb* and hasty and blundering reforms, this revolt was an expression of popular protest against the favour accorded by the sultan to the Europeans, and against the many forms which the foreign penetration took. The occupation of Tuat by France in 1900 and 1901 in particular had made a profound impression on Moroccan public opinion. There is no other explanation for the xenophobic character of the propaganda of certain religious fraternities, and the many attacks made on Europeans. Disorder reigned in Morocco; the progress of Bū Ḥmāra merely made the helplessness of the *Makhzan* more obvious. The way was prepared for the intervention of Europe.

In fact France, which had long aimed at establishing herself in Morocco, had not waited for Moroccan anarchy to pursue on the frontier with Algeria a policy of 'peaceful' penetration which she justified by the necessity for maintaining order. Parallel with this intervention, French diplomacy aimed to neutralize any eventual opposition to its Moroccan policy by concluding a series of agreements based on the principle of bartering recognition of imperial gains with interested powers: Italy (1902), Great Britain and Spain (1904). It seemed that these agreements, and the development of the French commercial and financial enterprises in Morocco (with a loan from a consortium of French banks in 1904) would quickly lead to a French protectorate. It might have begun with the 'plan of reforms' presented at Fez in January 1905. However, France was forced to retreat by the unexpected opposition of Germany, whom the French foreign minister, Delcassé, had imprudently excluded from the Moroccan affair, and who considered that she had political and economic interests to assert. After William II's ostentatious visit to Tangier (31 March 1905), Delcassé had to resign, and Germany insisted on the holding of an international conference, with the connivance of the Moroccan sultan, who hoped thus to be able to avoid the threat of a French protectorate. Regarded as an episode in the diplomatic history of Europe, the Algeciras Conference (16 January–7 April 1906) resulted in a partial failure for Germany. From the point of view of Moroccan affairs, it was a setback for France. It proclaimed the independence of the sultan, the integrity of his empire, and economic equality among the powers; and thus placed Morocco under a sort of international guardianship. Nevertheless special rights were accorded to France and Spain, who were entrusted with the organization of the police, which allowed them wide possibilities of action.

Between 1907 and 1911 Morocco was the theatre of increasing anarchy, for which French intervention, less and less dissimulated, was partly responsible. The progressive nibbling away of Morocco brought the unpopularity of the sultan to its height: the south proclaimed his brother, Mawlāy 'Abd al-Ḥāfiẓ, who succeeded in getting himself recognized as sultan by Morocco and by the powers (January 1909). After some success (Bū Ḥmāra was captured and put to death in 1909) the situation under the new sultan deteriorated. Obliged to endorse the commitments entered into by his predecessor, reduced to raising new loans to pay the debts, the costs of public works and the indemnities which were exacted from him, and forced to tolerate foreign intrusions into Moroccan affairs, Mawlāy 'Abd al-Ḥāfiẓ became as unpopular as 'Abd al-'Azīz had been. He had no alternative but to ask for French military support against the revolt of the tribes which besieged him in Fez. While French troops were operating in the neighbourhood of Fez, the Spaniards were beginning in May 1911 to occupy the zone which had been allotted to them in 1904. At this point, Germany, observing the failure of the plans for Franco-German economic co-operation which were worked out in 1909, and fearing that the Moroccan question would be settled without her, provoked a new crisis in July 1911, obliging France to buy her freedom of action in Morocco by consenting to concessions in the Congo by the agreement of 4 November 1911. All that now remained for France to do was to negotiate with the *Makhzan* a treaty of protectorate, largely inspired by that of the Bardo. It was signed on 30 March 1912 at Fez. But the conquest of Morocco which then began was not to be completed until 1934.

ALGERIA TO THE FRENCH CONQUEST (1830)

With the deys there was established in Algiers a monarchy moderated by the insubordination of the Janissary militia, every member of which could aspire to the highest office and for which each revolution was the pretext for substantial gains. Of the twenty-eight deys who succeeded each other from 1671 to 1830, half were assassinated. Only eleven times did the succession take place normally, the revolutions proceeding according to an invariable pattern: the assassination of the dey by a group of Janissaries who occupied the Janīna (the residence of the deys) and its approaches, and proclaimed their candidate who was then officially invested. These violent actions, which had become almost habitual, explain the growth of legends such as that of the 'seven deys' who were said to have been chosen and massacred on the same day, and whose seven tombs were pointed out in early nineteenth-century Algiers.

Nevertheless, the regency of Algiers weathered the crises of the beginning of the eighteenth century to progress towards a more stable form of government, the deys being increasingly chosen from among the dignitaries who shared the power: the treasurer, the commander of the troops, and the receiver of tribute. Between 1724 and 1791, except for a brief period of unrest in 1754, the power was held by only six deys who succeeded each other without violence, the reigning dey often nominating his successor, sometimes even from among his own family. During the same period the western province was, for nearly twenty years (from 1779 to 1796), under the enlightened government of Muḥammad Bey al-Kabīr, the conqueror of Oran; while Constantine experienced, if not quite a 'golden age', at least a restorative period of tranquility and prosperity under the five beys who governed it between 1713 and 1792, and in particular under Ṣāliḥ Bey (1771–92). The long reign of the Dey Bābā Muḥammad b. 'Uthmān (1766–91), who was the contemporary of the two beys mentioned above, was on the whole peaceful, any insubordination of the militia being kept in check by the severity of the dey. The development of trade, which was particularly apparent in the west of the regency, was the sign of real progress in the economic life of the country. From many points of view therefore this last quarter of the eighteenth century can be considered as a period of Algerian renaissance.

In foreign affairs, the situation of the regency appeared equally satisfactory. In order to solve the problems presented to them by Algerian privateering, the European powers, rather than resorting to naval demonstrations, which in any case had little effect, either attempted to conclude treaties with the Regency, which were not always adhered to, or (and this was often the case with the smaller states) submitted themselves to the rather humiliating practice of paying tributes and giving presents. Towards the end of the eighteenth century, the Algerians achieved a series of successes which impressed Europe with a high idea of their power, and convinced them of their own invincibility. In July 1775 a Spanish expeditionary force which arrived off Algiers (344 ships and 22,000 men) was beaten back into the sea. In 1792 Oran was definitively retaken from the Spaniards, and became the capital of the western province. Algerian territory was thus freed from foreign occupation. In its relations with the two neighbouring Muslim countries, the *ojak* of Algiers maintained an almost constant military superiority. After the Algerian troops had three times defeated those of Mawlāy Ismā'īl there were no further difficulties with Morocco. The deys launched a series of victorious campaigns against Tunisia at the end of the eleventh/seventeenth and beginning of the twelfth/eighteenth century, and they succeeded, after the campaign of 1756, in reducing the regency of Tunis to tributary status.

In the last years of the eighteenth century, however, the stability of Algeria came to an end, and the Regency went through a new period of crisis shortly before its encounter with France. The two fundamental institutions of Algiers, privateering and the militia, were both in danger. The decline of privateering, which in the previous century had been a flourishing occupation in Algiers, and the main source of revenue for the treasury, became marked in the eighteenth century. The fleet was smaller (twenty four ships in 1724, about ten in 1788), the crews of inferior quality, and the raids less profitable. The number of slaves held in Algiers, which in the middle of the seventeenth century had exceeded 25,000, fell a century later to 3,000 and to 1,000 in 1788. The population of the town of Algiers followed the same descending curve as that of the revenues obtained from privateering. At the same time the power of the militia declined. Recruitment became more difficult: between 1800 and 1829, only slightly more than 8,000 recruits were brought from the Levant, and the total number of the effective forces of the militia diminished after the middle of the eighteenth century. These troops no longer possessed their previous quality as fighters, and were concerned chiefly with the advantages which they could obtain from their political role. As the financial difficulties which the deys were experiencing were reflected in some irregularity in the payment of the militia, their insubordination increased.

In order to clear off the deficit, and to satisfy the demands of the militia, the deys were forced to resort to dangerous commercial expedients (monopolies), and to exploit the local population. It was at this time that an intense religious ferment led to the creation or the reformation of many religious fraternities: the order of the Ṭayyibiyya, founded at the beginning of the eighteenth century and very widespread in Oran; the Darqāwa, a branch of the Shādhiliyya which detached itself from them at the beginning of the century; the Tijāniyya, founded by Aḥmad al-Tijānī (1150–1230/1737–1815), with its centre at 'Ayn Māḍī to the west of Laghwat; the Raḥmāniyya, founded by the Kabyle, Muḥammad b. 'Abd al-Raḥmān al-Gushtulī (d. 1208/1793/4). In many cases these fraternities catalysed the discontent of the population and gave a formidable religious interpretation to its anti-Turkish sentiments.

From the end of the century, the power in Algiers was again unstable, affected by the indiscipline of the militia: between 1798 and 1816 seven deys were put into power by revolutions and then perished through them. In 1816, 'Alī Khūja, in order to escape from the domination of the militia, decided to leave the Janīna and to go to live in the Qaṣba with a guard of 2,000 Kabyles. His successor, Ḥusayn Dey (1818–30), followed his example in this. A change was taking place, big with consequences which could have turned the state of Algeria into an hereditary monarchy relying on the non-Turkish elements of the population. Its immediate consequence however, was that the deys deprived themselves of the help of the militia without being able to count on support within the country. The early years of the nineteenth century were marked by continual internal revolts, which were nothing new in Algeria (the Kabyles were in a permanent state of rebellion), but the bitterness of which is perhaps explained by their religious character: the Darqāwī revolt in Kabylia (1803–7) and in Oran; further difficulties with the Kabyles (1810–15); and conflict between the beys of Oran and the Tijāniyya between 1820 and 1828. In the meantime the Regency's position abroad was weakening. In 1807 Tunisia put an end to half a century of Algerian domination. Relations with a rapidly developing Europe were undergoing a marked change. Following a period of renewed privateering activity, which coincided with the Revolutionary and Napoleonic wars, a series of naval operations demonstrated Algeria's true weakness. After an American squadron had forced Algeria to sign a treaty, Lord Exmouth, who had come in 1816 to procure the abolition of slavery, forced the Dey 'Umar to submit to his conditions, following a bombardment which demolished the forts of Algiers. Although Algiers could still on occasion produce an illusion of power, and even believe in it itself, it no longer possessed the means to resist a determined assault.

Although the formalities which implied the position of the deys as vassals of the Ottoman sultan continued to be scrupulously respected, the Regency of Algiers in fact possessed an autonomy which was recognized by the foreign powers who signed treaties with it. The reason why the masters of Algiers could never contemplate breaking the links which united them to the Sublime Porte was that the organization of the state rested on the Janissaries, who could be recruited in the Levant only with the consent of the sultan. Rather than a real monarchy, the Regency continued to be a sort of republic dominated by the Turkish military *élite*. The quasi-colonial antagonism which existed between a minority of foreign masters and the indigenous masses prevented Algeria from becoming a real nation, and was a major weakness in its Turkish government.

Although he held absolute power, the dey was nevertheless only one of the Janissaries (he continued to draw pay and a bread ration), elected from among his equals, and he had difficulty in escaping from the control of the militia, as was proved by the violent disturbances which occurred at the beginning of the century. In addition to his stipend, the dey received very many perquisites, such as fees for the investiture of important dignitaries, tribute from the beys, and presents from consuls, and he had at his command the public treasury. He had his own official house with a *khaznadār* (treasurer), a *turjumān* (interpreter), scribes and ushers. There had gradually grown up around him a sort of government, with five 'powers' (*puissances*) who performed the function of ministers: the *khaznajī*, in charge of the treasury, who was often chosen as the dey's successor; the *agha* of the *sipāhīs* (or of the *maḥalla*) who was in charge of the land forces; the *wakīl al-kharj*, a sort of minister of sea-power; the *bayt al-māljī*, the steward of the dey's household; the *khūjat al-khayl*, who administered the territories of the Regency and received the tribute from the beys. The '*agha* of the two moons', the chief of the militia, held only a secondary and representative role, as did the *Dīvān* of about sixty members, who in principle elected the dey, and from whom the majority of the high officials were chosen. A certain number of clerks (sing., *khūja*) kept the principal registers, and attended to the correspondence.

The militia which dominated and exploited the state was recruited in the Levant, for the most part in Anatolia. On his arrival in Algiers, the Janissary private was entered in the registers of the militia, in which were later recorded his increase in pay and his promotions. The Janissaries were divided into 424 groups of about twenty men, distributed into rooms (sing., *oda*) within eight barracks. Their active service was divided into garrison duty and service in the field. The *yoldash* very often followed a trade, and, with increasing frequency, married Algerian girls; but their children, the *Kul oghlus*, were not admitted to the militia until a later date, and they remained excluded from the highest offices, and from the majority of the prerogatives of the pure Turks. As the *ojak* was renewed by recruitment from outside, it did not in Algeria form a hereditary aristocracy. To these Turkish forces were added Turkish and Arab cavalry *sipahis*, paid Kabylian troops, and contingents of cavalry supplied by the *Makhzan* tribes. Privateering almost disappeared after 1815; the Algerian fleet, destroyed by Exmouth in 1816, and later involved in the Turkish naval disaster at Navarino, consisted in 1827 of no more than about ten ships.

The administration of the country was characterized by a great local variation in administrative usage, and by a wide decentralization, which even extended to a semi-autonomy for the professional, religious or ethnic groups. The Regency was divided into four provinces. That of Algiers (*Dār al-Sulṭān*) came directly under the authority of the dey. The three others were governed by beys: the *beylik* of Titteri (Tīṭarī) with its capital at Medea, the first in rank but the smallest in size, the *beylik* of the West with its successive capitals at Mazouna, Mascara and Oran; and the *beylik* of the East (Constantine). The beys, who were appointed and dismissed by the dey, had around them actual little governments, and had armed forces at their disposal for police operations. They enjoyed wide powers, and some of them were very important persons. Algiers supported them by sending three *maḥallas* (expeditionary forces) a year, in return for which it expected them to send regular tribute, which was brought twice a year by the lieutenant (*khalīfa*) of the bey, and once every three years by the bey himself. The insufficiency of the tribute was a frequent cause of the dismissal of the beys. The provinces were themselves divided into *waṭans* administered by *qā'ids*, who were appointed and usually Turks, and by shaykhs, who were elected. But the actual situations varied greatly between the *Makhzan* tribes, which contributed to the police, supplied military contingents and enjoyed various privileges in return, and the regions which were partially or totally independent, such as Kabylia or the Aurès. Where they were unable to install an effective local administration, the Turkish authorities (whose actual control extended over only a part of Algeria) made use, according to the circumstances and their relative strength at the time, of severity, diplomacy or cunning, for example in taking advantage of the divisions among clans, or ethnic or religious quarrels.

The basic taxes, which weighed especially heavily on the peasants, were traditionally the tithe (*'ushūr*) on the harvests, the *zakāt* on animals, the *lazma*, a sort of poll-tax which replaced the tithe in Kabylia and in the south, and the *kharāj* paid by the *ra'iyya* (subject peoples) in conquered territories. The tribes, who in greater or less degree escaped the government's authority, were made to pay a tax in kind or in money, the *gharāma*. To these taxes, which moreover varied according to the region, were added many other taxes and arbitrary levies. The dey's resources (tributes from the provinces, fees and other perquisites) supplied the budget of the regency. The expenses consisted basically of the pay of the militia, for the officials bought their appointments and afterwards recouped themselves with perquisites, while much of the expenditure on matters of public interest, such as worship and education, was met by private initiative. The dey's treasury seems to have been well filled: it is estimated at 100 million francs in 1830. This system possessed undoubted advantages which were due to its very simplicity: the payments in kind, which were very frequent, were less onerous on the taxpayers, and well adapted to a country lacking in specie, while they provided direct support for the high officials. Nevertheless, because of much waste in the fiscal system and the exactions which were added to the normal levies, the taxation was heavy without in fact contributing very much to the state.

Of the probably three million inhabitants of Algeria in 1830, the rural population represented more than nine-tenths. Because of methods and equipment which in general were rather primitive, and a complex and unsatisfactory system of land-tenure little more than the absolute minimum was produced. It is true that agricultural techniques were well adapted to natural conditions, and that the produce was destined mainly for consumption by a relatively small population: there was much arable soil, which allowed the extensive use of the land by the tribes in the grazing of sheep and goats. Life in the towns seems to have decreased at the end of the period of Turkish rule: there were few real towns apart from Algiers (30,000 inhabitants), Constantine (12,000) and Oran

(9,000). The urban population differed profoundly from the rural population, as much in the diversity of its composition (Turks, Moors and *Kul oghlus* all lived there and sometimes quarrelled; there were also substantial Muslim minorities, Mzabites, Kabyles, and large Jewish communities) as in the variety of its occupations: artisans, traders and '*ulamā*'. The artisans disposed of a relatively restricted internal market, and limited themselves to the processing of agricultural products, and the manufacture of objects of everyday use. They did not contribute to Algerian exports, and internal trade was hampered by the lack of geographical unity of the Regency, the difficulty of communications and the diversity of weights and measures in use. Foreign trade, based on the sale of a few raw materials (wheat, oil, animals) and the purchase of manufactured products (cloth) and some foodstuffs (sugar, coffee) remained rather small in volume. Its profits were concentrated in the hands of some European merchants and a few Andalusian[1] and Jewish families.

The concentration of political power exclusively in the hands of a foreign ruling class, and the often brutal exploitation of the population would to a certain extent justify the description of the Turkish régime in Algeria as 'colonial' if there had not existed between governors and governed strong links, such as the possession of a common religion, culture and social structure, which covered over the antagonism and if, furthermore, any idea of a massive human colonization or of exclusive exploitation of the land had not been completely foreign to the Turkish conquerors. Because of this ambiguity, the revolts of the people against the excesses of the Turkish domination could not assume a truly nationalist character. The Turks had founded the territorial framework of Algeria, but it was French colonization, established on the ruins of Ottoman domination, which was, through the country's reaction, to form the Algerian nation.

The origin of the French expedition of 1830 is found in the very involved affair of the credits held by Jewish merchants in Algiers, for deliveries of grain made to France between 1793 and 1798, partly thanks to the money lent by the dey. Ḥusayn Dey attempted for several years to get his demands heard in Paris, but without success. Finally, tired of the procrastinations of the French government and of the insolent behaviour of the consul Deval, the dey gave the latter the famous 'blow with the fly-whisk', which caused diplomatic relations to be broken off (29 April 1827). There followed three years of blockade of

[1] By 'Andalusian' is meant the descendants of Muslim refugees from Spain.

Algiers with very little result, interspersed with unfruitful negotiations. In August 1829 the French truce ship was fired on by cannon from Algiers, which put an end to the negotiations.

The Polignac government, which had at one time considered using Muḥammad ʿAlī Pasha to conquer the Maghrib, then decided to send an expedition against Algiers (31 January 1830). Actually it was less concerned to defeat Algiers than to succeed in a matter of internal politics: it intended by reinforcing the prestige of the monarchy with a success which it hoped would be outstanding, to strangle the opposition, and obtain favourable elections. It was only the business circles of Marseilles which were truly interested in the actual colonization of Algeria. From 14 June 1830, 37,000 men were landed at Sidi Ferruch near Algiers. On the 19 June the Algerian forces attacked the expeditionary force at Staweli, but were defeated. On 29 June the French army resumed its march on Algiers, and on 4 July it occupied the Emperor Fort which commanded the town. Negotiations entered into with some of the important officials ended in the capitulation of the dey, who accepted the conditions of General de Bourmont. On 5 July at 12 o'clock French troops occupied Algiers. This success came too late to save the Restoration monarchy, and France found itself engaged in a colonial enterprise which it had neither really wanted nor seriously prepared.

TUNISIA

Husaynid Tunisia to 1830

The capture of the Bey Ibrāhīm al-Sharīf by the Algerian troops produced a profound reaction in Tunis, where the memory of the two expeditions of 1686 and 1694 was still quite fresh. The unanimity with which the high officials, the officers of the militia and the important citizens of Tunis entrusted the vacant office to the *agha* of the Turkish *sipahis*, Ḥusayn b. ʿAlī, considered to be the most capable of saving Tunis, can be regarded as one of the first manifestations of national awareness in Tunisia (Rabīʿ I 1117/July 1705). Ḥusayn, the son of an Ottoman trooper, born in Candia, who had settled in Tunisia and founded a family there, justified this confidence: before the end of the year 1705, the Algerian troops, abandoned by their allies among the Tunisian tribes, were forced to recross the frontier. Soon afterwards Ḥusayn b. ʿAlī thwarted an attempt by the Dey Muḥammad Khūja al-Aṣfar to seize power. The absolute power which the bey held from then on was later to be sanctioned by the Porte, which issued a firman entrusting to him the government of Ifrīqiya (1708). A later attempt by the Porte to re-establish its authority in Tunis failed completely (1127/1715), and after this it contented itself with the demonstrations of submission which reached it from this distant province, without contesting the semi-autonomy which its rulers enjoyed. After the long period of disturbances at the end of the eleventh/seventeenth century, Tunisia first experienced under Ḥusayn b. ʿAlī a period of calm in which to recover. The construction by this bey of very many buildings of public utility (wells, cisterns, reservoirs, bridges), markets and places for worship and education (three *madrasas* in Tunis and several in the towns of the interior), is evidence of this effort at reconstruction. It was particularly active at Qayrawān, which had been destroyed by Murād Bey: the walls were rebuilt and a *madrasa* and two markets erected.

The solidity of the Husaynid monarchy was put seriously to the test during the second quarter of the eighteenth century, during a series of crises which partook of the double character of dynastic struggles and foreign wars. Their origin was the frustrated ambition of Ḥusayn's nephew, ʿAlī Pasha, who had been deprived of the succession to the throne by the late birth of the bey's sons (Muḥammad in 1711 and ʿAlī in 1124/1712). Their seriousness arose from the help which the claimants received in Algiers, where every opportunity was seized to reassert the vassal status of the neighbouring Regency while obtaining profit from it in the form of tribute or of the spoils of war. The failure of the first revolt of ʿAlī Pasha having obliged him to seek refuge in Algiers in 1729, the prince succeeded in persuading Ibrāhīm Bey to support his cause. The Algerian troops marched on Tunis and installed ʿAlī Pasha there (September 1735). Ḥusayn and his sons continued the struggle in the Sahel and at Qayrawān until the town was taken and the bey died (16 Ṣafar 1153/13 May 1740). It was now the turn of his sons to seek refuge and support in Algeria.

A prince of ostentatious tastes (witness his buildings of the Bardo, which had become the habitual residence of the beys) and an enlightened ruler (he was responsible for four *madrasas* in Tunisia), ʿAlī Pasha had to fight in order to impose his authority. The revolt for which he had been responsible resulted in the permanent division of Tunisia into two parties (sing., *ṣaff*), the Ḥusayniyya and the Bāshiyya, whose opposition was in fact based on earlier quarrels. In particular the bey had to subdue powerful tribal confederations on the Algerian frontier in the south of the country. His own son, Yūnus, revolted against him in 1165/1752. Above all he had to face the danger from Algeria which reappeared this time in support of Ḥusayn's sons. The Algerian expedition of 1159/1746 failed, but in 1169/1756 the Algerians seized Tunis, and sacked the town. 'Alī Pasha was put to death, and the Ḥusaynīs were re-established, though not without experiencing some difficulty in ridding themselves of the encumbrance of their protectors. The crises which 'Alī Pasha had had to face (and to which there had been added in 1742 a conflict with France, after the recovery of Ṭabarqa from the Genoese) had obliged him to increase the man-power of the Turkish militia, in spite of the little confidence that he placed in it, especially since the revolt of 1156/1743.

After 1756 the descendants of Ḥusayn b. 'Alī succeeded one another almost without incident: Muḥammad Bey (1169/1756), 'Alī Bey (1172/1759), Ḥammūda Bey (1196/1782), 'Uthmān Bey (1229/1814), Maḥmūd Bey (1230/1814), Ḥusayn Bey (1239/1824), Muṣṭafā Bey (1251/1835). Contrary to the normal order of succession, however (by order of seniority within the family of the bey) 'Alī Bey had his son Ḥammūda (born 1173/1759) as his successor, passing over Maḥmūd, his nephew (born 1170/1757); 'Uthmān, having succeeded his brother Ḥammūda in 1814, was assassinated soon afterwards, and Maḥmūd finally came to the throne after having been twice frustrated.

The Husaynid beys eradicated the traces of the disturbances which Tunisia had suffered. The severe punishment meted out to the turbulent population of the Ousseltia, which was expelled from its *jabal* and dispersed (1759–62), served as an example, and for half a century there was no serious revolt in Tunisia. The second rebuilding of Qayrawān, which had been destroyed by Yūnus, is a positive example of this effort towards internal reconstruction. Under 'Alī and Ḥammūda the country experienced a certain economic prosperity, which was somewhat marred by a series of natural disasters, in particular the epidemics of plague in 1783–5 and 1818–20. During the disturbances of the following century, the reign of Ḥammūda, that 'Tunisian Charlemagne' was often referred to as a golden age. On several occasions the beys affirmed their quasi-autonomy in their relations with the Porte. Ḥammūda did this with a certain amount of *éclat*, first by intervening on his own account in Tripoli, to re-establish the Qaramānlī dynasty there (1794–5), then by his obvious unwillingness to break with France in 1798. This same bey attempted to free Tunis from its humiliating situation as a tributary of

Algiers. Ḥammūda's expedition of 1807 against Constantine was not successful, but the victorious resistance of the Tunisian troops near the frontier (14 July 1807) marked the end of Algerian raids into Tunisia until the definitive peace could be signed, under the auspices of the Ottoman government, in March 1821. In its relations with the European powers, a fair number of which had concluded direct treaties with it (16 in 1816), the Regency also held its own: offering resistance to France in 1770, standing up to the Venetians in 1784–6, pursuing a privateering war against the smaller maritime powers, or exacting from them humiliating tributes or gifts. It was not until September 1819 that the action of the powers taking part in the Congress of Aix-la-Chapelle forced the bey permanently to abolish privateering.

At the beginning of the nineteenth century, the Husaynid beys had become Tunisian princes, Arabic in language and culture, who often allied themselves in marriage with the great families of Tunis. The office of chief minister was filled by Tunisians as well as by *mamlūks*: among them were the shaykh and historian Ibn 'Abd al-'Azīz (under 'Alī Bey and Ḥammūda Pasha), the al-Aṣram, natives of Qayrawān who were hereditary *bāsh kātibs*, or Muḥammad al-'Arabī Zarrūq, under Maḥmūd Bey. The Turkish militia declined rapidly after 1750: in spite of the caution with which Ḥammūda Pasha treated them, it was quite clear that the troops had lost all political influence. It was perhaps an attempt to regain it which led them to revolt in 1811 and 1816. These revolts, and the vigorous repression which followed them, only hastened the decadence of the militia, while the beys naturally tended more and more to have recourse to the local troops. Thus was completed, shortly before the occupation of Algiers, the evolutionary process which had transformed the Regency of Tunis, dominated by the Turkish *ojak*, into a quasi-monarchic national state.

The political and administrative structure of the state of Tunisia immediately before the conquest of Algeria was at the same time very primitive, if we consider the means employed, and very complex, if we take into account the great variety of institutions which had been inherited from the ancient or the more recent past. Whatever may have survived of Ottoman rule, the bey was, at the beginning of the nineteenth century, practically an independent ruler. The hereditary character of the régime was in no way affected by the formality of the double investiture (*bay'a*) which associated the *Dīvān* and the important dignitaries with the enthronment of the ruler, nor by the request for investiture by the sultan, which was granted automatically, carrying with it the title of pasha, and regularly renewed. There were only a few external signs which continued to witness to the fact that in principle the bey was a vassal: it was in the name of the sultan that coins were struck, and that the *khuṭba* was said. The fact was also still expressed in some demonstrations of respect, and in occasional military aid: some Tunisian squadrons joined the Ottoman fleet in 1821 and 1826, which resulted in the destruction of the Tunisian navy at Navarino. Apart from this the bey governed without reference to the Porte. Even the use of Turkish, which had been a symbol of belonging to the Ottoman world, was abandoned in treaties about 1830 and in correspondence with Istanbul in 1838.

Without officially possessing the title of ministers (it was Aḥmad Bey who first appointed *wazīrs*) or exactly their functions, a certain number of high officials surrounding the bey did in fact hold this sort of position: the *ṣāḥib al-ṭābi'* (keeper of the seals), who was often the chief minister; the *khaznadār* (treasurer); the *kāhiya* (commander of the troops); the *kāhiya* of La Goulette, who was also *amīn al-tarsakhāna* (director of the arsenal), in charge of the navy and of foreign affairs. The chief secretary (*bāsh kātib*) also played an important role in the bey's entourage, for he had in his hands all the correspondence of the Regency; he was assisted by Arabic and Turkish secretaries, about ten in number, but enough for the business to be transacted.

To fulfill important political functions and to command the troops, the beys chose *mamlūks*, slaves who were bought in the East and brought up in the palace. In this way they assured themselves of a staff which was relatively competent and generally loyal: the beys gave Husaynid princesses in marriage to the most important of them. The *mamlūks* formed a caste, the highest rank of which was occupied by the Circassians and the Georgians, who had the greatest contempt for their Greek and Italian fellow-slaves (who had become very numerous at the beginning of the nineteenth century), and also for the native Tunisians, whom the exercise of the functions of *kātib* assured of a certain amount of influence over affairs. The Tunisians had also the monopoly of the judicial and religious offices, but the traditional jurisdiction of the *qāḍīs* and of the *majlis shar'ī* (religious court) suffered competition from the justice which was dispensed by the bey and a number of high officials.

The Turkish personnel which had formerly governed the Regency no longer played more than a secondary or honorary role; an example was the dey, who had become a sort of chief of police in Tunis, or the former chief of the militia, the *agha al-kursī*, or the formerly all-powerful *Dīvān*. This decline was reflected in that of the militia, which in about 1830 consisted of scarcely more than 2,500 men. The rulers, who surrounded themselves by a guard of *mamlūks* (four *odas* of twenty-five men) employed mainly native troops (3,000 recruited in Kabylia, four *ojaks* of 500 Arab *sipahis*) and, in case of need, contingents furnished by the *Makhzan* tribes. The regular army, reduced for reasons of economy to about 7,000 men, was of mediocre quality, but nevertheless sufficient to impose order on the tribes, who were even worse armed (and above all lacked cannons) and very poorly disciplined.

To establish his authority in the interior of the country, collect taxes and maintain order, the bey sent two annual columns (sing., *maḥalla*), one in summer to the west, and the second in winter to the south. The local administration was entrusted to governors (sing. *ʿāmil, qāʾid*) who bought their offices and subjected their provinces to an exploitation which was limited only by their concern not to be removed from office and divested of their spoils by the bey. The hold which the government had over the populations, which was exercised through elected shaykhs, varied according to the regions: it was strong in the settled agricultural regions near to the capital and in the Sahel of Sousse, and weak in the mountain areas and in the steppe, which were under the domination of the great tribes.

The calm and stability which the country had enjoyed since 1169/1756 had brought with it a relative economic prosperity which showed itself in various ways: a tendency for the tribes to settle in the high steppes, the formation of new villages, an increase in the cultivation of olive trees in the neighbourhood of Sfax, and an extension of the area of cultivated land (about 750,000 hectares, were under cultivation in about 1840). The country continued to live according to the rhythm of the traditional commercial currents: north-south exchanges between the nomads with their flocks and the growers of wheat and of olives, relations with the Sahara and trade with Algeria and the Levant, in which the local artisan class still played an important part (e.g. the making of 'chechias', woollen caps, which employed 15,000 persons in the eighteenth century, the manufacture of woollen cloth and leather goods).

Foreign trade was expanding and the exports (mainly of oil from the Sahel) definitely exceeded the imports.

At the beginning of the nineteenth century, however, there appeared an increasing number of signs pointing to economic and financial difficulties. The abolition of privateering in 1819 had certainly affected the bey's finances, although its role in Tunis had never been of more than secondary importance. More serious for Tunisia had been epidemics and famines which had impoverished and depopulated it. Following the example of Ḥammūda, the beys attempted to obtain new resources from a policy of monopolies, which hindered trade and was a burden on agriculture. Some efforts were made to improve the system of taxes (which were made heavier by the abuses and the extortions of the *qā'ids*) and, to encourage the peasantry; there was introduced (in November 1819) a tithe (*'ushūr*) on the produce of the olive plantation of Sousse, in place of the fixed *qanūn*, and in 1825 a reform in the system of collection of the tithe on cereals. But the results were not what the beys had hoped. In about 1830, the farmers of the Sahel, overwhelmed by a series of bad harvests, and by the harmful consequences of the commercial monopoly of oil, were on the brink of ruin: the crisis produced the downfall of the minister, and cost the government heavy indemnities to the French merchants. About the same time, monetary difficulties led Ḥusayn Bey to devalue the *riyāl* (piastre) yet a little further. The meagre profit which this operation brought him was largely cancelled out by the aggravation of the monetary and economic troubles: the piastre continued to fall in value, and gold and silver coins became very scarce in the country.

The crisis which was beginning to affect the Regency was in part the effect of European commercial penetration, which was to increase after 1830. Sea trade, which was relatively extensive from Tunisia, took the form of an exploitation of its natural, agricultural resources by the Europeans and their local agents, who had this trade under their control and received all the profit from it. Whereas Tunisia was strengthening most of her commercial relations with Europe (whose merchant navies held a monopoly of the Mediterranean traffic), the traditional outlets towards the Maghrib and the Near East were declining, and with them the economic activity which supplied them, the products of the artisan classes. The break-up of the Ottoman empire in the Mediterranean, beginning with the French conquest of Algiers, was to accelerate the political and economic decline of Tunisia.

Tunisia in the nineteenth century from the reforms to the protectorate

The Algerian expedition was welcomed by the bey of Tunis who at first saw it only as an event which rid him of hated neighbours: he even considered joining with France in the reorganization of the neighbouring Regency. Negotiations led to the project of installing in Constantine and Oran Tunisian princes, tributaries of France. After beginning at Oran, the enterprise was interrupted, the French government having refused to ratify the agreements (1831). In reality a new era was beginning for Tunisia. Isolated, especially from the world to which she had belonged for ten centuries, after the occupation of Constantine in 1837, Tunisia gradually changed into a mere commercial dependency of Europe, to the detriment of its traditional economic equilibrium. Further, the beys tried to counter the political pressure which was exerted directly on them by an attempt at reconstruction and progress which was only to accelerate the process of internal disintegration.

The diplomatic situation of the Regency was immediately and profoundly altered by the conquest of Algiers. In Paris (and still more in Algiers) it was thought that Tunisia was destined to fall sooner or later under French influence, and that it was in France's interest to maintain there a weak and isolated authority: thus French policy tended to break what remained of the links between Tunisia and the Ottoman empire, to consolidate Tunisian autonomy, envisaged as a state of quasi-independence. On the other hand Great Britain, alarmed at the progress of French influence, was led, in order to protect effectively the *status quo* in Tunis, to advocate a *rapprochement* with the Porte, and tried to make the somewhat theoretical dependence of the beys into a reality. At the same time, because of the re-establishment of their authority at Tripoli (1835), the Ottomans were in a favourable position to defend their rights in Tunis, and eventually to try to consolidate their position there. The beys (and in particular Aḥmad Bey), who were truly alarmed by the pressure from France but who were also anxious to stress their autonomy, were forced by circumstances to play a diplomatic game, the subtlety of which was apparent in 1836 and 1837 when French squadrons appeared off Tunis, ostensibly to prevent the Ottomans from repeating there the operation in which they had succeeded at Tripoli. The same situation later recurred almost every year. In the end, as France's ideas on the status of Tunis were more realistic, and above all closer to the wishes of the beys, and as in addition she was in a position to exert an almost irresistible pressure on Tunisia, it was French policy which prevailed. Tunisia continued to detach itself progressively from the Ottoman empire, at the risk, should the British policy change, of finding herself alone face to face with France.

The attempts at reform in Tunis, as in Egypt and Turkey, at first took the form of modernization of the army. In 1830, Ḥusayn Bey had asked for and obtained help in modernizing his troops: thus there were organized the first *Niẓāmī* units, for the creation of which he requested the Porte's approval after the event (1831). This effort was later continued at great expense by the minister, Shākir, an admirer of Muḥammad ʿAlī Pasha, and in particular by Aḥmad Bey (1837–55) when he came to power. The formation of a European-style army appealed to his liking for prestige, and was intended to serve his main ambition—to obtain the recognition of the quasi-independence of Tunisia, and to have it respected by the Ottomans. Thus within a few years seven regiments of infantry, two of artillery and one of cavalry were formed, although the quality and the number of these troops did not entirely correspond to the bey's hopes, or to the financial expenditure authorized. Greatly influenced by the example given by Egypt, the bey established a military school in the Bardo (March 1840), and tried, but without much success, to create an industry to support his military effort by a textile mill, a gunpowder factory and a foundry.

However modest this army was (not more than about 10,000 men), it was still disproportionate to the resources of the country: military expenditure ended by absorbing two thirds of the budget. In addition Aḥmad Bey allowed himself to spend money on luxuries, such as the building of a Tunisian 'Versailles' at the Muḥammadiyya near Tunis. He was the victim of European adventurers, or of high officials who pilfered from the treasury. Tunisia thus resorted to financial expedients and seemingly attractive yet disastrous enterprises, such as the creation of a bank and of paper money in 1847, which were to lead to catastrophe. About 1852 it was threatened with bankruptcy: the flight to France of Maḥmūd b. ʿAyyād, the concessionary of the majority of the farms and monopolies, taking with him considerable state funds, and the effort made in 1854 to send some 10,000 men to the aid of the sultan, helped to make the situation even worse.

This rather disorganized attempt at progress was not however entirely without results. It was Aḥmad Bey who by degrees abolished slavery between 1841 and 1846, and who put an end to the humiliating position of the Tunisian Jews. The School of the Bardo produced an *élite* of officers and high officials with modernist ideas, while even the teaching at the great mosque of the Zaytūna was reorganized in 1842. The bey persistently refused to adopt the Ottoman Tanẓimāt because of the diplomatic implications of such a decision; but he did not deny that reform was necessary. The foreign influences to which he opened his country (his visit to Paris in 1846 was from this point of view a particularly spectacular gesture), and the more exact knowledge of the modern world which the Tunisians obtained in the course of many missions to Europe, helped to increase Tunisia's progress.

The period of the real reforms began with Muḥammad Bey (1855–9) who was a traditionalist ruler, but anxious to improve the lot of his subjects. He began his reign by replacing a certain number of taxes by one single tax, the 'subsidy' (*i'āna* or *majba*) of 36 piastres a year (1856), and by abolishing certain abuses in the collection of the tax in kind. But it required the joint pressure of the French and British consuls which was made possible by the temporary *rapprochement* between France and Great Britain, to force the bey to adopt, on 10 September 1857, the Fundamental Pact (*'Ahd al-amān*), which was the starting point for actual political reform. Inspired by the Ottoman Tanẓimāt, the text granted to all Tunisians, Muslims and Jews, equal guarantees and rights, and accorded to foreigners the right to hold property in Tunisia. The reformist movement then continued under the impetus of a modernist *élite* (among them the minister Khayr al-Dīn Pasha al-Tūnisī and the historian and minister Ibn Abi'l-Ḍiyāf) and under the vigilant control of the consuls, who expected it to facilitate foreign economic penetration. In 1857 there was established a Commission of Reforms, and in August 1858 a Municipal Council at Tunis. The accession of Muḥammad al-Ṣādiq (1859–82), more definitely modernist than his predecessor, gave new impetus to the movement. After founding the official journal of Tunisia (*al-Rā'id al-Tūnisī*), and promulgating the law on recruitment (March 1860) and the decrees on the organization of Tunisian ministries (February and April 1860), the bey proclaimed in January 1861 a constitution which established a limited monarchy, the bey sharing his legislative powers with a Grand Council (*al-Majlis al-akbar*) of sixty members; regular tribunals were to be instituted, with legal codes based on European models.

This was an experiment without precedent in the Ottoman world. Some of the foreign powers which had advocated modernization found in practice that an assembly in which the public interest had spokesmen was less malleable than an absolute potentate: the granting of new concessions and privileges encountered serious difficulties. Furthermore the Tunisians, inspired by their attainment of civilization and progress, demanded that foreigners should henceforward come under the jurisdiction of the regular tribunals, a claim which the majority of foreign governments would not accept. While France and Italy opposed the reforms more and more openly, Great Britain was the only country to support the development of the new institutions. She signed in 1863, a convention with the bey which, in exchange for the freedom to trade granted to the British, submitted them to the *lex loci*. Within Tunisia, the reform policy also encountered great difficulties: it disturbed the habits of the peasantry and bedouin (particularly in matters of justice); there was a lack of loyal and competent officials to make the new institutions work: finally the majority of the '*ulamā*' were hostile to these innovations. But it was primarily the financial difficulties, with their international implications, which caused the policy of reform to collapse. The beys aggravated the financial crisis by launching into expenditure of doubtful value, sometimes suggested by untrustworthy European businessmen. In order to obtain the money it required, the government at first borrowed locally at usurious rates of interest. Then it turned to Europe. In 1863 the bey borrowed from the banking house of d'Erlanger in Paris. He actually received a small proportion of the nominal sum, and it was soon dissipated. In need of money once again, the bey decided to double the *majba*. This measure brought the country's discontent to a head: in the spring of 1864, the great tribes of the centre of the country refused to pay the tax, and the revolt became general.

The revolution of 1864 was more than a mere bedouin revolt. The rebels presented a list of precise complaints and chose leaders among themselves. The movement spread to the region of the Sahel, and, in the coastal towns where the European penetration had made itself most felt, it took on an indisputably nationalist character. The revolution failed, however, for lack of unity and clear perspectives. It was nevertheless to have considerable consequences. First of all the bey made it the pretext for bringing the reforms to an end, as he was in any case being encouraged to do by the French consul. The military efforts and then the repression hastened the financial and economic ruin of the country. In 1865 the government contracted a second loan, still more disastrous than the first. The drought, famine and cholera which followed in 1866 and 1867 finally overwhelmed Tunisia. In 1866 the government had to make heavy payments in various annuities and was practically deprived of resources. The bey, faced with bankruptcy, was finally forced to accept the tutelage of an International Financial Commission (5 July 1869). Thus there began the process of internationalization of the Tunisian Question.

This agreement established a sort of triple protectorate of France, Italy and Great Britain over the finances of Tunisia, with France predominating: a French inspector of finances sat on the executive Committee. But the defeat of 1871 forced France to adopt a cautious policy in Tunisia, and the Commission on the Debt finally contributed to halting the Italian efforts at penetration. For several years the superior influence of Great Britain ensured a virtual state of equilibrium at Tunis, the British consul even taking advantage of the circumstances to settle, with the agreement of Khayr al-Dīn, the problem of relations with the Porte: but the firman of 23 October 1871, which reaffirmed the Ottoman sovereignty at Tunis, was to remain a dead letter.

The few years of respite from diplomatic complications which Tunisia experienced after 1871 saw a final attempt to rehabilitate the country. On becoming prime minister in October 1873, Khayr al-Dīn attempted to apply successfully a realistic policy of internal improvements, more fruitful than ambitious but premature constitutional reforms, thus following the principles which he had enunciated in his work *Aqwam al masālik*, published in 1867. Khayr al-Dīn was able to re-establish financial stability, while paying Tunisia's debt. His intense legislative activity contributed greatly to the making of modern Tunisia: it covered the organization of the administration of the 'habous' (*ḥubus*, i.e. *waqf*), the reorganization of justice, the statute concerning share-cropping, the codification of the rules for the corporations, the organization of the teaching at the Zaytūna Mosque, and the foundation of the Ṣādiqiyya College (1875) with a syllabus which was both traditional and modern. Thanks to more favourable harvests, the economic situation improved and trade revived. The experiment, which seemed as if it would succeed, was, however, short-lived. Given less and less support by the powers, who rejected his project of mixed courts, and who were irritated by his resistance to their enterprises of economic penetration, and subjected to contradictory pressures over the Eastern crisis, Khayr al-Dīn was abandoned by the bey, and had to resign (1877).

Henceforward nothing could prevent Tunisia's becoming a protectorate. The decisive step was taken at the time of the Congress of Berlin

(1878) when Great Britain decided, in order to ensure its possession of Cyprus, to place no further obstacles in the way of France's ambitions in Tunisia. Having obtained Germany's support, France had only to overcome the opposition of Italy, and to await a favourable opportunity. In the years 1879 and 1880 there was carried on a bitter struggle between France and Italy, each attempting to develop its influence in Tunisia by means of concessions wrung from a powerless and corrupted Tunisian government. Since April 1880, however, French policy received little support by London, where Granville had replaced Salisbury as foreign secretary. It seemed to be at a standstill in Tunis.

Within a few weeks, however, the French government was to resolve the Tunisian Question to its advantage and according to the wishes of the Quai d'Orsay, the politicians and the business circles in France, where it was considered a matter of urgency to put an end to Italian 'obstruction'. An incursion into Algerian territory (30–31 March 1881) by mountain tribes, who habitually paid very little heed to frontiers, provided the necessary pretext. The president of the Council, Jules Ferry, requested from the Chamber of Deputies, and obtained on 4 April, sums for a punitive expedition to the frontiers, in collaboration with the Tunisian authorities. The operation took quite a different direction however. After three weeks of unopposed advance, the French troops arrived at the gates of Tunis, and the bey was made to sign the Convention of the Bardo (12 May 1881) which tacitly established a French protectorate in Tunisia.

CONCLUSION

Thus the three countries of the Maghrib were led, by different historical evolutions and at different moments in European expansion, towards the same end as colonies. The reasons for this are many: the inability of these states to adapt themselves to the modern world, the backwardness of the economy, stagnation in the social organization and the archaism of their political institutions, the lack of any national cohesion, except in the case of Tunisia, but above all the irresistible force of the European penetration, whether they attempted to canalize it as in Tunisia, or to repel it as in Morocco.

On the whole the destructive effects of the contact with Europe far outweighed any progress that resulted from its influence. In the economic sphere, the expansion achieved seemed in fact to make the local situation still worse. Improvements affected only the system of trade without changing the basic situation, i.e. the methods and means of production, the over-equipment of exploitation contrasting more and more with the under-equipment of production. On the other hand, economic colonization brought with it the alteration of the basic structures of the countries.

In the political sphere, the pressure exerted by the European powers was fundamentally ambiguous. They denounced the abuses and the archaisms of the local administration, and commended 'reform'; but at the same time they hid behind these abuses to obtain the continuance of privileges which prevented reform. Furthermore reform was itself an agent in the dissolution of the countries, and inevitably involved the downfall of precisely those traditional structures which attempts were being made to save. In fact, from a more general viewpoint, the question arises whether in the under-developed countries at the beginning of the twentieth century, 'reform' as it was then envisaged was really possible, and whether the alternative was not between a complete revolution which would have overthrown the whole of the political, economic and social structure, and a semi-protectorate imposing a limited reform.

Algeria had been conquered almost by accident in the first stages of European expansion. Half a century later neither Tunisia nor Morocco was in a position clearly to understand the terms of this dilemma, still less to solve it. Salvation could not come from within: the two countries could have escaped colonization only if the foreign pressures which weighed on them had neutralized each other, as happened in the case of Persia. In a North Africa which was dominated by the presence of France in Algeria, they had no alternative but to succumb.

CHAPTER 4

NORTH AFRICA IN THE PERIOD OF COLONIZATION

ALGERIA (1830–1962)

The occupation of Algiers (1830) led at first to the conquest of Algeria and then to that of the whole of the Maghrib by the French; the conquest was limited until 1834 to a few points on the coast but progressively extended towards the interior in spite of some spectacular reverses. The treaties which were concluded in 1834 and 1837 with the most representative chief of western and central Algeria, the *Amīr* ʻAbd al-Qādir, seem to have left the French freedom of action in the east. Thus they occupied Constantine in October 1837. The expedition of the Duc d'Orléans which linked Constantine to Algiers without any armed opposition, far from indicating the pacification of Algeria, as the French government maintained, was the beginning of a period of ruthless conflict. On the one side there was General Bugeaud, governor-general from the end of 1840, who obtained from the government men, supplies, credit, and above all complete freedom of movement; on the other, ʻAbd al-Qādir, whose authority was based on his personality, his readiness to use force to reduce opposition, his desire to create, in imitation of Muḥammad ʻAlī, if not an Algerian nation at least an Algerian state, and finally his good relations with Mawlāy ʻAbd al-Raḥmān of Morocco. The latter gave him substantial help until his defeat at Isly (1844). Bugeaud hounded ʻAbd al-Qādir and his partisans. Everywhere where the *amīr* could offer resistance, the general used the methods of total war; devastating the country, and massacring or carrying off women and children. In 1843 the *amīr* lost his own retinue, and was thus deprived of his mobile capital. In 1844 Moroccan help was withdrawn. He failed to gain the *beylik* of Constantine. ʻAbd al-Qādir surrendered to the French in 1847, and Bugeaud left Algeria in 1848. From 1852 to 1871 the war continued locally: in Kabylia (1852–64) and the region south of the Sahara (1864–70); in spite of some spectacular reverses French authority spread. The revolt of Muḥammad al-Ḥājj al-Muqrānī (1871) gave the French the opportunity to crush several hundred tribes belonging to Algiers, Constantine, and the south. The last uprisings took place in 1879 and 1880.

The effects of the conquest were twofold. In the first place the war produced destruction and losses in men and in money. The rural economy declined, as did that of the towns, which were totally or partially abandoned as soon as they were occupied by the French. The forced contributions, fines and taxes levied, added to the increase in the traditional taxes, deprived the Algerians of a large part of their financial reserves. But this was nothing beside the irreparable loss of human lives. The population of Algeria fell from about three million in 1830 to 2,600,000 in 1866 and 2,100,000 in 1872; to the losses of the war were added those caused by the destruction of food supplies, by epidemics of cholera or typhus in 1837, 1849–52, and 1866–70, and by famine.

In the second place, the armies were followed by colonization, which produced major changes in the economic life of the country. The European population increased from 3,228 in 1831 to 272,000 in 1870. The colonists settled at first in the towns, then were able to occupy increasing areas of land (they took over 481,000 hectares between 1830 and 1870 and 402,000 hectares between 1871 and 1880), because of the confiscations which resulted from the conquest. A body of legal measures and the policy of 'cantonment' (at first from 1846 to 1848, then from 1856 to 1860), allowed the demands of the concessionaries, whether individuals or companies, to be satisfied, and official or private colonization projects to be carried out. The first efforts met with some serious failures: first, because the concessionaries speculated in land instead of working to improve it; secondly, because the concessions were either too small or too large; thirdly, because the inexperienced colonists lacked basic resources and suffered from economic or climatic crises. Nevertheless, from 1855 their worst trials seem to have been over, and the number of births exceeded that of deaths; even the serious crisis of 1866–70 affected them relatively little. Among the immigrants the majority were Spanish and Italian until 1855, after which the number of French immigrants was greater. All of them lived mainly in the towns, which grew up at an astonishing rate along the coast.

Colonization upset the traditional economy. The price of food rose by an average of 200 to 300 per cent. Financial speculation and the thrusting of the Algerian economy, without protective tariffs, first into the French, and then into the international field of commerce, laid a heavy burden on the peasantry, who perhaps suffered from the hazards of their climate more severely than they had hitherto done. Thus, first in the period from 1845 to 1850 and again from 1866 to 1870, Algeria experienced serious price-rises and famines, which added their effects to those of epidemics. The underground reserves, which normally enabled the peasants to get through the years of drought, had been emptied when grain was fetching a high price (e.g. during the Crimean War), and particularly after the new commercial law of 1851 made it easier for goods to be exported from Algeria. In addition, the *Senatus Consultum* of 1863 broke the links of solidarity among the members of the tribes. Finally, the tribes which depended on the forests for wood, rights of pasturage and cultivated enclaves were, at the end of the Second Empire, partly driven out from these zones. Nor did colonization modify to any extent the agricultural techniques of the peasants or the implements which they used.

In the towns, the *madīnas* (native quarters) were disrupted, and the influx of European immigrants led firstly to increased rents, which resulted in inordinate building and speculation in property, producing an enormous housing crisis in 1848 in Algiers, in Blidah and in Bône. Secondly, it had the effect of changing the basic elements and the emphasis of urban commerce. Thirdly, it gave the Algerians the impression that their normal way of life in their towns was crumbling. Without the support of the *ḥubus*, the traditional centres of education, the *zāwiyas*, *madrasas* and *kuttābs*, were in jeopardy.

The conquest altered the administrative organization of Algeria from top to bottom, especially after 1834. 'The French administration acted exactly as if it believed that the population of Algeria consisted only of an agglomeration of individuals without any common link or any social organization'[1]. In 1833, a parliamentary commission recommended that Algeria should be retained; the royal ordinance of 22 July 1834 therefore announced the decision to entrust the administration of the possessions in North Africa to a governor-general, responsible to the minister of war. A new central administration was installed in Algiers, staffed partly by civilians but consisting chiefly of military personnel. These formed, after the creation of the Arab Bureaux in 1844, a solid administrative framework which included Arab dignitaries, and thus permitted vast territories to be controlled by only a small staff. These territories were divided into circles, the 'Arab territories', within which the tribes lived. The 'civil territories' were defined in 1845 as

[1] Pelissier de Reynaud, *Annales algériennes*, I, 74.

'those in which there exists a European population sufficiently numerous for all the public services to be, or to be capable of being, completely organized'. Finally the 'mixed territories' had a small European and a large Arab population. This demarcation was superimposed on the division of the country into three provinces, Algiers, Oran and Constantine, which in 1848 became three departments.

The brief revolutionary episode of 1848 was followed by the Second Empire. The French in Algeria did not cease to show their opposition to it, and they received support both in Paris and also even from the governors-general. They worked against the Arab Bureaux, and the military government of Algeria which restricted their ambitions and their appetites. Napoleon III and his 'Arabophile' entourage attempted to restrain the movement; but the cause of the colonists who advocated a civil régime was reinforced by the crisis of 1866–70, and by the liberalization of the régime in France. The civil régime triumphed in September 1870. The Empire, however, to a greater extent than the régimes which preceded it, had provided Algeria with the groundwork of a modern range of essential public services.

The Third Republic carried on this progress. The railways increased from 296 kilometres in 1870 to 3,337 kilometres in 1914. All the great French banks established branches in Algeria, and the Bank of Algeria became an issuing house, and above all a central organization and regulator of credit. The value of trade increased from 79 million francs in 1831 to 259 million gold francs in 1870, and reached 1,292 million gold francs in 1913, in spite of the crises of 1846–52, 1865–70, 1875–8 and 1888–95. Imports always exceeded exports, and the major part of Algerian trade was with France; at first because the commercial relations between Algeria and France were based increasingly on reciprocal and absolute freedom from duty, and later because French shipping enjoyed a monopoly. Cereals and livestock, which until 1870 formed the main items of export, were overtaken in 1913 by wine and its by-products, and by iron and phosphates. The chief imports were coal and consumer goods. This change is linked with the economic transformation which took place in Algeria between 1870 and 1914.

The working of the mines, which had begun under the Second Empire, continued actively, particularly in the Constantine area, and the value of mineral products, iron and phosphates in particular, increased from 4,586,000 gold francs in 1872 to 261 million gold francs in 1913. After

1875 the area of vineyards increased regularly. This appeared to be the ideal crop for the colonists; but the freedom with which credit was available, imprudent speculation, and an excessive planting of vineyards produced a serious crisis in Algerian agriculture after 1890. There were various consequences. The small proprietors of vineyards were ruined, and most of the large proprietors were in difficulties, but were on the whole better able to overcome them, and even to buy up abandoned land. The re-establishment of the vineyards demanded much capital and led to a concentration of property in too few hands. Some centres of colonization deteriorated in spite of the many inducements offered by the administration, which provided the country with a medical and public health service, freed the colonists from direct taxes, granted them credit facilities, and equipped the villages at the expense of the native sub-districts, which for this purpose were attached to the colonization centres.

From September 1870 onwards, the colonists had the administration in their power. They were thus able to impose a series of measures; which, in December 1870, gradually transferred all the military territories in which the Arabs lived into civil territory under their authority, and facilitated the sequestration and purchase in 1871, after the revolt of Muqrānī, of Arab personal and tribal holdings of land.

Between 1881 and 1900 the official colonization received from the administration 296,000 hectares. The European population grew considerably, from 272,000 in 1870 to 681,000 in 1911. It was larger in the towns than in the country, forming thirty-three per cent of the total population in 1872, and thirty-five per cent in 1906, and it was feared that still more settlers would abandon the country districts. The towns developed mainly along the coast, and, as they grew more and more enormous, they resembled the Mediterranean towns of European countries. The ratio of French to non-French inhabitants increased as a result of the law of 26 June 1889, which provided that foreign children born in Algeria were automatically naturalized. There arose a new type of person, the Algerian Frenchman, who was different both from the Europeans, whether French or non-French, and from the Algerians. Being French citizens, they were electors, and controlled the whole of the political and administrative life of the country, with the exception of a few high officials who came from France. Thus they were not concerned about French public opinion. The Europeans imposed and maintained the *indigénat*, a discriminatory legal system, which disregarded French common law, and surrounded the native Algerians with a network of restrictions, fines and prison sentences. These were often very severe, and were remitted only at the discretion of the administrative officials, who, in the mixed communes, exercised the powers of judges. This iron régime existed also in the assize courts and the criminal tribunals, where the French magistrates judged without pity, and the juries were entirely French.

Although they had suffered severely during the crisis of 1866–70 and the revolt of 1871, between 1881 and 1891 the Algerian population regained, and even exceeded, its former numbers; although certain observers thought that it would shortly disappear, in 1911 it numbered in fact 4,686,000. Although many Algerians returned to the towns, the majority lived in the country districts. Those in the towns, apart from a few merchants and artisans, formed a class of unskilled workers, which benefited from none of the French social laws. From 1870 to 1913 the peasants lost important areas of land in the north and in the high plains. They were forced back towards the south or towards the mountain regions, and fell into difficulties even more quickly than before. Their economic and social condition deteriorated; the small landowners became hired workers, who, in years of crisis, joined the vagabond army which was a source of anxiety to the colonists and the administration. The problem was all the more serious because the land-legislation from 1863 to 1887 had broken up the tribal system which enabled the poor to survive in times of hardship. The severe crisis which struck them at the end of the nineteenth century led to the sending of a parliamentary commission. Shortly afterwards the administration decided to create native provident societies to succour their members in times of crisis, and to assist them to improve their agricultural equipment (1893). In 1897 it also modified the law of 1887, applying it in a way which was less favourable to the colonists, and made the forest regulations less harsh.

Admiral de Gueydon, who arrived in the spring of 1871 and restored order after the colonists had set up the Commune of Algiers, was the first civilian governor-general. He controlled the whole of the administration of Algeria, which in the departments devolved upon the prefects, in the arrondissements upon the sub-prefects and in the communes upon the mayors. The native Algerians, who were French subjects, were governed in the mixed communes by administrators. From 1881 to 1896 the Algerian administrative services were attached directly to the appropriate ministries in Paris, and the Algerian government was no more than a 'decoration as expensive as it was useless, at the most an inspector of colonization in the palace of an idle king' (J. Ferry). There were delays in settling any matters, even when they were in the hands of the Algerian members of the French parliament, who had now become the real masters of Algeria. This administrative deficiency, added to the crisis in the Algerian economy, gave rise to violent anti-Jewish riots in the towns. Order was restored by the suppression of the attachments, the restoration to the governor-general of real authority over the whole country, the creation of the Financial Delegations representing various economic interests to vote the budget and above all the appointment of an energetic governor-general.

The colonists and the European civilians had imposed on the Algerians a humiliating political situation. They were French subjects, and contributed very substantially to the budget, but the colonists maintained that they were not fitted to occupy seats in the deliberative or consultative assemblies. The *indigénat* and the absence of resources denied the masses any other course than that of resignation, especially after the suppression of the revolts of the Aurès (1879) and of Bū 'Amāma (1880), the conquest of Tunisia, and the British occupation of Egypt. All that the Algerians obtained was the sending, in 1898, to the Financial Delegations of twenty-one delegates who were nominated by the administration (there were forty-eight European delegates) and completely under its power. But pilgrims returning from Mecca brought news from the Middle East of the exile of leaders like Shaykh Muḥammad 'Abduh, and echoes of the Salafiyya reform movement, or of the Young Turk Revolution of 1908. A number of historical or pseudo-historical works sought to 'make known to the descendants the history of their ancestors'. Between 1907 and 1912 political agitation grew; its causes being the project of applying in Algeria the separation of Church and state, compulsory military service, or simply the impression that a Muslim Algerian could no longer live in this country 'accursed by God'. Thus after some affrays in 1907, 1909 and 1911, scores of families fled from Tlemcen to reach Islamic soil, first in Morocco, and later in the Levant. In 1912 certain Algerian newspapers launched a press campaign in which they proposed that Algerians should be able to surrender their rights as French citizens, but without prejudice to personal status, in return for release from compulsory military service. These demands were supported by the Paris newspaper *Le Temps*, but opposed by the Europeans in Algeria.

In spite of promises, the political situations of the Algerians had scarcely changed by 1914.

From 1914 to 1962, Algeria, like the other countries of the Maghrib, and to an even greater extent, went through several phases of tension and of apparent relaxation. From 1914 to 1954, the European population increased, but less rapidly than it had previously done (in 1872–1911 it had increased by 472,000, in 1911–54 by 232,000) because of the losses of the two World Wars and the ageing of the population: in 1911, 435 per 1000 were less than nineteen years of age; in 1953, 350. The Europeans lived mainly in the towns, especially in the ports, which thus grew considerably; the urban population in 1906 was 446,000, and in 1954, 760,000. The creation of colonization centres became very rare, and the villages often lost their European inhabitants entirely; the proportion of non-French decreased still further, from thirty-eight per cent in 1901 to five per cent in 1954, although they occupied 2,700,000 hectares in 1951. The new type of colonist became hardened in a racialism which sometimes took violent forms against the native Algerians. The number of the latter rose spectacularly from 4,686,000 in 1911, to 6,201,000 in 1936, and 8,360,000 in 1954, in spite of the wars, the economic crisis and also the years of partial famine followed by deadly epidemics from 1921 to 1945. It was a very young population (in 1954, 525 per 1,000 were under nineteen years of age) and its rate of growth was high (28 per 1,000 in 1954). It too became increasingly urban, particularly after 1930, and thus formed shanty-towns which became larger and larger.

The Algerian economy suffered from the First World War with its mobilization of men, requisition of goods and property, rise in prices and inflation. The difficulties in obtaining supplies of coal, iron, steel, chemical products and food, resulting from bad sea communications and the difficulty in obtaining credit, weighed heavily on both the colonists and the peasants. 1917 was a year of serious crisis, and by November 1918 Algeria was threatened with economic disaster. From 1919 to 1929 the administration attempted to resume a policy of colonization. It launched vast enterprises (e.g. barrages), and encouraged the colonists to modernize their equipment. For the peasants these years were still difficult.

When the great world economic crisis struck the Maghrib, they suffered more than the colonists, for whom the crisis was mainly one of overproduction and the consequent collapse of prices. Having fallen into debt, the colonists found themselves in an impasse, and began to consider the most violent solutions. The administration attempted to solve the problem by obtaining an increase in credits and improving the quality of the products sold, but only the largest proprietors survived. For the Algerians, the crisis meant the collapse of prices, hence the diminution of resources and financial reserves; and the impossibility of weathering years when the harvest was inadequate. The crisis which forced the colonists, the mines and the various industries to reduce their labour-force meant unemployment for the day-labourers. Algerian workers employed in France returned to Algeria, where they became a liability, whereas they had previously sent back large sums of money. Among the few artisans there was also unemployment; thus every household knew the threat of famine. The administration sought a solution in a very inadequate increase in the credit made available, in measures against excessive interest (1936), and in a guaranteed price for wheat.

The recovery during the years 1936–9 was too short to enable Algeria to face the Second World War without danger. The country was forced to make a tremendous effort, and to send to France and to the Axis powers a large part of its food reserves. After November 1942 sea communications with Europe were broken, and the Allies had too many other tasks to be able to concentrate their attention on the Maghrib alone. These harsh years were characterized chiefly by colossal monetary inflation, general mobilization, and very low levels of agricultural and mining production: 1945 was a year of acute crisis and of epidemics. After 1945 industrial enterprises developed in the areas around the ports, in spite of the resistance of the French industrialists: thus the number of workers increased from about 30,000 in 1914 to 200,000 in 1954, to which should be added the 200,000 who worked in France. In 1954, the banks and almost the whole of the industrial and mining production were in the hands of the Europeans, as was sixty-five per cent of the agricultural production. In 1956 the discovery of petroleum and of gas in the Sahara strengthened the hold of the Europeans on the Algerian economy, in spite of the large-scale participation of the whole of Algeria in the petroleum industry.

The disparity between the growth of the population and that of resources led to an ever-increasing migration of Algerians to Europe, from 21,684 emigrants in 1920 to 148,700 in 1952, which was temporarily stopped only by the crisis and the wars. In an effort partially to solve this problem, the CFLN (*Comité français de libération nationale*) considered a long-term programme dealing with every field; later, in 1959, the Constantine Plan attempted to close this gap which was increasing with the years. In fact all that was achieved was an increase in education, which, from 1950, reduced illiteracy.

Politically, until 1954, the Europeans refused any concessions. They did not recognize the military and financial efforts of the Algerians in the First World War. They reduced as much as possible the already trifling concessions granted by the law of 4 February 1919. The Europeans formed a resolute barrier which intimidated the various French governments. Nevertheless Algerian opinion was influenced by several factors. Among these were external events, such as the struggle being carried on by ʿAbd al-Karīm in Morocco (1923–5), and the Muslim Congress of Jerusalem (1931). Communist, socialist and trade union propaganda was exerted both in Algeria and on the emigrant Algerian workers in France. There was a partial renaissance of Islam, thanks to the ʿ*ulamā*ʾ, who opened Qurʾanic schools from 1930, and were anxious to restore to the Algerians the sense of their glorious past. Certain French-educated and liberal Algerians who claimed equal political rights, had the support of some liberal French thinkers. Finally, Messali Hadj demanded the independence of Algeria, from the congress held in 1927 in Brussels by the League against Colonial Oppression.

The administration replied by demonstrating the submissiveness of its supporters, the marabouts and the notables, and attempted to suppress all hostile propaganda. From 1933 Algeria was in a ferment, with both Europeans and Algerians in agitation, and the demonstrations sometimes turned into bloody riots. The Regnier decree (March 1935) and an increase in the police forces did not stop the movement. The governor-general, Le Beau, who was charged with the task of re-establishing contact with the educated *élite* among the native Algerians, and who later had the support of the Blum government, encountered opposition from the majority of the Europeans, who admired the régimes of Mussolini, Hitler and Franco. In response to the demands of the Algerian Muslim Congress (June 1936) the Blum government adopted a certain number of liberal measures, and sought to improve the political situation of some Algerians. The Blum-Viollette project caused the violent expression of opinion among the Europeans. Strikes by mayors, violent press campaigns, riots and incidents involving bloodshed, and interventions in Paris paralysed the will of the government, so that when the war began in 1939 the situation had changed very little for the Algerians since 1919.

After the French defeat in 1940, the majority of the Europeans collaborated with, and admired, the Vichy régime. They applauded the very harsh treatment to which the Algerian Jews were subjected, thinking thus to gain the approval of the native Algerians, nearly all of whom remained very reserved. The Anglo-American landings of November 1942, and the new effort demanded of Algeria, resulted in a renewal of Algerian political demands in a message from the Muslims to the responsible authorities in December 1942, a manifesto of the Algerian people in March 1943, and an addition to the manifesto in June 1943. Without claiming independence, these various documents demanded 'the recognition of the political autonomy of Algeria as a sovereign nation', which went far beyond the views and the minor reforms conceded in 1943 and 1944 by the CFLN. The Algerians' disappointment was all the greater because Muslim public opinion had been rendered sensitive by the fall of France, by the principles of the Atlantic Charter, and by the propaganda emitted variously by the nationalist leaders Messali and Abbas, of the Communists and of the '*ulamā*', all of whom based their teaching on the right of the people to decide their own destiny—a right which was denied by the majority of the Europeans.

This refusal coincided with the departure of the CFLN from Algiers and the culmination of the economic crisis. In May 1945 there was a series of demonstrations which in some regions took a dangerous turn. The assassination of a number of Europeans was followed by bombing, skirmishes, the massacre of several thousands of Algerians, and the arrest and imprisonment of the Algerian leaders. After much discussion the Statute of Algeria was passed in 1947, but all its promises of political evolution were cynically overridden by the administration, by means of an almost universal rigging of elections from 1947 to 1954, to the great satisfaction of the Europeans. Having no means of expressing itself, a part of the Algerian opposition went underground from 1948. The OS (*Organisation spéciale*), which had arisen from the PPA (*Parti populaire algérien*), now the MTLD (*Mouvement pour le triomphe des libertés démocratiques*, led by Messali), attacked and plundered the post office of Oran (1949), and in 1952 organized the escape of the imprisoned nationalists, Ben Bella, Ait Ahmed and Khider. In 1954 it changed into the CRUA (*Comité révolutionnaire d'unité et d'action*) which on 1 November 1954 commenced open warfare.

The French government was then obliged to proceed from police operations to actual war. The 'fellaghas' (revolutionaries) could rely on an inexaustible supply of recruits, on the secret importation of arms from abroad, on the unremitting political and diplomatic action at the United Nations Organization and in the Arab League, of Morocco and Tunisia who were able to help them after 1956, on their intimate knowledge of the country, and on the sympathy (and later on the participation) of the Algerian population. There also worked in their favour the horror at the excesses committed by the French troops, which were publicized by the French and foreign press, and the racialism of the Europeans in Algeria, who refused to allow any political concessions. The latter hardened their position still further as the result of a series of murders; and imposed their intransigence, first on J. Soustelle and then on R. Lacoste, who had become their spokesmen within governments which grew progressively weaker and less and less capable of resisting the pressure of the military leaders. In spite of certain reforms, the rigorous dividing up of towns and country districts, and the transfer of hundreds of thousands of peasants into regroupment centres, the war continued and spread. The French military machine was too cumbersome for this incessant guerilla warfare. The FLN (*Front de libération nationale*) made the following statement of its war aims: 'National independence through (1) the restoration of the sovereign democratic and social State of Algeria within the framework of Islamic principles; (2) respect of all the fundamental liberties without distinction of race or creed'. It organized the action of the FLN and the ALN (*Armée de libération nationale*) at the Congress of Soummam (August 1956) and rallied those who were undecided to its cause. The arrest of some of its leaders in October 1956 did not stop the war, which was a ruthless opposition between the Europeans and the Algerians. The former had the strength, violence and energy of despair; partisans of *l'Algérie française*, they nevertheless accepted the bill (February 1958) which made Algeria an 'integral part of the French Republic'; helped by the army, they had no hesitation in rebelling against their government in order to impose their ideas on the French nation.

The Algerians were convinced that the just cause of independence, which had the support of world opinion, was that of all the Algerian Muslims, they therefore rejected all proposals of negotiation. Convinced that they alone were the legitimate rulers, they set up in Tunis in September 1958 the GPRA (*Gouvernement provisoire de la République Algérienne*), under the leadership of Ferhat Abbas, and formed relations with several states. In the face of the failure of the insurrection of the generals (April 1961), of France's anxiety to end the war in Algeria, and the strengthening of the authority and widening of the following of the GPRA and the FLN, the Europeans, with the help of certain parts of the army, launched, between 1961 and 1962, a campaign which was basically terrorism. Nevertheless the final negotiations were completed at Evian in March 1962, where a political and an economic agreement, signed by France and a delegation of the GPRA, gave Algeria its independence. These agreements were ratified by others concluded between the OAS and the GPRA (June 1962), and in July 1962 the GPRA was installed in Algiers.

TUNISIA (1881–1956)

In spite of the entry of French troops and the Convention of the Bardo (12 May 1881), the first French resident minister in Tunisia, Paul Cambon, realized the weakness of his position. He obtained from the French government a 'treaty establishing the Protectorate, guaranteeing the debt and suppressing the capitulations.'[1] This was the Convention of La Marsa, of 8 June 1883, signed by Cambon and the Bey 'Alī. This formula allowed 'the continuation of the bey's rule, everything being done in his name and on his responsibility',[2] and the evading of French parliamentary opposition. The ruler retained absolute power, chose his own ministers, and appointed members of the administrative services. The legislative acts and beylical decrees were not valid until his seal had been affixed. The bey chose his prime minister, his minister of the pen, but not his ministers for war, the navy and foreign affairs, who were French generals or admirals, or the resident-general. From the time of the Treaty of the Bardo, and still more from that of La Marsa, the bey reigned but did not rule: he had pledged himself 'in order to assist the French government in accomplishing its protectorate ... to carry out such administrative, judicial and financial reforms as the French government shall consider expedient' (Convention of La Marsa, article 1). In addition, the French government sent to Tunisia a resident minister, who became in 1885 the resident-general, and 'had under his authority all the administrative services concerning both the Europeans

[1] P. Cambon, *Correspondance 1870–1924* (Paris, 1940) T. 1: letter from Cambon to d'Estournelles de Constant, 11 June 1882.

[2] *Ibid.*, letter of 2 March 1882.

and the natives' (decree of 23 June 1885), and without whose endorsement the bey's decrees had no force. From 1883 there were created general administrative departments, and in 1883 there was created a General Secretariat, the holder of which soon came to occupy a very important place, and to fill the role of a minister of the interior and lieutenant to the prime minister, and above all to the resident general, for whom he deputized in the administrative field.

The local administration remained in the hands of the *qā'ids*, who had administrative, judicial and financial powers. They were chosen from old land-owning families, and were assisted by the shaykhs, the *khalīfas* created in 1889, and the *kāhiyas* created in 1912. Between 1881 and 1914 their number decreased. The controllers of civil affairs, first appointed in 1884, supervised the native administration in their district. The number of these controllers of civil affairs grew from three to nineteen. In Tunis itself, the equivalent of the *qā'id* was the *shaykh al-madīna*, but matters of municipal interest were dealt with by a consultative commission. From 1 January 1885 it became possible to appoint municipal councils in the principal districts. In 1892, the chamber of commerce which had been formed in 1885 was divided into two, one for the north and one for the south. The first Chamber of Agriculture, formed in 1892, and representing strictly French interests, was followed by four other such Chambers in 1895 and 1902. Thus the Consultative Conference, created in 1896 to advise on financial problems, had only French delegates.

The Convention of La Marsa ensured the settlement of the Tunisian debt and thus created a healthy financial situation. In 1891, the Tunisian budget, which until then had been in piastres, was drawn up in francs; it retained the taxes which had existed before the protectorate and added taxes and contributions imposed by the new administration, which was thus enabled to launch and support colonization. This, in the form of large societies, had begun before 1881 in some important areas; but until this time all the properties had been subject to Muslim law. Cambon declared that if the country wished to 'attract and retain capital, it is necessary to protect those who acquire land from their ignorance of the language, laws and customs of the country, and to shelter them from unforseen claims; in short to guarantee the facility and the security of the transactions made'. Hence the beylical decree of 1 August 1885 decided that there should be non-compulsory registration of land, and that of 23 May 1886 authorized the transfer of *ḥubus* property against the payment of a perpetual rent. In 1892 the colonists owned 402,000 hectares, and the non-French settlers 27,000. The further acquisition of land for colonization continued, assisted by legislation, in the following years. The Consultative Committee of Colonization, which was created in 1903, and later became the Colonization Commission, played a major economic and political role. In addition the efforts of the colonists were supported by tax concessions and the organization of mutual agricultural credit. By 1913, twenty-five banks were issuing each year short-term loans of more than 12 million gold francs. The societies and the large landowners who possessed most of the land possessed modern implements and equipment. In 1911, 4,088 landowners owned 853,000 hectares, devoted at first to cereals and later to olives, which became from 1892 a spectacularly successful crop in the Sahel and round Sfax.

From 19,000 in 1881 (11,200 Italians, 7,000 Anglo-Maltese, 708 French), the number of Europeans rose in 1911 to 143,000 (88,000 Italians, 46,000 French). The Italians benefited from the proximity of Italy, and the privilege granted by the agreements of 1896. There were few Europeans in the country districts, while the commune of Tunis alone had, in 1911, 69,500 inhabitants (17,800 French and 34,200 Italians). From 1881 France had provided Tunisia with roads, railways and ports, having always only the interests of the Europeans in mind. The discovery of phosphates in 1885, and the granting of the first concessions, encouraged prospecting among the Europeans. The production of phosphates increased from 70,000 metric tons in 1899 to two million metric tons in 1913, that of iron from 98,000 metric tons in 1908 to 590,000 metric tons in 1913, and 59,000 metric tons of lead were produced in 1913.

The customs system as modified in 1898 gave privileged treatment to French products, while avoiding any reduction in the receipts, and any disturbance of the usual commercial relations between Tunisia and purchaser countries. In addition, French shipping had a monopoly of the carrying trade. The volume of trade increased from 37·2 million gold francs in 1880 to 322·9 million in 1913; in the latter year France was Tunisia's chief customer.

European settlement met with very vigorous resistance from the Tunisians. In the field of colonization the opposition showed itself over the seizure of 'waste land' by the Beylical Decree of 1896, and the *ḥubus* property. The political opposition drew its membership from various sources: from Tunisians who had fled to, or were in contact with, the east, from intellectuals from the east who were staying temporarily in the Maghrib, such as Shaykh Muḥammad ʿAbduh in 1884–5 and 1903, and who spread information about the Salafiyya reform movement. There were those in Tunisia who wished to restore to the Tunisians the sense of their past. Others criticized French policy openly and vigorously. Some showed conservative tendencies, while others relied on French help for the development of their country. Most of them considered that the best hope for Tunisia's future lay in education. The improvement of education at the Ṣādiqiyya or Zaytūna schools, the spread of French education, the creation of the Khaldūniyya (1896), and the press all played their part in this development. The number of newspapers increased, particularly after 1904, added to those which came from France or abroad; among them was *Le Tunisien*, which had appeared in French in 1907, and in 1909 became *Al-Tūnisī*. At the North African Conference held in Paris in 1908, the Young Tunisians set out their criticisms and their programme.

In 1907 some Tunisian members were admitted to the Consultative Conference, which until then had consisted only of French. In 1910, it was divided into two sections, French and native Tunisian, and a Higher Government Council was formed with a predominantly French membership.

Public opinion, in Tunis particularly, had become so greatly aroused that in 1911 there occurred incidents involving bloodshed. The war between Italy and the Ottoman empire gave the Tunisians the opportunity to demonstrate actively their opposition to the Italians in particular and to the Europeans in general, and their sympathy with the Ottomans. In 1912 further incidents set the administration and the Tunisians against each other, resulting in a state of siege, arrests, and the imprisonment or the banishment of the Tunisian leaders. This unrest in the towns was followed by unrest in the country districts. The Tunisian peasants were driven from their land, though often not without resistance. They also suffered from the long period of depression (1888–1900) which affected Tunisian agriculture. Forced back into areas with an indifferent water supply, they suffered severely during years of drought. In the more fertile areas the rents of the land increased. Their agricultural techniques had scarcely changed. Finally, the peasants, plunged into the currents of French and international trade, were unable to stand up to the fluctuations of a capitalist economy for which they were not equipped. Obliged to settle in one place, and impoverished, they had abandoned their tents, so that they were no longer able to rely on the traditional help from the richer members of the tribes. The former small landowners sometimes became mere agricultural employees without any protection. In 1907 the administration organized native provident societies (later called Tunisian provident societies) to combat excessive interest and help the smaller peasants in times of crisis. In spite of these efforts, the situation of the Tunisian peasantry in 1914 was difficult.

The number of Europeans grew from 146,000 in 1911 to 255,000 in 1956 (180,000 French, 67,000 Italians). This increase in the number of French and decrease in the number of Italians was connected with the law of 20 December 1923, which made it easier to obtain French nationality, and with the defeat of Mussolini's Italy, which enabled the French authorities to denounce the agreements which had given the Italians a privileged position. Thereupon some of them returned to Italy. In 1911, 4,088 Europeans owned 853,000 hectares; in 1949–50, 3,079 European landowners possessed 756,000 hectares, the greater part of it in northern Tunisia. From 1920 to 1929, the Europeans enjoyed wide credit facilities which enabled them to equip themselves with machinery. The number of landowners decreased and production increased. The average harvest of soft and hard wheat from 1910 to 1914 was 320,000 quintals, while that from 1921 to 1925 was 752,000 quintals.

Mining production and commerce also increased between 1913 and 1930: phosphate from 2·044 million metric tons in 1913 to 3·326 in 1930; iron from 0·590 million metric tons in 1913 to 0·978 million metric tons in 1929. Commerce rose from 322·9 million gold francs in 1913 to 678·6 million gold francs in 1929. Trade was largely orientated towards France, especially after the law of 30 March 1928, which gave the latter the advantage of preferential treatment for her imports and of a semi-monopoly of sea transport.

In spite of war, the population of Tunisia seems to have increased. From 1921 to 1931 it increased by 277,575: in 1921 it was 1·938 million. The drift of population from the country to the towns and to the north tended to overcrowd the land and the towns there; after 1930, the north developed still more.

The political demands made by the Young Tunisians were repeated between 1914 and 1919. The reasons for this were the length of the war, the contribution in men and in money demanded from Tunisia by France, the resistance of the Ottoman empire, the German victories and

Islamic propaganda, and the Italian and French withdrawal in southern Tunisia and Libya. Remoter factors included the revolt of the *Sharīf* Ḥusayn of Mecca, the arguments concerning the promises which were said to have been made to him by Great Britain, and President Wilson's Fourteen Points. In 1919, the survivors of the Young Tunisians made further representations to the powers and to France in order to produce a new equilibrium based on the re-establishment of the Constitution ('Destour', i.e. *Dustūr*) of 1861. They founded in 1919 a new party, *al-Ḥizb al-Ḥurr al-Dustūrī al-Tūnisī* (the Destour party), among whose members was 'Abd al-'Azīz al-Tha'libī. *La Tunisie martyre,* ascribed to him,[1] denounced with some exaggeration the evils in Tunisia since 1881, and presented a programme which would transfer the political preponderance to the bey and the Tunisians, within the constitutional framework of a liberal democracy, and would then limit or halt the progress of colonization. The new resident, L. Saint, was faced with the demands of the Destour, supported by the bey; he was a man of liberal ideals, and met with opposition and mistrust from the French in Tunisia. After the failure of the discussions, Saint took measures against the Destour, and intimidated and isolated the bey. While determined to maintain French authority, he introduced certain administrative reforms in 1922. The reforms were accepted by the bey and the reformers, and refused by the Destour. This party had dwindled through the departure of Tha'libī, and the prosecution and imprisonment of its leaders. An attempt to revive political action under cover of trade union action in 1924 failed. The Tunisian opposition appeared to be annihilated for a long time.

The crisis of 1929 was the beginning of a long period of difficulties for Tunisia. The prices of agricultural products fell, in spite of the devaluation of the franc in 1928. The colonists, indebted by their earlier purchases, asked the administration to protect them, which it partly did, through advances on crops, credit facilities, and temporary suspension of the sale of estates. The vine-growing areas decreased from 51,000 hectares in 1934 to 27,000 in 1948, because from 1936 the vines were attacked by phylloxera, and had to be uprooted. Thus colonization suffered setbacks from the crisis and the Second World War, and the ownership of land became concentrated in the hands of a small number of colonists.

[1] A careful reading of *La Tunisie martyre* leads one to believe that, in spite of the generally held opinion, al-Tha'libī is not its author.

The crisis and the Second World War also affected the production of the mines, which did not recover until after 1946. In order to reduce competition between Tunisian, Algerian and Moroccan phosphate production, a depot was set up in 1933 with the task of dividing sales among the three countries. Tunisian trade declined between 1929 and 1947. The balance of trade continued to show a deficit. The chief exports were agricultural and mining products (four-fifths of the total value), and the chief imports manufactured goods, fuel and clothes. Tunisia's principal customer was still France. Industrial and commercial enterprises were almost entirely in French hands; a number of Italian banks which between the wars had attempted some projects were eliminated, to the profit of the French banks.

During the Second World War, inflation, the increases in prices, and the difficulties in obtaining food, accelerated the drift from the land by those Tunisians who had the least resources. The rural population fell from eighty-three per cent in 1931 to seventy-one per cent in 1946, whereas the total population increased from 2,086,000 to 3,441,000. It was a young population, 500 per 1,000 being under nineteen years of age. Tunis grew from 106,800 in 1926 to 272,000 in 1956, and became surrounded by shanty-towns, inhabited by people from the countryside, who had no special skills, and were either partially or completely unemployed.

Nevertheless the majority of Tunisians still lived in the country districts, using traditional methods of cultivation. They produced cereals north of the Dorsal, oil in the Sahel, raised animals in the centre and the south, or grew citrus fruit or market-garden crops on Cape Bon, in the outskirts of the towns, and in the oases. The number of wage-earners increased and the old types of contract-relationship tended to decline. Agricultural workers were driven from the land by mechanization, and suffered more than others the harsh effects of crises or wars.

In the towns the artisans, faced with competition from European products and with the economic crises, were forced to close their shops, the corporations were in jeopardy, and a whole urban society was disintegrating in the same way as the rural society.

The crisis and the Second World War refashioned the political scene in Tunisia, especially as the Ṣādiqiyya College, the Zaytūna and the French educational establishments received many pupils, and as the French trade unions and left-wing parties—both in France and in Tunisia—supported the Tunisians in their claims. The latter, profoundly shocked by the Eucharistic Congress at Carthage (1930), paid much attention to movements in the Islamic world and to newspapers such as *La Voix du Tunisien* and *L'Action Tunisienne*. A group of newcomers, led by a young lawyer Ḥabīb Bourguiba (Bū Ruqayba), formed a new party in 1934, *al-Ḥizb al-Dustūrī al-Jadīd* (the Neo-Destour party) and presented new objectives. These were:

> The independence of Tunisia, completed by a treaty of friendship and unity with the great French Republic and guaranteeing to France the safeguarding of the interests of the foreign colony; to turn the French protection into a spontaneous alliance between two free peoples, free from any idea of preponderance or of domination, which should not exist with the great unity of interests of these two peoples, to influence the mass of the Tunisian people.

Peyrouton, the new resident-general, had Bourguiba and his friends put under house-arrest along with a number of militant communists and suppressed the opposition press. His successor, A. Guillon, and the government of the Front Populaire were anxious to inaugurate a new policy, and some liberal measures led to a lessening of tension; but both P. Vienot, who was responsible for Tunisian affairs in the Blum government, and Guillon stated that there was 'no question of France's abandoning her rights as a protecting power'. Furthermore the violent hostility of the colonists to all liberal measures, and the will of the Neo-Destour party, the influence of which was spreading and which sought a further advance, ended in an impasse which resulted in strikes and bloodshed in 1937 and 1938. At Tunis, faced with a gathering, which, when a shot was fired, turned into a riot, the resident announced a state of siege, and it seemed that the arrests and condemnations which followed must hinder any action by the Neo-Destour.

The fall of France in 1940, the accession of the Bey Moncef (Muḥammad al-Munṣif) in 1942, the occupation by German and Italian forces, and the liberation by the Allied armies started up political action again. No sooner was Bourguiba freed than he invited the Tunisians to forget the struggles of the past and to join Fighting France, in spite of the deposition of the bey, who was considered too independent, in May 1945. From 1943 to 1956 the French authorities alternated between reforms and repression, while the Neo-Destour and its supporting organizations continued to seek the independence of Tunisia. The reforms did not prevent the Bey Lamine (Muḥammad al-Amīn) in 1949 from demanding officially 'the introduction of substantial and necessary reforms such as to satisfy the aspirations of all the inhabitants of our kingdom'. The new resident, Perillier, was, in June 1950, 'charged to understand Tunisia, and to lead it towards the full development of its resources and towards independence, which is the final objective for all the territories within the French Union'. At the same time the action of the Neo-Destour spread, through the cells which it had established in the towns and in the country, and also its action at the Arab League and the United Nations.

Strikes and violent clashes clearly illustrated that the local French authorities were willing to yield nothing. The bey might announce in May 1951 'the reorganization of the executive and its method of establishment on the basis of a representation of our people in elected bodies', but the resident and his auxiliaries, supported by the French ministries and the French in Tunisia, refused to yield. On the contrary, the latter aimed at participating equally with the Tunisians in the functioning of the political institutions of the country. The conflict reached its most dramatic phase with the arrival of the new resident, Hautecloque, when there took place police raids, arrests, and summary executions which went unpunished. The strikes and demonstrations, the exile of Bourguiba and the Neo-Destour leaders, the hostility of the bey, who refused to sign the decrees proposed by Hautecloque, the boycott of the municipal elections and armed resistance all showed that the way chosen by the French could not succeed.

The departure of Hautecloque, and the decision of the government under Mendès-France to recognize unconditionally 'the internal autonomy of the Tunisian state', and hence 'internal sovereignty', made discussion easier. The personal action of Bourguiba, and the anxiety of both sides to come to an agreement gave internal autonomy a concrete meaning. On his return to Tunisia in June 1955, Bourguiba announced that this constituted 'an important stage on the way to independence'. Ṣalāḥ b. Yūsuf, who was hostile to Bourguiba and excluded from the party, attempted to launch a movement of armed resistance. This was crushed, and he fled to Cairo. The independence granted to Morocco led Bourguiba to demand the same for Tunisia, and it was conceded on 20 March 1956.

MOROCCO (1912–56)

The Treaty of Fez which was signed between France and the sultan, Mawlāy 'Abd al-Ḥāfiẓ, (1912) permitted France to act officially in the latter's name. Henceforth all Morocco's dealings with other powers were transacted through the French government, which delegated its powers to the resident-general, General Lyautey, who insisted that the ruler should retain all the appearances of power; this was the protectorate in its true sense. Nevertheless, the country was very far from accepting the treaty of Fez, and resisted it vigorously, the more so as Mawlāy 'Abd al-Ḥāfiẓ encouraged this resistance. Lyautey acted quickly: he replaced him by Mawlāy Yūsuf, who was more amenable, in August 1912. This change did not put a stop to the fighting. At the beginning of the First World War the mountain districts were still unsubdued. In order to prevent the recently subdued areas from joining the revolt, Lyautey directed all his military efforts towards the mountain regions. In addition, he applied a policy of carrying out major works, such as would impress foreigners and Moroccans. He thus on the one hand demonstrated France's intention of remaining in Morocco, and on the other maintained bases from which to effect later the submission of the rest of the country. When the war was over, the conquest was continued, and at the same time the administration was organized. The Middle Atlas and the Rif formed the two barriers of resistance led by Abd el Krim ('Abd al-Karīm). After having defeated the Spaniards, the latter was directly threatening Fez and Taza, but he was defeated by a great combined Franco-Spanish military effort (1925), and some years later (1934) further operations suppressed the last pockets of resistance in the High Atlas.

From the first, Lyautey had stated that 'the protectorate must be considered as a permanent régime'. He thus retained the traditional administration (*Makhzan*) with the sultan at its head; but a certain number of services copied from the French model had a controlling function. Some of them with time acquired a dominating political role, others an economic one. At their head, the resident-general was

> the trustee of all the powers of the Republic in the Sharifian Empire; he is the sole intermediary between the sultan and the representatives of foreign powers; he approves and promulgates in the name of the government of the Republic the decrees issued by His Sharifian Majesty; he controls all the administrative services; he has the high command of the army and the disposal of the naval forces (Decree of 11 June 1912, art. 2).

Until 1925 it was Lyautey who impressed on all the administration his very personal style, composed of dynamic efficiency and theatrical ostentation; careful not to repeat the mistakes which had been made in the past, he was anxious to produce an exemplary achievement which would make Morocco the symbol of a successful colony.

This administrative framework did not change greatly. The resident was assisted by a deputy minister at the Residency and by a secretary-general; his acts had no force until sealed by the sultan as 'dahirs' (i.e. *ẓāhirs*), though conversely the dahirs had no effect until the resident had countersigned them. Not until the end of the protectorate was there a disagreement between the sultan and the resident about reforms proposed by the latter. At the local level, the French officials exercised a close control over the Sharifian administration proper, and gave it the necessary impetus and guidance. In practice it was on them that the application of the protectorate rested, and they had all the necessary powers. The country was divided into regions, territories, circles and annexes. The dahir of 8 April 1917 created municipalities in certain towns, but both the French and Moroccan members were appointed by the residency, and merely offered advice. Fez and Casablanca had special régimes of their own. In the tribes, the dahir of 21 November 1916 set up the *Jamāʿa*, presided over by the *qāʾids*, and that of 27 April 1919 placed the Moroccan communities under control. The *qāʾids* were the agents of the central power: as judges and tax-collectors, and not very well paid, they were open to corruption. In the towns the place of the *qāʾids* was filled by the pashas.

Lyautey set up advisory chambers of commerce, of industry and of agriculture whose members were at first only French, but later Moroccans also. He also formed a higher agricultural council, then another of commerce and industry. Later he introduced into the governmental council representatives of the colonists, then of the Moroccans, and finally of the French inhabitants who were engaged in neither agriculture nor industry: these representatives of economic interests gave their opinions on the resident's financial projects.

Foreigners had not waited until the Treaty of Fez to gain an economic foothold in Morocco. In 1880 the Convention of Madrid recognized their rights of ownership within certain limits. The Convention of Algeciras increased these facilities, especially in the ports and in some of the towns and their immediate surroundings. In 1913, the Europeans owned more than 100,000 hectares. Between 1913 and 1915, measures introduced the optional registration of land, as a result of which several hundred thousand hectares were transferred to the possession of the French, even though the Moroccans registered vast areas. In spite of the dahir of July 1914, which declared collective tribal land to be inalienable, another of April 1919 allowed the tribes to sell to the state, if land was required for public utilities, or in order to create colonization areas. In 1916 a Colonization Committee was commissioned to distribute the rural estates. In spite of the 1914–18 War and the Rif War, private and official colonization throve. At the end of 1927, 2,044 European colonists, 1,847 of them French, were cultivating 650,000 hectares. Their numbers were few, they were well organized, and enjoyed various advantages: help from the administration, agricultural co-operation, agricultural mutual insurance banks, and above all credit arrangements, to enable them to equip and improve the land. At the same time the phosphate deposits were worked by the Sharifian Office of Phosphates: 8,200 metric tons in 1921, increasing to 1,850,000 metric tons in 1930. From the beginning of the protectorate, and even during the First World War, the French administration provided the country with a network of roads, railways and with a transport system. Casablanca thus arose from nothing. Sheltered by the Convention of Algeciras and by the protectorate, foreign enterprises developed and flourished. The number of Europeans increased from 11,000 in 1911 to 104,700 in 1926; they lived chiefly in the rapidly growing towns.

The Rif War, and above all the crisis of 1929, slowed down colonization and the development of the country. In 1935 private colonization occupied an area of 569,000 hectares divided into 1,754 estates. The area of vineyards increased after 1927 but did not exceed a few thousand hectares. Administrative aid, a more judicious choice of crops (market-garden crops and citrus fruits), an improvement in the trade channels, and the opening of the European markets, facilitated a recovery in 1936, later interrupted by the Second World War. The production of phosphates also decreased between 1930 and 1933, and did not regain its former level until 1945. The exploitation of non-ferrous metals and of iron began immediately before the Second World War, which interrupted it almost completely. The war also resulted in the influx of large numbers of Europeans (who increased from 191,000 in 1936 to 295,000 in 1947), and a spectacular rise in prices.

The Europeans increasingly ignored the country areas inhabited by the Moroccans. These, who numbered perhaps five million between 1912 and 1926, increased by 1947 to more than eight million, including the Jews, who increased from 161,000 in 1936 to 200,000 in 1947, and who lived mainly in the towns. Colonization restricted the area available to some of the tribes, and caused them to become wholly or partially sedentary: it certainly reduced the pasturage in the Atlantic regions, leading to a reduction in the size of the herds. The herds of the nomads in the south or in the steppes also decreased, as their movements from place to place were more strictly controlled. Finally, the traditional methods of transport had to compete with the motor. The agricultural techniques had scarcely changed, nevertheless there was a reduction in the area of unploughed land. To the traditional cereals (hard wheat and barley) were gradually added soft wheat, oats and maize; peas and crops grown for fodder or for industry alternated with beans; forestry and market-gardening spread; but these changes affected only a minority of medium or wealthy landowners.

In spite of the Moroccan provident societies which were formed in 1917 to help the peasants and to protect them from excessive interest-rates, the majority of them lacked means. When difficulties arose, such as the 1930 crisis, the bad harvests of 1945, the inflation of money and the rise in prices between 1940 and 1945, the small farmers sold their land, left it and went to the towns. The old family estates and the rural land owned in common broke up, and gave place to the employment of paid day labourers. The new arrivals, often from the south, filled the native quarters, and overflowed into shanty-towns, which grew up in a disorderly and unplanned fashion. In this way Casablanca spread to enormous proportions: from 20,000 inhabitants in 1900 to 320,000 in 1947. The artisan classes were unable to compete with imported products, and, lacking financial means, were in danger of bankruptcy. Only those with the best resources survived, among them the merchants who were able to force a way into the new channels of trade. Former artisans, unskilled workers, and former peasants who had emigrated to the towns made up the lower proletariat of the new Moroccan industry, which was mainly manufacturing. It was not an organized proletariat, for its members were forbidden to join the French trade unions. The inhabitants of both town and country had to pay increased taxes, linked with the service of debts incurred before the treaty of Fez, with the formation of a more complicated system of administration superimposed upon the *Makhzan*, and with the devaluations of the French franc. The farmers were not able, with the techniques at their disposal, to face the changes in the situation, which were particularly great between 1912 and 1956. Trade appeared to increase: from 221 million gold francs in 1913 to 344 million gold francs in 1947; but the town and country dwellers used more and more imported products, and most of these came from France.

On the death of Mawlāy Yūsuf he was succeeded by Sīdī Muḥammad b. Yūsuf (1927), whose reign saw the beginning and growth of Moroccan political claims. The Berber Dahir of May 1930 aroused Moroccan and Islamic opinion, for it brought under French jurisdiction 'the repression of crimes committed in Berber territory, whatever the status of the person who commits the crime'. It appeared to break the legal unity of the kingdom, and it coincided with other French acts—in Algeria the ostentatious celebration of the centenary of the French occupation, and in Tunisia the Eucharistic Congress at Carthage. The Moroccans saw it as a more or less open attack on Arabism and Islam. The protest took various forms, and drew its forces from the middle-class and the *'ulamā'* of the Qarāwiyyīn mosque. It was manifested at the first royal celebration in 1933, and during the sultan's visit to Fez.

In 1934, the opposition, grouped into the *Comité d'Action Marocaine*, presented to Paris and to Rabat a plan of reform which advocated a number of reforms in administration, justice and education, and presented an economic and social programme. It had the support of certain elements of the French left-wing, but was rejected by the Residency and the French in Morocco. After 1936 (Blum's government being in power), the nationalist leaders extended their action widely throughout the country and carried on negotiations with Vienot, the member of the Blum government in charge of Moroccan affairs. In the spring of 1937 there was a hardening of the French attitude, and the *Comité d'Action Marocaine* split into the Nationalist party and the Popular Movement. Fever was mounting in the country; agitators resorted to violence in the autumn of 1937, and the nationalist leaders, 'Allāl al-Fāsī and al-Wazzānī were arrested and deported. But Franco's victory in Spain and the French defeat in 1940, made Spanish Morocco into a centre of intensive Nazi propaganda and of nationalism until the Anglo-American landings of November 1942.

After 1940 official colonization made little progress, while private colonization continued to increase. The greater part of it was situated in the neighbourhoods of Fez, Meknes, Rabat, Casablanca and the majority of the properties consisted of more than 300 hectares. The colonists concentrated on cereals for export, vines, citrus fruits and vegetables, and their farms were highly mechanized. The influx of foreign capital, the experience of the war-years, and the desire to provide

North Africa with an industrial framework independent of Europe resulted in mining and industrial enterprises, which employed many Moroccan workers controlled by a few European specialists. In spite of its being officially forbidden, the Moroccans joined the French trade unions, and in 1946 the General Union of the Confederated Trade Unions of Morocco was formed with two secretaries—one Moroccan and one French, the latter disappearing in 1951. Removed from their family or tribal background, the workers crowded together in the shanty-towns on the outskirts of the great cities, whence they took part in political and social action.

The Second World War resulted in many difficulties for the peasantry: rises in prices, bad harvests, with famine in 1945, and epidemics. The construction of barrages and the creation of the districts of peasant modernization affected only a very small number. The improvements brought by the Moroccan provident societies could not prevent the land from being increasingly overcrowded by a growing population, and the consequent migration of peasants to the towns.

At the time of the Allied landings, the sultan refused to follow the resident to the interior, and this first gesture of independence was followed by his interview with President Roosevelt who was passing through Morocco in January 1943. Encouraged by this attitude, and realizing that the position was changing, the nationalists led by al-Fāsī and the Popular Movement led by al-Wazzānī united, forming the Istiqlāl party. On 11 January 1944 they presented to the sultan, the resident and the Allies the manifesto of the Istiqlāl party, demanding Moroccan independence and democratic government. Later they stated that they had 'absolutely no intention of realizing their ideal by the use of violence'. The French Committee of National Liberation (CFLN) refused to consider Moroccan independence; it merely granted some minor reforms and, perhaps by means of a conspiracy, deprived the nationalist movement of its leaders. There then began a trial of strength, with street demonstrations and strikes, which were sometimes violent, between, on the one hand the nationalists supported by the Moroccan population and the sultan, and, on the other, the French government and the Residency with the support of a few important Moroccans and the Europeans, who were opposed to any real concession. This state of affairs continued until 1956. By means of its cells planted throughout the country, its action outside Morocco in France, at the United Nations and the Arab League, it support from the Spanish zone, and its unceasing propaganda, the Istiqlāl convinced its audience. The resident attempted to introduce some basic reforms, but they were not welcomed by the French, and did not prevent the sultan from refusing to render homage to France (April 1947). The latent crisis became worse when the sultan, on a visit to France, tried in October 1950 to negotiate with the French government over the head of the resident, Juin, and refused to sign some proposed dahirs. Juin's policy was to ignore the nationalists, excluding them from the assemblies, and threatening to depose the sultan (1950–51). He and his successor, Guillaume, acting independently of Paris, left the field free for a police force and an administration which were favourable to French extremists. The violent strikes of 1952 created an atmosphere of tension, and in August 1953, in the absence of a government, Guillaume took it upon himself to depose the sultan, who was much too intractable. The arrest of the key members of the Istiqlāl, the installation of a new sultan, Muḥammad b. 'Arafa, the departure of Guillaume, and the coming to power of the administration of Mendès-France did not put an end to the struggle, which was carried on from Spanish Morocco, from Algeria and from the secret organization of the resistance, under the guidance of the trade unions and a provisional executive committee of the Istiqlāl. Acts of terrorism continued in the towns, French products were boycotted, and there was activity within the tribes. Between 1953 and 1955 there was built up a Liberation Army which went into action in the autumn of 1955. Further violent action, in the summer of 1955, hastened the solution of the crisis. Negotiations began at Aix-les-Bains. The sultan was recalled from exile in October 1955, to serve as a mediator between the nationalists and the French government. Muḥammad V received a triumphant welcome to Morocco and appointed a government which, on 2 March 1956, procured the independence of Morocco.

CHAPTER 5

THE NILOTIC SUDAN

THE COMING OF THE ARABS

The central axis of the eastern *Bilād al-Sūdān* is constituted by the River Nile. In the north, this is a single stream from the confluence of the Blue and White Niles by the modern town of Khartoum (*al-Kharṭūm*) to the First Cataract above Aswān. Except in certain districts, where rocky cliffs close in on the river, the main Nile is fringed by a narrow strip of irrigable land, which supports numerous villages and a few small towns. The riverain settled area, as far south as the Sabalūqa Cataract, a few miles below the confluence of the Niles, is the historic Nubia (*Bilād al-Nūba*), the seat of the most ancient civilization in what is now Sudanese territory. To its south, around the confluence, on the banks of the Blue and White Niles, and in the peninsula (*al-Jazīra*, the Gezira) lying between them, is another area of settlement, where the greater annual rainfall makes more extensive cultivation possible. In this region, known to the medieval Arabic writers as 'Alwa, the only ancient urban site lay at Sūba, on the Blue Nile, not far from Khartoum. East and west of the main Nile, the sandy deserts of the north merge imperceptibly into seasonal grasslands further south. This is herdsman's country, and a Hamitic-speaking group of nomad tribes, the Beja (*al-Buja*) have occupied the eastern desert from time immemorial. Their territory (*Bilād al-Buja*) covers the rolling plains, which rise to the arid escarpment of the Red Sea Hills. Below, in the sultry and uninviting coastal plain, are scattered harbours, around four of which in succession, Bādi', 'Aydhāb, Suakin (Sawākin) and Port Sudan, substantial towns have grown up.

The Nubian corridor has, throughout history, been a mingling-place of peoples, but since pharaonic times its culture has been strongly tinctured by the successive phases of civilization in Egypt. At the time of the Muslim conquest of Egypt, Nubia had, within the previous century, been converted to Christianity by missionaries from Egypt. South of Nubia proper, the kingdom of Alodia (i.e. 'Alwa) had also accepted Christianity. In view of the recent introduction of Christianity, however, one may query whether it had struck very deep roots among the mass of the people. The nomadic Beja remained pagan, except in fringe districts adjoining Nubia or the Red Sea coast, where they were accessible to Christian influences.

The Christian kingdom of Nubia, known to the medieval Arabic writers as al-Muqurra, at first opposed effective resistance to the Muslim Arab conquerors of Egypt on far from unequal terms. The first clashes seem to have been little more than border-raids. A more serious expedition, commanded by the governor of Egypt, ʿAbd Allāh b. Saʿd b. Abī Sarḥ, invaded Nubia and besieged the capital, Dunqula (i.e. Old Dongola). He was unable to win a decisive victory, and withdrew, apparently after concluding an armistice. A Fatimid source gives the text of a treaty alleged to have been concluded between ʿAbd Allāh and the king of Nubia, by which, *inter alia,* the Nubians undertook to pay an annual tribute of 360 slaves to the Muslims. The treaty, almost certainly legendary, represents an attempt to retroject conventions of Muslim-Nubian relations which had developed by the fourth/tenth century. Other evidence indicates that the supply of slaves was an element in the reciprocal trade of Nubia and Egypt.

It is possible, but unlikely, that ʿAbd Allāh b. Saʿd had at first intended to conquer Nubia. His experience, the long and exposed lines of communications, and the difficulties of the terrain, served to discourage any further attempts for centuries.[1] In 568/1172, Tūrān Shāh, the brother of Saladin, led an expedition into Lower Nubia for combined punitive and reconnaissance purposes, but achieved no lasting conquest. Under the Mamluk sultans several further expeditions were made, but although these succeeded in weakening the Nubian kingdom, they did not result in the annexation of Nubia to Egypt.

The submergence of Christian Nubia was really due to the steady pressure of Arab tribes from Upper Egypt. By the middle of the third/ninth century, a frontier society had come into existence east of the First Cataract, composed of Arabs from the tribes of Rabīʿa and Juhayna, who had escaped from the pressure of government, and sought wealth in the gold-mines of the northern Beja territory. Intermarriage with both Beja and Nubians ensued. During the early fifth/eleventh century an arabized and islamized Nubian principality was formed south of the First Cataract. Its princes bore the title of *Kanz al-Dawla*, first conferred by the Fatimid Caliph, al-Ḥākim, in 396/1006, whence they are known as the

[1] It has been suggested (in a private communication) that the Arabs may have found it more convenient to leave Nubia outside the Muslim empire, as a source of slaves and especially eunuchs, since enslavement and mutilation within the frontier were forbidden.

Banū Kanz. The Mamluk expeditions enabled the Banū Kanz to extend their power upstream in the early eighth/fourteenth century, and in the subsequent dark age the Nubian kingdom foundered. A brief reference by Ibn Khaldūn (d. 808/1400) indicates that Nubia had been fragmented into petty states, which suffered the incursions of Juhayna. The ruling dynasties intermarried with the Arabs, to whom authority passed by female succession.

Present-day tribal genealogies show the majority of the Arabic-speaking Sudanese as coming from one or other of two lines of descent. The nomads claim to be Juhayna, while most of the settled clans of the main Nile are regarded as descendants of a certain Jaʿal, who is, furthermore, stated to have been an ʿAbbasid. Disregarding this assertion (a typical genealogical sophistication), we may reasonably see in these Jaʿaliyyūn the descendants of the arabized Nubians of the late Middle Ages. Other groups and tribes claiming to be Jaʿaliyyūn (or ʿAbbasids) bear witness to a diaspora, which can be traced in recent centuries, but which may well have commenced before the arabization of Nubia.

The fate of ʿAlwa is even more obscure than that of Nubia. It was still flourishing in the early seventh/thirteenth century, while a modern Sudanese tradition dates the fall of Sūba, and final subversion of the kingdom, to 910/1504–5. This rests, however, on a false synchronism with the establishment of the Funj capital at Sennar (Sinnār), and Sūba may have fallen at an earlier date. Traditional sources further describe the capture of Sūba by an Arab tribal host under a chief named ʿAbd Allāh Jammāʿ, and the flight and dispersion of its inhabitants. The descendants of ʿAbd Allāh Jammāʿ, the ʿAbdallāb, exercised a hegemony over the nomads who occupied the region around the confluence and the northern Gezira, as well as over the arabized Nubians living north of the Sabalūqa Cataract. Their own residence was on the main Nile.

THE FUNJ SULTANATE

The fall of Sūba represents the final break-through of the nomad Arabs into the grasslands of the Nilotic Sudan. By a curious and fateful coincidence, their southern expansion synchronized with a migration northwards, down the Blue Nile, of cattle-nomads who were neither Arabs nor, at first, Muslims. These people, the Funj, first appear on the Upper Blue Nile at the beginning of the tenth/sixteenth century. Their remoter origins, which are obscure, have given rise to luxuriant speculation. Sennar, which became their dynastic capital, is traditionally stated, with curious precision, to have been founded in 910/1504–5. A nineteenth-century recension of a Sudanese chronicle asserts that the Funj chief, 'Amāra Dūnqas, allied with 'Abd Allāh Jammā' to overthrow Sūba, but the alliance, if it existed, was precarious. A tradition (related by James Bruce) speaks of a battle between the Funj and the 'Abdallāb near Arbajī in the Gezira. Since Arbajī seems to have been the most southerly Arab settlement at that time, the tradition implies a conflict between two groups of nomads for the grazing of the central Gezira. That the immediate victory fell to the Funj is clear from the resulting situation, since the 'Abdallābī chief, although autonomous, was vassal to the Funj king, and bore the non-Arab title of *mānjil* or *mānjilak*.

Lower Nubia, between the First and Third Cataracts, lay outside the area under the Funj-'Abdallābī hegemony. About the middle of the tenth/sixteenth century, this region was annexed to Ottoman Egypt by Özdemir Pasha, a Circassian Mamluk in the service of Sultan Süleymān. It was constituted as a *kashiflik* under the name of Berberistān (i.e. the land of the Berberines), and garrisons of Bosniak troops were installed in the three fortresses of Aswān, Ibrīm and Sāy. The *kashiflik* became hereditary in a clan of Mamluk descent, while the descendants of the Bosniaks also formed a privileged caste.

Özdemir, who, in order to oppose the Portuguese threat to the Red Sea, aimed at the conquest of Abyssinia, also brought under Ottoman rule a strip of the African coast of the Red Sea, including the important ports of Suakin and Massawa (Maṣawwa'). In the earlier Middle Ages, the principal town in this region had been 'Aydhāb, which, at least as early as the third/ninth century, had been a port for pilgrims coming from the Nile Valley. Its commercial importance increased in consequence of the development of Egyptian trade with the Yemen from the fifth/eleventh century. It was destroyed during the first half of the ninth/fifteenth century, and Suakin, which had long existed as a harbour, succeeded to its importance. The development of Pilgrimage and trading-routes between Upper Egypt and the Red Sea contributed to the islamization of the Beja. Their degree of arabization varied: the 'Abābda of the north adopted the Arabic language, while the southern tribes retained their Hamitic speech but acquired Arab genealogies.

The early Funj period witnessed the effective islamization of Nubia and the Gezira. The immigrant Arabs who brought about the dissolution of the Christian kingdoms had, of course, been Muslims, and a dated inscription at Old Dongola shows that the church was converted into a mosque in 717/1317. Nevertheless, there was much scope for Islamic teaching, among the formerly Christian peoples, and among the laxly Muslim nomads and the pagan Funj. This was accomplished by religious teachers, who were also adherents of Ṣūfī orders. The prototype of these *fakīs* (as they are colloquially called) was a Yemeni Arab, Ghulām Allāh b. ʿĀʾid, who settled in Dongola, about the second half of the eighth/fourteenth century. The early Funj period saw a great increase in the number of Muslim teachers. Some of these were aliens, but most were men of local origin. They fall into two main categories: those who were primarily concerned to teach and administer the *Sharīʿa*,[1] and those who were more interested in initiating disciples into Ṣūfī mysticism. A hard and fast division is impossible; the former class never consolidated into an official hierarchy of *ʿulamāʾ*, although there is some evidence of the appointment of *qāḍīs* and cult-officials by the Funj or ʿAbdallābī rulers.

The Ṣūfī teachers enjoyed enormous prestige. Many of them had the reputation of thaumaturges, and they acted as advisers of, and intercessors with, the chiefs. There are, however, some indications of another attitude, that of the dissident *fakīs*, whose mission was to warn and reprove the rulers. In the light of later Sudanese history it is significant that the best known of these, Ḥamad al-Naḥlān (d. 1116/1704–5) proclaimed himself to be the *mahdī*.

The importance of the *fakīs* was enhanced by the grants of land which they received from the Funj or ʿAbdallābī chiefs. There was also a strongly hereditary tendency at work, since a *fakī* transmitted not only his material possessions, his *khalwa*,[2] his books and his land, to his descendants, but also his *baraka*, the mystical power of his holiness. Dynasties of holy men were thus not uncommon.

During the first two centuries of Funj rule, the dynasty at Sennar consolidated its position. Its early conversion to Islam is indicated by the Muslim name (ʿAbd al-Qādir) of a king who died in 965/1557–8. The acquisition (perhaps in the eleventh/seventeenth century) of a genealogy demonstrating the descent of the Funj from the Umayyads

[1] As in the western *Bilād al-Sūdān*, the Mālikī *madhhab* predominated.

[2] A *khalwa* is, primarily, a retreat of Ṣūfī devotees. In the Sudan, it has acquired the meaning of a Qurʾanic school.

symbolized the arabization of the dynasty. Serious clashes between the Funj and the ʿAbdallāb took place in the late tenth/sixteenth and early eleventh/seventeenth centuries, but after a crushing defeat sustained by the ʿAbdallāb in 1016/1607–8, the *status quo* was restored through the intercession of an influential *fakī*. Meanwhile the Funj kings had been expanding their power westwards across the Gezira to the White Nile, where they established a garrison and bridgehead at Alays, among the Shilluk. These were a powerful pagan tribe who raided down the White Nile in canoes: they may have been ethnically connected with the Funj.

Possession of the White Nile bridgehead enabled the Funj king, Bādī II Abū Diqan (1054–91/1644–80), to make an expedition against the Muslim hill-state of Taqalī, lying south of the Kordofan plain. The ruler of Taqalī was made tributary, and the slaves obtained from the pagan Nūba of the hills (not to be confused with the riverain Nūba of Nubia proper) were formed into a slave-guard to protect the Funj ruler and his capital.

While the Funj monarchy was establishing itself in the Nilotic Sudan, another dynasty, further west, was undergoing a similar process of arabization and conversion to Islam. The traditions of the Kayra suggest the marriage of an Arab Muslim into the originally pagan royal clan of Darfur. Sulaymān *Solong* (i.e. in Fūr, 'the Arab'), the first of the historical rulers, probably flourished *c.* 1050/1640. There is little definite information about the dynasty for another hundred years, but it seems to have been connected with the contemporaneous sultanate of Waday[1] (with which it was repeatedly at war), and, more certainly, with the Musabbaʿāt, who established their rule in the Kordofan plain.

During the twelfth/eighteenth century, the Funj-ʿAbdallābī hegemony over the Gezira and Nubia declined. The process had indeed been initiated much earlier, when the Shāyqiyya, a tribal group living on the great bend of the Nile, downstream of the Fourth Cataract, gained their independence of the ʿAbdallāb. The critical battle probably took place in the reign of the Funj king Bādī I Abū Rubāṭ (1020–5/1611–17). The Shāyqiyya appear to be of a different origin from the arabized Nubians who are their neighbours. Although their territory was an important centre of Islamic learning in the early Funj period, the Shāyq-

[1] Waday was the cultural watershed between the eastern and western parts of *Bilād al-Sūdān*.

iyya later became notorious as predatory warriors, forming a confederacy of clans under four chiefs.

As ʿAbdallābī power declined, the Saʿdāb Jaʿaliyyūn, living to the north of the Sabalūqa Cataract, emerged from obscurity. Their tribal capital, Shandī, became an important centre of trade. At Dāmir, near the confluence of the ʿAṭbarā with the main Nile, was a little tribal theocracy, the home of the Majādhīb clan of hereditary *fakīs*, whose prestige extended to the Red Sea coast. North of the ʿAṭbarā lay the tribal territory of the Mīrafāb, the name of which, Berber (Barbar), probably indicates the late survival in the region of non-Arabic speech. As the bellicosity of the Shāyqiyya increased, during the eighteenth century, their neighbours suffered, notably the ancient Nubian principality of Dongola. This most northerly part of the ancient Funj-ʿAbdallābī dominions was further harassed when the survivors of the Mamluk grandees, fleeing in 1811 from proscription in Egypt, established their camp[1] where New Dongola now stands, and fought the Shāyqiyya.

While the control of the ʿAbdallābī viceroy over the north was thus palpably diminishing, his suzerain, the Funj king, was in no better case. The establishment of a slave-guard by Bādī II, in the late eleventh/seventeenth century, seems to have marked a turning-point, since it created tension between the monarch and the free Funj warriors. They revolted against Bādī III al-Aḥmar (1103–28/1692–1716), who, however, succeeded in overcoming his opponents. The appearance of the *mahdī*, Ḥamad al-Naḥlān, in this region is another indication of unrest. The next king was deposed by the Funj warriors in 1132/1720, and the succession passed to another branch of the royal family, inheriting through the female line.

Tensions soon reappeared. Bādī IV Abū Shulūkh (1136–75/1724–62) antagonized the Funj notables. The former royal clan was proscribed, and the king began to supplant the old ruling group by men of Nūba origin, probably slaves, and Fūr refugees at his court. Following victory over the Abyssinians in 1157/1744, he sent an expedition against the Musabbaʿat of Kordofan. After initial defeats, this expedition attained success under the generalship of a certain Muḥammad Abū Likaylik in 1160/1747. This man came from the Hamaj, the section of the population which was probably descended from the old inhabitants of ʿAlwa, and was thus ethnically distinct from both the Funj and the Arabs.

[1] In Turkish, *ordu*, which has become arabicized as a place-name, *al-ʿUrḍī*.

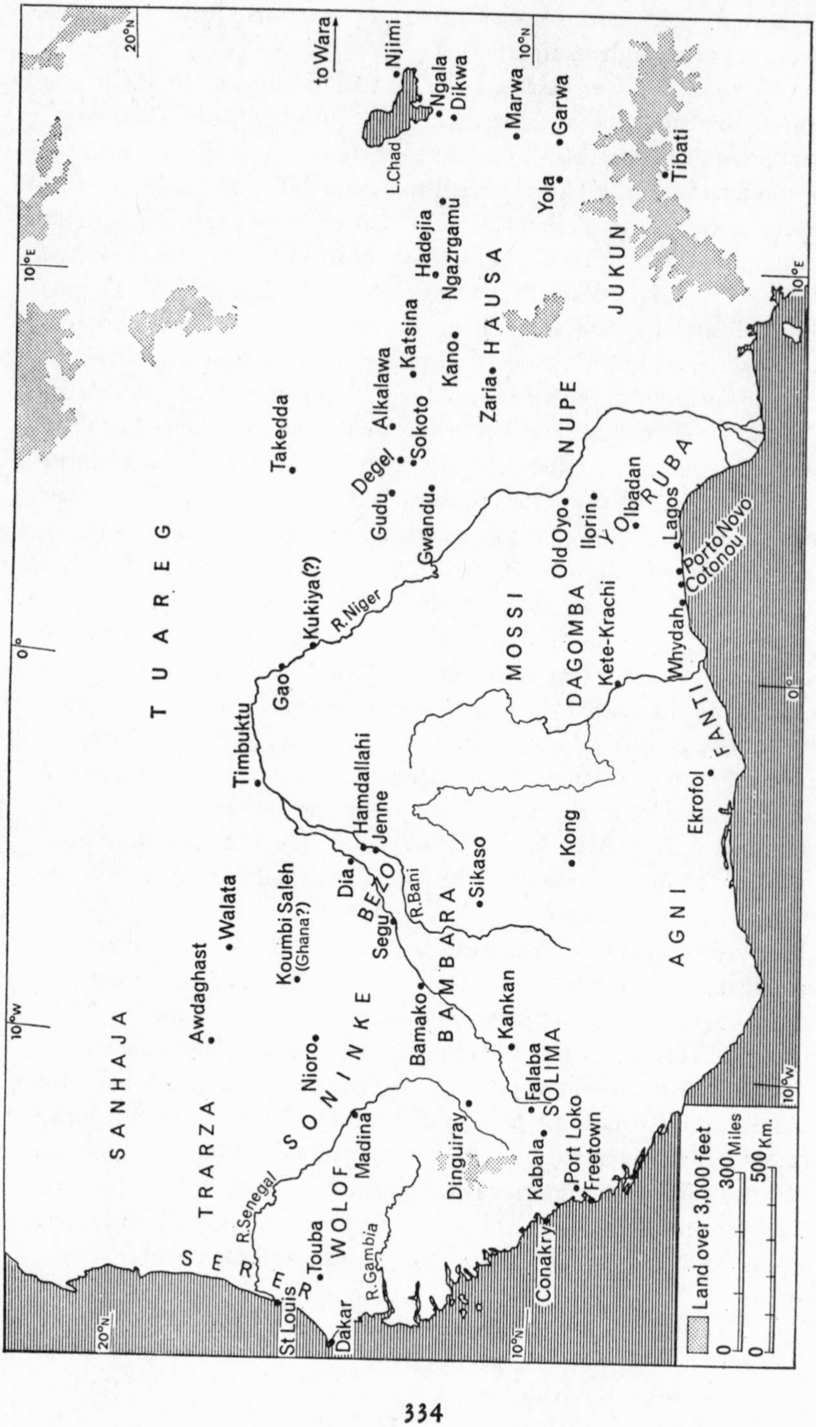

Map 12. Trans-Saharan Africa.

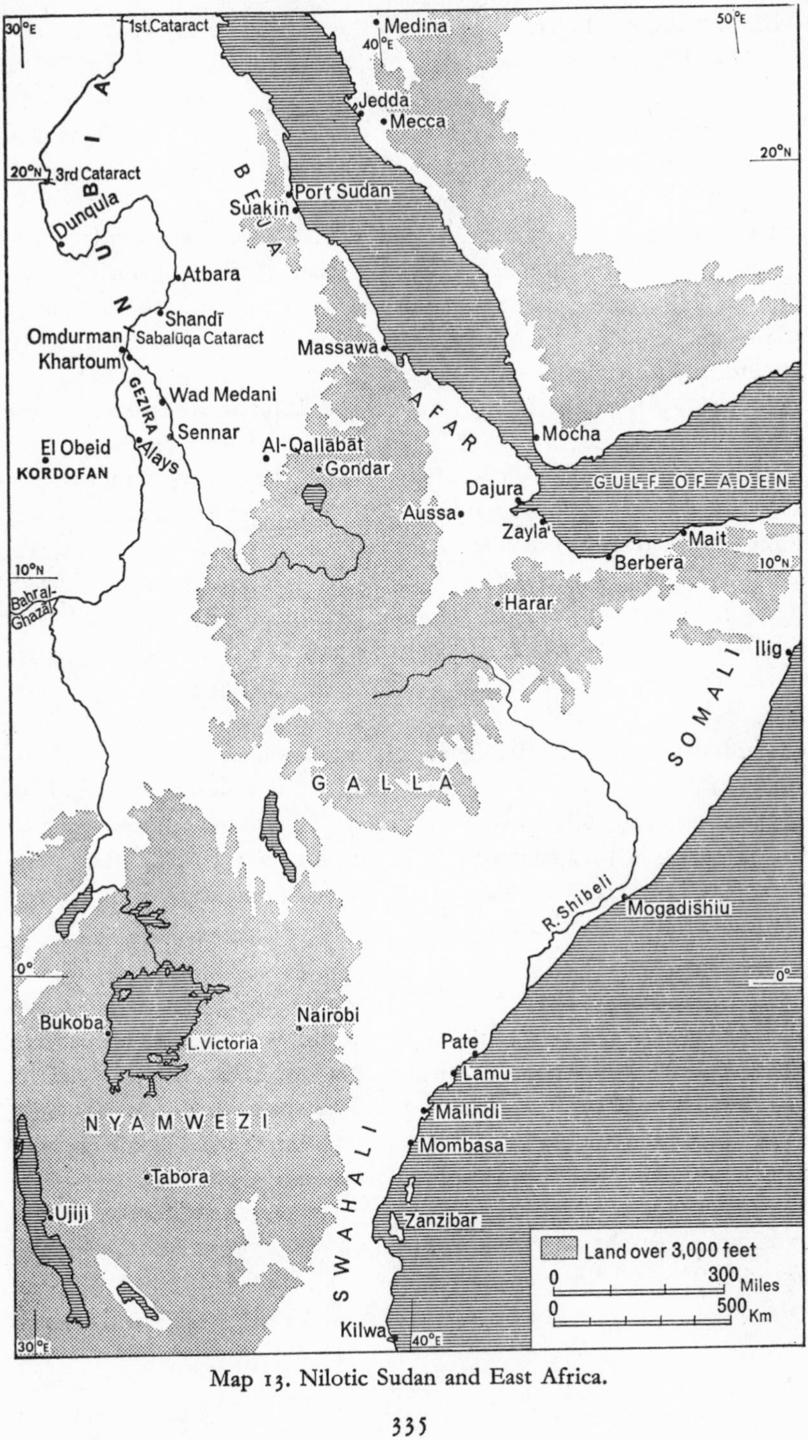

Map 13. Nilotic Sudan and East Africa.

Bādī IV did not himself accompany the expedition to Kordofan, and it may well be that he wished to rid himself of the Funj warriors. Some years after the defeat of the Musabba'at, the king's persecution of their families aroused the Funj chiefs in Kordofan, and, with Abū Likaylik at their head, they marched on Sennar. He was deposed without a struggle in 1175/1769, and the throne passed to his son.

The real power, however, rested with Shaykh Muḥammad Abū Likaylik, who ruled the kingdom of Sennar until his death in 1190/1776–7. He established an hereditary regency which lasted for nearly half a century. The later Funj kings were pawns in the struggle for power, which occupied the last decades of the kingdom. The internecine struggles of the descendants of Abū Likaylik contributed to the decline of the state.

In Darfur, meanwhile, the Kayra sultanate was growing in importance. After the death of Abū Likaylik, the Musabba'at briefly regained power in Kordofan, but the province was conquered by Muḥammad Tayrāb, sultan of Darfur, who died in 1202/1787. A dynastic struggle followed, in which the eunuch, Muḥammad Kurra, procured the accession of 'Abd al-Raḥmān al-Rashīd as sultan. Darfur was at this time becoming better known through trading caravans which went to Egypt by the Khārja Oasis and Asyūṭ along the Forty Days' Road (*Darb al-Arba'īn*), exporting slaves, ivory and ostrich feathers. This commercial activity was in the hands of Nubians of the diaspora. On 'Abd al-Raḥmān's death in 1215/1800–1, Muḥammad Kurra installed the new sultan, Muḥammad Faḍl, but the two became estranged, and Kurra was killed four years later. The long reign of Muḥammad Faḍl—he ruled nearly forty years—saw a decline in the power of Darfur.

THE TURCO-EGYPTIAN PERIOD

The remote and self-contained life of the Nilotic Sudan was brusquely affected by the expedition sent by Muḥammad 'Alī Pasha. The viceroy had various motives: to expel the remnant of the Mamluks from Dongola, where they constituted a potential threat to his rule in Egypt; to restore trade, which had suffered from the growing anarchy in the Nile valley; above all, perhaps, to acquire control of the Sudanese slave trade, which would provide him with military recruits,[1] and the legendary gold of the Sudan.

[1] Russian conquests in the Caucasus had dried up the traditional source of military slaves.

The main expedition advanced up the Nile, and obtained the submission of Berberistān and the riverain states to the south. The last Funj sultan recognized the conqueror in 1821. The only armed opposition came from the Shāyqiyya. A second expedition occupied Kordofan, but failed to annex Darfur. Meanwhile the heavy and unaccustomed taxation imposed on the Nilotic Sudanese provoked a desperate revolt, which was brutally suppressed. Thereafter, for nearly sixty years, there was no general resistance to Turco-Egyptian rule. The Sudanese territories were divided into provinces, administered and garrisoned by Turco-Egyptian officials and troops. A new town, Khartoum, strategically situated at the confluence of the Blue and White Niles, became the residence of the governors-general. Under this régime, the Nilotic Sudan attained a far higher degree of political unity and administrative centralization than it had possessed under the Funj-ʿAbdallābī hegemony.

Towards the end of Muḥammad ʿAlī's reign, a foothold was obtained at Kasala among the Beja tribes. Expansion towards the Red Sea logically entailed possession of the ancient ports of Suakin and Massawa, but although these were briefly leased to Muḥammad ʿAlī, the sultan did not make a permanent cession of them until the time of Khedive Ismāʿīl. The way up the White Nile beyond Alays, the limit of Arab territory, was discovered by three official expeditions under an intrepid Turkish sailor, Selīm Kapudan (Salīm Qabūdān), between 1839 and 1842, and during the decade that followed, the government monopolized the trade of the newly discovered regions. From 1851 onwards, however, European and Ottoman merchants poured into the riverain areas of the Upper Nile, in search of ivory. Their uncontrolled irruption had two evil consequences: the disintegration of tribal society, and the extension of the slave-trade to new areas, and on an increased scale. Similar results followed the rather later penetration of the Baḥr al-Ghazāl, the vast western region, drained by tributaries of the White Nile.

During the reign of Khedive Ismāʿīl (1863–79) the process of expansion was carried further, and a sustained attempt was made to bring the remoter territories under effective control. To achieve this aim, and also to suppress the slave-trade, which had aroused European indignation, Ismāʿīl appointed European and American officials. While the courage and integrity of these aliens temporarily strengthened khedivial rule, their invidious position as Christian servants of a Muslim power, their ignorance of local languages, and their frequent incompatibility with their Egyptian or Sudanese colleagues, all contributed to increase tension.

A prominent figure at this period was the Ja'alī merchant-prince, al-Zubayr Pasha Raḥma Manṣūr. He had made himself the chief operator of the ivory and slave-trade of the western Baḥr al-Ghazāl, where he had enormous political influence. Ismā'īl, having failed to procure his overthrow, recognized him as governor of the Baḥr al-Ghazāl in 1873. A trading-dispute with the Baqqāra or cattle-herding Arabs, through whose territory al-Zubayr's caravans passed, developed into hostilities with their overlord, Sultan Ibrāhīm Muḥammad of Darfur. In 1874, al-Zubayr defeated and killed the sultan, but was prevented by the hasty arrival of a Turco-Egyptian force from carrying out a unilateral occupation of Darfur, which was annexed to the Egyptian Sudan. The vast increase in khedivial territory during Ismā'īl's reign, however, laid an impossible burden on an administration which was renowned neither for its efficiency nor its honesty. The prestige of the khedive, and the energy of the British governor-general, General Gordon, appointed in 1877, postponed the collapse for a few years.

THE MAHDIA

After the deposition of Ismā'īl (1879), which was followed by the resignation of Gordon, the revolutionary situation in the Sudan became apparent. The signal for revolt was given by a widely reverenced *fakī* of Dunqulāwī origin, who dwelt at Abā Island in the White Nile. His name was Muḥammad Aḥmad, and in June 1881 he publicly announced himself to be the Expected Mahdi. His opposition movement was nourished by a variety of resentments: that of the *fakīs* against the hierarchy of orthodox *'ulamā'* introduced by the Turco-Egyptian régime; that of the pious and conservative Sudanese against the administration's westernizing innovations; that of the Nubian diaspora against the repression of the slave-trade; that of local and personal factions against the holders of power and influence in the tribes, the Ṣūfī orders and the provincial towns.

The Mahdia which ensued began as a religious movement for the revival of Islam, primarily in the Sudan, but with universal implications; it developed into a theocratic polity, and this in turn was transformed into a territorial Islamic state.

The Manifestation of the Mahdi in Abā began a period of revolutionary war against the khedivial administration in the Sudan. The Mahdi quickly withdrew from Abā to the distant hill of Qadīr in southern Kordofan, where he recruited tribal forces (mainly Baqqāra) beyond the effective reach of the Turco-Egyptian régime. Emerging from Qadīr he won his first major success with the capture of El Obeid (al-Ubayyiḍ), the provincial capital of Kordofan, in January 1883. A last attempt to mount a large-scale offensive against him was defeated with the annihilation of the Hicks Expedition in the following November. The collapse of the khedivial administration in Darfur and the Baḥr al-Ghazāl followed, while the flame of revolt was carried to the Beja tribes, who dominated the important route from Suakin to the Nile. Gordon, who returned in 1884, ostensibly to carry out the evacuation of the Egyptian garrisons, committed himself to a hopeless resistance in Khartoum. When the city fell, in January 1885, the Mahdia had eaten the heart out of the Egyptian Sudan.

This period saw the elaboration of the characteristic ideology and institutions of the Mahdia. The Mahdi aimed to restore the primitive Islamic *Umma*, and to end the innovations and tyranny of the Turco-Egyptian régime. The strong Ṣūfī tradition of the Sudan imparted to his ideas an eschatological tinge. He envisaged his new *Umma* as a recapitulation of early Islam. He himself was the Successor of the Prophet, as his chief followers were the Successors of the Companions. His letters stress his divine election as Mahdi.

The revolutionary army on which he depended was largely tribal in origin, and consisted of three divisions, under his three chief companions. Pre-eminent among these was *Khalīfat al-Ṣiddīq*, the Successor of Abū Bakr, 'Abd Allāhi b. Muḥammad, a man of Baqqārī origin, who had joined him at Abā before the Manifestation. 'Abd Allāhi commanded the Black Flag division, composed of the levies of the Baqqāra Arabs of Kordofan and Darfur—restless nomads, who found in the Mahdia a release from the growing pressure of the Turco-Egyptian administration.

After the fall of Khartoum, the Mahdi established his residence at Omdurman, where an immense, straggling camp-city grew up. Here he died, in June 1885, to be succeeded as head of the theocratic state by 'Abd Allāhi, who assumed the title of *Khalīfat al-Mahdī*, the Successor of the Mahdi. Once he had secured his position, the Khalifa 'Abd Allāhi pursued a policy of *jihād* against his neighbours. Between 1886 and 1889, there was warfare in three principal areas: the Abyssinian frontier, Darfur and the west, and the Egyptian frontier. Although important temporary successes were gained, the Mahdist state could not make far-reaching conquests. The turning-point came in August 1889, when the long-awaited invasion of Egypt was crushingly defeated at the battle of Ṭūshkī (Toski). The great expanses of the southern Sudan, precariously held by Khedive Ismāʿīl, eluded the Khalifa's grasp. The Baḥr al-Ghazāl had no Mahdist governor after 1886, while the river-line of the Upper Nile was retained only with difficulty.

After Ṭūshkī, the policy of the *jihād* was tacitly abandoned by the Khalifa, who sought instead to strengthen his personal autocracy within his limited territorial state. A rift developed between the Khalifa and the tribesmen belonging to the main Nile and the Nubian diaspora, who filled the cadres of his bureaucracy. The situation was aggravated by the Khalifa's attempt to bring in the Baqqāra, and settle them in Omdurman and the Gezira. Meanwhile, the Khalifa endeavoured to secure his autocracy by appointing his kinsmen and clients to the principal military governorships and key offices of state. Resentment flared out in a revolt, in November 1891, centring around the Mahdi's family. ʿAbd Allāhi temporized, and subsequently destroyed the leaders piecemeal. His former colleague, *Khalīfat al-Karrār* (i.e., the Successor of ʿAlī) Muḥammad Sharīf, a cousin of the Mahdi, who had been the figure-head of the revolt, was tried and imprisoned. There was no other serious internal challenge to the Khalifa during the remainder of his rule.

The Khalifa's sovereignty seems to have gained in popular acceptance, and he began to groom his son for eventual succession. The Mahdist state collapsed only when its conquest was decided upon by the British government. In making the decision, the government was moved by considerations of policy in Europe: the claims and interests of Egypt were a negligible factor: the actual state of affairs in the Sudan had no weight at all.

The reconquest was planned and directed by Sir Herbert (later Lord) Kitchener, then *serdār* of the Egyptian army. Kitchener met with no serious setbacks, and attained his objectives with a notable economy of both lives and money. His success was due to his own administrative and organizing capacity, and to superiority of armament and transport, which depended on railway-construction. The province of Dongola was reconquered in 1896, and the main campaign began in the following year. In September 1898, the Khalifa was decisively defeated at Karari, near Omdurman. With the fugitive remnants of his followers, he fell in battle in November 1899.

THE ANGLO-EGYPTIAN CONDOMINIUM

Although the Mahdist state ceased to exist in 1898, the work of occupying and pacifying the Sudan still remained. A French attempt to establish a foothold on the Upper Nile, by the Marchand expedition, was prevented by Kitchener's prompt action, but complete control over the tribes was not established for a generation. When the Mahdist state collapsed, the sultanate of Darfur was re-established by ʿAlī Dīnār, a member of the Kayra dynasty. Nominally a vassal of the new Sudan Government, he excluded its agents from his territory, until he was overthrown by a military expedition in 1916, when Darfur was re-annexed. Some fringe territories which had recognized the rule of the khedive in 1881 were not regained in 1898; while agreements with France, Abyssinia and the Congo Free State substituted acknowledged frontiers for vague territorial claims.

The status of the reconquered territories was determined by a convention concluded between Britain and Egypt in January 1899. This was drafted by Lord Cromer, as British agent and consul-general, wholly in accordance with British policy. Its principal purpose was to exclude from the Sudan both international institutions, such as the Mixed Courts, and the authority of the Egyptian government. The Sudan was formally a condominium, under joint British and Egyptian rule. In practice, the governor-general, in whom the supreme military and civil command, was vested, was invariably a British subject, as were the chief administrative officials. The Egyptians were restricted to subordinate posts, to which competent Sudanese were also admitted in due course.

Lord Kitchener, the first governor-general, was succeeded in December 1899 by Sir Reginald Wingate. During Wingate's long governor-generalship, ending in 1916, two characteristic institutions of the Sudan government developed: the Sudan Political Service, a corps of civilian administrators, recruited in Britain, who passed the whole of their working careers in the Sudan; and the Governor-General's Council, constituted in 1910, and composed of senior officials, which formed the supreme legislative and executive body. An administration so recruited was naturally paternalist and somewhat parochial in its outlook. But it was efficient and incorruptible, and its members served devotedly the interest of the Sudanese, as they saw it. The country was governed with the utmost economy; even so, revenue did not exceed expenditure until 1913.

Under Wingate and his successor, Sir Lee Stack (1917–24), the economic and educational foundations of the modern Sudan were laid. Kitchener's military railway was expanded to link the provinces of the north. The White Nile, with its regular steamer-services, was the highway to the south. Khartoum rose from its ruins to be, once again, the capital. Omdurman remained the largest Sudanese urban settlement. Suakin and Berber, the old termini of the Red Sea-Nile route, were supplanted by new towns at Port Sudan and Atbara, the railway headquarters. In the Gezira, Wad Medani was not only a provincial capital, but also, after the First World War, the centre of the cotton-producing scheme controlled by the Sudan Plantations Syndicate.

The educational system was at first on a very small scale. It was intended to supply the government with clerks and minor officials, and was not conceived in any spirit of enlightenment. Literacy in Arabic was provided in the elementary schools, while English was taught at the next (intermediate) level. Secondary education was slow to develop: even by the Second World War, there was only one government secondary school. In the southern Sudan, the schools were provided by Christian missionaries, and Arabic was not taught. This religious and educational differentiation, superimposed on underlying geographical and ethnic distinctions, was to promote tensions between north and south.

The golden age of paternalism ended after the First World War. As militant nationalism grew in Egypt, the Condominium in the Sudan was called into question. Inside the Sudan, paternalism no longer satisfied the educated *élite*, and the first signs of Sudanese nationalism appeared in 1921. Then, in November 1924, the assassination of Sir Lee Stack in Cairo was followed by British insistence on the withdrawal of all Egyptian troops from the Sudan. The evacuation was accompanied by a mutiny of Sudanese troops, which was forcibly suppressed. Egyptian civilian officials were subsequently withdrawn, and the share of Egypt in the Condominium diminished to vanishing point.

During the next two decades, paternalism ceased to be an ideal, and turned into an expedient. The Sudan government looked for the future, not to the educated *élite*, but to the traditional tribal leaders, whose authority was extended and codified in pursuance of a policy of 'native administration'. In the southern Sudan, the fostering of native administration was accomplished by the exclusion of northern Sudanese, and a strenuous attempt to combat Islam and Muslim influences. Education was viewed with suspicion, and parsimoniously financed. The great depression of the early 1930s provided retrospective justification for retrenchment.

The Second World War saw the beginning of new political developments. There were two distinct but connected problems. The first was of conciliating the growing nationalist feeling in the Sudan; the second, of reaching agreement with Egypt. The spearhead of Sudanese nationalism was the educated *élite*, most of whom were in government service, and demanded, with varying degrees of moderation, a share in the running of their country. They had organized in 1938 the Graduates' General Congress, and they were able to enlist mass-support, through links with the two chief Muslim religious orders, the Khatmiyya and the *Anṣār*. The head of the Anṣār, ʿAbd al-Raḥmān al-Mahdī, the posthumous son of the Mahdi, was an overtly political figure; while his counterpart in the Khatmiyya, ʿAlī al-Mīrghanī, refused a public political role. The nationalists connected with the *Anṣār* became spokesmen of Sudanese independence, while those with Khatmiyya affiliations advocated union with Egypt.

The problem of the status of the Sudan had been shelved in the Anglo-Egyptian Treaty of 1936. No Egyptian government could abandon the claim that the Nile Valley legitimately formed an indissoluble political unity. On this rock successive negotiations foundered; while, since one Sudanese nationalist group was ostensibly committed to the Egyptian claim, the attempts to associate the Sudanese with the Sudan Government evoked only a partial response.

The first such attempt was made by the inauguration, in 1944, of the Advisory Council of the Northern Sudan. Since its functions were purely advisory, it was not taken seriously by many nationalists, who, moreover, saw in its restriction to the northern provinces, a deliberate attempt to divide the country. In 1948, the Sudan Government set up a Legislative Assembly, representing the Sudan as a whole, and an Executive Council, half Sudanese in composition. These developments took place against the protests of the Egyptians and their Sudanese allies.

In 1943, the rival nationalist groups were organized as political parties. Those under ʿAbd al-Raḥmān's patronage became the *Umma* party—a name which to their opponents had ominous hints of a new Mahdist monarchy—while the pro-Egyptian group, affiliated to the Khatmiyya, were known as the *Ashiqqāʾ*. Their leader, Ismāʿīl al-Azharī, became the most popular and formidable of Sudanese politicians.

While the deadlock between Britain and Egypt over the status of the

Sudan continued, the Sudan government, with British backing, promulgated a Self-Government Statute in April 1952. Three months later, the revolution in Egypt made possible a fresh approach to the problem.

Understanding was reached among the Sudanese nationalist parties, and between the Egyptian and British governments. The Anglo-Egyptian Agreement of 12 February 1953 adopted the Self-Government Statute as the basis for Sudanese constitutional advance. While the Egyptian régime abandoned the demand for the unity of the Nile Valley, and accepted the principle of Sudanese self-determination, the British permitted amendments to the Statute. These set up an international commission to limit the governor-general's powers and another to control the election of the projected Sudanese Parliament.

The new Parliament met in January 1954. Ismā'īl al-Azharī, whose supporters (reorganized in 1951 as the National Unionist party) had won a majority of seats, became prime minister. The sudanization of the army, police and civil service proceeded rapidly. As the British withdrawal proceeded, al-Azharī changed his attitude towards Egypt, in deference to the obvious feeling of Sudanese nationalists. The idea of union was dead: the only issue was by what process, and how soon, the Sudan would become independent. The Anglo-Egyptian Agreement of 1953 had laid down an elaborate procedure, but, under al-Azharī's guidance, the Parliament took more summary measures. These enabled him to proclaim an independent republic, on New Year's Day, 1956.

The republican government succeeded to the entire territory of the former Condominium, but did not command a united people. The split between the nationalists had left a legacy of factionalism in party politics. Al-Azharī handled both his supporters and his opponents astutely, but Sudanese parliamentary democracy was inaugurated in an atmosphere of political opportunism rather than statesmanship, and depended on personalities rather than principles. Still more serious was the rift between north and south, which was demonstrated in August 1955, when a military mutiny led to a breakdown of public security in the southern provinces. Events were to show that the coming of independence was in itself no solution to either of these problems.

CHAPTER 6

THE WESTERN AND CENTRAL SUDAN AND EAST AFRICA

A. THE WESTERN AND CENTRAL SUDAN IN THE EARLY PERIOD

The Sudan (more precisely, *bilād al-Sūdān*, the land of the blacks) is the Arabic name for the trans-continental savannah belt, several hundred miles wide, lying between desert and forest. The Sudan has been the principal theatre for African Islamic history below the northern coast. Only rarely have Saharan movements exercised critical influence—e.g. the Almoravids (fifth/eleventh century) or the Sanūsiyya (nineteenth century). Only recently has Islam taken root in the forest: this is primarily a characteristic of the European colonial period, which checked local wars, opened roads, and encouraged trade and migrant labour—a situation equally true for Muslim penetration south from the savannah, or inland from the East African coast.

The Sahara, with its Berber population, has, however, been of crucial importance as an avenue of approach. The northern Sudan cities, Timbuktu, Gao and others, were ports facing the desert just as the eastern coastal cities faced the Indian Ocean. Gold for export, salt for import, were staples of Saharan trade. Several major routes crossed the Sahara: from Morocco to the goldfields of the upper Senegal and Niger; from Tunisia to the area between the Niger and Lake Chad; from Tripoli to Lake Chad; from Libya to Waday. The eastern Sudan, though closest to the heartlands of Islam, was penetrated last, perhaps because of difficulties of communication along the Nile, and the persistence of Christian states astride the river. Below the northernmost Sudanic strip, called the *Sāḥil* or Coast, another pattern of Muslim mobility developed, chiefly east-west. Here the east coast, lacking any penetrable hinterland, differed fundamentally. The mobility of men and ideas within the Islamic world, across the Sahara or within the Sudan, founded upon trade but stimulated by religious duties, is the most important geographical fact of African Islamic history.

Islam south of the Sahara has followed a threefold development:

first, as represented by foreign Muslim residents; second, commanding some local support but forced to compromise with local custom; and third, able to impose reform at will. The pattern did not begin in all areas at the same time, nor advance at the same rate, so differing stages may exist side by side.

Ghāna

Ghāna is first mentioned by al-Fazārī in the eighth century; al-Bakrī, writing in 460/1067–8, supplies our first detailed description. It is typical of Islam in the first, foreign stage. The capital then included two main quarters, one royal (called *al-Ghāba*, the forest, because of its sacred groves) and one Muslim (presumably mainly for foreign merchants). The Muslim quarter had twelve mosques, including a cathedral mosque, with mosque officials and learned men. The royal quarter had also a mosque, for Muslim ministers constantly attended the king. The king was pagan, hedged with divinity.

The Muslim quarter shows already the mosaic character of Sudan society. Still today many towns have such quarters. So deeply ingrained is the concept that some African traditions, recorded in this century, describe a pagan quarter in Mecca. Muslim separateness was expressed in other ways also. Pagans prostrated themselves and poured dust on their heads before the king; Muslims showed respect by clapping hands, rendering prostration to God alone, and shared with royalty the exclusive right to wear tailored clothes.

Muslim traders were present in other towns as well as the capital; they were respected in some districts when they only passed by. Perhaps their example was already appreciated locally—a woman of Sama, where the inhabitants paid little attention to dress of any kind, asked a passing Muslim for his beard to clothe herself.

This phase of Ghāna history came to an end with the Almoravid conquest (*c.* 468/1076). Almoravid control lasted scarcely a decade. What happened to Ghāna in the twelfth century? It may have been a period of decline; the capital may have revived on the same site; or it may have flourished on a new, riverside site; a Berber dynasty, claiming *sharīfī* origin, may have taken over. All these and other theories have been advanced. It appears that the rulers of Ghāna became Muslim, and that the movement of peoples, particularly Soninke, stimulated by the Almoravid conquest led to the spread of Islam in new areas.

Takrūr

In the fifth/eleventh century, other states already had Muslim rulers. Al-Bakrī records a king of Malal (a Mande state), converted to Islam by the successful prayers for rain of a passing *'ālim*. Later historians said the first Muslim king of Mali was Barmandana, a pilgrim. We do not know if these two were the same. In Malal the commoners remained pagan; but in Takrūr, on the Senegal, we are told that both king and people converted. Takrūr has throughout its Islamic history been inhabited by two main groups, united by a common language: the one nomadic pastoralists, light-coloured, now called Fulani; the other sedentary, of mixed racial origins but mainly Negro, dark, now called Tokolor—that is, people of Takrūr. The Tokolor have been the champions of Islam. Torodbe, a name originally of religious clans, has been virtually another name for Tokolor. Takrūr troops, vainly, helped the Almoravids.

Later writers, in Egypt, began using Takrūr as equivalent for Mali, though Mansa Mūsā (early eighth/fourteenth century) protested that Takrūr was but part of his domains, and scholars knew that to use Takrūr for Mali was a mistake of the commoners. How did this wider, looser Middle Eastern definition arise? Was it pilgrimage usage, as later Java became a collective name for South-East Asian pilgrims? Were there West African communities in Cairo, who popularized the name? Ibn Khaldūn (1332–1406) received information from the *turjumān al-Takrūr*, the interpreter of the Takrūr, in Egypt: was this the head of an immigrant community, perhaps genuine Takrūrīs? Takrūr and *fuqarā'* prayed for the sultan Baybars. Confusion may have arisen from the repeated use, by Arab geographers, of Takrūr as a name linked also with the Gao area. West African Muslims, beginning later to write their own history, adopted this wider sense. Askiya al-Ḥājj Muḥammad was styled *khalīfa* for the land of the Takrūr; Aḥmad Bābā of Timbuktu was called al-Takrūrī; Muḥammad Bello entitled his study of the Fulani *jihād*, 'a study in the history of the country of Takrūr'; and so forth. In the heartlands of Islam, Takrūrī (plural Takārna or Takārīr) came to be applied to every West or Central African visitor. Despite the famous name, Takrūr and Tokolor in the west were of secondary importance until after 1700.

The Almoravids

Early efforts to unite the leading Ṣanhāja clans of the western Sahara were unavailing. Awdaghast, a principal Saharan town, passed under

Ghāna control. In the eleventh century a new Ṣanhāja confederacy was formed under Tarsina, a pilgrim and leader of *jihād*. He was killed, after a short career.

In 1035 or later, Yaḥyā b. Ibrāhīm, son-in-law and successor of Tarsina, left on Pilgrimage with several fellow chiefs. Returning through Qayrawān he heard Abū 'Imrān, from Fez, teaching there. Apparently for the first time, Yaḥyā realized the defects of his Saharan Islam: one of many instances in African Islamic history in which experiences on the way to and from Mecca are at least as important as what is observed in Mecca. Yaḥyā complained about the *'ulamā'* at home, and begged Abū 'Imrān for a missionary. Abū 'Imrān, as impressed with Yaḥyā's intentions as he was dismayed by his ignorance, found none of his students both willing and suitable. He recommended Yaḥyā to another teacher, Wajjāj b. Zalwī, near Sijilmāsa. Among Wajjāj's students a missionary was found, 'Abd Allāh b. Yāsīn, his mother a Jazūlī Berber from the Ghāna borders.

'Abd Allāh b. Yāsīn accompanied Yaḥyā b. Ibrāhīm to the desert. 'Abd Allāh, refusing the milk and meat of his Ṣanhāja hosts, lest their property be legally impure, dissociated himself from unreformed local Islam. Like John the Baptist, he lived on wild food only. He wore the mystic's woollen dress.

'Abd Allāh's witness and preaching won disciples, the *Murābiṭūn*, people of the *ribāṭ*, Almoravids; the word *ribāṭ* seems here to mean 'military service' or perhaps even 'sect'.[1] He attacked reluctant Ṣanhāja, and compelled them to come in. He purified their possessions by annexing one-third, serving financial and religious policy. 'Abd Allāh built a town, Aratnanna, where no house was taller than another. Adultery, lying and drinking were punished with the whip. Anyone entering the *ribāṭ* suffered for past offences. Musical instruments were broken, wine-shops closed.

He enforced the limit of four wives. Keeping within this, he himself married and divorced unceasingly. He never gave more than four *mithqāls* in dowry: his marital life may have made such economy imperative, but low dowries may also be a measure of social reform, such as was enforced for example by the Sudanese Mahdi Muḥammad Aḥmad. Supplementary prayers made up for those omitted in the convert's

[1] Al-Bakrī, our only contemporary observer, does not mention the island *ribāṭ* to which 'Abd Allāh is said to have withdrawn when first training his disciples. Later authorities disagree as to where the *ribāṭ* was, who built it and who went to it.

earlier life. Lateness at prayer, neglect of part of the prayer, even raising one's voice in the mosque, the whip rewarded all.

Dissatisfaction developed. A local *faqīh* and two chiefs overthrew 'Abd Allāh, who fled to Wajjāj. Wajjāj decreed that those who resisted 'Abd Allāh were outside the congregation and outside the law. Dealing death to opponents and wrong-doers alike, 'Abd Allāh fought his way back to power in the Sahara.

With a well-disciplined army, 'Abd Allāh conquered Sijilmāsa and Awdaghast, main terminals of trans-Saharan trade. Both towns had Zanāta colonies or garrisons, Berbers but deadly enemies to the Ṣanhāja. Awdaghast had further offended by acknowledging a Negro governor. When Awdaghast fell (446/1054–5), property was seized, women raped, and a learned pilgrim killed.

Yaḥyā b. Ibrāhīm, a Juddālī, had died; Yaḥyā b. 'Umar, a Lamtūnī, replaced him as temporal *amīr*. Now the Juddāla rebelled. 'Abd Allāh b. Yāsin, called north by trouble in Sijilmāsa, left Yaḥyā b. 'Umar to hold the fort in the Sahara. Yaḥyā, reinforced with Muslim troops from Takrūr—an interesting case of religious alliance across racial frontiers—hazarded battle with the Juddāla (448/1056). He fell, defeated, on Tabfarilla field, haunted afterwards by the crying of ghostly muezzins, so that the dead were left undespoiled. His brother, Abū Bakr b. 'Umar, succeeded him. 'Abd Allāh b. Yāsīn fell fighting in North Africa. Full command passed to Abū Bakr.

Faced with new dissension in the desert, Abū Bakr reconciled the quarrelling parties by leading them against the Negroes. Hitherto, the *jihād* had been against erring or rival Muslims, an ominous precedent. When he tried to return north, his cousin, Yūsuf b. Tāshufīn, to whom he had entrusted Morocco, refused to admit him. Henceforth the movement was split. Yūsuf reduced Morocco, taking Fez in 462/1070, when 3,000 Zanāta are said to have died in the mosques. Muslim Spain was also occupied. Abū Bakr also conquered the capital of Ghāna (*c.* 468/1076). He died soon after; the Almoravid adventure in West Africa concluded.

Mali

The core of Mali was the Mande state of Kangaba, near modern Bamako on the upper Niger; the actual capital moved many times. This southern, agricultural foundation strengthened prosperity, though trade, especially in gold and kola, was important too. In the seventh/

thirteenth century, Sunjata of Mali conquered Ghāna; the Soninke dispersion received another impetus, and the glory of Ghāna finally departed.

The greatest ruler according to written records—that is, from a Muslim point of view, Sunjata dominating oral tradition—was Mansa Mūsā (1312–37 or later). In his time, Mali expanded north to incorporate Walata and Timbuktu; east, to bring in the Songhay of the middle Niger; south and west, to influence Futa Jallon and Takrūr.

In the fifteenth century, as Songhay rose, Mali declined. Tuareg, Wolof, Tokolor and Mossi harassed the frontiers. Mali appealed vainly for Portuguese help. By the seventeenth century, Mali was once again confined to Kangaba, which still exists and is still ruled by the Kayta dynasty, the family of Barmandana.

The rulers of Mali were Muslim, but in the conversation between Islam and the divine kingship, neither side had prevailed. Prostration and dusting before the king were still required. Indeed, while in Ghāna Muslims (probably all foreigners) were exempt, in Mali even pilgrims, even the chief *qāḍī*, had to do this. Such exemption as was granted seems to have been a racial privilege for foreigners, not a religious one for Muslims. Other features of the traditional monarchy also remained: special dress (as in Ghāna, Muslims had a privileged position here), special eating arrangements, rights to the daughters of subjects, etc. *'Ulamā'* depended on royal largesse, distributed particularly in Ramaḍān.

Ibn Baṭṭūṭa visited Mali in 753–4/1352–3. His description of the Muslim festivals, when both the Muslim *khaṭīb* and the pagan poets addressed the kings, shows clearly the intermingling of the two faiths. He complained also about violations of Muslim rules of dress and eating. But the witness to a purer faith survived. In the capital, the cathedral mosque was crowded to overflowing on Fridays, and great stress was laid on youths memorizing the Qur'ān. Even *vis-à-vis* the king, *'ulamā'* maintained a certain detachment. The mosque and the *khaṭīb's* house were sanctuaries in the capital; and outside, Jaba (perhaps the modern Dia) was a religious town, ruled by a *qāḍī*, where the king's writ did not run.

Islam was probably largely upper class and urban, with a strong foreign element. Ibn Baṭṭūṭa stayed in the white quarter at the capital. The white community had two chiefs, one from Egypt, one a Jazūlī Berber from the tribe of Ibn Yāsīn's mother. Ibn Baṭṭūṭa, having trouble with the change of diet, was doctored by another Egyptian. But the chief *qāḍī* was a Negro, and Ibn Baṭṭūṭa was favourably impressed with Negro pilgrims in several villages. His comment that a man with but one shirt would wash it for the Friday prayer suggests that, in the capital at least, Islam had begun to penetrate among poor as well as rich. On the other hand, al-'Umarī reports that, except among persons of rank, no burial was performed, an intolerable procedure for Muslims.

Mali's foreign relations reflect the religious tension. To the south were innumerable pagans. When the imposition of Islam in the gold-producing areas reduced output, the pagan miners were simply placed under tribute, and left undisturbed in their traditional beliefs. Magic was practised in ivory-hunting. When cannibal delegations from the south visited Mali, the *mansa* provided unfortunate victims as a welcome feast. Occasional political incidents suggest that perhaps relations with the south were still closer. At least once the south was a place of exile: Mansa Mūsā sent there a dishonest *qāḍī* from Morocco, who returned after four years, uneaten because 'unripe'. And once (792/1390) a usurper emerged from the south, claiming descent from Sunjata, and seized power.

Relations with North Africa and the Middle East were the counterweight. Embassies passed between Mali and Morocco: Mansa Mūsā sent one (*c.* 1337) to congratulate Abu'l Ḥasan 'Alī, the Marinid sultan, on the capture of Tlemcen. Ibn Baṭṭūṭa attended a memorial dinner in Mali for Abu'l-Ḥasan, at which the Qur'ān was read, and prayers offered for the rulers of Mali and Morocco. Mansa Mūsā's grandson sent another with presents, including a giraffe, which caused great excitement. Once a deposed sultan of Morocco travelled to Mali, where he joined a pilgrim caravan. Barmandana, Sunjata's son and successor Uli, and other Mali kings went on Pilgrimage; that of Mansa Mūsā in the 1320s is the most celebrated in West African history.

Songhay

The Songhay empire was born of the union of river and desert. Traditions recount the early imposition of desert Berbers upon riverain Negroes. Kukiya was the first capital. In the fifth/eleventh century, the capital moved north to Gao, and the *za*, or king, adopted Islam. Early accounts are contradictory; perhaps not all refer to Gao. It seems, despite the *za*'s conversion, that Gao remained two towns, like the Ghāna capital, one for Muslims, one for the king and his people. Elaborate rituals surrounding royal meals show the divine kingship tradition still strong. Kukiya remained a powerful pagan centre, and *zas* resorted thither for part of their inaugural ceremonies. Muslim funeral steles date from 499/1106, if not earlier, in Gao, but do not appear in Kukiya until the fifteenth century.

In the seventh/thirteenth and eighth/fourteenth centuries, Mali exercised intermittent authority over Songhay. The Pilgrimage perhaps provided the Mali rulers with occasion to receive Songhay homage. Mali *'ulamā'* crossed Songhay into Hausaland. By 1400 Songhay had eclipsed Mali. 'Alī, last but one of the *sonnis* (successors of the *zas*), 869–97, 1464/5–1491/2, established Songhay as a great power. His conquests included Jenne and Timbuktu. His main antagonists were Fulani, Tuareg and Mossi.

The Muslim chroniclers, in awe of Sonni 'Alī's military success, abuse him as an impious tyrant. They were apologists for the Askiya dynasty, which deposed Sonni 'Alī's son. They had also genuine grievances, about Sonni 'Alī's lax observance of Islam, his oppression of some *'ulamā'*, particularly those of Timbuktu, and his cultivation of paganism. His words were those of one strong in Islam, as were some of his actions. But in other respects he behaved as an unbeliever. The chroniclers called him a *Khārijī*, here probably used loosely to mean heretic. For the first time, the problem of the 'mixers' was consciously posed.

Sonni 'Alī died; his son, Sonni Baru, replaced him. Askiya Muḥammad, a leading official under Sonni 'Alī, thrice summoned Baru to conversion, the first emissary being a *sharīf*. Baru, already Muslim, probably regarded this summons as a political challenge. He refused. Muḥammad fought and defeated Baru, and ascended the throne in 898/1493, first of the *askiyas*.

Oral tradition affirms Askiya Muḥammad to have been a nephew of Sonni 'Ali—the chronicles make him a Soninke stranger from the west. Oral tradition describes Muḥammad murdering the last *sonni* (apparently 'Alī) as the *sonni* led the festival prayers. The chronicles say Sonni 'Alī died in mystery, at the height of his powers, drowned returning from a campaign—none knows his grave. His death they attribute to the prayers of *'ulamā'* against him.

Whatever Muḥammad's origin, whatever the details of his revolution, his responsibility for the overthrow of the *sonnis* is clear. He at once wooed the Muslim party, paying special regard to *'ulamā'*, *qāḍīs, sharīfs* and pilgrims. Later, when he was firmly established, some of these privileges lapsed. A mysterious passage in the chronicles may relate to

Muḥammad's need for the intercession of religious men. The *qāḍī* of Timbuktu, we are told, later reminded Muḥammad that he had come to the *qāḍī*, beseeching the *qāḍī* to hold him by the hand lest he fall into hell; Muḥammad acknowledged this.

In 902/1496–7, Muḥammad went on Pilgrimage, oral tradition says in penance. Muḥammad was appointed *khalīfa* of Takrūr, probably by the 'Abbasid caliph in Cairo, having first symbolically laid aside his kingly estate. On Pilgrimage, Muḥammad met al-Maghīlī, who later visited Gao, and whose advice greatly helped Muḥammad in justifying the revolution.

The influence of Muḥammad b. 'Abd al-Karīm al-Maghīlī, a Berber *'ālim*, spans four centuries of West African Islam. In Tuat, al-Maghīlī reversed the hitherto tolerant policy towards the numerous Jews of the oasis. The *qāḍī* opposed him. But al-Maghīlī, with supporting opinions from religious authorities elsewhere in North Africa, destroyed (*c.* 897/1492) the synagogue, massacring many Jews and forcing others to wear distinctive dress and badges.

From Tuat, al-Maghīlī visited Takedda, Katsina and Kano, teaching. One of his pupils at Takedda became *qāḍī* of Katsina. In Kano and Katsina, commercial and Islamic centres of Hausa, al-Maghīlī stimulated religious revival.

From Hausa, al-Maghīlī travelled, *c.* 907/1502, to Askiya al-Ḥājj Muḥammad, in Gao. Al-Maghīlī advised the *askiya*, particularly about Sonni 'Alī and his religion and government. Hearing that the Jews had killed his son, and failing to persuade the *askiya* to take vengeance, al-Maghīlī returned to Tuat. He died in 910/1504.

Al-Maghīlī judged both Sonni 'Alī, and his people, as 'mixers'—despite the profession of faith, Ramaḍān, royal largesse in alms, they continued to venerate pagan shrines, and invariably sought the guidance of pagan priests. Against 'mixers', al-Maghīlī decreed, *jihād* is more urgent than against pagans, for 'mixers' lead ignorant Muslims astray.

Sonni 'Alī was also condemned for injustice, but injustice, unlike 'mixing', is only disobedience, not unbelief. What is unbelief is to maintain that injustice is right. Here al-Maghīlī condemned the venal *'ulamā'* (*'ulamā' al-sū'*), who approve whatever the king wishes them to approve. Al-Maghīlī introduced the distinction between good and bad *'ulamā'*, contrasting the *mujaddid*—perhaps the first mention in Sudanese literature of this apocalyptic figure sent each century by God—with the *'ulamā'* of his time. Al-Maghīlī's political recommendation was a centralized *jamā'a* under a strong *imām*, administering the *Sharī'a*, using force if need be.

These advices answer the *askiya*'s queries. Did the *askiya* know sometimes what answers to expect? For example, when he asked if he should follow ignorant *'ulamā'*, or recompense from state funds those whom Sonni 'Alī had wronged, was he perhaps preparing to consolidate his position by dropping those whose support was no longer essential? We know that his attitude towards the *'ulamā'*, at first deferential, later hardened.

On his return from Pilgrimage, Askiya al-Ḥājj Muḥammad launched a *jihād* against the Mossi. This was his only formal *jihād*. His later wars, like those of Sonni 'Alī, were against all neighbours, Muslim and pagan. Expeditions penetrated Mali, Masina, Agades, Hausa, and elsewhere.

Muḥammad, blind and enfeebled, was deposed by his son Mūsā at the *Aḍḥā* festival in 1529. Of all *askiyas* after Muḥammad, only Dā'ūd b. Muḥammad, 956–991/1549–83, enjoyed a long and effective reign. Especially damaging was civil war in the late 1580s. The Muslims backed a rival candidate for *askiya*. They were defeated, and cruelly repressed, as in Sonni 'Alī's time.

Some *askiyas* were good Muslims, but even these were 'mixers' in one way or another. An *'ālim* was astonished to find Dā'ūd observing rituals of the divine kingship; Dā'ūd explained that only so could he control his subjects and protect the Muslims. Dā'ūd used sympathetic magic to kill an opponent. Another *askiya* was a soothsayer. *Askiyas* continued to use the free daughters of their soldiers as concubines.

The position of *'ulamā'* was also ambiguous. They approved measures to enforce Islam, yet sought to preserve a certain religious distance. The chronicles abound in examples of religious defiance and imperial deference. Sometimes *'ulamā'* refused appointment by the *askiyas*, though some were appointed forcibly nonetheless, others taking sanctuary in the mosque. Some *'ulamā'* even cursed the *askiyas*. Timbuktu, proud of its autonomy, championed religious independence, but this autonomy was limited. The *qāḍīs* of Timbuktu itself, drawn from one family, were appointed by the *askiyas*: one *askiya* refused for seventeen months to appoint any *qāḍī* at all in Timbuktu.

Bornu-Kanem

Kanem (whence sprang Bornu) apparently arose through the imposition of Saharan pastoralists, particularly Zaghāwa, upon smaller Negro states, from early in the Muslim era. Only in the sixth/twelfth century was a settled capital established, at Njimi.

Various reports suggest Umayyad influence in early Kanemi Islam, as on the east coast and, to a lesser extent, in Ghāna. The first missionary to Kanem claimed descent from the Caliph 'Uthmān—tradition says the caliphate passed from the Umayyads to Kanem—in the fifth/eleventh century descendants of Umayyad refugees were said to live there.

Links with North Africa and the heartlands of Islam were especially close. The first Muslim king (*mai*), Hume, who lived in the late eleventh century, founder of the Sefawa dynasty, died in Egypt, presumably on Pilgrimage. His son and successor went thrice on Pilgrimage, each time settling slaves in Cairo; finally the Cairenes became suspicious, as in that time of Fatimid disorder they might, and drowned the king. In the seventh/thirteenth century, the reign of Dabalemi, friend of the Tunisian Hafsids, marked the climax of trans-Saharan connexions. Valuable presents from Kanem, again including a giraffe, reached Tunis: Kanem Muslims founded a Mālikī hostel for travellers in Cairo.

Influence abroad but no peace at home. Dabalemi opened the talisman, as in his father's time the sacred snake had been killed; both these acts, sacrilegious in pagan eyes, were perhaps steps towards purer Islam. Dabalemi's father was a black sultan, after a succession of red nomads, so religious reform and racial assimilation may have marched together. Hume was also called 'the son of the black.'

The broken talisman provoked ambition, intrigue, and civil war. Most serious was war with the Bulala, a branch of the royal dynasty. Several Kanemi *mais* were killed. Nomad Arabs moving west joined in. In 794/1391–2, the Mamluk sultan of Egypt received a letter from the *mai* (who claimed Qurashī descent) complaining that Arabs were enslaving Kanemi Muslims. Just afterwards, the *mai*, on the advice of his '*ulamā*', abandoned Kanem and fled southwest to Bornu.

The Bulala ruled in Kanem. Originally perhaps pagan reactionaries, by 1500 they apparently traded with Nile towns, exchanged gifts with Egyptian rulers and merchants, and received with honour learned men and *sharīfs*.

The establishment of the refugee dynasty in Bornu helped to end Hausa isolation. Fulani '*ulamā*', it is said, visited Kanem from Mali about 1300. Now such east-west connexions became closer. One early Bornu *mai* may have had a Hausa mother.

In the late fifteenth and the sixteenth centuries Bornu power waxed.

A new capital, Ngazargamu, was built. Njimi was retaken from the Bulala, but never reoccupied. Idrīs Alawma, *c.* 1580–1610, whose biography by his *imām*, Ibn Fartuwa, survives, is our most detailed example (though perhaps not otherwise the most important) of these Bornu *mais*. He cultivated the north: an embassy went to Tripoli, a large caravan brought horses to Bornu, Alawma went on Pilgrimage and founded a pilgrim hostel. Guns came from the north. Alawma's wars were many and ferocious. Men were killed (save the Bulala, who were Muslims and kinsmen); women and children, usually, saved alive as slaves. Alawma supplemented war with the destruction of crops and trees, enlisting even '*ulamā*' for this, encouraging the work with music and dancers. Sometimes Ramaḍān is singled out as an efficacious time for fighting. Ibn Fartuwa cites the example of Muḥammad's wars. Alawma acted sternly against moral offences; the *Sharī'a* was more generally applied; disputes were referred to *qāḍīs*, no longer to chiefs or the *mai*. Brick mosques replaced thatch. Weights and measures were standardized. People were encouraged to settle and farm.

The eleventh/seventeenth and twelfth/eighteenth centuries were a period of decline. Hausa dominated the Saharan trade. Tuareg pressure increased. The Jukun raided from the south: there are many Jukun stories of Jukun magic pitted against Bornu Islam, the honours always equally divided. The last three rulers before the Fulani *jihād* took refuge in religion and paternity.

Hausa

Hausa, like Kanem, experienced the imposition of nomadic immigration (perhaps associated with the unsuccessful revolt of Abū Yazīd, the Kharijite of the Zanāta, against the Fatimids in the fourth/tenth century) upon an earlier Negro population. Hausa society then developed in relative isolation until the eighth/fourteenth century.

Then the situation altered. The settled city states, characteristic of Hausa from an early date, began to jostle one another. Mali's power was felt in Hausa. And from Mali came Islam: Mandingo immigrants converted the rulers of Kano and Katsina, main trade centres, in the early eighth/fourteenth century.

In Kano, the first Muslims apparently observed prayer, slaughtering regulations, and burial rites. The mosque was built under the sacred tree. Despite this conciliatory gesture, the guardians of the pagan heritage defiled the mosque each night, until struck blind through special prayers of the Muslims.

Yaji, ruler of Kano, perhaps impressed with the punishing power of prayer, enlisted Muslim support in war to the south. The military and political utility of '*ulamā*' to the Hausa rulers (for which rulers sometimes paid handsomely) continues clear until 'Uthmān dan Fodio's conquest. And when Islam seemed ineffectual, the ruler might restore paganism, as Kanajeji b. Yaji did in his war against Zaria. The basic pattern however is not alternation between two extremes, but the judicious counterpoint beloved of the 'mixers.' '*Ulamā*' served also as peace-makers, interceding with invaders to prevent the destruction of cities, or arranging a truce between warring states.

Islam came to Hausa first from Mali. Western religious influence persisted, partly through the Pilgrimage. In the ninth/fifteenth century, for example, Fulani '*ulamā*' brought books on theology and grammar to Kano, and passed on to Bornu. '*Ulamā*' came to Hausa from Bornu-Kanem also, and from North Africa. Political influence was more from the east. By 1400, the Sefawa had moved to Bornu, west of Lake Chad, and Mali was declining. A Bornu prince took refuge in Kano in the ninth/fifteenth century, introducing among other things the first market. Bornu soon brought Kano under tribute, to control the dissident branch of the Bornu dynasty there. Kano, despite occasional wars with Bornu, became the main channel for Bornu influence upon Hausa. Bornu and Songhay struggled to control Hausa. Under Askiya al-Ḥājj Muḥammad, Songhay apparently triumphed, but briefly. The revolt of Kebbi disrupted Songhay communications. Bornu predominance in Hausa revived until the twelfth/eighteenth century.

From Bornu, it seems, Hausa learnt ceremonious despotism. Muḥammad Rumfa, ruler of Kano (late ninth/fifteenth century), first applied Bornu examples wholeheartedly: state councils, eunuchs in high office, a palace, another market, royal regalia, slaving, forced labour and the requisition of property. Subsequent rulers enlarged their prerogatives. In the eleventh/seventeenth century *jangali*, cattle-tax on Fulani, began. In the twelfth/eighteenth, one ruler of Kano taxed '*ulamā*'.

Some of these developments towards centralized authoritarian government were almost certainly associated with Islam. At the same time, several incidents suggest that Hausa shared the continuing, if often impotent, awareness of tension between faith and kingship. 'Umaru b. Kanajeji (early ninth/fifteenth century), once an '*ālim* earnest in prayer, succeeded to the Kano throne. His friend, Abū Bakr, upbraided him, and went to Bornu for some years. 'Umaru ruled well and peacefully. Then Abū Bakr returned, warning of the snares of this world and punishment hereafter. So 'Umaru abdicated, and led a life of penitence. Again, in the tenth/sixteenth century, a deposed ruler of Kano refused to resume the throne even when asked, preferring study among the '*ulamā*'. Again, an eleventh/seventeenth century prince, fearing civil war after his father's death, prayed for his own death, and was heard. Other rulers were so occupied with religious affairs that they were unable to govern effectively. Many, of course, combined faith and rule without qualms.

This awareness seems less vivid east of Hausa. Only here and there do traces appear. A sixth/twelfth century Kanemi *mai* was imprisoned by his mother for executing a thief instead of administering the Qur'anic punishment. He also elaborated royal ceremonial: several Arab writers describe the *mais* screened from public view, their subjects prostrate before them. Alawma's biographer that '...a king's justice quotes the dictum for one day is equal to service of God for sixty years.'[1] For its effectiveness, or its rarity? Might this apparent difference—granting the evidence for it is fragmentary—be associated with the fact that two main groups disseminating Islam in the west, Berbers and Fulani, were in some sense opposition groups, Berbers against Arabs, Fulani against Negroes, while eastwards the example of Middle Eastern Muslim despotism was more pervasive?

Bagirmi and Waday

In the tenth/sixteenth century, states began to emerge in Bagirmi and Waday. The Kenga dynasty in Bagirmi, originally pagan, became Muslim later in the century when 'Abd Allāh ousted his elder brother. 'Abd Allāh's government resembled the Bornu monarchy—he was probably a contemporary of Alawma—but Bagirmi Islam apparently derived from Fulani '*ulamā*' who had entered the country (together with cattlemen) even before the Kenga.

In Waday, the Tunjur dynasty may have been superficially Muslim, but was overthrown in the early eleventh/seventeenth century by 'Abd al-Karīm, perhaps originally of the Nilotic Ja'aliyyūn: he claimed 'Abbasid descent. According to one tradition, 'Abd al-Karīm learnt a

[1] Ahmed ibn Fartua (tr. H. R. Palmer), *History of ... the reign of Mai Idris Alooma of Bornu (1571–1583)* (Lagos, 1926), 9–10.

more ardent faith from the Fulani *'ulamā'* in Bagirmi: according to another, his uncle or father, a pioneer preacher in Waday, inspired him: yet another says that he displaced the leading *'ālim* in Waday (the ancestor of the Kapka Zaghāwa) by removing and reburying a tablet of Qur'anic inscriptions. 'Abd al-Karīm founded the capital, Wara; North African builders may have helped him and his successors.

The political history of Bagirmi and Waday in the eleventh/seventeenth and twelfth/eighteenth centuries centred on resistance to powerful neighbours, Bornu and Darfur. In the later twelfth/eighteenth century, both Bagirmi and Waday succeeded. The ruler of Bagirmi then, Muḥammad al-Amīn, went on Pilgrimage, usually a sign of security. Despite wars, pupils and *'ulamā'* continued to move about. *'Ulamā'* went between Bagirmi and Hausa, perhaps as early as the third quarter of the sixteenth century. Refugee *'ulamā'* from Bornu about 1600 went both to Hausa and Bagirmi. Waday looked east: teachers and traders came there from the Funj kingdom of Sennar, and pupils went to the Nile from Waday.

The Moroccan conquest and the rule of the pashas

Disagreement over the Saharan salt-mines, even fighting, continued between Morocco and Songhay throughout the sixteenth century. It came to a head under the Sa'did Sultan Aḥmad al-Manṣūr (986–1012/1578–1603), son of a Negro concubine. He reopened negotiations with Songhay about the mines, fortified with legal opinions from his *'ulamā'*. In 992/1584 a Moroccan embassy, perhaps a reconnaissance, visited Songhay with rich gifts. In 996/1588, Askiya Isḥāq II ascended the throne. Al-Manṣūr renewed his claims. The *askiya* defied him. Al-Manṣūr, pointing to the wealth of Songhay, and adding that the *askiya*, not being a Qurayshite, had no right to rule, persuaded his notables to support an expeditionary force. In Dhu'l-Ḥijja 998/October 1590, the expedition marched, about 4,000 troops, mostly Spanish musketeers. The muskets were to prove decisive.

Divided counsels ruled in Songhay. A suggestion of the Timbuktu *'ulamā'*, that their city be evacuated south of the Niger, was rejected, since *'ulamā'*, though scholarly, cannot plan war.[1] Jawdhar Pasha, the Spanish renegade commander, advanced on Gao, calling on the *askiya* to

[1] This may reflect a widespread attitude—among Somali, for example, *wadāds* or men of religion have usually only limited influence in political counsels, but are pre-eminent in making peace and reconciling enemies.

acknowledge the sultan, the *Sharīf*, his sovereign. Isḥāq refused. In Jumādā I 999/March 1591 the armies met at Tundibi. During the battle, the *askiya-alfa*, apparently a senior *'ālim* in Isḥāq's service, succeeded after several attempts in persuading the *askiya* to flee. Isḥāq's departure signalled the disintegration of the Songhay army. Only a picked *élite*, who had bound calf to thigh at the beginning, remained and were slaughtered, vainly protesting that they were Muslims. Isḥāq abandoned Gao, leaving only the *khaṭīb* to receive Jawdhar. Jawdhar, finding Gao poor and unhealthy, withdrew to Timbuktu, where he was received quietly by the *qāḍī*, and built a fortress in the Ghadames merchants' quarter.

Some of the Songhay forces abandoned the fleeing Isḥāq, and set up his brother, Muḥammad Gao, as usurper *askiya*. Muḥammad Gao's reign was brief and distracted. His main advisers were the *askiya-alfa*, Bukar, and the *hi-koy* or admiral of the river fleet, Laha Sorkia, representing the older semi-pagan tradition. Time and again, Laha Sorkia counselled resistance, Bukar collaboration. Muḥammad Gao followed Bukar's advice. Finally, the usurper and his colleagues, under safe conduct, were murdered by the Moroccans. Only Bukar went free. The Moroccans set up a third brother as puppet. The *askiya-alfa* seems to have played a traitor's part; perhaps Islam generally, appealing to a literate, urban class, divided the Songhay nation against itself.

In Dhu'l-Ḥijja 999/October 1591, fighting broke out in Timbuktu: the Moroccan garrison lost many killed. What part the Timbuktu *'ulamā'* played is not clear: it is difficult to imagine a general outbreak without at least the tacit approval of 'Umar, the *qādī*. This was the opinion of Maḥmūd Zarghūn Pasha, Jawdhar's replacement, and he wrote reproachfully to 'Umar.

Peace was restored, but in 1593 Maḥmūd Zarghūn summoned the *'ulamā'* of Timbuktu to renew their oath of allegiance. Once gathered in the Sankore mosque, they were arrested. In a scuffle outside, some *'ulamā'* were killed. Several others, the *qāḍī* and the celebrated Aḥmad Bābā among them, all apparently of the 'Aqīt family, were exiled to Marrakesh.

Later Aḥmad Bābā was granted an interview with al-Manṣūr. Finding al-Manṣūr concealed behind a curtain, Aḥmad Bābā refused to talk with him, complaining that by speaking without being seen, al-Manṣūr was imitating God. The curtain was removed. Aḥmad Bābā taught in the mosque at Marrakesh, and even gave *fatwās*, but he never accepted appointment as *muftī*. In 1016/1608 he returned to Timbuktu, alone; in 1036/1627 he died. Among his writings is a book on the avoidance of unjust rulers.

Songhay resistance continued downstream, towards Dendi, under Nūḥ, legitimate successor to Isḥāq who was killed. The Moroccans suffered through illness and guerilla warfare in the forests. Maḥmūd was killed. In 1007/1599 Askiya Nūḥ was deposed, and Jawdhar Pasha recalled to Morocco: vigorous campaigning ceased on either side. Northern Songhay remained under the Moroccans; Dendi, divided into several chieftaincies, continued independent.

The usual explanation today of the Moroccan conquest is economic. Certainly al-Manṣūr wanted gold, but the formal justification for conquest, in the letters of al-Manṣūr and Maḥmūd, was religious. When Aḥmad Bābā charged al-Manṣūr with aggression, the sultan replied that he, as a *sharīf*, wished to unit the Islamic world. For a time, the sultan of Morocco controlled his new province directly, making all principal appointments himself. But close supervision across the desert was impossible. Moreover, income from Songhay did not justify the heavy cost in men, money and supplies. The Moroccans had not conquered the gold-fields: even in Timbuktu they had to trade for gold, and trade depended on peaceful conditions. The most interesting item of income, in its religious consequences, was an elephant, whose Negro keepers are said to have introduced tobacco to Morocco, thus igniting the agitated controversy about the legality of smoking.

Morocco gradually lost interest. One of the last acts done at the sultan's order was in 1035/1626, when a senior Moroccan official was tortured to death in Timbuktu. In 1070/1659–60, the *khuṭba* ceased to be recited in the sultan's name. Occasional embassies from Morocco continued. As late as 1893 Timbuktu appealed to these ancient links, for help against the French, but in vain.

The pashalic of Timbuktu quickly became an elective office dependent on the will of the army. By 1750, nearly a hundred pashas had ruled, many several times, as compared with sixteen puppet *askiyas*, and only eleven Timbuktu *qāḍīs* despite an average age of well over fifty on appointment. The pashas collected taxes, but did not interfere with local institutions.

Timbuktu under the *askiyas* had been a religious citadel. *'Ulamā'* continued to serve the pashas, reconciling adversaries, administering an ineffectual oath of peace to a Tuareg chief, and so on. Yet, though it was thought irregular for a pasha directly to appoint a *qāḍī*, it seems that *'ulamā'* did not enjoy much independence of status. Violation of sanctuary at a saint's tomb, but not at the *imām*'s house, was visited by divine vengeance. *'Ulamā'* were faint-hearted in proclaiming the law. Occasional pashas refused alms to *'ulamā'*.

Islam was in some ways strictly observed. Al-Bukhārī was read to the pasha in Ramaḍān. The Prophet's Birthday was especially gaily celebrated. Free women were secluded. One pasha tried to apply *jihād* rules in his wars, but his officials concealed the enemy's acceptance of his appeal to be converted and submit, so that the attack might proceed. Later a rival preached *jihād* against this same pasha.

Relations between conquerors and conquered improved. But vassal revolts and enemy attacks soon restricted effective control by the pashalic to the main centres, Jenne, Gao and Timbuktu. Mali, now once more a chieftaincy only, attacked Jenne in 1007/1599, but was beaten off: the last convulsion of a long overshadowed empire. The Fulani of Masina raided, a portent of their future heritage. In the twelfth/eighteenth century particularly, Tuareg harrassed the pashas, and at last occupied both Gao (1770) and Timbuktu (1787). Nevertheless the Arma (Ar., *al-rumāh*, the shooters), descendants of the Moroccan invaders, are still an influential caste.

The Bambara

Following the Moroccan conquest of Songhay, a new power rose to dominate much of the western Sudan—the Bambara. These are a Mande-speaking people, centred on the upper Niger valley, once subject to Mali, then to Songhay. In the eleventh/seventeenth century, independent but not yet organized in states, they grew in strength. Mamari Kulubali (1712–55) founded the main Bambara state, Segu, while dissidents established Karta. Masina, even Timbuktu paid tribute to Mamari.

It was the essential religious characteristic of the Bambara, sometimes regarded as the champions of paganism, that Islamic elements were absorbed without displacing the pagan. The Bambara are an excellent, if extreme, example of the 'mixers.'

'Ulamā' were active in court life, helping to arbitrate in succession disputes, advising rulers, healing, reconciling officials and kings. Da, king of Segu (1808–27), in whose time arose Shehu Aḥmadu, had been warned by a local *sharīf* not to provoke the Muslims. Rulers themselves became at least superficially Muslim, another branch of their spiritual repertory.

Some, as the Kulubali clan, regarded themselves as Muslim: when al-Ḥājj'Umar called the king of Karta to conversion, he, holding himself already a Muslim, interpreted this as an ultimatum and killed the messenger. But Islam must not compromise clan independence: this was the mistake of Turo-koro Mari, king of Segu (1854–6), for which he paid with his life. Popular religion, observing Muslim festivals as honouring ancestors, employing Muslim and pagan divination, and so forth shows the same pattern. Certain tribal groups within Bambara country, all linked with ancient Soninke Islam, are particularly fervent Muslims.

The Mande dispersion

Dominant among the diverse, widespread, Mande peoples at this time were the Bambara, little influenced by Islam. But a simultaneous Mande dispersion begun long before, west and south to the Atlantic, east across the savannah, was profoundly significant for Islam.

Different Mande groups took part, including pagan cultivators. The traders, however, commonly called *dyula*, were Muslim. So of course were the '*ulamā*', esteemed by Muslims for whom they provided Qur'anic schools and other services, and by pagans whom they served as diviners, advisers, and so forth. Traders and clerics were complementary. Amulets were an important trade good. Supernatural authority safeguarded the commercial traveller: Owen, an eighteenth-century slave-trader in Sierra Leone called the Mande '...wandering pilgrims, who for their holyness is suffer'd to pass and repass, where others would not.'[1] A Mande emigrant (later a great chief under the Bambara king N'golo), intending to trade in Segu, found conditions too unsettled for commerce but did very well with making amulets.

Forms of settlement differed. Jobson, trading on the Gambia in the early seventeenth century, described Muslim towns as carefully separated from the pagan. Muslims married only among themselves. Such towns were staging points for travellers: Mahome, a particular friend of Jobson, '...did diverse times lodge and entertain strangers, that came, especially of his own profession...'[2] Larger commercial centres grew up in the savannah, as Kankan in upper Guinea, Kong in the Ivory Coast, and further east. Without separation, Muslims might be absorbed utterly by the local environment. Sometimes Mande immigrants became chiefs over local people. Such chiefs might abandon their original

[1] Nicholas Owen, *Journal of a Slave-Dealer* (London, 1930), 56–7.

[2] Richard Jobson, *The Golden Trade* (London, 1932), 93–4.

Islam; elsewhere Muslim chiefs ruled pagan commoners. Trading agents introduced by Europeans, or *'ulamā'* introduced by local chiefs, might become chiefs.

Trade was generally peaceful, but violence occasionally marked the city states. A Mande revolution founded Kong about 1730. Kankan was temporarily destroyed about 1765. Susu (a Mande people) seized Port Loko from the Temne, who regained it (under another Susu leader) about 1816. Mande rivals fought on the Liberian plateau and elsewhere. Refugees fled to new districts: Islam was further diffused.

B. THE WESTERN AND CENTRAL SUDAN IN THE EIGHTEENTH AND NINETEENTH CENTURIES

Introduction

The twelfth/eighteenth century was the birth time of the theocracies, which in a series of revolutions engulfed almost the whole Sudan before European control was imposed. For the most part, the relationships among these, and between them and the wider world of Islam, are obscure. It is tempting to postulate direct Wahhābī influence, but where our knowledge is sufficient to judge this seems unfounded. In 1784 the thirteenth Islamic century began. There was an air of apocalyptic expectancy, but no eminent leader in west or central Sudan emerged as *mahdī*. Two principles underlie reformist doctrine. First, 'mixing' is forbidden. Those who combine pagan and Muslim practices are infidels. And second, as no accommodation between infidel and Muslim practices is permissible, so there can be no association between infidel and Muslim people. An infidel king means an infidel kingdom, and *hijra*, emigration, is obligatory for Muslim citizens of such a kingdom. Between emigrant and stay-at-home Muslims there are no signs of love. The property of stay-at-homes may be confiscated; and, *hijra* should lead to *jihād*. Equally an alliance between an infidel and a Muslim ruler convicts both of infidelity. These two principles, that 'mixers' are infidels and that those who associate with 'mixers' are infidels, are related, whether as cause or effect, to the fact that the *jihāds* were mainly against professing Muslims.

A political revolution complemented the doctrinal. Everywhere the reformers established states, usually incorporating smaller, former states. The Fulani, and the closely related Torodbe, the Tokolor religious class from which both 'Uthmān and al-Ḥājj 'Umar came, were the chief agents. Spreading from the ancient area of Takrūr on the Senegal, they entered Masina perhaps in the fifteenth century, and reached Bagirmi and Adamawa in the 18th. In Futa Toro and Masina, the reformers overthrew existing Fulani dynasties, but certain rules of the game here moderated war among brothers.

The Fulani everywhere were immigrants, sometimes of centuries' standing, sometimes nineteenth-century invaders. Al-Ḥājj 'Umar and al-Kanamī were both foreigners, relying on imported troops. It was an age of Islamic imperialism. Only the later leaders, Samori for example and Lat Dior, appear as nationalists, often in response to European encroachment, and their purely Islamic fervour is in doubt.

Thus the reformed faith, and the revolutionary government, spread over the western and central Sudan, recoiling at the forest beyond Ilorin, at the European presence on the Senegal, at the turbulence of desert nomads around Timbuktu, or where the distance was too great in Bornu and beyond.

Futa Jallon

Militant Islam first revived in Futa Jallon, the highlands where the Senegal and Gambia rivers rise, an area of mixed peoples among whom the Solima were important. In the eleventh/seventeenth century Fulani pastoralists, with *'ulamā'*, began entering Futa Jallon. In 1725, Ibrāhīm Mūsā, a Fulani cleric, took the title *almami* (*al-imām*) and proclaimed against the local rulers *jihād*. About 1776, Ibrāhīm Sori, the Fulani war-leader, himself now *almami*, ended the *jihād*.

Politically, the imamate of Futa Jallon failed. Civil strife was endemic. Finally the descendants of the two Ibrāhīms agreed that the office of *almami* should alternate between them every two years, a precarious arrangement. Yet Futa Jallon had considerable religious influence. The half-century of war encouraged many Muslims, individuals and groups, to move south and west. Pagan tributaries of Futa Jallon learnt of Islam. Most important perhaps, Futa Jallon was a centre of education. The Mandingo king of Forecaria studied there: so also Sulaymān Bal of Futa Toro: a prudent Sierra Leone ruler in 1769 sent one son to learn from the Christians, another to Futa Jallon.

Among some, the sword earned hatred not submission. The Solima, at first allies of the Fulani, their leaders converted to Islam, later broke with Fulani domination. Driven from Futa Jallon, the Solima founded a new capital, Falaba, to the south. Every trace of Islam was abandoned, even Muslim dress, even fashion—Solima women now wore a gold earring in the left ear only, '... in which they will sometimes carry two or even three, in order to show that it is not poverty but purpose, and as a distinction from the women of Fouth Jallon'.[1]

Even here, the power of education held. The king of Falaba in 1822 still cherished the Islam he had learnt in his youth in Futa Jallon, though because of popular feeling he had now to pray secretly. Falaba preserved its independence till crushed by Samori in 1884.

Futa Toro

The Fulani Denyanke dynasty ruled Futa Toro, on the middle Senegal, from the tenth/sixteenth century. At first with strong Mandingo connections, and probably Muslim, the Denyanke later became identified with a pagan Fulani aristocracy, contrasted with the Muslim, more racially mixed, Futa Toro Tokolor. Yet Denyanke princes continued to study under '*ulamā*' in the *Sāḥil*; one '*ālim*, a *sharīf*, healed and converted a Denyanke ruler, father of his pupil.

After the *jihād* began in Futa Jallon, Sulaymān Bal, a Futa Toro '*ālim*, went there to study. He asked his teachers to invoke God against the Denyanke. Once more in Futa Toro, Sulaymān won disciples. He disquieted the Denyanke, but did not attack them. Instead, he fought the Trārza Moors, traditional scourge of the valley.

After seven years' war, he announced that an *almami* should rule Futa Toro. His followers acclaimed him *almami*, but he refused. So did the next popular choice. Finally 'Abd al-Qādir, a Tokolor of reputed Qurashī ancestry, reluctantly accepted, though he was not invested until 1189/1775–6, after Sulaymān had fallen fighting the Trārza.

'Abd al-Qādir continued the Trārza wars, adding civil war and war to the south. In the civil war, aided by a disputed succession, the religious party overthrew the Denyanke. Even so, the Denyanke refrained from murdering 'Abd al-Qādir when they once might, and 'Abd al-Qādir reserved an enclave where a Denyanke *almami* might rule.

In the southern wars, 'Abd al-Qādir fought Futa Bundu, where another *almami* ruled. 'Abd al-Qādir captured and killed him. A Moor, who had come to the Negroes seeking purer religion, returned in disgust at this murder of a Muslim. Attacking the Wolof state of Cayor, 'Abd

[1] A. G. Laing, *Travels ... in western Africa* (London, 1825), 359.

al-Qādir was captured, but was released in respect for his supernatural powers. About 1805, 'Abd al-Qādir faced revolt at home, attacks from abroad. Warned by *'ulamā'* that his salvation was assured only if he was killed on his own soil by his own people, he asked a shaykh to pray for this. 'Abd al-Qādir was killed, some say by the new *almami* of Futa Bundu.

The imamate continued until the French occupation, a religious Tokolor aristocracy supplanting the Denyanke warriors. Elections rivalled the Timbuktu pashas: one *almami* ruled nine or ten times. Al-Ḥājj 'Umar's visits in mid-century increased confusion.

'Uthmān dan Fodio

'Uthmān was born in Gobir in 1167/1754, of a family of scholars. His early life was spent in study, travelling from one teacher to another. One of the most important was Jibrīl b. 'Umar, by oral tradition a Hausa, who initiated him in the Qādiriyya order. Jibrīl had already alarmed the Hausa kings by preaching reform, even attempting *jihād*. About 1775, 'Uthmān began preaching and teaching himself, wandering widely in Kebbi, Zanfara and elsewhere.

'Uthmān's prestige soon attracted the attention of the kings. Oral tradition says he became court tutor under Bawa, king of Gobir. Written records, on the contrary, portray 'Uthmān as very much apart, cautioning his followers not to go to the kings of this world. When Bawa summoned the *'ulamā'* to Magami in the late 1780s, 'Uthmān attended, but he and his party (unlike the other *'ulamā'*) refused the royal alms. This meeting may perhaps have been to ask prayers for the forthcoming campaign against Katsina, after which Bawa died of grief at the death of his son. In the contrast between the oral and written reports, the former, reflecting popular conservatism, seems to stress continuity between the old and new régimes, while the latter, reflecting official apologia, favours the 'new broom' interpretation. Both versions may indeed be correct for different stages in 'Uthmān's career.

In the early 1790s, 'Uthmān settled at Degel in Gobir. Tension mounted. 'Uthmān and his brother 'Abd Allāh wrote religious poetry of great popular effect. The Timbuktu Kunta sent a friendly emissary. 'Uthmān instructed his people to begin arming. The Gobir king attempted to curb the growing independence of 'Uthmān's party, the *Jamā'a*, by forbidding emblems such as the turban and the woman's veil. Fighting broke out between the Hausa *'ālim*, 'Abd al-Salām, a partisan of 'Uthmān, and Yunfa king of Gobir. Yunfa threatened Degel. In February 1804, 'Uthmān and the *Jamā'a* emigrated to Gudu, on the Gobir border.

The emigrants began raiding. The kings began persecuting their Muslim subjects. The first main battle was at Kwotto water, 'Abd Allāh defeating the Gobir forces. Hausa and Fulani fought on both sides, Tuareg also aiding Gobir. After this, 'Uthmān established a new base in Zanfara, then friendly because of vivid recollections of recent war with Gobir. Later, violent resistance to 'Uthmān arose in Zanfara. The tribal character of the *jihād* is debated. Official Fulani apologetic may neglect the contribution of Hausa Muslims. Doctrine, seeking general principles, sometimes reinforced tribal distinctions: 'Uthmān ruled that the enslavement of any Fulani was wrong because most Fulani were Muslim; and that all Hausa kings might be overthrown, despite the rare serious Muslim among them. Very rare were Hausa holding military or political office in the *jihād*; a few achieved religious eminence; there may have been some popular support by Hausa Muslim commoners.

The fighting spread. *'Ulamā'* and warriors hurried to 'Uthmān, received banners from him, and returned to lead the *Jamā'a* in their various homes. The fall of the Gobir capital in 1808 meant that the *jihād* was out of danger. Reformed Islam, under Fulani *amīrs*, spread over most of Hausaland and beyond.

The reformed doctrine, sometimes assumed to be Wahhābī, may have had a medieval inspiration.[1] In constitutional theory, the Fulani empire was much more complex than the Medinese *umma*: the sources quoted are often late 'Abbasid. In doctrine, the Fulani respected *ijmā'*; for example, the Fulani attitude towards tomb observances, though puritan, was milder than the Wahhābī. The Fulani were scrupulous about Mālikī orthodoxy: they did not become schismatic. Jibrīl, twice on Pilgrimage, may have been more Wahhābī: 'Uthmān, his son Bello, and 'Abd Allāh were never in Mecca.

The Fulani were deeply concerned with doctrinal precedent. Their writings, largely imitative, were not, however, entirely so. 'Uthmān denied that Muslims through grave disobedience became unbelievers, thus differing, though respectfully, from Jibrīl. Bello affirmed that

[1] M. Hiskett, 'An Islamic tradition of reform . . .', in *BSOAS*, 1962 (3), 577–96.

Muslims helping unbelievers in war against Muslims became unbelievers, 'Abd Allāh denied it. Disputing an opinion of Aḥmad Bābā, 'Uthmān said every scholar decides according to the knowledge of his own time.

The basic argument was not with paganism, but with the 'mixers'. Al-Maghīlī's strictures on Sonni 'Alī were repeatedly cited. 'Abd Allāh argued that the similarity between fifteenth-century Songhay and eighteenth-century Hausa made the *jihād* legal.

Fulani political theory condemned many practices then current. Kings were criticised for abusing the rights of women; but social freedom for women was also reproved. Discipline of women was a favourite point of reformers: a Bornu *'ālim* once objected to women attending 'Uthmān's public preaching. Fines in place of Qur'anic punishments were condemned. Royal titles, royal music, abject reverence to royalty, all came under the ban; customary inheritance and uncanonical taxation likewise. Among the objectionable taxes were the *jangali* or cattle tax, and a tax on meat at the market. Complaints about commandeering livestock, and about penalties for stray animals, confirm a cattle-owning strand among the reformers.

In place of the fractious Hausa kingdoms, 'Uthmān proposed a united polity, the *Jamā'a*, under the *amīr al-mu'minīn*. The *wazīrs* should wake the ruler if he sleeps, make him see if he is blind, remind him if he forgets. Other officials, particularly *qāḍīs*, are specified. All officials should strive for justice and compassion. A good deal of 'Uthmān's political writing attempts the proper regulation of *jihād*.

What happened in practice? After the fall of Alkalawa (1808), 'Uthmān left practical affairs mainly to 'Abd Allāh in the west, and Bello in the east, Gwandu and Sokoto becoming the respective capitals. Was 'Uthmān perhaps already distressed by the materialism of the *jihād*? There is a report that his declining years were haunted by remorse for the many Muslims he had killed. 'Abd Allāh certainly had serious doubts: even while marching on Alkalawa, suddenly filled with revulsion at the selfishness of his colleagues, he started off for Mecca. In fact he went only to Kano. Later, when Bello ousted 'Abd Allāh for the succession to 'Uthmān (d. 1817), 'Abd Allāh overcame in scholarship his disappointment.

Bello's succession signalled widespread Hausa revolts. Indeed, some areas of Hausa resistance continued in arms throughout the century. The Fulani rulers found it politic to compromise with Hausa traditions of government, while they also quarrelled among themselves.

Adamawa

Pastoral Fulani, mainly from Bornu, probably arrived in northern Adamawa in numbers only in the later eighteenth century. Perhaps for this reason, they still speak their own language, and are relatively distinct racially. Few strong, organized societies existed to check their encroachment. Even before the *jihād*, several Fulani lamidates (i.e. amirates) were founded, often peacefully.

Modibbo Adama—he refused out of humility the title *lamido* (i.e. *amīr*)—was born in northern Adamawa, studied in Bornu, and became a teacher. Visiting Sokoto, he received a flag for Adamawa from 'Uthmān, to the chagrin of some who already ruled parts of the country. In 1809, Adama proclaimed *jihād*.

The main early conquests were north of the Benue: important was the Marwa plain, south of Mandara, rich in horses. The sultans of Mandara had been converted early in the eighteenth century, it is said through '*ulamā*' from Fez returning from Mecca. Faith did not save Mandara: Adama occupied the capital. But his troops quickly forgot religion for plunder. Adama, dismayed by their greed, prayed that the Mandarans might regain their city. His prayer was answered. The Fulani were expelled. Mandara was later a buffer between Bornu and Adamawa.

Adama's own campaigns were principally north and east, where Fulani had already penetrated. The plateau country to the south had first to be invaded, then conquered. Begun about 1825, this was speedily accomplished.

Little is known of early Adamawan Islam. Amulets and charms were widespread in Barth's time (1851). Friday and festival prayers were favoured occasions for important announcements—concerning forthcoming expeditions, or the succession—even for capturing an intractable *lamido*.

Adama died in 1848. Four sons succeeded him. Open dissensions among the lamidates appeared. Tibati in particular, defied neighbours and Yola, the capital of Adamawa, alike.

Yola paid tribute to Sokoto, and important questions, often concerning succession, were referred thither. Yola in turn received tribute from lesser lamidates. The Fulani lived in towns and settlements, like colonies; even those with town residences were often absent with herds and flocks. Hausa became increasingly important, exploring new areas through trade, working as artisans, acting as financiers for the *lamidos*.

Kanuri, Shuwa, and some local people closely allied to the Fulani, also shared free Muslim status. Other local people were dependent tributaries. Still others resisted: fighting continued into the twentieth century. There were large slave settlements.

Adamawa was a principal slave reserve. Recaptives far away in Sierra Leone told of Fulani slaving there. Tribute to Sokoto was mainly slaves: often, Sokoto agents came to collect these. Drafts on Yola for slaves were given and honoured. About 1852 a *sharīf*, al-Ḥabīb, came to Sokoto begging. He was given letters for horses in Zaria, and for 200 slaves in Adamawa, which he collected. Later he was involved in Kano politics. Occasionally the demand, external and internal, for slaves so increased that even Fulani, even *'ulamā'*, were enslaved.

Nupe and Yoruba

References to Nupe begin in Hausaland with the eighth/fourteenth century. In the ninth/fifteenth, Nupe exported eunuchs and kola, and imported horses. Later, even guns came from Nupe. Bawa of Gobir exchanged horses and *vedettes* for Nupe slaves and cowries. Bello remarked on the strange and beautiful merchandize of Nupe. Islam probably penetrated with trade, affecting Yoruba as well as Nupe. In the 1580s, an *'ālim* from Nupe is said to have healed a quarrel between king and nobles in Yoruba. A little later, a Katsina *'ālim* wrote in answer to questions from Yoruba *'ulamā'*. The first recorded Muslim ruler (*etsu*) of Nupe is in the twelfth/eighteenth century. With the *jihād*, Islam became more thrusting. Fulani *'ulamā'* and cattlemen had already penetrated Nupe. A court *'ālim*, Mallam Dendo, who became a flag-bearer of 'Uthmān, confirmed Fulani influence by exploiting a disputed succession. The Fulani were few, so Dendo maintained puppet Nupe *etsus*. His son, 'Uthmān Zākī, 1832–59, was the first Fulani *etsu*. Later, disputes among Fulani dynasties led to interventions by Gwandu.

In Yoruba, groups were already splitting from the old Oyo empire, and Dahomey was raiding. About 1817, the Oyo governor of Ilorin, Afonja, revolted, supported by a Yoruba Muslim chief, Alimi a Fulani *'ālim* (whence probably his name), and by Muslim bands, Yoruba, Hausa and Fulani, which were encouraged to come to Ilorin. Traditions differ about Alimi: was he devout, anxious to curb his supporters, refusing a chieftancy; or did he aim at political power? His son, 'Abd al-Salām, who succeeded him in 1833, and whose prayers had formerly helped Afonja against Oyo, did seek power. Afonja fought, but too late. He was killed. Ilorin became the south-western bastion of the Fulani, as Adamawa the south-eastern.

The Yoruba retreated south from old Oyo. The Fulani boasted of dipping the Qur'ān in the Atlantic. Internecine war, fostered by the Fulani, racked Yoruba. Slaving was widespread: in 1852 Muslim traders, mainly in slaves, were in Ibadan, and highly regarded. But 'Abd al-Salām died in 1842; the Fulani were checked in 1843; and Ibadan, triumphant in 1862 over its main Yoruba rival, emerged the scourge of its neighbours and a barricade against the Fulani.

Bornu, Bagirmi and Waday

Eastward 'Uthmān's *jihād* met Muslim resistance. The Fulani, long infiltrating western Bornu, responded to 'Uthmān's inspiration; fighting broke out between them and the *mai*. Twice the Bornu capital, Ngazargamu, fell to Fulani religious warriors; twice the fleeing *mai* appealed to Muḥammad al-Amīn al-Kanamī, a Kanembu *'ālim* recently returned from Mecca; twice al-Kanamī repulsed the Fulani. Al-Kanamī, maintaining a puppet *mai*, founded a new capital, Kukawa, on the spot where he once finished reading the Qur'ān, his habit when travelling.

The *mais* were powerless against their dominating saviour. Al-Kanami's favourite troops were his Kanembu spearsmen. Shuwa and Arabs were among other foreigners whom he encouraged to settle, and in whom he placed chief reliance. Al-Kanamī's sword was not temporal only: a vision called him to war with the Fulani.

The *mais* chafed. In 1817 a conspiracy between the *mai* and Bagirmi, against al-Kanamī, failed. Further fighting followed. In 1824 al-Kanamī, invoking 'Abdal-Qādir, and helped by British cannon, crushed Bagirmi at Ngala. Emboldened, he turned west and marched on Kano. The *amīr* of Bauchi (who before the battle put 200 men to guard his concubines, lest in defeat they disperse and he be thought poor) threw him back in 1826. Thereafter, despite raiding and subversion, spheres of influence were apparently observed between Sokoto and Kukawa.

Al-Kanamī died in 1835 or 1837; his son 'Umar succeeded. 'Umar made peace with Bagirmi, his mother's country. Henceforth the main rivals were Bornu and Waday, often fighting over a prostrate and ravaged Kanem. Bagirmi was a slave reservoir. In 1846 the *mais* made a last attempt to regain authority with help from Waday, but failed. The last Sefawa fell in battle. 'Umar became official, as well as effective, ruler.

In 1856–7 Sharīf al-Dīn, a Fulani ascetic, passed slowly through Bornu towards Mecca. ʿAbd al-Qādir, king of Bagirmi, tried to prevent him entering Bagirmi, first by persuasion, then by force. Sharīf al-Dīn, accompanied by many thousands of pilgrims, possessed of such supernatural resource that some called him *mahdī*, defeated and killed ʿAbd al-Qādir. Sharīf al-Dīn went on, his following growing, and with it problems of discipline and supply. Some pilgrims turned back: one of ʿAbd al-Qādir's sons took vengeance on these, hence his nickname *Abū Sikkīn*, 'father of a knife'. Then Sharīf al-Dīn himself was killed, and his convoy dissolved.

Correspondence survives between al-Kanamī, and ʿUthmān and his colleagues. Fulani apologetic accused Bornu of various offences: injustice, such as bribery and embezzlement; sin, such as free women uncovering their heads; pagan practices, including sacrifices at sacred spots, and river rites; and of aiding the Hausa against the Fulani. Sin and injustice, ʿUthmān admitted, do not constitute unbelief. Al-Kanamī, having lived long in Medina, Cairo and Fez, and having studied history, knew well that no Muslim realm, no Muslim epoch, was free of wrong, yet did not thereby become pagan. Pagan practices, however, ʿUthmān continued, are unbelief: since the *mai* observed these, Bornu was a land of unbelief. The existence of Muslims there made no difference. ʿUthmān urged *hijra* upon al-Kanamī. It was the final charge, of aiding the Hausa, that was the cause of the Fulani attack on Bornu. To aid an unbeliever is to become one. ʿUthmān and al-Kanamī respected each other's learning. Al-Kanamī accused Bello of acting against ʿUthmān's writing. Bello, more sarcastic than ʿUthmān about al-Kanamī, nevertheless disliked such war between religious leaders, and suggested a negotiated peace.

Islam in al-Kanamī's Bornu was quite strict. Al-Kanamī and ʿUmar, having like ʿUthmān the title shaykh, renounced dynastic pomp, though Muslim festivals continued occasions of state ritual. The Prophet's Birthday was gay, the women dancing with especial verve. Al-Kanamī severely enforced Ramaḍān, and feminine morality. Once an *ʿālim* intervened, successfully, to prevent him hanging two girls for fornication. On another occasion, al-Kanamī overruled a *qāḍī*, and applied the tribal custom of a life for a life. Prayer and food regulations were observed: the *qāḍī* disallowed the oath of a Muslim who had eaten the Christian bread of the first European visitors. Qur'āns copied by Bornu scribes were exported to North Africa.

Bagirmi Islam was not highly regarded. In Waday, the Sanūsiyya made the route through Kufra to Cyrenaica culturally, and perhaps commercially, the most important Saharan crossing in the later nineteenth century. Bornu similarly looked to the Fezzan and Tripoli. The Waday rulers cultivated Sanūsī connexions. The Sanūsiyya probably strengthened Waday, but did not reform Islam there. Dud Murra, the last free king, was enthroned in 1901 with ceremonies combining the divine kingship and Islam. The marriage of these incompatible concepts, against which the Muslims of Ghāna had witnessed in the eleventh century, survived here in the twentieth.

Rābiḥ

Rābiḥ b. Faḍl Allāh had served under al-Zubayr Pasha Raḥma Manṣūr in the Nilotic Sudan. In 1879, to escape growing khedivial authority, Rābiḥ and several hundred rifles vanished into the Baḥr al-Ghazāl. Ten years later he re-emerged, going west. He failed to conquer Waday, but did set up a client state to the south-east. Bagirmi was overrun, and in 1893 Bornu fell. Here Rābiḥ settled; he established his capital at Dikwa, to become a populous, impressive city.

We know little of Rābiḥ's government, or his religion. He was in touch with three main Islamic powers: the Mahdia, the Sanūsiyya, and Sokoto. The Sudanese Mahdi and later the Khalifa 'Abd Allāhi urged Rābiḥ to join them; but Rābiḥ, though he adopted the Mahdist patched *jubba* for his troops, and carried a banner with a Mahdist device, never went. Rābiḥ's relationship with the Sanūsiyya was hampered by his hostility towards Waday. As for Sokoto, Rābiḥ traded west, particularly to Katagum, for ammunition, despite Sokoto efforts to check such trade. And Rābiḥ was once allied with Ḥayātu, a Mahdist, great-grandson of 'Uthmān dan Fodio, from Adamawa, who married Rābiḥ's daughter. One story says Ḥayātu served as Rābiḥ's *imām*, but was later killed by Rābiḥ's son for suspicious contacts with Gombe.

Shehu Aḥmadu

Fulani pastoralists, moving east from Futa Toro from perhaps the eighth/fourteenth century, gained ascendancy in the Masina region. They apparently included '*ulamā*' from an early date. Vassals to Mali, later to Songhay, the Masina Fulani defied the Moroccans in 1598, and sustained their independence. Later Mamari Kulubali (1712–55) of

Segu established suzerainty over Masina. Shehu Aḥmadu was born in 1189/1775–6, in Masina, of a Fulani scholarly family. He combined study and teaching with a shepherd's life. Attracted to Jenne, he quarrelled with the Arma *'ulamā'* there, who banned him from the mosque. Marka and Fulani *'ulamā'* were advised in dreams of Aḥmadu's destiny as leader: a vision, after four months' retreat, confirmed this for Aḥmadu himself. The first bloodshed occurred when Aḥmadu's pupils killed a son of the Fulani *ardo* (ruler) of Masina. Aḥmadu withdrew north to await consequences.

Forces from Fulani Masina and Bambara Segu (still the overlord) attacked Aḥmadu at Noukouma in 1818.[1] The Fulani were not eager to attack, and Aḥmadu defeated the Bambara. Masina was free. Aḥmadu besieged and took Jenne. The Fulani of Kunari, across the Bani, submitted. The leader here, Galadyo, was never a reliable adherent, and at last found refuge eastwards under Sokoto. In Kunari the new capital, Hamdallahi (Ḥamd Allāhi), was built.

Timbuktu was taken. A governor was sent, a new *imām* (a *sharīf*) appointed. But the city's traditional independence was not broken: under Aḥmadu's successors the Kunta established a virtual protectorate, though tributary still to Masina. Even less successful were efforts to control the Tuareg. Raiding continued between Masina and the Bambara. Some Bambara died heroic martyrs for their pagan faith.

The new state, the *dina*, from the Arabic *dīn*, 'religion', was governed by a grand council of forty *'ulamā'* with legislative, executive and judicial authority. Every local capital had a salaried *qāḍī*. There were conciliation councils, censors of public morality (almost spies), clerks, and a sort of advocate. The standard administrative title, from the village upwards, was *amīr*. All main centres had state-supported schools and compulsory education. Aḥmadu himself taught. Ngorori, the only converted *ardo*, enrolled in Aḥmadu's school but showed himself to be more diligent than academically gifted. Students specially qualified in Qur'ān recitation might come to Ḥamd Allāhi for examination by Aḥmadu. State finance was Qur'anic, plus a tax on harvests and a military tax on those not taking direct part in war. Weights and measures were standardized. Society comprised free men, whether of the nobility or of the various castes, and captives. Aḥmadu refused the grand council's request that castes be abolished for the sake of Islamic

[1] Different dates are given for the beginning of the *jihād*; I follow A. H. Ba and J. Daget, *L'Empire peul du Macina* (Paris, 1962).

brotherhood. A touch of mildness concerns free women, who were never struck; judicially decreed beatings were given instead to their huts or possesions.

Many Masina Fulani were nomads. Aḥmadu himself had been a shepherd—the first man to swear allegiance had found him resting on one leg, the Fulani shepherd's habit. At Noukouma horned cattle heads are said to have descended from heaven upon the Bambara: and indeed the Bambara did lose one fight because they were unable to handle cattle. Ngorori was converted sincerely when one stormy night he found Aḥmadu alone, seeking a wild beast among the cattle, and knew him therefore a leader as well as a man of religion. *'Ulamā'* blessed the herds, and the *dina* carefully regulated transhumance. Nevertheless nomads were unmanageable. Aḥmadu encouraged settlement, celebrations at the return of the cattle were banned (apparently ineffectually), and it was known that the shepherds, once beyond Muslim oversight, reverted to pagan rites.

Shehu Aḥmadu died in 1844; his son, Aḥmadu II, ruled 1844–52; his grandson, Aḥmadu III, was killed by al-Ḥajj 'Umar. 'Umar never controlled Masina himself: eventually his cousin, al-Tijānī, mastered the area, and the state survived until the French conquest.

Al-Ḥājj 'Umar

'Umar b. Sa'īd Tal was born in 1793–4,[1] at Halwar village in Futa Toro. He was a Tokolor, of the Torodbe or religious clan. In 1826–7, he left on Pilgrimage, visiting Mecca, Medina and Jerusalem. He formed intimate links with Muḥammad al-Khalīfa al-Ghālī, the Tijānī representative in the Ḥijāz. Returning, 'Umar halted long in Cairo, Bornu and Sokoto. In Sokoto, he participated fully in Bello's court—a severe judge, a mighty man of prayer in war. He married Bello's daughter Maryam, and later took some part in the election of 'Aṭīq, Bello's successor. Slaves and followers from Hausaland were his first and most loyal disciples.

About 1838, passing more quickly through Masina and Segu, he ended his Pilgrimage in Futa Jallon. As his following increased, and his military strength—he was the first *jihād* leader to concentrate systematically on firearms—relations with the Futa Jallon authorities became strained. About 1848, 'Umar made his *hijra* to Dinguiray, just east of Futa Jallon. In 1852, he proclaimed *jihād*.

[1] Many early dates in 'Umar's career are disputed; in such cases the text follows Mohamadou Aliou Tyam, *La vie d'el Hadj Omar* (Paris, 1935).

His first main campaign was northwards, against the Bambara rulers of Karta. Their capital, Nyoro, fell in 1855. 'Umar then proposed to Aḥmadu III of Masina, an alliance against Segu, another Bambara state. Aḥmadu, suspicious perhaps of 'Umar's association with dissident Fulani, sent an army against 'Umar. 'Umar defeated this in 1856. The wounded were tended and returned, in recognition of their faith. 'Umar's wars were often ferocious: once prisoners were killed to observe the Festival of Sacrifices. In 1856 Turo-koro Mari, king of Segu (1854–6), was murdered. He had become so friendly with 'Umar that the Segu people, fearing for the independence of their state, killed him.

Until now, there had been no sign that 'Umar wished either to fight the French, who were increasingly influential in his homeland Futa Toro, or to attack established Islamic states such as Futa Jallon (against which he attempted no victorious return from his *hijra*) or Masina. But his eastern policy had received a double check. Perhaps encouraged by extremist followers, he turned west and attacked Madīna, highest French post on the Senegal, in 1857. He was repulsed.

'Umar might now pursue *jihād*, either westwards against the French, leading probably to defeat, or eastwards against Segu, possibly clashing with Masina. He chose the latter. In 1860, 'Umar agreed with the French a demarcation of spheres, along the upper Senegal and Bafing rivers.

Turning east, 'Umar committed himself to a career of colonization. His visits to Futa Toro, though he could interfere with the imamate there, were not preliminaries to conquest. Rather, he encouraged emigration, so that Muslims might escape European domination, and that his foreign conquests might be secured by settlement. Emigrants, primarily Tokolor, were his most reliable troops. Sometimes 'Umar burnt villages and food stores to force people to follow.

'Umar preached the example of co-operation shown by the *Anṣār* and *Muhājirūn*. The Tijānī bond also helped reconstitute the new communities. Early initiated by a Futa Jallon *'ālim*, he renewed his initiation with al-Ghālī, receiving all the secrets of the order. He became deeply versed in Tijānī doctrine, writing in detail about such concepts as *jihād al-nafs*, the self-conquest which should precede military *jihād*. His command of Tijānī mysteries established his reputation: though not a prophet, he had the habitual gifts of prophets. Time and again, in Hausaland under Bello, or on his own campaigns, he went into *khalwa* (retreat) seeking God's guidance before giving battle. His prayers were effective in finding water or stopping rain. He prayed too to assure his followers and colonists of paradise. This was a lively hope: his troops went into battle confident of conquering here, or of winning Paradise. Rivalry between the Tijāniyya and Qādiriyya *ṭarīqas* spiced 'Umar's conflicts with Masina and Timbuktu.

'Alī, king of Segu (1856–61), sought the aid of Aḥmadu III, given on condition that 'Alī adopt Islam. 'Umar defeated the combined Segu-Masina forces, and in March 1861 entered the capital of Segu. Attempts to negotiate between Aḥmadu III and 'Umar failed. On 15 May 1862 occurred the final battle. Aḥmadu was defeated. 'Umar occupied Hamdallahi. 'Umar's justification for the Masina War followed the Fulani precedent for the Bornu War. As Bornu had supported the Hausa kings against 'Uthmān, so Masina had joined Segu. 'Umar collected the idols which remained in Segu despite 'Alī's conversion, and took these to Masina, to convince the '*ulamā*' there that the alliance had been corrupt.

'Umar's triumph was fleeting. The Kunta, protectors of Timbuktu against the Masina Fulani, now found the Tokolor the main threat, and joined with Balobbo, leader of the Masina resistance. 'Umar was besieged in Hamdallahi. Attempting to escape, he was trapped at Déguembéré, in February 1864, and killed.

Considering the rapidity of 'Umar's conquests—seven years from Nyoro to Hamadallahi—and the disastrous circumstances of his death, it is surprising that anything was salvaged. Yet his successors continued to rule until the French conquest (1890–3). 'Umar himself never settled, or made himself a king: al-Ghālī had warned him against mixing with the rulers of this world. In 1862–3, he confirmed his eldest son, Aḥmadu Seku (born at Sokoto, but not Bello's grandson), as his successor. Aḥmadu Seku, ruling from Segu, faced disaffection from other 'Umarian governors, and from subject peoples. However, the Tokolor regained control of Masina, aided by renewed mistrust between Balobbo and the Kunta. They took vengeance by the execution of 300 Masina '*ulamā*' bound one to another with their turbans. In 1874, Aḥmadu Seku proclaimed himself *amīr al-mu'minīn*.

French policy towards 'Umar was rarely hostile. His first meetings with French officials, in 1846–7, were friendly. Later Faidherbe, governor of Senegal (1854–61, 1863–5), seriously considered extending French influence down the Niger through an alliance with 'Umar.

An embassy arrived in Segu to negotiate this in 1864, but the treaty was never implemented. Later, the French hesitated between posing as liberators of conquered people under the Tokolor yoke, and trying co-operation again. Another embassy brought back another treaty (1880–1); this also was not implemented. British rivalry, and Samori's resistance, turned the French southwards.

The Senegambia and Samori

The European challenge from the coast, the Muslim inspiration from the interior, and the weakening of traditional institutions generally, encouraged the emergence of many Muslim champions in west Africa in the later nineteenth century. On the Gambia, the misnamed 'Soninke-Marabout' wars—'Soninke' here used for pagans and 'mixers', 'Marabout' for stricter Muslims—marked the gradual advance of reformed Islam. Fodi Kabba was a notable marabout: the British twice carried his capital on the lower Gambia by storm in the 1850s, but he was not killed by the French until 1901. Ma Ba, another *'ālim*, in 1862 declared a *jihād* against the rulers of Badibu, and made it for a time the strongest Muslim power on the Gambia. The British had invaded Badibu in 1860–1, but withdrew, perhaps creating a vacuum.

Lat Dior, ruler of Cayor deposed by the French, had adopted Islam as part of the defence of Wolof independence. He took refuge with Ma Ba, and the two worked in concert until Ma Ba's death in 1867. Lat Dior then made peace with the French, and returned to Cayor. Later, when the French decided to build a railway in Cayor, Lat Dior renewed hostilities. He was killed in October 1886, having had the presentiment that he would that day say the evening prayer with Ma Ba. Another religious leader was al-Ḥājj Mamadu Lamin, the Soninke champion whom the French killed in 1887.

These religious wars were fought on three fronts. The war against paganism and degenerate Islam seems clearest on the Gambia: Ma Ba at first invited harmonious relations with the Europeans. The war against European colonialism was chiefly against the French. Finally, there was the war of Muslim against Muslim. Ma Ba was unusually co-operative: he had consulted with al-Ḥājj 'Umar in 1850, and later supported Lat Dior. But Lamin, who had been with Aḥmadu Seku in Segu before going on Pilgrimage in 1874, later found his supporters attacked by Aḥmadu. Defeated himself by the French, Lamin retired to Futa Bondu and fought the *almami* there. In Futa Toro, the *almami* warred with the 'Mahdi of Podor', whose son later resisted the French.

Samori Ture, greatest of the western leaders, was born in a village, south of Kankan, about 1830, of Mandingo parents. His father, once a trader, was a prosperous herdsman, marrying locally, gradually identifying himself with local paganism. Samori broke this pattern. First, he became a trader. As a trader, he practised Islam. Some of his contacts were *'ulamā'*, representing the peaceful accommodation of Muslim traders among pagans—the Mande dispersion already described.

About 1851–2, Samori's mother was enslaved by a local warrior chief. Devoted to her, Samori served the chief for several years, raiding and studying the Qur'ān with him until his mother was released. Thus Samori was introduced to militant Islam, already expressed in several chieftaincies in the area. Popular lore today, however, attributes his redoubtable prowess to a liaison with a female *jinn*.

Samori then built up his own state, this first phase of expansion culminating in the capture of Kankan about 1879. Samori was commonly called *almami*. Whether he took also the title *amīr al-mu'minīn* is uncertain: perhaps he did, and later renounced it. For each village, an *imām* was appointed. *'Ulamā'* advised government officials. Samori particularly required that the children of leading families be educated, sometimes examining pupils himself.

In 1882, Samori moving north clashed with the French advancing east against al-Ḥājj 'Umar's successors. This diversion preserved the 'Umarian empire for a decade. In 1886–7, the French signed 'spheres of influence' treaties with Samori.

Samori's most resilient African rival was Tyeba of Sikaso, whose brother and predecessor was a client-convert of Aḥmadu b. al-Ḥājj 'Umar. In 1887–8, Samori besieged Sikaso. The siege failed. Angry that the French had not helped him, Samori renewed his quarrel with them, meanwhile proposing an alliance, which came to nothing, to Aḥmadu. Samori was quickly defeated; and Kankan was occupied in 1891.

Hitherto, Samori had operated in the Mande heartlands. The first of the principal Muslim champions not relying on an immigrant community, he has come to symbolize Mande national resistance to European imperialism. But in the 1890s he had to create a new, eastern empire, in the upper Ivory Coast and beyond. Kong fell in 1895. Refugees, Muslim and pagan, fled in all directions. One, who went south, tells of the wretched, oppressed condition of the dispossessed when they reached French protection—of their gradual establishment, mosques being built, teachers and '*ulamā*' multiplying, until countless animals were slaughtered at the Greater Festival and all wore silk at the Lesser.

European advance, once it reached the Sudan interior, swept the Muslim states like prairie fire. The 'Umarian empire fell to the French (1890–3), Aḥmadu Seku and the irreconcilables fleeing to Hausaland. Samori's sixteen year defiance ended in 1898. Rābiḥ, helped it is said by Bagirmi '*ulamā*', destroyed the first French force in Bagirmi, but his death in 1900, fighting them in Bornu, established them in both countries. Waday was occupied in 1909. The British Royal Niger Company took Ilorin in 1897; the sultan of Sokoto died resisting the British in 1904. Germans occupied most of Adamawa (1899–1901); the British took Yola, and the Anglo-German boundary decapitated the state.

C. EAST AFRICA

The east coast before the tenth/sixteenth century

Early Islam in Africa south of the Sahara was often a religion of ports. In the western Sudan, the cities which first welcomed Islam were harbours facing the desert ocean of the Sahara. On the eastern coast, the towns looked out upon the Indian Ocean. And, as both the northern and southern littorals of the Sahara shared some degree of common culture, so the East African coast was part of the world of the Indian Ocean. But whereas the western Sudan towns were parts of great states, which could absorb and in some sense use Islam, the eastern coastal towns remained until the nineteenth century disunited, without imperial achievement. It is as if in tropical Africa, Islam, though in its 'mixed' form buttressing existing states, had to wait for the actual creation of states by people for whom Islam was a primary consideration until the theocracies of the eighteenth and nineteenth centuries. The superior protection offered by the Sahara may have contributed, while the east coast was repeatedly distraught by sea-borne interlopers. On the other hand, the east coast became unambiguously a part of the Muslim world much earlier than the western Sudan. Another difference is that the southern Saharan 'ports' backed on to open, savannah country, across which Islam gradually spread, while the eastern ocean ports were pinned to the coast by the forest, a barrier not breached until the nineteenth century. Only the south, where the arrival of the Portuguese in the tenth/sixteenth century perhaps interrupted Islamic penetration on the Zambesi, and the north, where Islam crossed the Horn of Africa and lapped the foothills of Ethiopia, were exceptions.

Even before the Prophet's *Hijra*, some of his Meccan supporters had found refuge in Ethiopia. The East African coast was apparently a frequent sanctuary for the oppressed in the early centuries of Islam. The followers of Zayd, great-grandson of ʿAlī, are said to have been the first to flee thither. Later came refugees from al-Aḥsā; these are said to have founded Mogadishu. Still others fled from ʿUmān.

Trade continued to be important: ivory, particularly for India; slaves (the Zanj who revolted in ʿIrāq in the later third/ninth century were East Africans); perfume, one of the luxuries in which even severe Muslims may indulge; gold; and other things. By the mid-twelfth century, the people of Zanzibar were predominantly Muslim; several Islamic inscriptions survive in Mogadishu from the seventh/thirteenth century. But still the overall character of the coast was pagan.

The most fully documented of the early coastal settlements is Kilwa. Its founding is usually attributed to immigrants from Shīrāz in the fourth/tenth century, but recently it has been argued that *c.* 1200 is a better date, and that the immigrants, though they may have shared some elements of Shīrāzī culture, came from the Banādir coast.[1] The chronicle details, circumstantial and sometimes conflicting, of the founding of Kilwa are perhaps mainly imaginative. The island on which Kilwa was founded was bought from the local people for cloth, suggesting the recurrent link between trade and early Muslim settlement. There were already other immigrant Muslims in the area, and before long fighting broke out between some of them and Kilwa; Kilwa was temporarily conquered, and the Friday prayers were said in the name of a usurper. Then the government returned to the line of the founder, who was, according to one account, the son of an Ethiopian slave woman, and emigrated to Africa because his half-brothers jeered at his descent.

In the early eighth/fourteenth century, benefitting from the gold trade with Sofala, and apparently under a new dynasty, Kilwa prospered. Ibn Baṭṭūṭa visited the town in 731/1331, in the reign of al-Ḥasan b.

[1] N. Chittick, 'The "Shirazi" colonization of east Africa', in *Journal of African History*, vi, no. 3, 1965, 275–94; J. S. Trimingham, *Islam in East Africa* (London, 1964), 10–1.

Sulaymān, surnamed Abu'l-Mawāhib, 'the giver of gifts', for his generosity. Al-Ḥasan is the first of the Kilwa rulers whom we know to have gone on Pilgrimage; on the way, he spent two years in Aden studying. Al-Ḥasan frequently raided the pagan Zanj; these raids were called *jihād*, and a later king killed on such an enterprise was deemed a martyr. Al-Ḥasan divided the booty according to Qur'anic injunction, and *sharīfs* in particular frequented his court, from 'Irāq, the Ḥijāz, and elsewhere. Ibn Baṭṭūṭa visited also Mombasa, Zayla', where many of the people were heretics, (perhaps descendants of earlier refugees), and Mogadishu.

From the mid-eighth/fourteenth century until the coming of the Portuguese at the end of the fifteenth, Kilwa declined politically. During the ninth/fifteenth century, various Islamic offices are mentioned, some of them innovations. The sultans lost control of the great officials, and there was a succession of civil disturbances, depositions, foreign interventions and puppet rulers. But commercial prosperity continued, and on the coast as a whole new powers were rising, first Pate, then Mombasa. In 1498 Vasco da Gama arrived, and within a few years the Portuguese had conquered almost the entire coast.

The Horn of Africa before the tenth/sixteenth century

The towns of the Somali coast, such as Zayla' on the Gulf of Aden, and Mogadishu on the Banādir coast of the Indian Ocean, share to a considerable extent the characteristics of the Swahili culture further south: trading centres, welcoming Arab and other immigrants, evolving distinctive amalgams both of population and of language, witnessing to some form of settled government and to Islam. But, while Swahili culture has throughout been confined to the coast—its very name derives from the Arabic, *sawāḥil*, coasts—the Somali seaboard and hinterland have much in common. Muslim states in the interior were loosely federated with sultanates on the coast, nomadic Somalis shared the townsmen's faith, and all confronted a common challenge in Christian Ethiopia, though in the earliest centuries Ethiopia was exempt from *jihād*.

Perhaps as early as 283/896–7, Arab immigrants established a Muslim state far inland, in Shoa. Late in the seventh/thirteenth century (1280–5) this was absorbed by Ifat, one of seven Muslim kingdoms, all tributary to Christian Ethiopia. Early in the eighth/fourteenth century, Ifat controlled also the port of Zayla'. Students from Zayla' at this time had their own hostel at al-Azhar, and a section of the Umayyad mosque at Damascus. These Muslim territories, sometimes loosely called Adal, were frequently in revolt against their titular overlord. In 1329 the Emperor Amda Seyon undertook a particularly severe campaign against Ifat, indirectly a result of Muslim pressure on Christians in Egypt, and seems to have cleared Ethiopia proper of Muslim influence. Such wars had many religious overtones. Early in the ninth/fifteenth century full-scale war was again being waged. The Emperor Yeshaq (1414–29) killed the ruler of Ifat, Sa'd al-Dīn, in his last stronghold, an island off the Zayla' coast. Sa'd's sons fled to Yemen, but later returned. The *jihād* of the *Imām* Aḥmad Grāñ was the climax of these repeated conflicts.

Ibn Baṭṭūṭa, in Mogadishu in 731/1331, gives us our best description of Muslim society on the Horn at this time. He describes a deeply islamized court, around the ruler or shaykh. Elaborate hierarchy governed precedence. He was lodged in the comfortable students' hostel of the *qāḍī*'s school. The *qāḍī*, the shaykh's secretary, the *wazīrs* and four principal *amīrs* sat as a court, the *qāḍī* dealing with religious law; the shaykh's advice, when necessary, was sought and given in writing. The shaykh could speak Arabic, but this was not his own language. Many details suggest Middle Eastern influence: cloth was exported to Egypt, the *qāḍī* was Egyptian, a eunuch sprinkled Ibn Baṭṭūṭa with rose-water from Damascus, the shaykh wore a cloak of Jerusalem stuff, and so on. A purist might quibble over the golden birds surmounting the royal canopy, an excessive purist over the royal band, but it is clear that here was orthodox Islam.

The Muslim states were threatened not only by their Christian foe, but also by their turbulent nomadic neighbours. It has been widely accepted that the Galla inhabited the Horn at the beginning of the Muslim era, and that they were then gradually expelled by the Somali, who pushed south and west, having perhaps found the Aden Gulf coast overcrowded with Arab settlers. The Somali, steeled by conversion to Islam, were generally victorious. This analysis has recently been questioned, partly on linguistic grounds.[1] It is suggested that Afar (the northern neighbours of the Somali), Somali and Galla all originated in the area of southern Ethiopia. The Afar moved out first, north and east into the Horn, followed by the Somali. The first mention of the name Somali

[1] H. S. Lewis, 'The origins of the Galla and Somali', in *Journal of African History*, vii, no. 1, 1966, 27–46.

is in the time of the Emperor Yeshaq, though a Somali tribe is described near Mogadishu in the seventh/thirteenth, perhaps even in the sixth/twelfth century. In the tenth/sixteenth century, the new interpretation continues, the Galla, expanding into Ethiopia and challenging too the Swahili area as far south as Malindi, also trod on Somali heels towards the Horn: this is the origin of traditions of Galla-Somali conflict, not an earlier expulsion of Galla from the Horn by Somali.

Whichever view is finally accepted, by the tenth/sixteenth century it is clear that the nomadic Somali were a principal Muslim force in the Horn. They are prominent in Grāñ's *jihād*. Somali genealogies insist on an Arab ancestry, preferably within the Prophet's family. Whatever the doubt about the historicity of these claims, they reveal the great importance of Arab immigrants in bringing Islam. Supposed tribal ancestors are revered as saints, and many other Arab missionaries are remembered.

Aḥmad Grāñ

Like two thunder clouds the Portuguese and the Ottoman Turks approached each other in eastern Africa. In 922/1517 the Ottomans took Cairo: in the same year the Portuguese burnt Zaylaʿ. One burst of lightning in this overcharged atmosphere was the *jihād* of Aḥmad Grāñ. In the ninth/fifteenth century, a militant, reforming Muslim movement developed in Adal, under leaders styled *amīrs*, opposed to the traditional Muslim aristocracy. The militants wished to challenge Ethiopia, the traditionalists appreciated peace and commerce. Maḥfūẓ, one dominant *amīr*, proclaimed a *jihād*, but was defeated and killed. For some years no one succeeded in gaining lasting authority in Adal. One ruler enforced piety for three years, but was killed by a rival, Abū Bakr. Finally Aḥmad b. Ibrāhīm (1506–43)—Aḥmad Grāñ—emerged. He was styled *imām*, not *amīr* or sultan. He married the daughter of Maḥfūẓ, and began to challenge Abū Bakr.

The *ʿulamāʾ* attempted to exercise their traditional role as peacemakers, but failed. Perhaps, since Grāñ was himself an Islamic champion, the *ʿulamāʾ* did not enjoy the prestige usually derived from the contrast between themselves as men of religion and the warrior leaders.

Grāñ killed Abū Bakr, and replaced him with a puppet. In 1527, with his headquarters at the inland city of Harar, Grāñ began serious fighting with Ethiopia. In 1531, he invaded, and scourged Ethiopia unmercifully for the rest of his life. Churches and monasteries were ravaged, and huge numbers of Ethiopians forced to accept Islam. These wars were *jihād*, but Grāñ was unable to enforce full legal control over the division of booty. The fugitive Ethiopian king cried out for Portuguese aid, and when Portuguese gunmen appeared Grāñ appealed to the Ottomans for help. In 1543 Grāñ was killed, and the invasion collapsed. Grāñ's widow tried to carry on the struggle from Harar; her new husband was made *amīr al-mu'minīn*. He was succeeded by a man of slave origin, 'Uthmān, who pandered to the traditionalists and offended the purists. Civil strife ensued; a final attempt at *jihād* failed.

After the sixteenth century

The Portuguese, and the *jihād* of Grāñ, both weakened the cause of Islamic government in the area. To the south, though the struggle against the Portuguese, a struggle religious as well as economic and military, may have prepared the ground for nineteenth century attempts to unify the coast of Zanzibar, it was not in itself sufficient to bring coastal Muslims together. In the north, the *jihād* led to the final disintegration of Adal, the main sphere of relatively settled Islamic life in the interior. In 1577 the capital was moved from Harar to Aussa, in order to be further from the Ethiopian menace. The dynasty was at last overthrown by the Afar at the end of the seventh century. Earlier in the same century the dynasty of Mogadishu, closely linked with Somali settled on the Shebeli River, collapsed before the challenge of Somali newcomers.

Ironically, and for quite different reasons, the decline of the interior Muslim states was followed by a strengthening of the influence of coastal Muslims. Under the Emperor Susenyos, Roman Catholic missionaries in Ethiopia, inheritors of the soldiers who had fought Grāñ, overplayed their hand. Some Ethiopian chiefs complained that they would prefer Muslim to Portuguese rule. Under Susenyos's son, Fasiladas (1632–67), reaction became policy: he made an agreement with the Ottoman governors of Suakin and Massawa to execute Catholic priests trying to enter Ethiopia. Islam seemed now an ally against the Portuguese, a reversal of the previous position.

While the political power of inland Muslim bases declined—and even at the best of times their authority over the nomads was incomplete—they nevertheless maintained a considerable degree of religious authority. Harar is still regarded by Somalis as a centre of Muslim learning just as Zaylaʿ and Mogadishu. The *ʿulamāʾ* of Aussa were able to intervene to protect their town from an attack by an Arab force. In the early nineteenth century the sultan of Tajura felt obliged to accept their arbitration in a controversy over the marriage of his son. Mukhā Arabs assaulted Harar, encouraged by a disgraced member of the ruling family who represented his countrymen as apostates, but were beaten off.

Two new Muslim powers entered the area. The Ottomans occupied Massawa in 1557, unsuccessfully attacked Ethiopia, and seemed to promise firmer Muslim intervention; but they withdrew in 1633. Apart from stray raids, and two expeditions in the 1580s which were perhaps not officially sanctioned, there was little Ottoman interference further south. Ottoman domination continued in shadowy form—Zaylaʿ and Berbera came under the *sharīfs* of Mukhā in the eleventh/seventeenth century, and were thus nominally within the Ottoman empire. Effective outside Islamic intervention did not come in the south until the mid-seventeenth century, when ʿUmān was invited in by Mombasa Muslims. In 1698 Fort Jesus at Mombasa, the seat of Portuguese government on the coast, fell to them.

In origin, both the Turkish intervention in the north, and the ʿUmānī further south, resulted from appeals by local Muslims for support against a Christian threat. Religion, however, may be more effective in prompting such alliances than in maintaining them. During the twelfth/eighteenth century, there were recurrent suggestions by various coastal rulers that the Portuguese might return, and early in the nineteenth century Mogadishu and Brava sought, unsuccessfully, to exchange ʿUmānī protection for British. Neither Ottoman nor ʿUmānī, the latter with considerably more direct links, was able effectively to control representatives in Africa. Early in the nineteenth century eunuchs held office in Zanzibar, ʿUmān hoping these would be less prone to set up their own principalities.

In the nineteenth century both distant suzerains took a more active interest. In 1840 Sayyid Saʿīd of ʿUmān came and settled in Zanzibar; his authority extended over Mogadishu and the Banādir coast. In the mid-eighteenth century, the first caravans began trading into the interior; these became prominent under Sayyid Saʿīd. But there was still little penetration of Islam beyond the coast. The coast itself, though speaking Swahili (a language with a Bantu grammar but heavily arabicized in vocabulary) and sharing a distinctive Swahili culture, was undeniably part of the *dār al-Islām*. In West and Central Africa, we can visualize Islam as a foreign element introduced into the local African setting, while on the East Coast it is rather African people, through migration, slaving and intermarriage, that are being drawn into an essentially Islamic setting. The persistence too of the eastward orientation of the coast may be seen in Sayyid Saʿīd's encouragement of Indian immigrants, many of them Muslim. All, including Hindus, enjoyed religious freedom. Saʿīd himself was an ʿIbāḍī.

Ottoman claims revived later in the century, through the agency of Egypt, over the coast from Suakin to Berbera and inland to Harar. Despite community of religion, the Egyptians had trouble with the hinterland nomads, and were able to establish their authority partly because the Somali were not united. One Egyptian expedition, intending to penetrate Ethiopia, was annihilated by the sultan of Aussa. Among public works erected during the brief Egyptian period (1870–84) were several mosques.

The Galla

The Galla, perhaps originally from south central Ethiopia, began expanding in the early tenth/sixteenth century, and are today found over nearly half the area of Ethiopia. The Galla expansion was at the expense of Muslim as well as Christian: the Galla devastated Harar (where the ruler, ʿUthmān, attempted the interesting policy of encouraging them to take part in Muslim markets) and attacked Aussa. Some Galla adopted Islam, perhaps through the example of the Muslim residue of Grāñ's invasion. By the early nineteenth century, certain groups were largely Muslim, like the Wallo in the north whom Krapf, travelling among them in 1842, found determined Muslims.[1] He met some on pilgrimage, and at least one chief was entitled *imām*. The Wallo claimed conversion by an Arab called Debelo, for which we may perhaps read Dibuli, traditionally among the first Shīrāzī settlers on the coast.

Among such Galla, Islam affected political and social organization but little. The tribes remained fiercely individualistic and fissiparous. Noticeably out of step with the general Galla pattern, however, were the five despotic Galla kingdoms which emerged in the nineteenth century south-west of the Gibe River—Enarea, Guma, Goma, Gera and Jimma. Perhaps these drew on the local Sidama heritage, or even looked back to

[1] J. L. Krapf, *Travels, researches, and missionary labours* . . . (London, 1860), 82 ff.

pre-sixteenth century Muslim states. Probably trade contributed considerably: revived demand on the Red Sea and in Arabia prompted Ethiopian traders, mostly Muslim, to organize caravans in search of luxury items such as slaves, ivory, gold and civet. A principal route was Massawa-Gondar-Gojam and into the Gibe region. Enarea, under Abba Bagibo, who reigned from about 1825, became the principal resort of merchants trading in the area, and at the same time a centre of Islam. A proposal from Abba Bagibo, for an alliance, was refused by the Christian ruler of Gojam because Abba Bagibo was a Muslim and traded in slaves. But Abba Bagibo's gift of a hundred horns of civet and fifty female slaves was accepted, and firearms together with men skilled in their use were sent in return. Muslim traders are not in themselves adequate explanation why Islam should win local converts: in Kafa, for example, just to the south, they are well regarded, and may perhaps be traced back to the tenth/sixteenth century, but Islam has little local following.

How far Islam was immediately effective is uncertain. Abba Bagibo had twelve official wives. The government of Enarea, even its judicial system, seems in his time to have taken little explicit account of the new faith followed by the ruler, his court, and many of his subjects. Even in the later nineteenth century, though there were several hundred '*ulamā*' at the capital there were virtually no mosques: one hut, called a mosque, near the royal cemetery, was respected as a sanctuary. The common faith did not always unite the new kingdoms: Jimma and Enarea fought for control of the trade-route north; in the later nineteenth century Jimma was pre-eminent. The *jihād*, which in the 1880s a confederacy of four of the Muslim kingdoms declared on their pagan rivals, was perhaps only a continuation of age-old squabbling.

But there is evidence of a recurrent effort after a more effective faith. The dynasty of Goma tried to islamize itself by claiming descent from a Mogadishu shaykh. There was the influence of Sudanese and Egyptian traders, and later of the Mahdists, who allied themselves with Galla Muslims, but were expelled by the Shoans representing central Ethiopian authority. With the Shoan conquest of the Gibe area, begun in 1886, Firissa, heir to the throne of Guma, fled to Massawa. There he joined Shaykh 'Abd al-Raḥmān, a refugee from Goma. The two went frequently on Pilgrimage. In 1899–1900 anti-Shoan agitation arose in Guma: Firissa returned, claimed the throne and proclaimed a *jihād*. He forbade his troops to castrate prisoners (the common Galla custom) or to take prisoners expecting great ransoms, for such profane trophies defiled the *jihād*. Rebuked by *'ulamā'* for observing traditional sacrifices after killing nine enemy horsemen, Firissa gave expiatory alms to the poor. Meanwhile 'Abd al-Raḥmān founded *zāwiyas* of the Mīrghaniyya order in Firissa's domains. An attempt to convert a neighbouring ruler led to Firissa's falling into Shoan hands. He was executed, clasping the Qur'ān. Local Muslims today revere him, last prince of Guma, as a *walī*.

The Gibe Galla story shows again the importance of mobility within Islam: coastal origins are claimed, traders are sometimes effective missionaries, refugees find consolation and friends in the heartlands of Islam and then return. Movements like the Mahdia reach from one area to another, and the orders continue their peaceful penetration: in this century, the Tijāniyya has come from Algeria and the Qādiriyya from the Somalis.

Within Christian Ethiopia, Galla acquired increasing influence at court. 'Alī, a Galla prince (d. 1788), founded a Galla dynasty in Begamder province, and began pilgrimages to the tomb of Grāñ. The internal progress of Islam seemed likely to receive external support. In 1838 Muḥammad 'Alī first attacked Ethiopia, and later the Egyptians thrust in from the coast. Harar, still independent, was captured in 1875, and pagan Galla in the area were forcibly converted. The enlarged challenge brought a more acid response. Ethiopian emperors in the later nineteenth century several times tried to impose Christianity upon their Muslim and pagan subjects. Menelik (1889–1913), the architect of modern Ethiopia, was less ruthless: when Jimma submitted to him, he incorporated the principality bodily, apparently promising not to build churches there.

Arabs in the interior

The earliest caravan traders to the Swahili coast were certain peoples of the interior, as the Nyamwesi and Yao. But throughout the nineteenth century Arabs and Swahili (hereafter in this section called Arabs) gradually moved inland, to Tabora, Ujiji, Nyangwe, to Buganda and Lake Nyasa, to Katanga. At first, the interests of these pioneers were commercial, chiefly in ivory and slaves, but soon, partly through entanglement in local politics, travelling merchants evolved into colonists. During the years 1884–8, throughout East Africa, Arab efforts to build up, or win over, principalities in the interior intensified. The main example was Buganda, discussed below, but similar though lesser instances might be multiplied. A major stimulus was European, particularly German, encroachment on the coast, and many of the Arab political pretensions in the eastern interior were anti-European.

On the coast itself, as the German presence became increasingly felt, Muslim irritation sharpened, and in 1888 Abūshīrī b. Sālim al-Ḥārthī took up arms. Behind this resistance economic motives may have been influential, particularly concern over the slave trade. But the flash-point came in Ramaḍān, over incidents like lowering an Islamic flag, defiling a mosque by bringing dogs in, and interference with festival prayers. A Muslim diviner was called in, and a similar reliance on divination was attributed to German policymakers. The resistance spread: Yao and Kilwa, for example, joined in. But it was crushed, and in 1889 Abūshīrī was hanged.

Further west, in the Congo area, the break did not come until later. The Congo Free State at first found the Arabs of the upper Congo helpful in supplying ivory, finding labour, and as a buffer. Tippu Tib, an outstanding Swahili colonist and slaver, was for a time a Free State official. Had this attempt at indirect rule succeeded, the consequences for Islam in Central Africa might have been far-reaching. But neither Tippu Tib nor the Free State headquarters could control men in the field. In 1892 war broke out—as perhaps it was bound to do at some time, particularly over the slaving question—and within two years Arab power was broken.

The extent to which these events were encouraged from Zanzibar is uncertain. Probably the unrest of the 1880s was so stimulated; but, although Tippu Tib had once been the sultan's agent on the upper Congo, by the 1890s Zanzibar's bolt had been shot. Whatever Zanzibar's part, there was never among the Arabs an authority capable of imposing unity.

The degree of Arab culture established in the interior was sometimes considerable. The Nyangwe area, where Livingstone in 1871 observed most savage slave raiding, was later brought under extensive plantation colonization which maintained a leisured ruling class. A Free State official, European, shortly before 1892, described meetings with Arabs, wearing snowy robes, turbans, and vests of gold and silver braid, drinking coffee from china cups, discussing Napoleon's wars, Turkey's government, and Manchester's cotton. Less is known about the specifically religious aspect: some of the Arabs were devout men, and there were apparently some Wahhābīs among them. There was little or no proselytizing, but considerable imitation, at least among the entourage of the Arabs, of religious practice.

The Yao

The Yao are the only major people south of the Somali to have adopted Islam before the colonial period. Living then midway between Lake Nyasa and the Indian Ocean, the Yao were by the later eighteenth century sending caravans to the coast, part of a trading network stretching from the ocean to Katanga. By the later nineteenth century, with fire-arms they had become a major slave-raiding people. Yao children used to play a game with beans representing traders and slaves going to the coast. The Yao expanded westward into the Nyasa region.

The coast had not only a material effect, demanding slaves and offering guns and other trade goods: it set also a cultural example. Dhows and bedsteads were copied, fashions of dress adopted, mangoes and coconuts planted, all in imitation of the coast. Religion followed. Sixty boys and girls were buried alive at the funeral of one Yao chief, who had traded much to the coast and planted mangoes at his capital. His cousin and successor, summoned home from the coast, was buried in his turn beside the mosque.

The first Yao Muslims went to the coast for initiation; later coastal '*ulamā*' and teachers came to Yaoland; later again Yao '*ulamā*' themselves took the main role. Islam, spreading particularly in the late nineteenth and early twentieth centuries, became a distinguishing feature of Yao nationality. Islamic influence on Yao social life has been curtailed by firm matrilineal traditions, but here and there changes may be seen: Islamic rather than customary marriage, for example, allows a husband to demand that his wife live with him in his village.

Buganda

In East Africa, Buganda is, in its relations with Islam, perhaps the closest parallel to the earlier, greater states of Central and West Africa. It is remarkable how often, in the relatively short story of Buganda Islam, themes already familiar confront us. The faith arrived with trade. The earliest long-distance imports came perhaps in the eighteenth century. In the mid-nineteenth century, under Kabaka Suna, the first Muslims appeared, from Zanzibar and the coast. As the first Muslim visitors to eighth/fourteenth century Kano helped the king in his local wars, so these Arabs marched with the Buganda forces. And, as in Ghāna the immigrant Muslims had held somewhat aloof from the king, so the Buganda Arabs condemned the king's slaughter of his subjects, warning him that the same God who had given him his kingdom had created these his people. The reproof apparently impressed Suna; but later, for reasons now unknown, he expelled the Arabs.

In the 1860s, under Mutesa, Suna's successor, the Arabs returned. Mutesa even more than Suna became interested in Islam. Though never a convert, he adopted the Islamic calendar and Arabic dress, observed Ramaḍān, enforced Muslim greetings, and encouraged mosque building in town and country. But, as in Mali Negro Muslims had not the same privileges as Berber or Arab Muslims in Ghāna, so Mutesa could not grant the same licence to the newly converted Buganda Muslims that Suna had allowed to the Arabs. Tension mounted when Buganda Muslims dressed presumptuously, and refused the royal food as uncleanly slaughtered. A visiting Muslim cautioned the Buganda that Mutesa, despite his interest, was not a full Muslim—he was, for example, uncircumcised—and should not lead the prayers as he had been doing. He was a 'mixer'. In 1875–6 Mutesa struck back. A hundred or more Buganda Muslims were martyred.

No more for Buganda than for Ghāna or Songhay earlier, was Islam a domestic problem only. Mutesa might use Islam in local diplomacy—he sent an unsuccessful mission to convert the ruler of neighbouring Bunyoro, bearing among other gifts shoes suitable for taking off on entering the mosque—but he soon felt the squeeze of larger-scale power politics, particularly Egyptian ambitions. In place of Morocco's Spanish eunuchs, the khedive employed a variety of European officials (one of whom tried, but failed, to build the first brick mosque in Buganda). The khedive was scarcely more likely than Aḥmad al-Manṣūr successfully to administer an empire far to the south. But before annexation could be seriously attempted, the arrival in 1877 of Christian missionaries fundamentally altered the situation.

For a decade, Muslims and Christians, neither possessing political authority, argued their case before the court, but in 1888 Muslims and Christians united to expel Mwanga, Mutesa's successor. He was too much a pagan for either. Within a month, the Arabs, with Buganda Muslim support, had driven out the Christians, and installed almost a puppet *kabaka*, Kalema. As elsewhere in East and Central Africa, Christian European encroachment on the periphery led the Muslim Arabs to attempt political power in the interior. Civil war in Buganda followed. In 1890, the Christians finally triumphed. Very soon after, Buganda passed into the colonial period.

Muḥammad b. ʻAbd Allāh

The Somali leader, Muḥammad b. ʻAbd Allāh (1864–1920/1), found his country distracted on three fronts: Ethiopia, from 1887, expanded east, conquering such Muslim centres as Harar and Aussa, bringing both Galla and Somali under Ethiopian rule; on the opposite side, the pace of British, French and Italian penetration on the coast increased in the 1880s; and the Somali clans were quarrelling among themselves. Ethiopian and European ambitions were fostered by the withdrawal of Egyptian garrisons as a result of the Mahdist rising in the Sudan. The British, taking over from the Egyptians on the coast, met some opposition from Sanūsī and Mahdist agents, who were themselves at odds.

Muḥammad, a precocious Qur'ān scholar, soon embarked on wide-ranging travels for knowledge, visiting Harar, Mogadishu, the Sudan, even Nairobi. While on Pilgrimage, he joined the Ṣāliḥiyya order, a militant and puritan wing of the Aḥmadiyya. He was to apply Shāfiʻī law strictly, with punishments, even mutilation and death, for defaulters at prayer and other such backsliders. The Aḥmadiyya and the Qādiriyya were the main orders in Somaliland. Perhaps because of a ready correspondence between saints venerated by the orders, and ancestors venerated by the clans, to be a Muslim came to involve for almost every Somali membership in an order.

In 1899, from the interior of Somaliland beyond European zones, Muḥammad launched his *jihād*. He was still waging it, often defeated but never captured, when he died some twenty years later. His discipline excelled in severity even that of the Almoravids. He did not, apparently, proclaim himself *mahdī*, as is sometimes said.

His *jihād* challenged four antagonists. First, he fought the other orders. The Qādirīs were his especial enemies. His followers murdered the leading Qādirī shaykh among the southern Somalis in 1909: the Qādirīs asserted it was more meritorious to kill one *darwīsh* heretic than a hundred infidels. Also in 1909 one of Muḥammad's disillusioned supporters secured a letter from the founder of the Ṣāliḥiyya, reprimanding Muḥammad for his excesses.

Second, he fought the British, resisting both foreign and Christian encroachment. Perhaps sensing European rivalries, he was more co-operative with the Italians; they in their turn giving him a small state under their protection in 1905, used him as a buffer between Somali factions. The British occupation of the interior was, however, more the result than the cause of Muḥammad's *jihād*.

Third, he fought the Ethiopians. In 1913, there was a dramatic reversal in Ethiopia. Menelik died, and was succeeded by Lijj Iyasu, son of his daughter and a Galla chief. Iyasu, encouraged by German and Ottoman diplomats, showed great inclination towards Islam. He moved his court to Harar, and adopted many Muslim customs. Among his wives were a niece and a daughter of the Muslim ruler of Jimma. The '*ulamā*' declared him a *sharīf*. In 1916 he proclaimed his conversion and Ethiopia's religious dependence on the Ottoman sultan-caliph, and summoned the Somalis to *jihād*. It was arranged that he should marry a daughter of Muḥammad b. 'Abd Allāh. But the marriage never occurred, for a Christian counter-revolution in 1917 deposed Iyasu, and checked the Galla-Muslim resurgence.

Finally, Muḥammad fought other Somali clans. He applied all the devices of pastoral Somali politics, as of Islam, to build up his following. He was a renowned poet, both in Arabic and the vernacular. Though clan lines broadly demarcated his supporters and opponents, he did have unusual supra-clan appeal, and is revered today as pioneer of a united Somali nationalism.

Muḥammad's career, as that of al-Ḥājj 'Umar, responded to two stimuli. Both moved within an independent Muslim tradition: early study and travel, Pilgrimage leading to special dedication to a particular order and this leading in turn to rivalry with other orders. Both drew inspiration from other reform movements—'Umar from Sokoto, Muḥammad from the Mahdist Sudan. Neither seems to have sought a settled, permanent theocracy for himself, though 'Umar made arrangements for his succession which Muḥammad did not. But both found the Muslim tradition distorted by a second stimulus, that of the European presence. Both tried to keep abreast technically. 'Umar could turn his back on the Europeans; it was too late for Muḥammad to do that. Perhaps because Muḥammad could no longer withdraw, but had to make his stand at home, he seems now, like Samori, a nationalist forerunner.

D. THE MODERN PERIOD

The effects of European colonization

The effect of European colonial control upon the development of Islam in tropical Africa is far from fully analysed. It was in part the effect of a hostile challenge: various Muslim champions fought the Europeans, but often these Muslims felt able to negotiate, and sometimes the Muslim leaders quarrelled among themselves as much as with the Europeans. Some learned Muslims advocated a pacific attitude. Perhaps more important, for the spread and strengthening of Islam, was the association of the faith, in the minds of some, with modern nationalist sentiment. The fact that so many Muslims accommodated themselves to European rule led to new tensions within the Muslim community. In part also, and this was the greater part, the effect of European colonialism was to enlarge Islamic opportunities, in three main ways: indirect rule, direct employment of Muslims, and generally increased mobility.

Indirect rule was clearest in northern Nigeria, where British authority was exercised through the Fulani amirates established by 'Uthmān dan Fodio's *jihād*. Similar systems operated elsewhere, for example in northern Cameroon under Germans and then French. Sometimes Europeans, wishing to organize and simplify, enlarged the realms of the traditional Muslim rulers through whom they chose to govern. Thus the Zaghāwa of Waday were brought under a single sultan by the French in the 1930s; the British confirmed Muslim authority over pagans in Nupe and Ilorin; while in Cameroon the French assignment of certain pagan cantons to Muslim amirates led to such violent resistance that in 1937 one *amīr* was nearly killed and the cantons had to be freed. Indirect rule often implied a complete ban on Christian mission work, as in northern German Cameroon or British Somaliland, or its stringent curtailment, as in northern Nigeria. European authority in indirect rule somewhat limited the operation of Islamic law: some of the more severe punishments for example were forbidden, and slavery was gradually abolished. But *qāḍīs* sometimes found their influence increased by government backing, for instance in turbulent Somalia.

Indirect rule was not confined to traditional Muslim states. The French, at first suspicious of the autocratic control which the leaders of the Ṣūfī orders, especially the Murids, had over their disciples, later found this control another channel for indirect rule, a channel the more important since, with the decline of chiefs, people tended to regroup around religious leaders. Even the short-lived attempt of the Congo Free State to utilize the governing power of Tippu Tib and other Arabs on the upper Congo may be interpreted as an experiment in indirect rule. Indirect rule, while it strengthened traditional forms of Islam, generally hindered new Muslim developments, so that both amirates and Ṣūfī orders seemed increasingly old-fashioned.

European colonialists everywhere relied extensively on the direct employment of the most educated and experienced African groups. These were by no means always Muslim. In Sierra Leone, Christian Creoles were widely employed; in Nyasaland, pagan and Christian Nguru immigrants went more willingly to school and soon outdistanced the Muslim Yao; in Nigeria, the whirlwind sown by Ibo dominance in the Muslim north is still being reaped today. But in some areas, particularly East Africa, and in some callings, particularly the military, Muslims enjoyed considerable influence as the employees of Europeans.

In East Africa, many of the early government officials, foremen on European farms, and so on, were Muslim Swahili from the coast. This was particularly true in German East Africa, where the Germans took over the old Zanzibari pattern of administration, and extended it far into the interior. The fact that the Maji-Maji revolt in German East Africa in 1905 was against Arabs and Swahili as well as Europeans suggests the extent to which the Germans had entrusted power to these subordinates. In East Africa too the early military garrisons were Muslim, Sudanese or Swahili, but this feature was not confined to the east.

The colonial troops of all European powers in Africa were often Muslim. Occasionally such troops were used against other Muslims: Muslim Galla served Italians against Arabs and Turks in North Africa, Hausa served the Free State against the Congo Arabs, Sudanese and Somalis served Germans against Abūshīrī, and more recently Senegalese served the French against the Algerian nationalists. Muḥammad ʻAbd Allāh bitterly criticized those who fought for 'the uncircumcised heretic'. The *Union culturelle musulmane* of French West Africa in 1958 condemned sending Muslim troops against Muslims in Algeria. But such troops might also contribute to the spread of Islam. Non-Muslim recruits were often converted.

As for the third opportunity of the colonial period, mobility, this, as indirect rule and direct employment, had some disadvantages. Some underlying patterns were disrupted: the push from Zanzibar into the

Congo was blocked, and links between the western Sudan and North Africa weakened. New boundaries dissected established states: Yola was severed from the rest of Adamawa. Occasionally Muslim trading communities declined, by-passed by new railways and roads.

But in general Muslims were able to take advantage of the new opportunities. Muslims and Europeans shared a common interest in trade. Once colonial rule was established, communications greatly improved. In the earliest days, Europeans sometimes relied on already established Muslim communications: various explorers remarked the relative ease of travel in Muslim areas. Islam spread from town to country. Muslims moved into new areas. Equally, pagans moved into Muslim areas: Bambara infiltrating Fulani regions near Jenne, no longer having to fight the Fulani, ended by becoming Muslim; Mossi were converted when they went to work on Gold Coast cocoa plantations. Even deportations sometimes played a positive part in the pattern of mobility.

Separatists and reformers

The fringes of Africa, north and east, have shared in the major schisms and heresies of the Muslim world. These did not, apparently, penetrate the western or central Sudan to any significant extent. Instead, a new heresy developed there, that of the 'mixers'.

Probably the best known and most important example of modern 'mixing' is the Murids of Senegal, an offshoot of the Qādiriyya. The founder, Aḥmad Bamba, received his call in 1886. Although he was himself in origin part Tokolor, the mass of Murids are Wolof, and the brotherhood has been called the 'Wolofization' of Islam. The founder and his descendants constitute a lineage of saints. Adherents become direct disciples of one leading marabout or another, often a member of the founder's family. The disciple surrenders himself, body and soul, to the teacher. The disciple works for the teacher; the teacher prays in place of the disciple; salvation is assured to both. Manual labour, particularly on the land, is sanctified. Most of the profits go to the teachers, in whose luxurious estate the disciples take vicarious satisfaction. The main festivals of the Islamic calendar are observed at the Murid headquarters, Touba, but more popular than these is the Magal festival, commemorating the return of Aḥmad Bamba from exile.

Although the 'mixing' heresy continued into this century, the arrival of Christianity, of European colonial rule, and of Western civilization, introduced entirely new factors into the African equation. Muslims had to adjust themselves, not only to the local African heritage, but to the Christian and Western challenge also. The Muslim response was twofold: external, a matter of foreign relations between Muslims and the West; and internal, a matter of domestic reform—the adjustments necessary within the Muslim community to enable it to meet the new challenge. As Muslims disagreed among themselves about the proper attitude at both levels, opportunities for divergent, and sometimes heretical, opinions increased. The situation was additionally complicated because heresy, even if defined, could no longer be disciplined as in the old days. Further, most of our information comes from European observers, sometimes inclined to overstate the case. It seems better, therefore, for the modern period to borrow from African Christianity the term 'separatism' for all those Muslim movements which have separated from other Muslims, or from existing Islamic traditions, in order somewhat differently, and perhaps more appropriately, to express the faith.

In the early colonial period, some degree of resistance or aloofness was a mark of orthodoxy, and to co-operate closely with the infidels was a symptom of separatism. Thus the well-known judgment on early heresy in Islam, that the one constant criterion was subversion, was reversed by colonialism. Aḥmad Bamba at first considered *jihād*; he did not put this to the test, but the French were suspicious, and twice exiled him, treatment greatly enhancing his repute. Gradually, however, an unusual degree of co-operation developed. The French, as we have seen, came to use Murid discipline for a form of indirect rule. Economics were important in reconciling Murid marabouts to French rule, and the Murids were soon producing more than half the total groundnut crop, Senegal's main export.

The Murids were in three senses separatist: as 'mixers', as having too close an association with their non-Muslim rulers, and as exploiting their religious organization for economic ends. Tijānī and Qādirī leaders began to imitate the Murids, until what had once been separatist became almost standard. A new separatism arose in reaction, the Hamallists.

Shaykh Ḥamāllāh (Ḥamā Allāh) began preaching in Nioro in the 1920s. He used the shortened prayer, allowed to Muslims in urgent danger, to symbolize the incompatibility of Islam and infidel overrule. He and his followers were repeatedly charged with involvement in violent disturbances. He died in exile in France in 1943. Ḥamāllāh, teaching a reformed Tijānī rite and condemning the temporal comportment of many marabouts, was on angry terms with other Muslims, especially traditionalist Tijānīs.

Neither Murids nor Hamallists proceeded to the second level of Muslim response, that of internal adjustment. One of the earliest examples of this occurs in a variety of separatist episodes, apparently unrelated but much alike, in Freetown, Porto Novo, Cotonou, Lagos, and elsewhere, to which I give the general name 'coastal fever'. Beginning often in the late nineteenth century, it became acute in several places in the 1920s. In Porto Novo, it took the form of tension between Creole Muslims returned from South America, and Nigerian Yoruba and Hausa immigrants. Making allowance for local variations, it is possible to trace certain broad outlines of argument: on the one side a traditionalist party, defending local Islam in its existing form, and on harmonious terms with the colonial authorities; and on the other reformers, wishing to modernize Islamic organization, and to maintain more distance from the colonial régime. The main focus of controversy was the imamate. There were frequently rival *imāms*, and also rival concepts of the imamate, the traditionalists regarding the office as sacred, and succession to it as governed by custom, the reformers regarding it as an elective, representative office. In Lagos, the reformers wished a written constitution for the Muslim community. Both sides showed remarkable willingness to submit to colonialist interference in religious affairs: many reconciliation meetings were sponsored by colonial officials; in Porto Novo twenty-three candidates for the imamate were tested by an official, in Freetown and Lagos ownership of the Friday mosque was thrashed out before colonial courts.

Although the Aḥmadiyya, founded in India by Ghulām Aḥmad late in the nineteenth century, stands partly in the tradition of Shīʿī mystical separatism, it is also perhaps the clearest example of all of response to the Western and Christian challenge, both in external relations and internal adjustment. Ghulām Aḥmad made three major claims: to be the Mahdi waging peaceful *jihād*; to be the Messiah; and to be a prophet. The doctrine of the peaceful Mahdi was rendered suspect in orthodox eyes by the religious romanticism of the Aḥmadīs over the British Empire, regarding it as a step towards a divinely-willed world order, one of the more mysterious ways in which God moves to perform His wonders. As Messiah, Ghulām Aḥmad drew strength from his positive identification with Jesus. The centralized organization of many Christian missions, with professional missionaries, schools, publishing houses, scripture translations, and other modern features, was copied by the Aḥmadiyya. These are to be employed in the struggle against Christianity, for the Aḥmadiyya is more anti-Christian than syncretist. The third claim, that Ghulām Aḥmad was a prophet after Muḥammad, is the ultimate heresy: that he should have ventured this is perhaps a measure of the difficulties which he thought confronted Islam.

The Aḥmadiyya first appeared on the West African coast during the First World War, when several young men in Lagos and Freetown joined by mail. In 1921, the first Indian missionary arrived. Too unorthodox to gain a footing in the Muslim interior, the Aḥmadiyya remains confined principally to southern Nigeria, southern Gold Coast, and Sierra Leone. It strengthened the ranks of those Muslims actively loyal to the British, and it contributed to the modernization of Islamic organization in the area. But its numbers remained small, and its effectiveness was weakened by successive internal schisms. Its chief importance, to be discussed in the next section, has been its pioneering contribution to Muslim-Western education in Africa. It joined the arguments about the nature of the imamate, and the necessity of a constitution; it attempted to regularize finance, forbidding for example extravagant celebrations and thus clashing with the ancient heresy of 'mixing'.

Muslim separatism in Africa is an attempt to maintain a balanced relationship between the faith and the practical circumstances in which the faith exists. If the faith seems too foreign, it will be adapted; if too acclimatized, it will be reformed. In the nineteenth and twentieth centuries, the practical circumstances have included both the African traditional heritage, and the Christian, colonial and Western presences. National independence changes the detail of the practical circumstances somewhat, but in no way removes the tension between them and the ideal faith. Indeed, the demands of nationalism may stimulate new separatisms, whether for or against the state. Another future source of separatism may be the Qur'ān translated. Many leaders of Christian separatism argue their case, partly at least, from the Bible. Such use of the Qur'ān is much less common in Muslim separatism. In Africa hitherto, the standard of reference has been more the Pilgrimage, and the teaching of the *'ulamā'*. The Aḥmadiyya, while still believing that the Qur'ān is essentially untranslatable, has popularized its own English versions, and has encouraged people to think of reading the Qur'ān in their own language, or at least in a language they can readily understand. In East Africa, an Aḥmadiyya Swahili translation appeared in 1953, followed in 1962 by an orthodox version as riposte. It would be surprising if some of the readers of these did not formulate convictions which are at odds with the accepted practices of Muslims round about them.

Education

The European colonial period brought new challenges to African Islamic education, with new subjects and new qualifications needed. The endeavour to adjust education to include the new disciplines without sacrificing the positive Islamic element continues until today. The colonial governments themselves, on a limited scale, embarked on this endeavour before many Muslims took it up. But such European initiatives never really overcame the suspicions of the pious, while students who were committed to Western education preferred the more widely recognized qualifications of fully Western schools.

The French established *madrasas*, advanced schools combining western and Islamic education, in several Muslim centres, using local teachers often trained in North Africa. In the *madrasa* of Timbuktu, set up in 1911, the chief *imām* was one of the teachers. He had led the Timbuktu delegation to Morocco requesting help against the French invaders—last echo of the trans-Saharan ambition of Aḥmad al-Manṣūr in the sixteenth century. He had gone on to Mecca, but later returned home and settled under the French. Arabic, Berber and French languages were taught: one of the Arabic texts was *A Thousand and One Nights*. A similar German school was established at Garwa, in Adamawa, in 1906, to train junior civil servants. This school also offered Arabic, and had compulsory mosque attendance on Fridays. But in 1915, when German rule ended, there were only fifty-four pupils. French officials attempted to regulate traditional Qur'anic schools from as early as 1857. But what the French justified as a means of raising standards, the Muslims condemned as unwarranted governmental interference in religious affairs, and the regulations were only partially effective. The clearest example of Muslim resistance to colonial meddling in education is in British Somaliland. Christian mission schooling had been one of the irritants leading to Muḥammad b. 'Abd Allāh's *jihād*, and from 1910 it was banned. In 1920, British plans to introduce schools financed by a tax on livestock led to a riot in which a district commissioner was killed.

The plans were dropped. In 1936 such proposals were revived, to be blocked by another riot. It was, however, possible for the British government to give grants to a few Qur'anic schools, which taught Arabic and arithmetic, and a few boys went to the Sudan for secondary education. A curiosity among these colonial experiments in Muslim education is the school reported in 1906 from Murzuk, then still a Turkish outpost. The school was maintained and staffed voluntarily by Young Turks, political prisoners banished to the Sahara.

In the long run, the reconciliation of Muslim and Western education depended on African initiative. Edward Blyden (1832–1912), active in various attempts to bring together Muslim and Western, and Muslim and Christian education, in Liberia, Sierra Leone and Nigeria, marks the transition. Though a West Indian and a Christian, he was more identified with local Muslims than European officials could be.

The earliest spontaneous Muslim effort seems to have been the school founded in Ekrofol in southern Gold Coast in 1896, by two Fante Muslims, converts from Methodism. After some years, this school failed. The effective inaugurators of Muslim-Western education in tropical Africa were the Aḥmadīs. Many of the Nigerians and Sierra Leoneans who welcomed the Aḥmadiyya after the First World War, just as many of the Gambians who welcomed it after the Second, were more interested in educational help than doctrinal innovation. When doctrinal innovation was found inherent in the Aḥmadiyya, some African Muslims set up their own, more orthodox, educational groups. The *Anṣār-ud-dīn*, founded in Nigeria in 1923, is now a much larger organization than the Nigerian Aḥmadiyya. The Muslim Brotherhood in Sierra Leone, founded in 1959, is rapidly overtaking the Sierra Leonean Aḥmadīs in educational work. The Brotherhood is heavily backed by the United Arab Republic. This is a great help, since Arabic occupies a prominent place in most modern Muslim school plans. Both the *Anṣār* and the Brotherhood were established by former Aḥmadīs. Similar 'voluntary agency' Muslim educational progress developed later in East Africa, where again Aḥmadīs have contributed, and the Muslim Welfare Association of the Ismāʿīlī community.

French-speaking tropical Africa was more influenced by North African developments. The Salafiyya movement, attempting both to reform and to defend Islam, stressed modern Muslim education. The Free Schools of Morocco, flourishing in the 1920s, were a direct result of Salafī teaching. In North Africa, politics often swallowed education;

but in tropical Africa reforming Muslims continued to advocate Salafī ideas until the end of the European period. Reformist schools began about 1950. The principal organization encouraging such work was the *Union culturelle musulmane*, set up in 1953.

Although the French-speaking countries have not had to digest Aḥmadī heresy, the new schools have occasioned considerable controversy and, for example in Bamako, some violence. Three main Muslim viewpoints emerge: the reformist, the purely traditionalist, and that of certain traditional leaders who acknowledge the need for some modernizing and purifying of African Islam. In seeking to purge accretions and reform corruptions, these reformers—and the Aḥmadīs, the *Anṣār*, the Brotherhood, and others—stood in the succession of those who, from the Almoravids onwards, have waged war against 'mixing'. But the class-room has replaced the armed camp; in place of military dedication, these schools offered academic learning. Those, like the reformist schools in French West Africa, or the Brotherhood schools in independent Sierra Leone, with strong North African connexions, could offer also Arabic as an effective, living language.

APPENDIX

South Africa

Slaves and political prisoners, from the Dutch East Indies, were the first Muslims in South Africa, arriving in the late eleventh/seventeenth and early twelfth/eighteenth centuries. Some, such as Shaykh Yūsuf, who had championed Bantam resistance to the Dutch, were men of political and religious stature. Stories of many miracles adorn his memory, and his tomb is still a place of pilgrimage, one of a circle of tombs of early saints, surrounding and guarding the Cape peninsula. In 1767, the Dutch ceased sending political exiles to the Cape.

As for the slaves, their numbers increased during the eighteenth century, and Cape law and customs stiffened against them. Those slaves, for example some from East or West Africa and from Madagascar, who were not already Muslim inclined to the example of their Malay colleagues. A *sharīf*, Sa'id, is said to have come to the Cape after Shaykh Yūsuf's death, and to have taught the slaves, miraculously entering their locked quarters at night to read the Qur'ān and to bring them food. Not until the early nineteenth century were Muslims allowed a regular mosque in Cape Town.

A third wave of Muslim immigration came from 1860 on, when Indian labourers came to the plantations in Natal and Transvaal, followed by Indian traders, especially Bombay Muslims. Muslims from elsewhere in Africa have drifted in too, for instance a few Somalis.

The Cape Malays became skilful artisans; and, in common with various other Muslim groups in Africa, the army was among their vocations. Malay artillerymen distinguished themselves in the defence of the Cape against the British in 1804.

The Cape Malays are frequent pilgrims to Mecca. In the second half of the nineteenth century, ties with Istanbul developed, partly through a controversy among the Cape Malays over the religious respectability of a Malay sword dance—an Asiatic example, perhaps, of the 'mixing' heresy. As in East Africa, Islam in South Africa is represented by several traditional orders; but resistance to novelties, such as the Aḥmadiyya, is keen.

CHAPTER 7

THE IBERIAN PENINSULA AND SICILY

I. ISLAM IN THE IBERIAN PENINSULA

The Muslim conquest

The weakness of the Visigothic monarchy and the apathy of the oppressed Hispano-Roman population offered an easy prey to the Arabs recently established on the other shore of the Straits of Gibraltar. Mūsā b. Nuṣayr, who had just triumphantly overrun Morocco, and his lieutenant, Ṭāriq b. Ziyād, governor of Tangier (Ṭanja), with the complicity of the legendary Count Julian, were the fortunate conquerors of Spain. The first landing of a detachment of 400 men sent to reconnoitre by the Berber, Ṭarīf b. Mallūq, took place in Ramaḍān 91/July 710, and the booty obtained without resistance induced Mūsā to give to his freedman, Ṭāriq, command of the expedition guided by Count Julian which encamped at Calpe (Jabal Ṭāriq, i.e. Gibraltar) and took Cartaja in Rajab 92/spring 711.

King Roderick, who was putting down a Basque revolt, hastened to Cordova, and, after gathering an army together, advanced towards the Algeciras region. Here Ṭāriq awaited him with 12,000 Berbers and a number of partisans of the sons of Witiza, a former king, who were rebels against Roderick. The battle took place on 28 Ramaḍān 92/19 July 711 on the banks of the river Barbate. It is not certain whether Roderick lost his life in the encounter, but, on the dispersal of his troops, Ṭāriq, contrary to the instructions which he had received to return to Africa, or at least to remain where he was until further orders, attacked Écija and took Cordova. Toledo, almost evacuated by its authorities, offered him no resistance, and so he was able to advance with his irresistible cavalcade as far as Guadalajara and Alcalá de Henares. In the face of such extensive conquests, he asked for reinforcements from Mūsā b. Nusayr. Mūsā, jealous of the glory acquired by his freedman, and indignant at seeing himself disobeyed, landed at Algeciras with 18,000 men and after taking Medina Sidonia, Carmona, and Alcalá de Guadaira by assault, captured Seville with no great effort. Only before Mérida, where Roderick's chief supporters had assembled, did he have to keep up a siege of six months. Once he had obtained its submission, he made for Toledo, where Ṭāriq, whom he had met and lashed with his scorn at Talavera, handed over to him the treasures of the Visigothic dynasty. He wished to carry on by way of Saragossa to Lérida, but the Umayyad Caliph al-Walīd ordered him to present himself with Ṭāriq at Damascus in order to give an account of his conquests.

Before his departure he completed the subjugation of the sub-Pyrenean region as far as Galicia, and left for Syria at the end of 95/summer 714, handing over the governorship of Andalus to his son ʿAbd al-ʿAzīz, who pacified the whole of south-eastern Spain, and signed a treaty of submission with the Visigothic lord of the Murcia region, Theodomir. He married Roderick's widow. In 97/716 he was assassinated at Seville by order of the Caliph Sulaymān, after a short rule of two years. Before his death, the conquest of the peninsula was for practical purposes finished. It seems that Muslim garrisons had already been established in the chief towns and that a great number of Hispano-Romans had accepted conversion to Islam in order to enjoy full rights of citizenship under the new régime. These converts on becoming the great majority of the population of Andalus, gradually acquired a very original character, for they combined the culture brought by the invaders from the Orient with their native characteristics, which included the preservation of their Romance language, spoken by them as well as by the Mozarabic communities (which continued to be Christian) in the big cities such as Toledo, Cordova, Seville, and Valencia.

The military morale of these invaders, who did not balk at the barrier of the Pyrenees and, disregarding the danger to their line of retreat, invaded Gaul, offers the most vivid contrast with the passive surrender of the native people, who, in spite of their great numerical superiority, their knowledge of the terrain, particularly suited to guerrilla warfare, and their occupation of the strongholds, offered no more than the belated resistance of a few fanatical mystics, who braved Islam and its Prophet only to suffer martyrdom.

The governors dependent on Damascus

The period of roughly forty years, 716–58, which intervened between the murder of ʿAbd al-ʿAzīz and the establishment of the Umayyad amirate in Spain, is characterized by the rivalry and struggles with which the Qaysites and Kalbites revived Arab factionalism in the Iberian peninsula, and by the rapid succession of governors nominated and dismissed by the *wālīs* of Qayrawān, or the caliph in Damascus. Their task was to consolidate the conquest, to put down rebellion, and to launch expeditions against Gaulish territory. These were finally brought to a halt at Poitiers, where Charles Martel defeated and killed the governor of Cordova, ʻAbd al-Raḥmān al-Ghāfiqī, in Ramaḍān 114/end of October 732. The fugitives fled to Narbonne, whence another expedition set off in 116/734, invaded Provence, and did not withdraw until four years later. Charles Martel laid siege to Narbonne, and again succeeded in defeating, in 120/737, another column commanded by ʻUqba b. al-Ḥajjāj. Finally his son, Pepin the Short, re-took Narbonne in 133/751, thereby forcing the Muslims definitely to give up the conquest of Gaul. Civil war and the character of the invaders themselves, who were for the most part ignorant soldiers, did not create a propitious climate for the development of culture. Burning with the ardour of their new religion, they needed no more than the Qur'ān, the sole fount of law, to impose their religion without provoking ideological conflicts. During this first period, they contented themselves with the division and organization of the huge patrimony which had fallen into their hands. Not only did they live alongside the vanquished Christians, but they accepted their conversion to Islam; and, as they had crossed over to the peninsula as a military force, and not as immigrant tribes, they suffered from a shortage of women, and so took wives among the vanquished. This fashion was inaugurated by ʻAbd al-ʻAzīz, son of Mūsā b. Nuṣayr, when he married Roderick's widow. It became almost the general rule, especially as the Umayyad *amīrs* themselves, and even the caliph and the *Ḥājib* al-Manṣūr, preferred Basques, Galicians, and Frankish women, although they had women of their own nationality within easy reach.

About 720 a few Visigothic aristocrats and the natives of Asturias began the *Reconquista* with the proclamation of Pelayo and the battle of Covadonga, which later acquired a legendary tinge. When the Berbers evacuated the sub-Pyrenean regions of Galicia and Asturias, this state under Alfonso I succeeded in extending as far as the valley of the Duero. With a patriotism unknown to their Mozarab co-religionists, and with unquenchable valour, these Iberians put a brake on the Islamic advance, and began to recover their ancestral lands. The disproportionate power of their adversaries, with their devastating raids and their assaults on citadels and cities, failed to impose sovereignty on the modest kingdoms of Oviedo, Pamplona, and later León, which were to resist the attacks of the Cordovan power with stoical firmness. Though they may sometimes have acknowledged themselves to be feudatories, they were never to relinquish their sovereignty, and were to show their obvious superiority in battle as soon as the caliphate began to decline.

As regards the law of land-tenure in conquered Andalus, the sources are very scarce and contradictory. The majority state that the division of land was begun by Ibn Nuṣayr, according to law, reserving the 'Fifth' (*al-Khums*) for the state, but Ibn Ḥazm, who betrays the national sentiment of the *muwallads* (native Muslims), assures us that the régime was based on the law of the strongest. The conquerors, arriving from the Maghrib, Ifrīqiya, and Egypt, occupied agricultural properties by force; only to be themselves in their turn, and not much later, evicted by the Syrians brought in to suppress a Berber revolt, without there being in any of these cases any regular and lawful procedure.

The establishment of the Umayyad Amirate of Cordova

The spectacular collapse of the Umayyad Caliphate in Syria, and the accession of the 'Abbasid dynasty, finally loosed the bonds which linked Andalus to Damascus through frequently dismissed governors.

'Abd al-Raḥmān b. Mu'āwiya, grandson of the Caliph Hishām, managed to escape from the extermination of his family, and took refuge in North Africa. Through his faithful *mawlā*, Badr, he made contact with Umayyad clients in Andalus, where he arrived on 1 Rabī' I 138/14 August 755. He entered Seville, and took the road for Cordova, in the neighbourhood of which he achieved a resounding victory, which opened to him the gates of the capital. He was recognized in its mosque as *amīr* of all Andalus.

In the thirty-two years of his reign (138–72/756–88) he showed his great qualities. Surrounded by a court of Umayyad *émigrés*, he devoted himself to the consolidation of his power, and to the energetic suppression of the continual uprisings of his subjects, both Arab and Berber. These bathed almost all his reign in blood, and alternated with the intrigues of his relatives who, though welcomed at his court, attempted repeatedly to dethrone him, and paid for their treachery with their lives.

These internal complications did not allow him to devote all his efforts to the *jihād* on the frontier of the little kingdom of Asturias, with which he kept a truce of twenty years from 150/767 to 169/786. In this interval Charlemagne undertook, in 161/778, his celebrated expedition against Saragossa, which ended in his defeat at Roncesvalles. This disaster showed Charlemagne that uncertain alliances with dissident Muslim chiefs made success against Spanish Islam very doubtful. For this reason he preferred to found the kingdom of Aquitaine to watch and maintain the Pyrenean frontier, and he succeeded, in 169/785, in making the inhabitants of Gerona submit to the Frankish authority.

ʿAbd al-Raḥmān I preserved and extended the organization which the governors appointed from Damascus had established in the new province. He made Cordova the seat of his government, and refrained from adopting any other title but that of *amīr*. At least at the beginning of his rule, he allowed the *khuṭba* to be recited in the name of the ʿAbbasid caliph. About the middle of his reign, he organized an army of mercenaries, Berbers, and *mamlūks* bought in northern Europe. ʿAbd al-Raḥmān I died in Cordova on 25 Rabīʿ II 172/30 September 788 before reaching his sixtieth year. According to the Arabic chronicles, which eulogize him in the warmest terms, he was one of the best rulers of his dynasty. The native population caused ʿAbd al-Raḥmān I no anxiety, for both the country people and the town-dwelling proletariat, who had not forgotten Visigothic tyranny, lived on good terms with the central power. Homesickness for his distant homeland caused him to establish a country residence near Cordova, which he called al-Ruṣāfa after the summer palace between Palmyra and the Euphrates, where, as a boy, he had stayed for long periods with his grandfather, Hishām.

From ʿAbd al-Raḥmān I onwards, all the history of the Umayyad amirate of Cordova is influenced, not to say dominated, by the instability of the various ethnic groups—Arab, Berber, neo-Muslim, Mozarab, and Jewish—whose passionate rivalries made impossible the pacification of the country until the time of ʿAbd al-Raḥmān III. By contrast, the population of the nascent Christian states was much more homogeneous and stable, for the inhabitants of the territory evacuated by the Berbers had once more adopted their old religion, if indeed they had ever abandoned it. Alfonso I and Fruela I would not tolerate Muslim communities within their dominions, and it was not until the beginning of the sixth/twelfth century, when the Reconquest was already far advanced, that Christian rulers allowed nuclei of Moriscos (i.e. Muslims) to remain, in view of the impossibility of peopling the newly conquered territory with their own few subjects.

The successor to ʿAbd al-Raḥmān I was not his first-born, Sulaymān, but his second son, Hishām, whose proclamation provoked a dynastic war, in which Sulaymān and another of his brothers, ʿAbd Allāh, had to emigrate to North Africa. The reign of Hishām I (172–80/788–96), in contrast with that of his father, was characterized by general internal peace and by the official adoption of the Mālikī *madhhab* in the peninsula. Various Andalusian pilgrims had heard Mālik b. Anas (d. 179/795) expound his chief work, *al-Muwaṭṭaʾ*. When these disciples returned to Andalus, the information which they gave on the development of Islamic culture in the East interested Hishām I, and contributed to the fact that he, as also his successor, al-Ḥakam I, established the Mālikī *madhhab* on an official basis. The Mālikī teachings soon crystallized into an unchangeable doctrine, opposed to any attempt at innovation, and so made of Andalus a firm stronghold of orthodoxy.

This interlude of peace at home, which Hishām I enjoyed during his brief reign, enabled him to press the religious war against the Asturian kingdom almost every summer. Two armies, one following the Ebro up to Álava, the other marching to the north-west along the Bierzo, won two victories. In 178/791 Álava and Asturias were again the object of a counter-attack, but the column which succeeded in sacking Oviedo was taken by surprise and suffered heavy losses on the way back in a marsh, even though Alfonso II was almost captured on the banks of the Nalón. Hishām died prematurely at the age of forty, after nominating as his successor his second son, al-Ḥakam I (180–206/796–822), whose succession to the throne ushered in a long period of trouble in the country. His two uncles, who had come out against his father, renewed their attacks. The first, Sulaymān, advanced towards Cordova, failed in his attempt to enter the capital, and finally was killed in the Mérida region. The second, ʿAbd Allāh, after seeking the support of Charlemagne, whom he visited at Aix-la-Chapelle, was pardoned on condition of residing at Valencia until his death.

Meanwhile uprisings in the three marches of Saragossa, Toledo and Mérida occupied almost all the attention of al-Ḥakam I. Saragossa, where an agitator had declared himself independent, was reconquered, and in order to secure its frontier the fortress of Tudela was established on the right bank of the Ebro. Toledo, always inclined towards dissidence, was brought to heel by terrorism on the famous 'Day of the Ditch' (*Waqʿat al-Ḥufra*, 181/797) when the Toledan bourgeoisie was treacherously decimated.

In the Lower March the *amīr* had to struggle for seven years in order to reduce Mérida, and to this series of provincial uprisings was added the plot set on foot to dethrone him, and to put his cousin in his place. The plot was discovered, and savagely repressed. The repression in its turn provoked new disorders, and the excitement of the people boiled over in the revolt of the Arrabal,[1] which came near to costing al-Ḥakam his throne and his life. The vengeance of the *amīr* is vividly remembered

Map 14. The Iberian peninsula and the Maghrib in the late third/ninth century.

in the annals of western Islam. After unheard-of rapine and butchery the survivors of the Arrabal were exiled, and the whole area with its houses was razed, and ploughed, and sown again. Some of the emigrants peopled the quarter of the Andalusians in newly founded Fez, while

[1] I.e. *al-Rabaḍ*, a suburb of Cordova.

others adopted piracy, and were even able to take Alexandria, and found a kingdom in Crete.

Such serious disturbances did not prevent al-Ḥakam from attacking the region which formed the nucleus of Castile, taking Calahorra in the Ebro valley, and raiding the borders of Álava. But even this placed no obstacle in the way of the Christian advance into Muslim territory all over the north, to conquer Lisbon in the north-west, and form the Hispanic March in the east, with the taking of Barcelona by the Franks.

The reign of the cruel al-Ḥakam I coincides paradoxically with the humanization of Andalus, and the first signs of the influence which the ʿAbbasid culture of Baghdād was to exercise on the Iberian peninsula. At the same time, there began to take place a fusion between the Arab aristocracy and the neo-Muslims of Hispanic origin, now that numerous non-Arabs, even Berbers and Slavs, occupied important posts at court and in the administration of the amirate. At the end of his life, after a reign lasting almost a quarter of a century, al-Ḥakam I's outlook grew embittered and his mistrust increased, a fact which the *ʿulamāʾ* attributed to remorse for his crimes, especially against the people living outside Cordova. He shut himself away in his palace, surrounded by Christian mercenaries, and ignoring his subjects' discontent and his own unpopularity, devoted himself solely to the maintenance of political unity in his kingdom. On 10 Dhu'l-Ḥijja 206/6 May 822, he solemnly proclaimed not only a successor but also the latter's heir presumptive, should his successor die prematurely. Fifteen days later al-Ḥakam I died at the age of fifty-three. On his deathbed, he urged his son to be just and firm.

On succeeding to the throne, ʿAbd al-Raḥman II (206–38/ 822–52) enjoyed thirty years of relative peace in the interior, gained by the harsh energy of his father. In this period of political calm, the intellectual revival flowing from the Orient continued to develop. His paternal great uncle ʿAbd Allāh who, besides being the practically independent governor of Valencia, had designs on the Tudmīr region, died in 208/823–4, and, after putting down at Lorca the unrest provoked by the hostility between Qaysites and Kalbites, ʿAbd al-Raḥmān founded the new city of Murcia.

He left his brother, al-Walīd, to suppress without great difficulty an obscure rebellion which broke out at Toledo, and devoted his activity for the most part to fighting the Christians in the north. In three successive campaigns he attacked the regions of Álava and Old Castile. These campaigns were followed by frequent incursions into Galician territory where Alfonso II reigned. He also launched a number of summer expeditions against Barcelona and Gerona, which he was unable to take; and not until the death of Louis the Pious in 841 did a Muslim army penetrate into France, sacking the Cerdagne, and reaching as far as Narbonne.

Three years later, in 229/844, the Scandinavian pirates reached the Atlantic coast of the peninsula. They disembarked opposite Lisbon, and, after bloody battles, re-embarked to reappear at the mouth of the Guadalquivir, take Cadiz, and attack defenceless Seville, which was sacked, and such inhabitants as did manage to escape, were killed or enslaved. ʿAbd al-Raḥmān II mobilized all his forces and completely defeated the invaders. The demoralized survivors re-embarked, and though in 859 and 866 they repeated their attempts, they were easily repulsed.

The Mozarabs, although subject to severe taxation, were tolerated and no *dhimmī*, as such, was condemned to death until the formation of the party led by the fanatics Eulogio and Álvaro, whose mystic exaltation led them to seek martyrdom in insulting the Prophet, and blaspheming against the Muslim religion. This wave of provocation lasted until 245/859 when, during the amirate of Muḥammad I, Eulogio, its prime mover, was beheaded.

Meanwhile diplomatic relations where instituted between Cordova and Constantinople at the instigation of the Emperor Theophilus, who proposed a treaty of alliance to carry on the struggle against the ʿAbbasids, the natural enemies of the Umayyads as of the Byzantines. The Cordovan *amīr*, however, who sent in his turn an embassy to Theophilus, refused to come to an agreement.

ʿAbd al-Raḥmān II, one of the wealthiest monarchs of the Mediterranean world, was an efficient administrator, who, by generous distributions of wheat, eased the two great famines which desolated Spain in 207/822–3 and 232/846. He perfected the administrative organization and hierarchy in imitation of the ʿAbbasid governmental structure, with monopolies of the mint and of the manufacture of precious fabrics. The army and navy were two of the major preoccupations of this *amīr*, who expanded his fleet, and instituted an arsenal at Seville as a result of the incursions of the Northmen.

He was, moreover, a great builder and, surrounded by unheard-of luxury, encouraged music and art. The Umayyad amirate of Cordova now had no fear of sedition fomented by Baghdād, so ʿAbd al-Raḥmān II not only copied the customs of his old enemies, but even decided to imitate their manner of life. His tastes, his refined luxuries, his art, his poets, his musicians, and even his commerce looked towards ʿIrāq. This was an orientalization of which the most notable exponent was Ziryāb who, born in Mesopotamia and warmly welcomed at the Cordova court, was the unquestioned arbiter of taste, and able to impose his refinements and his innovations.

At the end of his life the *amīr* made no official choice of an heir among his many sons. A plot aimed at poisoning him failed, but he died within two months. Muḥammad I (238–73/852–86), his son and successor, was proclaimed by various *fatās*[1] of the palace in a *coup d'état*. He followed the same political and administrative lines as his father, and did not compare unfavourably with him in intelligence, loftiness of ambition, and energy in suppressing the almost permanent unrest in the Marches, above all in that of Toledo, which led to the battle of Guadazalete. In Mérida, the capital of the Lower March, ʿAbd al-Raḥmān b. Marwān al-Jillīqī (i.e. the Galician) raised a rebellion, and made himself for many years the independent lord of Badajoz. At the same time ʿUmar b. Ḥafṣūn fomented a serious insurrection in the districts of Reyo and Tākurunna in the south of Andalusia. Muḥammad I died while trying to clip the wings of Ibn Ḥafṣūn's brigandage, which was extending every day, and al-Mundhir, on succeeding his father, could not master the situation during the two short years which his rule lasted (273–5/886–8). He left no sons.

His brother ʿAbd Allāh (275–300/888–912) succeeded him, only to find himself involved in a confusion of family crimes and continuous insurrections, in which the enemies of the Umayyad régime often combined into unstable leagues. The Muslims of Spanish origin (*Muwallads*) had created little independent principalities in the south-west of the peninsula and found themselves in conflict with the Arabs of the province of Elvira, whose internecine struggles were desolating the region. The seamen of the Mediterranean coast between Alicante and Águilas created the semi-independent federation of Pechina, while in Seville Arab patricians and *Muwallads* began a long period of civil strife. This terminated in the creation of a quasi-independent state ruled by the Arab,

[1] The *fatās* were palace officials recruited from the ranks of slaves.

Ibrāhīm b. Ḥajjāj, who later became a relative by marriage of Ibn Ḥafṣūn.

The latter, despite his brilliant but disorganized efforts, was unable to co-ordinate the general dissidence of the country. He was beaten at Poley and then, having forsworn Islam, was further weakened by repeated defeats, and finally succumbed to the pressure of ʻAbd al-Raḥmān III. Just as confused as the situation in the south of Andalusia was that in the Marches, where a mosaic of independent states, subject to a purely formal protectorate, encircled the region of Cordova from Badajoz on the west, to Toledo on the north and Saragossa on the east. By contrast, the kingdom of Asturias, which had shown such activity under Alfonso II against Muḥammad I, launched no attacks of any scope against ʻAbd Allāh, while the Banū Qasī, although weakened by domestic rivalries, kept up the struggle against the Basques of Pamplona. In Catalonia, liberated from Carolingian tutelage, the dynasty of the marquis-counts of Barcelona was founded.

In the first three centuries of the *Hijra* there appeared no philospher among the Spanish Muslims, and it was only contact with the famous Eastern schools which caused Muʻtazilite ideas, considered heretical, to enter Spain, in spite of the rigid official Malikism. With Ibn Masarra these ideas were hidden under a veil of asceticism, and led to the creation of a philosophical and theological system, and finally to Sufism. The most eminent personage of this movement was the Murcian, Muḥyī al-Dīn b. al-ʻArabī, whose pantheistic mysticism spread throughout Andalus, and gained for him in the Orient a reputation as a miracle-worker, almost a prophet.

ʻAbd al-Raḥmān III (300–50/912–61) is the outstanding figure among the Umayyad princes. In a long reign of almost fifty years, he made his country the most flourishing in all Europe, with a prestige rivalled only by that of Constantinople. He succeeded to a toppling throne when he had scarcely attained his majority, and immediately plunged into the struggle against Ibn Ḥafṣūn, inflicting continual defeats on him, until he died hemmed in in his fortress of Bobastro. The four sons of Ibn Ḥafṣūn continued the now hopeless struggle, and at last, in the spring of 316/928, ʻAbd al-Raḥmān III entered the eyrie which had resisted him for so long. With this, Andalus was pacified, and immediately afterwards the Algarve and Levante submitted. Toledo resisted for three years, but finally had to surrender unconditionally. The king of León, Ordoño III, took advantage of the initial difficulties of ʻAbd al-Raḥmān III in putting down these risings, but soon the victory of Valdejunquera and the campaigns of Muez and Pamplona made the Leonese and Navarrese respect him, until the aggressive Ramiro II of León defeated him with great slaughter, and routed him at the Ditch of Simancas (327/939). But with the death of the Leonese king in the winter of 339/950 and the outbreak of discord among León, Castile, and Navarre, ʿAbd al-Raḥmān III reached the apogee of his power, and saw the Christian kings hastening to do homage at his court. However, in spite of his overwhelming superiority in men and riches, he did not succeed in annexing any important territory, far less in suppressing any of the Christian principalities with which he had to fight.

In order to counter the danger of a Fatimid invasion of the southern part of his states, the Cordovan ruler intervened in North Africa, occupied Ceuta, and succeeded in making a large part of the north of Morocco, and a considerable area of the central Maghrib, recognize his protectorate.

Towards the end of 316/928 ʿAbd al-Raḥmān III reached the triumphant culmination of his political career by adopting the caliphal title of *amīr al-muʾminīn*. He took the appellation of *al-Nāṣir li-Dīn Allāh* and founded Madīnat al-Zahrāʾ, where he dazzled the Muslim and Christian embassies who sought audience of him by magnificent receptions. In the course of an unusually long reign he succeeded by his political genius and untiring energy in strengthening authority in his dominions, organizing his administration, and enforcing respect for his frontiers.

The Umayyad state now witnessed a great development of scientific culture, under the influence of the Orient and the personal effort of the heir apparent, al-Ḥakam. Medicine had hardly been studied at all until, from the days of ʿAbd al-Raḥmān II onwards, doctors who had received training in ʿIrāq, created a school where the works of Galen were studied, and later the *Materia medica* of Dioscorides was translated and utilized. The same was true in the field of history, until Aḥmad al-Rāzī, who had been left in Andalus at the age of three by his father, a native of Persia, codified the rules of historical composition. In the third/ninth century, and even more in the second/eighth, few were the occasional annalists who had gathered together collections of items of anonymous information, contaminated with legends relating especially to the remote period of the conquest. Such as the *Akhbār majmūʿa*, a very poor history of little documentary value, as was observed by ʿĪsā b. Aḥmad al-Rāzī, who also earned fame as the official chronicler of the dynasty, in the service of the Caliph al-Ḥakam II.

Al-Ḥakam II (350–66/961–76) succeeded his father at forty years of age. His reign was one of the most peaceful and fruitful of the dynasty. He attained his greatest glory through his love of literature and the arts, in assembling an exceedingly rich library, and enlarging and embellishing the incomparable mosque of Cordova.

A landing of Northmen in the region of Lisbon was easily repulsed, and frequent Leonese and Navarrese embassies seemed to affirm the submission of the Christian states of the peninsula. But when León, Castile and Navarre formed an alliance with the counts of Barcelona, al-Ḥakam II was obliged to direct in person an expedition against Castile in the summer of 352/963. The Christian princes had to sign a truce, and for several years new embassies from different regions of the peninsula filed through Cordova along with the envoys of the Holy Roman Emperor Otto II, and the Byzantine Emperor John Tzimisces.

Garci Fernández, count of Castile, taking advantage of a seizure, which kept the caliph inactive for several months in 364/974, with Galician and Basque reinforcements, besieged Gormaz, but was put to flight under its walls by the general Ghālib b. ʿAbd al-Raḥmān. In North Africa, al-Ḥakam II followed the risky policy of his father even though there now remained in his hands only the two citadels of Ceuta and Tangier. When the Fatimid caliph established himself in Egypt, al-Ḥakam was able to subdue the Idrisid princes, who were transferred to Cordova and emigrated to Egypt a little before he died.

On the accession of Hishām II (366–99/976–1009), who was very young and unable to direct the helm of the Cordovan caliphate, the way began to open out for the dictatorship of Muḥammad b. Abī ʿĀmir, who was to be called on account of his victories *al-Manṣūr* (Almanzor, 'the Victorious'). He countered all the plots woven against him, and was dictator of Muslim Spain for twenty years. He annihilated all his old collaborators without pity, and enlisted great Berber contingents in his army. He undertook continental campaigns against the Christians of the north, even as far as Santiago de Compostela and Barcelona, so that a number of counts recognized his sovereignty. It was only in the battle of Peñacervera that he came near to being defeated, after a desperate battle against Count Sancho García, with whom the Leonese and the Basques from Pamplona to Astorga had allied themselves. The sexagenarian al-

Manṣūr died in 392/1002 at Medinaceli on returning from his last expedition against Rioja.

Al-Manṣūr's tireless activity in the peninsula did not prevent him from continuing al-Ḥakam II's North African policy. He tried to conciliate the Zanāta Berber *amīrs* with generous gifts and put an end to the sporadic resistance of the remaining Idrisids. After successive triumphs and defeats in his struggle against the Fatimids he managed to establish a viceroyalty in Fez, which he entrusted to his son 'Abd al-Malik al-Muẓaffar. On succeeding his father, al-Muẓaffar (392–9/1002–8) maintained for six years, until his premature death, the peace at home which was so tragically destined to yield to anarchy and lawlessness. In his campaigns against the peninsular Christians he continued his father's work zealously; he attacked the region of the Spanish Marches, whose count had violated the truce signed but little before, and he defeated the Castilians. However, after suffering some time with a chest complaint, he returned to Cordova to die.

His brother, 'Abd al-Raḥmān, known as Sanchuelo because of his close resemblance to his maternal grandfather, Sancho Garcés II, king of Pamplona, succeeded him in the regency, but after a few months he provoked the tragedy in the history of Muslim Spain, the *fitna* or Andalusian revolution.

Licentious and vain, he demanded that the puppet ruler, Hishām II, name him officially as heir to the caliphate. The Cordovans were outraged and organized a plot to put on the throne an Umayyad pretender, Muḥammad II. Sanchuelo, returning from Toledo, was treacherously taken prisoner and murdered (399/1009), and with this episode there begins the complex and deplorable sequence of nine proclamations, dethronements and reinstatements which in the brief space of thirty years led to the suppression of the caliphate and the sudden collapse of a régime which had imposed its hegemony over the whole peninsula.

Muḥammad II, the victim of a Berber rebellion, was replaced for a moment by Sulaymān, the son of 'Abd al-Raḥmān III, only to be restored and then replaced again by Hishām II, who was killed by Sulaymān, at his new enthronement by the Berbers on their sacking of Cordova (403/1013). Idrisids from Morocco, the Hammudids (Banū Ḥammūd) succeeded Hishām II, with an interregnum by another Umayyad, al-Murtaḍā. Finally in 422/1031, the Cordovans, after fresh but unfruitful attempts at restoration, decided to do away with the caliphate, and formed a council of nobles to administer the reduced territory which was still in their power.

It was only the prestige and the extraordinary ability of 'Abd al-Raḥmān III, al-Ḥakam II, and al-Manṣūr, coupled with the importation of large Berber contingents, which had enabled the Muslims to get the upper hand over the small and divided Christian states. But their victory had not been durable, and no sooner had this sequence of three great leaders come to an end than the superiority of the Christians showed itself as decisively as had that of the Muslims at the invasion. The Arabs of the amirate depending on Damascus had succeeded in rapidly islamizing a great number of Hispano-Romans, but they were unable to annihilate the islets of native resistance in the Pyrenees. Conversely, the reconquerors, who had maintained their resistance heroically, were not successful, despite spectacular territorial advances, in reconverting to Christianity those very neo-Muslims whose ancestors had so easily released themselves from the bonds of the Catholic faith.

The high cultural level attained by the Spanish Muslims during the Umayyad Caliphate, in the confused days of the *fitna*, and the formation of the Party Kingdoms, finds its outstanding exponent in Ibn Ḥayyān in history, and in Ibn Ḥazm in literature and philosophy. Ibn Ḥayyān, the son of Khalaf, the secretary of al-Manṣūr, is the prince of historians of the Umayyad period. His two masterpieces are *al-Matīn*, in sixty volumes, known to us by a few quotations only, and *al-Muqtabis*, in ten volumes, which gives a rich and magnificent panorama of the Cordovan amirate from its beginnings until the time of the author. Three volumes only have been preserved.

Worthy to be associated with him is the famous polygraph Ibn Ḥazm, author of *Tawq al-ḥamāma* ('The Necklace of the dove'), which has been translated into several European languages, and the *Fiṣal*, a history of religions, in which he gives a critical exposition of all the attitudes of the human spirit in the religious sphere. It is an extraordinary work, without predecessor, and was unique of its kind until modern times.

The Party Kingdoms

The state of more or less permanent conspiracy, which disturbed the life of the Muslims of the peninsula until the end of the Umayyad Caliphate, became even more permanent, as a necessary consequence of the *fitna* by the formation of the Party Kingdoms. The slave-troops were largely of Slav origin. Many of them rose to become the most important officers of the caliphal government and of the ʿAmirid dictatorship, and made themselves masters of the Levante. Along the Upper Frontier formed by the valley of the Ebro, with Saragossa as its capital, at first, the Tujībīs and later the Hudids (Banū Hūd), took possession. In spite of dynastic rivalries, the Hudids prospered, and allied themselves with the Cid Campeador against the count of Barcelona and the kingdom of Aragon. On the Lower Frontier, formed by the valleys of the Tagus and the Guadiana, two independent kingdoms established themselves with Toledo and Badajoz as capitals. At Toledo the king, al-Ma'mūn (429–67/1037–74) of the Dhu'l-Nunid (Banū Dhī'l-Nūn) dynasty, attached himself to Alfonso VI of Castile and managed to take possession of Cordova and Valencia. The latter city had been ruled by the ʿAmirid, ʿAbd al-ʿAzīz, the son of Sanchuelo, and on his death (453/1061) by his son. Al-Ma'mūn's son and successor was the incompetent Yaḥyā al-Qādir, who had to submit, and, abandoning his capital, moved to Valencia under the protection of the Castilians. The Castilians, with the Cid Campeador, finally took possession of Valencia (478/1075), and it remained in their power until it was retaken by the Almoravids. Badajoz was ruled by the Aftasids (Banu'l-Afṭas), a Berber dynasty, which maintained a continual state of war with the ʿAbbadids (Banū ʿAbbād) of Seville. When Alfonso VI took Coria (471/1079), King ʿUmar the Aftasid sought the help of the Almoravids. He was finally beheaded with his two sons for having allied himself again with Alfonso VI against the Almoravids (487/1095).

Seville, governed by the Hispano-Arab dynasty of the ʿAbbadids, is the most important and best known of the Party Kingdoms. On expelling the Ḥammudid caliph, the Sevillians formed a republican government under the presidency of the *Qāḍī* Muḥammad b. ʿAbbād, who ridded himself of his colleagues and made himself *de facto* king. His son, al-Muʿtaḍid (433–61/1042–69), extended his dominions, annexing without scruple the little principalities which had sprung up between Seville and the ocean. But, in spite of his conquests and annexations, he had to pay tribute like the kings of Badajoz, Saragossa, and Toledo to Ferdinand I, who had united León and Castile. Although his son, Muḥammad al-Muʿtamid (461–84/1069–91), took possession of Cordova, he was unable to resist Alfonso VI, and had to ask for the help of the Almoravids. He finally lost his throne, betrayed by the Sevillians, and was exiled to Aghmāt at the foot of the High Atlas, where he died in obscurity. His fame as poet and the pomp of his court won for him the attention and eulogy of Arab *littérateurs*, who made of him an idealized figure with exaggerated virtues.

The Ṣanhāja Berbers, coming from Ifrīqiya, set up a kingdom in Granada when the Umayyad pretender, al-Murtaḍā, was defeated under its walls. Zāwī b. Zīrī, the conqueror, did not believe it possible that his fellow-tribesmen could survive in Andalus, and left the rule to his nephew, Ḥabbūs, whose son, Bādīs, consolidated the Zirid power during a long reign (430–66/1038–73). He repulsed the attacks of the ruler of Seville, al-Muʿtamid, who followed a frankly anti-Berber, Arabo-Andalusian policy. ʿAbd Allāh, Bādīs's grandson and successor, was a coward who was loth to draw his sword, and could not make himself respected within his realm, nor resist the attacks of al-Muʿtamid and the pecuniary demands of Alfonso VI, whose protection he sought after having been present at the battle of Zallāqa and the siege of Aledo (see below). In 483/1000 he was deposed by the Almoravid Yūsuf b. Tāshufīn and exiled to Aghmāt, where he wrote the memoirs of his not very brilliant reign.

The Party Kings inherited, and imitated to the best of their abilities the pomp of the caliphate, and in their little courts, amidst disorder and war, art and culture flourished. This disorder and war prevented them from resisting the Christians in the north, and obliged them to seek help from the Almoravids, who by that time had taken possession of all Morocco and part of Algeria. This extreme measure caused much disquiet and repugnance on the part of these kings and their immediate collaborators, but when the Christian danger became even more grave, they sent ambassadors to Yūsuf to obtain confirmation of his decision to wage Holy War, and to sign the treaty by which the Andalusian kings promised to unite their forces to fight side by side with him. Yūsuf promised to respect their sovereignty and guaranteed not to meddle in their internal affairs; moreover, a term was fixed within which he and his troops undertook to evacuate Andalus.

The era of the Party Kings is characterized by an intellectual liberty considered legitimate by rulers who devoted themselves wholeheartedly to scientific and religious studies. Ṣāʿid (born 420/1029) attributes this renaissance, of which he was a witness, to the cessation of the intolerance imposed by al-Manṣūr, and the dispersal of books and scholars, which the Berber *fitna* provoked at Cordova. These books and scholars created a fertile soil for the 'ancient' studies cultivated by the Greeks and the Romans, i.e. philosophy, mathematics and natural science.

Seville, Badajoz, Almería, Granada and Saragossa were the new intellectual centres born of the decentralization of Cordova.

The Almoravids in Andalus

Yūsuf b. Tāshufīn crossed from Ceuta to Algeciras, which he occupied by force. He reached Seville, whence he proceeded towards Badajoz, accompanied by the Party Kings, in order to face the army of Alfonso VI on Friday, 12 Rajab 479/23 October 1086 at Zallāqa on the right bank of the Guadiana. The defeat of the Christians has a peculiar importance in the medieval history of Spain, not because in itself it was much more than another indecisive battle, but for what it symbolized. It was an unmistakable sign that the interplay of forces and the course of the Reconquest had suffered a change as sudden as it was complete.

Its effects became obvious immediately. The Levante, which had submitted to the protectorate of Alfonso VI, shook off the yoke of Castile, and the Cid Campeador was charged with its recovery. His successes, and incursions from Aledo, provoked repeated calls for help, and al-Muʿtamid succeeded in exacting a promise from Yūsuf b. Tāshufīn to lay siege to Aledo. Yūsuf crossed over to Andalus for the second time and the siege got under way (480/1088). The Muslim camp, however, was a hive of intrigues which prevented a prolonged encirclement, until finally the Almoravid *amīr* lost patience with the Party Kings, who had reopened their treacherous parleying with the Christians, and decided to dethrone them all.

Granada and Málaga were annexed during his third visit to the peninsula; then it was the turn of the king of Seville, al-Muʿtamid, whose capital surrendered in 484/1091, after his son al-Ma'mūn had been killed in an assault on Cordova. Almería and Badajoz yielded to the *Amīr* Sīr, a relative of Yūsuf, but in Levante his advance was blocked by the Cid, who took possession of Valencia in 1094, and defeated the Almoravids in the battle of Cuarte. After the death of the Cid (492/1099) Valencia was taken by the Almoravid *amīr*, Mazdalī; in 503/1110, the Almoravids occupied the kingdom of Saragossa and, in 1115, the Balearic Islands.

Yūsuf died at the beginning of 500/2 September 1106, and his son and successor, ʿAlī, continued his offensive policy. The only son of Alfonso VI was defeated and killed on 16 Shawwāl 501/29 May 1108. In the following year ʿAlī crossed over to Andalus, and took Talavera de la Reina. His cousin, Mazdalī, made an attack on Oreja and Zorita, only to be defeated and killed in the following year at Mastana. ʿAlī arrived in

Andalus for the third time in 511/1117 and besieged Coimbra without result; Alfonso I of Aragon, on the contrary, made clear the premature decadence of the warlike spirit of the Almoravids in his famous year and a half's expedition through the heart of Andalusia, and took Saragossa in 512/1118.

The defeat suffered by 'Alī at Cullera in 522/1129 decided him to send his son Tāshufīn as governor of Granada and Almería, in order to raise morale and reinforce the defences of the frontier against the young and energetic Alfonso VII in Castile, and Alfonso I in Aragon. Tāshufīn showed unfailing courage in a struggle that was as prolonged as it was unequal, until he returned to Morocco, to be nominated hereditary *amīr* on the death of his brother Sīr. In the spring of 533/1139, with his faithful Catalan general Reverter, he undertook the ill-fated military operations which ended in his falling to his death from the cliffs near Oran, in 537/1143.

The Almohads

The collapse of the Almoravid empire brought in a second period of Party Kings, which began in 539/1144, a little before the death of Tāshufīn. Everywhere in Andalusia the new kinglets swarmed. But the resounding triumph of the Almohads in Fez and Marrakesh caused most of these new rulers to send deputations with their recognition to 'Abd al-Mu'min.

Once organized resistance in the Maghrib had ceased an Almohad army crossed over to Andalus, subdued all Algarve, and entered Seville. The new Party Kings, however, seeing the Moroccan rebellion of al-Māssī against 'Abd al-Mu'min, broke their oaths of fidelity, only to submit with the same inconstancy as soon as they learned that 'Abd al-Mu'min had mastered the situation, and was sending more troops to the peninsula.

At the end of 544/spring 1150, 'Abd al-Mu'min undertook the foundation of Rabat. He summoned the turncoat lords of Andalus to Salé and decided to keep them at his court in order that he might be able to carry out with greater security the campaign of 546/1151–2 against Bougie and Constantine. On his return he instituted hereditary rule, and with his customary harshness suppressed the rebellion of the brothers of the Almohad Mahdi, and the tribes of Hargha and Tinmāl.

Seeing his political horizon thus cloudless, he was able from 549/1154 onwards to devote all the resources of his empire to the *jihād* against the kingdoms of Portugal, Castile and Aragon. These had had ten years (539–49/1144–54) in which to reopen their offensive against the feeble Party Kingdoms and against the other territories subject to the almost nominal authority of the Almohads which could offer no serious resistance to the Christian advance. But the picture of this struggle changes completely from 549/1154 onwards. The lost fortresses in the Llano de los Pedroches and in the region of Cordova were retrieved by the Almohads; Portuguese territory was attacked; La Beira was razed to the ground; the castle of Trancoso was attacked. The Almoravids of Granada, impressed by these successes, asked for peace, and offered to hand over the city. This surrender was accepted and ʻAbd al-Mu'min proceeded immediately to lay siege to Almería, which was taken in the summer of 552/September 1157.

After these triumphs, ʻAbd al-Mu'min devoted all his efforts for two years, 553–5/1158–60, to his campaign in Ifrīqiya, but his absence had grave consequences for Andalus. Ibn Mardanīsh, the Party King of Murcia, and his father-in-law, Ibn Hamushk, who had allied themselves with the Christians and showed open hostility to the Almohads, laid siege to Cordova, made themselves masters of Jaén, took Granada by surprise, and defeated an army which had come to the help of the city in the Vega; but they were defeated in their turn at the battle of Sabīka, and Granada came again under Almohad occupation.

ʻAbd al-Mu'min had undertaken great fortification works at Gibraltar, in order to make it a base for his operations. He assembled a large fleet, and recruited the mighty army which was to attack the four kingdoms of Portugal, León, Castile and Aragon, but, at the very moment of preparing this expedition, he fell ill and died at Rabat on Jumādā II 558/May 1163.

His son Abū Yaʻqūb Yūsuf (558–80/1163–84) reconquered Murcia, having defeated Ibn Mardanīsh. He undertook and personally directed several campaigns, but his successes were few, and his reverses extremely serious. The conquest of Murcia was due in great part to the defection of Ibn Hamushk, the lieutenant of Ibn Mardanīsh, and the death of the latter, whose sons accepted Almohad doctrine. Meanwhile Alfonso Enriquez of Portugal and his famous general Giraldo made some spectacular conquests when they assaulted various fortresses in Estremadura. If he failed to take possession of Badajoz, it was only because of the opposition of Ferdinand II of León, who had allied himself with the Almohads.

In order to prove to Yūsuf that they had broken definitely with Castile, the Murcians persuaded him to organize a great offensive against Huete, which was a pitiful failure. Ten years later he undertook a vast campaign against the small but aggressive kingdom of Portugal, choosing as his objective the fortress of Santarem, the base of operations for Portuguese lightning raids. The siege and attack lasted for only five or six days. When the king of León approached to help the besieged, panic seized the Almohad army and made them recross the Tagus in frightful confusion, leaving Yūsuf, almost alone, to be mortally wounded, and withdrawing without fighting toward Seville.

Abū Ya'qūb Yūsuf, although the son of a Zanātī father and a Maṣmūdī mother, and born at Tinmāl in the heart of the High Atlas, was a cultivated monarch, who was well versed in all the subtleties of Arabic literature, and, educated in Seville, surrounded himself with Andalusian literary men, physicians and philosophers. He made Ibn Ṭufayl, the author of the philosophical novel *Ḥayy ibn Yaqẓān*, his medical attendant, and suggested to Ibn Rushd (Averroes) the idea of studying and commenting on the work of Aristotle. These commentaries, translated into Latin and Hebrew, exercised an extraordinary influence on medieval thought. His father had given orders that Cordova should be the capital city of Andalus, but when he died Abū Ya'qūb Yūsuf caused the central administration to return to Seville, and during the years of his residence there as ruler he beautified and enriched it with many buildings.

Abū Yūsuf Ya'qūb al-Manṣūr (580–95/1184–99) was proclaimed on the day following the death of his father, while he was on the road from Évora to Seville. As soon as he arrived at Marrakesh he undertook the foundation of the imperial quarter of Ṣāliḥa as a residence for himself and his successors; but hardly had the work begun, than the ominous news reached him of the landing of the Majorcan Almoravids, the Banū Ghāniya, at Bougie. The very serious consequences of this landing were to disturb the whole of his reign and that of his successor, al-Nāṣir.

With the energy and swiftness which were characteristic of him, Ya'qūb embarked on a large-scale campaign in which, after retaking Bougie, he defeated the Majorcans and obliged them to withdraw into the desert. But the habitual slowness with which the Almohads proceeded, and the necessity for resting his troops after so long and arduous a campaign, gave the Christians time to intensify their attacks in the peninsula. The hardest blow was dealt by the king of Portugal, Alfonso Enriquez, who, in the summer of 585/1189, took Silves with the help of a fleet of Crusaders who were on their way to Palestine.

Ya'qūb crossed over to Andalus, bent upon vengeance. He attacked Torres Novas, to the north of Santarem, but could not take Tomar, which was defended by the Templars. Dysentery and fever played havoc in the Almohad camp, and the caliph himself fell ill. In the summer of the next year, 587/1191, he took Alcacer do Sal, to the south of the Tagus, and regained Silves, a victory which obliged the Christian kings to sign a four-year truce.

On the expiry of the truce Alfonso VIII of Castile made a violent assault on the region of Seville, and Ya'qūb accepted the challenge. At the foot of the citadel of Alarcos on the frontier of Castile the battle took place (591/1195). The Almohad victory was judged by the Muslim chroniclers to be even more brilliant than that of Zallāqa, and the Christian losses were so heavy that in the campaigns of the two following years, 592–3/1196–7, in which Ya'qūb made such great advances through Estremadura, Toledo and Guadalajara, the Castilian king dared not stand in his way, but signed a truce for ten years.

The caliph returned to his capital sick and exhausted by the fatigues of his long campaigns, and had his son, al-Nāṣir, proclaimed as his heir. His frequent intercourse with Andalusian literary men and philosophers very early made him lose 'Abd al-Mu'min's simple faith in the infallibility and impeccability of the Mahdi. He was a warm admirer of Ibn Ḥazm and his Ẓāhirī doctrine; he declared war on Malikism, which was so well-rooted in the peninsula, and showed the same favour towards Ibn Rushd as had his father, although he found himself obliged for a time to exile him as a result of the intrigues of the jurists. The Arab chroniclers paint the reign of Ya'qūb al-Manṣūr as the culmination of Almohad power. But the fact is that he bequeathed to his son a much less enviable heritage than that which he had received from his father. The struggle on two fronts, which forced him to leave Ifrīqiya in order to hasten to Andalus and vice versa, was the first severe setback, which very soon, with the Castilian victory at Las Navas de Tolosa, the Marinid invasion, and the independence of the Hafsids in Tunisia, was to hasten the downfall of the Almohads and put an end to the dynasty in the midst of continuous strife and subversion.

When al-Nāṣir (595–611/1199–1214) succeeded to the throne at the age of seventeen years, his tutors put a large-scale plan into execution. They took possession of the Balearic islands, suppressed the rebellion of Ibn Ghāniya, and left the government of Ifrīqiya in the hands of the wise and faithful Hafsid, 'Abd al-Wāḥid. Meanwhile the truce signed with

Castile had expired, and Alfonso VIII, burning with desire to avenge the defeat of Alarcos, took the offensive. In the spring of 1212, he and al-Nāṣir, who had now crossed over to the peninsula, led their forces to Las Navas de Tolosa (*al-ʿIqāb*), where the battle took place on 15 Ṣafar 609/16 July 1212. This was the most famous battle of the Reconquest. In it disappeared the last Muslim hope of consolidation in Andalus with the support of the great African empires.

With the untimely death of al-Nāṣir and the proclamation of his son, who died without offspring at twenty years of age, civil war became endemic and the caliphs were deposed or assassinated with cold impunity. Al-ʿĀdil, the son of Yaʿqūb al-Manṣūr, rebelled in Murcia, while ʿAbd Allāh b. Muḥammad, the great-grandson of ʿAbd al-Muʾmin, known as al-Bayāsī, proclaimed his independence in Baeza. ʿAbd Allāh allied himself with Ferdinand III and handed over to him Martos and Andújar, for which the Cordovans put him to death. At the same time the Almohads in Marrakesh murdered al-ʿĀdil. Al-ʿĀdil's brother, al-Maʾmūn, proclaimed himself in Seville in 624/1227, but crossed over to Morocco to fight with his rival Yaḥyā, the son of al-Nāṣir, abandoning Andalus to new Party Kings, who rose against the Almohads, and gave birth to three kingdoms, of which only that of Granada was able to survive for two centuries and a half.

The most ephemeral of these little states was that of Valencia, occupied in 636/1238 by James I of Aragon, who had already made himself master of Majorca. Slightly more durable was the government of Ibn Hūd and his successors in Murcia. Ibn Hūd raised the banner of insurrection in al-Ṣukhūr (Los Peñascales) of the Ricote valley and personified and directed the general insurrection of the Spanish Muslims. When al-Maʾmūn withdrew to Morocco, he was recognized with equal speed and fickleness by almost the whole of Andalus, but when he was defeated at Mérida by León, there rose against him the founder of the Nasrid dynasty of Granada, Muḥammad b. Yūsuf b. Naṣr, and Ibn Hūd, after alternate recognition and rejection, was murdered at Almería in 635/1238.

The union by Ferdinand III of the crowns of León and Castile gave a special impulse to the Reconquest. He proceeded to the conquest of the valley of the lower Guadalquivir, which led to his taking of Seville in 1248. Ibn Hūd was succeeded on his death by his son, al-Wāthiq, who was twice dethroned and restored. The Murcians undertook to pay tribute to Ferdinand III, and handed over their citadel, but finally rose once more, and recognized the king of Granada, so that he might come to their aid. But when this aid proved of no avail, Murcia had to yield.

The Kingdom of Granada under the Nasrids

The rising of Ibn Hūd and the departure of the Caliph al-Ma'mūn for Morocco induced Muḥammad b. Yūsuf b. Naṣr, a member of the Arab family of the Banu'l-Aḥmar, to proclaim himself king in his turn. This he did on 25 Dhu'l-Qa'da 627/5 October 1230 in the little town of Arjona and so founded the dynasty which reigned in Granada until 1492.

Muḥammad I in his kingdom of Granada seemed destined to end as had his rival Ibn Hūd, for the new state had little depth, and its frontiers were eminently vulnerable to Castilian invasion. Ferdinand III took possession of Arjona, devastated the Vega of Granada, and besieged Jaén, whereupon the new king, with an unexpected dramatic gesture, presented himself before Ferdinand, and recognized him as his overlord. He surrendered Jaén, and signed a truce for twenty years in consideration of an annual payment of 150,000 maravedíes. Thus the new Nasrid king won recognition, though he had to contribute to the siege and taking of Seville and to watch passively the submission of the whole of lower Andalusia. His continual and confused struggles with his rival, Ibn Hūd, and the constant threat of the Reconquest, caused him on his deathbed in 671/1273 to recommend his son and successor Muḥammad II, nicknamed *al-Faqīh*, to seek the protection of the Marinids, whose *amīr*, Abū Yūsuf Ya'qūb, in order to rid himself of his rebellious nephews, had made them cross the straits in 660/1261–2 with 3,000 volunteers to wage the Holy War.

Presently Ya'qūb himself landed at Tarifa, which Muḥammad II had ceded to him along with the fortress of Ronda as a base for his operations. He made raids on the regions of Almodóvar, Úbeda and Baeza, and before Écija defeated and killed the *adelantado* of the Frontier, Don Nuño Gonzalez de Lara, who had barred his way with scanty forces. The archbishop of Toledo was also defeated before Martos by the Granadans, who took him prisoner and killed him. Alfonso X of Castile attempted to make good these disasters by laying siege to Algeciras, but the Castilian fleet, which had been watching the straits since 1277, was surprised and scattered almost without struggle by fourteen Marinid galleys. This catastrophe forced Alfonso to lift the siege. The spectacle of these victories, and of Málaga handed over to the Marinid *amīr*, and the fear of being dispossessed by the Africans as the Party Kings had been, made the *amīr* of Granada, negotiate with Alfonso X and with Yaghmurasān, the Zayyanid lord of Tlemcen, against Abū Yūsuf Ya'qūb, though Ya'qūb had been his main support against the Christians. Ya'qūb in his turn received an embassy from Alfonso X, who was asking for his help against his rebel son, Sancho, and seeing himself abandoned by his tributaries, had recourse to his principal enemy.

The *amīr* crossed over to the peninsula, and had an interview with Alfonso, who handed over his crown on receiving a loan of 100,000 gold dinars. Together they attacked Cordova, and raided the districts of Toledo and Madrid. Muḥammad II, a victim of endless apprehensions, feared that the two monarchs might decide to dethrone him, so he treated with Alfonso; but then, seeing the Marinids laying siege to Málaga, thought himself lost, and applied to the Moroccan heir apparent to bring about a reconciliation with Abū Yūsuf. The latter then attacked the Cordovan district, passed through Baeza and Úbeda, but did not reach Toledo. He came back laden with booty and returned to Marrakesh at the end of October 682/1283. In the spring of 684/1285, he repeated his raids through lower Andalusia, but with more energy, and such was the devastation caused during the summer, that Sancho IV decided to meet with him near Jerez, and sign a new pact.

In 701/1302 the third king of Granada, Muḥammad III surnamed *al-Makhlū'* ('the Dethroned'), succeeded to the throne but after seven years was deposed in favour of his brother, Abu'l-Juyūsh Naṣr ,who ruled only five years before being replaced by a collateral. Al-Makhlū' recognized Abū Ya'qūb Yūsuf, who was besieging Tlemcen, and took advantage of the minority of Ferdinand IV to take Bezmar and various fortresses, while his troops hurled themselves through Andalusia. But when Ferdinand IV attained his majority, he arranged a three-year truce with Castile, which brought about a breach between Morocco and Granada. The Granadans took possession of Ceuta in 705/May 1306, but lost it in 709/1309, and reconciled themselves with the Marinids.

Meanwhile Castile and Aragon composed their differences in order to continue the Reconquest. Ferdinand IV and James II made a concerted effort to deal a mortal blow to the kingdom of Granada by besieging the Algeciras and Almería respectively. Both failed, although the Castilians won Alcaudete. While this was going on, the confused internal situation in Granada stimulated a new plot by which Abu'l-Walīd Ismā'īl, one of the most capable and energetic of the Nasrid *amīrs*, came to the throne. After twelve years he fell a victim to assassination, after inflicting a bloody defeat on Castilian troops. As a result of this victory Ismā'īl recovered the fortresses of Huéscar, Orce, Galera, and (in the following years) Martos. Ismā'īl was succeeded by his son, Muḥammad IV. His reign was disturbed by continual rebellions, and he was obliged to ask for help from the Marinid ruler, with whose assistance he besieged and took Gibraltar. He was murdered, like his father, in 733/1333. He was succeeded by his brother, Abu'l-Ḥajjāj Yūsuf I, who reigned for twenty-three years before he too was assassinated. During his reign he had to face Alfonso XI of Castile, and had to seek assistance from the powerful Marinid *amīr*, Abu'l-Ḥasan, but he and his ally were defeated at the battle of the Salado in 741/1340, and Abu'l-Ḥasan returned hastily to Morocco. The threat of Marinid intervention in the peninsula was now definitely ended. After taking Alcalá la Real, Priego, Rute and other citadels, Alfonso XI contrived to find resources in Castile to undertake successfully the arduous siege of Algeciras and prevent a second crossing by Abu'l-Ḥasan. He died of plague during the siege of Gibraltar, for the loss of which in 1333 he had never been able to console himself, and which he needed as the last base necessary for the conquest of Granada.

The son and successor of Yūsuf I, Muḥammad V, left the government in the hands of the renegade Riḍwān, his father's *wazīr*, and maintained good relations with Castile, whose king, Pedro I, buffeted by many political upheavals, could only intermittently address himself to the Reconquest. Muḥammad V was forced by a plot to abdicate, leaving the throne to his brother Ismā'īl II, who was assassinated by Muḥammad VI, the ally of Aragon. Pedro seized the opportunity to take possession of Iznájar and other fortresses, penetrating as far as the Vega of Granada. Muḥammad VI, seeing that Málaga was in revolt against him and that Muḥammad V had many partisans, sought an interview with Pedro I, during which he was treacherously stabbed in 763/1362. The second reign of Muḥammad V lasted for thirty years, during which there was a complete reversal of roles between Morocco and Granada, since, through the decadence of the Marinid dynasty, influence and the direction of public affairs at the court of Fez passed into the hands of Muḥammad V. Both kingdoms were the scene once more of family rivalries and civil wars, of which the most outstanding victim was the celebrated *wazīr* and writer Ibn al-Khaṭīb. He was forced to flee from Granada, only to be murdered in Morocco by the henchmen of Muḥammad V.

From this moment onwards, information, and even chronology, become uncertain. The Christian chronicles scarcely pay attention to the Reconquest until its last phase.

With the enthronement of the Catholic Kings, Ferdinand II of Aragon and Isabella of Castile, the distressing death-throes of the Nasrid kingdom begin. In 887/1482 began a long and difficult war which lasted ten years, and might have lasted even longer but for the continual internal struggles, in which Muḥammad XI Abū ʿAbd Allāh (Boabdil), his father, ʿAlī Abu'l-Ḥasan, and his uncle, Muḥammad XII al-Zaghall, were involved. Abū ʿAbd Allāh had come to an agreement with Ferdinand and Isabella by which, when al-Zaghall gave himself up, he should hand over Granada, which was then 'the best fortified city in the world', but he preferred to resist to the end. He tried to provoke an insurrection of the Muslim subjects of the Catholic Kings, and also attacked the fortresses in the hands of the Christians, but very soon the influx of refugees, and the consequent scarcity of provisions forced him to parley. This he did in great secret, but the terms of the capitulation became known, and when a riot put his life in danger, he had to bring forward the date of the handing-over. The Catholic Kings made a solemn entry into Granada on 2 Rabīʿ I 897/2 January 1492, thus putting an end to the Muslim domination in the Iberian peninsula which had lasted for 780 years.

II. MUSLIM SICILY

At the height of the Middle Ages, when Muʿāwiya succeeded to the caliphate at Damascus, the Arabs, after attacking the islands of Cyprus and Rhodes, launched their first raid against Sicily from the Syrian coast in 32/652. Their forces were small but impetuous, and having spread terror, and encountered no resistance, gathered much booty, and returned to their starting point. The second attack, which also lacked the preparation necessary for a conquest, and had no immediate object beyond that of obtaining loot, was undertaken from Alexandria in 49/669. A landing was made at Syracuse, a great deal of booty was collected in the course of a month, and then the raiders withdrew, in fear of being blockaded by the Byzantine fleet.

Subsequent attacks did not depart from Syria or Egypt, but from the North African coast, where the Arabs had been definitely settled since the foundation of Qayrawān. Pantellaria fell into their hands about 81/700, though meanwhile the Byzantines had concentrated their naval forces in Sicily, and had retaken Barqa in 68/687 and Carthage, for a time, in 78/697. With the arrival of Mūsā b. Nuṣayr as governor of Ifrīqiya, the raids on Sicily became more frequent, but the Byzantines multiplied their coastal defences, and their fleet blocked the way of the African Muslims, and hampered their trade. Moreover, the conquest of Andalus caused a diversion of forces, and the schisms and rebellions which broke out among the Berbers gave a respite of half a century to the oppressed Sicilians, who, though no longer sacked by the Muslim corsairs, were still fleeced by the Byzantine tax-collectors.

The first Aghlabids of Qayrawān maintained diplomatic relations with the patrician who governed the island, and signed a truce, so that the true conquest of Sicily did not begin until 211/827. It was due to the treachery of the Greek governor, Euphemius, who, having been dismissed, revolted in Syracuse, and, in order to avenge himself, crossed the sea, and offered sovereignty over the island to the Aghlabid *amīr*, Ziyādat Allāh. He promised him the co-operation of his numerous partisans, and undertook to pay tribute, on condition of being granted the title and insignia of an emperor.

The *amīr* decided to accept so favourable an offer, once he had put down the rebellions which he had to face in Ifrīqiya. He declared a *jihād*, and sent a fleet and army under the command of the celebrated jurist Asad b. al-Furāt which won a signal victory when it landed at Mazara. Syracuse was on the point of yielding, but the invading general, Asad, died (213/828). The Muslims, seeing their retreat cut off by the Byzantine fleet, gave up the siege, burnt their ships, and, decimated by plague, interned themselves starving in the island. They attacked Mineo and Girgenti, but had to give up the siege of Castrogiovanni. Within two years of the landing at Mazara, the invaders faced the failure of their plan, being reduced to the precarious possession of Mazara and Mineo, while Euphemius had been murdered by the inhabitants of Castrogiovanni.

Although the first steps of the invasion of Andalus and of Sicily were similar, their future course of development was very different. In both cases the morale of the Muslims was greatly superior to that of their enemies, but while the Hispano-Romans gave up without resistance, and embraced Islam, the Greeks and Latins of Sicily offered a tenacious opposition, and, in spite of bloody defeats, neither gave up their cities, nor embraced the invaders' religion so easily.

In the summer of 215/830, Ziyādat Allāh equipped a new fleet with powerful landing forces, and resumed the offensive. The Muslims adopted a new approach from the west, and laid siege to Palermo. Its inhabitants defended themselves heroically for a year until hunger, plague and continuous attacks obliged them to capitulate in the autumn of 216/831, and accept the status of *dhimmīs*. The firm occupation of Palermo, and the great number of African Muslims who hastened to populate it (attracted by the advantages offered by its position, its port, and its fertile countryside), enabled the definite conquest of the island to be begun with the continuous support of the government in Qayrawān. On the death of Ziyādat Allāh, his brother, Abū 'Iqāl, continued to send reinforcements, who pursued the invasion of the island along the coast between Palermo and Messina, and in the interior in the Etna region.

The Greeks could find no better expedient than to transfer the seat of their administration from Syracuse to Castrogiovanni. Although the new governor of Palermo tried to besiege this impregnable fortress, and defeated the Byzantines in the open field, his *coup* against the fortifications failed, and it was not occupied until twenty years later. Meanwhile Muslim domination was being extended, and when it had covered a third of the island, the republic of Naples, without reckoning the gravity of the step, allied itself with the invaders against the Lombards of Benevento. This opened the Italian peninsula to Arab raids during the fifty years for which this alliance lasted.

Its first ill-omened result was the capture of Messina with the co-operation of the Neapolitan fleet. The Byzantines initiated a counter-offensive, which brought about a dreary succession of lootings and alternate local victories and defeats, in which the Muslims, with their bravery and aggressiveness, came off best. The Sicilians, accustomed to the Byzantine yoke and the despotism of the patricians, saw no great difference between paying tribute to the emperor of Constantinople, and to the *amīr* of Palermo, who represented the Aghlabids. In the summer of 239/853 the new governor, al-'Abbās b. Faḍl, after a savage raid which laid waste the whole of the eastern region as far as Catania and Syracuse, forced Butera, after a siege, to give him 6,000 captives. He also took Castrogiovanni by a sudden *coup*.

During this time the Muslim fleet of Palermo, accustomed to sea warfare, and allied with the Neapolitans, had begun to attack the Adriatic coast. In 223/838 it occupied Brindisi and Taranto, beat the Venetian fleet, and extended its advances along the coasts of both the

Adriatic and the Tyrrhenian. On the island itself, after the unsuccessful attempts of 251/865 and 255/869, the Muslims began the final siege of Syracuse in the summer of 264/877. After an heroic defence, having been hemmed in for almost a year by sea and land, and abandoned by Constantinople, (since the Byzantine fleet could not break the blockade and free it from hunger), it was taken by assault and sacked with frightful carnage on Wednesday, 4 Ramaḍān 264/21 May 878.

The serious disturbances which were provoked in Ifrīqiya by the fall of the Aghlabid régime, and the insurrection of Abū Yazīd, 'the man on the donkey', at the head of the Kharijites (332–6/943–7) left Sicily to the mercy of Berber adventurers in the southern part of the island, while many towns which had submitted, declined to pay tribute. This state of affairs persisted until the Fatimid dynasty had become firmly established, and the Kalbī family of the Banū Abī Ḥusayn had gained recognition as the *de facto* independent and hereditary governors of Sicily. Then the war against the eastern part of the island was renewed, and Taormina was besieged and taken within four months at the end of 351/962. In the following year Rameta, the last Greco-Roman *municipium*, where the fugitives from the conquest of Messina and its province had gathered, was besieged. Its inhabitants sought the aid of the Emperor Nicephorus Phocas, but his large fleet and forces suffered a crushing defeat. Nevertheless it resisted until the beginning of 355/966, in which year the city was taken by assault and sacked, its defenders slaughtered, and the women and children taken captive. A further defeat of the Greek navy in the straits of Messina, and raids against the coastal towns of Calabria, which desolated the country and impeded commerce, obliged the Byzantines to sign a peace, and to acknowledge the Muslim right to exact tribute from all the Christians of the island.

The first three Kalbī *amīrs*, had not to resist Byzantine attacks nor civil wars, but frequently intervened by invitation in the struggles of the small and disunited states of southern Italy. Their profitable raids on the mainland enabled them to enrich themselves, and to encourage the development of Muslim culture, which until that time had been limited to the study of the language and Qur'anic exegesis by Mālikī jurists under the influence of the celebrated Saḥnūn. A very clear example of this progress was the collaboration of a Sicilian scholar, 'Abd Allāh, versed in technological and philological matters, in the Arabic translation of Dioscorides's treatise on botany, made for 'Abd al-Raḥmān III, the Umayyad caliph of Cordova.

At the beginning of the eleventh century the Sicilians sacked the cities of Cagliari and Pisa (1002), but the doge of Venice, Orseolo, obliged them to withdraw before Bari in 1003 and the Pisans gained an important naval victory before Reggio. The Sicilians had their revenge in 1009 when they took possession of Cosenza. In 1015 they were besieging Salerno, which was ready to submit to the payment of tribute, when an unexpected episode marked an astonishing turn in the history of Muslim Sicily. A handful of Normans returning from Palestine as Crusaders, outraged at the inactivity of the Christians besieged in Salerno, effected a sudden sally against the besiegers, who, taken by surprise, were put to flight, abandoning their encampment.

It is almost incredible how the morale of the Muslims collapsed when Norman contingents, under the orders of Robert de Hauteville and his brother Roger, intervened, and how easily they allowed themselves to be defeated by a detachment of knights brought together by chance, and with no resources but their personal bravery. Although at first they were so few, almost all being leaders, the Normans managed very soon by their military prestige, their incomparable personal bravery, and their iron discipline, to form a nucleus of French, German, and (above all) Italian adventurers, who, fired by their example, followed them with unusual faithfulness. Even the Muslims themselves, on accepting to be vassals of the Norman dynasty, helped them with intrepidity in their campaign, and contributed in no small fashion towards the establishment of the grand duchy of Apulia, and the new kingdom of Sicily.

Once the principality of Calabria, from which the Byzantines were expelled, had been created, Robert and his brother Roger took advantage of the civil war between the Muslims in Sicily, and crossed the straits. They took possession of Messina, which yielded in terror without resisting, invaded Val Demone, and gained a decisive victory before Castrogiovanni. In the following year, Robert advanced towards Girgenti, and, although the Sicilian Muslims saw a ray of hope when they allied themselves with the Fatimids, he succeeded in defeating them at Cerami. After frustrating an attempt by the Pisan fleet to attack Palermo, the courageous Roger began the difficult siege of this city.

Roger first slowly subdued the little rebel states which had grown up in the interior of the island, and within three years had placed the people of Palermo in so intolerable a situation that they decided to try their luck at the battle of Misilmeri. They were defeated with enormous losses. Five months of rigorous siege, hunger, the defeat of a fleet sent from

Ifrīqiya to render assistance, and the savage assaults of the besiegers, forced the capital of Sicily to yield to the Normans at the beginning of 1072. The conditions concerning personal liberty, respect for property, and the exercise of Islamic law under Muslim judges were relatively humane.

The elder brother, Robert, lord of the Norman territories on the mainland, remained ruler over Palermo, Messina and Val Demone. Roger, with the consent of the whole army, kept the remainder of the territory, already or yet to be conquered. Profiting by the absence of Roger, who was helping his brother in his campaign against the Byzantines and the Holy Roman Emperor Henry IV, the Muslims of Val de Notto staged an armed rebellion, but the tireless Roger attacked Trapani and Taormina, and, after occupying Girgenti, encircled and took Syracuse in 1085, while the Pisans and Genoese were besieging and sacking Mahdiyya on the African coast.

A kinsman of those Hammudids who had occupied the caliphate of Cordova between 1015 and 1027, crossed to Sicily. He was the last, ill-fated *amīr*, who, in cowardly fashion, surrendered the impregnable fortress of Castrogiovanni, and turned Christian, only to end his life in exile in Italy. Butera still offered armed resistance, but when it and Noto surrendered, the whole island passed into Roger's power in 1091. In the same year, in spite of his being sixty years of age, and newly married for the third time, Roger determined personally to undertake the conquest of Malta, which had been captured by the Aghlabids in 869. He met no resistance and liberated many Christian captives, to whom he gave possession of the island.

His military prowess was refined by a political prudence and moderation, by which he kept in balance all the antagonisms of the varied island population. Realizing clearly that the Muslims exceeded the Greeks and Latins in numbers and talents, he treated them in their civil life with a kindness till then hardly heard of. Thus he had at his disposition a social force which hitherto had been wasted. Recognizing his impartiality and moderation, the Muslims obeyed him blindly, and with their support, he was able to impose his will on the other Norman lords, who possessed fiefs to the south of the Tiber. Once the Sicilians were liberated from the continual devastation of war and the consequent unbridled rapine, they could develop their intellectual life, and devote themselves to the cultivation of their literature, poetry, legislation, and the scientific knowledge which they had received from the East. Roger I, though a convinced

Christian, was free from prejudice, and even at the risk of being considered a Muslim, encouraged them to cultivate their gifts. Through the concourse of two mentalities as different as the Greek and the Arab, the works of Plato, Aristotle, Ptolemy, and Dioscorides were translated and studied as they were in Andalus.

Roger II, having reached his majority, succeeded his father in 1105 and transferred his court to Palermo. He declared war on the Zirids of Mahdiyya. This campaign ended in a naval disaster, but, far from discouraging him, it made him determined to renew his attacks against the African coast. He had now been recognized as duke of Apulia, and proclaimed king of Sicily. He attacked the island of Djerba, took Tripoli, and, by the time he had taken possession of Mahdiyya, Sousse and Sfax, it seemed that the conquest of Ifrīqiya by the Normans of Sicily was to be the revenge for the Arab invasion. The arrival of the Almohads frustrated such ambitious plans.

Roger II died on 27 February 1154. He was a worthy successor to his father, from whom he inherited the courage and political skill which allowed him to make of Sicily one of the most powerful and wealthy states of southern Europe, feared equally in southern Italy, on the coasts of Greece, and along the African littoral. The interest which he took in organizing the administration, while preserving the forms of Muslim life, gained for him a fame and a glory only equalled by his celebrity as an open-handed patron. Science and letters flourished in Sicily in the fifth/eleventh and sixth/twelfth centuries on a par with the cultural progress of the Umayyad Caliphate of Cordova, although the court of Palermo did not produce geniuses to be compared with Ibn Ḥayyān in the field of history, or with Ibn Ḥazm in literary and philosophical studies.

Thanks to the close contacts between Muslims and Christians, and the fact of Greek and Arabic both being well understood on the island, it was possible for the *Optics* of Ptolemy to be translated and published. Geography was studied with extraordinary success and is symbolized in the famous *Book of Roger* which was dedicated to Roger II by al-Idrīsī. In his prologue, al-Idrīsī eulogizes Roger's untiring efforts to encourage scientific studies. Philosophical questions were learnedly treated when Frederick II elaborated the *Quaestiones Sicilianae*. The physicians of Palermo contributed to the progress made by the school of Salerno, while mechanical and military arts were made known in Italy by the weapons employed by the Muslim engineers at the sieges of Syracuse and Alexandria.

There could be no greater contrast than that between the tolerance, and scientific and administrative interaction, which the Sicilian Muslims, as subjects, enjoyed, and the conquering rage with which the Norman princes waged war on all the Islamic states in order to subdue them and sack them without pity. When William II married Princess Constantia of Sweden, the new political orientation opened the gates to German domination. This, with the aggressive and warlike spirit created by the Crusades, destroyed the atmosphere in which the Oriental culture of the island, potently fertilized by Latino-Norman activity, had flourished. The conquered people found themselves day by day worse treated; the cultured classes emigrated to Africa, and the rural masses, in revolt so as ultimately to exhaust the patience of their masters, were exiled to the mainland. Soon discredit and finally oblivion overcame the Arabic language and Muslim culture in Sicily.